Hume's Imagination

Hume's Imagination

TITO MAGRI

OXFORD
UNIVERSITY PRESS

Great Clarendon Street, Oxford, OX2 6DP,
United Kingdom

Oxford University Press is a department of the University of Oxford.
It furthers the University's objective of excellence in research, scholarship,
and education by publishing worldwide. Oxford is a registered trade mark of
Oxford University Press in the UK and in certain other countries

© Tito Magri 2022

The moral rights of the author have been asserted

First Edition published in 2022

Impression: 1

All rights reserved. No part of this publication may be reproduced, stored in
a retrieval system, or transmitted, in any form or by any means, without the
prior permission in writing of Oxford University Press, or as expressly permitted
by law, by licence or under terms agreed with the appropriate reprographics
rights organization. Enquiries concerning reproduction outside the scope of the
above should be sent to the Rights Department, Oxford University Press, at the
address above

You must not circulate this work in any other form
and you must impose this same condition on any acquirer

Published in the United States of America by Oxford University Press
198 Madison Avenue, New York, NY 10016, United States of America

British Library Cataloguing in Publication Data
Data available

Library of Congress Control Number: 2022940844

ISBN 978–0–19–286414–7

DOI: 10.1093/oso/9780192864147.001.0001

Printed and bound in the UK by
TJ Books Limited

Links to third party websites are provided by Oxford in good faith and
for information only. Oxford disclaims any responsibility for the materials
contained in any third party website referenced in this work.

Contents

Preface and Acknowledgements   xi
A Note on References   xv

1. Introduction: A Magical Faculty   1
   1.1 An Interpretive Blind Spot and a Philosophical Problem   1
   1.2 The Imagination in Hume's *Treatise*   5
       1.2.1 The Works of the Imagination   5
       1.2.2 Hume's Problem: Cognitive Gaps   7
       1.2.3 Imagination and Inference   9
   1.3 Imagination, Naturalism, and Scepticism   10
       1.3.1 Imagination and the Science of Human Nature   10
       1.3.2 A New Foundation of Science   13
       1.3.3 Scepticism   14
   1.4 The Scope of the Discussion   16
   1.5 Summary   17

PART I. THE ELEMENTS OF THIS PHILOSOPHY

2. The First Principle   21
   2.1 Kinds of Perceptions   21
       2.1.1 Phenomenology   25
       2.1.2 Elements   26
   2.2 Two Viewpoints and Hume's Ontology of Perceptions   28
       2.2.1 Two Viewpoints   28
       2.2.2 Perceptions as Mental Existents   32
       2.2.3 Impressions as Objects, Objects as Impressions   36
       2.2.4 Hume's Ontological Pluralism   39
       2.2.5 Equivalence   41
   2.3 The First Principle   43
       2.3.1 Content   43
       2.3.2 Point and Status   45
   2.4 Existence and Reference   50
       2.4.1 Representing Existence   50
       2.4.2 Manners of Conception   52
       2.4.3 Representation, Reference, and Reality   56
   2.5 Summary   61

3. Our Second Principle   63
   3.1 The Natural Limits of Object Representation   63
       3.1.1 Enter Imagination: The Missing Shade of Blue   63

	3.1.2 Cognitive Gaps and the Natural Mind	67
	3.1.3 Cognitive Gaps: A Taxonomy	70
	3.1.4 Representational Naturalism, Scepticism, and the Imagination	72
3.2	The Second Principle	75
	3.2.1 The Liberty of the Imagination	75
	3.2.2 Perfect Ideas	78
	3.2.3 Principles of Association and Transitions of Ideas	79
3.3	The Nature of Hume's Imagination	84
	3.3.1 The Structural Principle: 'In the larger or more limited sense'	85
	3.3.2 Natural and Philosophical Relations	91
	3.3.3 Cognitive Gaps and the Structural Principle	93
3.4	Inferentialist Naturalism	96
	3.4.1 Non-Mixture	96
	3.4.2 Inference and the Structural Principle	99
	3.4.3 Transitions and Conceptions: The Important Footnote	104
3.5	Summary	108

PART II. THE INTELLECTUAL WORLD OF IDEAS

4. As if It Were Universal		113
4.1 Concerning Abstract or General Ideas		113
	4.1.1 A Cognitive Gap: Representational Naturalism and Generality	113
	4.1.2 Hume's Abstraction: Resemblance, Naming, Custom	117
	4.1.2.1 Resemblance	119
	4.1.2.2 Naming	120
	4.1.2.3 Custom	121
	4.1.3 Generality and the Structural Principle	122
	4.1.3.1 Names–Ideas Inferences	122
	4.1.3.2 Revival of Custom	123
	4.1.3.3 Custom-revival and Generality	124
	4.1.3.4 Generality and Inference	126
	4.1.4 Application in Reasoning and Possibility of Error	128
4.2 We Accompany our Ideas with a Kind of Reflection		131
	4.2.1 Distinctions of Reason	131
	4.2.2 The Readiness, with which the Imagination Suggests Its Ideas	135
4.3 Summary		139
5. Nothing we Imagine is Absolutely Impossible		141
5.1 Whatever the Mind Clearly Conceives Includes the Idea of Possible Existence		142
	5.1.1 The Cognitive Gap of Modality	142
	5.1.2 The Established Maxim: Content and Point	145
	5.1.3 Imagination and Modality: Separability and Determination	152
5.2 Hume's Philosophy of Modality		162
	5.2.1 Metaphysical and Physical Possibility	163

		5.2.2 Absolute and Epistemic Possibility	167
		5.2.3 Humean Modalities and Sceptical Realism	171
	5.3	To Consider the Matter A Priori	176
		5.3.1 Hume's A Priori	176
		5.3.2 From Metaphysical Necessity to the A Priori	179
		5.3.3 Explaining A Priori Maxims	182
	5.4	Summary	184

PART III. A NEW SYSTEM OF REALITIES

6. A Just Inference			189
6.1	The Cognitive Gap of Causation		190
	6.1.1	Causal Reasoning and Causal Content: Inferring the Unobserved	190
	6.1.2	The Missing Idea of Cause: Necessity	194
	6.1.3	From Necessity to Inference	196
	6.1.4	From Inference to Experience	201
	6.1.5	From Experience to the Imagination	204
6.2	The Nature of that Inference		207
	6.2.1	Causation as a Natural Relation	208
	6.2.2	Customary Transitions	210
	6.2.3	Causal Ideas	217
6.3	Summary		221

7. That Intelligible Quality			223
7.1	The Missing Idea of Necessary Connexion		223
7.2	Imagination and the Necessity of Causes		227
	7.2.1	From Causal Inference to Necessary Connexion	227
	7.2.2	From Necessary Connexion to the Imagination	229
		7.2.2.1 The Inferential Core	229
		7.2.2.2 The Impression of Determination	233
		7.2.2.3 Causal Necessity and the Imagination	234
	7.2.3	Transitions and Conceptions: Spreading in the Mind, Spreading on the Objects	235
		7.2.3.1 Conceiving Connexions	235
		7.2.3.2 Spreading in the Mind	237
		7.2.3.3 Spreading on External Objects	239
7.3	Hume's Philosophy of Causation		243
	7.3.1	The Two Definitions: Structure, Rationale, and Implications	243
		7.3.1.1 The Complexity of Causal Content	243
		7.3.1.2 Inferentialism and the Two Definitions	244
		7.3.1.3 The Ontology of Causation	248
	7.3.2	True Meaning and Wrong Application	252
7.4	Summary		259

PART IV. AN EXTERNAL AND INTERNAL WORLD

8. The Ideas which are Most Essential to Geometry — 263
   - 8.1 Representing Space and Time — 264
     - 8.1.1 Manners of Disposition of Visible and Tangible Objects — 264
     - 8.1.2 Finite Divisibility and Adequate Representation — 269
   - 8.2 Imagining Space and Time — 274
     - 8.2.1 An Abstract Idea of Time and Space — 275
     - 8.2.2 The Definitions and Demonstrations of Geometry — 275
       - 8.2.2.1 The Cognitive Gap of Geometrical Equality — 276
       - 8.2.2.2 Closing the Gap: Geometrical Equality — 278
       - 8.2.2.3 The Illusion of Perfect Equality — 282
     - 8.2.3 A Vacuum or Pure Extension — 284
       - 8.2.3.1 The Missing Idea of a Vacuum — 285
       - 8.2.3.2 We Falsely Imagine We Can Form such an Idea — 291
       - 8.2.3.3 A Vacuum is Asserted — 294
   - 8.3 Summary — 296

9. The World as Something Real and Durable — 299
   - 9.1 The Missing Idea of Body — 299
     - 9.1.1 The Principle Concerning the Existence of Body — 299
     - 9.1.2 The Cognitive Gap of External Existence — 303
       - 9.1.2.1 The Senses — 303
       - 9.1.2.2 Reason — 305
     - 9.1.3 Refining the Individuation of the Gap — 306
   - 9.2 Imagining a Real and Durable World: Coherence and Spreading — 308
     - 9.2.1 'Spreading out in my mind the whole sea and continent' — 309
     - 9.2.2 The Hysteresis of the Imagination — 312
     - 9.2.3 'A principle too weak to support so vast an edifice' — 314
   - 9.3 Imagining a Real and Durable World: Constancy and Identity — 316
     - 9.3.1 The Cognitive Gap of Perfect Identity — 317
     - 9.3.2 The Cognitive Gap of Imperfect Identity — 322
     - 9.3.3 From Imperfect Identity to Continued and Distinct Existence — 325
       - 9.3.3.1 The Opposition of Two Principles — 325
       - 9.3.3.2 How to Reconcile Such Opposite Opinions — 326
   - 9.4 The External World: Perceptions, Bodies, Qualities — 328
     - 9.4.1 Perceptions without the Mind, Objects within the Mind — 329
     - 9.4.2 Bodies Existing with the Qualities of Impressions — 334
   - 9.5 Scepticism with Regard to the Senses — 338
     - 9.5.1 The Vulgar and the Philosophical Belief — 339
     - 9.5.2 The Sceptical Malady and Hume's Realism — 342
   - 9.6 Summary — 347

10. A Mind or Thinking Person — 350
    - 10.1 The Missing Ideas of Soul and Self — 351
      - 10.1.1 The Soul as Substance — 351
      - 10.1.2 Selfless Perceptions — 353

10.2	Imagining the Self and Personal Identity	356
	10.2.1	Identity of Successive Perceptions	356
	10.2.2	The True Idea of the Human Mind	360
	10.2.3	The Same Thinking Person	366
10.3	Hume's Recantation	370
	10.3.1	The Labyrinth	370
	10.3.2	United in our Thought or Consciousness	374
	10.3.3	A Difficulty too Hard for my Understanding	381
10.4	Summary	384

PART V. THE IMAGINATION OR UNDERSTANDING, CALL IT WHICH YOU PLEASE

11.	One of the Greatest Mysteries of Philosophy	389
11.1	Belief as Attitude: Assent	389
	11.1.1 The Cognitive Gap of Assent	389
	11.1.2 Assent, Sensible Representation, and the A Priori	394
	11.1.3 Imagination, Probability, and Assent	396
11.2	Belief as a Mental State	400
	11.2.1 The Missing State of Belief	400
	11.2.2 Imagination, Belief, and Doxastic Deliberation	403
11.3	Scepticism and the Imagination	409
	11.3.1 Hume's Sceptical Concerns: Sources and Varieties	410
	11.3.2 Reflection, Imagination, and the Possibility of Belief	413
	11.3.3 The Dangerous Dilemma	422
11.4	Summary	426

12.	The Ultimate Judge of All Systems of Philosophy	429
12.1	The General and More Established Properties of the Imagination	430
	12.1.1 An Unjust Blame	431
	12.1.2 The First Question: 'Principles, which, however common, are neither universal nor unavoidable in human nature'	433
	12.1.3 Rules of Judgement	435
12.2	Reasonable Foundations of Belief	437
	12.2.1 The Test of the Most Critical Examination	437
	12.2.2 The Truth and Fidelity of our Faculties	440
	12.2.3 Truth, Imagination, and Belief	443
	12.2.4 The Improvement of the Human Mind	447
12.3	Love of Truth	450
	12.3.1 The Second Question: 'In the same sense, that a malady is said to be natural'	450
	12.3.2 The Cognitive Gap of Value and Hume's Naturalistic Sentimentalism	452
	12.3.3 The Satisfaction We Derive from the Discovery of Truth	453

  12.4   Oblig'd by Our Reason   459
    12.4.1   The First Source of All Our Enquiries   459
    12.4.2   The Title of Reason   462
  12.5   Summary   467

Appendix: Principles of Hume's Theory of the Imagination   471
Bibliography   475
Analytical Index   487
Index of Names   492

Preface and Acknowledgements

In this book, I aim to propose a new and unitary interpretation of the nature, structure, functions, and systematic importance of the imagination in Book 1: *Of the understanding*, of Hume's *Treatise of Human Nature*. The interpretation I propose has deeply revisionary implications for Hume's philosophy of mind, as well as for his naturalism, epistemology, and stance to scepticism. My principal claim is that we can best, and perhaps only understand Hume's imagination as a mental natural kind if we consider it as the source of a distinctive and necessary sort of mental contents; as the source of new original ideas, like those of cause, body, or self. A basic insight of Hume's philosophy in Book 1 of the *Treatise* is that we can be in cognitive contact with objects, their properties, and their relations only sensibly; that we can only represent sensible objects. Impressions of sensation or objects of sense are all we can be acquainted with. Hume complements this radically empiricist commitment with another insight (one which drew Kant's attention): the ideas and cognitions issuing from object representation fail to explain and to support most of our best-established, ordinary and philosophical cognitive practices.

This combination of claims brings Hume's philosophy to the verge of paradox. The restriction of object representation to sensibility (impressions of sensation, objects of sense) is both an expression and a condition of the program of naturalization of mind and cognition pursued in the *Treatise*. This means that the limits Hume detects in object representation are natural to it, are an aspect of our cognitive nature. Therefore, our ordinary and philosophical practices, including the kind of reflection that underlies the experimental method of reasoning and Hume's naturalism, seem to involve a cognitive impossibility. This sort of paradox could and did motivate either resorting to some special sort of object representation, by intellectual ideas (this is how Hume conceives of rationalist philosophies), or giving up any claim to complex, distinctively human cognition (scepticism). For Hume, this would be the unpalatable choice between a false reason (rationalism) and no reason at all (scepticism). Hume's way out of this dilemma is not to drop naturalism, or to embrace scepticism. It is to drop the identification of content and cognition with object representation. We can preserve naturalism (object representation is only sensible) without threat of scepticism (conceptual thought and reasoning are possible) by complementing sensible representation with a different, equally natural, but non-representational kind of cognitive content. Contents that are missing from sensible representation and seem to be impossible or spurious can and do perform their cognitive roles without having to represent objects at all. This is the place and function of the imagination in human nature. Hume's imagination is our natural faculty of inference and the source of a distinctive kind of ideas, which allow us to overstep the limits of our sensible representation of objects consistently with naturalism. (A reading along similar lines could perhaps be given of the place and function of sentiments in Hume's morals.)

The book reconstructs how Hume's naturalist and inferentialist theory of the imagination develops this fundamental insight. Its five parts deal with the dualism of representation and inference; the inferential character and the cognitive structure of the imagination; the explanation of generality and modality; the production of causal ideas; the production of spatial and temporal ideas and of the distinction of an external world of bodies and an internal one of selves; and the replacement of the understanding with imagination in the analysis of cognition and in epistemology. In this way, I aim to remedy to a sort of blind spot in Hume scholarship, because precisely the complexity and the apparent lack of unity of Hume's imagination seem to be responsible for a relative lack of interpretive attention to this topic. One somewhat surprising conclusion I come to draw is that, at the core of Hume's philosophy, we find a partial but significant form of inferentialism about mental content. Rather than as a card-carrying representationalist, as he is often considered, we should look at Hume as an early, but important and committed inferentialist. This, at least, if the role of imagination in his philosophy is well understood. In this connection, the study of Hume's theory of the imagination can also contribute to the current, lively philosophical debate on imagination. Hume's philosophy can give suggestions about how to treat imagination as a mental natural kind, despite its cognitive complexity and the variety of its roles.

Work on this book has taken quite a stretch of my life. All along these years, I have presented my views about Hume's imagination and related topics at International Hume Conferences in Canberra, Rome, Las Vegas, and Budapest; at Hume conferences in Rome, Assos, Belo Horizonte, and at the Oxford Hume Forum (online); at the Modern Philosophy Conference at New York University and at the NY/NJ Modern Philosophy Seminar; and at talks at the University of Pittsburgh; University of Florida (Gainsville); University of Reading; Union College (Schenectady); University of Wisconsin (Milwaukee); and at the University of Toronto. All along these years, I profited from helpful discussions with many people about Hume's philosophy, naturalism and normativity, and mental representation. I here remember D. Ainslie, A. Baier, H. Beebee, A. Bilgrami, J. Biro, S. Blackburn, M. Boehm, R. Brandom, E. Chavez-Arizo, R. Cohon, J. Cottrell, S. Darwall, P. Donatelli, M. Frasca-Spada, C. Fricke, D. Gauthier, A. Gibbard, L. Greco, P. Kail, E. Lecaldano, L. Loeb, B. Longuenesse, S. Marchetti, E. Mazza, J. McDowell, J. McIntyre, P. Millican, D. Norton, O. Oymen, S. Pollo, H. Price, E. Radcliffe, P. Railton, J. Richardson, C. Rovane, A. Schmitter, D. Tamas, J. Taylor,

A. Vaccari, A. Varzi, and two Readers for OUP. Peter Momtchiloff, from OUP, has taken special care of my project. My philosopher friends, Julia Annas and David Owen, have had an important part in this effort. David was perhaps the first philosopher with whom I discussed seriously about Hume's views on knowledge and reason. Together with Julia, they have so many times provided a wonderful environment for my study and writing. Finally, I have the greatest debt with Don Garrett, whose friendly criticism, suggestions, and encouragement have been a constant and indispensable support for my work.

A Note on References

In the text, I refer to passages in the main text of Hume's *Treatise* by Book, Part, Section, and Paragraph. For instance, the form: '1.3.6.5' refers to Book 1, Part 3, Section 6, and Paragraph 5 of the *Treatise*. I refer to passages in the *Introduction* and the *Appendix* of the *Treatise* in the form: '*Introduction*' and '*Appendix*', followed by paragraph number; and to passages in the *Abstract*, with '*Abstract*' and paragraph number. All quotations are from: D. Hume, *A Treatise of Human Nature*, D.F. Norton and M. J. Norton, eds., 2 Volumes, Clarendon Press, Oxford 2007 (also includes: *An Abstract of A Book, A Letter from a Gentleman*). I refer to my own text by chapter, section, and subsection. For instance, the form: '§ 1.2.2', refers to Chapter 1, Section 2, and Subsection 2 of this book.

1
Introduction: A Magical Faculty

[A] kind of magical faculty in the soul, which, tho' it be always most perfect in the greatest geniuses, and is properly what we call a genius, is however inexplicable by the utmost efforts of human understanding.
(1.1.7.15)

1.1 An Interpretive Blind Spot and a Philosophical Problem

No text of modern philosophy comes close to Hume's *Treatise of Human Nature*, especially its Book 1: *Of the understanding*, in the variety, complexity, and systematic importance of the roles it gives to the imagination. Because of our cognitive nature, we can have ideas with general and modal contents only if they are conceived, transposed, and changed by the imagination. All sorts of reasoning, both a priori and a posteriori, compare ideas conceived by the imagination and depend on its primitive transitions. In this way, what might appear as the 'whole intellectual world of ideas', open to our understanding and intellectual agency, is nothing but the result of how 'the imagination suggests its ideas, and presents them at the very instant, in which they become necessary or useful' (1.1.7.15). It is the imagination that puts in place the 'foundation of mathematics' (1.4.2.2). It 'peoples the world', making us 'acquainted with such existences, as by their removal in time and place, lie beyond the reach of the senses and memory' (1.3.9.4). This makes it possible for us to have a view of the world as a connected system of continuedly and independently existing objects; it forms all the 'ties of our thoughts' and is '*to us* cement of the universe' (*Abstract* 35). The transitions of the imagination are the source of our worldview. 'I paint the universe in my imagination, and fix my attention on any part of it I please' (1.3.9.4). Even the distinction between the external world of bodies and the internal world of our self or mind comes from the imagination (1.4.7.3). This is the sense in which Hume talks of the 'empire of the imagination', of its 'great authority over our ideas' (*Abstract* 35), claiming that on its principles 'all the operations of the mind must, in a great measure, depend' (*Abstract* 35). It is no surprise, then, that by the simplest word counting and apart from the ubiquitous 'impression' and 'idea', 'imagination' and related words are the theoretically laden lexical area with most occurrences in Book 1 of the *Treatise*.[1]

It is thus only fair to say that the imagination, in Book 1 of the *Treatise*, jumps to the eye. But if we consider Hume scholarship, we find a very different situation. The role, importance, and nature of the imagination in Hume's philosophy has long been an interpretive blind spot. Two classic studies, Kemp Smith's *The Philosophy of David Hume* (1941) and Barry Stroud's *Hume* (1977), fail to give proportionate space and attention to the imagination. Kemp Smith's well-known individuation, in the philosophy of Hume's *Treatise*, of Hutchesonian and Newtonian strands, the first biological in character, with an insistence on instincts, passions, emotions, and sentiments, the second mechanistic, with perceptions treated as simples and association as the sole mechanism, confines the imagination to the latter one.[2] Insofar as the imagination plays any role in Kemp Smith's interpretation, it is almost exclusively a negative one: the hinge on which Hume's failed explanatory programme in terms of association of ideas turns.[3] Kemp Smith contrasts the imagination with the important category of natural beliefs, which he regards as one of Hume's achievements. He recognizes that natural (irresistible, causally determined, justification-independent) beliefs have their grounds in the imagination; but he holds that the phenomenon of natural belief is more important and less hypothetical than such explanation.[4] Hume's all-things-considered position should have been what he ended up with in the first *Enquiry*: dropping the search for associative mechanisms underlying, say, the natural belief in the external world; and treating such belief 'as being, like the moral sentiments, in itself an ultimate'.[5] The importance of the imagination in Hume's philosophy is no greater than that of a 'corollary to his early theory of belief'.[6]

With Stroud we take a huge step forward. Stroud has a much more balanced understanding of the role of the imagination in Hume's philosophy. Still, rather than discussing it thematically, on a par with the theory of ideas and with passions and moral sentiments, Stroud only addresses imagination in passing. In his conclusive, important reflections on Hume's naturalism, Stroud concentrates his criticisms on the explanatory shortcomings of the imagination. The 'act of

---

[1] 'Imagination' and related words like 'fancy', 'imagine', 'imagining', 'imaginary', 'fiction', 'feign', 'feigning', and 'fictitious' sum up to 374 occurrences in Book 1. To get a sense of how much this is, consider that 'belief' and related verbal forms have 203 occurrences; 'sensation', 'sensations', and 'senses', 216; 'reason', as name and as a verb, 211; and 'feeling', 46. Only if we consider 'impression'/'impressions' (respectively, 224 and 191 occurrences) and, of course, 'idea'/'ideas' (respectively, 655 and 439) do we find philosophically important words with more occurrences.
[2] N. Kemp Smith, *The Philosophy of David Hume* (1941), Palgrave Macmillan, New York 2005, 550.
[3] Kemp Smith, *Philosophy of Hume*, 533, 535.
[4] Kemp Smith, *Philosophy of Hume*, 409, 449, 493.
[5] Kemp Smith, *Philosophy of Hume*, 535.
[6] Kemp Smith, *Philosophy of Hume*, 462-3.

feigning the continued existence of bodies' fails to add anything significant to the coherence and constancy of our experience and thus 'does not seem to make any difference to any of our thoughts'.[7] In the same vein, Stroud denies that Hume has any 'satisfactory account' of the complex modal implications of causal inference and causal cognition.[8] His assessment culminates in reproaching Hume, because of his 'theory of ideas', for failing to understand that having an idea is 'a matter of having a certain ability, capacity or competence'.[9] Which is precisely what I would say is the distinctive cognitive contribution of Hume's imagination. There is some similarity between Stroud's and Kemp Smith's overall assessments of Hume's imagination. Both point to deep confusions, even inconsistencies, in Hume's conception of it. Stroud in particular individuates a 'curious tension' between Hume's view of the imagination 'as the home of the "sensitive" or "passionate" rather than the "cogitative", part of our nature' and the 'very strong "intellectual" or "cognitive" flavour' (particularly in the account of the idea of body) he imparts to it.[10] One is then left wondering what sense to make of Hume's obstinate, almost perverse concern with the imagination.

Much has changed in Hume scholarship since 1941, even since 1977, also in connection with Hume's theory of the imagination. In a classical work from 1983, J. P. Wright, in antithesis to Kemp Smith and Stroud, points out that association and imagination, rather than feeling or the passions, should be given pride of place in interpreting Hume.[11] And recent and very recent scholarship has done and is doing important work to bring into view the pervasive and important explanatory roles of Hume's imagination, as well as the philosophical problems they raise. To mention only a few names, I have in mind the work of scholars like Garrett, Owen, Loeb, Rocknak, Cottrell, Ainslie, and Costelloe.[12] However, I think that there is much interpretive and philosophical work still to be done in this area. Because, as Kemp Smith and Stroud witness, careful and intelligent readers may conclude that Hume's imagination is beset with confusions, tensions, even inconsistencies. That in Hume's philosophy the imagination is like a

---

[7] B. Stroud, *Hume*, Routledge, London 1977, 235.   [8] Stroud, *Hume*, 235.
[9] Stroud, *Hume*, 232.   [10] Stroud, *Hume*, 108.
[11] J. P. Wright, *The Sceptical Realism of David Hume*, Minnesota University Press, Minneapolis 1983, 209–10.
[12] D. Garrett, *Cognition and Commitment in Hume's Philosophy*, Oxford University Press, New York 1997; D. Garrett, *Hume*, Routledge, Oxford/New York 2015; D. Owen, *Hume's Reason*, Oxford University Press, New York 1999; L. Loeb, *Stability and Justification in Hume's Treatise*, Oxford University Press, New York 2002; S. Rocknak, *Imagined Causes: Hume's Conception of Objects*, Springer, Dordrecht/New York 2013; J. Cottrell, 'Hume: Imagination', in Internet Encyclopedia of Philosophy http://www.iep.utm.edu/hume-ima/; J. Cottrell, 'A Puzzle about Fictions in Hume's *Treatise*', forthcoming; D. Ainslie, *Hume's True Skepticism*, Oxford University Press, New York 2015; T. M. Costelloe, *The Imagination in Hume's Philosophy*, Edinburgh University Press, Edinburgh 2018. Before this recent surge, the one monograph dedicated to Hume's imagination was J. Wilbanks, *Hume's Theory of the Imagination*, Nijoff, The Hague 1968.

wastepaper basket, where all sorts of otherwise unaccounted for phenomena find some accommodation. A magical faculty in the worst sense of practical magic, without true systematic role and conceptual unity.

I think that this interpretive problem is still in many ways open. Interestingly, concern about the unity and the functions of the imagination has emerged also in contemporary philosophical discussion. The last two decades have witnessed a resurgence or, more exactly, a surge of philosophical interest in the imagination. This, however, has been accompanied with reservations about whether there is any significant common factor, any sort of unity of kind underlying the different applications of the concept (or name?) of the imagination. So, for instance, in the entry on imagination for the *Stanford Encyclopedia of Philosophy*, we find the remark that 'There is a general consensus among those who work on the topic that the term "*imagination*" is used too broadly to permit simple taxonomy.' Peter Strawson is also quoted to this effect.

> The uses, and applications, of the terms 'image', 'imagine', 'imagination', and so forth make up a very diverse and scattered family. Even this image of a family seems too definite. It would be a matter of more than difficulty to identify and list the family's members, let alone their relations of parenthood and cousinhood.[13]

This diversity or even confusion of uses seems to unveil an irreducible and hardly manageable multiplicity in the concept of imagination. In a recent article, Amy Kind has argued that it is not an accidental matter, or an expression of the different aims philosophers and cognitive scientists have in their research, that the imagination proves to be so recalcitrant to a unitary treatment. The heterogeneity of the imagination, as she points out, is determined by deep, possibly unavoidable tensions among its explanatory roles (engagement with fiction, pretence, mindreading, and modal cognition) and the demands they make on its features (for instance, whether supposing is a variety of imagining; whether and how imagining has motivational import).[14] This is the philosophical problem with the imagination: whether, to what extent, and in what sense it has theoretical unity and marks a cognitive and perhaps an epistemic kind. Reflection on Hume's theory of imagination may perhaps allow us to make progress with this problem.

---

[13] See http://plato.stanford.edu/entries/imagination/ (authored by Shen-yi Liao and Tamar Gendler). Strawson's quotation is from P. Strawson, 'Imagination and Perception', in *Experience and Theory*, L. Foster and J. W. Swanson (eds.), University of Massachusetts Press (Amherst) (31–54), 31.

[14] A. Kind, 'The Heterogeneity of Imagination', in *Erkenntniss*, 2013, 78 (14–159).

1.2 The Imagination in Hume's *Treatise*

There are thus pressing interpretive and philosophical reasons for addressing in a systematic way Hume's imagination. In fact, the theory of the imagination is in many respects the key to understanding Hume's philosophy in the *Treatise*.

1.2.1 The Works of the Imagination

At all the important steps of the analyses and arguments of Book 1, Hume refers to ideas and capacities which are deployed in our cognitive practices but cannot be explained with sense experience or a priori, but only with the imagination. To get a sense of the cognitive work of Hume's imagination, it may be convenient to have them present at a glance.

Perfect Ideas: Imagination can detach all ideas from the context of their first occurrence in sense experience; because of this capacity, it can separate all its ideas (1.1.3.1)

Association: The imagination combines the perfect ideas it has separated, forming whatever complex contents it pleases. It proceeds according to 'universal principles', so as to put in place the ideas that are the 'common subjects of our thoughts and reasoning' (1.1.4.1)

Generality: Imagination explains how general words get their meanings and how particular ideas are applied 'beyond their nature', allowing us to reason to general conclusions. This also explains 'distinctions of reason', aspectual thoughts, as well as the intentionality of thinking (1.1.7.7)

Modality: Imagination allows thinking of the same objects as existing in different situations and with different properties from the ones actually given in experience. This is also the root of a priori, demonstrative reasoning (1.2.4.11)

Space and Time: The ideas of space and time as general frames or structures of our experience, possibly existing without being occupied by things or events, are owing to the imagination (1.2.5.29)

Geometric Equality: The imagination explains the idea of a standard of equality of size on which we rely in geometry. Imagination in general produces the 'ideas which are most essential to geometry' (1.2.4.24)

Inference to Unobserved Objects: Only the imagination explains how from the present experience of an object we can conclude to the past or future existence of another one (1.3.2.2)

Uniformity of Nature: The 'principle' that '*the course of nature continues always uniformly the same*' is owing to imagination, not to sense, memory, or reason (1.3.6.11)

Belief: The imagination, in particular its power to enliven ideas, puts in place the contents and the attitudes that constitute cognition of matters of fact neither perceived nor remembered, but only inferred (1.3.8.7)

Causation: The idea of cause issues from a complex response of the imagination to repeated patterns of observed objects. This also explains the belief in the necessity of a cause for any beginning of existence (1.3.7.14–15)

Doxastic Deliberation: We can get to causal conclusions by reflective causal reasoning, by comparing causal ideas, and by applying rules of causal judgment, because of the contents made available by the imagination and in the cognitive context it defines (1.3.8.14)

Degrees of Probability: With the 'fancy', by conveying and distributing assent to different ideas, we come to the idea of the likelihood of events and of its degrees (1.3.12.22)

Causal Necessity: The 'new original idea' of causal necessity derives from the multiplicity of observed successions, only by way of their effects on the imagination and on its transitions (1.3.14.20)

Powers: The natural 'biass' to assume that causation consists in powers located in bodies depends on imagination's spreading internal impressions on external objects (1.3.14.25)

General Rules: The general rules by which we ought to judge of causes and effects are formed by the imagination (1.3.15.11)

Belief-Revision: We can effectively reflect on and correct beliefs based on reasoning, without any threat of regress, because of the embedding of this practice in the imagination (1.4.1.10)

External Existence: Our natural, unshakeable belief of a real and durable world is produced neither by the senses nor by reason, but by the imagination (1.4.2.14)

Identity: The principle of the individuation and identity of objects is possible because the imagination, in relation to the idea of time, can occupy different viewpoints on objects taken as unchanging (1.4.2.29)

Epistemic Evaluation: Functional and causal differences between principles of the imagination fix the reference of our distinctions between regular and irregular patterns of reasoning, all equally grounded in the imagination; imagination is the 'ultimate judge of all systems of philosophy' (1.4.4.1)

Self: We have no impression and idea of the self as what our several perceptions inhere to; but we have a natural propensity to imagine our internal simplicity and identity (1.4.6.16)

In a nutshell, the explanation of conceptual thinking, of a priori and a posteriori reasoning, of the structures of the external and internal world, the method of moral and natural philosophy, the objects and criteria of epistemic evaluation all ultimately depend on the properties and activities of the imagination.

1.2.2 Hume's Problem: Cognitive Gaps

The list of the works of imagination is certainly impressive. But it may look like a mixed bag. It spans across *modes of thinking* (context-independence, generality, modality), *cognitive capacities* (reasoning, doxastic deliberation and belief-revision, epistemic evaluation), *cognitive structures* (space and time, uniformity of nature, causal connections, powers, external existence, identity, self), and *mental states* (belief). However, I think that Hume's imagination harbours an important, unifying theoretical pattern, which hinges on a complex view of our acquaintance with objects, of its limits, and of the nature of mental activity.

As it emerges from the list, the imagination makes its entrance and operates where sense experience and the understanding or reason cannot explain ideas and cognitive capacities deployed in our ordinary and philosophical cognitive practices.[15] Furthermore, and most importantly, in all the cases I have listed, no matter how different the ones from the others, it is not by accident but a matter of natural necessity if sense experience or the understanding fail to provide us with such ideas and capacities. The contents of the relevant ideas and the corresponding capacities cannot be reduced to objects and properties; therefore they cannot in principle be explained with sense experience or intellectual insight. These cognitive gaps are unavoidable and irreparable; they are marks of human cognitive nature.

Hume's response to the limits of our natural representation or apprehension of objects is neither to explain away the relevant ideas nor to resort to some non-naturalistic cognitive faculty. There is no hint, in Hume, of any devaluation of the sensible sources of content; no hint of the rationalist thesis that objects are given in sensation only in a confused and indistinct manner. The input of sense experience forms a primitive, irreducible, and perfectly sound layer of the natural mind. Hume, rather, accurately individuates the ways in which ideas and cognitions issuing from sense experience or available a priori fail to match our cognitive practices and our worldview. Against this background, he advances alternative explanations of the missing elements by resorting to a complex of mental operations which he (quite appropriately, I would say) refers back to the faculty of imagination. *The primary role of Hume's imagination is to fill the cognitive gaps left open by ideas representing sensible objects or by the understanding with the naturalistic, empirically explainable production of new ideas and of cognitive changes.* In Hume's philosophy, the imagination has a unitary, positive, and constructive

---

[15] On the gap-filling function of Hume's imagination see Wilbanks, *Hume's Theory of the Imagination*, 154–5.

theoretical role: integrating our sensible representations of objects and our understanding with contents of new kinds and, in this way, explaining and vindicating (many of) our ordinary and philosophical cognitive practices.

In this connection, I think that Kant's interpretation of the fundamental inspiration of Hume's philosophy (whose misunderstanding by the common sense school he bitterly complains about in the *Prolegomena*) is deep and insightful.

> Among philosophers, David Hume came nearest to envisaging this problem ['How are *a priori* synthetic judgments possible?'], but still was very far from conceiving it with sufficient definiteness and universality. He occupied himself exclusively with the synthetic proposition regarding the connection of an effect with its cause (*principium causalitatis*), and he believed himself to have shown that such an a priori proposition is entirely impossible. If we accept his conclusion, then all that we call metaphysics is a mere delusion whereby we fancy ourselves to have rational insight into what, in actual fact, is borrowed solely from experience, and under the influence of custom has taken the illusory semblance of necessity.[16]

Hume came nearest to recognizing the problem of the synthetic a priori, because he realized, at least with reference to causality, that the necessity of the causal nexus excluded that causal thought and cognition had their sources either in sensibility or in simple concepts.[17] Kant thus agrees with Hume that there is a necessary cognitive gap corresponding to causal content and cognition and that this raises a special problem of constitutive explanation (a how-possible? problem). And he correctly identifies the imagination as Hume's response to this newly discovered, systematic problem, even though he rejects such response as mistaking 'subjective necessity (i.e., habit) for an objective necessity (from insight)'.[18]

> Since [Hume] could not explain how it can be possible that the understanding must think concepts, which are not in themselves connected in the understanding, as being necessarily connected in the object [...], he was constrained to derive them from experience, namely, from a subjective necessity (that is, from *custom*), which arises from repeated association in experience.[19]

---

[16] I. Kant, *Critique of Pure Reason*, Palgrave, London 2003, 55 (in 'Introduction', 6: 'The general problem of pure reason'). See also 127 (in 'Transcendental Deduction', 14: 'Transition to the transcendental deduction of the categories'). See, for a careful and informative account of Kant's reading and interpretation of Hume's philosophy, A. Anderson, *Kant, Hume, and the Interruption of Dogmatic Slumber*, Oxford University Press, New York 2020, 8–9, 87–89, 145–60.

[17] See I. Kant, *Prolegomena to any Future Metaphysics*, Cambridge University Press, Cambridge 2004, 7 (in 'Preface'): 'He indisputably proved that it is wholly impossible for reason to think such a connection *a priori* and from concepts, because this connection contains necessity; and it is simply not to be seen how it could be, that because something is, something else necessarily must also be.'

[18] Kant, *Prolegomena*, 7.   [19] Kant, *Critique of Pure Reason*, 127.

1.2.3 Imagination and Inference

Hume makes very strong claims about the role of the imagination in the production of ideas and in cognitive change. It is thus important to take a first look at what allows Hume's imagination to perform such a role. The first, crucial point is that he indissolubly connects the function of filling the gaps of object representation with the inferential character of the activity of the imagination. Representation of objects is confined, for human nature, to sense experience and to its storage in memory. (Hume dismisses the rationalist view of reason as a priori object-representing faculty.) The imagination can overcome the necessary, natural limits of object representation precisely because, as a cognitive faculty of human nature, it is *inferential* and *not object representing*. Because of this, it is not under the constraints of our natural representation of objects.[20] It can widen and change the scope and the patterns of our thinking and cognition because it consists in transitions of ideas and not in acquaintance with objects.

The second point (which I can only mention here) is the complex internal structure of Hume's imagination. It operates inferentially in the guise of implicit or explicit, immediate or reflective comparisons of available ideas, based on their contents and relations. In this guise, the imagination realizes our general capacities for reasoning. But its inferential character also consists in immediate mental transitions, which change ideas by their concurrence with its own primitive dispositions and put in place contents that would otherwise be missing and that we compare in reasoning. The dual character of Hume's imagination and its unity as a faculty will be examined in due course, when we come to discuss what I call the Structural Principle. What is important, right now, is that the production of new kinds of ideas and cognitive capacities is realized by the imagination in the different ways or levels at which it engages in *transitions among ideas*, based on empirically ascertainable, non-representational inferential principles. It is in connection with these transitions, or considered dynamically, that the principles of association and association itself are cognitively important and make for a radical change in what ideas and cognitions are available to our minds.

The foundation of Hume's philosophy in Book 1 of the *Treatise* is thus the natural distinction of kind between object-representing contents, ideas, and faculties (sense and memory) and inferential ones (imagination). And the distinction, within this latter, between inferences grounded on the contents and relations of ideas, with the character of reasoning, and mental transitions caused by the interaction of ideas with its non-representational principles. Nothing short of this conceptual pattern seems up to explaining how natural cognitive gaps can be

---

[20] For an interpretation of Hume's views on mental content very close to the one I am proposing, see K. Schafer, 'Hume's Unified Theory of Mental Representation', *European Journal of Philosophy*, 23, 4, 2015 (978–1005).

filled in a naturalistic way. Such gaps are inherent to our natural capacity of object representation. If the mind could not tap some other, radically different but equally natural source of content, there would be no remedy to such incompleteness.

It is also enormously interesting that Hume's imagination, in this way, comes in many respects close to our views of it. Four central features that contemporary philosophy and cognitive science identify as distinctive of imagination—its essential imagistic character, its proceeding in a broadly inferential way, its making available information about the world without explicitly representing it, its enacting or simulating mental states and properties—have clear counterparts in Hume. It is also widely recognized that, in these ways, imagination contributes in important and irreducible respects to our cognitive outreach and to its improvement. I will introduce and discuss these matters as we go on. But we can say that its overall function and its close connections with contemporary views retrospectively sanction Hume's identification of the imagination as 'a kind of magical faculty in the soul' (1.1.7.15).

1.3 Imagination, Naturalism, and Scepticism

Because of its central importance for Hume's philosophy overall, the theory of the imagination provides essential conceptual keys for its interpretation. I want to outline briefly how the theory of imagination is systematically significant for Hume's naturalism, his epistemological ambitions, and his stance on scepticism.

1.3.1 Imagination and the Science of Human Nature

The philosophical programme of the *Treatise* is well expressed by its full title: *A Treatise of Human Nature: Being an Attempt to Introduce the Experimental Method of Reasoning into Moral Subjects*. The 'science of MAN' (*Introduction* 4), the 'science of human nature' (*Introduction* 9), the empirical study of human nature, is the execution of this 'attempt'. We can gain a comprehensive and deep understanding of all that is relevant for philosophy only from the standpoint of human nature. ''Tis evident, that all the sciences have a relation, greater or less, to human nature; and that however wide any of them may seem to run from it, they still return back by one passage or another' (*Introduction* 4). This is because our nature includes the cognitive resources which can account for our success in all the sciences, even those with little or no relation to it ('Mathematics, Natural Philosophy, and Natural Religion', *Introduction* 4). Of course, the sciences that have human nature as their object ('Logic, Morals, Criticism, and Politics', *Introduction* 5) are also only appropriately understood from the perspective it affords. Constructing and vindicating this sort of naturalism is thus the general aim of the *Treatise*: 'Human Nature is the only science of man; and yet has been hitherto the most neglected' (1.4.7.14).

The science of human nature is, of course, empirical. 'As the science of man is the only solid foundation for the other sciences, so the only solid foundation we can give to this science itself must be laid on experience and observation' (*Introduction* 7). In fact, experimental moral philosophy, the 'application of experimental philosophy to moral subjects' by 'some late philosophers in *England*': 'Mr. *Locke*, my Lord *Shaftsbury*, Dr. *Mandeville*, Mr. *Hutchinson*, Dr. *Butler*, &c.', as Hume recalls in a footnote (*Introduction* 7 fn. 1), has followed the steps and taken up the method of experimental natural philosophy. Deferring to this tradition, Hume makes his case for a 'reformation' of moral philosophy in the spirit of natural philosophy.

> For to me it seems evident, that the essence of the mind being equally unknown to us with that of external bodies, it must be equally impossible to form any notion of its powers and qualities otherwise than from careful and exact experiments, and the observation of those particular effects, which result from its different circumstances and situations (*Introduction* 8).[21]

Against this background, the importance of the imagination for Hume's naturalism is perfectly clear. 'Logic' is the subject matter of Book 1 of the *Treatise*, the explanation of 'the principles and operations of our reasoning faculty, and the nature of our ideas' (*Introduction* 5); or, as Hume summarizes it conclusively, the full explanation of the 'nature of our judgment and understanding' (1.4.6.23). Hume's imagination is central to this explanation and crucially contributes to its naturalist and empiricist character. Restricting our attention to Book 1, the most serious threat to Hume's naturalism is the option, chosen in the Cartesian, rationalist tradition, to infer from the limits of our sensible cognition of objects the need for a different, non-sensible kind of object-representing ideas. Hume makes this point with initial reference to the ideas of mathematics, but then extends it to philosophy in general.

---

[21] Hume's experimental approach to the mind is one we are nowadays familiar with, both in philosophy and in cognitive science. Hume would subscribe to the following programmatic statement, which refers, significantly, to the imagination: 'Our suggestion is that philosophers interested in the imagination shift their methodology from the traditional paradox-and-analysis model to a more empirically-oriented phenomena-and-explanation model', J. Weinberg & A. Meskin, 'Puzzling Over the Imagination: Philosophical Problems, Architectural Solutions', in S. Nichols, ed., *The Architecture of the Imagination*, Clarendon Press, Oxford 2006 (175–202), 177.

> 'Tis usual with mathematicians, to pretend, that those ideas, which are their objects, are of so refin'd and spiritual a nature, that they fall not under the conception of the fancy, but must be comprehended by a pure and intellectual view, of which the superior faculties of the soul are alone capable. The same notion runs thro' most parts of philosophy, and is principally made use of to explain our abstract ideas, and to shew how we can form an idea of a triangle, for instance, which shall neither be an isosceles nor scalenum, nor be confin'd to any particular length and proportion of sides.   (1.3.1.7)

This important, programmatic text deserves our attention. The core of the contrast between Hume and the Cartesian tradition is not metaphysical or epistemological; rather, it is a contrast between the nature of ideas and of mental activity. Hume agrees with the rationalists (and with Kant) that our sensible acquaintance with objects does not provide us with all the ideas that support our overall cognition. It does not provide us with the conceptual contents required for cognitive rationality. But, against this background, Hume's (and Kant's) path radically diverges from that of the rationalists. These latter, admittedly in different ways, identify the source of the cognitive limits of object representation in its sensible character. The content of sense experience is confused and obscure, fundamentally because of the mediation of body and the senses. What is required is a different, clear, and distinct mode of object representation; and reason and the understanding can secure it. These faculties, which are free from the constraints of sensibility, afford the 'pure and intellectual view' and deliver the ideas 'of so refin'd and spiritual a nature' that acquaint us with the right kind of (intelligible, rational) objects for mathematical and in general a priori knowledge. By contrast, Hume (and, to some extent, Kant) understands the cognitive limits of sense and memory in terms of limitedness rather than of confusion and obscurity. Sense and memory are not the locus of obscure and confused ideas; their content is not a defective, undetermined form of what would be clear and distinct to the intellect. Sense and memory are marked by the natural limits of our primitive cognitive contact with objects; but within such limits, they are as clear and distinct as human cognition can be. The cognitive gaps that sense and memory leave open can be filled only by a separate, non-representational cognitive faculty. If sense and memory are not intrinsically flawed, the task they set is one of articulation and integration, not of extraction by the intellect of a rational core of content. This task is performed by the imagination, a perfectly natural, empirically scrutable, content-productive faculty. Of the ideas presumed to be of 'so refin'd and spiritual a nature', we should rather say that they fall 'under the conception of the fancy'. In this way, the imagination not only contributes to fully explaining the nature of our ideas and the principles of our understanding: it acts as a closure (that's all) clause in Hume's naturalistic logic.

1.3.2 A New Foundation of Science

Hume's naturalism, precisely by including the cognitive faculty of imagination, makes room for substantive epistemic ambitions. The science of man is barred access to the 'essence of the mind'. We cannot 'discover the ultimate original qualities of human nature', the 'ultimate principles of the soul' (*Introduction* 8). But this is perfectly consistent with making 'all our principles as universal as possible, by tracing up our experiments to the utmost, and explaining all the effects from the simplest and fewest causes'. And with the view that, if 'we can give no reason for our most general and most refined principles, beside our experience of their reality; which is the reason of the mere vulgar', this latter is still a 'reason' (*Introduction* 9). There cannot be reasons beyond all the facts of experience; but facts of experience count as reasons. In this respect, the susceptibility to empirical enquiry of the principles and operations of the imagination is a fundamental factor in the success of Hume's philosophical programme.

Hume's science of man pursues a 'reformation' of moral philosophy and aims to bring about 'changes' and 'improvements' in all the sciences.

> There is no question of importance, whose decision is not compriz'd in the science of man; and there is none, which can be decided with any certainty, before we become acquainted with that science. In pretending therefore to explain the principles of human nature, we in effect propose a compleat system of the sciences, built on a foundation almost entirely new, and the only one upon which they can stand with any security   (*Introduction* 6)

The science of human nature is thus in the service of a foundational programme.[22] It can set up and empower the 'tribunal of human reason' (*Introduction* 1). Even in the sceptical mood of the *Conclusion* of Book 1, Hume sounds a final note of epistemic confidence. The expectations of the *Introduction* to the *Treatise* are recalled and essentially confirmed. 'We might hope to establish a system or set of opinions, which if not true (for that, perhaps, is too much to be hop'd for) might at least be satisfactory to the human mind, and might stand the test of the most critical examination' (1.4.7.14). Such hope is grounded on the same considerations of historical progress that loom large in the *Introduction* (and one should keep in mind that the *Introduction* might well have been written last).

> Two thousand years with such long interruptions, and under such mighty discouragements are a small space of time to give any tolerable perfection to the

---

[22] See M. Boehm, 'Hume's Foundational Project in the *Treatise*', *European Journal of Philosophy*, 24, 2016 (55–77). 'Advocating and pursuing inductive, causal science' is rightly recognized by P. Millican as one of the fundamental aims of Hume's philosophy. See P. Millican, 'Hume, Causal Realism, and Causal Science', *Mind*, 118, 2009 (647–712), 701–7.

sciences; and perhaps we are still in too early an age of the world to discover any principles, which will bear the examination of the latest posterity. (1.4.7.14)

In the *Conclusion* of Book 1, Hume's hope is to 'contribute a little to the advancement of knowledge' (1.4.7.14); just as in the *Introduction* his aim is to bring remedy to the 'present imperfect condition of the sciences' (*Introduction* 2). The examination of the latest posterity is not so different from the 'mutual contentment and satisfaction' which can be obtained 'betwixt the master and the scholar' (*Introduction* 9). The science of man therefore harbours a cautiously progressive view of human knowledge and aims to contribute to such progress.[23] This appreciation of the cognitive practices of natural philosophers can be extended, at least in some measure, to our ordinary cognitive practices. Philosophical and everyday cognition are not so distant from one another. The 'schools of philosophers' and the 'shops of the meanest artizans' draw on the same resources: observation, experience, experimenting (*Introduction* 10).

Hume's theory of the imagination therefore is a central aspect of a reformation of philosophy with marked epistemological ambitions. Shifting ideas with conceptual contents, a priori reasoning, and a posteriori reasoning and belief from the understanding or reason to the functions and structure of the imagination is the way to constrain and at the same time secure the ambitions of experimental method in moral philosophy. Of course, this raises the fundamental question whether the naturalistic character of the imagination is consistent with its supporting epistemic normativity. This question will be addressed in due course.

1.3.3 Scepticism

Hume's cautious epistemic optimism must be consistent with his understanding of and concern for scepticism, certainly one of the most significant features of the *Treatise*. As Hume himself remarks, 'the philosophy contain'd in this book is very sceptical, and tends to give us a notion of the imperfections and narrow limits of human understanding' (*Abstract* 27). I will examine Hume's grounds for and response to scepticism later in the book: right now, I only want to say something about how Hume's concern for sceptical issues is related to the central position of the imagination in mind and cognition.

Hume's scepticism is often aimed against philosophical and religious orthodoxy. It supports the critique of many instances and domains of presumptive—and typically dispensable—cognition. The derivation of ideas from impressions of sensation is here the leading thought, the ground for Hume's critical scepticism. It

---

[23] 'This treatise therefore of human nature seems intended for a system of the sciences. The author has finished what regards logic, and has laid the foundations of the other parts in his account of the passions' (*Abstract* 3).

allows him to show that there is only pretence of cognition in these domains, because of the flawed status of certain ideas and of the ensuing unjustness of certain reasonings. This is, of course, an important strand in Hume's philosophy. But there is no deep trouble, here; and no negative or paradoxical implications for Hume's epistemic aims. The problems are with some views incautiously advanced by philosophers and by the vulgar, not with the basic cognitive functioning of the mind. (Except, of course, in regard of why and how we come by those views and beliefs; but this is a matter for the empirical enquiry into the mind and cognition.)

Hume's concern for scepticism also has a different character and role, which raise deep and interesting problems for his own philosophy. There are sceptical difficulties that plague, in apparently inescapable ways, the *possibility* and the *authority* of thoughts and cognitions that, as he is ready to recognize, we need and we seem to possess. These sceptical difficulties spring from a twin source. One is the natural limits, the cognitive gaps of object representation and of a priori reason. The detection of such limits or gaps raises a question about the possibility of general and indispensable features of our cognitive practices and our worldview, like generality, modality, geometry, causal reasoning, induction, causal necessity, existence of body, and existence and identity of self. The other is the way in which, according to Hume's philosophy, the natural mind responds to such cognitive gaps. Hume's main claim is that no further, superior kind of spiritual and refined ideas representing objects is possible or necessary. What supports our cognitive practices and our worldview, in the relevant respects, are ideas produced by and capacities instantiated in transitions of the imagination. Since the contents and capacities put in place by the imagination are not explainable with the existence and properties of their objects, doubts can arise as to whether resorting to them can help our search for truth and the improvement of our mind. The basic commitments of Hume's radical naturalism about mind and cognition seem thus to generate deep sceptical paradoxes and the need to engage with them.

The pattern of Hume's concern for and engagement with sceptical issues thus matches exactly the pattern of his interest for and theorizing about the imagination. The detection of cognitive gaps, via philosophical reflection on their conditions and consequences, is the grounding of Hume's sceptical paradoxes. By reflecting on what of our worldview and ordinary cognition we cannot explain with acquaintance with objects, we come to recognize some apparently impossible tasks in which our minds are engaged. The primary role of Hume's imagination is to respond, in a non-representational way, to cognitive gaps open in object representation. Sceptical paradoxes thus at the same time indicate where the mind must resort to a non-object representing source of content. Hume ends up in this way with a deeply revisionary account of what makes our natural mental activity possible as well as of what is its epistemic import. Rightly this fundamental aspect of his philosophy individuates scepticism as a fixed feature of our cognitive lot.

Given how we can advance beyond the limits of sensible acquaintance or of a priori reasoning, given the nature of our contents and attitudes of belief, we must be constantly alert to the risk of mistaking and overstepping our warrant, or, even, of systematic cognitive delusion. Much the same holds of how the imagination makes it so that scepticism is contained; that it does not disrupt our cognitive practices. Because of its very nature, the imagination is immune to the conclusion of sceptical arguments based on reflection and on the apparent need for certain sorts of justification; since the imagination is also the source and the rule for much of our cognition, we are in general sheltered from actual sceptical threats. Sceptical troubles are here to stay: they are the mark of how much of our thought and cognition depends on the imagination. But, again because of the cognitive role of the imagination, they do not threaten the tenability and, to some extent, the soundness of our ordinary and philosophical cognition. Hume's reliance on the faculty of imagination thus dovetails with the central aspects of his theoretical engagement with scepticism.

1.4 The Scope of the Discussion

I have chosen to concentrate my research and my discussion on Hume's *Treatise of Human Nature* almost to the exclusion of his *Enquiry Concerning Human Understanding*; and on Book 1 of the *Treatise*, with only some mentions of Books 2 and 3.

About the first choice: the relations between the *Treatise* and the later philosophical works of Hume are at present the object of much interpretive attention. I think it can be fairly said, with respect to our present concerns and to the first *Enquiry*, that Hume's decision to remedy 'some negligences in his former reasoning' and 'in the expression' (in the *Advertisement* to the *Enquiry*) and to avoid 'all unnecessary detail' required dropping most of the systematic and explanatory apparatus of the *Treatise*.[24] This involved in particular a dramatic restriction of the theoretical role of the imagination. The first *Enquiry* marks a shift from the 'science of human nature' to a 'mental geography, or delineation of the distinct parts and powers of the mind'.[25] The trade-off seems to be between the explanatory ambitions of the application of the experimental method of reasoning to moral subjects and the more modest but (in the view of the older Hume) more feasible aim of telling apart 'truth and falsehood' in 'all propositions' concerning the 'several', 'really distinct' 'powers and faculties' of the mind.[26] Imagination is

---

[24] D. Hume, *An Enquiry concerning Human Understanding*, T.L. Beauchamp, ed., Oxford University Press, New York 1999, 1.17 (94). I refer to this text by section, paragraph, and page number.
[25] Hume, *Enquiry*, 1.13 (93).
[26] Hume, *Enquiry*, 1.14 (93). See, on the relations between Hume's *Treatise* and his first *Enquiry*, the careful, deep, and well-balanced discussion in Hsueh Qu, *Hume's Epistemological Evolution*, Oxford University Press, New York 2020, chapters 1 and 2. Overall, the focus of Hume's philosophical program shifts from the philosophy of mind to epistemology.

the first and principal victim of this redefinition of Hume's philosophical project. In place of the systematic and ubiquitous reference to the imagination that we encounter in the *Treatise*, in the first *Enquiry* we find mention of a family of interchangeable notions: 'imagination' and 'fancy', of course; but also 'thought', 'thinking', 'conceiving', 'understanding', and 'mind'.[27] The fact that all these disparate notions are on a par, that they are all equally involved in inferences and transitions of ideas, is an indication of the limited explanatory ambitions of the *Enquiry*—of Hume's renunciation of his complex, controversial, but deeply original attempt to establish certain sorts of inferences as a distinct and natural source of contents. Insofar as in the *Enquiry* any distinctive, specific role is left to the imagination, it is mainly a negative one. Imagination is a source of error; its inventions are arbitrary; it delights itself with whatever is remote and exotic.[28] In a more theoretical perspective, the freedom and indeterminateness of imagination are contrasted with belief and judgement; the reveries of imagination are contrasted with the transitions of thought.[29] In this way, another important explanatory claim of the *Treatise*, the connections between imaginative transitions and attitudes and states of belief, is lost. Since the eclipse of the imagination goes together with the downfall of the systematic and explanatory ambitions of the *Treatise*, this indirectly confirms my claim that the imagination is theoretically fundamental for that work. But it also indicates how limited the relevance of the first *Enquiry* is for this study.

About the second choice: I think that there is a systematic unity in Hume's conception of the imagination throughout the *Treatise*. But the relevant pattern of unity is extremely complex, since it involves the heterogeneity of the perceptions or mental particulars with which the imagination interacts (ideas, passions) as well as partially different sets of principles of imaginative inferences. This would require careful examination. In order not to make an already long book even longer and because it is in Book 1 that the foundations of Hume's philosophy as a whole, including his theory of imagination, are laid out, I have chosen to concentrate only on this Book of the *Treatise*.

1.5 Summary

In this introductory chapter, I outline the interpretive and conceptual questions raised by Hume's theory of the imagination, sketching its main features, connecting it to other central themes of Hume's philosophy, and defining the focus and limits of my interpretation.

---

[27] Hume, *Enquiry*, 2.5 (97); 5.20 (128); 6.3 (132); 7.28 (145); 8.5 (149); 8.27 (160).
[28] Hume, *Enquiry*, 4.10 (111); 12.25 (208).
[29] Hume, *Enquiry*, 5.10–12 (124–5); 5.20 (128–9).

§ 1.1 introduces the dramatic contrast between the pervasiveness and fundamental importance of the imagination in Book 1 of the *Treatise* and the comparatively little attention that interpreters have paid to it. The classic studies by N. Kemp Smith and B. Stroud are a point in case. While recent Hume literature has given much more attention to Hume's imagination, an attitude still somehow prevalent is that his conception of the imagination lacks theoretical unity. Interestingly, the recent surge of philosophical interest in the imagination also bears witness to persistent doubts about its unity as a mental kind.

In § 1.2, I outline the functions of Hume's imagination. § 1.2.1 provides a list of the principal works of the imagination in Book 1 of the *Treatise*, which correspond to the main turning points of its theory of ideas and cognition. Then, in § 1.2.2, I suggest that the best way to understand the unity of Hume's imagination is by focusing on its natural function: closing the cognitive gaps of sensible representation and a priori and probable reason, in correspondence with contents and capacities deployed in our ordinary and philosophical cognitive practices. Such gaps are necessary, given the nature of our faculties of object representation and reasoning. Therefore, only a non-rational source of non-object representing ideas can close them. § 1.2.3 gives some indications about how the imagination performs this function. One consideration is that it operates with transitions or inferences, which can change the contents and properties of mental existence of the ideas (ultimately derived from sensibility) they involve. Another one is that the inferential activity of the imagination is of two kinds. One is by comparison of ideas and simulates the operations of understanding or reason. The other is more primitive, driven by non-representational principles of the imagination, and produces the ideas we compare in reasoning.

In § 1.3, I link the function and nature of the imagination with other general aspects of Hume's philosophy. One, in § 1.3.1, is its naturalistic and empiricist orientation. The imagination is a crucial aspect of Hume's naturalization of the mind. By suggesting an alternative account of how ideas missing from sense experience come in place, it pre-empts any explanation of them that would support rationalist philosophies. In § 1.3.2, I outline the epistemological concerns and aims of Hume's naturalistic philosophy, which are constant across Book 1 of the *Treatise*. Hume's qualified epistemological optimism in good part depends on his individuation and characterization of the cognitive roles of imagination. § 1.3.3 indicates that the pattern of Hume's engagement with scepticism fits with his conception of imagination. Sceptical doubts about sensible representation and a priori and a posteriori reason depend on the detection of their cognitive gaps. The deeply revisionary outcomes of the closing of such gaps by the imagination allow the silencing of such doubts, while not completely answering them. Scepticism is our ordinary cognitive lot.

Finally, in § 1.4, I explain why my study of Hume's imagination is restricted to the *Treatise of Human Nature*, and to its Book 1, *Of the understanding*.

PART I
THE ELEMENTS OF THIS PHILOSOPHY

Hume describes the subject matter of Part 1 of Book 1 of the *Treatise* as 'the elements of this philosophy' (1.1.4.7). Such elements include a taxonomy of perceptions (impressions and ideas; simple and complex impressions and ideas; ideas of memory and of the imagination) and a first survey of operations and products of the imagination (association of ideas; ideas of relations and other complex ideas; generality and abstraction). They also include—most importantly—two fundamental principles that identify, respectively, the conditions and character of our cognitive contact with objects and the role and way of operating of the imagination. Hume calls them simply 'the first principle' and 'our second principle'. These principles have implications that ramify throughout Hume's account of the nature of mind, giving shape to and putting constraints on all the cognitive capacities of human nature.

The outline of Hume's imagination given in Chapter 1 requires making precise the notion of cognitive gap and providing more textual support for it. This also begins to individuate the principles and operations of Hume's imagination. Cognitive gaps mark our representation of objects, which can be had only in sensible experience. The First Principle specifies the conditions for this primitive layer of content and cognition and its limits. In particular it allows seeing that cognitive gaps, rather than only accidental and situational, relative to particular bodies of information, are a general feature of object representation and of our cognitive nature. I address these issues in Chapter 2, *The First Principle*. The Second Principle provides a framework for identifying and explaining a vast family of important cognitive contents and capacities, with which we respond to cognitive gaps, as properties and operations of the imagination, a faculty of our natural mind. The Second Principle outlines a unitary conception of this diverse faculty, as cognitive but not primitively object representing. This conception is centred on cognitive change, on a content- or idea-generating role, and on a primarily and recognizably inferential structure. This is the subject matter of Chapter 3, *Our Second Principle*.

2
The First Principle

> All our simple ideas proceed, either mediately or immediately, from their corresponding impressions. This is the first principle I establish in the science of human nature; nor ought we to despise it because of the simplicity of its appearance.
>
> (1.1.1.11–12)

The primary task of any interpretation of Hume is to discuss his 'first principle': '*all our simple ideas in their first appearance are deriv'd from simple impressions, which are correspondent to them, and which they exactly represent*' (1.1.1.7). I will address this task mediately, by first tackling other general and related questions. The 'elements' of the philosophy of the *Treatise* are a complex collection of claims about the nature and kinds of perceptions and the relations between perceptions and their objects. These claims define Hume's conception of representation: how objects are given to our thought and our thought is of and about objects. The First Principle is the summary of these claims and becomes fully intelligible only in their context. In this way, we can also begin to individuate the limits of object representation and make room for the operations of the imagination.

2.1 Kinds of Perceptions

Hume classifies different sorts of mental items as 'perceptions'. Perceptions can be discrete mental particulars, both thing- and event-like, sort of thinly conceived substances.

> Since all our perceptions are different from each other, and from everything else in the universe, they are also distinct and separable, and may be consider'd as separately existent, and may exist separately, and have no need of any thing else to support their existence. They are, therefore, substances, as far as this definition explains a substance. (1.4.5.5)

Hume's perceptions, in this fundamental sense, are individuated by their qualitative or phenomenal features, which have their ultimate source in sensorial experience. The sensorial phenomenology of perceptions determines both what it is for perceptions to exist (perceived or unperceived, as we will see) and what they present or represent, their contents. Hume's perceptions can also be mental states or activities: 'To hate, to love, to think, to feel, to see; all this is nothing but to perceive' (1.2.6.7). But mental particulars are more fundamental. Mental activities and processes are completely explained by impressions and ideas together with the operation of certain structuring factors. Such structuring factors are in the mind but are *not* classified by Hume as perceptions. Their explanatory work is that of a 'disposition' to engage in a transition from an impression to an idea or to regard a succession of related objects as the persistence of an invariable one (1.3.8.2; 1.4.2.33). Or of a 'propensity' to form hasty general rules, to spread internal impressions on external objects, to feign the continued existence of objects, or to complete the union of related objects (1.3.13.9; 1.3.14.25; 1.4.2.41–2; 1.4.5.12). Or of a 'principle', explaining association of ideas and belief, extending and connecting together our factual cognitions, motivating action, shaping general rules or the idea of chance or belief in external existence (1.1.5.5; 1.3.7.4; 1.3.9.4; 1.3.10.1; 1.3.11.12; 1.3.13.8; 1.3.13.12; 1.4.2.22). Additionally, completely general capacities of the mind, like experience and habit, or a faculty like imagination, are called principles (1.4.7.3–4). Perceptions and mental principles together explain our mental contents and activities naturalistically and constitutively (that is, making sense not only of their occurrence but also of their character and possibility). They are the subject matter of Hume's 'logic': 'the principles of and operations of our reasoning faculty, and the nature of our ideas' (1.1.1.5); 'the nature and principles of the human mind' (1.1.2.1); 'the original nature and constitution of the mind' (1.1.3.7).[1]

Hume's theory opens with the distinction of perceptions into impressions and ideas:

> All the perceptions of the human mind resolve themselves into two distinct kinds, which I shall call IMPRESSIONS and IDEAS. The difference betwixt these consists in the degrees of force and liveliness, with which they strike upon the mind, and make their way into our thought or consciousness. Those perceptions, which enter with most force and violence, we may name impressions; and under this name I comprehend all our sensations, passions and emotions, as they make their first appearance in the soul. (1.1.1.1)

---

[1] Therefore, the basic ontology of Hume's theory of mind, on my reading, consists of thing-like and event-like, thinly substantial perceptions (activities or processes express the event-like dimension of perceptions as mental existence), and of causal and functional principles of union, transposition, and change of ideas. I. Johansson, 'Hume's Ontology', in *Metaphysica*, 13, 2012 87–105, 89, distinguishes four top genera in Hume's ontology of mind: perceptions, faculties, principles, and relations. I think that two of these categories are not fundamental in Hume's theory: faculties are individuated by and consist of causal and functional principles; relations are complex perceptions and again depend on principles.

The distinction is reiterated at the opening of Book 2: 'all the perceptions of the mind may be divided into *impressions* and *ideas*' (2.1.1.1). The novelty of keeping impressions distinct from ideas is recalled in the *Abstract*: 'When we feel a passion or emotion of any kind, or have the images of external objects conveyed by our senses; the perception of the mind is what he calls an *impression*, which is a word that he employs in a new sense' (*Abstract* 5). In the *Advertisement* that opens Book 3, the main connection with Books 1 and 2 is rightly the distinction of impressions and ideas. '*It must only be observ'd, that I continue to make use of the terms, impressions and ideas, in the same sense as formerly; and that by* impressions *I mean our stronger perceptions, such as our sensations, affections and sentiments; and by ideas the fainter perceptions, or the copies of these in the memory and imagination*.' Hume makes it clear that the distinction has a central role in the science of man. 'No discovery cou'd have been made more happily for deciding all controversies concerning ideas, than that above mention'd, that impressions always take the precedency of them, and that every idea, with which the imagination is furnish'd, first makes its appearance in a correspondent impression' (1.2.3.1).[2]

The distinction that is important for Hume's 'logic' is that between ideas and impressions *of sensation*. There is a distinction also of impressions. 'Impressions may be divided into two kinds, those of *Sensation* and those of *Reflexion*. The first kind arises in the soul originally, from unknown causes. The second is derived in a great measure from our ideas' (1.1.2.1). The same distinction opens Book 2.

> Original impressions or impressions of sensation are such as without any antecedent perception arise in the soul, from the constitution of the body, from the animal spirits, or from the application of objects to the external organs. Secondary, or reflective impressions are such as proceed from some of these original ones, either immediately or by the interposition of its idea. Of the first kind are all the impressions of the senses, and all bodily pains and pleasures: Of the second are the passions, and other emotions resembling them.   (2.1.1.1)

Impressions of reflection or secondary impressions depend on original impressions with some hedonic feature or on the corresponding ideas.[3] They constitute

---

[2] Hume makes claims of originality for the impressions–ideas distinction. In a footnote he remarks that he uses 'these terms, *impression* and *idea*, in a sense different from what is usual', adding that he is in this way restoring 'the word idea' to its 'original sense, from which Mr. *Locke* had perverted it, in making it stand for all our perceptions'. He adds: 'By the term of *impression* I wou'd not be understood to express the manner, in which our lively perceptions are produc'd in the soul, but merely the perceptions themselves'. He thus draws attention on his new concept of impressions, 'for which there is no particular name either in the *English* or any other language, that I know of' (1.1.1.1 fn. 2).

[3] 'An impression first strikes upon the senses, and makes us perceive heat or cold, thirst or hunger, pleasure or pain of some kind or other. Of this impression there is a copy taken by the mind, which remains after the impression ceases; and this we call an idea. This idea of pleasure or pain, when it

the primary and fundamental layer of passions, motivation, and sentiments. However, only impressions of sensation matter for explaining the nature of ideas and of our faculty of understanding.

Even circumscribed in this way, the impressions–ideas distinction raises some difficulties, the main one being whether it is one of kind or one of degree.[4] Hume initially distinguishes them as kinds of perceptions but immediately adds that their difference is one of degree of force and liveliness. He also recognizes that they can be easily confused.

> The common degrees of these are easily distinguished; tho' it is not impossible but in particular instances they may very nearly approach to each other. Thus in sleep, in a fever, in madness, or in any very violent emotions of soul, our ideas may approach to our impressions: As on the other hand it sometimes happens, that our impressions are so faint and low, that we cannot distinguish them from our ideas. (1.1.1.1)

However, similarity in force and vivacity would not turn impressions into ideas or vice versa, but only make it difficult to distinguish them. Therefore, the difference seems to be still one of kind. This view is supported by the fact that Hume sharply contrasts ideas of memory and ideas of imagination (see §§ 3.2.1–2). The distinction is, again, one of force and vivacity. But memory and imagination are also functionally different, performing different kinds of cognitive work, and Hume treats ideas of memory interchangeably with impressions of sensation (he occasionally refers to either both as impressions and as ideas). This suggests that, when ideas of imagination rather than of memory are considered, the difference with impressions of sensation is one of kind. Hume also characterizes the difference between impressions of sensation and ideas of imagination as the difference between feeling and thinking.

> Those perceptions, which enter with most force and violence, we may name *impressions*; and under this name I comprehend all our sensations, passions and emotions, as they make their first appearance in the soul. By *ideas* I mean the faint images of these in thinking and reasoning; such as, for instance, are all the perceptions excited by the present discourse, excepting only, those which arise from the sight and touch, and excepting the immediate pleasure or uneasiness it

---

returns upon the soul, produces the new impressions of desire and aversion, hope and fear, which may properly be called impressions of reflexion, because derived from it' (1.1.2.1).

[4] See Kemp Smith, *Philosophy of David Hume*, 232–6; S. Everson, 'The Difference between Feeling and Thinking', in *Mind*, 97, 1988 (in Tweyman, *David Hume. Critical Assessments*, Volume 1 (10–23), 16–17); W. Waxman, *Hume's Theory of Consciousness*, Cambridge University Press, Cambridge 1994, 27–42; J. Broughton, 'Impressions and Ideas', in S. Traiger, ed., *The Blackwell Guide to Hume's Treatise*, Blackwell, Oxford 2006 (43:58), 44–6.

may occasion. I believe it will not be very necessary to employ many words in explaining this distinction. Every one of himself will readily perceive the difference betwixt feeling and thinking. (1.1.1.1)

Now, it is rightly of feeling and thinking that Hume says that they can be easily confounded. However, the distinction between grasping contents in the context of reasoning and discourse (which is what the imagination does) and having such contents in occurring sensible experiences (impressions of sensation) seems to be both manifest and deep. The notion of feeling is itself complex and undergoes a development between the publication of Books 1 and 2 and the 'Appendix' published with Book 3. In the texts just quoted, Hume equates the feeling that distinguishes impressions from ideas with force and vivacity of conception and treats it as a matter of degree. But in the later material Hume modifies this view. Force and vivacity of conception is only one of the components of a more complex notion of feeling, which includes causal and functional dimensions like being stable, weighing on other perceptions, or making something present as real. Some of these features seem to make for a difference of kind between impressions and ideas. I conclude that Hume's considered position is that impressions of sensation and ideas of imagination differ in kind, even though there may be only a difference in degree in our experience of them.

An explanation of this somewhat uneasy start to Book 1 is that Hume is here trying to do two things at a time. He is giving a partial description of the immediate data of our consciousness, a selective phenomenology of our most primitive experience. But he is also proposing a doctrine of the elements, a theoretical taxonomy of the sources and kinds of mental contents which are going to govern all the analyses and explanations of the science of human nature. The two aims pull in opposite directions: the phenomenology of immediate awareness is marked by differences in force and degree, but it may be opaque when it comes to individuating different kinds of mental contents. The doctrine of elements builds on theoretical distinctions between perceptions and cognitive faculties, which may not be manifest to introspection. At the opening of the *Treatise*, Hume attempts to find evidence for his theoretical assumptions concerning contents and cognition in certain aspects of our immediate experience; but he is only qualifiedly successful in this aim.

2.1.1 Phenomenology

Donald Ainslie has pointed out that Hume takes for granted the phenomenology of ordinary experience—a sense of immersion in a three-dimensional world of persisting, public objects—throughout Book 1, finally explaining it at 1.4.2 with operations of the imagination. This sets the task of individuating, within such phenomenology, an immediate layer of sensible content that is deeper than imagination. Part of what Hume is doing in the opening of the *Treatise* is precisely to characterize this layer of content.[5] However, I conceive of that layer differently from Ainslie, who addresses it in terms of minimal constituents and their relations. 'A sensory impression taken in isolation presents merely an array of coloured tangible points.'[6] There is a sense in which, under analysis, the sensible manifestation of spatial impressions and ideas consists of coloured and tangible points. But there are problems with this way of understanding the *immediate* phenomenology of perceptions. Even restricting attention to spatial perceptions, which only lend themselves to such analysis, this does not seem to be how Hume characterizes their immediate manifestation in awareness. He rather resorts to the notion of their 'general appearance'. The contents involved in the most elementary forms of spatial cognition (recognizing proportional sizes, 1.2.4.23; distinguishing right and curve lines, 1.2.4.25; recognizing a plain surface, 1.2.4.28) correspond to the general appearance of spatial perceptions. This general appearance is explicitly contrasted with any awareness of points and arrays of points; and, considering how basic the cases of spatial cognition that involve it are, it is the most plausible candidate for characterizing our immediate awareness of spatial impressions. All the other kinds of spatial cognition (judgements of equality in size, revisions of these judgements, etc.) depend on this sort of awareness (1.2.4.28). Additionally, the awareness of simple ideas (blue or green) is characterized in terms of their general appearance, another indication that this notion is meant by Hume to express our immediate experience (1.1.7.7 fn. 5). Hume also calls the general appearance of spatial objects and impressions their 'united appearance'. They are present in experience, and individuated in sensible terms, as wholes rather than through their parts (1.2.4.25). All this seems to suggest that the phenomenology of the primary layer of our experience of impressions is richer than what Ainslie suggests. Perhaps we could think of it in terms of surface features of perceptions, consisting (in the visual case) of oriented coloured surfaces, inclusive of phenomena of occlusion, and present to us together with other, non-spatial qualitative episodes, with some awareness of temporal succession.[7]

2.1.2 Elements

From the viewpoint of Hume's doctrine of elements, the most important functional and explanatory feature of impressions of sensation is that, differently from ideas and impressions of reflection, they arise 'in the soul originally, from unknown causes' (1.1.2.1); 'without any antecedent perception' (2.1.1.1).

---

[5] Ainslie, *Hume's True Skepticism*, 42–4.   [6] Ainslie, *Hume's True Skepticism*, 63, 69.
[7] See C. Peacocke, *A Study of Concepts*, The MIT Press, Cambridge (Mass.)/London 1992, 61–7.

Impressions of sensation are not only immediate but *primitive*. Hume regards this as a necessary condition for any sort of mental activity. "'Tis certain, that the mind, in its perceptions, must begin somewhere; and that since the impressions precede their correspondent ideas, there must be some impressions, which without any introduction make their appearance in the soul' (2.1.1.2). This difference seems accessible to awareness (it is crucial for the First Principle).[8] Impressions of sensation are primitive also because they are individuated and they weigh on cognition independently of their causal ancestry. Hume is perfectly hospitable to the idea of mind–body causal connections. He holds that only his own theory of causation makes full sense of such causal connections (see 1.4.5.30–2). But he denies that his doctrine of elements requires an enquiry in the causation of impressions of sensation. The common method of reasoning does not prevent natural and moral philosophy diverging sharply in important respects. Hume remarks that questions of natural philosophy, say, concerning the anatomy and physiology of the brain, are out of the scope of moral philosophy. He is very keen to distinguish the two perspectives. 'The examination of our sensations belongs more to anatomists and natural philosophers than to moral; and therefore shall not at present be enter'd upon' (1.1.2.1). 'As these [impressions of sensation] depend upon natural and physical causes, the examination of them wou'd lead me too far from my present subject, into the sciences of anatomy and natural philosophy' (1.2.1.2). Hume holds that even though the causes of impressions, putatively the object of natural philosophy, are mostly out of our reach, this does not matter for moral philosophy.

> As to those *impressions*, which arise from the *senses*, their ultimate cause is, in my opinion, perfectly inexplicable by human reason, and 'twill always be impossible to decide with certainty, whether they arise immediately from the object, or are produc'd by the creative power of the mind, or are deriv'd from the author of our being. Nor is such a question any way material to our present purpose.
> (1.3.5.2)

Which of these is the right hypothesis is not for moral philosophy to decide. What Hume is looking for is an internal, undoubtable, immediate, phenomenal starting point, which can explain in a fundamental way all our thinking and cognition. Starting from physical, natural-philosophical considerations would threaten moral philosophy with unanswerable sceptical difficulties. Causal considerations are pertinent and important only from an internal perspective, as phenomenological,

---

[8] See Landy, 'Hume's Impression/Idea Distinction', *Hume Studies*, 32, 1, 2006 (119–40), 124–5, 129–30 on the copy of impressions by ideas (rather than force and vivacity) as the analytically grounded criterion of their distinction, based on considerations of explanatory role with reference to the commonly recognized distinction of impressions and ideas.

internally scrutable relations between the existence and the content of our perceptions, the building blocks of cognition. In particular, the causation of ideas by resembling impressions of sensation falls squarely within the scope of moral philosophy and is the subject matter of Book 1 of the *Treatise*.

2.2 Two Viewpoints and Hume's Ontology of Perceptions

2.2.1 Two Viewpoints

Perceptions, impressions, and ideas figure in Hume's doctrine of elements under two different respects: that of their *mental existence*, how they are in the mind; and that of their *contents*, what they present and represent. Explaining how perceptions and imagination contribute to the possibility of content and cognition requires distinguishing and appropriately connecting these two viewpoints. This is a fundamental, if mostly implicit, theoretical principle of Hume's philosophy: I will dub it *Two Viewpoints*.[9] Considered in their mental existence, perceptions are event-like and thing-like particulars, individuated by qualitative, sensorial features, with different degrees of force and vivacity; they are susceptible to incessant variation; they have causal relations to other perceptions and to the imagination; they are immediately present to awareness in their qualities, manners, and relations. Considered by their contents, perceptions are conceptions of certain subject matters, which can be but are not necessarily representations of sensible particulars; they are the elements of our judgements and of our idea-comparing reasoning; they stand in internal, logical relations; and it makes sense to think of them as not present to awareness.[10]

Hume develops his 'Logic', his theory of ideas and of the understanding, from both viewpoints. It is thus important to grasp the character and the point of this distinction. The important consideration is that it is not a difference in being between properties of perceptions. Quite generally, the properties of content of

---

[9] An accurate and insightful discussion of this distinction of viewpoints, more or less along the lines I am proposing, addressing the issues of representation and the impressions/ideas relation is in C. Kemp, 'Two Meanings of the Term "Idea": Act and Content in Hume's *Treatise*', *Journal of the History of Ideas*, 61, 2000, 675:690.

[10] There is a problem here. Pleasure and pain, good and evil, are explicitly regarded by Hume as impressions of sensation (1.1.2.1; 2.1.1.1). But they do not seem to have contents. Two Viewpoints would thus not apply to all impressions of sensation. However, (a) this difference between impressions is manifest to awareness: we do not think we apprehend a sensible object when we have a hedonic feeling. Differently from secondary qualities, not even the vulgar are inclined to ascribe distinct continued existence to hedonic sensations, 1.4.2.12; (b) non-object presenting impressions are anyway object-related: we can foresee good and evil; we have images of them; they can be the object of belief (1.3.10.2–3). Hume uses the phrase 'affecting object' to designate something that immediately excites a passion but is 'present' in impression and represented in idea (1.3.10.4). We may thus either tell pleasures and pains apart from object/presenting impressions or regard them as indirectly contentful. Either way, they do not seem to raise intractable problems.

Hume's perceptions are also properties with which they exist in the mind: such properties are necessarily jointly instantiated, as a basic fact of human cognitive nature. Perceptions are bearers of content because of their mental nature; they present and represent objects by the properties with which they exist in the mind. The striking case is that of visual and tactile impressions and ideas, which exist in the mind with extensions and spatial locations and which, precisely because of this way of existing in the mind, can represent extended objects and spatial states of affairs. Perceptions also exist in the mind with a temporal structure or duration and can represent temporally structured objects and situations precisely by these properties of mental existence (see § 8.1.1). The same holds in a different and less surprising way of qualities like smells and sounds. These are certainly properties of perceptions existing in the mind; if such perceptions present or represent any object, they do so precisely by these properties of their mental existence. Therefore, the distinction we are discussing is not existential (between properties) but conceptual (between ways of considering): a distinction of viewpoints. By natural necessity, properties of content and of mental existence are jointly instantiated by the perceptions that have them; but they differ in their conceptual and explanatory roles. In this way, the same perceptions can figure with different explanatory roles in Hume's science of human nature. This is made possible by what Hume calls a *distinction of reason*: an important conceptual operation of the imagination that falls short of individuating separately existing entities but makes sense of different cognitive roles (see § 4.2.1).[11]

Two Viewpoints thus makes possible a fine-grained articulation of the individuation and of the causal relations of perceptions. Hume's philosophy in Book 1, based on the detection of cognitive gaps and on the generation of contents by imagination, puts to work that difference and the interconnections between how perceptions exist in the mind and what they present and represent. The idea is that the principles of the imagination that respond to cognitive gaps and underlie cognitive change are sensitive to such difference and thus interact with perceptions in regard both of their existence and of their content. The basic pattern of the science of human nature is thus something like the following:

---

[11] In Hume's perceptions content and mental existence are conceptually and explanatorily distinct but not actually different. Hume takes a complex position in relation to the Arnauld–Malebranche controversy about the nature of ideas. Perceptions like impressions and ideas have representative nature: impressions *are* objects of representation; ideas *are* representations of impressions or objects. In this respect, Hume is close to Arnauld and opposed to Malebranche, who held that representational import is accidental to ideas and essentially pertaining to something else—God's ideas. (See E. J. Kremer, 'Arnauld on Ideas as a Topic in Logic', in P.A. Easton, ed., *Logic and the Workings of the Mind: The Logic of Ideas and Faculty Psychology in Early Modern Philosophy*, Ridgeview, Atascadero 1997 (65–82), 69–70.) On the other hand, Hume, just like Malebranche, is ready to ascribe substantial status to perceptions, qua mental existents. He also holds that, at least in the case of visible and tangible perceptions, it is rightly in virtue of the properties with which they exist in the mind that they can present and represent properties of objects. See Wright, *Sceptical Realism*, 79 fn. 10.

(a) Perceptions interact with the dispositions of the imagination on account of their properties of mental existence: their qualitative features; their relations and successions, repetitions and resemblances, interruptions and variations; as well as their force and vivacity.
(b) This interaction results in changes in the properties and manners of mental existence and presence to awareness of perceptions (like, say, different combinations of qualitative features; involvement in transitions of conception and attention; a feeling of their determination; different degrees of force and vivacity).
(c) The properties of the mental existence of perceptions are also properties of contents; therefore changes in their mental existence are also changes in their contents and cognitive import, with respect to those they have independently of interaction with the imagination.[12]

This is very schematic but indicates a recurrent pattern in Hume's philosophy and marks the importance of Two Viewpoints. Hume implicitly relies on this principle at crucial junctures of Book 1, which are also contexts where the imagination comes into play. For example, the explanation of causal ideas requires that we 'change our point of view, from the objects to the perceptions' (1.3.14.29). The shift from what perceptions allow to be conceived to how they are in the mind is necessary to explain the possibility, the origin, and the character of the idea of necessary connection, a central cognitive gap, and a paradigm of generation of

---

[12] This notion of content is familiar in contemporary philosophy: 'A *phenomenal content* of a perceptual experience is a representational content that is determined by the experience's phenomenal character', D. J. Chalmers, 'Perception and the Fall from Eden', in T. Szabó Gendler & J. Hawthorne, *Perceptual Experience*, Clarendon Press, Oxford 2006 (49:125), 49. Historically, Descartes' distinction between *materialiter* or *objective* considered ideas may be relevant here. 'Sed respondeo hîc subesse aequivocationem in voce ideae: sumi enim potest vel materialiter, pro operatione intellectûs, quo sensu me perfectior dici nequit, vel objective, pro re per istam operationem repraesentatâ, quae res, etsi non supponatur extra intellectum existere, potest tamen me esse perfectior ratione suae essentiae' ('Praefatio ad Lectorem', *Meditationes de Prima Philosophia*, in *Oeuvres de Descartes*, C. Adam & P. Tannery, eds., Volume 8, Vrin, Paris 1983, 8; 'I answer that the term "idea" here is ambiguous. It can be taken either in the material sense, as an operation of the understanding, in which case it cannot be said to be more perfect than myself, or objectively, for the thing represented by this operation; and this thing, even if it not supposed to exist outside of my understanding, can nonetheless be more perfect than me in virtue of its essence', 'Preface to the Reader', in R. Descartes, *Meditations on First Philosophy*, M. Moriarty, ed., Oxford University Press, Oxford/New York 2008, 7–8). This does not fit with how Hume conceives of representation but comes close to Two Viewpoints: perceptions can be taken in their formal reality or materialiter, that is, for what they actually are: mental acts or things; or in their objective reality: for what they represent, their contents. Descartes resorts to this view to explain, for instance, possibility of error. 'Nam profecto, si tantùm ideas ipsas ut cogitationis meae quosdam modos considerarem, nec ad quidquam aliud referrem, vix mihi ullam errandi materiam dare possent' ('Meditatio Tertia' in *Oeuvres de Descartes*, Volume 8, 37; 'Now, as far as ideas are concerned, if they are considered purely in themselves, and if I do not connect them with anything outside themselves, they cannot, strictly speaking, be false', 'Third Meditation', in *Meditations of First Philosophy*, 27.) The distinction has scholastic roots and was widely taken over in the rationalist tradition. Hume minimizes its ontological import. Properties of perceptions can have different explanatory roles without being different properties.

content by imagination. The explanation of the idea of external existence is another case. Hume denies that this idea can have a sensible origin because it presupposes a distinction based on Two Viewpoints. 'These faculties [the senses], therefore, if they have any influence in the present case, must produce the opinion of a distinct, not of a continu'd existence; and in order to that, must present their impressions either as images and representations, or as these very distinct and external existences' (1.4.2.3). The same perceptions would have to be considered for its content ('distinct objects') or for its mental existence ('mere impressions'). But this conceptual distinction is out of the reach of sense experience.

Hume's distinction between natural and philosophical relations of ideas, which is of paramount importance for his theory, is also framed in terms of the distinction between the viewpoint of mental existence and that of content:

> The word Relation is commonly used in two senses considerably different from each other. Either for that quality, by which two ideas are connected together in the imagination, and the one naturally introduces the other, after the manner above-explained; or for that particular circumstance, in which, even upon the arbitrary union of two ideas in the fancy, we may think proper to compare them.
> (1.1.5.1)

Proper comparisons of ideas depend on their contents; the natural introduction of one idea by the other is a property of mental existence. The same perceptions can be considered from either of two viewpoints: they can be connected with certain ideas in mental existence and compared with different ones in terms of content. In this way, they can perform different explanatory tasks. At the same time, the fact that there is no separation but only a distinction of reason between properties of content and properties of mental existence is the ground for their systematic concurrence in one causal and explanatory framework. The contents of ideas contribute to but do not determine natural relations; philosophical relations based on contents need not be natural relations; but changes in the contents of our ideas are also changes in what natural relations they can figure in; and changes in their natural relations bear on thought and cognition as changes in content.[13]

---

[13] Locke's naturalistic and closely related framework focuses almost unilaterally on ideas as contents: 'Whatsoever is the Object of the Understanding when a Man thinks...Whatever is meant by *Phantasm, Notion, Species*, or whatever it is, which the Mind can be employ'd about in thinking' (Locke, *Essay*, 1.1.8, 47); 'Whatsoever the Mind perceives in it self, or is the immediate object of Perception, Thought, or understanding, that I call *Idea*' (Locke, *Essay*, 2.8.8, 134). For Locke, what matters are '*determinate* or *determined*' ideas: 'By those denominations, I mean some object in the Mind, and consequently *determined*, i.e. such as it is there seen and perceived to be. This I think may fitly be called a *determinate* or *determin'd* Idea, when such as it is at any time objectively in the Mind, and so *determined* there, it is annex'd, and without variation *determined* to a name or articulate sound' (Locke, *Essay* 'Epistle to the Reader', 13–14). The psychological reality, the causal connections, and the explanatory work of mental episodes are less important than the semantic role of ideas with regard of language. This marks a very important difference with Hume.

2.2.2 Perceptions as Mental Existents

Two Viewpoints provides the conceptual framework for Hume's sparse but important ontology of perceptions that, in turn, is the key to his philosophy of mind and cognition, starting from the First Principle. From the viewpoint of existence, the most important claim in Hume's ontology of perceptions is that, for all perceptions, existence in the mind is a *contingent condition*. Perceptions, as existing particulars, can exist unperceived, that is, without the mind; and can exist perceived, exist in the mind, without any intrinsic modification and without this requiring the creation of a new perception. Impressions of sensation come to be present to the mind without the 'new creation of a perception or image' (1.4.2.38), 'without any real or essential change' (1.4.2.40). The very same things can exist within the mind and without the mind (1.4.2.39–40; 1.4.5.5). Of course, this claim does not follow from Two Viewpoints alone, which only gives expression to a distinction of reason between aspects of perceptions and does not sum up to an absolute modal claim. However, without Two Viewpoints, Hume would not even be in the position to formulate it. He would not be able to conclude that it is possible for perceptions to exist unperceived, from the fact that this is conceivable with reference to the same perceptions, if they are individuated for their contents rather than for how they exist in the mind (see § 5.1.1, for Hume's conceivability account of possibility).[14]

The claim that, for perceptions, being perceived or existing in the mind is a metaphysically contingent condition will be fully discussed when we examine Hume's theory of external existence (see § 9.4.1). Some points can, however, be anticipated. The first is that Hume's basic ground for that claim is that the difference between existing within the mind and without the mind depends on the obtaining of causal relations *among perceptions*. This metaphysical claim, in turn, gives expression to the third personal, reductionist conception of the mind, with little or no role for subjectivity, which is one of the fundamental and most original insights of Hume's philosophy in Book 1 (and the source of some of its most serious difficulties).

> We may observe, that what we call a *mind*, is nothing but a heap or collection of different perceptions, united together by certain relations, and suppos'd, tho' falsely, to be endow'd with a perfect simplicity and identity. Now as every perception is distinguishable from another, and may be consider'd as separately existent; it evidently follows, that there is no absurdity in separating any particular

---

[14] For an overview of the ontology of ideas in early modern philosophy, which puts the due emphasis on the pervasiveness of ontological commitments with respect to internal or mental existents, see M. A. Hight, *Idea and Ontology. An Essay in Early Modern Metaphysics of Ideas*, Pennsylvania State University Press, University Park 2008.

perception from the mind; that is, in breaking off all its relations, with that connected mass of perceptions, which constitute a thinking being. (1.4.2.39)

From the standpoint of metaphysical possibility, defined by the identity and nature of their ideas, the presence of perceptions in the mind is thus a bare fact consisting in and explainable with the obtaining of certain causal relations.

Hume also characterizes the mental existence of impressions and ideas as their being 'present with the mind' or appearing to 'our thought or consciousness' (1.1.3.1; App 20). This comes out clearly where he says that the conjunction of an object or perception (which are 'the very same thing') to the mind is its coming to awareness, its being 'seen, and felt, and become present to the mind' (1.4.2.39). Hume remarks that all sorts of impressions 'convey'd by the senses' have the same mode of existence. Colours, sounds, heat and cold, motion and solidity, even pleasures and pains, 'as far as appears to the senses, exist after the same manner'. 'All perceptions are the same in the manner of existence', 'as far as the sense are judges' (1.4.2.13). Reciprocally, we could say, for all perceptions to exist in the mind is to appear in certain ways, to be conscious.

> For since all actions and sensations of the mind are known to us by consciousness, they must necessarily appear in every particular what they are and be what they appear. Everything that enters the mind, being in *reality* a perception, 'tis impossible any thing shou'd to *feeling* appear different. This were to suppose, that even where we are most intimately conscious, we might be mistaken. (1.4.2.7)

The things that enter the mind and exist in it, exist by appearance and feeling; in the case of perceptions as individual particulars, consciousness and mental existence entail each other. This is very sketchy but it clearly indicates some problems in Hume's conception of the mental existence of perceptions. A serious one is that being perceived does not anymore seem to be a metaphysically contingent condition of perceptions (so that they could exist both perceived and unperceived). This is implicit in the equation of being in the mind and appearing to the mind and in the corresponding claim of impossibility of error. But Hume comes close to making explicitly this point when he says that it is 'scarce possible' or 'conceivable' that perceptions be different from how they appear, in their nature, relations, or situations (1.4.2.7). Since relations and situations are properties of existence, their existing in appearance or in the mind seems to be metaphysically necessary.[15]

We encounter here a serious and recurrent problem in Hume's philosophy of mind: the tension between a causal and third personal construal of mind, as a composition of individual perceptions, and the supposition that mental existence

---

[15] See, on the immediate presence, possibility or error, and corrigibility of perceptions, Qu Hsueh, 'Hume on Mental Transparency', *Pacific Philosophical Quarterly*, 98, 2017 (576–601), 577–82.

entails appearance to awareness. There is pressure in Hume's philosophy towards having perceptions, as individual mental particulars and as units of content, do all the important explanatory work. The pressure arises from Hume's commitment to experimental reasoning in philosophy as well as from his rejection of the role assigned by rationalist philosophers to the faculty of the understanding (typically regarded as a subject of intellectual agency). This leads Hume to give theoretical pride of place to causal relations among perceptions, held to be empirically ascertainable and third personal. But Hume seems committed to the view that the mental existence of perceptions also consists in their presence to consciousness, their appearance with intrinsic and extrinsic features. This view makes it difficult to maintain that the identity of perceptions is constant across their being perceived or unperceived. But this latter claim is non-negotiable in Hume's philosophy, because it forms the background of his overall naturalistic, empirical conception of mind.

This situation calls for interpretation and, perhaps, reconstruction. One framework for this is David Rosenthal's well-known distinction between *state consciousness* and *creature consciousness*. The first notion refers to what it is for a mental state to be conscious and to differ from a non-conscious one, the second, to what it is for a person or other creature to be conscious.[16] This framework allows arguing against the view that presence to awareness is intrinsic to mental existence, since the existence of a state with phenomenal, even sensorial features (like a pain) is not the same with the feeling or appearance of pain for a subject. It is natural to speak of a pain that lasted all day even though we were only intermittently aware of it.[17] More generally, within this framework we can outline a distinction between the individuating phenomenal qualities of mental states and the consciousness or experience of them, their what-is-it-like. That we individuate mental states based on the appearance of their sensory qualities does not entail that such states cannot exist unless someone is conscious of them and that creature consciousness rather than state consciousness is intrinsic to their existence. This framework could help Hume with his conception of the contingent mental existence of perceptions, by licensing differential ascriptions of conscious character. If state consciousness and creature consciousness are distinct and different, we can say that the existence in the mind of Hume's perceptions is their being creature-conscious. However, even though perceptions not existing in the mind could not be creature-conscious, they would still be state-conscious: they would have individuating phenomenal character. The features of state-conscious character would be the same as those with which perceptions are creature-conscious,

---

[16] See D. Rosenthal, 'A Theory of Consciousness' (1990), in N. Block, O. Flanagan, & G. Güzeldere, *The Nature of Consciousness*, The MIT Press, Cambridge (Mass.) 1998 (729:753), 729–30, 737.

[17] Rosenthal, 'Theory of Consciousness', 732–4.

therefore no change of their identity and no creation of a new perception would be involved in the shift from one condition to the other.[18]

Rightly with reference to Rosenthal's framework, however, we can also see how deep this difficulty runs into Hume's philosophy. The coherence of Rosenthal's position is secured by the fact that what he proposes is a higher-order theory of consciousness. On such a theory, state consciousness depends on creature consciousness, which comes to expression in a higher-order thought about a mental state. Whatever its other merits, this approach seems to allow keeping distinct subjective (creature) consciousness and the phenomenal, manifest features that constitute state consciousness. At the same time, it promises to deliver a unified view of consciousness across its subjective and phenomenal dimensions.[19] Whatever else we may say of Hume's views about the phenomenology and the consciousness of perceptions, he is certainly not a higher-order theorist. There is nothing higher-order in the experience or awareness of perceptions (even though Hume is ready to recognize that conscious perceptions can be represented in reflection). Quite the contrary, Hume regards presence to awareness as an aspect of the mental existence of perceptions. Pending further arguments on Hume's part, this makes for a possible conflict with the claim that perceptions can exist both perceived and unperceived. Hume leaves these issues badly undertheorized, almost untouched. There is no serious attempt, in the *Treatise* or elsewhere in his philosophical work, to come to terms with the nature of subjective experience and with its role in the explanatory programme of the science of human nature. Hume has nothing to say about how the fact that perceptions stand in certain causal relations to other perceptions is related to their appearing or being present to consciousness. This is a serious theoretical lacuna, with ramifications throughout Book 1 and no clear indication of how it can be filled consistently with other commitment of Hume.[20]

---

[18] This point is also forcefully made by T. Burge, 'Two Kinds of Consciousness', in Block, Flanagan, & Güzeldere, *The Nature of Consciousness* (427:433), 432. 'Phenomenal states can be phenomenally unconscious'; 'I distinguish what-it-is-likeness (phenomenally) from what is occurrently like for the individual'; 'Unfelt sensations remain sensations (phenomenal states) because there is a way that it is like feel them, and they are individuated in terms of their qualitative features; and because they meet empirical criteria of sensibility and sensation continuity'. This is akin to the position I am scribing to Hume. Hume's perceptions would have something like Williamson's *luminosity* or Ryle's *phosphorescence*.

[19] Rosenthal, 'Theory of Consciousness', 732–4.

[20] Hume's inattention to this issue has been a recurrent topic of interpretation and criticism: see (famously) D. G. C. McNabb, *David Hume. His Theory of Knowledge and Morality*, Blackwell, Oxford 1966 (1951), 26–7, 150–2. The state-consciousness aspect of Hume's theory does a lot of work and is often neglected. See J. Broughton, 'Explaining General Ideas', *Hume Studies*, 26, 2, 2000 (279–89), 287–8. Hume's lack of a full-fledged conception of subjective consciousness, as opposed to the presence or appearance of mental states, casts doubts on the phenomenological reading of his philosophy like that proposed in Waxman, *Hume's Theory of Consciousness* (see, for instance, 39, 114, 169). Ainslie shares the view I have advanced that Hume leaves badly undertheorized the consciousness or subjective experience of mental episodes or perceptions. See *Hume's True Skepticism*, 53–4: 'Hume is left

2.2.3 Impressions as Objects, Objects as Impressions

In Book 1 we find a systematic, interchangeable use of 'impression' (and occasionally of 'idea') and 'object'. Consider the following passages:

> To give a child an idea of scarlet or orange, of sweet or bitter, I present the objects, or in other words, convey to him these impressions (1.1.1.8)

> '[T]is confest, that no object can appear to the senses; or in other words, that no impression can become present to the mind, without being determin'd in its degrees both of quantity and quality. (1.1.7.4)

> Nay even when the resemblance is carry'd beyond the objects of one sense, and the impressions of touch are found to be similar to those of sight in the disposition of their parts; this does not hinder the abstract idea from representing both (1.2.3.5)

> The ideas of some objects it certainly must have, nor is it possible for it without these ideas ever to arrive at any conception of time; which since it appears not as any primary distinct impression, can plainly be nothing but different ideas, or impressions, or objects dispos'd in a certain manner, that is, succeeding each other. (1.2.3.10)

> Sensible objects have always a greater influence on the fancy than any other; and this influence they readily convey to those ideas, to which they are related, and which they resemble. I shall only infer from these practices, and this reasoning, that the effect of resemblance in inlivening the idea is very common; and as in every case a resemblance and a present impression must concur, we are abundantly supply'd with experiments to prove the reality of the foregoing principle. (1.3.8.4)

> Properly speaking, 'tis not our body we perceive, when we regard our limbs and members, but certain impressions, which enter by the senses; so that the ascribing a real and corporeal existence to these impressions, or to their objects, is an act of the mind as difficult to explain, as that which we examine at present. (1.4.2.9)

> We can never, therefore, find any repugnance betwixt an extended object as a modification, and a simple uncompounded essence, as its substance, unless that repugnance takes place equally betwixt the perception or impression of that extended object, and the same uncompounded essence. Every idea of a quality in an object passes thro' an impression; and therefore every *perceivable* relation,

---

without an account of our awareness of these objects [perceptions]', 61, 129. And he rightly identifies this as a source of theoretical difficulties.

whether of connexion or repugnance, must be common both to objects and impressions. (1.4.5.21)

In the contexts where these passages occur and in the passages themselves Hume is making disparate philosophical points. But this only indicates how inextricably and internally connected impressions and objects are throughout Hume's philosophy.[21] The lesson I want to draw from these texts is that impressions of sensation *are* sensible objects, objects sensibly *given* or *present*. Together with the recognition of a primitive and immediate layer of representational content, this is the real theoretical change brought about by Hume's impressions.

It is important to specify what concept of object is relevant here. Hume proposes a complex explanation of the ordinary and philosophical idea of body (an externally, continuedly, and independently existing object) at 1.4.2: *Of scepticism with regard to the senses*. This explanation, which I discuss further on, is an important case study of production of content and cognitive change by the imagination. Hume argues in a detailed way that impressions of sensation cannot put in place this complex cognitive construct (1.4.2.3–13). Therefore, if impressions are objects, we must understand their character of objects in some more restricted and primitive sense. Hume makes this point explicitly: 'My memory, indeed, informs me of the existence of many objects; but then this information extends not beyond their past existence, nor do either my senses or memory give any testimony to the continuance of their being' (1.4.2.20). A suggestion comes from what we have seen about the mental existence of perceptions. Impressions of sensation are individuated as different, distinct, and separable because of their phenomenal qualities or general appearance (inclusive of variations; and of spatial structures, in the case of visible and tangible impressions). Now, we have seen that this individuation is consistent with perceptions existing unperceived. What is constitutive of perceptions are their phenomenal qualities, their general appearance, not any subjective experience of them, their appearing. This explains, in the conceptual framework of Two Viewpoints, the internal relation between impressions and objects. Impressions of sensation can be considered for their mental existence *or* for their contents by a distinction of reason that leaves untouched their identity. Therefore, impressions of sensation, considered from the viewpoint of content, are conceived as qualitatively specified sensible particulars, different and separable from any other sensible particular. Under this conception,

---

[21] See M. Grene, 'The Objects of Hume's *Treatise*', *Hume Studies*, XX, 2, 1994, 163–77, for a careful and helpful examination of these issues. Grene distinguishes three main uses of 'objects' in the *Treatise*: objects of attention or intentional objects; objects as identified with impressions; external objects; recognizes that Hume's account of objects (and epistemology) is essentially unitary; affirms that impressions of sensation do not have but are objects. These are important interpretive insights. But (apart from Grene) the relation between impressions and objects has not drawn the attention it deserves.

their being perceived is only contingent. It is from this viewpoint and under this conception that Hume can claim that impressions of sensation are objects. If impressions, individuated by their general appearance, are conceived as to their contents, they just are individual sensible particulars. Impressions are objects, on this primitive, restricted concept of object, without any ascription of independent, external existence and any recognitional element. A fuller notion of object requires a special explanation in terms of imagination. It is not something we represent and it is not an element of Hume's philosophy.[22]

Impressions of sensation, from the viewpoint of their contents, are objects of sense; reciprocally, objects of sense, on the thin notion of them that is required at this fundamental level of Hume's theory, are individuated by their phenomenal qualities or general appearance. Just as impressions and perceptions in general are. This is a basic claim of Hume's ontology of perceptions and objects. Just as perceptions can exist unperceived, as (thinly individuated) objects, it must be possible for objects (on the same conception) to exist perceived, that is, to exist in the mind without the creation of a new perception. Therefore, simply based on the bare concept of object that we are at this stage considering, objects of sense must exist with the very same qualities with which impressions exist.

One thing this entails is that objects must be ascribed both primary and secondary qualities, in the same way as perceptions have non-problematically both kinds of qualities. Hume here draws on an aspect of ordinary sense experience. 'Colours, sounds, heat and cold, as far as appears to senses, exist after the same manner with motion and solidity' (1.4.2.13). In this respect, Hume's philosophy, as he thinks it is often the case with true philosophy, is close to our ordinary views (see for further discussion § 9.4.2).[23]

---

[22] Notice that on a plausible definition of 'external object': 'a space occupying (or spatially locatable) object which could, in principle, exist independently of being perceived' (P. Snowdon, 'How to interpret "direct perception"', in T. Crane, ed., *The Contents of Experience*, Cambridge University Press, Cambridge 1992 (48–78), 49), Hume's visual and tactile impressions of sensation would count as external objects. But this is not Hume's view of external existence.

[23] Hume's conception of objects of sense is not without counterparts in contemporary philosophy. In recent, important work, David Chalmers has called attention to the 'presentational phenomenology' of perceptual experience and has sketched a corresponding ontology as the starting point for a fundamental explanation of perception (Chalmers, 'Perception and the Fall from Eden', 64–5, 73). Hume's conception of objects of sense and of their appearance in experience bears some analogy to Chalmers's notion of an 'Edenic world'. This is a world of 'simple qualitative' properties 'with a distinctive sensuous nature' which are intrinsically possessed by objects; it is the world as it would be primitively encountered in sense-experience if the phenomenology of sense-experience were literally true ('Perception and the Fall from Eden', 66–9, 71–4). Essentially in the same way, Hume's objects of sense have intrinsic sensible qualities, both primary and secondary, and are ordered in phenomenal space and time; impressions of sensation are present and weigh on us as existents; and everything that is present in impressions of sensation is what and how it appears, when the conditions of our awareness are normal. This primitive, presentational phenomenology, in Hume's and in Chalmers' theories, has the main theoretical role of individuating sensible contents and articulating the ontology of sensible objects. Chalmers himself implicitly recognizes that Edenic worlds and properties are somewhat in the neighbourhood of Hume's views concerning sensible content ('Perception and the Fall from Eden', 83).

2.2.4 Hume's Ontological Pluralism

Hume's (minimal) objects of sense are individuated by the contents of everyday sense experience (again, minus the recognitional elements and the commitment to independent and continued existence): 'upon opening my eyes, and turning them to the surrounding objects, I perceive many visible bodies' (1.2.3.2). Objects present in impressions are, mostly, *things*: the city of Paris (1.1.1.4); a globe of white marble (1.1.7.18); a 'spot of ink upon paper' (1.2.1.4); the 'table before me' (1.2.3.4); 'my bed and table, my books and papers' (1.4.2.18); 'a hat, or shoe, or stone, or any other impression' (1.4.2.31). But also more or less specifically described *events*, like the killing of Caesar in the senate-house (1.3.4.2); engagement in a 'scene of action' (1.3.5.4); the onset of a real, conscious perception or 'action of the mind' (1.3.915); the throwing of a dye (1.3.11.12); 'twenty ships that leave the port' (1.3.12.11); the dying 'of a debauch' of a drinking mate (1.3.13.2); being abused by a person (1.3.13.14); 'particular conjunctions of objects', by contiguity or succession, which are the observational input of causal inference (1.3.14.15); 'the shock of two billiard-balls' (1.3.14.18); 'a sudden noise as of a door turning upon its hinges' and 'a porter who advances towards me' (1.4.2.20); and famously, one billiard-ball moving towards another and striking it (*Abstract* 9). We sensibly encounter particular qualities or *tropes*.[24] Scarlet or orange are present in experience as 'objects' (1.1.1.8). But we also encounter the 'taste of a pine-apple' (1.1.1.8); different shades of blue and a 'particular shade' of any colour (1.1.1.10; 1.3.7.5); the 'tone of voice' of the master (as heard by his dog) (1.3.16.6); 'a disagreeable taste in meats', 'colours reflected from the clouds' (1.4.4.3); the pressure of one object on our members (1.4.5.13).

Hume feels no pressure to draw deep ontological distinctions or to introduce strict priorities between objects of sense identified in these different ways. This is because the primary focus of his doctrine of objects is their import for representation. In Hume's doctrine of elements, impressions of sensation and objects of sense figure essentially in order to explain the primitive contents of our thought and cognition and their natural limits. This is not all Hume has to say about our cognition of objects; it is not all there is to the contents of ordinary sense experience. But it is what is needed to explain the primitive, representational layer of thought and cognition. No reductionist ontology of objects of sense and no

---

[24] See J. Hakkarainen, 'Hume as Trope Nominalist', *Canadian Journal of Philosophy*, 42, 2012, 55–66. While Hume certainly identifies some simple objects as tropes, I think it would be wrong to identify all simple entities, perceptions, or objects with particular instances of qualities. Visible and tangible points are a point in case: Hume conceives of such points as thing-like objects, concrete particulars that stand in spatial relations and have sensible qualities, rather than as particular qualities. The same point can have both visual and tactile qualities, thus cannot be identified with any of them. Tropes are included by Hume in the broad category of individual particulars rather than being the grounds of that category across the simple–complex (bundling) divide.

prioritizing some of their kinds is required or even recommended for the basic tenets of the science of human nature.

The distinction between simple and complex impressions or objects may seem to be an exception. As we will see, the distinction is crucial for the content of the First Principle; in the context of Hume's account of object-representing ideas, the simple–complex distinction therefore has an important theoretical role. The question is if it also indicates a deep distinction in the ontology of objects of sense, like a restriction of the status of object to simple ones. This does not seem to be Hume's take on the matter. For one thing, there is not even a psychological priority of simples over complexes, as if the awareness and the mental role of simple impressions and objects had to precede that of complex ones. For another, Hume does not restrict unity and objecthood to simplicity. He seems to link them to two conditions: one is that the relevant entities can 'exist alone'; the other is that they be 'perfectly indivisible' (1.2.2.3). The two conditions do not entail each other. They coincide in the case of space and time because finite divisibility entails spatial minima, that is, objects which both exist alone and are indivisible (see § 8.1.2). But Hume's overall requirements for unity, existence, and objecthood vary with contexts and can be wider and weaker. Wider, since not all kinds of impressions or objects are reducible to minima. Non-spatial impressions and objects (sounds, smells, tastes) cannot be reduced to minima, to indivisible and self-standing elements. In the case of non-spatial perceptions and objects therefore, there is no compelling connection between objecthood and simplicity.[25] Weaker,

---

[25] Donald Baxter, *Hume's Difficulty. Time and Identity in the* Treatise, Routledge, Abingdon 2008, has forcefully argued that in texts like the following Hume restricts existence to simples. "'Tis evident, that existence in itself belongs only to unity, and is never applicable to number, but on account of the unites, of which the number is compos'd. Twenty men may be said to exist; but 'tis only because one, two, three, four, &c. are existent; and if you deny the existence of the latter, that of the former falls of course.' 'That term of unity is merely a fictitious denomination, which the mind may apply to any quantity of objects it collects together; nor can such an unity any more exist alone than number can, as being in reality a true number. But the unity, which can exist alone, and whose existence is necessary to that of all number, is of another kind, and must be perfectly indivisible, and incapable of being resolved into any lesser unity' (1.2.2.3). Since objects are existing particulars, this would restrict objecthood to simples and assign to simple objects a special ontological status. However, this text should be read carefully. The point of the argument is to support the finite divisibility of space. By referring to 'unites', Hume makes the point that a whole cannot exist without its parts and that such parts must be actual, real entities (see T. Holden, 'Infinite Divisibility and Actual Parts in Hume's *Treatise*', *Hume Studies*, 28, 2002 (3–25), 11–15). The target is the illusion of attributing unity or existence to complex objects 'alone', that is, independently of the actual existence of their constituents or 'unites' (which, in the case of extension, are unextended points). This is the position of the upholders of infinite divisibility: attempting to conceive of extensions without real constituent parts. By contrast, any complex object conceived as composed of actual parts exists; it exists dependently on the existence of such parts. It cannot be considered a unity in the same sense in which its components are unities; but this is simply another way of saying that such components are its parts. In the case of extension, such actual parts must be simple and unextended ('perfectly indivisible'). But out of the context of this argument for finite divisibility, Hume has no requirement that actual parts or unites be simple. Twenty men exist in virtue of the existence of one, two, three, four individual men. But individual men are not simple and indivisible and still are assumed to exist as unites or objects. When duly generalized, therefore, the 'strong and beautiful' argument is simply a statement of Hume's

because Hume in general resorts, when discussing of existence and objects, only to the first condition: to exist as an object is to exist alone or to possibly exist alone. Any impression and object is distinct, therefore different, and therefore separable from any other; and this is for it to exist as a substance. This holds without restrictions. According to Hume, this condition is systematically satisfied by perceptions and objects as they sensibly appear. 'I do not think that there are any two impressions, which are inseparably conjoin'd' (1.2.6.3). The ontological mark of objects is not simplicity but rather distinctness and separability. The simple–complex distinction, which is so important for Hume's theory of content and representation, does not cut much ontological ice.[26]

2.2.5 Equivalence

Hume's complex conception of the relations between impressions and objects of representation is summarized in the following (somewhat difficult) text:

> I say then, that since we may suppose, but never can conceive a specific difference betwixt an object and impression; any conclusion we form concerning the connexion and repugnance of impressions, will not be known certainly to be applicable to objects; but that on the other hand, whatever conclusions of this kind we form concerning objects, will most certainly be applicable to impressions. The reason is not difficult. As an object is suppos'd to be different from an impression, we cannot be sure, that the circumstance, upon which we found our reasoning, is common to both, supposing we form the reasoning upon the impression. 'Tis still possible, that the object may differ from it in that particular. But when we first form our reasoning concerning the object, 'tis beyond doubt, that the same reasoning must extend to the impression: And that because the quality of the object, upon which the argument is founded, must at least be conceiv'd by the mind; and cou'd not be conceiv'd, unless it were common to an impression; since we have no idea but what is deriv'd from that origin. (1.4.5.20)

The context is Hume's ad hominem argument that the 'hideous hypothesis' of Spinozism is 'almost the same with that of the immateriality of the soul' (1.4.5.19). The text expresses a lemma in that argument, which Hume endorses and which is

---

mereological commitments. But mereological composition does not entail, by Hume's or by my lights, deep ontological differences.

[26] If I read him correctly, this is close to the reading of the simple–complex distinction proposed in Garrett, *Cognition and Commitment*, 60, 63–4. Wright, *Hume's A Treatise*, 68, remarks that perceptual atoms, visible and tangible minima, are not the kind of simple impressions that are involved in the First Principle.

based on the assumption, also explicitly endorsed by Hume, that "tis impossible our idea of a perception, and that of an object or external existence can ever represent what are specifically different from each other". We 'may suppose' such a difference; but it is 'incomprehensible to us'; 'a relation without a relative' (1.4.5.19). This text may seem to open a gap between impressions and objects: there is no good transition from the connection and repugnance of impressions to those of objects; even though there is one from conclusions concerning objects to impressions. But things are not so simple. The argument relies on Two Viewpoints. The first inference, which does not deliver certain knowledge of objects, proceeds from the 'connexion and repugnance' of impressions ('we form the reasoning upon the impressions'). Impressions are here considered from the viewpoint of mental existence, as mental episodes. Hume says that this reasoning is not reliable in its conclusions about objects. These are also considered from the viewpoint of existence, as existing without the mind. It is open to us to suppose, if not to conceive, that such objects are specifically different from impressions: different as to properties with which they exist ('an object is suppos'd to be different from an impression').[27] Therefore, we can suppose that the 'circumstance, upon which the argument is founded' fails to be 'common' to the impression and the object. It can be possible for impressions, considered in their existence in the mind or as perceived, to differ in some property from objects, considered in their existence without the mind or as unperceived.

By contrast, in the second inference we proceed from properties of sensible objects: 'we first form our reasoning concerning the object'. In this case "tis beyond doubt, that the same reasoning must extend to the impression". This radical difference is explained by the fact that in the second inference impressions and objects are considered from the viewpoint of content: the features by which impressions present objects and objects are apprehended. This is entailed by the very fact that it proceeds from the objects, since this requires that 'the quality of the object, upon which the argument is founded', 'at least be conceiv'd by the mind'. And this would in turn not be possible 'unless it were common to an impression': that is, unless it were the content of an impression, which is what impressions and objects have in common. From the viewpoint of content, there is no room even for supposing that objects be specifically different from impressions, or different for their internal properties or as to their relations, locations, and durations.[28]

---

[27] Hume seems to hesitate whether to frame the argument in terms of some (supposed but not conceivable) specific difference between impressions and objects ('quality'); or of some difference in internal relations ('connexion and repugnance'); or of some difference in external relations, durations, situations (see the later discussion of continued existence). These are of course radically different properties; but they do not make a difference to the point of this part of the argument, which is that we cannot infer qualities or relations of objects from qualities or relations with which impressions exist in the mind.

[28] See also P. Kail, *Projection and Realism in Hume's Philosophy*, Oxford University Press, Oxford 2007, 14–15: 'In effect, the vulgar view of the perceptual relation to "external object"—that the objects of perception are simply presented to the mind—is retained, but the objects are construed as sense impressions'.

Hume's discussion of the conditions of correctness of these inferences, which is premised on Two Viewpoints, gives some indication about how to frame the ontological relations between impressions and objects. I think that, at this stage of the argument, in the context of the doctrine of elements and in relation to the minimal conception of objects, we should understand the relation between impressions and objects as (at least) one of *equivalence*. Impressions and objects have the same properties of content: the general appearance that determines what an impression presents is the same with that which individuates the presented object. Impressions and objects are thus the same as to how they contribute to thought-contents and as to their overall role in mental activity. But we do not have to commit, in the context of Hume's doctrine of elements, to their identity. For all we know right now, the differences we may suppose, if not conceive, between perceptions and objects might have modal force and amount to a difference in existence. Only in Part 4 of Book 1, in the context of his account of the idea of body, Hume concludes that there is no consistent way to conceive of a modal difference, a difference in existence between perceptions and objects (see § 9.4.1). At that stage of the theory, he can commit to the doctrine of the numerical identity of impressions of sensation and visible and tangible bodies. The principle that I propose for impressions and objects, at this stage, is limited to equivalence. Equivalence (as I will call this principle) is restricted to impressions. Complex ideas that are not copies of impressions but can be completely analysed and explained in terms of simple elements given in impression (the golden mountain is the example) have objects as their contents. 'To form an idea of an object and to form an idea simply is the same thing' (1.1.7.6). But we would not say that they are equivalent to objects, because one intrinsic feature of what is to be an object, that is, presence, or reality is missing. They are equivalent at most to possible objects. By contrast, impressions of sensation present objects by being objects of sense; and the ideas derived from and corresponding to such impressions are representations of actual objects.

2.3 The First Principle

Two Viewpoints and the parsimonious ontology of perceptions summarized by Equivalence are the background for the First Principle, which gives expression to Hume's conception of object representation.

2.3.1 Content

The opening pages of the *Treatise* establish, with a deceitfully plain and perspicuous sequence of claims and arguments, a fundamental principle of the science of human nature. In Section 1.1.1: *Of the origin of our ideas*, Hume advances 'one general proposition' (1.1.1.7) or a 'general maxim' (1.1.1.10), which he formulates as follows:

> All our simple ideas in their first appearance are deriv'd from simple impressions, which are correspondent to them, and which they exactly represent.
> (1.1.1.7)

This principle he calls 'the principle of the priority of impressions to ideas' (1.1.1.11). He adds: 'This is the first principle I establish in the science of the human nature' and warns that 'the simplicity of its appearance' should not induce to 'despise it' (1.1.1.12). I will refer to it simply as the First Principle, to keep in mind the order and the importance of its introduction. Hume regards the First Principle as fundamental: it is expression of his naturalism and empiricism about contents and thought. It summarizes how impressions and ideas 'stand with regard to their existence, and which of the impressions and ideas are causes, and which effects' (1.1.1.6). And of this question, he says: 'the *full* examination of this question is the subject of the present treatise' (1.1.1.7).

The content of the principle is that all simple ideas stand in relations of *derivation* and of *correspondence* with simple impressions of sensation and that in this way the former *exactly represent* the latter. Two Viewpoints provides the conceptual framework for understanding the First Principle. Derivation is a relation pertaining to the mental existence of perceptions; correspondence, to their contents; representation is a function of both. Two Viewpoints allows us to explain the convergence of derivation and correspondence and, in this way, the nature and the importance of the ideas abiding by the principle.

The relation of derivation is causal. Impressions cause ideas and this requires, in Hume's philosophy, that there be constant conjunctions of resembling impressions and resembling ideas. (That is, impressions of sensation that resemble each other are constantly conjoined to ideas which resemble each other.) In presence of such a constant conjunction, we cannot think that the relation between impressions and ideas can 'arise from chance'; rather, it 'clearly proves a dependence' (1.1.1.8). This derivation, of course, relates to mental existence: the existence in the mind of simple ideas depends on that of simple impressions. Hume's characterization of the causal relation between impressions of sensation, at this initial stage of his argument, is sketchy (there is no hint of how the constant conjunction of impressions and ideas proves a dependence). The phenomenal difference of force and vivacity of conception allows determining the direction of the derivation or dependence of impressions and ideas. The most general ground for deciding of this is 'the order of their *first appearance*'. Other arguments, like those from obstruction or accidentally limited use of the organs of sensation, are less general (1.1.1.8). But to observe the order of appearance of kinds of perceptions we must first have a basis for distinguishing such kinds. Given their qualitative correspondence, force and vivacity of conception is the only basis for this distinction: impressions, marked by their distinctive feeling, can be observed to always precede ideas.

The relation of correspondence consists in the resemblance of the qualitative features of impressions and ideas. Such qualities individuate their mental existence as well as their content. From the viewpoint of what they present and represent, the resemblance of impressions and ideas determines their correspondence. The role of Two Viewpoints is, again, crucial. The resemblance of qualitative features is the common ground of the relations of derivation and of correspondence because it can be considered under different viewpoints and perform different explanatory roles. It allows us to observe and collect kinds or perceptions and, in this way, contributes to determining their causal dependence. But it can also determine that impressions and ideas present and represent the same conditions and thus correspond. This is an internal relation between those perceptions, consisting in the resemblance of their individuating features. It is a contingent fact whether from an impression of sensation a corresponding idea derives; but given this fact, their correspondence is not contingent: it is not susceptible to change unless the perceptions change. Two Viewpoints thus makes it possible to keep consistently together the dimensions of causation and of resemblance, or of existence and of content, of the First Principle and of representation. In this connection, it is interesting that Hume remarks that 'every idea, with which the imagination is furnish'd, first makes its appearance in a corresponding impression' (1.2.3.1).[29] Ideas are first present *in* impressions. This can only make sense under Two Viewpoints. If we think of ideas and impressions as mental existents, ideas cannot be part of impressions since they causally depend on them and thus are distinct beings. But this can be right with regard to relations of content, if an idea corresponds to an impression which precedes it.

2.3.2 Point and Status

Together, derivation and correspondence constitute the representational nature of ideas: determining the conditions of object representation is the point of the First Principle.

> When I shut my eyes and think of my chamber, the ideas I form are exact representations of the impressions I felt; nor is there any circumstance of the one,

---

[29] The context is a restatement of the First Principle: ' No discovery cou'd have been made more happily for deciding all controversies concerning ideas, than that above-mention'd, that impressions always take the precedency of them, and that every idea, with which the imagination is furnish'd, first makes its appearance in a correspondent impression' (1.2.3.1).

which is not to be found in the other. In running over my other perceptions, I find still the same resemblance and representation. Ideas and impressions appear always to correspond to each other. (1.1.1.3)

The ideas that satisfy the condition of derivation and of correspondence 'exactly represent' impressions of sensation; therefore, by Equivalence, they exactly represent *objects of sense*. Ideas represent impressions of sensation that *are* objects of sense and thereby *present* objects. Impressions of sense, considered in their contents, are in fact the same as sensible objects. This is the ground for considering as object-representing the ideas which satisfy the First Principle. Notice that correspondence establishes the representational relation only if taken together with the causal dependence of ideas on impressions. This latter makes for the order of representation, contributing to determining what represents what; and this order seems to be required for an idea to be the representation of an object.[30]

The point of the First Principle is thus to provide the basis of a naturalistic conception of object representation, or cognitive contact with objects, as this is realized in human nature and as the primitive ground of cognitive content and of mental activity in general. The First Principle has constitutive import. It says what is to be the representation of an object, given human nature, and how such representation is possible at all for us. Ideas that do not abide by the First Principle are metaphysically and physically possible. But given our cognitive nature, these ideas do not put us in cognitive contact with an impression of sensation or sensible object. No other kind of object representation is physically possible for us; but *this* kind certainly is possible. The relation between our impressions of sensation and our ideas realizes for us object representation.[31] I would add that Hume's concept of object representation involves an assumption of object-dependence. Contents that represent objects must depend on the objects they represent and represent them in virtue of such dependence. Such contents would not exist without their objects existing and they correspond to them by standing with them in

---

[30] For a good discussion of representation and copying of impressions by ideas, see Schafer, 'Hume's Unified Theory'. Schafer rightly emphasizes that representation by copying is fundamental among, but not exhaustive of, the varieties of mental content recognized by Hume.

[31] Therefore, impressions of sensation have representational nature: they are what only can be represented. See B. Stroud, 'Gilding or Staining' the World with "Sentiments" and "Phantasms"', in R. Read & K. A. Richman, eds., *The New Hume Debate* (Revised Edition), Routledge, London/New York 2007 (16–30), 25–8. Stroud remarks that (in order for the projective account of moral, aesthetic, and causal ideas to work; more deeply, in order for the working of imagination to be intelligible at all, 20–1) 'at least some impressions must be understood "intentionally"', that is, as having contents. He also claims that Hume is prepared to think of impressions in these terms, but that 'he is not really in a position to explain how we could ever have any thoughts at all of something's being so', because of his faulty identification of objects with combination of qualities and of his lack of an adequate notion of judgement. My reading of Hume's conception of impressions is more or less in direct contrast with Stroud's: in the light of Two Viewpoints, of Equivalence, and of their constitutive contribution to the relation of representation, Hume's impressions can be individuated in terms of content.

such existential relation. Hume explicitly recognizes the object-dependent aspect of object representation. In a gloss that specifies and articulates the First Principle, he makes the following remark, introducing a maxim concerning the conditions of representation:

> Ideas always represent their objects or impressions; and *vice versa*, there are some objects necessary to give rise to every idea. (1.3.14.6)

This maxim, *Representation*, sets Hume's basic constraint on the nature of ideas with representational import. To represent is to represent objects of sense. This is all there is, primitively, to object representation in Hume's philosophy; it is in this sense that ideas *always* represent objects or impressions. But what is really interesting here is the '*vice versa*' clause. This clause makes explicit something that the First Principle only implied. For ideas to represent objects, the objects forming their contents must themselves exist; otherwise, the corresponding ideas would not exist and no representational content would be available. Representation is a real relation; it cannot be a relation without a relative. The First Principle makes room in our nature for this concept of representation. By the First Principle, object representation, at the primitive and fundamental level, consists in the real relations of causation and resemblance in which ideas stand to objects or impressions of sensation. Thus, object-representing ideas depend by natural necessity on objects. Such ideas can exist only if the objects that form their contents are actual. This does not exclude that we can have ideas the contents of which are not actual objects or are not even as of objects. Also in this case, Hume is pursuing taxonomy rather than exclusion. 'Ideas always represent the objects or impressions, from which they are deriv'd, and can never without a fiction represent or be apply'd to any other' (1.2.3.11). Therefore, with a fiction, that is, by some operation of the imagination, ideas can represent (allow us to conceive) or be applied to objects (notice the broader characterization of their role) they do not depend on. Such ideas, as we will see, can be cognitively important and even epistemically valuable but they fail to acquaint us with objects and their properties.

The First Principle restricts exact representation to simple impressions and ideas. We have already seen that this restriction has no deep and general ontological implications. It is rather an aspect of Hume's 'Logic' or doctrine of elements. Simple perceptions, impressions, or ideas are 'such as admit no distinction and no separation' (1.1.1.2: no distinction and separation in relation to their internal, individuating properties, of course; as episodes, they are all distinguishable and separable). It is with this restriction in mind that Hume says that ideas are the reflection of impressions and vice versa, 'so that all perceptions of the mind are double, and appear both as impressions and ideas' (1.1.1.3). It is also only with reference to simple impressions and perceptions that we can 'know on which side this dependence lies', because it can be observed that simple

48 THE FIRST PRINCIPLE

impressions always precede the resembling simple ideas (1.1.1.8). The importance of the simple–complex distinction in relation to the First Principle becomes clear in the light of the (qualified) foundational programme of Hume's philosophy. Success in this programme requires identifying, in a naturalistic framework, a level at which the success of our ideas, the appropriateness of our contents, and their good cognitive standing are secure: at which point it is secured that our ideas represent objects. The problem is raised by Hume's assumption that ideas can be produced, or at least deeply transformed, by mental activity, specifically by the imagination; and that the ideas we ordinarily and mostly entertain and apply, ideas of complex things and events, might well have been put in place in this way. Complex ideas can fail to be representations of complex impressions.

Hume's response to this problem is to shift from complex to simple contents, to restrict the First Principle to simple ideas, and to argue that, with reference to simple ideas, representational character is necessary, because it is a condition for their very existence. (The necessity in question is physical: simple ideas without a preceding resembling simple impression would lack a causal condition of existence; according to Hume, it is a physical, not a metaphysical, necessity that everything coming to existence has a cause.) Simple ideas, with their necessarily representational character, secure the satisfaction of the demand for a fundamental if limited cognitive contact between mind and objects. On this reading, the simple–complex distinction is not manifest in the phenomenology of our experience. The input of our ordinary experience consists of complex impressions. The distinction of their simple components is a further exercise of the imagination ('Tho' a particular colour, taste, and smell are qualities all united together in this apple, 'tis easy to perceive they are not the same, but are at least distinguishable from each other', 1.1.1.2). But if we are to understand the concept of representation and how representation of objects is possible at all for human nature, we must resort to the First Principle; and, with it, to the mereology of simple and complex perceptions.

The First Principle is thus the basis for a theoretically important taxonomy of perceptions.

(1) Ideas deriving from and corresponding to impressions of sensation exactly represent the objects which such impressions are, or which are present as such impressions. Exact representation is secured at the level of simple ideas; but also complex ideas can perfectly well (but need not) derive from and correspond to complex impressions.

(2) There is a weaker sense in which complex ideas that do not exactly represent impressions or objects may still be considered representational. All such complex ideas are generated by the imagination. But some of those ideas have contents that depend only on combinatorial operations of the imagination, which transpose simple representational ideas. In these cases

the contents of these ideas are still such that they could *possibly represent* some object: they are ideas of possible existents. These ideas are still indirectly and potentially representational because their contents, were they actual, would individuate objects and given the right real relations would be exact representations of them. What bars them from being object representing is not any feature of their content, but its actuality, its being given in impression (the idea of a golden mountain is an example, 1.2.2.8).

(3) Other complex ideas produced by the imagination are such that they do not even potentially represent objects. This is not because they are inconsistent but because they essentially include some substantive element of content that could not be traced to any impression of sensation. These elements, and the ideas they contribute to, are instances of content and can be cognitively in order; but they are such not by representing objects. There are no conditions at which their contents could be actual as objects, as real existents and we could be so related to them as to represent them. Ideas like those of an empty space and time, of necessary connection, of body, of personal identity are the examples.

To have some labels at hand: the ideas, simple or complex, that are completely explained by the First Principle are *exact representations*. The ideas, simple and complex, whose contents are reducible to representations, modulo some operation of the imagination, are *potential representations*; the contentful ideas that are not so reducible are *non-object representing*, or *non-representational* for short. Non-representational ideas are the proper domain and exclusive product of the imagination; they essentially depend on it for their existence, contents, and cognitive roles. The First Principle therefore is not meant by Hume to confine us to a simple and absolute alternative between what has cognitive content and what lacks it. It has the task of distinguishing and ordering causally, logically, and epistemically different kinds of ideas and cognitions, within the context of an overall naturalistic account of the mind. The quantification that figures in the content of the First Principle must be understood as restricted to ideas actually or potentially representing objects. Since the alternative individuations and explanations of ideas and cognitions (by impressions of sensation and by the imagination) make room for possibilities of error, both in the ordinary application of such ideas and in their philosophical understanding, the First Principle is also a critical tool—as Hume describes and applies it.[32]

---

[32] Garrett, *Cognition and Commitment*, 57, is completely right about this: the 'primary importance' of the First Principle is its motivating 'more detailed investigations into the cognitive processes underlying the use of central yet problematic concepts'. The crux of the New versus Old Hume debate is whether there can be meaning or content outside the bounds of the First Principle. New Humeans are right in holding that there can be; although they fail to grasp the categorial difference between content conforming to the principle and imaginative content.

The status of the First Principle follows on its content and point. The interpretive debate has been whether it is an a priori principle or an a posteriori discovery and generalization; and whether it is a principle of meaning or has only epistemological import.[33] On my view, the debate makes the mistaken assumption that a priori and a posteriori, meaning-theoretical and epistemological considerations are in Hume mutually exclusive. As to the first point, what is distinctive of Hume's naturalism is precisely the combination of a priori conceptual principles and of a posteriori facts concerning the natural mind and cognition. Hume's naturalism does not aim to eliminate a priori principles but to locate them in the nature of our natural cognition, with its account of general and modal conceptual content. In this way, it also aims to vindicate the a priori claims that express conditions of conceivability, grounded on the identities of ideas. The science of human nature postulates the distinction between basic, deep regularities and merely accidental features of mind and cognition, as well as some sort of fit between such regularities and conceptual principles concerning thought and cognition (see § 5.3.1). Insofar as it gives expression to these conceptual principles in terms of the natural properties and relations of impressions and ideas, the First Principle has thus a *relatively* a priori status.[34]

2.4 Existence and Reference

2.4.1 Representing Existence

Since existential dependence is a necessary condition for ideas to represent impressions or objects, Hume must clarify how this condition figures in the explanation of object-representing content, of exact representation. Since, as it is clear from Hume's qualitative, phenomenal specification of content, the condition of existence cannot be purely externalist, its contribution to object-representing content must consist in its being somehow represented. But right here an important difficulty arises. Any perception with at least potentially representational

---

[33] See, for discussion, Garrett, *Cognition and Commitment*, 43–50. Garrett holds that the First Principle is a posteriori. However, he also remarks that, to account for the role of experience in our cognition, besides the view that representations are copies of impressions, one must also introduce the view that 'understanding—construed as a mental act—requires such representations and depends on their presented content' (47). If this, as Garrett remarks, is an 'additional premise', it is plausible that it is a priori. The First Principle turns out to be relatively a priori.

[34] D. Landy, *Hume's Science of Human Nature. Scientific Realism, Reason, and Substantial Explanation*, Routledge, New York/London 2018, 22–3, 149–50, distinguishes between the Copy principle and the Representational Copy principle. This comes very close to my ascription of relatively a priori status to the First Principle: an empirical condition (causal dependence and resemblance) is joined to a conceptual identification (representational import). See also, for a fuller, excellent discussion of this topic, D. Landy, *Kant's Inferentialism. The Case against Hume*, Routledge, New York/Oxford 2015, 30–1, 36–7.

character, any perception as of an object, includes an assumption of (at least possible) existence. (As the context makes clear, Hume is here considering perceptions in their contents, not in their mental existence.) 'There is no impression nor idea on any kind, of which we have any consciousness or memory, that is not conceiv'd as existent; and 'tis evident, that from this consciousness the most perfect idea and assurance of *being* is deriv'd' (1.2.6.2). Also in this case, the quantification must be understood as implicitly restricted. Not all perceptions with cognitive content have contents as of objects: some, like the idea of necessary connection, the idea of an empty space and time, the idea of self, and the idea of external existence do not (except by some illusion). But many of our ideas do have contents as of objects, that is, as of existents. With regard to such ideas, there is the problem of marking off the ideas with which we represent actual existence from those with which we only entertain possible existents, or exact from potential representations. The distinction between mere possibility and existence is itself a perfectly ordinary aspect of our cognitive practices. Hume's repeated reference to the 'reality' of 'existence' (1.3.8.6) and to 'real existence' (1.3.9.6; 1.4.4.11; 2.3.10.2; 2.3.10.11; 3.1.1.9) and to their importance (these phrases figure in his definition of truth) thus requires explanation.

Hume seems, however, to call into question any account of existence as a feature of content. Hume denies that impressions of sensation can give existence *as an object* or include an *existence trope*, which could be the cause and the model for ideas representing existence. Hume's arguments for this conclusion are a posteriori and a priori. A posteriori, differential ascriptions of existence could be explained if the idea of existence were derived 'from a distinct impression, conjoin'd with every perception or object of our thought' (1.2.6.2). Or if we had 'an abstract idea of existence, distinguishable and separable from the idea of particular objects' (*Appendix* 2). Hume rejects both these explanations. We do not find any such impression. 'Whoever opposes this, must necessarily point out that distinct impression, from which the idea of entity is deriv'd, and must prove, that this impression is inseparable from every perception we believe to be existent' (1.2.6.5). And, by the imagination, all individual impressions are separable: 'I do not think there are any two distinct impressions, which are inseparably conjoin'd.' Hume thus denies that there are particular ideas, with a distinct, separable content, which represent existence. Therefore, we cannot represent existence by a general idea either, which (on Hume's theory of abstraction) would require such particular ideas.

A priori, the ascription of (real, actual) existence could not make any difference to how we represent objects of sense. If there were a distinct property and a distinct impression of existence, to conceive of an object as existent, we would have to add something, a further property, to the content of the idea that individuates it. But then, no simple object could ever be represented as actual or existing, because such representation would always be complex. And no complex object could be exactly represented as existing because the representation of its existence would add a property to the content of the idea which already exactly represented it. Hume makes this point explicitly, in connection with the strictly related topic of belief.

> All the perceptions of the mind are of two kinds, *viz.* impressions and ideas, which differ from each other only in their different degrees of force and vivacity. Our ideas are copy'd from our impressions, and represent them in all their parts. When you wou'd any way vary the idea of a particular object, you can only encrease or diminish its force and vivacity. If you make any other change on it, it represents a different object or impression.   (1.3.7.5)

If representing existence changed the content of our idea of an object or impression, we would end up by representing a different one. Hume concludes that the idea of existence cannot be different from the idea we have of any object.

> The idea of existence, then, is the very same with the idea of what we conceive to be existent. To reflect on any thing simply, and to reflect on it as existent, are nothing different from each other. That idea, when conjoin'd with the idea of any object, makes no addition to it. Whatever we conceive, we conceive to be existent. Any idea we please to form is the idea of a being; and the idea of a being is any idea we please to form.   (1.2.6.4; see 1.3.7.2)

But this leaves us with the difficulty of explaining how existence (reality, actuality) can be a feature of representation. Existence should be sensibly manifest and represented but not as a distinct quality or object.

2.4.2 Manners of Conception

Hume provides an original and important account of how object-representing contents can represent existence. The account, which is one of the philosophical achievements of the *Treatise*, broadens the conception of the content and cognitive role of impressions along two dimensions: the mode and manner with which objects are present in impression; the fixedness or invariance of the order of objects, of the scenes given in sense and memory.

The contrast between feeling and thinking opens Book 1 ('Everyone of himself will readily perceive the difference betwixt feeling and thinking', 1.1.1.1) and closes the Appendix to the whole *Treatise* ('Had I said, that two ideas of the same object can only be different by their different *feeling*, I shou'd have been nearer the truth', *Appendix* 22). The contrast marks a difference in how perceptions exist in the mind but, per Two Viewpoints, has consequences for content. In this latter respect, perceptions, in the mode of thinking or as thoughts are only individuated by their objects and can only be differentiated in terms of their objects: different objects, different thoughts. But perceptions with the same objects can be felt differently and this can make a difference to what they overall present and represent and to their cognitive effects.[35]

The mode of feeling, differently from that of thinking, makes room for different manners or modes of conception of the same ideas. These manners of conception determine different cognitive roles for represented or conceived contents. The prime application of the notion of manners of conception is in explaining the differences between impressions and ideas, the similarities between impressions and ideas of memory, and the dissimilarities between ideas of memory and of imagination.

> And here I believe every one will readily agree with me, that the ideas of the memory are more *strong* and *lively* than those of the fancy. A painter, who intended to represent a passion or emotion of any kind, wou'd endeavour to get a sight of a person actuated by a like emotion, in order to enliven his ideas, and give them a force and vivacity superior to what is found in those, which are mere fictions of the imagination. (1.3.5.5)

The difference in manner of conception, in force and vivacity, between impressions of sensation and ideas explains that existence is ascribed only to the former or to objects of sense. It can also make a difference among ideas with contents as of objects, without being itself represented or, better, without counting itself as a distinct element of representation. Reality or existence can be given, ultimately, only by 'an immediate perception of our memory or senses' (1.3.4.1). But such perception is not the presentation of an object or quality; it rather consists in a variation in the manner of conception of some object or quality: 'the different degrees of force and liveliness, with which they strike upon the mind, and make their way into our thought and consciousness' (1.1.1.1). This manner of conception constitutes our apprehension of existence and contributes as an essential dimension to the exact representation of objects: as their actuality or existence, their being what is there and can be referred to. (I will discuss the feeling of reality, the associated modes of conception, and their cognitive effects more in detail when we come to treat of Hume's theory of belief, see §§ 11.1.1–3).[36]

---

[35] The importance of feeling in the philosophy of Hume has been widely recognized but not always accurately. Feeling in the present context is specified in terms of manners of conception with specific *cognitive* imports. Interpreters who, like Kemp Smith and Barry Stroud, give unilateral emphasis to a supposed non-cognitive character of Hume's feeling and its closeness to passions are on the wrong track.
[36] See Waxman, *Hume's Theory of Consciousness*, 33–9. This explanation of our discriminative sense of reality has left many interpreters unconvinced. However, there is something we can say in its favour. Self-intimating character (force) and sensorial thickness (vivacity), together with a sense of

There is a second way in which real existence is present in impressions of sensation and represented by ideas. While not prominent in the text and scarcely noticed by interpreters, it is philosophically interesting on its own. We can start from a difference between memory, a faculty of representation, and imagination, the cognitive but non-representational faculty (fuller discussion at §§ 3.2.1–2). Hume writes that 'the imagination is not restrain'd to the same order and form with the original impressions' and that memory as opposed to imagination preserves 'the original form, in which its objects were presented', the 'order and position' of objects of sense (1.1.4.3). This is a constitutive condition of memory: failing to preserve the fixed order of objects in sense is a 'defect or imperfection' of memory, a failing in its 'chief exercise' (1.1.3.3). The obvious implication is that impressions and objects of sense have and manifest such an 'original' 'order and form'. Since the ideas that represent impressions and objects are, primitively and necessarily, ideas of memory (by the First Principle), preserving the original order and form of impressions and objects is a condition and an aspect of their exact representation by ideas of memory.[37] In other words, such order and form, insofar as there is a representation of them, are and are manifest as fixed and invariant.

The fixed order of impressions of sensation and of ideas of memory is a substantive feature of sensible representation. Spatial impressions and spatial experience present us with complex sensorial *scenes*, which display partial spatial orderings of qualitatively specified objects.

> 'Tis likewise evident that, as the senses, in changing their objects, are necessitated to change them regularly, and take them as they lie *contiguous* to each other, the imagination must by long custom acquire the same method of thinking, and run along the parts of space and time in conceiving its objects. (1.1.4.2)

As Hume explicitly says, the order of spatial objects influences the transitions of the imagination. A fortiori, we can say, it is a constitutive condition of memory, and thus of object representation, that it is locked onto the order and form of

---

fixedness, seem to be essential to the phenomenology of perceptual experience, in contrast with dream or illusion. They seem to contribute to the feeling of what happens. Kant's principle of the 'Anticipations of Perception': 'In all appearances, the real that is an object of sensation has intensive magnitude, that is, a degree', where the 'real of sensation' is a 'merely subjective representation' and 'intensive magnitude' is 'a degree of influence on the sense' is along Hume's lines (*Critique of Pure Reason*, 201–2).

[37] Hume tends to assimilate perceptions of sense and of memory and to talk of 'an impression of the memory or senses' (1.3.5.1) or of 'an impression present to the memory or senses' (1.3.6.4). (See also 1.3.6.7: 'the immediate impressions of our memory and senses'; 1.3.9.2: 'immediately present to the memory or senses'; 1.3.10.9: 'impressions of the memory'; 1.3.16.6: 'some impression immediately present to their memory or senses'.) The cognitive and epistemic equivalence of sense and memory ('ideas of the memory...are equivalent to impressions', 1.3.4.1) is assumed in the explanation of causal cognition.

spatial impressions or objects of sensation. Such order and form contributes to object-representing content and to any further cognitive step by being represented as fixed and invariant, as the 'inseparable connexion, by which they [simple ideas] are united in our memory' (1.1.4.6).What holds of spatial sensorial scenes seems to be also true of the '*co-existent* parts' of an object, 'connected together by a strong relation' (1.4.3.5). Hume is even ready to talk of sense and memory as presenting inseparable objects. 'We have no other notion of cause and effect, but that of certain objects, which have been *always conjoin'd* together, and which in all past instances have been found inseparable' (1.3.6.15). Since Hume is distinguishing the output of imaginative processes from the input of sensible representations, he cannot have in mind the contents of our ordinary experience, which are shaped by associations and imagination. The inseparable connexion is between impressions of sensation or objects of sense as such. Hume has a rich view of the content of sense experience, which includes some sort of non-conceptual unity, unity given with the impressions of sensation and preserved in memory. This bears some resemblance to Kant's notion of a 'synopsis of the senses': a receptive (not spontaneous or synthetic) unification of the manifold of the senses.[38]

The fixedness and invariance of the order and form of objects, which contribute to the content and the cognitive import of memory, seem to be a way in which we represent objects as existing or actual. A problem might arise if we understood the fixed order and form of objects in impressions, or the inseparable connexion of ideas in memory, as a modal qualification of sensible contents. Modality, in Hume's philosophy, arises from the inferences of imagination; but we are now putting to one side the operations of the imagination and the senses and memory are not inferential.[39] And, as it is well known, Hume excludes any 'primary con-

---

[38] Kant, *Critique of Pure Reason*, 127 fn. 130. But even here Kant ascribes a synthetic function to imagination at a very primitive level, assuming the non-connectedness of sensible content—something Hume's theory simply does not require. Furthermore, Kant's synopsis refer to the manifold of intuition a priori, while Hume's order is a fact. Perhaps Fodor's worst interpretive mistake is to downplay the extent to which informationally rich impressions make available the idea of a system of realities, see Fodor, *Hume Variations*, 129. Fodor's strictures against Hume's recourse to imagination (as something-I-know-not-what), because of his lack of the notions of mental trace and of structural representation thus lack any compelling ground (130–1).

[39] See T. Crane, 'The Nonconceptual Content of Experience', in Crane, ed., *The Contents of Experience* (137–57), 149–52: perceptual experience lacks inferential structure (pro tanto it is nonconceptual) but it is not unstructured. For an articulation of the view that sensory awareness is 'most naturally understood as directed not at facts, but at spatiotemporal particulars, see, for instance, J. J. Valberg, 'The Puzzle of Experience', in T. Crane, ed., *The Contents of Experience*, Cambridge University Press, Cambridge 1992 (18–47), 20. See M. Johnston, 'The Function of Sensory Awareness', in Szabo Gendler & Hawthorne, eds., *Perceptual Experience* (260–90), 270. Johnston further contends that the function of sensory awareness is not to provide qualia or to present facts or propositions but 'to present truthmakers for the immediate judgments we make about the scenarios we are sensing' as 'new topics for thought and judgment'. And that sensory awareness can be of some structured state which corresponds to judgements (279–82). These remarks are relevant for the interpretation of Hume's representation of existence.

nexion betwixt the ideas' which would support causal inferences and which are by construction object-representing (1.3.8.13). However, there is a way out of this difficulty. The fact that the senses are 'necessitated' in their change of objects may not indicate a modal condition; such necessitation (or connexion) may not express the dual of possibility. Rather, it could be seen as the expression of the actuality of objects in their representation; the fact that insofar as sensorial scenes are present or are represented, we have not available the thought or even the sense that they could possibly be otherwise. To represent impressions and objects as actual or existent because of their fixedness is not to think that they in some way uphold themselves against some other possibility; it is rather that this is how such objects exist, how they actually are, nothing else being there for us to think.[40]

Notice also that Hume has a role in cognition for more or less elusive feelings like that of fixedness and invariance. He mentions a feeling of remembering, which includes a conception of an earlier action of the mind but which in its mode eludes any exact determination ('that certain *je-ne-scai-quoi*, of which 'tis impossible to give any definition or description, but which every one sufficiently understands'). This feeling is an aspect of what we think when we have an idea of our past thoughts (1.3.8.16). This *je-ne-scai-quoi* seems precisely a manner in which such ideas appear to the mind or exist with the mind and which gives us a conception of their pastness. In the present case, because of a feeling of fixedness and invariance, impressions and ideas derived from them and resembling deliver more than the individuating qualities of objects: they present and represent objects as actual or existent.

2.4.3 Representation, Reference, and Reality

This account of the representation of existence or actuality allows us to clarify Hume's conception of exact representation. David Owen has remarked that the ideas of 'existent entities' have judgmental character, since they involve an affirmation. Owen also importantly points out that this character does not consist in a propositional structure, as if they were the mental reflection of a sentence, but rather in their involving an existential commitment. Judgmental import does not consist in a structure or in some additional element of content, but in the manner of conception of ideas (1.3.7.5 fn. 20).[41] Hume's exact representations combine

---

[40] Somewhat in the spirit of the 'Actually' operator introduced by Davies and Humberstone, whose function is to restrict reference to a single world as the actual world, see M. Davies & L. Humberstone, 'Two Notions of Necessity', *Philosophical Studies*, 38, 1980 (1–30).

[41] See Owen, *Hume's Reason*, 91, 99, 103. Rejecting the view that complex ideas are formed by mirroring sentences is important for a correct understanding of Hume's association of ideas. See also C. Echelbarger, 'Hume and the Logicians', in Easton, ed., *Logic and the Workings of Mind* (137–51), 147: 'So, while many propositions may contain at least two terms united together by the understanding, the *psychologically and epistemologically simplest* of propositions will be single ideas

object-dependence, existential import, cognitive safety, and qualitative, phenomenal individuation. We can express this complex character by reading a dimension of demonstrative reference into such ideas; by regarding Hume's exact representations as *inner demonstratives*. Ideas abiding by the First Principle perform the general cognitive role of demonstratives: singling out individual particulars by standing with them in a relation (causation and resemblance) that makes them directly available as topics of thought and cognition. The inner character of the demonstrative relation consists in the fact that, for Hume, such particulars are equivalently objects and impressions. As well as in the fact that it is in virtue of properties of mental existence, causal derivation, and resemblance that ideas represent their objects. No external condition is admissible. Two Viewpoints secures the transition from properties of mental existence to properties of content; Equivalence secures that our ideas, if the right conditions are satisfied, do not fall short of representing objects, items that can exist unperceived. This also secures the cognitive safety of this sort of representation. To have an idea representing or referring to an impression or object is to have in mind something of the form: *This such*. Where: *Such* is a sensible, that is, a sensorially, qualitatively specified particular (without any conceptual recognitional element). Of course, no demonstrative would be possible without the reality of what it is addressed to, the existence of the object we are referring to by our: *This*. But this condition is secured precisely by the nature of impressions of sensation, by their forceful manner of conception and their fixedness, which form the existential dimension of the content of primitively representing ideas.[42]

of the *existence* of some kind of individual object and these will not have to be formed by any act of uniting ideas *other* than the ideas composing the idea of the object itself'. When we simply think of a tree we think of a-tree's-existing. (And when we have the impression of a three, we conceive of *this*-tree's-existing.)

[42] Landy, *Kant's Inferentialism*, 108, following Sellars, proposes a 'this-such' form for Kant's intuitions, identifying the 'such' dimension with a conceptual specification of the object demonstratively located. Leaving to a side the thorny issue of the conceptual character of Kant's intuitions, we can follow Hume in regarding such specification as non-conceptual. The idea of internal demonstrative import is familiar in contemporary discussions of the contents of experience. See Valberg, 'Puzzle of Experience', 21–2: presence and reference can be either internal or external; P. Snowdon, 'How to interpret "Direct Perception"', in Crane, ed., *The Contents of Experience* (48–78), 56,67,72 ascribes to Hume and qualifiedly endorses the view that the objects we can single out in a demonstrative way, in virtue of our experience, are perceptions in the mind—what we can directly perceive, what we can fix on as objects of demonstrative thought in virtue of our experience—not external, space-occupying bodies. Snowdon also remarks that Hume is committed to the fundamental epistemological position of demonstrative judgements as opposed to judgements as to what kind of object is currently perceived. Chalmers, 'Perception and the Fall from Eden', 109, holds that the experience of objects involves phenomenally determined demonstrative modes of presentation; in the Edenic world one is directly acquainted with and can demonstrate phenomenal *Thises*. See also D. Chalmers, *Constructing the World*, Oxford University Press, Oxford 2012, 286–7, for the notion of 'experiential demonstratives'. For an excellent discussion of how a step in our conceptualization of phenomenal properties consists in a demonstrative reference to an episode of experience ('introspective reference') issuing in a judgement of the form '*this* (phenomenal property) *is present*', see B. Gertler, *Self-Knowledge*, Routledge, London/New York 2011, 114–15, 118–19 (Hume's forceful and lively manner of conception substitutes introspective attending as the bearer of the demonstrative).

Hume claims that the 'reference of the idea to an object' is an 'extraneous denomination, of which in itself it bears no mark or character' (1.1.7.6). This may sound cryptic (and externalist), but, having discussed Hume's conception of object representation, we are in fact on familiar grounds. The context of this claim is the view that to conceive an idea simply is the same as conceiving the idea of an object. The concept of reference is introduced to mark the difference between the *simple conception* of an individual particular and the representation of its *real existence*. Reference does not add anything to the features that individuate objects as contents of representation; rather, it posits them and allows us to represent such objects as actual. Reference is an 'extraneous denomination' simply in the sense that the representation of existence is not realized with elements of content but with manners of conception. Against this background, the only primary kind of reference can be to qualitatively individuated, actual particulars, by a demonstrative of the form: *This such*.[43]

Hume's notion of reference is, as I said, a direct one. This, however, requires qualification. If we understand directness as cognitive primitiveness or immediateness, Hume's reference is as direct as one may want. There is no involvement of concepts or descriptions. But if directness is understood in the sense that reference does not consist in a qualitative presentation of objects, then there is no such thing as direct reference in Hume's philosophy. The point, as we know by now, is that the individuation and presence of particulars, which makes them count as objects of reference (of exact representation), is only naturally realized sensibly, that is, in impressions of sensation. For Hume, existents are only present to be represented or referred to as qualitative, sensible impressions, with modes of appearance like force and vivacity or fixedness and invariance.[44]

In this connection, it is interesting to consider the following important text:

> We can never have reason to believe that any object exists, of which we cannot form an idea. For as all our reasonings concerning existence are deriv'd from causation, and as all our reasonings concerning causation are deriv'd from the experienced conjunction of objects, not from any reasoning or reflection, the

---

[43] On singular reference and its problems for Hume, see D. Pears, *Hume's System. An Examination of the First Book of his* Treatise, Oxford University Press, New York 1990, 11–12, 33–4, 37. Pears remarks (a) that Hume's theory needs both a referential and a descriptive component of content and (b) that in the case of immediate perception, this is not problematic because impressions are self-intimating, speak for themselves, identify themselves. However, (c) the case of memory is problematic because reference can only be provided by the context of a task of recollection, but it is left unexplained; (d) singular causal reference works better, it is provided by the occurrent impression. I observe that point (c) applies to judgemental memory or recollection, not to memory as storage of information, which falls rather under (d).

[44] This in part explains the central relevance for representational import of the resemblance relations between impressions and ideas. See K. P. Winkler, 'The New Hume', in Read & Richman, *The New Hume Debate* (52:87), 76–7: 'Hume imposes this further requirement [resemblance; which is further than constant conjunction of impressions and ideas] because he remains attached to the ideal of intelligibility, at least in this special case. He wants the impression to render the conception intelligible – to make it comprehensible that we possess a conception of the sort in question'.

same experience must give us a notion of these objects, and must remove all mystery from our conclusions. This is so evident, that 'twou'd scarce have merited our attention, were it not to obviate certain objections of this kind, which might arise against the following reasonings concerning *matter* and *substance*. I need not observe, that a full knowledge of the object is not requisite, but only of those qualities of it, which we believe to exist.   (1.3.14.36)

The focus of this passage is causal reasoning and belief. But its point can be generalized to all the states which involve the real existence of an object, including sensation and memory. We have no reason for and even no way of inferring and believing the existence of objects without a phenomenally specifiable idea of it, an idea that could figure in impression. In the same way, we cannot in general conceive of something as real except in terms of presence in impression, therefore on a qualitative specification in a forceful and fixed mode. Without such a qualitative specification, reference is impossible because it is without object: we have nothing to refer to, with significant cognitive import. Notice that the role of such qualitative specification of object is not limited to *fixing* our reference. The very nature and possibility of the referential or representational relation are in question since the ontology of Hume's objects of reference is qualitative.

All this is relevant for the New Hume debate (I only hint here at a complex issue). A crucial tenet of the New Hume interpretation is that, beyond the resources summarized in the First Principle, (a) there is room for ascribing cognitive content to mental episodes or ideas and (b) such content is purely, non-descriptively, referential in nature.

There is after all no inconsistency or tension at all in the thought that we may refer to a thing of which we have no descriptively contentful conception, hence that we may have a 'relative' idea of it, in Hume's terms, although we do not in any way 'comprehend' it, in Hume's terms; an 'abstract description'—like 'the reason in reality of the conjunction of any two objects'—'suffices to *pick* causal power *out*—*it* provides and 'identifying description'—in such a way that we can go on to *refer* to it while having absolutely no sort of positively contentful conception of its nature, in terms of the theory of ideas.[45]

Strawson assumes that Hume's suppositions or relative ideas, while deprived of content or 'in a certain sense void', still can allow us to refer.[46] One could, however, point out that supposing or having relative ideas does not even potentially define a representational, referential relation to objects.[47] Relative ideas simply mark off, for purposes of discussion or refutation, certain philosophical views, in

---

[45] G. Strawson, *The Secret Connexion*, Oxford University Press, Oxford 1989, 121–2.
[46] See also G. Strawson, *The Evident Connexion*, Oxford University Press, Oxford 2011, 16.
[47] See P. Millican, 'Hume, Causal Realism, and Causal Science', 657–9.

particular the thought of real existence as specifically different from the qualitative, sensible individuation of perceptions. Relative ideas and suppositions of this sort are held to involve no absurdity and are the product of philosophical reflection.[48] But Hume only advances these views in order to dismiss them as explanatorily irrelevant and philosophically dangerous. And Hume regards this idea of external existence as involving an absurdity (see § 9.5.1). By contrast, qualitative contents, even if they fail to abide by the First Principle, can well be cognitively in good order.[49]

What is certainly right and important in the New Hume interpretation is the view that the First Principle delivers and is meant to deliver only an incomplete, if indispensable, conception of content and cognition. This is also the background of my idea of cognitive gaps. But the New Hume interpretation gives a wrong twist to this view and draws the wrong consequences from it. The basic point is that what the First Principle leaves unaccounted for is *not* some non-qualitative referential dimension of meaning. Rather, it is the imaginative, inferential kind of content, which integrates what we can represent naturally and primitively and extends our capacities for conceiving of objects and forming our worldview.[50] In Book 1, the theoretically important distinction is not one between descriptive and non-descriptive reference but between object-representing and inferentially

---

[48] See Winkler, 'The New Hume', 62: 'In forming a relative idea we take an idea of an object and an idea of a relation and we then form an indirect conception of *another* object that stands in the given relation to the given object'. A very good discussion and a powerful rejection of the New Hume reading of reference in Hume is in Landy, *Science of Human Nature*, 155–68.

[49] Wright, *Sceptical Realism*, 104–7, 112–13, has a partially different but convergent take on this point. Wright rightly contends that some aspects of the manifest and of the scientific image—for instance, that there is a vacuum, space without objects and time without changes, as we commonly believe and as it is assumed in Newtonian natural philosophy—are inconceivable if addressed in terms of clear and distinct, impression-based ideas. That is, if addressed in terms of the 'objective reality' of ideas or of what I would call their representational import. (The same holds of reflection on and rational analysis of such ideas.) This is a principled limit to what we can conceive and know. However, Hume (in contrast with Berkeley) does not conclude from this that there is nothing real answering to ideas that fail to achieve these standards of conception. Rather, he concludes that confused ideas, like that of a vacuum, rather than clear and distinct ideas, might be our guide to physical reality. 'We can *suppose* the existence of that which is *inconceivable*'. Irregular or confused ideas and reasoning are essential for forming beliefs about actual objects that do not extend to impressions. This is much in agreement with what I am saying. My basic complaint with Wright is that rather than a contrast between clear or distinct and irregular or confused ideas we should talk of a difference in kind (representational/sensible or inferential/imaginative) of contents.

[50] This is completely missed by Winkler in his otherwise extremely careful and intelligent assessment of the New Hume: see 'The New Hume', 64, 72–3; see the remarks in J. P. Wright, 'Hume's Causal Realism', in Read & Richman, *The New Hume Debate* (88–99), 89–90. Strawson, *Secret Connexion*, 243–4, also advances a view of causal content much closer to the one I am suggesting. ('The concept [of causal powers and so on] goes beyond the regular-succession experiential basis as a result of a process of essentially cognitive or intellectual elaboration. If the Humean framework is suitably stretched, this can be seen as a process of elaboration by the Imagination, resulting from the effect of custom on the Imagination'). Imagination, on this view, is not a source of error. But characteristically, he refrains from fully ascribing this view of the cognitive work of imagination to Hume. ('Hume cannot put things like this, of course', 244 fn. 19.) This is because the dualism of descriptive content grounded on impressions and non-descriptive, relational reference he ascribes to Hume leaves little room for the distinctive role of imagination.

grounded qualitative contents. Hume's key principle that the reference of an idea to its object is an 'extraneous denomination' also goes against ascribing referential import to relative ideas. The principle put forward by Hume is completely general. It is an aspect of his doctrine of what it is to think of something as existent or real. Now, if relative ideas had referential import—letting us refer to unobserved entities—the principle could not hold with complete generality. For all there is to the content of these ideas would be their referential import, fixed by a purely relative formula. Then, regarding this presumably important class of ideas, reference to objects would not be an extraneous denomination.[51]

2.5 Summary

In this chapter, I discuss the first of two principles that define the elements of Hume's philosophy. The First Principle explains the conditions and the limits of object representation, as realized in human nature. This sets the stage for individuating cognitive gaps and for the content-productive role of the imagination.

§ 2.1 introduces perceptions as thinly substantial mental particulars, individuated by qualitative features, and their division (which Hume regards as innovative) into impressions and ideas. The distinction is by the force and fixedness with which we conceive them. This is a matter of degree and Hume recognizes that we can mistake the ones for the others. However, with the distinction of ideas of memory and of the imagination, Hume seems to hold that impressions and ideas differ in kind. Only the first provide a primitive input to object-representing cognition.

In § 2.2, a complex of claims about perceptions and their objects provides a background for the First Principle. § 2.2.1 introduces an important principle underlying Hume's philosophy of mind, Two Viewpoints: perceptions, either

---

[51] See Kail, *Projection and Realism*, 34–5, 83–3, 90, on the link between Hume's genetic concerns and a weaker sense of 'meaningless' which excludes acquaintance but leaves room for a thin conception of what we cannot be acquainted with. The problem with this is not the conclusion—I am myself defending the view that cognitive gaps can be filled by non-representational content—but the presumed link with the genetic character of Hume's account. Such genetic character does not make Hume's conclusion weaker: so to say, epistemological rather than semantic or metaphysical. It is a semantic conclusion; it belongs to Hume's 'Logic'. It bars us from having a representational thought of some item (like causal power), by showing that its content cannot be given object-dependently, according to the First Principle. This genetic conclusion is, of course, semantic and metaphysical—as strong as this goes. If any epistemological concern is in some way present, it is of the form: if we cannot know what objects our thoughts are about, then we have no such thoughts at all. (Evans' 'Russell's Principle' is a version of this, see G. Evans, *The Varieties of Reference*, Clarendon Press, Oxford 1982, 90–120.) See, on the intrinsic link between intellectual content and cognition and the metaphysics of essences in post-Cartesian rationalism, G. Hatfield, 'The Workings of the Intellect: Mind and Psychology', in Easton, ed., *Logic and the Workings of the Mind*, (21–45), 28: 'In this doctrine [Descartes' doctrine of "intellectio pura"] the relations among essences, minds, and things become tightly bound, and hence the theory of intellectual cognition itself becomes a part of metaphysics.' The breach with rationalism thus involves a complete redefinition of the semantic and metaphysical underpinnings of mental activity. See Millican, 'Hume, Causal Realism, and Causal Science', 657–8, 666, 698–9.

impressions or ideas, figure in the science of human nature both for how they exist in the mind and for the contents they bear. The two features are conceptually distinct but jointly instantiated and this has a key role in the explanation of representation and of the transitions of the imagination. §§ 2.2.2–4 outline Hume's ontology or perceptions and objects. The fundamental claim is that perceptions only contingently exist in the mind. Perceptions can exist unperceived and objects can be in the mind without the creation of new perceptions. That mental existence is a matter of causal relations among perceptions is the ground of Hume's third personal, reductionist conception of the mind. § 2.2.5 introduces, against this ontological background, Equivalence: impressions of sensation are equivalent to sensible objects, on account of their contents and on a thin concept of object, well distinct from that of body.[52]

Two Viewpoints, Equivalence, and the impression-idea distinction, are the grounds of the First Principle, discussed in § 2.3. By the First Principle, object representation is by ideas caused by impressions of sensation and exactly resembling them. This gives a naturalistic rendering of the conditions and limits of thought and cognition of objects, the primitive input to thought and cognition in general. Given our cognitive nature, only ideas conforming to the First Principle give us access to objects. The logical status of this principle is controversial. Based on my reading of it as naturalistic constitutive condition of object representation, I suggest that it is relatively a priori. It allows sketching a Humean taxonomy of ideas as exactly (actually) representational, potentially object-representing, and non-representational. The First Principle is a critical tool aiming to taxonomy, rather than to exclusion of ideas.

Finally, in § 2.4, I discuss some philosophically important points in Hume's object representation. In § 2.4.1 I show that for Hume the existence of objects is not represented by some distinct element of content but by the mode of conception of their ideas. Such mode (§ 2.4.2) is a feeling, which Hume characterizes phenomenologically (force and vivacity) and functionally (fixedness and invariance). This makes it so that the representation of existents is not modal but locked on actuality. § 2.4.3 suggests that the cognitive nature of impressions is that of an inner demonstrative: *This such*. 'Such' expresses the qualitative individuation of a particular (equivalently object and perception). Demonstrative import ('This') finds support in the feeling of its reality. Hume thus holds a conception of reference as qualitative presentation of actual objects. Based on this, I criticize the New Hume interpretation, which looks in Hume for a non-descriptive notion of reference. However, those interpreters are right in holding that the First Principle does not exhaust Hume's conception of cognitive content.

---

[52] This thin concept of object has been carefully discussed, under the label of 'proto-objects', in Rocknak, *Imagined Causes*, 81–8.

3
Our Second Principle

> The same evidence follows us in our second principle, of the liberty of the imagination to transpose and change its idea.
>
> (1.1.3.4)

Hume's theory of object representation makes it possible to identify as its natural, necessary limits the cognitive gaps that give shape to Book 1 of the *Treatise*. The conclusion Hume aims towards is that in order to explain our cognitive practices, we must resort to kinds of contents or ideas that are cognitive but non-representational and to a non-object-representing mental faculty, the imagination, which can put them in place. The Second Principle of Hume's doctrine of elements outlines the function and the position of the imagination in mental activity and cognition. As we will see, this is also a crucial move in Hume's campaign against rationalism. In § 3.1, I introduce the topic of cognitive gaps with a discussion of the much debated case of the Missing Shade of Blue and then defend the idea of the natural necessity of the cognitive gaps which structure the argument of Book 1. This makes room and provides a grounding for a content-productive role of the imagination, coming to expression in the Second Principle. I discuss this principle and outline the related operations of the imagination in § 3.2. § 3.3 introduces an important principle about the structure of Hume's faculty of the imagination, the Structural Principle, which is crucial for a unitary understanding of the different ways in which it figures in Book 1. Finally, in § 3.4, I individuate the common feature of the ideas produced by the imagination and their difference from those given in sense and memory in their inferential character and ground.

3.1 The Natural Limits of Object Representation

3.1.1 Enter Imagination: The Missing Shade of Blue

Hume's imagination enters the scene right after the statement of the First Principle. No sooner is the discovery announced that all simple ideas, the primitive contents of our thinking, depend on impression of sensation, that Hume shows this fundamental explanation of content to be incomplete. 'There is however one contradictory phaenomenon, which may prove, that 'tis not absolutely impossible for ideas to go before their correspondent impressions.' (1.1.1.10). There can be ideas that are phenomenally simple and cognitively in order but not explained by the First Principle. The 'phaenomenon' is the following.

> Suppose therefore a person to have enjoyed his sight for thirty years, and to have become perfectly well acquainted with colours of all kinds, excepting one particular shade of blue, for instance, which it never has been his fortune to meet with. Let all the different shades of that colour, except that single one, be plac'd before him, descending gradually from the deepest to the lightest; 'tis plain, that he will perceive a blank, where that shade is wanting, and will be sensible, that there is a greater distance in that place betwixt the contiguous colours, than in any other. Now I ask, whether 'tis possible for him, from his own imagination, to supply this deficiency, and raise up to himself the idea of that particular shade, tho' it had never been conveyed to him by his senses? (1.1.1.10)

Relying on common opinion ('I believe there are few but will be of opinion that he can'), Hume answers in the affirmative and takes this as 'proof' that 'simple ideas are not always derived from the correspondent impressions' (1.1.1.10). The example is well chosen; it deals with what is unquestionably a simple idea, with our basic level of content. This passage has had its fair share of interpretive discussion, with special focus on whether and to what extent it is a counterexample to the First Principle.[1] I want to address this issue from the viewpoint of its background, the claims about impressions and ideas of colour and the arguments with which Hume supports his endorsement of the common opinion. From this angle, Hume's doctrine, a sort of mental experiment, appears carefully crafted.

> I believe it will readily be allow'd, that the several distinct ideas of colours, which enter by the eyes, or those of sounds, which are convey'd by the hearing, are really different from each other, tho' at the same time resembling. Now if this be true of different colours, it must be no less so of the different shades of the same colour, that each of them produces a distinct idea, independent of the rest. For if this shou'd be deny'd, 'tis possible, by the continual gradation of shades, to run a colour insensibly into what is most remote from it; and if you will not allow any of the means to be different, you cannot without absurdity deny the extremes to be the same. (1.1.1.10)

This text deserves attention. The conclusion Hume wants to draw from his mental experiment requires that what is raised in the described way is a distinct

---

[1] In partial dissent with the reading proposed in D. Garrett, *Cognition and Commitment in Hume's Philosophy*, Oxford University Press, New York/Oxford 1997, 51-2, I would not downplay but redescribe the contrast between the missing shade and the First Principle.

idea. If the Missing Shade of Blue is a distinct idea it is undoubtedly a simple one and Hume's overall argument succeeds. Now, suppose that the spectrum of blue consists of a number of distinct ideas: the blank spot (the 'greater distance in that place betwixt the contiguous colours', 1.1.1.10) would be the placeholder for a missing, distinct, and simple idea. Hume therefore must argue for the supposition that the spectrum of blue consists of distinct ideas.

Hume's argument for this supposition is not perspicuous, but I would reconstruct it as follows.

(a) The ideas of different colours are distinct: our 'several distinct ideas of colours' or of 'sounds', while 'resembling', are still 'really different from each other'. To see this, consider how they 'enter by the eyes' or 'are convey'd by the hearing', that is, the impressions or objects which cause them and which they resemble. All such impressions or objects, as we know, are distinct. The corresponding ideas must be distinct as well.

(b) The same holds of ideas of shades of the same colour, which, no matter how resembling, are 'distinct' and 'independent of the rest'. The ground for this is, again, a consideration concerning impressions or objects, 'shades of the same colour', each of which is represented by the idea it 'produces'.

(c) The consideration, in the case of shades of the same colour, is not phenomenological. Hume argues that, if impressions or objects that are shades are not really distinct, "'tis possible, by the continual gradation of shades, to run a colour insensibly into what is most remote from it'. This is impossible, since, by (a), different colours are really different and their ideas distinct. Therefore, some of the impressions of the shade of the same colour must be different ('if you will not allow any of the means to be different, you cannot without absurdity deny the extremes to be the same') and the same holds of the ideas they produce.

The detour taken by Hume at (c) can be explained if we consider that shades of the same colour are not easily discriminable at a phenomenological level so that it seems required to mount a backward induction to their non-distinctness.[2] Be this as it may, the ideas that represent shades of the same colour are distinct.[3]

---

[2] For the contrast between Hume's view and Newton's claim of the continuous character of colour spectra, see E. Schliesser, 'Hume's Missing Shade of Blue Considered from a Newtonian Perspective', *Journal of Scottish Philosophy*, 2, 2004, 164–75, 165–6. Notice that for Hume the distinctness of impressions of shades of the same colour is not a phenomenological datum. Such shades are not in general countable by us (just as spatial minima in general are not). Hume *argues* for their distinctness. The one phenomenological datum required by Hume's mental experiment is the gap, the 'greater distance' in the spectrum of blue.

[3] At least, there must be *some* distinct ideas in the spectrum of a colour: the absurdity follows on not allowing 'any of the means to be different' (1.1.1.10; my emphasis). See, on Hume's argument, R. J. Fogelin, 'Hume and the Missing Shade of Blue', *Philosophy and Phenomenological Research*, 45, 1984, 263–71, 265–6.

A fortiori, the idea of the Missing Shade of Blue is distinct and, in the described situation, it comes to exist without a preceding impression.

Hume's argument for the distinctness of ideas of different shades of the same colours is based on the conditions of object representation: colours and shades of colours as impressions or objects (as they 'enter by the eyes' or as each 'produces' an idea) individuate ideas; therefore distinct and different colours and shades of colours individuate distinct and different ideas. By Representation, ideas count as representations by having objects for contents and by existing and being individuated dependently on their objects (see § 2.4.4). Representation is thus at work in the argument. We can move between the properties of objects and the properties of ideas only because the ideas are representations of objects and the objects form the contents of ideas. Now, the relatively a priori First Principle is the realization of the possibility of representation, according to this concept of it, in human nature. Objects are present to the natural mind as impressions of sensation and ideas can represent objects by being caused by and resembling to impressions. Therefore, Hume's argument to the conclusion that the Missing Shade of Blue is a distinct, simple idea and that in the described situation it is without a preceding impression depends on the a priori principle Representation and on the relatively a priori First Principle. Therefore, that conclusion is based on the First Principle, which cannot be called in question by it. At least, this cannot have been Hume's intention in arguing for it.

This is not to say, however, that Hume's discussion is pointless. I think that we should rather rethink the point of the conclusion established in this way. In my view, the point is that ideas raised by a mental operation of this sort would *not* represent objects. We would have available such ideas and they would have cognitive content. But they would not represent an object since they would not exist and be individuated dependently on it. They would not be object representing. No actual shade of blue has caused the idea that resembles to it. Even though, of course, such a shade of blue could have existed; and the idea would then have represented it.[4] In this sense, the idea is the idea of an object, of a shade of colour; yet it does not represent one exactly but only potentially. The Missing Shade of Blue in this way does not count as a counterexample to the First Principle. To act as a counterexample, the missing idea should have been such as to represent an actual object, depending on and being individuated by it, while no such object is present in impression. But this, of course, is not how Hume says the idea is produced. The point of the example is thus not the falsification but the limitation of the First Principle as a source of content. It is an 'exception', rather than a counterexample, to it.[5]

---

[4] See K. Durland, 'Hume's First Principle, his Missing Shade, and his Distinctions of Reason', *Hume Studies*, 22, 1996, 105–21, 110.

[5] See Schliesser, 'Missing Shade', 169–70. This might help us to understand Hume's comment that the 'instance is so particular and singular, that 'tis scarce worth observing' (1.1.1.10). As it has been

Correspondingly, the idea is produced not by some mysteriously non-sensible relation to a shade of colour, but by a natural mental response to a certain pattern of visual experience. It is in this response that Hume sees a role for the imagination, thus introduced as a faculty producing ideas. The idea of the shade of blue, missing from visual impressions, is 'raised', by the subject of the mental experiment, 'from his own imagination'. This latter, prompted by and exploiting the representation of the similarities between the ideas of the different shades, fills in the blank with the relevant visual quality, spreads it with the right shade of blue. In its first appearance, thus, Hume's imagination takes up, very succinctly, its basic general character: a function from the conception of ideas directly or indirectly grounded in sense experience to the conception of new original ideas. But this is only a first, if highly significant, encounter with this 'magical faculty in the soul'. Hume says nothing about how imagination produces this new idea. Most importantly, the gap in representation is accidental: there is nothing in the idea of a shade of blue that makes it unavailable to representation. Hume is only giving a first hint of the incompleteness of the fundamental First Principle; of the need to complement it with another principle of content and mental activity. We need and have ideas that do not represent impressions or objects; that do not acquaint us with existing particulars; but which still contribute to how we think and what we can know about.[6]

3.1.2 Cognitive Gaps and the Natural Mind

The central role and fundamental position of the imagination in mind and cognition come in view if the cognitive gaps which it is its function to close by producing new ideas can be shown to be *naturally necessary* to object representation, rather than relative to specific bodies of empirical information. If such cognitive gaps mark the very nature of object representation, their closure and the explanation and (qualified) vindication of our cognitive practices and of our worldview

---

observed, the instance does not seem so particular or singular: lacunae in perceptual acquaintance seem to be easily replicable, see J. Morreall, 'Hume's Missing Shade of Blue', *Philosophy and Phenomenological Research*, 42, 1982, 407–15, 408–10. Hume could not have failed to notice this. If he concludes that it 'does not merit that for it alone we should alter our general maxim' (1.1.1.10), he might not have meant that the example is not weighty enough, but that it is out of the scope of the First Principle (the validity of which Hume's argument presupposes).

[6] I thank a reader for OUP for prompting me to correct an earlier version of my interpretation of this text. (I hope but I am not sure I have answered her/his concerns.) For a reading of the Missing Shade of Blue close to the one I propose, see D. Landy, 'Hume's Impression/Idea Distinction', *Hume Studies*, 32, 1, 2006 (119–40), 131–4 (the idea is indirectly caused by resembling impressions). However, Landy does not mention the role of imagination in this context. See also Fogelin, 'Missing Shade of Blue', 370–1; and Durland, 'Missing Shade', 112–14, for an interesting reconstruction of how Hume's imagination might proceed in generating the idea without violating the principle of representation.

require the operation of a *non-representational* but *cognitive* faculty. This introduces the deep dualism of mental contents and faculties that is distinctive of Hume's philosophy.[7]

The limits of object representation are natural if they reflect general facts concerning how our minds make cognitive contact with 'the real existence or the relations of objects' (1.3.2.2). Some such facts are the following.

(a) According to the elements of Hume's philosophy, objects are given *only sensibly* and sensibility can give us only objects; impressions and objects are equivalent. We primitively and fundamentally represent only '*real existence and matter of fact*' and such representation is only by impressions of sense and ideas derived from and resembling them. Hume's impressions of sensation are the only primitively representable objects; what is not given in sensibility cannot be an object for us.

(b) Representation is *only particular*: objects individuated by sensible qualities can only be particulars and their presence to the mind as perceptions individuated by those very qualities, which can thus weigh on thought and cognition, is only as particulars.

---

[7] Berkeley, in order to achieve a firmly anti-sceptical position, is prepared to recognize certain a priori limits of our cognition of objects. The limits of human sensibility must be individuated with the aim of uprooting error and scepticism. In Berkeley, this takes the form of a severe restriction of the ontology of the objects of sensible acquaintance. 'The various sensations or ideas imprinted on the sense, however blended or combined together (that is, whatever objects they compose) cannot exist otherwise than in a mind perceiving them'; 'the absolute existence of unthinking things without any relation to their being perceived...seems perfectly unintelligible. Their *esse* is *percipi*.' (G. Berkeley, *Principles of Human Knowledge*, 3, in *Philosophical Works*, M. R. Ayers, ed., Dent, London 1975, 78). Hume rejects this conclusion. But he seems to accept the views that only perceived ideas can have any bearing on thinking and judgement; that only sensible qualities, such as light, colours, sounds, tastes, odours, and 'tangible qualities' are perceived immediately; and that only what is perceived immediately is perceived at all (G. Berkeley, *A New Theory of Vision*, 10, 38, in *Philosophical Works*, 10, 18; *Three Dialogues between Hylas and Philonous*, in *Philosophical Works*, 138). Berkeley presses these general claims to establish specific, dramatic limitations of sensible cognition, some of which are also recognized by Hume: the heterogeneity of the senses of sight and touch, the radical contrast of visible and tangible objects and ideas, the lack of a visible, immediate idea of distance, of 'outness'. See *New Theory*, 41, 46 ('the ideas of space, outness, and things placed at a distance are not, strictly speaking, the object of sight'), 49, 95 (on the Molyneux Problem), in *Philosophical Works*, 21–2, 36. Hume claims, closely following Berkeley footsteps, that we have no immediate sense of outness (1.4.2.9); that without imagination we can be aware of the inner and outer distinction (1.4.7.3); and that, in our immediate experience, pain and pleasure are no more internal to the mind than colour or sound—or shape and mass (1.4.2.7). Just as it is with Hume, the limitations of Berkeley's ideas set a radical problem of explanation of cognitive change, with reference to the unity, connectedness, and generality of our perfectly in order cognition of *rerum natura*. The conceptual room for this cognitive change can be found in Berkeley's rejection of what Winkler aptly calls the 'content assumption': the assumption that the content of thought is only determined by its object—which Berkeley identifies with an idea (*Berkeley*, 39–43, 74). This is a very valuable interpretive insight, since it releases content-individuation from the exclusive hold of what thought refers to. The content assumption, as Winkler remarks, is rejected also by Locke. I would add that it is also, firmly rejected by Hume. Of course, the consequences of such rejection are different in the different philosophers.

THE NATURAL LIMITS OF OBJECT REPRESENTATION 69

(c) Representation is *object-dependent*: ideas can represent impressions or objects only by causal dependence and resemblance; their existence and their contents presupposes the existence of such impressions and objects.
(d) Representation is only of the *actual*; whatever we represent, we can only represent as contingently existing. There can be no representation of necessity and possibility; we do have ideas of the possible and the necessary but they are not object representing.

In the second place, some general facts concern our faculties of representation.

(a) Hume is not only open but deeply committed to the idea that the natural mind has a constitution and a structure: 'the nature and principles of the human mind' (1.1.3.1) or 'the original nature and constitution of the mind' (1.2.3.7). The necessity of such principles is physical and a posteriori. It makes thus sense to think of the operations of our natural faculties as necessary.
(b) Sense and memory are, out of natural necessity, the only faculties giving us cognitive contact with real existence. Hume occasionally labels them as 'perception' and contrasts them with 'reasoning'. The objects and the relations which form their contents are all 'immediately present', without 'any exercise of the thought, or any action, properly speaking'. The faculty of representation is not inferential, but only 'a mere passive admission of the impressions thro' the organs of sensation' (1.3.2.2).
(c) Representation by sense and memory is analogous to the physical phenomenon of mirroring. 'The first circumstance, that strikes my eye, is the great resemblance betwixt our impressions and ideas in every other particular, except their degree of force and vivacity. The one seem to be in a manner the reflection of the other; so that all the perceptions of the mind are double, and appear both as impressions and ideas' (1.1.1.3).

One thing that follows from the overall nature of Hume's faculty of representation is its *non-conceptual* character. Object representation, as it is realized in human nature, does not involve the application of concepts, not even in a recognitional role ('This such is a so and so').[8] Hume's representation also leaves no

---

[8] On non-conceptual content see (E. J. Lowe, 'Experience and its Objects', in Crane, ed., *The Contents of Experience* (79–104), 89–92(. Russell discusses the 'meaning' of images ('the simplest kind of meaning') along Humean lines, in terms of 'resemblance' to sensations or impressions: 'On propositions' (1919), in *Logic and Knowledge. Essays 1901–1950*, Allen and Unwin, London 1956 (285–319), 300–4. Johnston, 'The Function of Sensory Awareness', 270, 282–86, ascribes non-conceptual character to primitive acts of sensing. Natural representation, by the First Principle, is shared with subjects with minimal cognitive capacities, infants, and non-human animals: see (T. Crane, 'The Nonconceptual Content of Experience', in Crane, ed., *The Contents of Experience* (136–57), 141–3 (.However, I refrain from regarding this as a mark of its non-conceptual nature because it is shared

room for any dimension of intentionality or of aspectual thinking: an idea representing the corresponding impression or object *as* this or that. Hume is ready to recognize the intentional character of cognition, meaning by this simply that it can be different without any difference in the objects that form their contents but only in how they bear on conception and belief. However, as we will see (§ 4.3.2), intentionality in this sense depends on the imagination. There is no room for *representing as* in Hume's sensible representation.[9]

I want to suggest that the limits of object representation are the consequence of such general facts concerning our primitive acquaintance with objects; therefore, that they are determined by the original qualities of our minds and are inseparable from our species, from our cognitive nature.[10] In the light of Hume's obvious commitment to the conceptual—recognitional, inferential, aspectual, intentional—character of our ordinary and philosophical cognitive practices, this marks a deep, dramatic gap in our cognitive capacities.[11]

3.1.3 Cognitive Gaps: A Taxonomy

Hume's cognitive gaps fall into three main categories, which point to three basic functions of the imagination: (i) missing *modes of thought*: abstract, general, aspectual, compositional, inferential, modal; (ii) missing *worldview structures*: space and time, projectable regularities, causal connections, external existence, persistent minds; and (iii) missing *mental states*: mere conception, reasoning, belief.

(i) The first category of cognitive gaps is that of *modes of thought*. Ideas representing objects and the faculties of representation, sense and memory, are

---

with imaginative inferences and affective states. See 1.3.15: *Of the Reason of Animals*; 2.1.12: *Of the Pride and Humility of Animals*; 2.2.12: *Of the Love and Hatred of Animals*. It is a striking feature of Hume's philosophy that the fact that certain kinds of content and cognition are shared by humans and animals counts as evidence *in favour* of the account given of them.

[9] This is righty remarked in Landy, *Kant's Inferentialism*, 26, 44–5, 60–1. I agree that this makes for an indeterminateness in representational contents. Indeed, if we attempted to understand the overall contents of our cognitive practices in terms of Hume's conception of representation, we would fall prey of a very serious case of the Disjunction Problem. But this only means that a second, non-representational source of content, the transitions of imagination, must be involved.

[10] In this respect, the case for the scientific realism of Hume's science of human nature is particularly important; see Landy, *Science of Human Nature*, 57, 65–74.

[11] Price, among classic interpreters, has paid most attention to the incompleteness of the deliverances of sense perception: '[Hume] is impressed, as no other philosopher before him had been, by the *interrupted* and *fragmentary* character of human sense-experience.... Our sense-experience, though, of course, there is some continuity in it, is full of holes and gaps', H. H. Price, 'Hume's Theory of the External World' (1940), in *The Collected Works of H.H. Price*, Volume 1 (3–228), Thoemmes Press, Bristol 1996, 20. Compare Quine's 'relation between the meager input [sensorial input]and the torrential output [our world-description]' which is the core of naturalistic epistemology ('Epistemology Naturalized', in W. V. O. Quine, *Ontological Relativity and Other Essays*, Columbia University Press, New York/London 1969 (69–90), 82–3).

both fundamental and severely restricted. Hume's representation is receptive, sensible, particular, demonstrative, object dependent, and locked on actuality. It is non-inferential, non-conceptual, non-aspectual, and non-intentionally directed. These properties characterize the representation of objects as a primary, animal layer of human cognition. Our ordinary and philosophical thinking, our 'reflection and conversation' (1.1.7.1) cannot but engage in abstract, general, aspectual, compositional, inferential, intentional, modal modes of thought; we display all sorts of conceptual capacities. These modes and capacities mark so many respects in which sensible representation leaves open gaps with respect to our cognitive practices. Hume argues that such modes and capacities are in fact available to our minds but that they are not representational and must be explained differently than with the nexus of impressions, objects, and ideas. This is discussed in Part 3, Chapters 3 and 4.

(ii) The second category of cognitive gaps is that of the structures of our worldview. Our 'impressions or ideas of the memory' make available 'a kind of system, comprehending whatever we remember to have been present, either to our internal perception or senses'. We regard 'every particular of that system, joined to the present impressions' as a *'reality'* (1.3.9.3). The system of our representations, however, falls short of exhausting our worldview, the manifest and the scientific image. This system does not display a general spatial and temporal structure. The representation of spatial relations is only fragmentary; it does not determine an overall frame of space. The same holds of time: we represent objects in flux, with durations and temporal relations. But not a general frame of time, which includes their successions and durations. The elements of the first system of realities are unconnected to each other, except insofar as they are present together in sense and memory. Even more strikingly, this system of realities does not provide grounds for even conceiving, based on their relations with others, objects with which we are not acquainted (1.4.7.3). Furthermore, observed objects are not ascribed continuous and independent existence, distinct from the perceptions of them. And the internal perceptions we are aware of are not represented as elements of our persistent mind and self (1.4.7.3). Also in this case, the problem is not local or accidental. Sensible representation does not provide the cognitive resources for these structures of our worldview. What makes it possible for our ideas to be exact representations, to give us primitive and certain cognition of real existence, also restricts their contents in the ways just summarized. We *do* form a second system of realities, 'which peoples the world, and brings us acquainted with such existences, as by their removal in time and place, lie beyond the reach of the senses and memory' (1.3.9.4). But this is precisely the work of imagination.

Explaining it forms the bulk of Hume's philosophy in Book 1, discussed in Parts 4 and 5, Chapters 5–10.[12]

(iii) The third category of cognitive gaps is that of the *mental states* we are in when we think conceptually and when we grasp and assent to causal connections, external existence, and internal persistence. Conceptual thinking involves some measure of context-independence: this is the key to its inferential, productive, and systematic character. Conceptual thinking has also active and directed character, displays intentionality. But mere conception of ideas is unavailable to the sensible, object-representing mind. Within sense and memory, the contents and the existence of ideas are bound to their primitive presentation in impression; and the conception of objects is always constrained by their representation as present and with a fixed order and form. Correspondingly, reasoning is not a representational activity or state since it can be extended to non-actual objects. Furthermore, when we think in conceptual and inferential terms and draw conclusions in reasoning about substantive structures of our worldview, like causation, reality, and identity, we are in mental states which are not object-representating and do not involve the existence of their objects. Such states are inferential, not referential, but are nonetheless cognitive and modify and improve our cognitive practices. This kind of state Hume takes himself to have discovered and identifies with belief. Together with its expression in judgement, it realizes our cognition of the second system of realities. This is discussed in Part 5, Chapters 11 and 12.

3.1.4 Representational Naturalism, Scepticism, and the Imagination

Hume's theory of object representation and of its gaps has a relatively a priori status: it identifies the substantive shape taken by conceptual constraints on object representation, as they are realized in the nature of human and animal minds. I will call Hume's position about thought and cognition of objects (thing- or event-like particular existents) *Representational Naturalism*.[13]

The cognitive gaps of object representation are not only a stable and robust matter of fact, rather than a local and accidental one; they are limits issuing from of how our nature realizes the conceptual conditions of representation. From this

---

[12] See, for discussion of this passage, Rocknak, *Imagined Causes*, 52–8.
[13] That Hume states logical or, better, a priori truths about impressions (the most important of which is that they must be determined in their degrees both of quantity and of quality) is recognized by H. W. Noonan, *Hume on Knowledge*, Routledge, London 1999, 81–2.

viewpoint, the central task of Book 1, explaining how our cognitive practices and our worldview emerge from our own nature, becomes very complex, even bordering paradox. If cognitive gaps are natural to our object-representing faculties, only some deep cognitive change can give a naturalistic basis to ordinary and philosophical cognition. But such a change in our cognitive capacities seems to challenge their natural and necessary constitution, so that its very possibility seems to come in question. There is an interpretive tradition, from Kemp Smith onwards, which identifies the main problem of Hume's philosophy in the uneasy relation between naturalism and scepticism. I would say that this problem springs from a deeper one: the uneasy relation of Hume's naturalism *with itself*. Both our faculty of representation and our inclusive, connected, objective worldview are and must be explained as natural. But, as we have seen, human nature and object representation do not provide sufficient cognitive resources for ordinary and philosophical cognition—while these should have been grounded right on it, as their 'capital or center'. The paradox therefore would be that Hume seems to require human nature to overcome itself.

At the core of Hume's philosophy we find an alignment of Representational Naturalism, sceptical concerns, and the functions of the imagination. The cognitive impossibilities concealed in representational naturalism are the source of serious sceptical issues that threaten Hume's philosophy. However, evoking and contrasting such sceptical troubles is, rather, a crucial feature of Hume's campaign against rationalism. Rationalist philosophers exploit sceptical objections to sense experience with the aim of replacing sensible with intellectual cognition, ideas of sense and memory with ideas of a spiritual nature. Hume challenges rationalism in a subtle way. He does not refrain from identifying the necessary limits of sensible cognition and their troubling consequences (as Kant approvingly noticed). At the same time, he holds that no purely intellectual mental content and capacity is admissible, on account of its being non-naturalistic; everything mental must be grounded in human nature, empirically, and in terms of causation. Addressing scepticism in this way, based on Representational Naturalism and the detection of the necessary limits of object-representing cognition, gives dialectical strength to Hume's position. It makes it difficult to see how we can *avoid* rationalism; but, if the gaps in object representation can be successfully overcome, it establishes on a very strong basis that it *can* be avoided.

Cognitive gaps depend on the *limits* but not on the *disorder* or on the *obscurity* and *confusion* of sensible experience. Representational Naturalism fails to explain our worldview not because it restricts us to contents that are flawed, obscure, and confused but because our (perfectly in order) representational faculty is naturally limited to particular sensible existents. The former view is a fundamental tenet of rationalism: the only proper kind of mental content is intellectual, the rational apprehension of objects; sensibility only delivers such contents in an obscure and confused way; thus it is cognitively defective and it properly serves only non-cognitive purposes.[14] As Kant was later to say, the rationalists regard sensibility and the intellect as differing logically (by being distinct or confused) but not transcendentally (by their origin and content).[15] By contrast, for Hume, contents and cognitions delivered by sense and memory are irreducible, fundamental, and perfectly in order as they are. Sensible representation is by nature inherently limited—it does not exhaust our worldview—but it is not inherently defective. Representational Naturalism is a stable position and the sceptical concerns it raises do not motivate and warrant its replacement with some non-naturalistic construal of thought and cognition.[16] Restrict representationalism,

---

[14] For a paradigmatic statement of the rationalist conception of sensibility as confused intellect, see Descartes' *Second Meditation* (the conclusion of the analysis of our idea of a piece of wax): 'So then, what is this wax, which is perceived only by the mind? Certainly it is the same wax I see, touch, and imagine...But yet—and this is important—the perception of it is not sight, touch, or imagination, and never was, although it seemed to be so at first: it is an inspection by the mind alone, which can be either imperfect and confused, as it was before, or clear and distinct, as it now is, depending on the greater or lesser degree of attention I pay to what it consists of', R. Descartes, *Meditations on First Philosophy*, M. Moriarty, ed., Oxford University Press, Oxford/New York 2008, 23. The content of our intellectual consideration of an object is the same with that of its sensible apprehension. But now it is clear and distinct and allows us to grasp what the object consists of, its essential properties. For Hume, only sensibility is a faculty of object representation; what complements sensibility are cognitive contents of a different, non-object representing sort. Also Kant, if in a different way, denies that sensibility is only confused intellect (a position he traces in Leibniz). 'The concept of sensibility and of appearance would be falsified, and our whole teaching in regard to them would be rendered empty and useless, if we were to accept the view that our entire sensibility is nothing but a confused representation of things, containing only what belongs to them in themselves, but doing so under an aggregation of character and partial representations that we do not consciously distinguish' (*Critique of Pure Reason*, 83). See, for the early modern conception of the intellect and Descartes' breach with Aristotelianism on the cognitive independence from the senses or corporeal phantasms of the intellect as the only proper mental faculty, Hatfield, 'The Workings of the Intellect: Mind and Psychology', in Easton, ed., *Logic and the Workings of the Mind*, (21–45), 26 ff.

[15] I. Kant, 'Transcendental Aesthetic', Section 2, 8: 'General Observation on Transcendental Aesthetic', *Critique of Pure Reason*, 83–4.

[16] The commitment to Representational Naturalism is where Hume diverges from Berkeley. Berkeley rejects the representational import of our immediate perceiving, as Winkler points out with extreme clarity. Berkeley's ideas of sense do not represent, they only signify, in an essentially instituted way, other ideas. (Winkler also makes clear that there is no deep contrast between natural and conventional signification.) Only ideas of imagination can represent, as images of resembling ideas of sense. But still the representational relation is only between ideas, with different phenomenology; it is horizontal, not vertical (Winkler, *Berkeley*, 14–17, 21; 'Berkeley and the Doctrine of Signs', in *The Cambridge Companion to Berkeley*, K. Winkler, ed., Cambridge University Press, Cambridge 2005, 125–65, 134, 152). See also M. Brandt Bolton, 'Berkeley and Mental Representation', in *New Interpretations of Berkeley's Thought*, 77–106, esp. 89–3. Berkeley's topology of the mind, therefore, is ultimately different from Hume's, because it casts imagination also in a representational role. See also J. R. Roberts, *A Metaphysics for the Mob*, Oxford University Press, Oxford 2008, 43–69, who insists that 'Berkeleyan ideas of sense are not representations', in the context of a convincing meaning-as-use, non-cognitivist, and pragmatist interpretation of Berkeley's semantic and metaphysical views. By contrast, Hume attempts to reinstate a form of representational content of ideas with the Fist Principle, Equivalence, and the metaphysical possibility that perceptions exist without the mind. This has consequences for their respective views of how to respond to the limits of immediate perception: Berkeley's view of mediate sensible apprehension and Hume's conception of cognitive non-representational ideas. Berkeley does not regard the integration of the ideas of sense, by way of constant experience, custom, and habituation, and of sudden judgements or immediate mental transitions—which are much the same ingredients as Hume's—as summing up to the individuation of a new kind of cognitive content, or the generation of novel, cognitively significant, ideas. What goes beyond immediate

complement representation of objects with a different naturalistic kind of cognitive content, and in this way, you can preserve naturalism and tame sceptical threats. Hume's naturalistic response to scepticism is not to look for new kinds of objects of representation (embracing the rationalist illusion of ideas of spiritual, intellectual nature) but to resort to a naturalistic non-representational cognitive faculty. Hume's theory of the imagination is the crucial element in this philosophical strategy.[17]

3.2 The Second Principle

3.2.1 The Liberty of the Imagination

Hume introduces the imagination with a principle, 'our second principle', which states its function, thus complementing the First Principle and completing the doctrine of elements of the *Treatise*.

> The same evidence follows us in our second principle, *of the liberty of the imagination to transpose and change its ideas*. The fables we meet with in poems and romances put this entirely out of question. Nature there is totally confounded, and nothing mentioned but winged horses, fiery dragons, and monstrous giants. Nor will this liberty of the fancy appear strange, when we consider, that all our ideas are copy'd from our impressions, and that there are not any two impressions which are perfectly inseparable. Not to mention, that this is an evident consequence of the division of ideas into simple and complex.

---

perceiving, notions, are not ideas. And his inferentialism is more pragmatist than imaginative. Hume, by contrast, advances a radical and enormously detailed theory of empirical content that is cognitive without being representational.

[17] This preliminary characterization of Hume's imagination as *sui generis* cognitive faculty, which is at least in some respects more fundamental than other, possibly more familiar kinds of cognitive capacities, seems in sharp contrast with the account of the imagination proposed by P. Langland-Hassan, *Explaining Imagination*, Oxford University Press, Oxford 2020, 1, 8 11–14, 26–7, 116–17. According to this account, imagination is not a distinct faculty but is reducible to other basic folk-psychological mental states (beliefs, desires, and intentions). The reduction is mediated by changes in the contents of the states; but still, the relevant cognitive capacities consist of and can be explained by combinations of beliefs, desires, and intentions, without *sui generis* imaginative states. However (barring any fears of anachronism), I do not think that there is a deep contrast here. Langland-Hassan's main point is that the explanatory work that some take to be done by *sui generis* imaginative states is in fact done by beliefs and other familiar states; and that imaginings are at most parts or constituents of such states. Now, this may be a forceful point against views that factorize (functionally) cognitive activity into distinct compartments or 'boxes', but not against one like Hume's, which is primarily genetic and focused on the possibility of cognitive contents and states. For Hume, no less than for Langland-Hassan, we cannot tell apart the cognitive works of the imagination from the presence of contents and states of belief and of instances of reasoning; although, of course, the direction of explanation is opposite. (This is so in the *Treatise*; in the first *Enquiry* the familiar contrast of imagination and belief is prominent.)

Where-ever the imagination perceives a difference among ideas, it can easily produce a separation.   (1.1.3.4)[18]

The wording of the Second Principle and the immediately following explanations deserve close attention.[19]

First, the imagination is a faculty of mental 'liberty'. It is free in relation to its ideas, the contents it takes. It makes for our freedom in considering ideas and in directing our thoughts to what they represent. (As we will see in § 4.3.2, the intentional direction of mental processes is tied to the imagination.) The liberty of the imagination marks an active layer of the natural mind and stands in direct contrast with the fixed order the senses and memory.

Second, what the imagination is free to do is to 'transpose' and 'change' its ideas. Hume's choice of words is rarely gratuitous. Transposition and change seem two interrelated but distinct sorts of activity on ideas and two correspondingly different sorts of cognitive change. Imagination *transposes* ideas by conceiving them independently of their original context and rearranging them to form new contents for thinking. This is the main source of the complex ideas that are the subject of our thinking and conversation. It is why Hume here refers to the 'division of ideas into simple and complex'. *Change* of ideas, I would say, consists in a different sort of cognitive operation: one putting in place structures of substantive content that are not present and represented in sense and memory. Ideas are changed by imagination to generate new, substantive, non-representational contents and cognitive possibilities, which constitute the manifest and the scientific image.

Third, this liberty of the imagination is anchored in the basic principles of Hume's philosophy. Two Viewpoints in particular has an important role in dispelling any concern that 'this liberty of the fancy' is 'strange'. Ideas formed by the First Principle are 'copy'd' from impressions. They have the same contents with such impressions and thus, by Equivalence, their contents consist in the objects that such impressions are (from the viewpoint of content): actual, sensible particulars. Particulars, impressions, and objects all exist distinctly. 'There are not any two impressions which are perfectly inseparable'. The ideas representing them are also distinct, from the viewpoints of their contents. But the distinctness of ideas considered as to their contents is also their independent existence in the mind. Properties of content and properties of existence of perceptions are the

---

[18] See also 1.3.5.3: it is 'a peculiar property of the memory to preserve the original order and position of its ideas'; by contrast, 'the imagination transposes and changes them, as it pleases'.

[19] I am aware that the principle of the liberty of imagination is 'second' relatively to the immediately preceding and evident 'principle' that memory preserves the 'order and position' of simple ideas. But the reference to and the connection with the First Principle, while mediated, is strong. As we have seen, sense and memory are inextricably intertwined and both are strictly regimented by the First Principle: they are, in fact, the natural realization of the conceptual principles of representation that also underlie the First Principle.

same in actuality. Perceptions exist in the mind with the same qualities with the objects they represent and are individuated in the same ways. And the existence of ideas in the mind is a matter of their causal relations with certain other perceptions and therefore preserves their identities and distinctness. Perceptions existing in the mind are perceived and they are perceived as they are, as distinct beings. The imagination responds rightly to their perceived distinctness. 'Wherever the imagination perceives a difference among ideas, it can easily produce a separation'. This fact, that it can separate in conception what is inseparable in representation, is the root of the liberty of imagination.

Fourth, the liberty of the imagination is also one of the roots of its contrast with memory. Memory is a faculty of representation also because it shares with impressions of sensation the invariance of objects and their order; the imagination is free from such constraint and is variable in its contents; but then, it is also non-object representing.[20] A trait of deep originality of Hume's imagination is precisely that it does not interpose itself between objects of sense, sense experience, and memory. That is, that it does not operate in parallel with sensation to secure that those figures impressed in the organs of sense come to awareness as ideas and are then preserved in memory.[21] This is an aspect of the 'reformation' which Hume wanted to promote in philosophy by introducing the notion of

---

[20] See, for a different but (I think) consistent reading of the two ways in which Hume distinguishes memory and imagination, Landy, *Science of Human Nature*, 118–21. Hume is ready to recognize that this difference between memory and imagination is epistemically ineffective, 'it being impossible to recal the past impressions, in order to compare them with our present ideas, and see whether their arrangement be exactly similar' (1.3.5.3). But it marks a structural and functional difference between these faculties. For an overview of the functions and powers of the imagination, along somewhat different lines from mine, see T. M. Costelloe, 'Hume's Phenomenology of the Imagination', *The Journal of Scottish Philosophy*, 5, 2007, 31–45.

[21] Hume's stark contrast of memory and imagination marks a fundamental difference of his views with Aristotle's, who regards imagination as a function or work of the capacity of perception, subservient to the preservation of images or appearances and involved in memory, dreaming, and acting. See T. Kjeller Johansen, *The Powers of Aristotle's Soul*, Oxford University Press, Oxford 2012, 199–220. Also for Descartes, at least at a certain stage of his philosophical career, the imagination is connected rather than contrasted with memory, as the faculty that converts material impressions into images or ideas, 'les formes ou images que l'âme raisonnable considerera immediatement, lors qu'étant unie à cette machine elle imaginera ou sentira quelque object'. These are then stored in memory (*Traité de l'Homme*, in *Oeuvres de Descartes*, C. Adam & P. Tannery, eds., Volume 11, Vrin, Paris 1996 (3–215), 177; 'forms or images which the rational soul united to this machine will consider directly when it imagines some object or perceives it by the senses', *The Philosophical Writings of Descartes*, 2 Volumes, J. Cottingham, R. Stoothoff, & D. Murdoch, eds., Cambridge University Press, Cambridge 1984–5, Volume 1 (81–110), 106). Descartes' imagination is thus a cognitive faculty expressive of the union of bodily machine and rational soul and with the role of forming ideas, mental forms or images, out of corporeal figures. Memory is successive to and dependent on the operation of the imagination and common sense. See for a very good introduction to this aspect of Descartes' philosophy, G. Hatfield, 'Descartes' Physiology and its Relation to his Psychology', in *The Cambridge Companion to Descartes*, J. Cottingham ed., Cambridge University Press, Cambridge 1992, 335–70. It is true that Hume considers imagination as the foundation of memory (as well as of sense and memory) (1.4.7.3). But this must be understood with reference to the recognition of memories as such and to judgements based on such recognition; not to the primitive fact of our making and storing copies of impressions. At this basic level, memory and imagination stand in radical contrast with one another.

impression (§ 2.2.1). The starting point of Hume's philosophy is internal and mentalistic: it is the immediate presence of perceptions and, within the genus of perceptions, of impressions. At the root of Hume's philosophy, there is no psychophysical interface to explain; impressions do not have to be turned into episodes of awareness, imagination does not have to generate mental imagery in any primitive way. Images, qualitatively specified perceptions, are non-problematically assumed as data, without any need for a faculty of transduction. Imagination is essentially related to such data; but not as the faculty that makes available to awareness (like Locke's 'perception'). Rather, it is the faculty of their transposition and change, on the basis of principles of mental activity that can be individuated empirically, by observation.[22]

3.2.2 Perfect Ideas

Ideas are susceptible to transposition and change only if they are set free from their uniformly strong conception by memory and from its fixed order and connection. This consists in a manner of conception of ideas: an impression losing all its force and vivacity and turning into 'a perfect idea'. Perfect ideas are fainter ideas and the faculty by which impressions are conceived as perfect ideas is the imagination (1.1.3.1). Perfect ideas are those the imagination can transpose, make stronger and livelier, and change in their properties. The first and basic cognitive change brought about by Hume's imagination is thus the *detached conception* of ideas. Detached conception can be factorized in two dimensions, prominent in Hume's text: *disengagement* and *looseness*. Disengagement directly corresponds to the faintness of ideas. It is the capacity of the imagination to entertain ideas, with contents that are the same with impressions of sense and ideas of memory, without the compelling feeling of presence and reality in which representation of existence consist. This makes it possible for the natural mind to unlock itself, in imagination, from the demonstrative import and object dependence of sense and memory. Looseness is a property of the contents of imaginative states. In imagination the mind is not restricted to the order and connexion with which objects are

---

[22] See Garrett, *Cognition and Commitment*, 21, 25-6. Garrett remarks that Hume makes 'an exhaustive distinction of idea-forming faculties into *memory* and *imagination*, faculties whose representations differ not in fundamental character or content but only in causal history and in degree of "force and liveliness" or "vivacity"'. I accept the basic interpretive point: only memory and imagination deal with ideas or contents. But the differences between these two faculties must be given due recognition: their causal and phenomenal differences invest the character of their content, in connection with relation to and representation of objects. Memory is the only cognitive capacity which functionally conforms to First Principle. (My use of 'representation' is different from Garrett's.) Like Aristotle and Descartes, Spinoza also regards imagination as a precondition of memory, see P. Steembakkers, 'Spinoza on the Imagination', in L. Nauta & D. Pätzold, eds., *The Scope of the Imagination; 'Imaginatio' between Medieval and Modern Times*, Peters, Leuven 2004, 175:193, 181 (I thank Don Garrett for this reference).

present in sense and memory, one more trait of the hold of actuality on our thinking.

Perfect ideas are thus a natural complement of the Second Principle, which sums up to the following: 'whenever the imagination perceives a difference among ideas, it can easily produce a separation' (1.1.3.4). Hume's careful phrasing points to the complex relation between representation and imagination. Imagination 'perceives' differences represented by ideas of memory and has the capacity to 'produce' 'easily' a separation among such ideas. The easiness and the very possibility of the separation depend on impressions of sensation having gone all the way to perfect ideas, preserving the same (object-individuating) contents and shedding the force, vivacity, and fixedness that are essential to their representational import. Disengaged apprehension and loose hold of contents on the mind are mutually connected, just as the contrasting properties of feeling of reality and fixed order and form. Detached conception thus severs the link of the mind with present reality. It takes the natural mind out of the bounds and the bonds of objects representation, as well as of out of its relative cognitive safety. This sets in place the presuppositions for the further works of the imagination. The contrast between the self-intimating, firm, stable, locked conceptions of sense and memory and the faint and loose ideas of the imagination marks the threshold at which the mind can gain the capacity of transforming its contents and cognitive possibilities while losing its immediate contact with objects. This is also one of the basic roles ascribed to the imagination in contemporary philosophy and cognitive science: the potentiality for off-line conception, for thinking without assuming that one is engaging with the real thing. Counterfactual and modal reasoning in particular seem connected to the imagination's capacity for offline working.

3.2.3 Principles of Association and Transitions of Ideas

Against the background of perfect ideas, the basic explanatory role of Hume's imagination is thus that it can recombine, transpose, and change separately conceived ideas ('wherever the imagination perceives a difference among ideas, it can easily produce a separation'): 'All simple ideas may be separated by the imagination, and may be united again in what form it pleases' (1.1.4.1). Ideas, released from their primitive representational contexts, can be taken up into new, empirically explainable patterns of mental activity and thereby determine further contents.[23] Hume has made it perfectly clear that detached conception and

---

[23] Hume's doctrine of the interaction between ideas and between ideas and impressions is neatly summarized in Owen, *Hume's Reason*, 76: 'Ideas interact with each other, and with impressions, in three ways: impressions cause ideas, ideas are associated with each other, and ideas can be philosophically related to one another'. My only gloss is that, without falling back to faculty psychology, we should recognize that in the second and in the third case the interaction between ideas is essentially

recombination by the imagination, no less than the force and fixedness of object-dependent representation, can make a naturalistic understanding of understanding and cognition difficult to achieve. Simply assuming a capacity for detachment and recombination, without regulating principles, would leave mental contents underdetermined and fail to explain the manifest fact that we share the same kinds of complex ideas, 'the common subjects of our thoughts and reasonings' (1.4.4.7). Hume introduces the association of ideas and its principles to close this gap.

> As all simple ideas may be separated by the imagination, and may be united again in what form it pleases, nothing wou'd be more unaccountable than the operations of that faculty, were it not guided by some universal principles, which render it, in some measure, uniform with itself in all times and places. Were ideas entirely loose and unconnected, chance alone wou'd join them; and 'tis impossible the same simple ideas should fall regularly into complex ones (as they commonly do) without some bond of union among them, some associating quality, by which one idea naturally introduces another. (1.1.4.1)

The 'universal principles' of association of ideas—resemblance, contiguity, causation—ultimately account for our shared contents of thought and cognition, for the fact that 'languages so nearly correspond to each other' (1.1.4.1). More deeply, for the unity of our worldview, for the continuity of the second system of realities, grounded on imagination and judgement, with the first, delivered by sensible representation. 'These are therefore the principles of union or cohesion among our simple ideas, and in the imagination they supply the place of that inseparable connexion, by which they are united in our memory' (1.1.4.6).[24]

Hume lavishes praises on association of ideas, comparing it to the most celebrated Newtonian principle: 'Here is a kind of ATTRACTION, which in the mental world will be found to have as extraordinary effects as in the natural, and to shew itself in as many and as various forms' (1.1.4.6). He even bases his claim to philosophical fame on the discovery of association.

---

mediated by the original qualities and by the activities of imagination. (Sense and memory, by contrast, seem to be purely and primitively receptive.)

[24] That imagination is the faculty of compositionality is pointed out by Fodor, *Hume Variations*, 118. However, this must be taken with a pinch of salt. As Owen, *Hume's Reason*, 91, has remarked, we do not find in Hume the view that complex ideas, which are the general output of association, have sentential structure. Complex ideas are composed in an informal, synthesizing sense: they are put together by the imagination according to content-responsive principles. It is only in this broad sense that we can talk of compositionality. However, the main point I want to make here is left intact: by way of this sort of imaginative structuring, composition or association, a needful generalization of our natural cognitive capacities—new kinds of ideas: relations, substances, modes; new items of thought: the New Jerusalem—becomes possible.

Thro' this whole book, there are great pretensions to new discoveries in philosophy; but if any thing can entitle the author to so glorious a name as that of an *inventor*, 'tis the use he makes of the principle of the association of ideas, which enters into most of his philosophy.   (*Abstract* 35)[25]

The elements of content, once released from their primitive representational contexts, can enter into explainable and intelligible patterns of mental activity and thereby determine further contents of cognition and discourse.[26] The compositional operations of the imagination, driven by associations of ideas, are 'the cause why, among other things, languages so nearly correspond to each other; nature in a manner pointing out to every one those simple ideas, which are most proper to be united into a complex one' (1.1.4.1). And their output are complex ideas falling in certain kinds: modes, substances, and relations. 'Amongst the effects of this union or association of ideas, there are none more remarkable, than those complex ideas which are the common subjects of our thought and reasoning, and generally arise from some principle of union among our simple ideas' (1.1.4.7).

---

[25] Locke's disparaging attitude to association of ideas: 'wrong and natural Combinations of *Ideas*' (*Essay* 2.33.18, 401) is well known. This attitude reflects a conception of how we attain our ideas and cognitions that is very different from Hume's. Locke recognizes the need for complementing and integrating the ideas we receive from sensation and reflection in order to match the cognitions we generally and manifestly have (*Essay* 1.1.2, 43–4). But he has a more parsimonious and less dramatic view of the cognitive operations and changes which account for 'all those Notions', 'those sublime Thoughts', 'those remote Speculations', in which our knowledge and opinion in general consist. There is an 'ordinary method' of 'Nature' in the 'rise, progress, and gradual improvements' of the 'Faculties and Operations of the Mind' (*Essay* 2.11.14, 161). The pressing theoretical concern, for Locke, is precisely the continuity between the ideas and the cognition afforded by sensation and reflection and those owing to the operations of the understanding. Cognitive change in Locke's theory, thus, is not too deep: it does not presuppose or involve differences in kind between mental faculties, contents, and states. Correspondingly, Locke puts strong emphasis on the voluntary character of the operations of the understanding. This active and voluntary connotation of thinking and cognition is pervasive across Locke's categories of complex ideas: modes, ideas, and even substances (*Essay* 2.22.2,4,9 289–93; 3.5.5–7, 430–2; 2.30.3–4, 373). It is inextricably connected with naming and he pragmatic ends of language (*Essay* 3.3.11, 414; 3.5.6–7, 430–2; 3.6.48–49, 469–70; 3.10.18–19, 499–501). This is also a reason of the scarce importance Locke gives to imagination. Locke wants to make it do with only one kind of contents, the representational content delivered by sensation and reflection; and with their composition, variation, and abstraction. The cognitive faculty which is responsible for these operations and for the corresponding degrees of knowledge and opinion, the understanding, is itself representational. Thus, it comes to no surprise that imagination or fancy figures in the *Essay* in the minor and basically interfering of a faculty or capacity for framing chimerical ideas. And that it is does not even figure in Locke's list of 'Modes of Thinking'—inclusive of sensation, remembrance, recollection, contemplation, reverie, attention, intention or study, extasy, reasoning, judging, volition, and knowledge (*Essay* 2.19.1–2, 223–4).

[26] Hume's doctrine of the interaction between ideas and between ideas and impressions is neatly summarized in Owen, *Hume's Reason*, 76: 'Ideas interact with each other, and with impressions, in three ways: impressions cause ideas, ideas are associated with each other, and ideas can be philosophically related to one another'. My only gloss is that, without falling back to faculty psychology, we should recognize that in the second and in the third case the interaction between ideas is essentially mediated by the original qualities and by the activities of imagination. (Sense and memory, by contrast, are purely and primitively receptive.)

However, Hume's initial presentation of this important doctrine in 1.1.4 is so sketchy that it risks being misleading. The basic point of the doctrine is clear: non-object-representing contents of mental activity explain our widely shared and mutually recognizable thoughts and cognitions. Such contents originate in the transposition and change of perfect ideas, on the basis of principles which are identifiable not from the given contents of ideas but rather from empirically discoverable properties of the imagination. However, when it comes to specifying the character and the effects of the 'concurrence' of these principles with ideas with the relevant properties this early but programmatic discussion is found wanting. This is not only for lack of detail. Hume limits himself to indicate summarily how the representational relations of resemblance and contiguity in space and time operate on imagination so as to produce an association among ideas, very wisely only hinting to the 'stronger connexion' produced by the relation of causation (1.1.4.2). But one would never anticipate, on this sparse basis, the enormously complex network of broadly associative operations that is deployed throughout Book 1. Hume's doctrine of association of ideas, as it is put forward in 1.1.4, is barely an explanatory scheme. To really appreciate its importance one must track it in the detail of Hume's explanation of ideas and cognitive capacities. For instance, Hume's real treatment of the idea of substance is at 1.4.3: *Of the antient philosophy*; of the causal relation is at 1.3.6: *Of the inference from the impression to the idea*; and of identity at 1.4.2: *Of scepticism with regard to the senses*.

The phrase 'association of ideas' and the Newtonian metaphor of 'ATTRACTION' convey the image of units of content, like mental points, connected by linear forces acting at a distance and finding a dynamic equilibrium in certain patterns of aggregation. On this view, perfect ideas are associated because of (some of) their qualities and a uniting force, like atoms in a chunk of matter. Ideas gravitate towards and cohere with one another. Association is primarily a state, an arrangement of our ideas, which exemplifies a pattern of unity: 'bond of union', 'associating quality', 'uniting principle' (1.1.4.1). However, this would be a simplification and a distortion of Hume's view of association. Hume's doctrine is more focused on the processes that associate ideas than on their aggregate existence in the mind. Hume's association of ideas is best understood as a *transition of the mind*, a movement of the imagination from one idea to another.[27] The associative qualities of ideas are the bases for such transitions: they 'produce an association' in the sense that upon the 'appearance' of some idea they 'naturally introduce another' (1.1.4.1). But it is the imagination, as it 'runs easily' or can 'run along' ideas according to these principles, which constitutes the association (1.1.4.2). Elsewhere,

---

[27] The perplexities voiced by Kemp Smith, *Philosophy of Hume*, 245–8 about the interconnection of association of objects (contents) and of ideas (mental existents) stem from his downplaying the active role of imagination.

Hume treats association of ideas and transitions of the imagination as equivalent: 'a quality, which produces an association of ideas, and an easy transition of the imagination from one to the other' (1.4.6.7); 'producing an association or transition of ideas' (2.2.2.16). This suggests that the core of Hume's doctrine of association are mental transitions, supported by properties of ideas consisting in (in the case of resemblance and contiguity) or depending on (in the case of causation) observed relations among them. These transitions express original qualities of the imagination, the principles of its interaction with ideas. 'The very essence' of the 'three relations of resemblance, contiguity and causation' 'consists in their producing an easy transition of ideas' (1.4.6.16). This involvement of properties and relations of ideas in the transitions of the imagination, rather than their aggregation, is the realization in the natural mind of the 'ATTRACTION' of ideas.

In support of this reading of Hume's association, I remark that in the texts we are considering, along with the Newtonian ones, we also find a different set of metaphors. For instance, 'nature' 'pointing out to every one' what simple ideas 'are most proper to be united into a complex one'; this being the 'manner' in which the mind is 'convey'd from one idea to another' (1.1.4.1). This is prominent in the *Abstract*.

> But notwithstanding the empire of the imagination, there is a secret tie or union among particular ideas, which causes the mind to conjoin them more frequently together, and makes the one, upon its appearance, introduce the other. Hence arises what we call the *apropos* of discourse: hence the connection of writing: and hence that thread, or chain of thought, which a man naturally supports even in the loosest *reverie*   (*Abstract* 35).

This suggests a view of association as a content-responsive, differential, and content-directed mental activity; and thereby as a function of the imagination rather than a property of ideas. So, for instance, their qualities completely determine the resemblance of two ideas. But that an idea naturally introduces another resembling one is a further fact, which consist in a content-oriented operation of the imagination and depends on a primitive, original quality of it. The 'bond of union' among ideas consists primarily, both as to its character and to its effects, not in a link among ideas but in transitions among them.[28] Hume also explicitly identifies the principles of association with a 'rule or method' of mental activity.

---

[28] Hume derives this theme from Berkeley. In his discussion of our perception of distance and of the differences between the ideas of sight and touch, Berkeley replaces presumptive elements of the content of ideas with customary, experience-based, immediate transitions of the mind. 'Not that there is any natural or necessary connexion between the sensation we perceive by the turn of the eyes and greater or lesser distance, but because the mind has by constant experience found the different sensations corresponding to the different dispositions of the eyes to be attended each with a different degree of distance in the object, there has grown an habitual or customary connexion between these two sorts of ideas, so that the mind no sooner perceives the sensations rising from the different turn it gives to

The rule, by which they [our thoughts] proceed, is to pass from one object to what is resembling, contiguous to, or produc'd by it. When one idea is present to the imagination, any other, united by these relations, naturally follows it, and enters with more facility by means of that introduction. (2.1.4.2)

Hume remarks that the principles of such transitions must be 'resolv'd into *original* qualities of human nature, which I pretend not to explain' (1.1.4.6). Here, as it is often the case in the science of man, enquiry hits on empirical bedrock. However, this more re-orientates than blocks the enquiry. A 'true philosopher' should 'restrain the intemperate desire of searching into causes', which could 'lead him into obscure and uncertain speculations'. But this is because 'his enquiry wou'd be much better employ'd in examining the effects than the causes of his principle' (1.1.4.6).[29]

3.3 The Nature of Hume's Imagination

Association is thus Hume's generic label for the activity with which the imagination closes the gaps between the input of impressions of sensation and our worldview.

> 'Twill be easy to conceive of what vast consequence these principles must be in the science of human nature, if we consider, that so far as regards the mind, these are the only links that bind the parts of the universe together, or connect us with any person or object exterior to ourselves. For as it is by means of thought only that any thing operates upon our passions, and as these are the

---

the eyes,... but it withal perceives the different idea of distance.' *New Theory*, 17 (11). This is with the same immediateness with which hearing a word makes us think of its meaning, *New Theory*, 51, 64, 140 (22, 26, 49–50). These 'sudden judgements', based on experience, are all there is to our perception of distance, *New Theory*, 20, 24, 62 (12, 25). See *New Theory*, 25 (12): 'That one idea may suggest another to the mind it will suffice that they have been observed to go together, without any demonstration of the necessity of their coexistence, or without so much as knowing what it is that makes them so to coexist'; 145 (51): 'So swift and sudden and unperceived is the transition from visible to tangible ideas that we can scarce forbear thinking them equally the immediate object of vision'. Hume's imagination is in many respects the systematic development of these insights and their application to a more comprehensive view of the construction of human cognition.

[29] A striking indication of the differences between the *Treatise* and the first *Enquiry*, in relation to imagination, is the short work Hume makes in the latter of association of ideas as principles of the imagination. At the opening of Section 3 of the *Enquiry: Of the association of ideas*, Hume simply lists the principles of association, *Enquiry* 3.1–3 (101–2). When he moves to consider the 'effects' of these principles, however, we find nothing of the topics covered in Part 1 of the *Treatise*: complex ideas, relations, and abstraction. Rather we meet with a lengthy discussion of the unity of narrative works, *Enquiry* 3. 5–18 (102–7) that is inherently interesting but more than risks losing focus of contents and cognition. Interestingly, the 1777 edition of the *Enquiry*, which has traces of Hume's editorial work, omits all this discussion.

only ties of our thoughts, they are really *to us* the cement of the universe, and all the operations of the mind must, in a great measure, depend on them.

(*Abstract* 35)

This cognitive change seems to go beyond combining simple ideas into complex ones or some complex ideas into others. Generality and modality, cognitive structures like the connectedness of things and events and their external existence, cognitive activities like reasoning, point to possibilities of thought and cognition that do not seem amenable to the recombination of perceptions and units of mental content. The content-productive function of Hume's imagination is thus much more complex than what the Newtonian imagery with which Hume introduces association suggests. Hume addresses this functional complexity both in terms of the structure of the imagination as a faculty (which I discuss here) and of the general character of its production of content (which I discuss in § 3.4).[30]

3.3.1 The Structural Principle: 'In the larger or more limited sense'

The structure of Hume's imagination is outlined in the somewhat elusive characterization that Hume gives of this faculty at 1.3.9.19 fn. 22. In this important text, Hume explicitly identifies imagination as the faculty by which we engage in mental transitions; and he distinguishes two different ways in which such transitions contribute to cognition.

> In general we may observe that as our assent to all probable reasonings is founded on the vivacity of ideas, it resembles many of those whimsies and prejudices, which are rejected under the opprobrious character of being the offspring of the imagination. By this expression it appears that the word, imagination, is commonly us'd in two different senses; and tho' nothing be more contrary to true philosophy, than this inaccuracy, yet in the following reasonings I have

---

[30] It may seem anachronistic to employ the notion of mental content in interpreting the *Treatise*. But Hume's apparatus of cognitive gaps and of production of ideas which can close them certainly invites such a reading. Modes of cognition which differ in regard to the possibility of composition, generality, or modal qualification, to inferential structure, to including the thought of causally connected events, persistent bodies, and identical persons seem to differ precisely in relation to their different kinds of contents. Then we should accept as a fact that Hume's imagination is productive of new mental contents and new mental states. See, for an example of this, the controversial but often insightful reading proposed in J. Fodor, *Hume's Variations*, Oxford University Press, Oxford 2003, especially 91–4, 113–4. (Fodor grudgingly acknowledges that imagination is Hume's faculty of compositionality; but he does very little of it.) What matters, anyway, is avoiding, as most recent interpreters do almost unanimously, the interpretation originally proposed by Reid and echoed by the logical positivist according to which Hume has no firm grasp of, and no commitment to, the contentfulness of mental episodes.

often been oblig'd to fall into it. When I oppose the imagination to the memory, I mean the faculty, by which we form our fainter ideas. When I oppose it to reason, I mean the same faculty, excluding only our demonstrative and probable reasonings. When I oppose it to neither, 'tis indifferent whether it be taken in the larger or more limited sense, or at least the context will sufficiently explain the meaning. (1.3.9.19 fn. 22)[31]

This text has an interesting story. The footnote was added to 1.3.9.19 when Book 2 of the *Treatise* was in print. It was moved from its original location at 2.2.7.6 and inserted, with an expanded text, at its present location.[32] Quite clearly, Hume went through this hassle because he realized that such an important clarification about his conception of imagination had to be given much earlier in the text, if only in a footnote: rightly where the imagination was called upon to perform important and diverse explanatory roles. The new context of the footnote is the conclusion of a section where Hume discusses different causes of belief: association by causation, but also by resemblance and contiguity; custom based on experience, but also on education and hearsay. The diversity of the causes of different sorts of belief and their different epistemic standing call in question the unity and soundness of the explanation that the imagination offers of them and, thereby, of the imagination itself as a faculty.

In the newly placed footnote, Hume tracks down the causal and epistemic diversity of the cognitive effects of the imagination to its structural complexity. The text of the footnote is correspondingly expanded with the addition of the first lines, where Hume declares his aim of sheltering his theory of belief from the risk of mistaking whimsies and prejudices for assent to probable reasoning. The imagination is commonly conceived of in two different senses and, while this seems to go against true philosophy, there are good reasons for understanding it in this way. Hume even takes himself to be 'oblig'd' to resort to this duality.

---

[31] Talk of faculties, and of the imagination as a faculty, is completely non-problematic in Book 1 of the *Treatise*. What would be problematic is talk of non-reducible mental faculties, or powers in general. But Hume has available a perfectly intelligible idea of power, grounded on his inferentialist account of the ideas of cause and causal necessity (this is discussed in Chapters 6 and 7). What is required is that faculties or powers, in particular mental faculties, be scrutable a posteriori or from actions and experience: 'power consists in the possibility or probability of any action, as discover'd by experience and the practice of the world' (2.1.10.6). Therefore, Hume can perfectly well individuate a faculty of imagination, on the basis of empirically ascertainable properties and relations of perceptions, given that these can be conceived as a causally and functionally connected system (as our true idea of the mind is). We can also say that the idea of the faculty of the imagination is the abstract idea of a mental power, which is based on abstract ideas of powers of perceptions, which generalize on their empirically ascertainable actions and relations.

[32] The information is given in Volume 2 of the D.F. Norton & M.J. Norton edition of the *Treatise*, Clarendon Press, Oxford 2007, 593–4, 635, where the original text is given. In 2.2.7.5–6 Hume discusses a complication in how imagination contributes to compassion, that is, that the sympathetic passion may acquire strength from the weakness of the original. This prompts the distinction between the two senses of imagination; but the context is hardly a compelling one for such clarification.

Actually we can regard the two senses as distinguished and combined in a principle, the Structural Principle, which together with Two Viewpoints is crucially important for my interpretation. The main point of the footnote and the content of the Structural Principle is the distinction between:

(a) A *larger sense* of imagination, in which it is opposed to memory (an object-representing faculty) as the faculty of forming fainter, perfect ideas and of freely transposing and changing them; in its larger sense, imagination includes a reasoning and idea-comparing part, demonstrative and probable reason; by 'imagination in the larger sense' I will primarily refer to this idea-comparing part.

(b) Imagination in a *more limited sense* or opposed to reason. This is not a contrast between faculties but a limitation or contrast *within* the faculty opposed to memory. The imagination, as opposed to reason, is an idea-transposing and idea-changing but *not* a reasoning and idea-comparing capacity. This part is contrasted with the reasoning part but still acts as its necessary support.

Hume also holds (as hinted at the very end of the footnote) that in some theoretical roles, actually (as we will see) in many of them, the imagination figures in both ways or according to both senses; that is, as one faculty operating in both capacities. This will turn out to be crucial for understanding how Hume's imagination works.

With reference to the Structural Principle, we must ask three questions:

(i) How is imagination to be understood in its larger sense?
(ii) What are the nature and the role of imagination in the more limited sense?
(iii) How can the two senses coexist in one faculty?

Answering these questions takes us some way toward clarifying Hume's conception of the imagination.

(i) Imagination as contrasted with memory, or imagination in the larger sense, is the faculty of change, transposition, variation of ideas; of mental transitions or of inference. Imagination is taken in a larger sense if its potential for transitions of ideas is taken in the most inclusive way, to include our demonstrative and probable reasonings; that is, idea-comparing reasoning in general. Fainter ideas are ideas unlocked from the hold of sense and memory, perfect ideas that the imagination can transpose and change. Demonstrative and probable reasoning compare ideas with reference to their contents. 'All kinds of reasoning are a *comparison*, and a discovery of those relations, either constant or inconstant, which two or more objects bear to each other' (1.3.2.2). We ordinarily engage in idea-comparison with some implicit or explicit understanding of their contents and thereby of the roles they can take in reasoning. Idea-comparing reasoning—or Lockean reasoning, as Schmitt has aptly dubbed it—is reasoning, demonstrative or probable, as we practice it in philosophy and in everyday life.[33] Such comparison entails some transposition of ideas, an operation that only the imagination can perform with its faint and loose ideas. This is why the imagination, simply as the faculty of fainter ideas, is primed for reasoning.[34]

But reasoning, the idea-comparing operation of the imagination, requires well-understood ideas; and such understanding is in the first place to be achieved in relation to the source of these ideas in impressions.

> 'Tis impossible to reason justly, without understanding perfectly the idea concerning which we reason; and 'tis impossible perfectly understand any idea, without tracing it up to its origin, and examining that primary impression, from which it arises. The examination of the impression bestows a clearness on the idea; and the examination of the idea bestows a like clearness on all our reasoning.
> (1.3.2.4)

Here lies a difficulty. Reasoning presupposes well-understood ideas to compare. But a 'primary impression' for the ideas we reason with and about is not always to be found. The problem then is how in these cases (cognitive gaps) we can have available ideas that are understood well enough to support good reasoning. Hume must rely on the imagination to put such ideas in place, since there is no other cognitive faculty in human nature apart from sensible representation, which is here out of the question. Then, the operations by which the imagination puts in place the ideas required for our reasonings that are not present in impression cannot consist in comparison of ideas. This would either contradict the assumption that no impressions can be found that allow us to conceive such ideas or leave open a cognitive gap.[35] To break this impasse Hume resorts to principles

---

[33] F. Schmitt, *Hume's Epistemology in the* Treatise, Oxford University Press, Oxford 2014, 135–6.

[34] Hume offers two contrasting and seemingly inconsistent characterizations of the imagination: as 'the faculty, by which we form our fainter ideas' (1.3.9.19, fn. 22) and as 'the vivacity of our ideas' (1.4.7.3). The first is when he is contrasting the imagination with memory and when he is locating it within his general topology of mind. The second is when he is describing the general, inclusive cognitive role of the imagination as the foundation of memory, senses, and understanding. The dynamics of force and vivacity, the changes in their degrees, are fundamental for the works of imagination, because they constitute the transmission and the variation of our sense and acceptance of certain contents as real. This is required if imagination is to bring about radical cognitive changes relatively to sensible representation. While the contrast is real, however, the inconsistency is only apparent. Quite simply, unless ideas are conceived faintly, as perfect ideas, there can be no room for change in force and vivacity and therefore for belief formation and fixation. I thus agree with Garrett, *Cognition and Commitment*, 13, 2–28; contra the surprising reading of Kemp Smith (the two definitions are almost opposite in meaning).

[35] B. Winters, 'Hume on Reason', *Hume Studies*, 5, 1979, 20–35 (in Tweyman, ed., *David Hume. Critical Assessments*, I, 229–40), makes this point very clearly.

of association, which connect ideas, modifying our cognitive possibilities in ways not accountable by their given contents. But as we have seen association of ideas is better understood, rather than as an aggregation of contents, as a pattern of imaginative transitions among ideas and propensities to such transitions. If this is so, then there has to be a broadly inferential activity of the imagination that does not consist in a comparison of ideas. The contents available to the mind must be not only recombined but deeply transformed; and this cannot result from comparing ideas already available.

(ii) This is the point of Hume's articulation of the faculty of imagination. Imagination in the more limited sense is the seat of the whimsies and prejudices that Hume aims to tell apart from the reasoning part of imagination in the 'larger' sense. Since whimsies and prejudices belong to imagination in a 'sense' that is different from that in which it is the faculty of reasoning, Hume is apparently on safe ground. But this, as it stands, is only a defensive move, suggesting that we have and apply a disjunctive concept of imagination. The truth is that Hume's view of the structure and working of the imagination goes beyond this superficial disjunctive appearance. Hume's neat partitioning might give only an illusory solution to his problem, because the distinction between imagination in the more limited sense and the idea-comparing, reasoning-involving part of the imagination, both included in the inclusive faculty of fainter ideas, is superficial. As Hume makes clear throughout Book 1—for instance, at 1.3.6.12, 1.3.8.12, 1.3.12.22, 1.3.16.9, and again, thematically, at 1.4.1 and at 1.4.7—whimsies, prejudices (biases), and trivial properties of the imagination in the more limited sense are indispensable for the very possibility of demonstrative and probable reasoning. There is a deep conceptual, functional, and causal interconnection between the two senses of imagination, which is the real point of the Structural Principle.

It is in this context, as the necessary complement of idea-comparing reasoning, that we should understand the nature and the role of more limited imagination. Imagination in the more limited sense abides by the Second Principle and engages in transpositions and changes of its ideas. This is what imagination in general does. But more limited imagination does not operate by comparing antecedently well-understood ideas and discovering their constant and inconstant relations (it excludes demonstrative and probable reasoning). It operates in ways and on principles not individuated and put in place by the contents of impressions of sensation and ideas of memory and by their relations. The transitions of the more limited imagination are based on empirically discovered cognitive principles that are not reducible to object representation. For instance, repetition and habituation effects; propensities to confound resembling ideas; cognitive hysteresis; effects of resemblance between mental acts and mental objects; propensities to complete unions of ideas by adding other; propensities to turn manners of conception into traits of content; intransitivity effects of the complexity and length of chains of reasoning; intransitivity effects of limited span of attention; propensities to engage in transitions of manners of conception along transitions of ideas; propensities to form ideas in order to reduce cognitive conflict or dissonance. These principles will be introduced and discussed as we go on.[36] These 'whimsies and prejudices' are cognitive biases and belong to the more limited imagination. But it is rightly because of these propensities and biases that the imagination can be productive of the new ideas and cognitive changes that we apply in probable and demonstrative reasoning. More limited imagination is still, in a broad sense, inferential: its operations are transitions among ideas, empirically explainable and predictable (even though their principles may be difficult to access), responsive to the contents of ideas but also to independent patterns of mental movement. This is a primitive, non-idea-comparing layer of Hume's imagination and it is only with reference to it that we can completely characterize its function.[37]

(iii)   Hume remarks that there are uses of the concept of imagination where it is indifferent whether it is taken in the larger or the more limited sense. This is consistent with a disjunctive reading; but given Hume's other commitments, it is best understood with reference to cognitive operations of the imagination in which the functions that come to expression in reasoning merge with and are supported by those that can be labelled as biases. Quite simply, if the more limited imagination operates by propensities like those listed earlier and if in this way some of the ideas, relations of ideas, and mental capacities that are requisite for demonstrative and probable reasoning primitively come into place, there is a functional merging of more limited imagination with the reasoning part of imagination in the larger sense. With respect to these contents and modes of thinking, there is division of labour but no opposition between the two senses or parts of imagination.[38]

---

[36] For an interesting attempt to a systematization of the principles or functions of imagination, see R. P. Wolff, 'Hume's Theory of Mental Activity', *Philosophical Review*, 69, 1969 (in Tweyman, ed., *David Hume. Critical Assessments*, III, 158–75), 173.Wolff's table of categories for the propensities (dispositions to form dispositions) of the imagination includes a propensity to develop dispositions to reproduce ideas; a propensity to develop a disposition to conceive causally interrelated impressions as identical; a propensity to conceive absent objects as existent; a propensity to reproduce a discontinuous series as continuous; a propensity to conceive a perception with the greater firmness. This is close to the account proposed here.

[37] Loeb, *Stability and Justification*, 59, proposes to call imagination, in its most general cognitive role, 'the faculty of association' and to restrict 'imagination' to its more limited sense, as the locus of belief-forming processes lacking justification. Loeb also refers to the propensities that are different from (primitive) causal inference and that Hume regards as somehow irregular as 'imaginative propensities' (161). I think this is misleading in more than one way. At least in the central, causal case, as Loeb recognizes, association constitutes an inference (42). I would say that inference, rather than any sort of gluing of individual perceptions, is the mental reality of Hume's association. Therefore, imagination is in general the faculty of inference (primitive or reflective). There are also no grounds for secluding causal inference, primitive or reflective, from imaginative propensities. I think that it is important to preserve a sense of the unity of imagination in its different and even contrasting roles.

[38] By contrast, Langland-Hassan, *Explaining Imagination*, 4, 6, 28, 44, 49, 62, denies that imagination is a natural cognitive kind. But the two different concepts of imagination that mark its

I think that the Structural Principle is precisely what is needed to make sense of the general nature and function of Hume's imagination. Both more limited imagination and imagination in the idea-comparing sense determine cognitive changes, but in radically different ways: the second, by producing new knowledge and new beliefs, by increasing our epistemic purchase; the first, by producing new modes of thinking, new ideas, and new cognitive capacities, by changing and augmenting the mental contents and capacities we have available. (The tasks of epistemology and the theory of content are strictly connected in Hume's philosophy, but still distinct.) If the two parts of imagination did not functionally converge, the architecture of Hume's natural mind would be disrupted. The ideas presupposed by cognitive practices of all sorts and by our worldview would not be in place; and with this, the gaps of sensible representation would remain open. Another important consideration is that our engagement in inferential thinking and cognition, even when reflective and idea-comparing, is in general the operation of the imagination as a whole. This makes it possible to ascribe to our reasoning, belief-formation, and belief-revision certain properties, conditions, limits, and outcomes which would be out of place if they were the work of a distinct faculty of the understanding. As we will see, together with the production of new contents, this is the key to Hume's explanation of some of the most complex forms of probable reasoning and to his response to scepticism.

3.3.2 Natural and Philosophical Relations

Hume's doctrine of relations of ideas mirrors the structure of the imagination. As with association of ideas, Hume's initial presentation of this doctrine only dimly anticipates its complexity and its importance in the development of the theory. But the distinction between natural and philosophical relations of ideas is clear enough.

> The word *relation* is commonly used in two senses considerably different from each other. Either for that quality, by which two ideas are connected together in the imagination, and the one naturally introduces the other, after the manner above-explained; or for that particular circumstance, in which, even upon the arbitrary union of two ideas in the fancy, we may think proper to compare them.
> (1.1.5.1)

Hume adds that we use the word in 'common language' in the first sense, while 'in philosophy' we use it in the second. A natural relation is a 'quality' by which two ideas are 'connected together in the imagination' and the one 'naturally

---

heterogeneity, the capacity for mental imagery and that for thought about possibility and fictions, have nothing to do with Hume's articulation of the faculty of imagination.

introduces' the other. Natural relations are products of more limited imagination, which establish a 'connexion or association of ideas' (1.1.5.3): resemblance, contiguity, causation. Natural relations are primarily responsible for our forming all sorts of complex ideas. (The detailed working of imagination, in the different cases, is different.) Philosophical relations *are* complex ideas, falling in the Lockean taxonomy recalled at 1.1.4.7: 'These complex ideas may be divided into RELATIONS, MODES, and SUBSTANCES' (see Locke, *Essay*, 2.12.3, 164). They do not connect, associate, unite ideas; they do not work as 'principles of union and cohesion' among our ideas. Philosophical relations are 'any particular subject of comparison, without a connecting principle'. They are 'particular circumstances' in which, 'even upon the arbitrary union of two ideas in the fancy, we may think proper to compare them'. Philosophical relations are principles and subject matters of idea-comparing reasoning. The difference between natural and philosophical relations is thus also one between compelling movements of the mind, which only marginally involve the cognitive agency of a subject of thinking; and mental operations falling, to some extent, within the scope of reflection and doxastic deliberation. In both cases, what is at work is 'imagination' or 'fancy'. But in the case of philosophical relations we compare ideas as we 'think proper', considering their contents; we engage in reasoning with intentional, even normative guidance.

Also in the case of natural and philosophical relations, we have a clear psychological partition coupled with explanatory priority and functional continuity. Ideas of philosophical relations, like identity, space and time, and causation, are a 'source' of comparisons and reasonings and have an essential role in ordinary and philosophical cognition. But the seven philosophical relations depend on the natural relations for their possibility. The principles of comparison—the particular 'circumstances' in which we may think it proper to compare ideas—are themselves not all of them representational. Identity, general relations of space and time, quantity, and number, common qualities and their degrees, and cause and effect are not given in impression and therefore not represented in ideas. Therefore, they are based on the primitive content-producing relations—natural relations that in this respect merge with the philosophical ones.[39] And our practice of reasoning reflectively, in a more or less explicit way, by comparing ideas would not be possible or at least would not have the properties and conditions it has, if natural relations of ideas did not systematically embed our consideration of philosophical ones. Hume muddles the picture by presenting the contrast between natural and philosophical relations as one between passivity and activity of the mind, rather than one between different levels and ways of the activities of

---

[39] See, on the dependence of philosophical on natural relations, E. Schliesser, 'Two Definitions of Causation, Normativity, and Hume's Debate with Newton', *Journal of Scottish Philosophy*, 5, 2007, 83–101.

the imagination. But, again, the unity of Hume's imagination can be recognized if we look at relations as transitions among ideas.[40]

3.3.3 Cognitive Gaps and the Structural Principle

Closing the gaps of object representation involves a deep cognitive change. Since the gaps depend on Representational Naturalism, on the natural and necessary conditions of representation of objects, and as this is a fundamental layer of thought and cognition and an apparently unique source of content, such cognitive change borders paradox. Confronted with paradoxes of cognitive change, contemporary naturalistic philosophers would resort to an externalist move: contents and cognitions can be explained, in ways not accounted for by their modes of mental presence, with their dependence on external, environmental, physical, or social conditions.

Because of the inner character of representation and of the liberty of imagination, Hume cannot take this path. It is true that Hume occasionally resorts to natural-philosophical hypotheses.[41] Hume repeatedly suggests that the imagination—like sense and memory—is supported by the physiology of sense perception and of brain processes. He is ready to describe its working in quasi-physical, quasi-mechanical ways—in terms of inertia or attrition; of effects of distance in space and time; of 'pipes and canals' (1.3.10.7). Hume reiterates the explanatory limits of the science of man—introducing the 'relations of

---

[40] This aspect of the structure and working of Hume's imagination can remind us of dual process theories of reasoning. That is, of the distinction between 'system 1' processes ('a form of universal cognition shared between animals and humans', 'a set of subsystems that operate with come autonomy', inclusive of 'instinctive behaviors' and 'formed by associative learning') and 'system 2' processes (like logical reasoning which is 'slow and sequential in nature and makes use of the central working memory system'). See J. St. B. T. Evans, 'In Two Minds: Dual-process Accounts of Reasoning', *Trends in Cognitive Science*, 7 (10) 2003, 454–59, 454, quoted in K. Stenning & M. van Lambalgen, *Human Reasoning and Cognitive Science*, The MIT Press, Cambridge (Mass.)/London 2008, 124. Stenning and van Lambalgen remark that System 1 processes are connected to 'automatic, but defeasible, reasoning to interpretations' and to planning and that they are 'credulous' (as opposed to 'sceptical' system 2 ones). System 1 and system 2 processes also 'work together from early on in human development', with system 2 ones starting 'as repair processes when a system 1 process meets an impasse' (*Human Reasoning*, 124–30). The great relevance of this for the interpretation of Hume's philosophy is obvious.

[41] In linking imagination, error, and the brain, Hume was of course following an important modern tradition. We owe to J. P. Wright the uncovering and the detailed examination of the neurophysiological aspects of Hume's account of mental activity (of impressions of sensation and of imagination, in the first place; with particular regard to belief) and of their roots in Descartes and especially in Malebranche. See *Sceptical Realism*, 5–6, 15, 68–70, 73–4, 189–200, 204–06, 211–20. Wright's scholarship is admirable and the conceptual layer of Hume's philosophy he helped to dig out is certainly important. However, we should be wary of ascribing to Hume any aim of reduction of the mental to the physical (Wright recommends we see Hume 'as attempting some sort of reduction of mental to physical processes according to the theories which were available to him in his own day', 204). See also J. Hakkarainen, 'The Materialist of Malmesbury and the Experimentalist of Edinburgh. Hume's and Hobbes' Conceptions of Imagination Compared', *Hobbes Studies*, 17, 2005, 72–107.

resemblance, contiguity and *causation,* as principles of union among ideas, without examining into their causes' was 'in prosecution of my first maxim, that we must in the end rest contented with experience'. But he adds that there is 'something specious and plausible, which [he] might have display'd on that subject'. This is a natural-philosophical hypothesis. "Twou'd have been easy to have made an imaginary dissection of the brain, and have shewn, why upon our conception of any idea, the animal spirits run into all the contiguous traces, and rouze up the other ideas, that are related to it' (1.2.5.20). This is the sketched explanation. 'As the mind is endow'd with a power of exciting any idea it pleases; whenever it dispatches the spirits into that region of the brain, in which the idea is plac'd; these spirits always excite the idea, when they run precisely into the proper traces.' 'But as their motion is seldom direct, and naturally turns a little to the one side or the other; for this reason the animal spirits, falling into the contiguous traces, present other related ideas in lieu of that, which the mind desir'd at first to survey.' We may fail to notice this change and 'continuing still the same train of thought, make use of the related idea, which is presented to us, and employ it in our reasoning, as if it were the same with what we demanded. This is the cause of many mistakes and sophisms in philosophy' (1.2.5.20–1).[42]

---

[42] This seems to be based on Malebranche, for instance, on *Search after Truth*, Book 2, Part 1, chapter 5.iv: 'Or c'est dans cette facilité que les esprits animaux ont de passer dans les member de nôtre corps, que consistent les habitudes.... Il est visible par ce que l'on vient de dire, qu'il ya beaucoup de rapport entre la memoire et les habitudes. Car de même que les habitudes corporelles consistent dans la facilité que les esprits ont acquise de passer par certains endroits de nôtre corps: ainsi la memoire consiste dans les traces, que le mêmes esprits ont imprimées dans le cerveau, lesquelles sont causes de la facilité que nous avons de nous souvenir des choses. De sorte que s'il n'y avait point des perceptions attachées au cours de ces esprits animaux, ni à ces traces, il n'y auroit aucune différence entre la memoire et les autres habitudes', N. Malebranche, *De la Recherche de la Verité. Ou l'on Traite de la Nature de l'Esprit de l'homme, et de l'Usage qu'il en doit faire pour éviter l'erreur dans les sciences*, Pralard, Paris 1678 (4th edn.), 85–6; 'Now it is in this facility the animal spirits have of flowing into the members of our bodies that *habits* consist.... It is obvious from what has just been said that there is a great similarity between *memory* and *habits*, and that in one sense, memory can pass for a habit. For just as corporeal habits consist in the facility the spirits have acquired for flowing through certain places in our bodies, so memory consists in the traces the same spirits have imprinted upon the brain, which are the causes of our facility in recalling things to ourselves. Thus, if there were no perceptions attached to the paths of the animal spirits, nor to these traces, there would be no difference between the memory and the other habits', N. Malebranche, *The Search after Truth*, T. M. Lennon & P. J. Olscamp, eds., Cambridge University Press, Cambridge 1997, 108. A cursory comparison of Hume's explanatory resort to imagination with the lengthy and sustained discussion in Malebranche *Search after Truth*, Book 2, Part 1, chapters 2 and 3, makes very clear the radical differences in the orientation of the two theories. In particular Malebranche is interested primarily in how imagination, in strict continuity with the senses, is a major source of cognitive error, precisely on account of its essential connection with body. The focus of Malebranche's enquiry are thus the physical, mechanical causes of imaginative processes (animal spirits and brain traces). Malebranche keeps the discussion of the cognitive principles of imagination to a minimum: essentially, associations between traces and ideas based on resemblance, simultaneity, and convention (*Search after Truth*, Book 2, Part 1, chapter 5.i). This is integrated with the restriction of the cognitive import of imagination to the pragmatic requirements of self-preservation and the well-being of body (Search after Truth, Book 2, Part 1, chapter 4.iii). Nothing like Hume's painstaking and constructive attention for the cognitive principles of imagination.

Still, Hume is committed to keep moral and natural philosophy distinct and not to essentially resort to any specific neurophysiological explanatory construct. Hume's theory of imagination is motivated neither by a materialist metaphysics of mind (addressed, sceptically, in 1.4.5) nor by natural-philosophical interests (the dissection of the brain is easy and imaginary). Imagination is a topic in moral philosophy: the philosophy of mind and cognition. The solitary exception at 1.2.5.20 notwithstanding, it is very clear that the order of explanation is from mental actions to physical effects. The explanation is framed in mentalistic language. The mind is a causal agent. It is 'endow'd with a power of exciting any idea it pleases'. It 'dispatches the spirits into that region of the brain, where the idea is plac'd': some grasp of the idea is presupposed by the physiological activation. And the assessment of the results of the brain processes is from the viewpoint of content and intentionality—it depends on whether the idea presented by the animal spirits is that 'which the mind desir'd at first to survey'; whether it is 'the same with what we demanded'. This points to the explanatory irreducibility of the mental, of the internal. Quite generally, the primary and right level of description of Humean mental processes, a fortiori imaginative ones, is neither adaptive (as Wright rightly remarks, contra Kemp Smith) nor mechanical (as Waxman rightly remarks, contra Wright), but cognitive: articulated in terms of mental contents, manners of conception, and mental existence, based on Two Viewpoints.[43]

However, within this essentially mentalist and internalist framework, Hume addresses the paradox of cognitive gaps and cognitive change with a conceptual move that bears some (functional) resemblance to externalism. This move is resorting to the natural difference between the faculties of representation (sense and memory) and that of inference (imagination) and, within this latter, between imagination as inclusive of idea-comparing reasoning (larger sense) and as restricted to immediate associations and transitions (more limited sense): the Structural Principle. The principles that determine how more limited imagination interacts with ideas and support demonstrative and probable reasoning are distinct from and irreducible to representational contents as well as to comparisons of ideas. Even though these latter are also a function of the imagination. This introduces a natural difference in the structure and working of the mind and of the imagination. This difference makes it possible for Hume to take an explanatory standpoint that is in some sense external to sense and memory and to demonstrative and probable reasoning. This difference in standpoint is internal to mind and cognition but supports the indirect and empirical explanations that Hume proposes of new and original ideas. It provides Hume with a fulcrum for forcing the limits of sensible representation or of idea-comparing reasoning in a consistently naturalistic way, without falling prey of scepticism or giving support

---

[43] See *Sceptical Realism*, 225, 230–1; Waxman, *Hume's Theory of Consciousness*, 14–15.

to rationalism. The cognitive articulation expressed by Two Viewpoints and the Structural Principle is much more important, in my view, than the physiological underpinnings of imaginative activities.[44]

3.4 Inferentialist Naturalism

3.4.1 Non-Mixture

Aside from the considerations linked to the Structural Principle, the content-productive function of Hume's imagination and the problems it raises can be addressed also from another perspective. The Newtonian language with which it is initially characterized, in terms of the association of ideas, seems to indicate that the identity of ideas, as mental atoms or points, is preserved across the activities, the transpositions, and the changes of the imagination and in the resulting new contents. Just like that of physical atoms or points is preserved in their aggregation. This is, in fact, a commitment important both for Hume's theory of content and for his theory of the passions. Just like the Structural Principle, it is introduced, almost as an afterthought, in Book 2 of the *Treatise*. Differently from the footnote which introduces the Structural Principle, however, Hume did not move it to Book 1. Still, it is implicitly at work throughout Book 1, as we will see. Here is the text.

> Ideas may be compar'd to the extension and solidity of matter, and impressions, especially reflective ones, to colours, tastes, smells and other sensible qualities. Ideas never admit of a total union, but are endow'd with a kind of impenetrability, by which they exclude each other, and are capable of forming a compound by their conjunction, not by their mixture. On the other hand, impressions and

---

[44] In consideration of the complex structure and function of Hume's notion of imagination, the remark in the 'Introduction' to A. Kind & P. Kung, eds., *Knowledge through Imagination*, Oxford University Press, Oxford 2016, 9: the 'instructive', cognition-generating use of Hume's imagination is less significant than what it may appear, because its notion is much broader than the ordinary one, seems unwarranted. Hume's notion of imagination is broader than the ordinary one, or of that of many philosophers, as he himself recognizes in the footnote just discussed. But as the Structural Principle establishes, this broader notion is articulated in operations, principles, and systems that make sense of cognitive functions in many respects distinctive of imagination as we understand it. There is more than an echo of Hume's functional articulation of imagination in the contemporary distinction between voluntary and involuntary, intentional and spontaneous imagination (see P. Langland-Hassan, 'On Choosing what to Imagine', in Kind & Kung, *Knowledge through Imagination* (61–84) 61–2; T. Williamson, 'Knowing by Imagining', in Kind & Kung, *Knowledge through Imagination* (113–23), 115–16). Even more to the point, the consideration of the constrained character of imaginative processes, which is fundamental for the cognitive role and the epistemic assessment of imagination (see A. Kind, 'Imagining under Constraints', in Kind & Kung, *Knowledge through Imagination* (145–59), 146–7, 150–1, finds support in Hume's distinction between natural and philosophical relations. The former are a source of and a constraint on voluntary imagining; and in some cases, such source and constraint have epistemic value.

passions are susceptible of an entire union; and like colours, may be blended so perfectly together, that each of them may lose itself, and contribute only to vary that uniform impression, which arises from the whole.   (2.2.6.1)

The crucial claim is that, differently from 'reflective' impressions, that is, passions, 'ideas never admit of a total union, but are endow'd with a kind of impenetrability, by which they exclude each other, and are capable of forming a compound only by their conjunction, not by their mixture'. The identity of ideas, therefore, is preserved across the activities of the imagination; an idea does not 'lose itself' by being transposed and changed by the imagination (2.2.6.1). The persistent identity of ideas, of course, is the one ideas have before and independently from the interaction with imagination: before their transpositions and changes, their association, their involvement in imaginative transitions. Their identity therefore can only consist in their individuation in terms of the impressions of sensation which cause them and to which they resemble. Their individuation stems from the qualities with which they come to exist in the mind and by which they primitively represent objects.

This claim is important for the study of Hume's theory of passions. In fact, I think that the contrast between perceptions 'which exclude each other' and perceptions which 'may be blended so perfectly together, that each of them may lose itself' is the core of Hume's distinction between cognitive and non-cognitive states. Because of its importance for the understanding of cognitive content and activity, the claim that object-representing ideas preserve their identity across their composition ('forming a compound') deserves the status of a principle of Hume's philosophy: *Non-Mixture* ('forming a compound by their conjunction, not by their mixture'). Right now, however, this principle seems to raise a problem for Hume's theory of the imagination. It is difficult to see how the transitions of the imagination can preserve the identity of the ideas they involve, which consists in their original individuating qualities and object-representing import, while changing them so that they make available new and original mental contents, of a different kind from those by which they represent impressions and objects. The difficulty is not too different from the one we have discussed in connection with the Structural Principle. In either case, the problem is how the imagination can overstep what is given by our sensible contact with objects and comes to expression in the content of ideas, without postulating a different, non-sensible order of objects and representations.

To reconcile Non-Mixture with the dramatic cognitive changes that the transitions of the imagination are expected to explain we must take a closer look at the nature of these transitions. My general interpretive hypothesis is that Hume's imagination produces new contents and cognitive changes primarily as a *faculty of inference*. More precisely, it is a faculty with the function of producing transitions from the conception of certain ideas to the conception of certain others.

In such transitions, engaged with by the imagination, our minds move from certain perfect ideas (with cognitively detached object-representing contents) to perfect ideas with new and original contents. These transitions of the imagination consist in inferences because they are responsive to the contents of ideas, and can be understood and explained with reference to them, even though only non-reductively. The inferential character of the imaginative transitions producing contents and cognitive change is required by Hume's overall theoretical aim, which is that of giving a fundamental naturalistic explanation of our cognitive practices, with a potential for their 'foundation' or 'reformation'. This explanatory and partially vindicatory character requires that such transitions have cognitive import and be susceptible to some sort of assessment, in relation to the contents of ideas and to their own principles. That is, that in a broad sense, they count as inferences. Non-Mixture, the persistence of object-representing contents of ideas across the content-producing transitions of the imagination, is just the other side of their broadly inferential character. Without some continuity of content with the ideas that are their original, representational input, such transitions could not count as conclusions, or inferences. Notice also that the construction of our worldview, the unification of the first with the second system of realities, requires continuity with primitively object-representing ideas. At the same time, it is distinctive and constitutive of the inferences producing contents and cognitive changes that (differently from idea-comparing inferences) they are *not* reducible to the contents of the ideas they proceed from and that they do not presuppose the contents of the ideas they conclude to. There is an indispensable, causal, and cognitive role of the original principles of the imagination with which the ideas interact.

This begins to clarify the nature of imagination-produced cognitive change in Hume's philosophy. If Hume understood cognitive change on the model of rationalist philosophers, as the change of sensible ideas into intellectual ones, ideas, as individuated by their occurrence in relation to impressions of sensation, would lose themselves across such mental activity. Non-Mixture, together with the First Principle, sets the bar very high for rationalist philosophers. Positively, once Non-Mixture and the inferential character of content-producing transitions are recognized, we can see that the change in the content of ideas they bring about is not a change in their kinds of objects; it does not consist in a change of sensible with intellectual objects. It is a change in the cognitive role of ideas, caused by their inclusion in the inferential transitions of the imagination, which transpose them and change both their relations of content to other perceptions and their conditions of existence in the mind. This change makes it so that ideas bear new properties of content; but since these properties depend on the inclusion in such transitions of the imagination, they are consistent with their preserving their individuating, object-representing contents. Therefore, from the viewpoint of Non-Mixture, only an inferential account of cognitive change by the imagination can explain our worldview. Reciprocally, if cognitive change were explained along Humean lines, by transitions of the imagination, but ideas lost their object-representing identities in their mixture, the new and original contents produced by such transitions would lose any contact with particular existents. Inference and reference would fall apart and there would be no hope to explain our interconnected cognitive world of sense, memory, and judgement.

Non-Mixture therefore invites the consideration of Hume's theory of the imagination as a species of inferentialism, in the context of a deeply dualistic view of mental content and activity. Since the principles and operations of imagination are explained naturalistically, Hume's inferentialism is naturalistic. This position, *Inferentialist Naturalism*, complements Hume's Representational Naturalism, underlies his responses to the cognitive gaps this latter involves, and, supported by the Structural Principle and Non-Mixture, makes ultimate sense of the content-productive function of the imagination in Hume's philosophy.

3.4.2 Inference and the Structural Principle

One may find surprising or totally implausible that there is an important inferentialist layer in Hume's theory of the imagination and, thereby, in Hume's philosophy in general.[45] While a full articulation and defence of my interpretation must wait for the detailed exegesis and analysis of Hume's arguments in Book 1, I want to give now a sketch of it, as an aspect of the elements of Hume's philosophy. Of course, Hume's inferentialist commitments must be taken with some latitude; but they still fit well with a recognizable conceptual framework of inferentialism.[46]

I take my start from the notion of material inference; more precisely, from two senses in which one can talk of material inference. This notion is usually understood simply in contrast with formal inference—reasoning exemplifying a valid inferential scheme—as inference based on the grasp of conceptual contents, of the contents of the concepts that form the subject matter of reasoning. To stick to a trite example, an inference like 'If Delhi is east of Jaipur, then Jaipur is west of Delhi' depends, for its possibility and for its goodness, on our understanding of

---

[45] A prominent inferentialist like Brandom contrasts early modern rationalist inferentialism, as exemplified by Spinoza or Leibniz, precisely with the representationalism of the British empiricists; see R. Brandom, *Making it Explicit*, Harvard University Press, Cambridge (Mass.), 1994, xvi, 93–4; R. Brandom, *Articulating Reasons*, Harvard University Press, Cambridge (Mass.), 2000, 45–7.

[46] In my inferentialist reading of Hume's theory of the imagination I am relying, as a theoretical backdrop and as an interpretive tool, on the important work of contemporary inferentialist philosophers, like Brandom (see the works cited in fn. 45) and Huw Price, *Naturalism without Mirrors*, Oxford University Press, New York 2011. Of course, I am not saddling them with anything that my inferentialist reading of Hume implies. But in the case of Price, I would say that my interpretation is deeply consonant with his overall take on inferentialism and with what he says about Hume.

the subject matter and in particular of the concepts: East, West.[47] This content-based conception of reasoning—of explicit or implicit, reflective or immediate reasoning—certainly fits Hume's view of demonstrative and of mature probable reasoning (for this notion, see § 6.1.1): comparisons of ideas discovering, immediately or mediately, their content-grounded constant or inconstant relations. This also determines whether any instance of inference or transition is good or bad. This was the conception of reasoning that prevailed among Hume's predecessors, Descartes and in particular Locke.[48]

To move from here to a distinctive position of inferentialism, however, two crucial and interrelated claims must hold of material inferences. The first is a claim of asymmetry in the relations between formally valid and materially good inferences. Material inferences are not incomplete formal inferences and do not depend on formal inferences for their being possibly good or bad (and therefore to count as inferences at all). Quite the contrary, formal inferences should be derivable from material ones.[49] The second claim is that, as a condition for and as an aspect of the priority of material over formal inferences, the former should be regarded as activities, that is, from the viewpoint of the conditions for and the way of engaging in them, rather than from the viewpoint of their semantic conditions, reference and truth.[50] A generic position of inferentialism therefore springs from combining a commitment to material inference with the claim of its non-derivative cognitive character and of its primitively consisting in a cognitive activity. What is crucial, in this respect, is the shape that these claims give to how contents are involved in material inference. Such involvement goes in two directions. Material inferences not only *depend* on contents but also *individuate* contents. The contents involved in material inferences, on this view, cannot be individuated in advance of and independently from engagement in such inferences. That is, the contents of the concepts East and West not only determine the goodness of an inference 'If Delhi is east of Jaipur, then Jaipur is west of Delhi' but they are also individuated by the possibility and the goodness of the activity of performing such inference or cognitive transition. Suppose that we engage in mental transitions like 'If A is east of B, then B is west of A'; that this activity does not presuppose an explicit semantic identification of its elements; and that it still can be assessed in terms of good or bad performance, in relation to its instances, contexts, and point and aim, either pragmatic or cognitive. Then we can say that it not only applies but individuates the contents of the concepts: East, West. This of

---

[47] Brandom, *Making it Explicit*, 97–8.
[48] This is masterfully discussed in Owen, *Hume's Reason*, chapters 2 and 3.
[49] This point is forcefully made in Brandom, *Making it Explicit*, 104–5.
[50] 'Inferential relations among concepts are implicit in the practice of giving and asking for reasons', Brandom, *Making it Explicit*, 91. This thought is given enormous and fascinating development throughout Brandom's philosophical work. It goes without saying that Brandom's normative and rationalist inferentialism only gives suggestions for the interpretation of Hume's philosophy.

course raises a host of analytic and explanatory issues, concerning the conditions of possibility and goodness of inferential activity and therefore the nature or character of such activity. The divide among different sorts of inferentialism reflects different responses to these questions. In particular to those concerning the relations between the ex-ante and ex-post individuation of inferences: enough to get inferences going and be assessable but not to individuate their contents in advance to their roles in inference.[51]

On this minimal sketch of an inferentialist account of content, I think that Hume's theory of the imagination counts as a species of inferentialism. Hume has no formal conception of inference (he does not regard it as important, just as neither Descartes nor Locke did). Starting from his material conception of inference and his recognition of the imagination as the natural faculty of inference, Two Viewpoints, non-Mixture, and the Structural Principle make room, at the core Hume's philosophy, for an inferentialist explanation of content. The identification of cognitive gaps indicates that, in many cases crucially important for our worldview, the ideas presupposed by our idea-comparing reasoning cannot be object-representing and object-individuated. Pro tanto, they are necessarily missing. This kind of reasoning would therefore not be possible if we were restricted to ideas referring to sensible objects. But the required ideas, with the attending inferential potentials, can be made available by the inferences of more limited imagination. These do not consist on idea-comparisons and are not explained only by the contents of ideas antecedently given in impression or as objects. They depend on and are explained by the concurrence of such ideas with the non-referential principles of the imagination (biases, whimsies, or prejudices). This is an asymmetry of the sort required by the inferentialist order of explanation. The inferences of the more limited imagination do not mirror the contents of object-representing ideas and their relations, but rather express our immediate, non-reflective engagement in certain transitions of ideas, based on their contents and on certain original propensities of the mind. Within and on the ground of this natural, primitive activity, in ways that we will examine as we go along but that fundamentally abide by Two Viewpoints, ideas can take up contents of new kinds and new conceptual roles and the deep cognitive changes motivated by the limits of object representation become possible.[52] Ideas, individuated by the contents

---

[51] See D. Macbeth, 'Inference, Meaning, and Truth in Brandom, Sellars, and Frege', in B. Weiss & J. Wanderer, *Reading Brandom. On Making It Explicit*, Routledge, London 2010 (197–212). This way of understanding material inferences is primarily associated to Brandom who, differently from Sellars, recognizes as constitutive of the concepts they involve inferences based not only on necessary but also on accidental relations between concepts (and also on relations with non-inferential conditions, perceptions, and actions).

[52] In more recent work, marked by a more nuanced stance to naturalism, Brandom seems to give more emphasis to the primitively active character of material inference. See R. Brandom, *Between Saying & Doing*, Oxford University Press, Oxford 2008, 118–19: the underlying inferential practice consist of 'practical discriminative abilities', of some 'practical differential responsive ability'. To think

which they primitively have, can interact as mental existents with more limited imagination; the effects of such interaction modify the conditions and properties of their mental existence and, based on Two Viewpoints, their properties of content; the cognitive changes evidenced by our worldview can be explained in this.[53]

This is the core of Hume's inferentialist account of content: as I am suggesting, it is a recognizable inferentialist position and we will see examples of it as we go on. Of course, Hume has a highly peculiar take on these issues, because of his early position in the inferentialist tradition. His position is one of weak inferentialism: the inferentialist order of explanation is necessary, but not necessary and sufficient, to account for our contents. Hume's inferentialism is circumscribed by the fundamental dualism of representation by sense and memory and of inference by the imagination.[54] Of course, again, ascribing to Hume a form of inferentialism besides causing interpretive qualms, raises complicated conceptual questions, one of which is how to reconcile the normative dimension of the inferentialist framework (its presupposing that inferential activity is primitively discriminable as good or bad) with Hume's naturalism. Hume's inferentialism would be an empty effort unless there were ways of distinguishing materially good or bad transitions of the more limited imagination, without relying on the contents of the ideas that such transitions are meant to put in place. The assignment of non-object-representing contents to ideas depends on the possibility of such distinction, on pain of indeterminateness; but the natural character of the work of the imagination, no matter how performed, makes it difficult to see how the distinction itself is available. I will discuss this important topic thematically in Chapter 12. Notice, finally, that Inferentialist Naturalism, as we have seen, can reconcile Hume's claim that ideas preserve their identity across their interactions

---

in terms of abilities to respond differentially to some input is to shift some explanatory weight from the structure to the primitiveness of inferential practice. This fits with what H. Price, 'Expressivism for Two Voices', in J. Knowles & H. Rydenfelt, *Pragmatism, Science, and Naturalism*, Lang, Frankfurt am Main 2011 (87–113), has acutely remarked: Brandom has resort to two notions of doing, as the implicit inferential practice that come to expression in our explicit sayings. One is a plurality of activities, expressing our preferences and credences, which are only minimally normative; the other is the engagement in a unitary practice of asking and giving reasons.

[53] Contemporary discussions of imagination recognize its inferential structure and carefully tell apart the involuntary from the voluntary development of a transition (see Langland-Hassan, 'Choosing what to Imagine', 63–4; Williamson, 'Knowing by Imagining', 116). Hume's natural relations are conditions for and a form of spontaneous mental inference.

[54] Brandom, *Making it Explicit*, 131, distinguishes a strong from a weak form of inferentialist explanation. In the strong form, inferential practice is both necessary and sufficient for explaining conceptual content. My reading of Hume his is in partial agreement with the important discussion of naturalism and representationalism in Price, *Naturalism without Mirrors*, 9–15, 33. I do not think that inferentialist naturalism requires dropping, rather than restricting, representationalism. (Price presents his attitude to Hume as one of 'abandoning the representationalist residue in Humean expressivism', 20; but, as he goes on to point out, the deeper contrast is between representationalism and inferentialism, 20–3.) Representational Naturalism might be a tenable, if limited, view; and it certainly fits with the aims and structure of Hume's philosophy. Price also rightly remarks, *Naturalism without Mirrors*, 317–18 that a theory like Brandom's, if consistently developed in an 'anthropological' rather than a 'metaphysical' direction, comes close to a position of Humean (subject) naturalism.

with imagination and that such interactions can deeply change the contents they deliver. One might even suggest that the fundamental role of object-representing ideas in our thought and cognition both explains Hume's commitment to regard such ideas as preserving their identity across cognitive changes and motivates an inferential, rather than representational understanding of the mental activities underlying such changes.

It is interesting to compare the inferentialist reading of Hume's imagination I have sketched with the articulated, careful interpretation of Hume's views about content and representations proposed by D. Garrett: 'things represent other things by playing a significant part of their causal and/or functional roles, through reliable indication and/or modeling, by the generation of mental effects and dispositions'.[55] This is in sharp contrast with the dualism of representation and inference that I have outlined. That something like causal and functional role is involved in Hume's theory of content is very likely. It is a consequence of Two Viewpoints that there is a close fit between the causal and functional properties of perceptions and their properties of contents; and the activities of imagination produce contents equivalent in causal and functional roles with elements of ordinary and philosophical cognition, missing from sensible representation.[56] I think, however, that this cannot be the whole truth about Hume's conception of content. Impressions of sensation are contentful perceptions; but they cannot be understood in terms of indication or modelling, because they are utterly primitive in their representational (better, presentational) role. Ultimately, impressions present objects by *being* objects and falling under the scope of Two Viewpoints, not by taking up any roles.[57] The representational relations between impressions and ideas, in their turn, are grounded on causation and resemblance (the First Principle). Of course, successful object-representing ideas are likely to have causal and functional properties similar to those (if any) of the represented impressions or objects. But this seems to be a consequence rather than the constitutive condition of the representational relation.[58] The notion of a causal-functional network

---

[55] D. Garrett, 'Hume's Naturalistic Theory', 307–13, see in particular 313.

[56] This also emerges from Garrett's discussion of general ideas, 'Hume's Naturalistic Theory', 314.

[57] See Schafer, 'Hume's Unified Theory', 14–15.

[58] Garrett is ready to recognize that that of ideas is a special case of representation, 'Hume's Naturalistic Theory', 312, 318. In my view, the case is so special that it forms a kind of content of its own. In more recent work, Garrett is more explicit about the inferentialist dimension of Hume's conception of content, see D. Garrett, *Hume*, Routledge, London/New York 2015, 57. More generally, in the same work, Garrett has introduced the interpretively and philosophically important notion of sense-based concepts, which reshapes the notion of response-dependence in Hume-inspired ways (see Garrett, *Hume*, 117–45). Sense-based concepts like beauty, virtue, causation, and probability give conceptual articulation and thus potential application in reasoning to our natural senses or sentiments of moral or aesthetic goodness, connectedness of events, and cognitive weight. Garrett accounts for sense-based concepts in terms of a four-stage process of repeated activation (repeated episodes of sense or imagination), initial generalization (a repetition-grounded abstract idea), natural correction (of the idea, with reference to features of the repeated experience), and relational attribution (which specifies the inferential roles the ideas). I cannot engage here in a discussion of Garrett's views but will

of perceptions is an admissible reading of the working of Hume's imagination and can explain its crucial additions to our ideas and cognition. One could consider replacing the inferentialist interpretation of Hume's imagination with a causal-functional one, precisely as an alternative rendering of its non-representational character and in consideration of their broad theoretical equivalence.[59] I think one should still prefer an inferentialist to a causal-functional reading primarily because of textual considerations. Hume's says very little about the causation of imaginative processes; but he is ready to describe the inferential transitions that explain cognitive change.[60]

3.4.3 Transitions and Conceptions: The Important Footnote

There is at least another problematic aspect of Inferentialist Naturalism that deserves mention and some discussion. The inferences of more limited imagination are introduced by Hume to explain how ideas with 'new and original' cognitive content are produced: ideas with roles in ordinary and philosophical cognition.[61] The explanation of such ideas must also satisfy the condition that they be *conceivable*: that the new contents made available by the imagination be present to the mind with some sort of qualitative specification. Such contents and ideas must be seamlessly combined with object-representing ideas: it is in this sense that Hume talks of two connected systems of realities, one owing to sense and memory and the other, which is continuous with the first, owing to imagination and judgement (1.3.9.3). Or of the universe we paint in the imagination (1.3.9.4). Conception of ideas is in general qualitative.

But here is the rub. Hume's imagination is, taken most generally, a function from conception to conception of ideas. But inferential activities and their underlying propensities do not seem to include or to produce the qualitative specifications involved in conception. Qualitative conception of ideas and transitions

---

remark that it could be read as a plausible account of the content-constitutive operations of Hume's imagination, at least insofar as they define networks of conceptual contents, and that it is in many respects convergent with the one I am developing here. (One main difference lies precisely in the weight we ascribe to inferentialist considerations. Of course, sense-based non-conceptual contents (particular ideas) and non-sense-based concepts (like external existence or personal identity) will require different explanations.)

[59] See Price, 'Expressivism for Two Voices', 15–16.

[60] See, for an excellent discussion of this fundamental dualism and of the necessary cooperation of the two kinds of content of the overall hybrid character of Hume's views, Schafer, 'Hume's Unified Theory', 15–25. My only complaint with Schafer's interpretation is that it does not pay its due to the faculty of imagination and to its inferential nature. See also Price, 'Expressivism for Two Voices', 15–16, for an interesting distinction between external and internal representations, which might be adapted to provide an interpretation of Hume's dualism of content.

[61] See, for this conception of imagination, J. Church, 'Perceiving People as People', in Kind & Kung, *Knowledge by Imagination* (160–84) 171–2.

along ideas seem to be completely different mental operations. It is then not clear how by inference we come to new conceptions. The threat of an explanatory gap thus looms at the core of Hume's imagination. Hume, while recognizing the problem, does not seem too concerned. Consider the following text where Hume discusses the interconnections between different kinds of mental acts: conception, judgement, inference. This text—which David Owen aptly dubbed the Important Footnote—deserves full quotation[62] (I have inserted Arab numerals for ease of reference).

> We may here take occasion to observe a very remarkable error, which being frequently inculcated in the schools, has become a kind of establish'd maxim, and is universally received by all logicians. [1] This error consists in the vulgar division of the acts of the understanding, into *conception, judgment* and *reasoning,* and in the definitions we give of them. Conception is defin'd to be the simple survey of one or more ideas: Judgment to be the separating or uniting of different ideas: Reasoning to be the separating or uniting of different ideas by the interposition of others, which show the relation they bear to each other. But these distinctions and definitions are faulty in very considerable articles. [2] For *first,* 'tis far from being true, that in every judgment, which we form, we unite two different ideas; since in that proposition, *God is,* or indeed any other, which regards existence, the idea of existence is no distinct idea, which we unite with that of the object, and which is capable of forming a compound idea by the union. *Secondly,* As we can thus form a proposition, which contains only one idea, so we may exert our reason without employing more than two ideas, and without having recourse to a third to serve as a medium betwixt them. We infer a cause immediately from its effect; and this inference is not only a true species of reasoning, but the strongest of all others, and more convincing than when we interpose another idea to connect the two extremes. [3] What we may in general affirm concerning these three acts of the understanding is, that taking them in a proper light, they all resolve themselves into the first, and are nothing but particular ways of conceiving our objects. Whether we consider a single object, or several; whether we dwell on these objects, or run from them to others; and in whatever form or order we survey them, the act of the mind exceeds not a simple conception; [4] and the only remarkable difference, which occurs on this occasion, is, when we join belief to the conception, and are perswaded of the truth of what we conceive. This act of the mind has never yet been explain'd by any philosopher; and therefore I am at liberty to propose my hypothesis concerning it; which is, that 'tis only a strong and steady conception of any idea, and such as approaches in some measure to an immediate impression. (1.3.7.5, fn. 20)

---

[62] See Owen, *Hume's Reason,* 74–5 and fn.18.

In this complex text, Hume is making different but strictly interrelated points. For our present concerns, the main point is that there is no difference in how ideas, judgements, and inferences (ideas we conceive, judgements we make, inferences we draw) are present to awareness. This is claimed at [3]. But to proceed with order I want to distinguish this from other claims Hume makes in this text.

(i) The principal conclusion Hume wants to establish is at [4]. It is a general point about the difference between mental states with or without cognitive commitment. (The Important Footnote is appended to Hume's official definition of belief.) Hume claims that this difference does not consist in the number or arrangement of the ideas forming the content of mental states; in particular, in separating and uniting a plurality of ideas, which was the traditional understanding of affirmation and denial.[63] Rather, the difference is that 'we join belief' to the 'conception' of ideas: that we are 'perswaded of the truth of what we conceive'. This 'act of the mind', Hume adds, 'has never yet been explain'd by any philosopher'. He then recalls his deeply original 'hypothesis' that it consists in 'a strong and steady conception of an idea' which 'approaches in some measure to an immediate impression' (I discuss this in Chapter 11).

(ii) On the way to this conclusion Hume makes an important remark about the nature of the different 'acts of the understanding', introducing and criticizing, at [1], the 'vulgar division' of such acts into '*conception, judgment*, and *reasoning*'. He says that this doctrine is 'faulty in very considerable articles'; in particular because it draws an otherwise needful distinction in a mistaken way. Conception is regarded as the 'simple survey' of one or more ideas; judgement as the 'separating or uniting' of different ideas; reasoning as the separating or uniting different ideas 'by the interposition of others'. Hume's criticism of this view, at [2], consists in counterexamples to the assumption that the number of ideas individuates judgement and reasoning. We can make a judgement 'which regards existence' without combining two ideas: 'the idea of existence is no distinct idea, which we unite with that of the object'. And we can 'exert our reason without employing more than two ideas', without a third, mediating one, as when 'we infer a cause immediately from its effect': which inference is 'not only a true species of reasoning, but the strongest of all others'. Not differently from the cognitive import, the logical character of acts of understanding cannot be read off number of ideas.

(iii) Still, there *are* differences between such acts. It is not the same 'whether we consider a single object, or several; whether we dwell on these objects,

---

[63] Owen, *Hume's Reason*, 74, fn. 18.

or run from them to others'; there are cognitive and functional differences associated to the different 'form and order' in which we 'survey' ideas. Such differences might be regarded as consisting in some different 'act of the mind' with which contents are made present. Against this, Hume remarks, at [3], that when the mind is engaged in acts of conception, judgement, and reasoning it entertains contents always in the same manner, no matter whether it dwells on one idea or runs from one idea to another. 'The act of the mind exceeds not a simple conception'; the different acts of the understanding, in this respect, are 'nothing but particular ways of conceiving our objects' and they all fall within the genus of simple conception. Judgement and inference are present to awareness in the same way as individual ideas.

One implication of this is that individual perceptions, impressions, or ideas can have complex and structured contents just like judgements and inferences, without any change in the act of conception by the mind. Another implication is relevant. What Hume criticizes the traditional doctrine for is not the distinction of different 'acts of the understanding' but the attempt to capture such difference either by the number of ideas or by some property of their mental presence. Hume's position, by contrast, is that there are differences in structure of content, in static or dynamic character, and in cognitive role between different acts of the understanding; but that having ideas, making judgements, and drawing inferences are all varieties of 'simple conception'. Awareness with qualitative, phenomenal features is the only 'act of the mind'. Thus, whatever content is instantiated by mental transitions (be it judgemental or inferential), it is present to awareness as conception, in the same way as the passive admission of impressions with their rich phenomenology and as the retention of their contents in qualitatively specified ideas.[64] In this way, Important Footnote opens the path to a unified view of the presence to awareness of different mental episodes, within the genus of conception; and makes room for associating a qualitative specification of contents to the transitions of the more limited imagination. Hume's sparse indications of how imaginative inferences and propensities come to awareness as qualitative conceptions of ideas will be discussed when we come to the phenomenon of spreading (§ 7.2.3).

---

[64] This is a basic trait of imagination in general that has recently come to be recognized (after a long oblivion). Imagery has been put back into the imagination rightly as a distinctive, specific feature that distinguishes it from other mental processes and makes it recognizable from the inside, by their subjects. See A. Kind, 'Putting the Image back in the Imagination', *Philosophy and Phenomenological Research*, 62, 2001, 85–109, 93–5. Of course, imagery was important for Hume's predecessors, in particular Descartes; but in a different way than for Hume.

3.5 Summary

The Second Principle completes Hume's doctrine of elements. It outlines the function of the imagination: producing ideas that complement object-representing ones, closing the cognitive gaps in sense and memory, and enabling our ordinary and philosophical cognition.

§ 3.1 establishes that cognitive gaps can be necessary features of our natural representation of objects. § 3.1.1 introduces the concept of cognitive gap with the much discussed case of the Missing Shade of Blue. I read the case as limiting, rather than debunking the First Principle. The case is telling but the cognitive gap is only accidental. In §§ 3.1.2–3 I argue that, by nature, object representation is receptive, sensible, particular, object-dependent, and locked on actuality. It is non-inferential and non-conceptual. This is Hume's Representational Naturalism and it marks deep gaps with regard to our ordinary and philosophical cognition, which is abstract, general, aspectual, modal, and inferential; includes ideas of causal connections and material and mental continuants; and consists in mental states like mere conception, reasoning, and belief. As pointed out in § 3.1.4, this sets the almost paradoxical task of overcoming in a naturalistic way what are naturally necessary limits of thought and cognition. Hume rises to this challenge, avoiding both scepticism and rationalism, by complementing our naturally limited object-representing ideas with cognitive but non-representational ones, issuing from the imagination.

Against this background, § 3.2 discusses the Second Principle. § 3.2.1 introduces the liberty of the imagination of changing and transposing ideas. This marks a layer of activity and cognitive change in the natural mind, in contrast with sense and memory. The first stage in this activity is conceiving faint, loose, perfect ideas, disengaged from the feeling of force and invariance of impressions (§ 3.2.2). Hume then summarizes the compositional and transformative activity of the imagination with his theory of association, discussed in § 3.2.3. But this only hints at the richness and complexity of its production of new contents. At the initial stage, the theory focuses on the results of association, complex ideas, rather than on the associating transitions of the imagination, which, however, matter the most.

§§ 3.3 and 3.4 outline the nature of Hume's imagination: its structure and mode of working. § 3.3.1 introduces the important Structural Principle. The faculty of the imagination (imagination in the larger sense, opposed to memory) involves two parts or functions. One enacts comparisons of ideas and reasonings. The other (imagination in the more limited sense, opposed to reason), mental transitions supported by various sorts of cognitive biases. This principle is important because, as a fact of our cognitive nature, the two parts operate jointly and condition each other. If the corresponding impressions are missing, ideas are available to the idea-comparing imagination by being produced by the non-idea-comparing, more limited imagination, which in this way influences all our cognitive activity. In §§ 3.3.2–3 I show that this structure of the imagination is mirrored in the distinction between natural and philosophical relations of ideas and that together they explain how the imagination can tap cognitive resources not available to sense and memory, without any externalist or materialist assumption.

Finally, § 3.4 provides a fundamental functional characterization of Hume's imagination: Inferentialist Naturalism. In § 3.4.1 I introduce Non-Mixture. Ideas, differently from impressions, preserve their identities across their transpositions and changes. Such identity relates to their contents and is a constraint on content-producing transitions of the imagination, contributing to their inferential character, cognitive import, and potential foundational role. Hume is committed to a dualism of content, with inferential components integrating object-representing ones. Hume's inferentialism is naturalist (§ 3.4.2) because it merges with the Structural Principle. The transitions of the more limited imagination support and embed the idea-comparing ones and respond to non-representational principles or biases. These are the conditions of the production of ideas by the imagination. As I suggest in § 3.4.3, Hume at least indicates a way of understanding how the inferential transitions of the imagination can result in the conception of ideas.

PART II

THE INTELLECTUAL WORLD OF IDEAS

I turn now to the detailed exegesis and analysis of the works of Hume's imagination. The task in Part II is to specify how the imagination makes available conceptual modes of thinking. By this I mean cognitive phenomena like generality, aspectual distinctions, intentional directedness, modality, and the a priori. These are the first kinds of cognitive gaps that articulate Hume's philosophy. These conceptual capacities, which are missing from the primitive, object-representing layer of our cognitive nature, are pervasive in our ordinary and philosophical cognition. Accounting for them is crucial for Hume's philosophical campaign against Rationalism. The sensible, nonconceptual character of object representation *seems* to give a compelling ground for the anti-naturalistic, rationalistic step of relegating the senses to the status of confused perceptions and contrasting them to a faculty of understanding. This latter delivers 'ideas...of so refin'd and spiritual a nature' as 'must be comprehended by a pure and intellectual view, of which the superior faculties of the soul are alone capable' (1.3.1.7). Such intellectual view, according to the rationalists (actually, as Hume here says, to 'most parts of philosophy') gives access to the real world, only obscurely and confusedly expressed by the senses. Hume's Representational Naturalism thus seems to play into the hands of the rationalists. Hume must therefore give an alternative explanation of conceptual thought, which is that ideas with conceptual contents (like those of mathematics) 'fall under the conception of the fancy'. The imagination has the capacity to form general and modal ideas, with non-object-representing properties of content but cognitively in order. Since such ideas and the corresponding cognitive capacities do not require any sort of non-sensible, intellectual representation, but rather non-object-representing activities of the imagination, a compelling ground for Rationalism turns out to be merely apparent, a product itself of false philosophy. In a proper sense, there is *no intellectual world of ideas*; even though, by the imagination, it is *as if* we had such a world in view.

4
As if It Were Universal

> The image in the mind is only that of a particular object, tho' the application of it in our reasoning be the same, as if it were universal.
>
> (1.1.7.6)

The 'notion' of a 'refin'd and spiritual nature' and of a 'pure and intellectual view' is 'principally made use of to explain our abstract ideas, and to shew how we can form an idea of a triangle, for instance, which shall neither be an isosceles nor scalenum, nor be confin'd to any particular length and proportion of sides' (1.3.1.7). Correspondingly, generality is the first dimension of conceptual character that Hume explains with inferences of the imagination, conceived according to the Structural Principle. Strictly connected with generality are two other marks of the conceptual: the distinction of aspects in represented objects and the directedness of mental activity. These Hume also explains by resorting to the more limited imagination. Explaining generality was, of course, a main concern in the empiricist tradition and Hume is here following the steps of Locke and Berkeley. But his detailed account of the mental mechanism of abstraction is highly original, in particular because of the role of the imagination and of the thoroughly inferential ground and character of general content.

4.1 Concerning Abstract or General Ideas

4.1.1 A Cognitive Gap: Representational Naturalism and Generality

Our possession of general ideas sets complex explanatory tasks to Hume's philosophy. Hume marks the cognitive gap corresponding to generality by saying that general ideas are applied 'beyond their nature' (1.1.7.7) but 'without any danger of mistake' (1.1.7.9) and without 'talking nonsense' (1.1.7.14). This contrast requires explanation. Hume's discussion of the 'very material question' of general ideas falls neatly into two parts (1.1.7.1). In the first he addresses the nature of generality and identifies the corresponding gap. Like Locke and Berkeley, he denies that general objects are given to us and represented by ideas. Generality is produced by mental activity: abstraction. Following Berkeley, perhaps also Locke, he denies that abstraction modifies the nature of ideas, making them general entities.

Abstraction produces generality not by shifting ideas from the ontological category of particulars to that of universals but only by changing their properties of content. In the second part, Hume gives his positive account of how abstraction produces general ideas. While in many respects similar to Berkeley's and, arguably, to Locke's, Hume's positive account is importantly different from theirs. The difference, which has gone somewhat unnoticed, has to do not only with the psychological detail of Hume's account but also with his firm grasp of the inferential nature of abstraction. If generality were represented, by the First Principle and Equivalence, general contents would presuppose general objects. Generality would thus be an impossibility. But the inferential nature of the imagination allows the mind to have general contents which are non-object-representing.

The first part of Hume's discussion, as I just said, follows in Berkeley's and perhaps Locke's footsteps. 'A very material question has been started concerning *abstract* or *general* ideas, *whether they be general or particular in the mind's conception of them*.' Hume endorses Berkeley's answer, in its general tenor and main lines.

> A great philosopher has disputed the receiv'd opinion in this particular, and has asserted, that all general ideas are nothing but particular ones, annexed to a certain term, which gives them a more extensive signification, and makes them recal upon occasion other individuals, which are similar to them. (1.1.7.1)

He then proceeds to give arguments to confirm this position—'one of the greatest and most valuable discoveries that has been made of late years in the republic of letters'.[1] Hume's arguments are obviously indebted to Berkeley and Locke, but they are framed and articulated in terms of Representational Naturalism. He assumes that generality depends on abstraction: "Tis evident, that in forming most of our general ideas, if not all of them, we abstract from every particular degree of quantity and quality' (1.1.7.2). His argument for this is that, for any idea abiding by Representation, an object must exist that it represents; that, by the First Principle, only impressions of sensation are objects we can represent; and that all sensible objects are particular. This latter is a directly a priori principle of Hume's metaphysics, concerning things of nature in general.

> 'Tis a principle generally receiv'd in philosophy, that every thing in nature is individual, and that 'tis utterly absurd to suppose a triangle really existent, which has no precise proportion of sides and angles. (1.1.7.6)

---

[1] Given its importance for the explanation of conceptual content, it is striking that in the first *Enquiry* the explanation of generality by abstraction is confined to a footnote to the discussion of infinite divisibility, itself a lemma in the discussion of *Academical or Sceptical Philosophy*, *Enquiry*, 12.20 fn. 24 (205). See, on the explanatory task Berkeley sets to his own theory of general ideas, K. Winkler, *Berkeley. An Interpretation*, Clarendon Press, Oxford 1989, 26–7.

The principle is established by abstract modal reasoning. Determinables are not conceivable separately from their determinates: selective attention and inferential roles are all there is to their distinction; this does not establish possible separate existence (see § 5.2.2). Therefore, determinables and determinates are not really different and objects can exist only with completely determined properties, as individual particulars (1.1.7.3). The same holds a priori of perceptions and a fortiori of impressions as they exist in the mind, that is, as mental things or events. 'That [an impression having no particular degree nor proportion] is a contradiction in terms; and even implies the flattest of all contradictions, *viz.* that 'tis possible for the same thing both to be and not to be' (1.1.7.4). By Two Viewpoints, this has implications for representational content. It is a posteriori, a fact of human nature, that objects are present to us only as impressions of sensation. The difference between the properties with which perceptions exist in the mind and the properties of content they bear is only of viewpoint. And considered in their properties of content, impressions are equivalent to objects of sense. Therefore, it is relatively a priori that all the object-representing ideas we can have are particular.

> 'Tis confest, that no object can appear to the senses; or in other words, that no impression can become present to the mind, without being determin'd in its degrees both of quantity and quality. The confusion, in which impressions are sometimes involv'd, proceeds only from their faintness and unsteadiness, not from any capacity in the mind to receive any impression, which in its real existence has no particular degree nor proportion. (1.1.1.4)

If our access to objects were intellectual, we could represent something general. As things stand with our natural minds, however, supposing to have intellectual acquaintance with objects means losing any cognitive contact with existence. Therefore, there is no alternative to explaining general content by abstraction.

Hume then proceeds to show that, if abstraction functioned representationally ('The abstract idea of a man represents men of all sizes and all qualities'), it would involve an impossibility. This is argued for in terms of a 'plain dilemma'. Abstract ideas could *represent* generality in the *absence* of general objects in one of two ways: 'either by representing at once all possible sizes and all possible qualities, or by representing no particular one at all'. An idea aimed at representing all possible sizes and all possible qualities seems to be an absurdity, since it would imply 'an infinite capacity in the mind'. This is because this would mean either to represent an actual infinity of objects or to have the idea of a set of merely possible ones; both of which are out of the reach of our object representation. This takes us to the second horn of the dilemma, which has been commonly embraced: 'our abstract ideas have been suppos'd to represent no particular degree either of quantity or quality'. Hume, like Berkeley, also rejects the second alternative: ''tis utterly impossible to conceive any quantity or quality, without forming a precise notion of its degrees'. This makes of abstraction and generality an impossibility.

Hume's arguments against the second alternative of the 'plain dilemma' are the same with the arguments against the representation of general objects.

(1) Whether we can conceive of qualities and quantities without a determinate degree depends on 'whether abstraction implies a separation'; whether by abstraction we can separate from the qualities and quantities of objects their determinate degrees. Hume denies that this is possible, because separate conception presupposes the possibility of distinct conception; and distinct conception presupposes a difference to be represented. 'But 'tis evident at first sight, that the precise length of a line is not different nor distinguishable from the line itself; nor the precise degree of any quality from the quality. These ideas, therefore, admit no more of separation than they do of distinction and difference' (1.1.7.3).

(2) 'But to form the idea of an object, and to form an idea simply is the same thing; the reference of the idea to an object being an extraneous denomination, of which in itself it bears no mark or character' (1.1.7.6).

(3) The inference from the properties of objects to the properties of content of impressions and ideas is good. 'If this [indeterminateness] therefore be absurd in *fact and reality*, it must also be absurd *in idea*; since nothing of which we can form a clear and distinct idea is absurd and impossible' (1.1.7.6). And of course, by Two Viewpoints, the impossibility of contents is the impossibility of the existence of ideas. 'Now as 'tis impossible to form an idea of an object, that is possest of quantity and quality, and yet is possest of no precise degree of either; it follows, that there is an equal impossibility of forming an idea, that is not limited and confin'd in both these particulars' (1.1.7.6).

Hume's rejection of the second horn of the 'plain dilemma' obviously reminds us of Berkeley. Berkeley holds that generality is not perceived, imagined, or framed in the mind by means of or as an abstract idea, resulting from the separation of a constituent of an idea, a sensible quality—say, extension—from the other sensible qualities and circumstances which determine its particular existence.[2] We have a capacity for thinking in general terms and, in this sense, we can be said to have general ideas, but not general ideas which are abstract in the aforementioned sense.[3] The function of generality is realized by mental, imaginative

---

[2] See Berkeley, *New Theory*, 122–4 (44–45): we have no abstract ideas and thinking we have is a chief source of confusion. See Winkler, *Berkeley*, 30–1. (Winkler, 39–40, also remarks that there is no deep contrast between Berkeley's and Locke's accounts of general ideas: both explain generality with selective attention and neither accepts what he calls the 'content assumption', the identification of the content of an idea with its object.)

[3] Berkeley, *Principles*, 'Introduction', 12 (69): 'By observing how ideas become general we may the better judge how words are made so. And here it is to be noted that I do not deny absolutely there are general ideas, but only that there are any *abstract general ideas*'.

operations, which separate and combine ideas, consider them in a selective way, and allow them to stand the one for the other.[4]

While the similarity between Hume's and Berkeley's arguments is evident and acknowledged by Hume, there are differences that are worth remarking on. The focus of Hume's theory is the contrast between two ways, equally inaccessible, in which ideas might have general representational content (in the absence of general objects); not between two ways in which ideas could be present in the mind, as particular or general entities.[5] Hume's arguments draw on his (non-Berkeleyan) ontology of perceptions and on his (equally non-Berkeleyan) view of representational content. Hume is interested in the mental nature or existence of ideas only as a lemma in his arguments. Considered as mental episodes, all ideas are particular because everything is particular. The important issue for Hume is the nature of general content and in particular if it could have representational character; and abstraction comes into question not so much in terms of whether ideas can *exist* incomplete or indeterminate but whether by leaving out the degrees of quantities and qualities we can still have *objects* as the contents of ideas. It is in this sense that he regards the application of ideas 'beyond their nature' as the crucial question in the theory of generality and identifies it with a major cognitive gap in human nature.

4.1.2 Hume's Abstraction: Resemblance, Naming, Custom

In the second part of his account, Hume aims to show that the constraints of particularity on ideas are consistent with their having general contents by abstraction, *if* abstraction is understood rightly. 'Abstract ideas are therefore in themselves individual, however they may become general in their representation. The image in the mind is only that of a particular object, tho' the application of it in our reasoning be the same, as if it were universal' (1.1.7.6). This is possible if we drop the identification of cognitive content with object representation. Hume says that ideas that are 'in themselves individual' become 'general in their representation'. But representation, here as in other occurrences, stands for their having a cognitive role and possessing content in general. In this context Hume also talks of ideas, by abstraction, 'having a more extensive signification'; and of their forming 'a notion' (1.1.7.1–2).[6] This more extensive signification, this cognitive

---

[4] *New Theory*, 127 (45–6); *Principles*, 5 (78). The rejection of abstract general ideas supports Berkeley's other claims about ideas: that they sum up only to a disparate, heterogeneous view of reality; that they lack any necessary connection (because we cannot appeal to some abstract quality connecting them). It also supports immaterialism: no abstraction of existence of sensible things from their being perceived.

[5] 'Generality lies not in ideas themselves, but in the representative use made of them', Waxman, *Hume's Theory of Consciousness*, 94.

[6] Keep present, to avoid confusion, that *my* use of 'representation' (and 'object representation') is strictly *interpretive*: it designs an object-directed, object-dependent, sense-based layer and dimension

condition of generality, has an inferential character and is put in place by inferences of the imagination. As Hume remarks in the text just quoted, it is in their *application in reasoning* that the ideas in our minds are *as if they were universal*. Hume also suggests that general content involves (differently from representation) a specific activity of the mind, rather than the passive admission of objects of sense. An idea which 'in its appearance in the mind', in its mental existence, has 'a precise degree of quantity and quality', 'may be made to represent others, which have different degrees of both' (1.1.7.3). It may be *made* to represent, that is, it may allow us to conceive other objects, without itself representing anything indeterminate. The imagination as a whole, in its idea-comparing and more limited senses, is involved in this activity.

Hume establishes this position by defusing the 'plain dilemma' with the following claim.

> Tho' the capacity of the mind be not infinite, yet we can at once form a notion of all possible degrees of quantity and quality, in such a manner at least, as, however imperfect, may serve all the purposes of reflection and conversation.
>
> (1.1.7.2)

He repeats the claim at the end of his rejection of indeterminate representation.

> This application of ideas beyond their nature proceeds from our collecting all their possible degrees of quantity and quality in such an imperfect manner as may serve the purposes of life, which is the second proposition I propos'd to explain. (1.1.7.7)

Hume is only apparently embracing the first horn of the 'plain dilemma': forming an idea that represents all possible degrees of quality and quantity. As he emphasizes, such idea and collection are 'imperfect' and do not sum up to a representation of objects. Hume also connects this imperfect idea with the purposes of reflection, conversation, life; with cognitive practice and application in reasoning (see also 1.1.7.12–14). By contrast, the plain dilemma only refers to representational ideas. Hume's position, as anticipated, is thus to dissolve the dilemma by showing how the content of ideas can be extended 'beyond their nature' by extending it beyond object representation. Ideas are not representational in their general content. The ideas we have available in advance to the concurrence of imagination persist in their object-representing role, by Non-Mixture. This makes it possible for general thinking to be continuous with ideas referring to objects; but generality, while fully cognitive, is non-object representing in its sources and roles.

---

of content, as individuated and theorized in Hume's philosophy. It is *not* meant to render in all its details Hume's use of this word and cognates; much less our uses of them.

The operation by which the imagination brings about this change in the content of ideas is Hume's abstraction. Hume's theory of abstraction follows a path traced by Locke and Berkeley (and before them by Hobbes). The main ingredients are resemblance, naming, custom, and how they shape the operations of imagination. But Hume's account is much more detailed and much more explicit in its inferentialist orientation.

> When we have found a resemblance among several objects, that often occur to us, we apply the same name to all of them, whatever differences we may observe in the degrees of their quantity and quality, and whatever other differences may appear among them. After we have acquired a custom of this kind, the hearing of that name revives the idea of one of these objects, and makes the imagination conceive it with all its particular circumstances and proportions. (1.1.7.7)

4.1.2.1 Resemblance

Notice how Hume sets imagination at the core of his account of abstraction. We *find* resemblances: they are part of what we perceive in impression and represent with ideas. This is the necessary starting point of the account. But then we *respond* to these resemblances in ways which go beyond their representation, by an exercise of selective attention, by giving them pride of place with respect to their differences and even to the overall differences of the objects. This points to the primitive way in which the imagination is differentially responsive to resemblances, as a principle of transition and association. Therefore, even though resemblances supervene on represented properties of objects and are represented themselves, their role in the theory of abstraction is mediated by their involvement in mental activities that go beyond the representation of particulars.

This is just as well because theories of abstraction face a notorious problem with resemblance. If abstraction is to account for all sorts of general ideas and if the input to abstraction is to be rich enough to determine the sort of generality we deploy in ordinary discourse and cognition, then we confront a dilemma. Resemblances among particulars seem to be exactly the right input for abstractive processes. But to recognize resemblances and to think, to act mentally, on their basis, seems already to involve mastery of generality. Therefore, on this view, abstraction could and would not explain all general ideas, contrary to what Hume thinks.[7] Hume's framework of representation and imagination and in particular the explanatory combination of association and naming go some way toward easing this problem. Ascribing to imagination the *whole* weight of explaining generality (given Non-Mixture) loosens the link between representation and abstraction that could make this latter problematic, if not circular. The cognitive

---

[7] See S. Laurence & E. Margolis, 'Abstraction and the Origin of General Ideas', in *Philosophers' Imprint*, 12, 2012, 19, 1–22, for a clear statement and discussion of the difficulty. See also, for a good interpretive discussion, Broughton, 'Explaining General Ideas'.

influence of resemblance is not realized in further representations but in inferential propensities of the imagination. In this way, Hume can resort to resemblance without dangers of circularity.

4.1.2.2 Naming

Hume's resorting to naming is deflationary and non-problematic. Naming is simply an expression of the association established by imagination, in the guise of an easy transition, between resembling ideas. Hume hints at 3.2.2.10 to a conventional explanation of the origins of language, independent of any refined and sophisticated mental capacity. The associative activity of more limited imagination and our shared experiences make sense of communication, of naming, and of our uses of language without presupposing mastery of general ideas. Thus, there are no hindrances to take naming as available to the explanation of general ideas, and in particular to specifying the mechanism of abstraction. Such mechanism requires that, on account of their resemblance and under the prompt of imaginative transitions, each of us individually ends up applying the same names to resembling objects, whatever their other differences. On Hume's theory of conventions there are no principled problems in moving from here to names shared by a plurality of individuals for aims of communication.

Notice that Hume does *not* say that naming is by general names and that generality is first realized linguistically. The point seems rather to be that, because of the impact of resemblances on the imagination and of its associative and selective responses—and perhaps also because of the spatial and temporal contiguity between the observation of objects and our use of certain sounds or inscriptions—we individually acquire the propensity to name each and any of these objects in the same way, with resembling signs or sounds; and that this in turn has effects on imagination. That is, we *same-name* resembling objects: we give them names which are auditorily or graphically resembling the one to the other. All such same-sounding or same-looking names are names of particular objects, given in the light of their particular ideas. They are not yet bearers of general meanings; rather, they are candidates to such meaning, just as individual ideas are candidates to general content.[8]

---

[8] This is a complex interpretive point. One might suggest that generality enters in Hume theory with names, that is, as linguistic generality; and that general mental content follows suit. Waxman, *Hume's Theory of Consciousness*, 105–15, wisely cautions against putting too much emphasis on the role of language in the production of general ideas. Ainslie, *Hume's True Skepticism*, 64–8, remarks that, via the pervasiveness on abstraction and general ideas, that is, of conceptualization, language comes to play a central if somehow implicit role in the science of human nature. True: but this leaves intact the problem of what role language has in abstraction, by way of what sort of linguistic operation, and in what kind of relation to imagination. For a deep and careful account of Hume's theory of abstraction and of the role of abstract ideas, see Garrett, *Hume*, 52–9.

4.1.2.3 Custom

This is also indicated by how, within Hume's account of abstraction, custom is involved in naming. Hume explicitly likens the role of custom in naming with its role in causal thinking. Custom is a form of association, of the general propensity of the imagination to engage in transitions of ideas. 'When ev'ry individual of any species of objects is found by experience to be constantly united with an individual of another species, the appearance of any new individual of either species naturally conveys the thought to its usual attendant' (1.3.6.14). Customary transitions of ideas are the key to the functioning of names in abstraction.

> Thus because such a particular idea is commonly annex'd to such a particular word, nothing is requir'd but the hearing of that word to produce the correspondent idea; and 'twill scarce be possible for the mind, by its utmost efforts, to prevent that transition. In this case it is not absolutely necessary, that upon hearing such a particular sound, we shou'd reflect on any past experience, and consider what idea has been usually connected with the sound. The imagination of itself supplies the place of this reflection, and is so accustom'd to pass from the word to the idea, that it interposes not a moment's delay betwixt the hearing of the one, and the conception of the other. (1.3.6.14)

Names do not enter into Hume's abstraction as bearers of general meanings and the point of Hume's argument is not to substitute linguistic generality for mental generality. The explanation is wholly in terms of connections between particular words and particular ideas, realized not by a general meaning borne by the former but by a customary mental transition. Such a transition does not require (it actually excludes) the presence to the mind of a general content. Only the susceptibility of imagination to effects of repetition is at play. Hume also excludes that the connection between particular names and particular ideas requires reflection on past experience and consideration of the ideas usually connected with the words. Such reflection and consideration would likely involve some general idea of the involved ideas, sounds, and habits. By excluding it, Hume indicates that names do not enter as explanantia in the theory of abstraction qua general names. Rather, linguistic and mental generality are on a par and both require explanation. This, of course, raises the question of the role of naming in Hume's account of abstraction. I take up this question in what follows.

The three factors of Hume's abstraction—resemblance, naming, and custom—are thus inextricably connected with each other. In this way, the explanation of general content is thoroughly by the more limited imagination. Custom is the fundamental content-productive feature of Hume's imagination and, apart from a cursory mention in the short discussion of association by contiguity (1.1.4.2), it makes its entrance right in the explanation of generality. 'After we have acquired a custom of this kind, the hearing of that name revives the idea of one of these objects'. The imagination forges the link between names and ideas rightly because the link is based on custom and the cognitive effects of custom are restricted to the imagination. This is based on the Structural Principle and on Two Viewpoints: certain features with which perceptions, because of their contents, exist in the mind (their resemblance) interact with the propensities of the imagination; this interaction has effects on the existence in the mind of such perceptions, particularly because of their involvement in customary transitions; such change in the conditions of existence causes, in its turn, changes in their contents.

4.1.3 Generality and the Structural Principle

The next step of Hume's theory of generality establishes how resemblance, naming, and custom close the cognitive gap of generality by solving the 'foregoing paradox': *'that some ideas are particular in their nature, but general in their representation'* (1.1.7.10). The paradox is solved by defusing the 'plain dilemma': abstraction is impossible because it is impossible to conceive either all the different degrees of qualities and quantities or no determinate degree of them. Hume shows that we can in effect conceive with one individual and particular idea, persisting across its interactions with the imagination, a plurality of degrees of qualities and quantities of objects, *if* we do not understand such conception in object-representing terms. This is the inferentialist core of Hume's abstraction, which explains generality with the effects of customary transitions (from names to ideas) of more limited imagination on the imagination itself (primarily on more limited imagination, but also on imagination in the larger sense) and with how such effects come to awareness and conception.

> But as the same word is suppos'd to have been frequently applied to other individuals, that are different in many respects from that idea, which is immediately present to the mind; the word not being able to revive the idea of all these individuals, only touches the soul, if I may be allow'd so to speak, and revives that custom, which we have acquir'd by surveying them. (1.1.7.7)

4.1.3.1 Names–Ideas Inferences

The complex text just quoted unveils the role that naming has in Hume's abstraction, even without bearing general meanings. The key points are the relations of resemblance between the names (the episodes of naming) of certain ideas and those between the ideas that have such names; together with the inferential responses of the imagination to the perception of such resemblances. The first resemblance, between the names used in naming certain ideas, explains how the more limited imagination engages in transitions from the hearing of a name (a 'particular word') to the conception of one of the ideas to which names resembling that name have customarily been given. (An idea included in what Garrett has called the 'revival set' of that name.) '[B]ecause such a particular idea is commonly annex'd to such a particular word, nothing is requir'd but the hearing of that word to produce the correspondent idea' (1.3.6.14). Resemblances of acts of naming make it possible for the more limited imagination to perceive repetitions in name giving and to respond to such repetitions by eliciting one of the so-named ideas on hearing one such name. That is, the imagination responds to the resemblance and repetition of names with inferences to so-named individual ideas.

4.1.3.2 Revival of Custom
The crux of Hume's explanation is an effect of repetition-based name–idea inferences (which are performed by the more limited imagination) on the imagination itself. As described in the last text quoted, this further effect is the following: 'the word not being able to revive the idea of all these individuals, only touches the soul, if I may be allow'd so to speak, and revives that custom, which we have acquir'd by surveying them'. This requires some untangling and, possibly, some reconstruction. The further effect is the revival of the inferential custom that underlies the names–ideas inferences; a custom that is one of such 'habits' as 'may be reviv'd by one single word' (1.1.7.13).

What is to revive such custom is not immediately clear; but progress can be made by considering what Hume says about the causes of this further effect. As Hume remarks, in this connection, 'the same word is suppos'd to have been frequently applied to other individuals, that are different in many respects from that idea, which is immediately present to the mind'. What Hume has in mind here is an effect of the resemblance between the idea elicited by the occurrence of a name and the other ideas to which names resembling to the occurring one have been applied. This resemblance keeps this custom of inferring ideas from names working, even once an idea has been elicited by the occurrence of a name. In this way, an inferential potential (a propensity to engage in certain inferences) is associated with the occurrence of that name–idea pair and, on grounds of resemblance, it is distributed across same-named ideas. The propensity of the imagination, associated with the activity of giving resembling names to resembling ideas, is a propensity to 'the production of all the ideas, to which the name may be apply'd' (1.1.7.7). This effect of resemblance and repetition on the imagination is what the revival of the custom consists in.

This is the key to generalization, as we will see in a moment. It is interesting how important the role of naming is in this context. The transition from names to ideas, differently from the association between ideas and ideas, is not based on qualities: there is no resemblance between a word and the idea it names. It is based on *acts of naming* ('we apply the same name to them all') and, with the onset of a practice of naming, on the resemblance between the particular words used in naming. (It is not based, primarily, on contiguity, even though, in naming, ideas and occurrences of names are temporally contiguous; but this is a consequence of the act of naming itself.) Ideas are inferred from names on account only of the practice of naming: the names–ideas transitions do not depend on an association of qualities but on such practice. This makes possible an extension of the inferential potential thus associated to a name- idea pair to a plurality of resembling ideas; in particular to a plurality of ideas with different degrees of resembling qualities or also with different properties. If ideas are associated to ideas by resemblance, their associations and transitions are sensitive to the degrees of their qualities and quantities and to how they otherwise differ. Iconic or phenomenal resemblance is very exacting and intransitive; this may hinder the transitions of the imagination and block the revival of the custom. But if the association is realized by a sign, a word; and the transition is mediated by acts of naming performed by an individual and by his corresponding practice or custom; we may suppose that, once the association and transition between a name and an idea have been established, they can be easily spread across even partially resembling ideas. 'The word raises up an individual idea, along with a certain custom; and that custom produces any other individual one, for which we may have occasion' (1.1.7.7). Notice, again, that this does not postulate that names or ideas are general, but only that particular names are resembling and that they occur in a practice of naming particular ideas.[9]

4.1.3.3 Custom-revival and Generality

Hume describes the generalizing import of the revived inferential custom as follows: the occurrence of the word, which 'revives that custom, which we have acquir'd by surveying them', 'only touches the soul'. This suggests a way to understand the change produced in how ideas exist in our minds and the correlated change in the contents we have available. The crucial point is that the revival of the inferential custom falls short of making us conceive of all the resembling ideas and of all their qualities. What it consists in is rather a 'readiness' or propensity of the imagination to elicit resembling ideas associated with resembling names, on the hearing of one such name; as well as the experience of such 'readiness'. This

---

[9] On this reading, the revival of the custom of naming certain ideas by certain word or signs would be structurally similar to that of the probability of causes, which Hume addresses later in Book 1 (see § 11.1.3). On Hume's account, the probability of causes consists in the distribution of the imaginative transitions of forceful and lively conception across different, conceived ideas. The proportions in which such conception is distributed determine our ascription of credence and probability to such ideas. As Don Garrett has suggested to me (private communication), some ideas could be more likely to be elicited by the use of a name because more closely resembling the rest of ideas (or the average combination and degree of qualities) or because it has occurred more often in the context of the practice. This might help to explain how terms can be vague in their application and why thinking up a counterexample to a general conclusion can be difficult.

experience is a feeling that "twill scarce be possible for the mind, by its utmost efforts, to prevent that transition' (1.3.6.14). Or some sort of apprehension of a 'power of producing [ideas]' (1.1.7.12). I think that this gives us a clue to understanding how the revival of custom is connected to abstraction and generality. The revival of the custom is the more limited imagination being ready to elicit ideas resembling an actually elicited one. This potential for inferential activity cannot come to full actuality: because of the limits of our minds, the imagination cannot actually engage in all such transitions and elicit all the resembling ideas. Still, the more limited imagination is active in this respect and has the experience of its inferential readiness, in connection with a plurality of resembling ideas (individuated by Non–Mixture: ideas preserve their identity across the interactions with imagination). The experience of this readiness is, by the Important Footnote, equivalent to a mode of conception of such ideas. In particular, since the inferential potential cannot turn into a fully engaged transition, the mode of conception is an abridged or partial consideration of such ideas. This abridgement is *possible* for the imagination because it is not expression of the representational content of ideas but of their positions and roles in name–idea and idea–idea inferences. It is also something that is *naturally necessary* for it, since it is a causal consequence of those inferences. This is Hume's main hypothesis for explaining abstraction and generality.

> They [the individual ideas] are not really and in fact present to the mind, but only in power; nor do we draw them all out distinctly in the imagination, but keep ourselves in a readiness to survey any of them, as we may be prompted by a present design or necessity. The word raises up an individual idea, along with a certain custom; and that custom produces any other individual one, for which we may have occasion. But as the production of all the ideas, to which the name may be apply'd, is in most cases impossible, we abridge that work by a more partial consideration, and find but few inconveniences to arise in our reasoning from that abridgment. (1.1.7.7)

In addition to their primitive, particular object-representing contents (preserved by Non–Mixture), ideas come to have a further property of content, consisting in a partial conception of their objects. These properties are not representational but depend on how ideas figure in certain transitions of the more limited imagination. Through this complex process and because of this mode of conception, the contents of ideas become general and names become 'general terms' (1.1.7.10). There is no priority of generality of names on generality of ideas or vice versa. True, in the following text Hume seems to explain generality of ideas by their being annexed to a general term. But the definition he gives of a general term ('that is') makes clear that a term becomes general by the same process by which ideas become general.

However this may be, 'tis certain *that* we form the idea of individuals, whenever we use any general term; *that* we seldom or never can exhaust these individuals; and *that* those, which remain, are only represented by means of that habit, by which we recal them, whenever any present occasion requires it. This then is the nature of our abstract ideas and general terms; and 'tis after this manner we account for the foregoing paradox, *that some ideas are particular in their nature, but general in their representation.* A particular idea becomes general by being annex'd to a general term; that is, to a term, which from a customary conjunction has a relation to many other particular ideas, and readily recals them in the imagination. (1.1.7.10)

4.1.3.4 Generality and Inference

This is how Hume solves the problem of generality, by defusing the 'plain dilemma'. Generality does not consist *at all* in some special sort of ideas or in some special object–representing property.[10] It consists in a 'more partial consideration' of ideas, in a manner of conception and not in objects conceived. This 'abridgment' or 'partial consideration' is what for Hume counts as abstraction and constitutes generality of ideas: it is as if all the degrees of their qualities and quantities were conceived; *as if they were universal*. The inferentially caused abridged consideration makes possible conceiving (without representing as objects) all the qualities and quantities of certain kinds. It is what it is to have a general idea.

The traditional objection to the possibility of conceiving all the degrees of qualities and quantities is premised on a representational understanding of conception. Hume evades such objection by giving an inferentialist view of such conception. The revived custom of one of inferring an idea from a name. The effects of the revival are themselves inferential: the readiness to engage in other inferences involving ideas resembling the elicited one. The experience of this readiness is equivalent to an abridged consideration of the contents of such ideas, to abstraction; and such consideration makes available general contents. In other words, as per the Important Footnote, this inferential framework is present to consciousness as a *modified conception*—not a necessarily defective one—of the same ideas that were the input to the transitions and custom. Such ideas in

---

[10] 'I believe every one, who examines the situation of his mind in reasoning, will agree with me, that we do not annex distinct and compleat ideas to every term we make use of, and that in talking of *government, church, negotiation, conquest*, we seldom spread out in our minds all the simple ideas, of which these complex ones are compos'd. 'Tis however observable, that notwithstanding this imperfection we may avoid talking nonsense on these subjects, and may perceive any repugnance among the ideas, as well as if we had a full comprehension of them. Thus if instead of saying, *that in war the weaker have always recourse to negotiation,* we shou'd say, *that they have always recourse to conquest,* the custom, which we have acquir'd of attributing certain relations to ideas, still follows the words, and makes us immediately perceive the absurdity of that proposition; in the same manner as one particular idea may serve us in reasoning concerning other ideas, however different from it in several circumstances' (1.1.7.14).

this way are present to the mind only 'in power': not as fully determined representations of objects, as they necessarily would be if they were actually present; but only for how they are involved in the relevant inferences and for the effects that such inferences have on their conception. This dissolves the paradox of ideas with a cognitive role going beyond their nature. In general thought, individuals are 'only represented by means of that habit, by which we recal them, whenever any present occasion requires it'. There is no paradox, because this sort of representation (this sort of cognitive content) depends on imaginative activities dealing with ideas of objects and not on objects causing ideas that exactly resemble them. What of content and cognition goes beyond the nature of ideas does not have the nature of object representation but is inferential in source and application.[11]

Ideas are involved in generalizing inferences on account of their individuating qualities, which make for their internal relations of resemblances. Their individuation, by Non-Mixture, is stable across such inferences and a wide range of variation of their qualities and degrees. Correspondingly, the represented objects can preserve sameness of species. 'An object ceases not to be of any particular species on account of every small alteration in its extension, duration and other properties' (1.1.7.2). This makes it possible to keep referring to objects when thinking in general terms, even though what we think in such terms is not object-representing. Abstraction as described by Hume makes it possible for our general ideas to be non-arbitrary, as it is required by their role in reasoning and in our cognitive practices generally. (Of course, there is no assurance of this: transitions based on resemblance are highly fallible.)[12]

---

[11] Kemp Smith's criticism of Hume's account of abstraction (*Philosophy of Hume*, 259–64) misses its key features. Resemblance counts as explanans qua property of ideas and not qua idea of a property (this is the explanandum), as a natural and not as a philosophical relation. The direct effect of resemblance is to activate original qualities of imagination. General names are explained within the context of the explanation of general ideas.

[12] There are obvious similarities between Hume's and Berkeley's accounts of generality. Berkeley integrates and modifies Locke's theory (as he understands it) by reducing the presumptive faculty of abstracting, which would be based on possible separate existence, to the faculty of imagining, of representing to oneself particular ideas and compounding and dividing them. See *Principles*, 'Introduction', 10 (68): 'Whether others have this wonderful faculty of *abstracting their ideas*, they best can tell: for myself, I find indeed I have a faculty of imagining, or representing to myself, the ideas of those particular things I have perceived, and of variously compounding and dividing them'. On this basis, he explains generality as representational role, as standing for, as the use of an idea as a sign, with the concomitant indifferent suggestion, and as selective attention: '*universality*, so far as I can comprehend, not consisting in the absolute, *positive* nature or conception of anything, but in the *relation* it bears to the particulars signified or represented by it; by virtue whereof it is that things, names, or notions, being in their own nature *particular*, are rendered *universal*', *Principles*, 'Introduction', 15 (71). This is indeed very close to Hume's theory. But, apart from the lack of detail about the psychological mechanism at work in truly understood abstraction, what is missing in Berkeley's account and is well present in Hume is a full specification of the inferential grounding of general ideas.

4.1.4 Application in Reasoning and Possibility of Error

Hume explains generality of content as an abridged consideration of ideas, expressing customary, idea-to-idea inferential propensities. These latter, in their turn, depend on naming and on customary name-to-idea transitions. The abridged ideas are individual not only as to their mental existence but as to their contents, insofar as they represent their objects. Therefore, their generality issues from their involvement in operations of the more limited imagination. But the imagination figures in Hume's theory of abstraction also in its larger sense, that is, by the Structural Principle, as a non-representational cognitive faculty inclusive of idea-comparing inferences as well as of non-idea-comparing ones. The genesis of general ideas from the transitions of the more limited imagination is thus explanatorily complemented by their inferential *roles* and *application*, how they figure in reasoning or within idea-comparing imagination.[13]

Reliance on the conditions and acts of idea-comparing reasoning is systematic in Hume's explanation of generality. Hume remarks that our readiness to survey ideas is 'prompted by a present design or necessity'; that the custom revived by the use of a word associated to a particular idea in its turn 'produces any other individual one, for which we may have occasion' (1.1.7.7; 'whenever any present occasion requires it', 1.1.7.10; 'that custom, which so readily recalls every particular idea, for which we may have occasion', 1.1.7.11). Inferential potentials are put in place by the more limited imagination. But the design and necessity, the occasion, which determine whether such potentials invest particular ideas and our thinking takes up general character, are individuated within the practice of

---

[13] Ideas as images have central importance in Sedivy's carefully crafted but ultimately untenable reading (and criticism) of Hume's theory of abstraction, S. Sedivy, 'Hume, Images and Abstraction', *Hume Studies*, 21, 1, 1995 (117–34), 122–9. Sedivy points to the functional or inferential dimension of Hume's abstraction: application in reasoning determines the content of ideas, including its generality (119). This postulates that image-like ideas can be used for drawing inferences true of a general content (122). However, Sedivy denies that this is possible. Her main argument for this is the Witttgensteinian and Goodmanian one that pictorial properties of images cannot determine contents, even within an associative complex, because they are susceptible to an unbounded number of respects of similarity (124). 'The fact of their being associated together does not pick out or select a unique respect of similarity that they share.' Because of this, it is not possible to say what would count as a counterexample to the proposed reasoning, and therefore what is the general content which accrues of a certain individual idea. Sedivy is right that general content is firstly realized in general reasoning. But her argument to the radical indeterminateness of the content of images depends on assuming that associative links are merely a function of (supposed) intrinsic features of images. On this assumption, applying ideas-images in reasoning as if they were general is either an impossible cognitive feat or a circular move. But this completely neglects the role of imagination. The principles and biases of imagination discriminate between the respects of similarity in terms of salience or availability, of blocks and facilitations. It is these mental facts that break the tie among similarities of pictorial ideas. This is not a logical matter, but still a cognitively decisive one. In general, it is only if roles in reasoning are cashed out, at the most fundamental, content-determining level, as transitions of the more limited imagination (which are differentially content-sensitive), that Hume's account of generality is well understood. The image-like character of ideas, in this perspective, is less important than their concurrence with imagination.

idea-comparing reasoning; by the conclusions we aim to draw, the judgements we aim to make (or to revise, or to reject), the steps we accept or reject. An idea is applied 'beyond its nature' in virtue of its application in reasoning (as opposed to, say, memory or simple conception) and deploys properties of content beyond object representation. But, conversely, these properties of contents are individuated in terms of their roles or application in idea-comparing reasoning activity. 'The image in the mind is only that of a particular object, tho' the application of it in our reasoning be the same, as if it were universal' (1.1.7.6). The Structural Principe, which records and regiments the complexity and the unity of Hume's imagination, makes sense of this division of explanatory labour.

The involvement of the whole imagination as a faculty in the explanation of general content comes in view in the normative dimension of Hume's abstraction and generalization—a radically original twist of his theory. Hume needs to explain how a partial consideration of objects—partial relatively to the standards of object representation—can nonetheless be well suited for general reasoning, in any sort of domain. (Hume's example is from geometry; but it could be any sort of a priori or a posteriori reasoning: what matters here is only generality, not any specific subject matter or pattern.) This is obviously a crucial requirement on his theory, since we ordinarily draw distinctions between good and bad applications of general ideas and Hume's task is to explain our practice of general thinking without assuming general objects of thought. Possibilities of error and correctness seems to be intrinsic to reasoning activity; if the general contents of our reasonings, as explained in Hume's theory, were not susceptible to error, little could be made of the correct application of general ideas and thus of reasoning by comparison of such ideas. Reciprocally, in order to individuate and assess the different ways in which the consideration of ideas can be abridged, we must refer back to their roles in ordinary reasoning. The question thus is how to satisfy these requirements and to locate possibility of error in general thinking in the context of Hume's naturalistic, imagination-driven theory of abstraction, which seems to leave all applications of general ideas on a par. Hume's answer is strictly naturalistic.

> For this is one of the most extraordinary circumstances in the present affair, that after the mind has produc'd an individual idea, upon which we reason, the attendant custom, reviv'd by the general or abstract term, readily suggests any other individual, if by chance we form any reasoning, that agrees not with it. Thus shou'd we mention the word, triangle, and form the idea of a particular equilateral one to correspond to it, and shou'd we afterwards assert, *that the three angles of a triangle are equal to each other*, the other individuals of a scalenum and isoceles, which we overlook'd at first, immediately crowd in upon us, and make us perceive the falshood of this proposition, tho' it be true with relation to that idea, which we had form'd. (1.1.7.8)

Hume's solution of the problem is thus a further, empirical articulation of the revived inferential custom that determines the abridged consideration of ideas and thus their abstraction and generalization. The further property is a compelling inclination of the mind to the fast elicitation of ideas that fail to agree with some general conclusion. This ready suggestion of counterexamples is essential to explain how general contents can be present and active in the mind. It explains naturalistically how thinking activity can be sensitive to error in generalization, as a property of the imagination and thus without presupposing any general representation of objects. It should be seen as a further, indispensable explanatory factor of general content rather than an addendum to its explanation. The 'extraordinary circumstance' of this counterexample-eliciting propensity marks to the more limited imagination (the counterexamples 'crowd in upon us') and bears on the idea-comparing one. It is introduced by Hume as a remarkable fact about our cognitive nature. In this, he seems to be on reasonably safe ground. Identifying and accepting empirical facts is perfectly fitting to the experimental method of reasoning that Hume is extending to the philosophy of mind ('To explain the ultimate causes of our mental actions is impossible', 1.1.7.11). Most importantly, it is a fact psychologically well attested and with counterparts in contemporary cognitive science.[14]

This propensity marks a joint at which the two parts of imagination interact very closely. On the one hand, the idea-comparing activity of reasoning is immediately affected by this underlying propensity of the more limited imagination. On the other, the counterexample-eliciting propensity matters for the theory of abstraction and generality because general contents have application in idea-comparing reasoning. Only this latter context makes sense of the fact that such ideas, crowding on us, are counterexamples *at all*. Such ideas are incompatible with the proposition '*that the three angles of a triangle are equal to each other*', because they have a property (the inequality of their angles) that is the opposite of the idea on which the proposition is formed. This 'makes us perceive the falsehood of this proposition' and reject it on normative grounds (as false, as an error). But this, in turn, depends on the idea (the content of the proposition) not counting and not being taken as object-representing but rather on its expressing and being taken to express a role in reasoning. As Hume very insightfully remarks: 'tho' it [that proposition] be true with relation to that idea, which we had form'd'. If the content of the proposition consisted in the object that the particular idea we have formed represents, the proposition would be *true*. (Hume's non-quantified form allows for this.) That is, the proposition is true if the role of the idea in forming it is that of representing an object. In this respect, the ideas that crowd in on

---

[14] That natural reasoning works by way of search of counterexamples is today generally recognized in cognitive science. See P. N. Johnson-Laird & U. Hansson, 'Counterexamples in Sentential Reasoning', *Memory & Cognition* 2003, 31, 7 (1105–13).

us are not counterexamples: they are simply ideas of different objects and the proposition is not about them. To get a falsehood, we must consider the proposition as a quantified conclusion of reasoning and the idea that forms its content as to its application in such a reasoning; that is, according to its inferential role. At these conditions, the ideas *are* counterexamples. Therefore, the significance of such natural propensity depends on our practice of reasoning by comparing ideas and this crucially contributes to the inferential explanation of general content.[15]

4.2 We Accompany our Ideas with a Kind of Reflection

4.2.1 Distinctions of Reason

Hume extends his explanation of general content to 'that *distinction of reason*, which is so much talk'd of, and is so little understood, in the schools' (1.1.7.17) and which, we may add, seems to suggest an irreducible role for the understanding or reason. Distinctions of reason are distinctions without a difference, for example, between figure and body figured; or motion and body moved. They are ascribed to reason because they are purely conceptual, not being grounded in differences in reality.[16] These distinctions are at work and important in ordinary cognition, as aspectual modes of thinking: seeing or conceiving the same object *as* figured, *in* its figure; or *as* coloured, *in* its colour; thinking *of* the motion of a body and not *of* the body moved. They are also important for Hume's own philosophy: Two Viewpoints, the distinction between impressions and objects, and that between the idea of an object and the idea of its existence, are all distinctions of reason. Thinking as and related phenomena are well understood as conceptual

---

[15] See, for a closely related, well-argued interpretation of Hume's theory of abstraction, Schafer, 'Hume's Unified Theory', 8–12. Schafer remarks that two ideas, copied by the same impressions and with the same qualitative features, can stand in the mind for different things. His account of this difference in content is, however, in causal-functional terms, rather than in terms of inference and imagination. See, for a similar, functional reading, S. Sedivy, 'Hume, Images and Abstraction'. I think that understanding general content in terms of resemblance (see Landy, *Science of Human Nature*, 25–8, 109: 'The meaning of a general term consists *entirely* of a representation of the members of its revival set as resembling each other') misses the crucial inferential component that makes sense of the individuation and role of revival sets. This comes into light in Landy's earlier, fuller discussion of Hume's theory of general content (*Kant's Inferentialism*, 80–8). By neglecting the role of the inferences of the imagination and casting Hume's account of generality in the mold of his 'Representational Copy Principle' (that is, the First Principle) (81), Landy saddles Hume theory with a problem (the indeterminateness of the content of general ideas) that would certainly arise *if* Hume attempted to explain generality in terms of (some complication of) representations of objects *but* that does not arise given his inferentialist approach. While it is certainly true that extensions or revival sets, per se, do not sufficiently identify the content of general ideas, they are up to this task when taken together with the roles in reasoning and the transitions of the imagination that fix them.

[16] See Descartes' discussion of real, modal, and conceptual distinctions in *Principles of Philosophy*, I, 60–2 (*The Philosophical Writings of Descartes*, 213–14). Hume's distinctions of reason correspond to Descartes' conceptual distinctions.

exercises: what is not different and even cannot be different in reality can be conceived of under different aspects, to some cognitive advantage. But distinctions of reasons, the very thought of drawing a distinction without a difference, are deeply problematic in Hume's philosophy. This comes out in a modal argument (see Chapter 5 for discussion).

> The difficulty of explaining this distinction arises from the principle above explain'd, that *all ideas, which are different, are separable*. For it follows from thence, that if the figure be different from the body, their ideas must be separable as well as distinguishable; if they be not different, their ideas can neither be separable nor distinguishable   (1.1.7.17)

Where there is no difference (which belongs to the domain of impressions or objects and of representation), there can be no distinction and no separation (which belong to the domain of what is conceivable). Therefore, distinctions of reason seem to be unavailable to our thought. 'A person, who desires us to consider the figure of a globe of white marble without thinking on its colour, desires an impossibility' (1.1.7.18). This cognitive gap or impossibility, however, is owing to a too restrictive understanding of our cognitive capacities. The impossibility arises if we 'consider the figure and the color together, since they are in effect the same and undistinguishable' (1.1.7.18). That is, if we make our cognitive capacities strictly conditional on what representation gives us as an object. There *is* actually no difference in the object between colour and figure; this is the only way we can *represent* it; and this is the end of the story. Of course, the imagination can take steps well beyond representation and still make for a significant and regular cognitive change, as the case of general ideas has begun to show. What makes distinctions of reason problematic is that the liberty of imagination seems in this case to have no foothold at all in representation. The qualities and quantities of objects can have different degrees and complex ideas can represent them with different degrees; even though we cannot conceive of them without a determinate degree. This does not make for a separation of qualities or quantities from their degrees; but can mediate the reference of abridged ideas to particular objects. By contrast, colour and shape individuate a simple idea representing an object. There are no differences, in this case, that would support explaining and articulating distinctions in conception on the pattern of abstraction and generality. This cognitive gap is related to, but different from, that of generality. In the case of generality, lack of difference and separation between the length of a line and its exact measure threatens our attempts to think of multiple measures of the length of a line with indeterminateness. Attempting to form *one* idea that would *represent* different particulars (different degrees), we would end up with an indeterminate conception. In the case of distinctions of reason, the lack of difference and separation, say, between a surface and its colour threatens our attempts to think them separately with *emptiness*. Attempting to form *different* ideas that *represent* one and the same object, we would end up with no conception of that object. But in neither case are we restricted to representational contents. Imagination can in either case both complement representation and provide an account of the otherwise missing cognitive capacities.

Hume claims: 'to remove this difficulty we must have recourse to the foregoing explanation of abstract ideas' (1.1.7.18). Hume's abstraction accounts in an indirect way for the possibility of conceiving all the different degrees of the qualities and quantities of objects. Generality is attained without separation. Hume's theory of distinctions of reason accounts, in an indirect way, for the distinction of different aspects in one same object, without separation. Hume's explanation of distinctions of reasons is in two steps. In the first place, he points out that different simple ideas can bear different resemblances to each other without this implying any complexity (as if distinct but resembling particulars entered in their composition). Hume prepares this claim in a footnote added in the 'Appendix': "Tis evident, that even different simple ideas may have a similarity or resemblance to each other; nor is it necessary, that the point or circumstance of resemblance shou'd be distinct or separable from that in which they differ' (1.1.7.7 fn. 5). The point is repeated in the present context. "Tis certain that the mind wou'd never have dream'd of distinguishing a figure from the body figur'd, as being in reality neither distinguishable, nor different, nor separable; did it not observe, that even in this simplicity there might be contain'd many different resemblances and relations' (1.1.7.18). This observation provides the imagination with a basis for its work on undifferentiated sensible representation; more precisely, a basis in phenomenal resemblances and contrasts that fail to individuate objects but still make a differential contribution to conception.

> Thus when a globe of white marble is presented, we receive only the impression of a white colour dispos'd in a certain form, nor are we able to separate and distinguish the colour from the form. But observing afterwards a globe of black marble and a cube of white, and comparing them with our former object, we find two separate resemblances, in what formerly seem'd, and really is, perfectly inseparable. (1.1.7.18)

Individuating such separate resemblances in one simple idea of an object is not a separation by the imagination. The difference that is in this way brought into view is not a difference of impressions. This would give us a complex impression and idea, whose elements, once detached and turned into perfect ideas, could be easily separated and combined. Or one which would anyway support the application to objects of imagination-produced contents, like in the case of generality. This marks the difference between abstract ideas and distinctions of reason. The individuation of any relevant 'similarity or resemblance' within simple ideas is not given in impressions, represented by ideas, and further elaborated by imagination. Activities of the imagination—'observing', 'comparing', and finding—are already involved in the primary identification of such different resemblances; and these activities, which might even be of an idea-comparing kind, already spring from the concurrence of imagination and representation, rather than being an input to it. The representational dimension of distinctions of reason thus seems to be thin. Selective attention and comparison in the imagination have a place among the conditions for distinctions of reasons that has no counterpart in abstraction.

The resemblances that are found in this way are the ground for a further activity of the mind, the second step of Hume's explanation. Observing that simple ideas can be resembling to each other in different respects, comparing these resemblances, has complex effects on the imagination. In the first place, the repetition or custom of selective attention, which is itself an operation of the imagination, puts us in a position to reflect on such simple of ideas, in an immediate way: 'By this means we accompany our ideas with a kind of reflection, of which custom renders us, in a great measure, insensible' (1.1.7.18). By this reflection, in the second place, we come to have some measure of consciousness of and even of control on the operations with which the imagination responds to different resemblances of simple objects. If such operations become to some extent accessible, in reflection, then something like a differential conception of what are actually the same qualities of an object, and thereby the corresponding non-representational distinctions, becomes possible. These different ways of engaging in the consideration of such qualities, by custom-sensitive imagination rather than by representation, puts in place a conceptual articulation of our ideas.

> After a little more practice of this kind, we begin to distinguish the figure from the colour by a *distinction of reason*; that is, we consider the figure and colour together, since they are in effect the same and undistinguishable; but still view them in different aspects, according to the resemblances, of which they are susceptible. When we wou'd consider only the figure of the globe of white marble, we form in reality an idea both of the figure and colour, but tacitly carry our eye to its resemblance with the globe of black marble: And in the same manner, when we wou'd consider its colour only, we turn our view to its resemblance with the cube of white marble. (1.1.7.18)

Drawing such distinctions is thus not a matter of representing differences within simple ideas or objects (which is impossible) and not even of abridging the consideration of individual ideas but of considering or viewing simple ideas or objects, with their inseparable qualities, under different aspects. The imagination has moved from observing different resemblances among different simple ideas to regarding the same simple idea in different ways or guises. It is a matter of *carrying our eye* or *turning our view* from one to the other of two inseparable aspects of an object. A complex interplay of idea-comparing and more limited imagination is thus at the root of distinctions of reason, which are possible without requiring or establishing a real difference (and not even a modal one, as we will see). Hume is sparing of details in his account. His reference to our 'practice' of 'comparing' resemblances of objects may suggest a custom-revival style of explanation. The habit of observing and comparing different resemblances of simples prompts us to give selective attention to them also in the case of one single object. Be this as it may, this fills the cognitive gap of 'thinking as'. It makes it possible to dissolve the apparent impossibility of such an everyday phenomenon like aspectual thinking.

> A person, who desires us to consider the figure of a globe of white marble without thinking on its colour, desires an impossibility; but his meaning is, that we shou'd consider the colour and figure together, but still keep in our eye the resemblance to the globe of black marble, or that to any other globe of whatever colour or substance. (1.1.7.18)

4.2.2 The Readiness, with which the Imagination Suggests Its Ideas

Another important consequence of Hume's account of generality is the explanation of the intentionality of mental activities: their being directed or oriented to certain objects. The phenomena of generality, intentionality, and aspectual thinking are strictly connected. Hume remarks, in his account of abstraction, that it is possible to have different thoughts, with different conditions of correctness, in relation to the same represented object.

> Nay so entire is the [counterexamples-eliciting] custom, that the very same idea may be annext to several different words, and may be employ'd in different reasonings, without any danger of mistake. Thus the idea of an equilateral triangle of an inch perpendicular may serve us in talking of a figure, of a rectilineal figure, of a regular figure, of a triangle, and of an equilateral triangle. All these terms, therefore, are in this case attended with the same idea; but as they are wont to be apply'd in a greater or lesser compass, they excite their particular habits, and thereby keep the mind in a readiness to observe, that no conclusion be form'd contrary to any ideas, which are usually compriz'd under them. (1.1.7.9)

The one idea associated to different words is the core of representational content (by Non-Mixture), the individual idea elicited by the name-idea transitions of more limited imagination and made available, with a general inferential potential, to idea-comparing imagination. Only the persistence of this idea determines the reference, if there is one at all, of this whole network of thoughts. But the applications in reasoning of this idea can be radically different, depending on the different inferential potentials, the different customary inferential propensities connected with it. These potentials are individuated by the production of the more limited imagination of counterexamples relative to each application. In this way Hume can make sense of the different orientations that mental activity can take in relation to one and the same idea and, in this way, of the possibility that such activity be directed in different ways and to different cognitive purposes—both central phenomena of intentionality.

Intentionality, in this sense, is another crucial mark of conceptual character. It is also a further cognitive gap of representation that has to be filled. The representational relation between impressions or objects and ideas, as constitutively individuated by the First Principle, is a factual relation, causal and phenomenal, with a priority of impressions over ideas but no orientation and guidance of the representing function by the ideas. Such representation is the mirroring of one object or set of qualities by another object or set of qualities. Thus, also in the case of intentionality, we have a cognitive capacity which, on account of its conceptual character, cannot be tracked back to Representational Naturalism.[17]

The rationalist philosophers had a ready explanation of the phenomena of intentionality: the intelligible objects and properties represented by ideas determine what our thoughts are to be directed to. In this way, the objects apprehended by the understanding determine the internal and logical ordering of the thoughts of a subject. But Hume does not want to introduce a sui generis faculty of the understanding, or any non-reducible agency of thinking subjects, to explain how conceptual thinking, differently from sensible cognition, can be differently directed to its objects. The mental properties of intentionality are rather explained with the Second Principle and the associations and transitions of the imagination.

> Our imagination has a great authority over our ideas; and there are no ideas that are different from each other, which it cannot separate, and join, and compose into all the varieties of fiction. But notwithstanding the empire of the imagination, there is a secret tie or union among particular ideas, which causes the mind to conjoin them more frequently together, and makes the one, upon its appearance, introduce the other. Hence arises what we call the *apropos* of discourse: hence the connection of writing: and hence that thread,

---

[17] Landy, *Kant's Inferentialism*, 80–8, rightly remarks that the theory of generality and of distinctions of reasons are meant by Hume to address the problem of disambiguating the contents of ideas regimented by the Representational Copy Principle (in First Principle). I agree with this reading but, differently from Landy, I think that Hume is quite successful, in terms of his own theory, in the answer he gives to the 'thinking as' problem. The reason for this divergence is quite simply that, differently from Landy, I do not regard Hume's theory of generality as another instance of the application of the First Principle. There is a non-eliminable inferential component, owing to imagination.

or chain of thought, which a man naturally supports even in the loosest reverie. (*Abstract* 35)

The text where Hume advances his account of intentionality also provides an enormously interesting insight in the activities of the imagination.

> Nothing is more admirable, than the readiness, with which the imagination suggests its ideas, and presents them at the very instant, in which they become necessary or useful. The fancy runs from one end of the universe to the other in collecting those ideas, which belong to any subject. One would think the whole intellectual world of ideas was at once subjected to our view, and that we did nothing but pick out such as were most proper for our purpose. There may not, however, be any present, beside those very ideas, that are thus collected by a kind of magical faculty in the soul, which, tho' it be always most perfect in the greatest geniuses, and is properly what we call a genius, is however inexplicable by the utmost efforts of human understanding. (1.1.7.15)

Hume states clearly that the phenomena of intentionality *seem* to lend support to the rationalist postulation of an objective, necessary order of ideas: 'One would think the whole intellectual world of ideas was at once subjected to our view.' Intentionality would be easily explained as the apprehension of this intellectual world which (differently from the obscure and confused conceptions provided by the senses) allows us to 'pick out' the ideas forming our thoughts and to be guided by them in the pursuit of our cognitive aims ('as were most proper for our purpose'). This would explain the directedness and intelligible ordering of thinking. Hume's alternative explanation, in terms of the transitions of the imagination as a whole, allows him to reject this account of the phenomena of intentionality, without having to assume that sensible representation is already selectively and purposively *directed* to its objects (rather than simply *having* them or *being of* them). There is no intellectual world, no order and totality of ideas; but there is also no need to have and represent one. And there is no thinking agent doing this representing. The only ideas present are those collected, elicited by the imagination; the only guidance is that of the internal organization of the imagination and of its principles. This also explains why and how it may appear that a totality of ideas is present to us and guides our intellectual pursuits. Even though there is no intellectual world of ideas, 'the fancy runs from one end of the universe to the other in collecting those ideas, which belong to any subject' to *simulate* one such world and to *simulate* an intellectual subject. The intellectual world of ideas is *enacted* by the imagination. This is the magic of Hume's imagination.[18] One of the senses

---

[18] Hume's description of imagination as 'a kind of magical faculty in the soul', 'inexplicable by the utmost efforts of human understanding', comes very close to Kant's description of schematism, which

in which, as Hume says, imagination is 'a kind of magical faculty in the soul' is precisely that it simulates in the natural mind the working of a faculty of the intellect and its obligatory objects, representational conceptual ideas. This is a fiction but not an illusion, in any potentially debunking sense. The appearance of contemplating a complete collection and ordering of ideas, to which we only have to adapt or correspond, is the simulation of such intellectual state by the non-intellectual faculty of imagination, through its regular and explainable working.[19]

Also in this case, the Structural Principle makes it possible to differentiate and connect the explanatory contribution of the two parts of the imagination. The necessity and usefulness of ideas is defined by their roles in ordinary and philosophical thinking (ideas are suggested when they 'become necessary or useful', 'belong to any subject', or are 'most proper for our purpose'). The interaction between the contents of impressions and ideas and the inferential propensities of the imagination, the ensuing transitions of the imagination and their results (constructed in terms of Two Viewpoints) explain how such ideas can be ready at hand, as required by their roles in reasoning, without being already present. Just like general contents and aspects of objects, the relevance and pertinence of ideas is their presence in power. Not a matter of existence and representation. The fact that the action of the imagination is 'inexplicable by the utmost efforts of human

---

he regards as essentially involving imagination: 'an art concealed in the depths of the human soul, whose real modes of activity nature is hardly likely ever to allow us to discover' (A 141/B 180–1). The connotation of magic or art that is common to Hume's and Kant's imagination is interesting. This faculty appears at the same time familiar, indispensable, and puzzling to both philosophers. Both have recourse to the imagination as a productive faculty—productive of cognitive content. In this regard, it would not be correct to say that while Kant introduces imagination in order to account for the possibility of experience, also in the presence of perceptual representation, Hume only has recourse to it when perception is absent. See P. Strawson, 'Imagination and Perception' (1971), in R. C. S. Walker, ed., *Kant on Pure Reason*, Oxford University Press, Oxford 1982 (82–99), 86–7. There are cases where perceptual input is missing and imagination has to provide it. However, the role of Hume's imagination is typically not that of replacing impressions and ideas of memory if we lack them; but that of overcoming the natural particularity, object-dependence, and modal invariance of sensible representation—that is, of representation *tout court*. Even if—what is hardly conceivable—we were sensibly acquainted with all empirical objects, still the non-representational cognitive modes and structures deployed in our worldview, including intentionality, would remain out of our grasp.

[19] In this respect, in respect of its capacity to simulate mental states and whole mental landscapes, Hume's imagination come close to some views in contemporary theorizing. Think of Goldman's distinction between 'supposition-imagination', the mental act of supposing, typically involved in fiction, which has conceptual character, and 'enactment-imagination', which is 'a matter of creating or trying to create in one's own mind a selected mental state, or at least a rough facsimile of such a state, through the faculty of imagination' (A. Goldman, 'Imagination and Simulation in Audience Responses to Fiction', in Nichols, *Architecture of the Imagination* (41–56), 41–2). Goldman addresses enactment imagination in the context of a theory of mental simulation: mental processes issuing in states duplicating, replicating, resembling (that is, simulating) their ordinary, 'authentic' counterparts—like first-order processes of perception and belief formation. Goldman importantly suggests that enactment imagination is not confined to low-level tasks, like mirroring one's own or another's basic emotions, but is linked with higher and central cognitive activity (Goldman, *Simulating Minds*, 131–2, 142–3, 147–80). This seems to be the case for Hume's whole intellectual world of ideas. Goldman also contends that the pretend states issuing from imaginative processes are projected, meaning by this, inter alia, that they are somehow mixed with or treated as non-pretend states (this what Goldman's 'quarantine violation' amounts to) (Goldman, *Simulating Minds*, 164–5).

understanding' depends, on the one hand, on the lack of detailed and reliable psychophysical explanations, and on the other, on the general fact that explanations of the nature of the mind come soon to a halt. Certain principles must simply be accepted as primitive. Still, not only the work of imagination is susceptible to empirical enquiry: its cognitive and epistemic architecture is also recognizable. We are at least tacitly familiar with the cognitive requirements and roles deployed in our worldview; and these give us a thread to follow in our enquiring imagination and its products.[20]

4.3 Summary

Conceptual modes of thought like generality, aspectual distinctions, intentional directedness, modality, and the a priori are the first kind of cognitive gap that we encounter in Book 1 of the *Treatise*. We do ordinarily engage in such modes of thinking, but they are not reducible to object representation. Their explanation is crucial for Hume's campaign against Rationalism.

This chapter addresses Hume's explanation of generality and of aspectual and intentionally directed thinking. In § 4.1 I take up the issue of generality, starting (§ 4.1.1) from the individuation of the corresponding cognitive gap in object representation. Such gap depends on combination of the First Principle (only sensible objects or impressions are given to us) with the a priori principle that sensible objects or impressions are particulars. General, object-representing ideas would be impossible.

Against this Berkeley-inspired background, I address Hume's essentially original view of generality and abstraction, which closes the cognitive gap of generality by replacing the presumptive object-representing content of general ideas with an inferential, imagination-grounded one. In the first step of his account (§ 4.1.2), Hume claims that ideas can allow conceiving, for 'all the purposes of reflection and conversation', all possible degrees of qualities and quantities. This is through the combination of resembling representational ideas, acts of naming, and custom-based patterns of transitions of ideas.

---

[20] My general view of the content-productive activities of imagination and of the contents it produces has affinities with that advanced in Loeb, *Stability and Justification*, 162–72. Loeb fully recognizes that Hume's conception of content and of the conditions of meaning go beyond what is licensed by the First Principle. He explains this content in terms of propensities of the imagination and categorizes it in terms of illusions springing from such propensities and of quasi-contents forming ideas like those of external existence or body. The indirect genesis of such contents and their deviation from the First Principle explain Hume's reservations about their appropriateness. On the other hand, illusions and quasi contents are susceptible to perfectly natural psychological explanation. A flaw in Loeb's treatment of these issues is the seclusion he operates of causal from other kinds of imagination-grounded contents. He restricts the qualification of quasi contents to the latter. Had he recognized the affinity between all sorts of imaginative contents, he would have gained a less dim view of the strains that issues of justification put on imagination and its production of content.

In § 4.1.3 I discuss how the imagination changes object-representing contents into general ones. The imagination responds to resemblances of names and of ideas by shifting to an 'abridged', partial conception of ideas. This partial conception defines an inferential potential associated with contents of ideas preserved by Non-Mixture. This inferential potential constitutes generality: the explanation of generality by the consideration of their application in idea-comparing inferences (§ 4.1.4). This empirically unveils a propensity of the imagination to elicit counterexamples to general conclusions of reasoning. The two parts of the imagination converge in the individuation and our mastery of general contents.

In § 4.2 I extend Hume's imagination-based, inferential account of abstraction to two other, strictly related conceptual features of cognition, aspectual and intentional thinking. § 4.2.1 discusses Hume's account of distinctions of reasons, or aspectual modes of thinking, which are perfectly ordinary but deeply problematic for Representational Naturalism. Hume's response to this cognitive gap is to shift distinctions of aspects from representation to conception by the imagination. Hume accounts for aspects by allowing that resemblances of qualities of simple ideas, rather than represented, are conceived by the imagination. By reflection on such conceptions, the imagination forms a custom of selective attention, which gives access to aspectual thinking, the distinct conception of inseparable qualities.

§ 4.2.2 discusses Hume's account of the intentionality of mental activity: its possibly directing itself in different ways to the same objects. This is not a feature of representation, which simply mirrors objects given as impressions. The unity and identity of ideas (by Non-Mixture) consists in the objects they represent. But the same idea can figure in idea-comparing reasoning with different roles, owing to its involvement in different transitions of the more limited imagination. Reflection on such alternative cognitive possibilities is the ground for the directed character of mental activity, without any supposition of intellectual agency.

5
Nothing we Imagine is Absolutely Impossible

> 'Tis an establish'd maxim in metaphysics, That whatever the mind clearly conceives includes the idea of possible existence, or in other words, that nothing we imagine is absolutely impossible.
>
> (1.2.2.8)

The pattern of cognitive gaps and inferences of the imagination can be extended to Hume's account of two important and closely interrelated modes of conceptual thinking. The first is modality: our ideas of possibility and necessity. Modal ideas, allowing us to consider what could exist or could not fail to exist, are central to ordinary and philosophical cognition and cannot be explained with object representation. Modality thus indicates a major gap in Representational Naturalism and sets an especially pressing explanatory problem. The second conceptual mode is the a priori. Hume holds that, because of our nature, we can only represent objects a posteriori, by ideas causally dependent on impressions of sensation and sharing their qualities. However, we do have a priori knowledge of arithmetical truths and of the simplest truth of geometry. And some conclusions of the science of human nature rely on a priori principles and are relatively a priori. Hume's philosophy must therefore account of the a priori in order to make good its own presuppositions. Such account is internally linked to that of modal ideas, in particular to the distinction of metaphysical and physical modalities. Both rely on the imagination to achieve the naturalization of conceptual thinking and further Hume's anti-rationalist programme. My discussion is in three parts. In the first I outline the cognitive gap of modality and Hume's approach to modality in terms of conceiving and imagination. I also distinguish two fundamental kinds of modality-constituting transitions of the imagination. In the second, I examine Hume's distinction of two kinds of modality, metaphysical and physical, which is of fundamental importance for all his philosophy. I also discuss the conceptual and epistemic status of Humean modalities. Finally, in the third part, I examine Hume's recognition and explanation of the a priori in the light of his account of modality.

5.1 Whatever the Mind Clearly Conceives Includes the Idea of Possible Existence

The core of Hume's theory of modality is expressed in his famous dictum.

> 'Tis an establish'd maxim in metaphysics, *That whatever the mind clearly conceives includes the idea of possible existence,* or in other words, *that nothing we imagine is absolutely impossible.* (1.2.2.8)

The Established Maxim has constitutive import: the idea of possible existence is included in—that is, instantiated in and produced by—whatever the mind clearly conceives. The Established Maxim thus commits Hume to a conceivability claim about modality: what we can conceive is connected in a crucially important way (which I leave for now unspecified) to possibility. The relevant kind of conception is by the imagination: it is not restricted to the First Principle but formed according to the Second Principle. The idea of possible existence is not to be explained as the representation of an object. Hume's theory thus belongs to the family of the Conceivability accounts of modality—it is in fact the first account that attempts to reduce modality to conceivability in a thorough way.[1]

5.1.1 The Cognitive Gap of Modality

Conceivability accounts of modality have been endorsed since Descartes and are central to our contemporary views of modality. Hume's Established Maxim is distinctive because it primarily expresses a doctrine about the nature and possibility of modal content, rather than an epistemological one. According to Descartes, the ultimate ground of modal qualification are the essences or natures of things, inherently endued with modal force and represented by clear, distinct, and adequate ideas. The rationalists, who do not restrict representation to sensible actuality, are ready to admit objects of representation—like forms, essences, natures—with an in-built modal dimension defining an a priori space of possibilities. We have intellectual representations of such objects and it is only because of this that conceivability is relevant for possibility. (The analysis of the content of our idea of a piece of wax, in the second of the *Metaphysical Meditations*, is the exemplary case.) The conceivability of certain ideas unveils what is possible with regard of certain objects because these ideas represent the modal (necessary,

---

[1] 'Hume employs this principle with great conviction, telling us both that it is a necessary truth and that it is impossible seriously to deny it', T. Holden, 'Hume's Absolute Necessity', *Mind*, 123, 2014 (377–413), 388.

essential) properties they have.[2] Today's discussions of conceivability and its forms, implications, and validity focus on the epistemological question whether it is a safe guide to what is possible.[3]

By contrast, the Established Maxim, Hume's imagination-based version of conceivability, gives expression to a fundamental, constitutive account of modal content, of the modal articulation of our ideas and cognitions. A difficulty for the interpretation of Hume's theory of modality is that, differently than in the case of generality, Hume does not address modality in a compact text or sequence of texts. (This might be because Hume's theory of general ideas is firmly and explicitly embedded in the tradition of Locke and Berkeley while, in discussing modality, Hume is largely breaking new ground.) Still, it is possible to argue that Hume recognizes a modality gap. Hume's account of modality has bottom-up character: it is driven by and comes to expression in the discussion of plurality of specific, modality-involving problems, which are pervasive and important in Book 1. Important examples are general ideas;[4] the ideas of space and time;[5] the idea of

---

[2] This is precisely Descartes's position: conceivability does not count as a constitutive criterion of modality; it rather unveils what is per se, as a matter of God's creation, possible or necessary. It represents, does not constitute, necessity. 'Non quòd mea cogitatio hoc efficiat, sive aliquam necessitatem ulli rei imponat, sed contrà quia ipsius rei, nempe existentiae Dei, necessitas me determinat ad hoc cogitandum' ('Meditatio Quinta', in *Oeuvres de Descartes*, Volume 8, 67; 'It is not that my thought brings his [God's] existence about, or that it imposes any necessity on anything, but, on the contrary, that the necessity of the thing itself, namely the existence of Good, determines me to think it', 'Fifth Meditation', in *Meditations on First Philosophy*, 48). See 'Descartes. Modal Metaphysics', in *The Stanford Encyclopedia of Philosophy*, 25–6 (the author of the voice is D. Cunning). Kripke may be read as holding that the modal intuitions on the basis of which we stipulate whether something holds in a possible situation give us direct knowledge of irreducible modal facts, see M. Della Rocca, 'Essentialism versus Essentialism', in Gendler & Hawthorne, *Conceivability and Possibility* (223–52), 233. But of course Hume's anti-representationalism about modality can be set against a whole tradition of philosophy of modality. The traditional paradigms of statistical modality (temporal frequency: necessity as always being, possibility as being sometimes); of possibility as potentiality; and of referential multiplicity (possible worlds) are all, more or less directly, realistic: the thought of possibility is modeled after an objective order of things or some objective condition. See S. Knuuttila, *Modalities in Medieval Philosophy*, Routledge, London/New York 1983, especially chapters 1 and 4. See A. J. Vaidya, 'Modal Knowledge: Beyond Rationalism and Empiricism', in B. Fisher & F. Leon, eds., *Modal Epistemology after Rationalism*, Springer 2017 (85–114), 89: 'The core idea [in Descartes' Conceivability] is that clear and distinct perception of modality provides one with knowledge of modality.'

[3] See, of course, the articles collected in T. Gendler & J. Hawthorne, eds., *Conceivability and Possibility*, Clarendon Press, Oxford 2002; and other literature quoted in the footnotes of this chapter. Expressivists about modality of different, Humean and non-Humean sorts, like Blackburn, Brandom, Gibbard, and Price, are of course the exception.

[4] 'It has been establish'd as a certain principle, that general or abstract ideas are nothing but individual ones taken in a certain light, and that, in reflecting on any object, 'tis as impossible to exclude from our thought all particular degrees of quantity and quality as from the real nature of things' (1.3.14.13).

[5] 'Our system concerning space and time consists of two parts, which are intimately connected together. The first depends on this chain of reasoning. The capacity of the mind is not infinite; consequently no idea of extension or duration consists of an infinite number of parts or inferior ideas, but of a finite number, and these simple and indivisible: 'Tis therefore possible for space and time to exist conformable to this idea: And if it be possible, 'tis certain they actually do exist conformable to it; since their infinite divisibility is utterly impossible and contradictory' (1.2.4.1).

cause;[6] the uniformity of nature and induction;[7] psychophysical interaction;[8] as well as external existence and personal identity. In these contexts, Hume resorts to modal claims precisely to establish that our ordinary cognition and worldview involve elements unavailable by the First Principle.[9] The modal character of the ideas involved in these cognitive contexts is therefore fundamental for the individuation of limits to object representation. Quite generally, the kind of representation of objects that is possible and fundamental for our nature is modally blank (as we have seen in § 2.4.3). What we can primitively represent are only existent particulars, in their actual fixed order and connection. This kind of content is prior in the order of explanation and indispensable to our minds but it is not susceptible to modal variation and does not support modal thinking. Any idea or mental activity the content of which includes some modal dimension is thus out of the scope of object representation. In fact, modal considerations seem to be the most general ground of Hume's identification of cognitive gaps.[10]

Thus, talk of a cognitive gap of modality in Hume's philosophy is perfectly in order, at least in the sense that modal considerations are systematically at work in the identification of most if not every cognitive gap. Correspondingly, the Established Maxim summarizes Hume's account of how modal cognitive gaps are closed: the idea of possible existence is included in whatever we clearly conceive; modal ideas, ideas of possibility and necessity, derive from some sort of transition involving such clear conceptions. Since the relevant conceptions are formed by the imagination, not received by sense and memory, Hume's conceivability does not presuppose the representation of possibilities and can complement object

---

[6] 'The separation, therefore, of the idea of a cause from that of a beginning of existence, is plainly possible for the imagination; and consequently the actual separation of these objects is so far possible, that it implies no contradiction nor absurdity' (1.3.3.3).

[7] 'Our foregoing method of reasoning will easily convince us, that there can be no *demonstrative* arguments to prove, *that those instances, of which we have had no experience, resemble those, of which we have had experience*. We can at least conceive a change in the course of nature; which sufficiently proves, that such a change is not absolutely impossible. To form a clear idea of any thing, is an undeniable argument for its possibility, and is alone a refutation of any pretended demonstration against it' (1.3.6.4).

[8] 'But as this latter conclusion [that position of bodies cannot produce motion] is contrary to evident experience, and as 'tis possible we may have a like experience in the operations of the mind, and may perceive a constant conjunction of thought and motion; you reason too hastily, when from the mere consideration of the ideas, you conclude that 'tis impossible motion can ever produce thought, or a different position of parts give rise to a different passion or reflection' (1.4.5.30).

[9] Actually, as we will see, modal considerations are applied recursively to identify cognitive gaps at the different layers of content or idea construction in Book 1 and to define how the imagination can close them. Here I concentrate on how the fundamental cognitive gap of modality in representation and on the content-constitutive role of conceivings and transitions of the imagination.

[10] Kail ('Conceivability and Modality in Hume', *Hume Studies*, 29, 2003, 43:6, 57) is right that the rejection of non-sensory representation is a posteriori. But it is a physical impossibility, which is the status of the strongest, relatively a priori conclusions of the science of man; there is no justification for accepting it. See, for a (highly qualified) defense of Hume's conceivability approach to modality, P. Millican, 'Hume's Fork and his Theory of Relations', *Philosophy and Phenomenological Research*, 95, 2017, (3–65), 33–7.

representation in this respect. By expressing the natural response to a natural limit of object representation, the Established Maxim is, as anticipated, not primarily an epistemological but a content-constitutive principle. The radical cognitive changes consisting in modalization are wholly owing to the imagination, Hume's faculty of modality. Hume's non-representational cognitive faculty is the imagination. By bringing modal contents, with regard to their individuation and constitution, under the scope of imagination, Hume makes room for arguments of Conceivability that close the gaps modalities open in representation.[11]

5.1.2 The Established Maxim: Content and Point

At the most basic level, imagination makes room for modal variation by its *detached conception* of ideas. Modal thinking consists in considering some subject matter for how it could be or for how it could not fail to be, rather than for how it actually is. In Hume's philosophy, this minimally requires the conception of perfect ideas. The hold on the mind of forceful and fixed impressions and ideas of memory constitutes our sense of reality. The detached and loose conception of perfect ideas by the imagination makes room for a sense of possibility, that what is actually so could be otherwise.[12] The Second Principle is correspondingly tailor-made to explain our capacity for offline thinking, which contemporary discussion also identifies as a basic cognitive function of imagination. Detached conception is thus the threshold of our natural modal competence.[13]

---

[11] See on Conceivability accounts of modality, T. Gendler & J. Hawthorne, 'Introduction', in Gendler & Hawthorne, *Conceivability and Possibility*, (1–70). S. Yablo, 'Is Conceivability a Guide to Possibility?', *Philosophy and Phenomenological Research*, 53, 1993, (1–42), especially in its Part X, accepts a moderate constitutive claim about imagination and modality. Of two contrasting alternatives—'(1) one cannot imagine an X unless it already appears to one that an X could exist; and (2) to imagine an X is thereby to enjoy the appearance that an X could exist'—it is the second that gives the point of Conceivability. I pause to remark a curious strabismus in Hume-related and imagination-focused discussions of modality: philosophers who give emphasis to Humean anti-realism about modality (Blackburn and Price) tend to neglect the mechanisms of imagination that generate modal contents; those who concentrate on the contribution of imagination to modal thinking (Gregory, Kung, and Williamson) neglect (or reject) the constructed character of modal contents. I find philosophically and interpretively important to keep the two perspectives together.

[12] See Blackburn, 'Morals and Modals', 64.

[13] Hume's imagination-based account of modal content bears *some* similarity to the recently advanced idea that modal thinking emerges primarily in the form of counterfactual reasoning, which is in turn an exercise of imagination. (See T. Williamson, The Philosophy of Philosophy, Blackwell, Oxford 2007, 134–178; see B. Kment, 'Counterfactuals and the Analysis of Necessity', *Philosophical Perspectives*, 20, 2006, (237–302), who however relies on explanatory reasoning rather than on imagination; but of course, for Hume such reasoning *is* an exercise of the imagination.) Hume's imagination is our natural faculty of counterfactual reasoning, by which we move from represented objects and situations to only conceived ones and then to views of how things could be or could not fail to be. The same principles and the same mental phenomena determine how we form and how we develop these suppositions. This somehow reminds us of Williamson's counterfactual-based modal epistemology; and even of Kment's emphasis on ordinary cognitive practices. Hume's theory, of course, is primarily about what puts in place modal ideas. But if we look at the link it establishes

Against the background of the conception of perfect ideas, the overall content and point of the Established Maxim can be articulated (and to some extent reconstructed) in terms of four inferences of conceivability: (1) Impossibility/Inconceivability; (2) Conceivability/Possibility; (3) Inconceivability/Impossibility; (4) Possibility/Conceivability. At least two of them, (3) and (4), are highly controversial, even disreputable. The content-constitutive reading of conceivability which I am giving of Hume's theory of modality allows us to make sense of all of them and (to some extent) of Hume's express or tacit acceptance of them. It is all-important, in this respect, to keep in mind that Hume's conceivability inferences are not to idea-comparing reasonings, much less formal entailments. *Once we have modally qualified and directly modal ideas available, our modal thinking can take the character of deductive reasoning, according to schemes just listed.* From this viewpoint, such inferences are pairwise logically equivalent by contraposition and share their logical properties. But the Established Maxim and the conceivability inferences are rather articulations of the work with which the imagination, primarily in its more limited part but operating as a whole faculty, puts in place modal components of content. It is only from this viewpoint that we can properly understand and assess Hume's version of Conceivability, as well as the point of different conceivability inferences.

(1) *Impossibility/Inconceivability*. This conceivability inference makes its appearance in the discussion of generality. Having claimed that it is absurd to suppose that a triangle can exist without a precise proportion of sides and angles, Hume says:

> 'Tis a principle generally receiv'd in philosophy, that every thing in nature is individual, and that 'tis utterly absurd to suppose a triangle really existent, which has no precise proportion of sides and angles. If this therefore be absurd in *fact and reality*, it must also be absurd *in idea*. (1.1.7.6)

---

between counterfactual thinking and modal thinking, we can see that this recent, important work on imagination, counterfactuals, and modality also takes a step in that direction. A main claim is that counterfactuals are logically equivalent to modal claims, so that the cognitive capacities that support our framing and assessing counterfactuals also explain our possession and mastery of modal concepts. Of course, there is no hint to modal logic in Book 1 and Hume's resorting to the imagination aims at a naturalistic reduction of modality. But the aim of providing psychological room and cognitive grounding for modal contents is shared by Hume and the counterfactual account. See T. Kroedel, 'Counterfactuals and the Epistemology of Modality', *Philosophers' Imprint*, 12, 12, July 2012, which gives importance to explaining the ability to make correct modal judgments as the byproduct of a more useful ability that is implemented more easily and has naturalistic, evolutionary grounds (2–3). This is a view that Hume certainly could endorse. Kroedel doubts that principles of logical equivalence can explain the epistemological connection between counterfactual reasoning and modalities. Rather, one should look at joint evaluation of beliefs about counterfactuals and modal beliefs, within the same cognitive processes (5–6). This is also an idea that Hume might accept.

The fact that a certain object cannot exist determines a failure to form the corresponding idea. This is the first strand of Hume's conceivability. The claim seems right: an impossible condition is one we cannot form a conception of in our minds, as an object or possible existent. (We can form a conception of it only in the sense that we may have an application of it in reasoning, like supposing it for reductio.) Of course, impossibility in fact or reality must be conceptually aligned with the right sort of inconceivability. In Hume's theory, there is a basic distinction between kinds of possibilities, with corresponding principles of conceivability, that is, sources in the imagination (see § 5.2.1). Impossibility involves inconceivability only relatively to this distinction. What we may call, following Hume, metaphysical impossibility is not problematic: absurdity in fact or reality deprives the mind of the capacity to form any idea at all. We can imagine we have such idea; but this is an illusion and a source of false philosophy. Other impossibilities require careful treatment. According to Hume, it is impossible for two objects to be such that, unless the one existed, the other would not exist. However, we seem to be perfectly able to conceive of such a condition. Impossibility thus would not imply inconceivability.

Rather than seeing this as a counterexample to the Impossibility/Inconceivability inference, we should simply recognize here a welcome consequence of Hume's naturalism and dualism about content and of his anchoring modalities on transitions of the imagination. This case would be a counterexample to the inference from impossibility to inconceivability if and only if the conception were object-representing. The conceivability of dependence relations between objects would then either be illusory (an illusion of content) or contradict the corresponding Impossibility/Inconceivability inference. And Hume, in his account of causal ideas, regards such relations as perfectly conceivable. The way out from this difficulty is that the conceptions we have of the relations of dependence among objects are not object-representing but by the imagination (see § 6.1.5). Now, conception by the imagination, differently from object representation, can be aspectual, intentionally directed, and (potentially) conceptual. Therefore, the two conditions of conceivability, if they are by the imagination, can address the same situation in different ways: more precisely in relation to the individuating features of their objects or to how such objects figure in ways the empirical world can be. Such conceptions are neither contradictory nor illusory and relate to different kinds of possibility (see § 5.2.1). Therefore, we can safely conclude, from the impossibility of a certain condition, that we cannot conceive any corresponding idea. This has application, for instance, in the detection of cognitive gaps.

(2) *Conceivability/Possibility*. As interpreters of Hume, we are centrally interested in this conditional, which immediately follows (1) in the text.

> Since nothing of which we can form a clear and distinct idea is absurd and impossible. But to form the idea of an object and to form an idea simply is the

same thing; the reference of the idea to an object being an extraneous denomination, of which in itself it bears no mark or character. (1.1.7.6)[14]

What is clearly and distinctively conceivable is not absurd and impossible. Again, we do not have to read this as a formal entailment or, in Hume's theory, a comparison of ideas. This pattern of inference is logically equivalent by contraposition to the preceding one. However, in the context of the Established Maxim, the two inferences have different roles and positions. This inference, as Hume formulates it, is best understood in terms of Two Viewpoints. We can form or conceive an idea; a certain idea, with certain qualities, can exist in our minds. The qualities with which the idea exists in the mind are also the properties of its content. A conceivable idea, we suppose, can individuate an object or existent: its properties of content can be the properties of an object or existent (if it is at least a potentially representational idea). An effect of such a conceiving is that we form a conception of the possibility of the object which forms its content. (This is by a quality of the more limited imagination, see § 5.1.3).

This is Hume's Conceivability at its clearest: it is a claim about how we come to have the idea of a *possible object*. The importance of this conceivability inference is also that it manifests what is prior in explanation ('since'): the non-modal content and the positive fact of conceiving an idea explain, with an act of the imagination, the modal qualification of the content of the idea thus conceived. In the quoted text, Hume seems to restrict conception to at least potential object representation and possibility to metaphysical possibility or simple possible existence. But the claim can be extended to ideas which include non-object-representing contents and to the corresponding physical possibilities. Hume is committed to the view that ideas of causal relations are conceivable and that it is possible for distinct existents to be causally related; and the first view is the cause of the second. Since the conceivability of causal ideas certainly is not exhausted by the conceivability of objects, Hume must hold that Conceivability/Possibility inferences can extend beyond the limits of object representation. This inference is therefore the main constitutive explanation of our modal contents.

(3) *Inconceivability/Impossibility*. There are obvious and general problems with this inference. Inconceivability might depend on accidental features of our cognitive capacities or positions. The goodness of any inference from inconceivability to impossibility depends on distinguishing between cases in which we fail to have any idea of an object because it escapes us from cases in which failure of conception indicates a flaw in the content of that idea. In the latter but not in in the former case, failure of conception allows inferring impossibility. Therefore, it is easy

---

[14] 'Whatever can be conceiv'd by a clear and distinct idea necessarily implies the possibility of existence; and he who pretends to prove the impossibility of its existence by any argument deriv'd from the clear idea, in reality asserts, that we have no clear idea of it, because we have a clear idea' (1.2.4.11).

to find counterexamples to this conceivability inference. However, I think that Hume has a use and a place for this conceivability inference, as a content-constitutive transition.[15]

The Inconceivability/Impossibility inference is not problematic if a conception is inconsistent or contradictory in its content. In this case, conceiving fails because it targets a content which is absurd or impossible. This blocks the act of conception, barring some illusion (but then the condition of clear conception is not satisfied); thereby, it blocks any further step toward viewing its (purported) content as possible. We fail to recognize any possibility. Hume explicitly commits to this species of inference of possibility when it involves a contradiction: 'We can form no idea of a mountain without a valley, and therefore regard it as impossible' (1.2.28). The Inconceivability/Impossibility inference in this way would be restricted to logical inconceivability. However, I think that this specification of the inference is too restrictive for the modal needs of Hume's philosophy. Restricting Inconceivability/Impossibility to contradictory contents does not match the diversity of modal gaps, tasks, and arguments that structure Hume's theory.

Hume's arguments in Book 1 typically aim to establish what ideas we have available on the basis of some Impossibility/Inconceivability inference. For instance, if no objects are such that one cannot exist without the other, we cannot have ideas of objects so related. Or, if no objects can exist externally and be specifically different from impressions, we cannot have such idea of external existence. Or, if no object can be strictly identical across change, we cannot have such idea of identity. This is Hume's method for identifying cognitive gaps: we proceed from some condition on objects that cannot be satisfied and conclude that perceptions with such condition for content cannot exist. There is, correspondingly, a gap in our minds (bundles of perceptions). Now, in order to conclude that certain conditions on objects cannot obtain, as the ground for the Impossibility/Inconceivability inferences that detect cognitive gaps, we must engage in some Inconceivability/Impossibility inference. We have to assess whether it would be possible to conceive (to have the idea of) a certain object: whether a certain at least potentially object-representing content can be formed. If such an idea is inconceivable, we can conclude to the impossibility of the content or object. Therefore,

---

[15] D. Tycerium Lightner, 'Hume on Conceivability and Inconceivability', *Hume Studies*, 23, 1, 1997, 113:132, 114–22, denies that Hume is committed to the Inconceivability/Impossibility inference. Hume only endorses weaker Inconsistency/Impossibility arguments (what Tycerium Lightner calls Contradiction), alongside the Conceivability/Possibility. Tycerium Lightner's careful discussion seems, however, to miss what I take to be Hume's main concern. This is also the position endorsed by Millican, 'Hume's Fork', 37. For an account of these issues closer to mine and from which I have learnt see Holden, 'Hume's Absolute Necessity', 389–91; see, for a contrasting view (about inconceivability), Ainslie, *True Scepticism*, 175–6 (however, Ainslie's treatment of Separability, 166–73, is closer to my overall take on Hume's modalities, if without my focus on the corresponding cognitive gaps).

Inconceivability/Impossibility inferences embed Impossibility/Inconceivability ones, in the context of Hume's individuation of cognitive gaps.

Notice that by proceeding in this way Hume would not move in a circle. Two Viewpoints secures the conceptual differences between the terms of the inferences, the objects and ideas, which make them viable and informative. Impossibility/Inconceivability inferences proceed from perceptions viewed in their contents, that is, from the objects individuated by those contents, to a conclusion about ideas considered as mental existents: we cannot conceive, form, or have such ideas. Hume explicitly endorses these inferences: 'whatever conclusions of this kind [about their connexion and repugnance] we form concerning objects, will most certainly be applicable to impressions' (1.4.5.20). By contrast, Inconceivability/Impossibility inferences proceed from ideas as mental existents, that is, from (failed) acts of conception or idea-formation, to conclusions about objects individuated by the content of such (purported) ideas (such objects cannot exist). Hume does not commit fully and generally to these latter inferences ('any conclusion we form concerning the connexion and repugnance of impressions, will not be known certainly to be applicable to objects', 1.4.5.20). But since this combination of conceivability inferences seems to be fundamental to Hume's arguments throughout Book 1, rightly because it is the most general way to identify cognitive gaps, some Inconceivability/Impossibility inferences must be possibly good. To make these arguments work, some wide condition determining whether ideas are inconceivable would be required.

Hume's text leaves this matter seriously underdetermined. And there is scarcely any *explicit* mention (much less a principled statement) of this conceivability inference in Book 1.[16] But what has just been said points to the need Hume has for Inconceivability/Impossibility inferences that do not depend on the contradictory character of certain ideas. I think that the case can be made that Hume *implicitly* resorts to such an inference in connection with his arguments for the finite divisibility of space and time. Hume draws this conclusion by explicitly resorting to Inconceivability/Impossibility: 'The plain consequence is, that whatever *appears* impossible and contradictory upon the comparison of these ideas, must be *really* impossible and contradictory, without any farther excuse or evasion' (1.2.2.1). What appears impossible and contradictory, or inconceivable, are 'parts of extension' 'inferior to some ideas, which we form', our minimal ideas of extension. The inconceivability of such parts makes us conclude that they are impossible; that the division of space or extension comes to an end. The point to discuss is whether the inconceivability, which is the ground for the modal conclusion, is by inconsistency or contradiction (and the ensuing impossibility is a

---

[16] See Millican 'Hume's Fork', 38–39, about the lack of good evidence for interpretive choices, with the need to resort to arguments *e silentio*. The 'mountain without a valley' implies a contradiction on Millican's reading of it: 'a mountain (i.e. a slope up) without a valley (i.e. a slope down)'.

metaphysical one). Hume, of course, explicitly talks of what appears 'impossible and contradictory'. But we should look closely at the context. The reasons for the inconceivability of ideas of sub-minimal parts of extension, that is, for the non-existence of such ideas, are, of course, strictly connected to those for the existence of ideas of minimal parts of extension. I would even say that the logical status of the former is the same as that of the latter. Now, Hume derives his argument for the existence of ideas that represent minimal parts of extension from a necessity of our cognitive nature. What secures that such ideas exist is the a posteriori fact (given by Hume at 1.2.1.3–5) that there is a limit to the phenomenal size of ideas of extension. At that threshold, right at the limit beyond which such ideas would not be perceived any more, the content they represent is a minimal part of extension (see, for a full discussion, § 8.1.2). The conceivability of ideas with such content thus depends on our cognitive nature. Therefore, the inconceivability of ideas inferior to that threshold does not depend on any inconsistency or absurdity they would imply, but on a necessity of our cognitive nature, of the nature of our visual experience. The limit to conception is not set by any intrinsic property of the object space (there is no such object) or by any intrinsic property of spatial objects but by the nature of visual experience and imagination. Therefore, there is no inconsistency in the thought of an object that is smaller than one represented by a minimal idea (1.2.1.2). But an idea with a content smaller than such a minimal idea is inconceivable: such content cannot be formed by our mind. On this basis, we can infer what is *really* impossible from what *appears* impossible (thereby, is inconceivable). The inconceivability is not by logical necessity, but relatively a priori. All other ideas of extension are composed out of such minimal ones; therefore, Inconceivability/Impossibility holds generally of spatial ideas and objects.[17]

Hume's identification of cognitive gaps does not necessarily involve contradictions: a vacuum, sui generis external objects, real powers, and connexions are inconceivable not by being inconsistent but by falling short of the causal and phenomenal conditions that would make of them the contents of ideas. At the same time, there are non-representational ideas in the same areas—ideas of a vacuum, of external existence, of a necessary connexion—which we can have and use in

---

[17] I thank Don Garrett and a reader for OUP for prompting me to clarify my view of this difficult interpretive point. (With what success, I don't know.) Millican, 'Hume's Fork', 37, asks and answers in the affirmative whether Hume countenances matters of fact that are not distinctly conceivable. I agree that he does, but in the sense that Inconceivability/Impossibility inferences also hold of ideas of matters of fact and of the corresponding conditions on objects. Hume also claims that beings with cognitive faculties different from ours might come to know physical possibilities that escape us and vice versa (*E* 2.7; see, for a different but related point, *Dialogues*, 9.6). But this epistemological restriction leaves intact the constitutive point that the satisfaction of certain naturalistic conditions on representation and conception (as realized, instantiated, in the human faculties of sensibility and imagination) are necessary and sufficient to put in place modal contents and belief. And the exercise of our faculties of idea-formation is the ground for safe if defeasible inferences to modal conclusions.

our reasonings rightly in the ways deployed in our good cognitive practices. I tentatively conclude that Hume has a use for Inconceivability/Impossibility and construes it in a way that is wide enough for that use and hedged enough to resist some obvious objections.[18]

(4) *Possibility/Conceivability*. This inference is generally and rightly rejected. It does not follow from something being possible in fact and reality that we have a conception of it. We might never have thought of it. It does not even follow that we can have a conception of it. It might be something out of the reach of our cognitive capacities. I am not aware that Hume accepts this inference and applies it. This inference is also highly problematic in his philosophy. In order to conclude with generality and without circularity from possibility to conceivability we should have access to conditions of possibility independently from conceivability. But this would raise vexing metaphysical and epistemological questions. There would have to be some sort of representational access to modality to come to know what is possible. This would go against Hume's conception of representation and would anyway make unrealistic assumptions about our cognitive capacities. Notice that we could not solve or sidestep this problem by distinguishing and aligning different modes of conceivability and possibility: the problem has to do with the core of Hume's philosophy, his theory of the natural limits of representation. Still, there could be conceptual room in Hume's philosophy, for an implicit commitment to Possibility/Conceivability. Possibility is *sufficient* for conceivability if conceivability is *necessary*, in a constitutive sense, for possibility. Possibility/Conceivability inferences would give expression to the Established Maxim as a fundamental explanation of the idea of possible existence; they would be meta-theoretical principles of modality. If clearly conceiving something includes the idea of its possible existence, if this is the only way in which modal contents are available at all, then the possibility of an object is certainly sufficient for its conceivability. The content-constitutive rather than epistemological reading of Hume's Established Maxim thus supports, if only to different degrees, all the conceivability inferences he accepts or could accept.[19]

5.1.3 Imagination and Modality: Separability and Determination

Hume's programme is to naturalize modal contents and explain their import for cognition, by discovering the underlying mental mechanisms. He identifies two principles of the imagination that explain the transitions holding together

---

[18] This could be used to correct the view that Hume has examples of inconceivability without impossibility; see Tycerium Lightner, 'Conceivability and Inconceivability', 122–5; Millican 'Hume's Fork', 39–40.

[19] See, on the constitutive rather than only evidential role of Conceivability, Holden, 'Hume's Absolute Necessity', 394–7.

conception and modality. These principles also define two different kinds of modal concepts, deployed in our ordinary and philosophical cognition. Hume thinks that philosophers have not recognized this difference and this has been the source of much confusion.

The first principle of production of modal contents is Separability.[20] Hume introduces Separability, just as he does with the Established Maxim, in the context of his theory of abstraction.

> We have observ'd, that whatever objects are different are distinguishable, and that whatever objects are distinguishable are separable by the thought and imagination. And we may here add, that these propositions are equally true in the *inverse,* and that whatever objects are separable are also distinguishable, and that whatever objects are distinguishable are also different. For how is it possible we can separate what is not distinguishable, or distinguish what is not different?
> (1.1.7.3)

Hume resorts to this principle—in the direct and converse form—at many places in Book 1. For instance, when discussing the finite divisibility of space;[21] the denial of the idea of a vacuum;[22] the rejection of the a priori principle that a cause is always necessary;[23] the rejection of a priori causal necessity;[24] the redefinition of the unity of things and of the idea of substance;[25] and the account

---

[20] See Garrett, *Cognition and Commitment*, 58–75.

[21] 'What consists of parts is distinguishable into them, and what is distinguishable is *separable*. But whatever we may imagine of the thing, the idea of a grain of sand is not distinguishable, nor *separable* into twenty, much less into a thousand, ten thousand, or an infinite number of different ideas' (1.2.1.3). 'A real extension, such as a physical point is suppos'd to be, can never exist without parts, different from each other; and wherever objects are different, they are distinguishable and *separable* by the imagination' (1.2.4.3).

[22] 'For as every idea, that is distinguishable, is *separable* by the imagination; and as every idea, that is *separable* by the imagination, may be conceiv'd to be separately existent; 'tis evident, that the existence of one particle of matter, no more implies the existence of another, than a square figure in one body implies a square figure in every one' (1.2.5.3).

[23] 'Now that the latter proposition is utterly incapable of a demonstrative proof, we may satisfy ourselves by considering, that as all distinct ideas are *separable* from each other, and as the ideas of cause and effect are evidently distinct, 'twill be easy for us to conceive any object to be non-existent this moment, and existent the next, without conjoining to it the distinct idea of a cause or productive principle. The separation, therefore, of the idea of a cause from that of a beginning of existence, is plainly possible for the imagination; and consequently the actual separation of these objects is so far possible, that it implies no contradiction nor absurdity; and is therefore incapable of being refuted by any reasoning from mere ideas; without which 'tis impossible to demonstrate the necessity of a cause' (1.3.3.3).

[24] 'There is no object, which implies the existence of any other if we consider these objects in themselves, and never look beyond the ideas which we form of them. Such an inference wou'd amount to knowledge, and wou'd imply the absolute contradiction and impossibility of conceiving any thing different. But as all distinct ideas are *separable*, 'tis evident there can be no impossibility of that kind. When we pass from a present impression to the idea of any object, we might possibly have separated the idea from the impression, and have substituted any other idea in its room' (1.3.6.1).

[25] 'Hence the colour, taste, figure, solidity, and other qualities, combin'd in a peach or melon, are conceiv'd to form *one thing*; and that on account of their close relation, which makes them affect the

of the independent existence of perceptions.[26] In all these cases, the activity of more limited imagination is expressed in the modal qualifications of certain ideas: whether spatial minima *can* be extended; whether material objects *can* exist independently; whether objects and events *must* be causally connected; whether there *can* be unity across diversity; and whether objects and perceptions *can* be the same.[27]

By Separability, the imagination moves from what is conceivable as an object to its possibly existing as object, independently, 'in fact and reality'. Of this sort is the argument showing that all perceptions can exist independently.

Whatever is clearly conceiv'd may exist; and whatever is clearly conceiv'd, after any manner, may exist after the same manner. This is one principle, which has been already acknowledg'd. Again, every thing, which is different, is distinguishable, and every thing which is distinguishable, is separable by the imagination. This is another principle. My conclusion from both is, that since all our

---

thought in the same manner, as if perfectly uncompounded. But the mind rests not here. Whenever it views the object in another light, it finds that all these qualities are different, and distinguishable, and *separable* from each other; which view of things being destructive of its primary and more natural notions, obliges the imagination to feign an unknown something, or *original* substance and matter, as a principle of union or cohesion among these qualities, and as what may give the compound object a title to be call'd one thing, notwithstanding its diversity and composition' (1.4.3.5).

[26] 'Our perceptions are all really different, and separable, and distinguishable from each other, and from every thing else, which we can imagine; and therefore 'tis *impossible* to conceive, how they can be the action or abstract mode of any substance' (1.4.5.27). 'But farther, what must become of all our particular perceptions upon this hypothesis? All these are different, and distinguishable, and *separable* from each other, and may be separately consider'd, and may exist separately, and have no need of any thing to support their existence' (1.4.6.3). ''Tis still true, that every distinct perception, which enters into the composition of the mind, is a distinct existence, and is different, and distinguishable, and *separable* from every other perception, either contemporary or successive' (1.4.6.16).

[27] Hume's Separability has a clear predecessor in Descartes. In the *Sixth Meditation* Descartes argues for the distinct existence of body and mind on the basis of our clear and distinct understanding of the one without the other. 'Et primò, quoniam scio omnia quae clare & distincte intelligo, talia a Deo fieri posse qualia illa intelligo, satis est quòd possim unam rem absque alterâ clare & distincte intelligere, ut certus sim unam ab alterâ esse diversam, quia potest saltem a Deo seorsim poni.' ('Meditatio Sexta', *Oeuvres de Descartes*, Volume 8, 55; 'First, since I know that whatever I clearly and distinctly understand can be produced by God such as I understand it to be, then if I can clearly and distinctly understand one thing without another, this is sufficient for me to be certain that the one is distinct from the other, since they can at least be produced separately by God', 'Sixth Meditation', *Meditations on First Philosophy*, 55.) The reference to God's power is inessential ('& non refert a quâ potentiâ id fiat, ut diversa existimetur'), because it only serves to mark that actually co-instantiated entities can possibly exist independently. Descartes clarifies his principle in the 'Replies' to the First Objections, where he insists that he has in mind a 'real distinction', rather than a 'modal one': a distinction between substances and not modes and substances ('Primae Responsiones', *Oeuvres de Descartes*, Volume 8, 120–1; 'First Objections and Replies', *Meditations on First Philosophy*, 83–4). This has further emphasis in the 'Reply to the First Part' of the Fourth Objections. Here Descartes makes it clear that inference to real distinction does not require an adequate knowledge but only a 'complete' one, that is, that we understand them enough to know that they are complete, self-standing things: substances. And that things can be complete, or substances, even if they are incomplete in relation to a unity which they form with some other substance, which is 'a single entity in itself'. (Reference to God's power again simply expresses the modal import of the clam.) ('Quartae Responsiones', *Oeuvres de Descartes*, Volume 8, 220–8; 'Fourth Objections and Replies', *Meditations on First Philosophy*, 140–7.)

perceptions are different from each other, and from every thing else in the universe, they are also distinct and separable, and may be consider'd as separately existent, and may exist separately, and have no need of any thing else to support their existence. They are, therefore, substances, as far as *this* definition explains a substance. (1.4.5.5)

Notice how Hume distinguishes Separability from the Established Maxim while embedding the first into the second. Possibility is grounded on conceivability; a specific condition on conceiving is the ground of a distinctive way of being possible. Separability allows us to move from how we conceive the contents of impressions to the possible distinct existence of objects represented by ideas that depend on those impressions.

In order to know whether any objects, which are join'd in impression, be separable in idea, we need only consider, if they be different from each other; in which case, 'tis plain they may be conceiv'd apart. Every thing, that is different, is distinguishable; and every thing, that is distinguishable, may be separated, according to the maxims above-explain'd. If on the contrary they be not different, they are not distinguishable; and if they be not distinguishable, they cannot be separated. (1.2.3.10)

It is important to consider how the imagination works in Separability. Separability realizes the Established Maxim in relation to the conditions for object representation. Difference is a way of existing: it is to exist as a self-standing, individual particular. Separation, in this context, is a property of conception: it is the reciprocal independence of ideas as to their contents and presence to the mind. Distinction mediates difference and separation because it is the presentation of differences to the mind. To distinguish, I would say, insofar as it is not simply to record or mirror real, observed differences, is to treat them as potential grounds for further cognitive steps. (This is not necessarily or even primarily reflective or explicit.) To separate is to take one such step: to exert the liberty of imagination, by the Second Principle, in telling apart distinguishable ideas and transposing them. Actual impressions or objects contribute contents to the ideas representing them and make such ideas exist. Such contents and the corresponding perfect ideas, being different and distinguishable, can be separately conceived. The separate conception extends to the objects or existents the ideas represent. Therefore, we come to conceive of such objects as separately existing, as existing by themselves, however, they are present in impressions of sensation. This condition of conceivability is owing to the imagination (it presupposes cognitive detachment) and is supported by Two Viewpoints (we move from a condition on contents to one on ideas to a further one on contents) and by Equivalence (impressions and ideas representing them are equivalent to objects as to their contents).

At first sight, one might suppose that only simple impressions and ideas realize the condition of Separability. Hume might seem to restrict to them the condition of separate conception and existence ('all our ideas are copy'd from our impressions, and...there are not any two impressions which are perfectly inseparable', 1.1.3.4; notice the reference to the First Principle, which only necessarily applies to simple perceptions). He also seems to restrict inseparability to simple perceptions: distinctions of reason, which exclude separation, apply to 'what formerly seem'd, and really is, perfectly inseparable', the features of simple perceptions (1.1.7.18). This, however, would be too thin a representational basis for modality-constituting transitions of the imagination that we are now considering. Per the Important Footnote, both simple and complex contents fall under our conception of ideas. It thus makes sense that we can conceive of either of them in the same modal terms and on the same grounds. In fact, Hume provides for an extension of Separability to complex contents with a distinction between kinds of relations of ideas.[28]

> These relations may be divided into two classes; into such as depend entirely on the ideas, which we compare together, and such as may be chang'd without any change in the ideas. 'Tis from the idea of a triangle, that we discover the relation of equality, which its three angles bear to two right ones; and this relation is invariable, as long as our idea remains the same. On the contrary, the relations of *contiguity* and *distance* betwixt two objects may be chang'd merely by an alteration of their place, without any change on the objects themselves or on their ideas; and the place depends on a hundred different accidents, which cannot be foreseen by the mind. 'Tis the same case with *identity* and *causation.* Two objects, tho' perfectly resembling each other, and even appearing in the same place at different times, may be numerically different: And as the power, by which one object produces another, is never discoverable merely from their idea, 'tis evident *cause* and *effect* are relations, of which we receive information from experience, and not from any abstract reasoning or reflection.   (1.3.1.1)

This text combines, in a complex pattern, considerations of logic (Hume's logic: the nature of ideas) and epistemology (how we 'discover' what) with modal points (what 'may be chang'd' in ideas or objects) and points about the a priori (about 'information' from 'abstract reasoning or reflection'). The crucial step connects the nature of relations of ideas with modality and Separability. Certain relations of ideas—internal relations—strictly depend on the identities of the related ideas, individuated by their qualities both as to content and as to existence in the mind. These relations are '*resemblance, contrariety, degree in quality,* and *proportions in*

---

[28] I doubt that the contrast drawn in H. Beebee, *Hume on Causation*, Routledge, London/New York 2006, 26, between comparisons of ideas and inferences from one idea to the other goes very deep.

quantity or number' (1.3.1.2). This dependence on the identity of ideas makes it so that such ideas cannot be clearly and distinctly conceived without their standing in such relations to other ideas. More precisely: given that we conceive of them at all with such relations, given that we form the corresponding complex ideas, they cannot be clearly and distinctly conceived in any different way.[29]

The point now is to see how this condition on conception can produce a modal qualification of ideas. Thinking of objects as separately existing in relation to their distinct conception as different is not yet to think of them in modal terms: it is not to think of their possibility or impossibility. Modal import is a further and distinct feature of contents and we still have to see how Hume accounts for it on the basis of Separability. The crucial consideration is that the conditions defined by Separability, the alignment or lack of alignment of difference, distinction, and separation, besides defining conditions of conception, influence the imagination also in a different way, which only bears on its more limited part. By the Structural Principle, the more limited imagination is a part or function of the imagination, which interacts with perceptions in ways that respond to their contents but are not reducible to them. In the case of modality, the structure of contents and conceptions defined by Separability can ease, hinder, or block the imagination in its forming ideas of objects or existents. This depends on whether difference, distinction, and separation are aligned: whether we conceive separately of contents that are present to the mind as distinct, because of the difference of their objects. The ease or difficulty of such conception is conscious; it is experienced or felt. This consciousness or experience, in turn, comes to be conceived as the possibility of the contents considered; as the possible existence of the conceived objects. Hume is far from specific about the conditions and character of this conception, which, however, is in the scope of the Important Footnote. (I give some details about how a transition of ideas can turn into a feature of content, along Hume-friendly lines, in § 7.2.3).

The ease or difficulty of a conception with contents regimented by Separability is a phenomenon that makes sense only in connection with the imagination, as described by the Structural Principle. In particular, it is the more limited imagination, a capacity for mental conceptions and transitions marked by biases and susceptible to intransitivities, which seems to be susceptible to effects of ease of its processes. Conception by understanding or as involved in idea-comparing reasoning only mirrors the structures of its contents. Such conception, again considered only in relation to its contents, can be logically more or less complex, without being more or less difficult. (In this sense, it is not difficult to conceive or form an idea with inconsistent content.) By contrast, engaging in such conception with the imagination, which is a properly mental, psychological activity, can be

---

[29] This is a point of debate between D. Owen, *Hume's Reason*, 103–5 and H. Beebee, *Hume on Causation*, 24–32.

easy or difficult. (Hume is here drawing on a traditional theme in the philosophy of the imagination, the quasi-bodily character of the imagination itself, famously revived by Descartes.)[30] The experience of the ease of conceiving an idea and its object (by Separability) causes a further transition of the more limited imagination, to conceiving of such object as something that could well be the case; as something not excluded from being or reality. Per the Important Footnote, a mental transition like that is present to the mind by simple conception, as a change in the conception of an idea. The perfect idea of an object, which is the same with that of its existence, comes thus to be qualified as a possibility. Conversely, we take and treat as possible what we can easily conceive as separately existing, by forming a clear idea of it as a distinct object or particular.

The contrapositive is also important. Attempted conceptions of ideas by the imagination, under the conditions of Separability, can fail to individuate objects existing by themselves. This may be because we attempt to conceive separately what is neither different nor distinct (a mountain and its valley) or to form one idea of what is different and distinct (the shape and the taste of a fruit). The conditions of Separability are not satisfied and this blocks the activity of the imagination in conceiving contents and forming the corresponding ideas. The awareness of this block comes to conception as the exclusion of such contents from reality. The more limited imagination turns its experience of the failure of a conception into the modal qualification of the objects of relevant ideas as impossible. These transitions of ideas of the more limited imagination are the link that connects Separability to the modal qualification of ideas. To sum up: ideas with at least potentially object-representing contents and abiding by Separability (difference, distinction, and separation are aligned) are easily conceived by the imagination. The experience of such easiness causes the more limited imagination to conceive as the possibility of the objects of those ideas. Ideas contravening Separability are not conceivable and such a block of conception causes the imagination to conceive the relevant contents as impossible, as excluded from existence. Non-Mixture secures that ideas with those modal qualifications go on referring to their objects; that such ideas do not lose themselves in the interaction with the imagination. Modal contents by Separability therefore primarily take the form of qualifications of ideas of objects.[31]

---

[30] See *Meditationes de Prima Philosophia*, 72–3 (*Meditations of First Philosophy*, 51–2).

[31] The role of imagination in producing modal contents by Separability outlines an answer to the objection that the latter principle fails for entities composed of parts. The whole is different and distinguishable from each of its parts but cannot be separated in thought or reality from any of it, since the 'proper idea' of the whole includes such parts (see P.D. Cummins, 'Hume on Possible Objects and Impossible Ideas', in Easton, *Logic and the Workings of the Mind* (211–27), 218–19; Cummins rejects the objection, on grounds different but consistent with mine). This depends on whether the proper idea is representational or imaginative—involving and determined by modality-constituting inferential transitions. In the first case, of course, the modal issue of separation, in contrast with the existential one of difference, does not even arise. But in the second case, we can perfectly well form the idea

This is summarized in the following extracts, the second of which also introduces a further modality-producing principle of the imagination.

> Whatever is absurd is unintelligible; nor is it possible for the imagination to conceive any thing contrary to a demonstration. (1.3.7.3)
>
> Thus as the necessity, which makes two times two equal to four, or three angles of a triangle equal to two right ones, lies only in the act of the understanding, by which we consider and compare these ideas; in like manner the necessity or power, which unites causes and effects, lies in the determination of the mind to pass from the one to the other. (1.3.14.23)

Separability is only one of the modality-constituting principles of the more limited imagination; it does not exhaust the modal needs of ordinary and philosophical cognition. There are intuitively in order and theoretically important modal ascriptions not explainable by Separability: the possibility of minimal spatial and temporal perceptions and parts of space and time and the relations of dependence between objects are examples. Hume's explanation of them resorts to a different reason why conceptions of ideas are easy or difficult and the corresponding experience moves the more limited imagination to conceive their contents as possible or impossible.

Where the 'absolute necessity' issuing from Separability does not take place, 'the imagination is free to conceive both sides of [any] question' (1.3.7.3). This is, paradigmatically, the case of causal ideas.

> The separation, therefore, of the idea of a cause from that of a beginning of existence, is plainly possible for the imagination; and consequently the actual separation of these objects is so far possible, that it implies no contradiction nor absurdity; and is therefore incapable of being refuted by any reasoning from mere ideas; without which 'tis impossible to demonstrate the necessity of a cause. (1.3.3.3)

But this does not mean that the imagination cannot be determined to conceive in one way or the other. Quite the contrary, causal ideas are modally qualified, precisely because of a channelling of the activity of the imagination in conceiving of ideas.

> Either we have no idea of necessity, or necessity is nothing but that determination of the thought to pass from causes to effects and from effects to causes, according to their experienc'd union. (1.3.14.22)

---

of wholes as possibly existing without one of the parts; and this modal content—if genuine—unveils a metaphysical possibility.

160 NOTHING WE IMAGINE IS ABSOLUTELY IMPOSSIBLE

This explanation of modalities is the same in general style with Separability. To think of something as necessary is to find it difficult to conceive of a situation in which it fails to obtain or to be compelled to conceive of it as obtaining. To think of something as possible is to find no such difficulty or compulsion; rather, it is to find easy to conceive of situations in which it fails to obtain, under the supposition that it actually obtains; or situations in which it obtains under the supposition that it actually does not obtain. But the principle of the imagination at work is not Separability. Rather than to the alignment or failure to align of difference, distinction, and separation, the more limited imagination responds, with respect to the easiness or difficulty of its conceptions, to other properties of mental existence and contents of ideas, like their repetition and resemblance.

> For after a frequent repetition, I find, that upon the appearance of one of the objects, the mind is *determin'd* by custom to consider its usual attendant, and to consider it in a stronger light upon account of its relation to the first object. 'Tis this impression, then, or *determination*, which affords me the idea of necessity.
> (1.3.14.1)
>
> In like manner the necessity or power, which unites causes and effects, lies in the determination of the mind to pass from the one to the other.   (1.3.14.23)

Drawing on these texts, I will dub this modality-constituting principle, alternative to Separability, Determination. By Determination, the conceptions of the imagination can be channelled, made easy or difficult, in more than one context and by a variety of imaginative propensities: sensitivity to repetition; cognitive inertia; the shift between resemblance of ideas and of mental acts; and drives to complete relations. Given that the experience of easiness or difficulty of conception causes a transition of the more limited imagination from the conception of ideas to that of the possibility of their objects, this makes for a variety of respects in which contents come to have modal features (of course, not all of them have an equally good epistemic standing). Determination is philosophically important, because it explains how we can have ideas of necessity that are wider and ideas of possibility that are narrower than those explained by Separability and how modal force can come in degrees. The central case in which this sort of modality-constituting mechanism is at work is that of causal necessity, of course. But also the ideas of a vacuum, of external existence, and of the identity of self are shot through with modal elements, which must be explained along similar lines (and certainly not by Separability). We will study the different ways in which Determination figures in Hume's theory as we progress.[32]

---

[32] We must keep modal ascriptions totally distinct from beliefs. We can ascribe modal force without thereby forming beliefs about the possible or necessary condition; just as we can form non-modal beliefs. In Hume's philosophy, belief diverges from the detached conception of perfect ideas as a sense

Hume is sparing in the details about the process that produces modal contents. On his account, a property of conceiving (the experience of its easiness or difficulty) causes a further conception and becomes a property of what is conceived. Such experiences are distinctively cognitive: difficulties in conceiving, or in accepting or even attending what one conceives, but not because of motivational or affective consideration (not a case of imaginative resistance). It is interesting that Hume's explanatory construct in the account of modality, the channelling of the transitions of the imagination by the experience of conceiving the relevant ideas, is amply recognized and studied in contemporary research.[33] A result in contemporary cognitive psychology of imagination is suggestive in connection with Hume's account of modalities. This is the existence and the role of *metacognitive experiences*, of the feelings of easiness and difficulty with which exercises of the imagination can be present to awareness. The phenomenology of imaginative processes can interact with biases that mark them in a favourable or adverse way. But most importantly, the feelings of easiness or difficulty of imaginative processes operate in an effective way as input to the inferences that in their turn determine their cognitive output. Such inferences depend on multiple factors and invest judgements about the likelihood of events, their distance in time and space, the informativeness of a representation. In general, metacognitive experiences modify the contents of imaginings and give and essential contribution to their cognitive import. Metacognitive experiences and the feelings of ease and difficulty in engaging in imaginations have important cognitive effects (to be kept well distinct from imaginative resistance). It is tempting to extend this approach to Hume's account of modality.[34]

---

of the reality of objects or relations of ideas, a forceful manner of conception directly or indirectly caused by the presence of such objects or the obtaining of such relations. By contrast, our sense of possibility and necessity are manners of conception only associated to perfect ideas and grounded on properties of our conception of them. Furthermore, while Hume excludes that belief is a distinct impression annexed to impressions or ideas, modal conceptions are realized in distinct internal impressions, which include feelings of easiness or difficulty. Reasoning and belief formation, of course, can be more or less difficult. But this is usually accountable in terms of content and computational complexity. Imaginative blocks are by contrast topic-specific and less predictable, also with respect to how they shape cognition. Reasoning can in its turn take up some features of imagination, as per the Johnson-Laird theory of mental models. In this case, computational complexity and topic sensitivity will be combined.

[33] See, for an overview and a strictly doxastic-inferentialist approach to imaginative blocks, S. Nichols, 'Imaginative Blocks and Impossibility', in Nichols, *The Architecture of Imagination*, 237, 255. But the theme of the productivity (of the indispensable productivity) of cognitive limitations and biases, which is central for an understanding of the imagination, has taken also different orientations, starting from the pioneering work of D. Kahneman and A. Tversky.

[34] See L. Sanna et al., 'Hard to Imagine: Mental Simulation, Metacognitive Experiences, and the Success of Debiasing', in Markman et al., *Handbook of Imagination and Mental Simulation*, Psychology Press, New York 2009, 197:210, 200–1. This kind of phenomenon is widespread. The phenomenology of simulated mental states makes it possible to process representations of the past and explains false memories (D. Bernstein et al., 'False Memories: The Role of Plausibility and Autobiographical Belief', in Markman et al., *Handbook of Imagination and Mental Simulation*, 89–102, 91, 97–8). It also contributes to explaining the cognitive differences between imaginings referred to the past and to the

5.2 Hume's Philosophy of Modality

Modal contents do not represent objects but express conceptions and transitions of the imagination. Therefore, at the level of their individuation and production, with reference to the Established Maxim, modal contents are mind dependent.

> This therefore is the essence of necessity. Upon the whole, necessity is something, that exists in the mind, not in objects; nor is it possible for us ever to form the most distant idea of it, consider'd as a quality in bodies. Either we have no idea of necessity, or necessity is nothing but that determination of the thought to pass from causes to effects and from effects to causes, according to their experienc'd union. (1.3.14.22)

> The necessity, which makes two times two equal to four, or three angles of a triangle equal to two right ones, lies only in the act of the understanding, by which we consider and compare these ideas. (1.3.14.23)

Therefore, the main philosophical difficulty with Hume's theory of modality is that, if the Established Maxim not only *guides* the use but *constitutes* the contents of modal thinking, this latter seems confined to subjective views about possibility. Modal contents individuated by inferences of the same kind with those that apply them do not seem to define objective conditions of correctness for modal thinking. No divergence seems to be in general possible between the individuation and the application of modal ideas. But Hume is also committed to some sort of modal objectivity: possibilities are ascribed to things, events, and states of affairs, not to our cognitive states; modal error and illusion are held to be possible; what is possible in existence and what is possible only in conception can be distinguished; modal conclusions can have the epistemic status of knowledge. Thus, we have a general and fundamental difficulty with Hume's theory of modality, which threatens to ramify throughout the accounts of generality, space and time, causality, external existence, and the self. This is essentially the same problem we met in Hume's account of generality: how can the application in reasoning of general ideas fail to conform to their contents, if such contents are inferentially determined? Just as in the case of generality, Hume is alert to this problem; also in the modal case, his solution has a broadly naturalistic character: identifying cognitive mechanisms that contingently realize the conceptual conditions deployed by our best practice of modal thinking.

---

future (L. Van Boven et al., 'Temporally Asymmetric Constraints on Mental Simulation', in Markman et al., *Handbook of Imagination and Mental Simulation*, 131–147, 132, 136).

5.2.1 Metaphysical and Physical Possibility

Our conceptions may variously fail to be clear: our awareness of impressions can be weak and uncertain; our ideas can only imperfectly resemble impressions; the transitions of the imagination can be irregular (especially when prompted by resemblance). Hume explicitly recognizes these obscurities in conceiving, which bear on the Established Maxim. But there is also a form of systematic modal error which is not determined by the contingencies of our conceiving but depends on the difference and confusion between two kinds of possibility. The two kinds are metaphysical and physical possibility (as I will call them) and their grounds are, respectively, Separability and Determination. This distinction and the possibility of modal error it opens are an important and original articulation of Hume's philosophy of modality. They are the key to Hume's conception of knowledge and probability and to his treatment of a priori and posteriori reasoning and of scepticism. A clear account of this distinction is one of the advantages of Hume's Inferentialist Naturalism about modality.

Modalities explained by Separability are *metaphysical*. In relation to contents structured by Separability and because of the easiness or block of its conceptions, the imagination moves from conceiving ideas of objects to conceiving the possible existence of such objects simpliciter, that is, without any condition or specification. This follows from the application of the modality-constituting transitions of the imagination to the very idea of existence.

> The idea of existence, then, is the very same with the idea of what we conceive to be existent. To reflect on any thing simply, and to reflect on it as existent, are nothing different from each other. That idea, when conjoin'd with the idea of any object, makes no addition to it. Whatever we conceive, we conceive to be existent. Any idea we please to form is the idea of a being; and the idea of a being is any idea we please to form. (1.2.6.4)

We conceive as existent only individual particulars and we conceive of individual particulars, by their ideas alone, only that they exist. By Separability, we conceive only individual particulars. Therefore, possibilities defined by conceivability by Separability only refer to the existence of objects. It is in this sense that I talk of possible existence simpliciter: our idea of existence simply consists in thoughts of individual particulars; possibilities defined in this way only relate to being.

What we exclude by Separability, we exclude from existence as such, from existence in its most general, barest sense: it is metaphysically impossible. Attempts to move from what is not conceivable as different or distinct to its existing by itself; or from what is the same to its separate conception, are blocked by the very structure of their contents. What is inseparable in existence cannot be conceived as distinct and different; what is conceived as different and distinct cannot exist as the same. To exist as an individual particular is to exist distinctly, that is, as different and independent from anything else. Separability in conception, therefore, anchors modal inferences to the conditions of individuation of objects or existence. The link between Separability, the ontology of objects, and metaphysical possibility is very strict. To fall in modal error or illusion in this domain is to be mistaken or deluded just about what there can be.[35]

In calling this kind of possibility metaphysical, I take a clue from something Hume says about effects taking place without their causes.

> The mind can always *conceive* any effect to follow from any cause, and indeed any event to follow upon another: whatever we *conceive* is possible, at least in a metaphysical sense: but wherever a demonstration takes place, the contrary is impossible, and implies a contradiction.   (*Abstract* 11)

In this text Hume is applying the Established Maxim to causal relations and claiming, on grounds of conceivability by Separability, that it is possible for effects to follow from any given cause or, in general, for any event to follow upon any other. This is to say that individual causal relations are not necessary, because the same causes could produce different effects and vice versa. On the other hand, as it is well known, Hume is committed to causal necessity ('the necessity or power, which unites causes and effects', 1.3.14.23). This is sufficient, by itself, to show that Hume does not mean to deny the modal force of causal relations but rather to tell apart a kind of modality on which they are necessary from one on which they are contingent 'at least in a metaphysical sense'. This notion of modality by Separability Hume contrasts with causal necessity and calls 'metaphysical'. Hume is far from consistent in this nomenclature. Mostly he describes Separability-grounded modalities as 'absolute' (1.2.3.14; 1.3.6.5; 1.3.7.14; 1.3.9.10; 1.3.14.13), occasionally pairing the two descriptions ('we may easily conceive, that there is no absolute nor metaphysical necessity, that every beginning of existence shou'd be attended with such an object', 1.3.14.35). However, I want to reserve 'absolute' for a different employment (see § 5.2.2).

---

[35] Think also of the following. A principle of Hume's metaphysics (one he says is 'generally receiv'd in philosophy') is that 'every thing in nature is individual' (1.1.7.6), which means (given that any natural individual particular is a sensible object or impression) that it must be 'determin'd in its degrees both of quantity and quality' (1.1.7.4). Supposing that some qualitative or quantitative feature of an object or perception 'in its real existence' can be indeterminate 'implies the flattest of all contradictions, viz., that 'tis possible for the same thing to be and not to be' (1.1.7.4). This is because that quantitative or qualitative feature could be and not be of a certain degree. To avoid this flat contradiction we must assume that all individual particulars, objects, and perceptions, can only exist distinctly and separately. Otherwise, if they existed not-separately, they would share some qualitative or quantitative feature; and such feature, being common to more objects or perceptions, would be a universal and could take different degrees. In this sense, Separability gives access to possible existence as such or simpliciter.

Physical modalities complement the metaphysical ones. The Established Maxim constitutively individuates them but not by Separability but by Determination. This is a principle of the more limited imagination that responds to non-representational properties of perceptions like repetition, order, distribution in time, intricacy, and resemblance with mental acts. These properties go beyond the individuation of particulars, either perceptions or objects. The non-object-representing ideas produced by transitions of the more limited imagination, like empty space and time, causality, external existence, and personal identity, essentially include modal dimensions. Hume is in a position to explain this. There is no general reason why we should not conceive clearly at least many of these ideas once we do not take them for representations of objects. Since such conceptions are by the imagination, they are likely to be experienced as easy or difficult, to channel the transitions of the imagination, and to give place to something like metacognitive experiences. In this way, they come to be possible as to their modal dimensions. With some hesitation, I call this second kind of Humean modality *physical*—principally because it is appropriate to express the possibilities and necessities which mark the natural mind and the world of bodies. Hume explicitly identifies causal necessity with physical necessity: "'Tis the constant conjunction of objects, along with the determination of the mind, which constitutes a physical necessity' (1.3.14.33). Modal ascriptions based on the mechanism of Determination may depend on propensities of the more limited imagination different from repetition and custom; however, the status of causal modalities is epistemically special (see § 12.2.2).[36]

A fundamental difference between Hume's physical and metaphysical modalities lies in what they qualify. In the case of metaphysical possibility, what is in question is possible existence simpliciter, the possible being of an individual particular (thing, event, or trope) or its non-exclusion from existence. Possible existence simpliciter is based on qualitative individuation and marks the outer limits of what can be thought as a possibility; reciprocally, what does not count as possible in this sense cannot be conceived at all as an object. The contents that are qualified by physical modalities differ from those of metaphysical possibility. What can count as physically possible are objects considered not simply as to their individuation and existence (the two conditions, in Hume, are equivalent), but as to their extrinsic qualities and relations, durations, and positions. Their identities are not in question. What we conceive of, as a physical possibility, is

---

[36] The distinction of these kinds of conceivability and modality is clearly connected to the distinction between representation by copying and by causal role drawn by Schafer, 'Hume's Unified Theory', 16–17 (this distinction is related to my distinction between representational and inferential content of ideas). The first presents the individuating features of objects; the second, their relations, or formal or structural aspects of the contents of ideas. This is close to the distinction between modalities dealing with the possible existence of individual particulars and modalities expressing general ways of the world.

some way of being of the empirical world. Some examples of such possibilities are (as we will see): whether certain objects could have certain spatial and temporal properties; whether a body could be located at certain place without moving the bodies around; whether certain objects would constantly and uniformly succeed one another; whether and how an object would influence another one; whether an object would be present if not observed; whether a person would have existed at certain times. What is in question is not whether some objects, with certain individuating qualitative specifications, can exist: this metaphysical possibility is presupposed. What comes into question with the idea of physical possibility is whether metaphysically possible objects can have certain further qualities, relations, locations, and durations.[37] Hume's distinction between kinds of modality is therefore substantive: a difference between the ways modal contents are produced by the imagination, between the subject matter and role of modal ideas, and between degrees of modal force.[38]

The distinction between metaphysical and physical modalities is, together with the First Principle, Hume's most important tool of philosophical criticism. Hume resorts to the distinction for giving expression to complex cognitive possibilities. For instance, causes and effects are separately conceivable and necessarily connected. Separate conception is the ground for the metaphysical possibility of their distinct existence: nothing is missing for these objects to exist by themselves. The necessity of their connection supervenes on their regular succession in the empirical world, which is the cause of the relevant modality-constituting inferences. To confuse such necessity and such possibility is to mistake the nature itself of causation. Something similar holds of external existence. By Two Viewpoints, there is a distinction of reason between objects of sense and impressions considered in their contents. This distinction fails to determine by Separability the metaphysical possibility of the different existence of objects and perceptions: their double, separate individuation and reality. By parity of reason, Equivalence fails to establish the metaphysical possibility that objects and perceptions be the same as to

---

[37] Hume's doctrine of the 'seven different kinds of philosophical relations' (1.3.1.1) is relevant here. Such relations can be divided 'into such as depend entirely on the ideas' and 'such as may be chang'd without any change in the ideas'. Conceiving of objects in terms of relations of ideas that constrain the ideas of them, and thereby the identities and the distinctness of their relata, has implications for their metaphysical possibility. External relations of ideas or objects, by contrast, are, so to say, pure relations, which can obtain or fail to obtain independently of the individuation of objects. These latter express how objects figure together in the systems of realities, rather than what they are or how they exist at all and are the subject matter of physical possibility. See, for an alternative account of the distinction of metaphysical and physical possibility, Boehm, 'Hume's Foundational Project', 13: objects whose inconceivability does not consist in a contradiction are not absolutely impossible but only relatively to us.

[38] See Kment, 'Counterfactuals and the Analysis of Necessity', 251–55, for discussion of the theoretical importance of distinguishing different degrees of modal force. Kment also argues that metaphysical, nomic, and conceptual necessity (the former two somehow corresponding to Hume's physical necessity, the third to his metaphysical one) are all absolute, differing only for degree along one single dimension of modal force (256–8, 266).

existence. This latter, the identity of objects and perceptions, is a metaphysical possibility but Hume establishes it on the different ground of the clear and distinct idea of external existence. At the same time, it is physically necessary that what are metaphysically the same things, perceptions and objects, exist, respectively, within or without the mind (see § 9.4.1). Finally, the successive and variable perceptions that constitute a mind are distinct and different. This makes the attempt to conceive of them as inseparably connected in a distinct, separable self or as inherent to it void. This idea of self is a metaphysical impossibility. But the perceptions that exist in a causally (and functionally) connected bundle succeed each other as a matter of physical necessity. On this basis, an idea of self as a causal system of perceptions, united by identifying transitions of the imagination, is conceivable and a physical possibility (see § 10.2.3).

The distinction of metaphysical and physical modalities is also the basis for an account of modal error and illusion. This matters enormously for Hume's theories of causation, the external world, and personal identity, which in crucial part consist precisely in disentangling modal errors and confusions. Of course, the possibility of modal error and illusion does not amount to modal scepticism. Once we are in possession, by inferences of conceivability, of the ideas of metaphysical and physical possibility, we can have reflective access to, examine, and correct our modal ascriptions, paying attention to the nature of their different objects and of the principles of imagination. This is, in itself, non-problematic in Hume's science of man; in fact, correcting such errors is one of its aims.

5.2.2 Absolute and Epistemic Possibility

We can address the objectivity and the epistemic import of Hume's modalities directly. The distinction of metaphysical and physical possibility is not one between objective and subjective modalities. With an eye to contemporary theorizing about modality and to recent interpretations of Hume, I will characterize the second distinction as one between absolute and epistemic modalities.[39] My claim is that not only in Hume's philosophy the two distinctions do not coincide, but that there is no robust sense in which modalities are epistemic. Hume's theory is committed to different grounds of exclusion of possibilities and to different degrees of modal force; but this commitment does not amount to a difference in terms of absoluteness or objectivity. Metaphysical and physical possibilities should be contrasted not in point of objectivity or absoluteness but

---

[39] Having reserved 'metaphysical' for modalities that abide by Separability, I am here employing 'absolute' to express an objective, non-subject relative notion of modality. This Hume also calls metaphysical; and it is so called in the discussion originating in Kripke. The reader should keep this well present.

on grounds of inferential conditions, subject matter, and degree of force. Doing otherwise would disrupt Hume's philosophical practice of combining in the same arguments physical and metaphysical modalities, as well as his treating physical modalities (that articulate the ideas of space and time, causality, external existence, self) as objective and susceptible to differential epistemological status. In general, saddling Hume with an epistemic reading of modalities would expose him to a threat of wholesale first-order scepticism, which is rightly one of his aims to avert.[40]

Hume is explicitly opposed to what one could regard as an epistemic approach to physical necessity: conditioning it (in its best instance, causal necessity) to some specific viewpoint. He denies that there are deep distinctions to draw within causal necessity. He contends that 'all causes are of the same kind'. There is no foundation for the distinction of efficient, formal, material, and final causation causes: 'our idea of efficiency is deriv'd from the constant conjunction of two objects', so that, 'wherever this is observ'd, the cause is efficient; and where it is not, there can never be a cause of any kind' (1.3.14.32). He then proceeds, by the 'same course of reasoning', to the conclusion 'that there is but one kind of *necessity*, as there is but one kind of cause, and that the common distinction betwixt *moral* and *physical* necessity is without any foundation in nature' (1.3.14.33). It is interesting to take a closer look at Hume's sketched argument. First, what is the 'common distinction' between moral and physical necessity? If Hume had Leibniz[41] or Clarke[42] in mind, moral necessity is a species of epistemic necessity: it is necessity relative to a subjective viewpoint, in this case, God's practical judgement in planning and creating the world. The point of the distinction is anti-deterministic, in opposition to the determinism of metaphysical necessity. But it is important that this is achieved by a sort of subjective relativization of necessity (if only to that peculiar subject which God is); and this is the core of the epistemic understanding of modality. Therefore, when Hume rejects the distinction of moral and physical necessity (or, in Leibniz's language, metaphysical necessity), he is not only taking a stance for causal determinism but also denying that necessity, physical necessity, can be viewpoint-relative. No 'weakening' of the constitutive factors of physical necessity can change 'the nature of necessity'. This is

---

[40] Garrett, *Cognition and Commitment*, 156–7 (and also 60, fn. 2), suggests distinguishing between two kinds and notions of absolute impossibility, one based on inconceivability by contradiction and the other expressing the cognitive grip of complete uniformity and proof. The former is what I call metaphysical impossibility, the latter, physical impossibility. As Don Garrett has reminded me, at *Enquiry*, 10.27 (181), the causal or physical impossibility of miracle is qualified as 'absolute'.

[41] See M. J. Murray, 'Pre-Leibnizian Moral Necessity', in *The Leibniz Review*, 14, 2004 (1–28).

[42] 'For this is a necessity, not of nature and fate, but of fitness and wisdom; a necessity, consistent with the greatest freedom and most perfect choice. For the only foundation of this necessity is such an unalterable rectitude of will, and perfection of wisdom, as makes it impossible for a wise being to resolve to act foolishly; or for a nature infinitely good, to choose to do what is evil', S. Clarke, *A Demonstration of the Being and Attributes of God: More Particularly in Answer to Hobbes, Spinoza, and their Followers*, James Knapton, London 1705, 140.

because such factors are perfectly objective. 'As objects must either be conjoin'd or not, and as the mind must either be determin'd or not to pass from one object to another, 'tis impossible to admit of any medium betwixt chance and an absolute necessity' (1.3.14.33). Notice how the determination of the mind, the mental source of physical necessity, is on a par with the constant conjunction of objects and, therefore, does not per se make for an epistemic relativization of necessity. Of course, causal necessity can be ascribed only on the basis of our experience; but once ascribed, it does not hold only relatively to our experience.

The objective, absolute status of physical possibility also emerges in Hume's complex explanation of probable reasoning in presence of a 'contrariety of past experiments' (1.3.12.13). The core of Hume's explanation are the claims that 'there is no probability so great as not to allow of a contrary possibility' and that 'the component parts of this possibility and probability are of the same nature, and differ in number only, but not in kind' (1.3.12.15). The combination of these component parts determines what belief we form about a single future event. The important point is that Hume is here combining two notions of modality: the physical necessity that is involved in the contents of causal judgements or probable cognition and the metaphysical possibility that such contents fail to hold. In Hume's argument, these two notions of modalities, one of which is by construction absolute, are on a par and are treated as both consisting of perfectly objective constituents, single experiments, combined imaginatively but in an objective, additive, and mechanical fashion so as to produce a cognitive 'compound effect' (1.3.12.17). This is an indication that Hume regards all modal ideas as equally susceptible to absolute, non-epistemic application and import.[43]

Taking a step back, we should recognize that it is very difficult to track down a notion of strictly epistemic modality in Hume's philosophy. The epistemic–absolute distinction is in general controversial and multifarious.[44] The only sense in which we can strictly talk of epistemic possibilities in Hume and contrast them

---

[43] See, on the non-epistemic character of Hume's conception of modality, Millican, 'Hume, Causal Realism, and Causal Science', 676–84. See Cummins, 'Hume on Possible Objects and Impossible Ideas', 217: '[Conceivability] is a maxim of metaphysics. The possibility of a state of affairs which can be perspicuously conceived is what Hume called absolute possibility and the impossibility of perspicuously conceiving an absolute impossibility is itself absolute. Even if one could form a simple idea without having a prior corresponding impression, one could not perspicuously conceive an absolute impossibility'. Garrett, 'Hume on Causation', 87, rightly remarks that the subjective source of causal necessity is consistent with the mind-independence of the causal relations in re, if these latter are fixed in actuality as what produces the impression of determination.

[44] We find in contemporary discussions of modality themes that are relevant for the interpretation of Hume. See, for one non-obvious instance, S. Roca-Royes, 'Conceivability and De Re Modal Knowledge', Nous, 45, 2011, 22:49, 32–3. In the course of a thorough critical discussion of Conceivability modal epistemologies, Roca-Royes holds that Conceivability can be addressed and discussed without having to decide about its epistemic or non-epistemic character (see § 6.2.2), if its non-modal assumptions (the contents of the conceiving) have the explicit character of 'pretenses' or imaginations. This fits with Hume's neither epistemic nor non-epistemic view of Conceivability, as I am outlining it.

with absolute possibilities is a sense in which *both* metaphysical and physical possibilities count as absolute and in which the modal force borne by epistemic positions is questionable.[45] To see this, keep in mind that the Established Maxim and Separability are introduced, at 1.1.7, rightly in order to *deny* that abstraction involves separation and that general contents, the contents of general ideas, are conceivable as objects or existents. At the same time, however, Hume, *by his own account*, formulates general content in modal terms. 'The abstract idea of a man represents men of all sizes and all qualities; which 'tis concluded it cannot do, but either by representing at once all possible sizes and all possible qualities, or by representing no particular one at all' (1.1.7.2). Hume even explains generality in modal terms, while denying that the Established Maxim applies to its case. 'Tho' the capacity of the mind be not infinite, yet we can at once form a notion of all possible degrees of quantity and quality, in such a manner at least, as, however imperfect, may serve all the purposes of reflection and conversation' (1.1.7.2). The only way I see to make sense of Hume's claims is to understand the possibilities that form the contents of our general ideas as merely epistemic, as different viewpoints we can take on the same objects or ideas; or as the targets of our selective attention. Not as something that could exist by itself. The same holds of Hume's doctrine of distinctions of reasons or abstract modes.

> The difficulty of explaining this distinction arises from the principle above explain'd, *that all ideas, which are different, are separable*. For it follows from thence, that if the figure be different from the body, their ideas must be separable as well as distinguishable; if they be not different, their ideas can neither be separable nor distinguishable. (1.1.7.17)[46]

Still, distinctions of reasons seem to constitute genuine conceptions and to include, or at least to entail, modal conditions that appear to be perfectly in order. To think of the figure as distinct from the body, when they are actually the same, is to think of possible situations in which they diverge, that is, say, of situations where this figure or this colour belongs to a different body (two different bodies with the same shape or colour). These possibilities cannot be established by Separability because there are no differences and distinct existences to be separated; and Determination and physical possibility seem to be out of the question. We should then consider them as merely epistemic, as differences that bear in some respects on our cognition, without individuating alternative conditions or ways of being. Therefore, there is room in Hume's philosophy for distinctly

---

[45] Picking up a useful label from Kment, 'Varieties of Modality', in *The Stanford Encyclopedia of Philosophy*, 1.1, we can thus say that Hume is a *monist* about epistemic and absolute modality.

[46] 'By an action we mean much the same thing, as what is commonly call'd an abstract mode; that is, something, which, properly speaking, is neither distinguishable, nor *separable* from its substance, and is only conceiv'd by a distinction of reason, or an abstraction' (1.4.5.26).

epistemic possibilities and for a distinction of epistemic and absolute possibilities. But it is a distinction between, on the one hand, possible beings or ways of being, metaphysical and physical possibilities and, on the other, differences in our cognitive positions or even focus. Hume takes care to keep them apart and to restrict proper modal import, metaphysical or physical, to the first. Of course, whether our specific modal claims, and the modally qualified ideas they are based on, are sound will depend on the actual way of working of the imagination in the different contexts and cases. In this respect, as we will see, there is large room for diversity, for illusion and error, even in relation to what are broadly the same content-constituting mechanisms. But we are not in principle confined to subjective, merely epistemic modalities.

5.2.3 Humean Modalities and Sceptical Realism

The sceptical realist reading of Hume has taken more than a step in the opposite interpretive direction. The Kripkean apparatus of absolute and epistemic modalities has not escaped the attention of interpreters who aim to individuate in Hume's philosophy, consistently with its other commitments, a layer of robust realism (about causal powers, about external existence). The problem is that Hume seems to commit with the Established Maxim to a conceivability account of modality and that, on this ground, he argues against real connections and the non-identity of objects and perceptions. The response to this has been that Hume's philosophy turns out to be hospitable to entities usually regarded as alien to it, like real connexions of objects or the double existence of objects and perceptions, if the modal claims against them are restricted to epistemic modality. Realism about powers and representational realism and Conceivability can be reconciled by resorting to something like Kripke's distinction of epistemic and absolute modality. We cannot conceive of such powers or existence and therefore we cannot assert their possibility, only in that we are in no evidential or experiential position to do this. But we can form notions that allow us to conceive of them and thus to assert their absolute possibility. The limits of our experience and modal cognition are not the limits of what is conceivable and possible. Of course, we are not in a position to frame any determinate, qualitative conception of real causal powers or double existence; but still we can conceive of them in such a way as to commit to such possibilities as absolute.[47]

---

[47] See, for an exemplary statement of this position, Kail, *Projection and Realism*, 89–90, 93–4, 96–8. Both there and in an earlier discussion ('Conceivability and Modality in Hume', *Hume Studies*, 29, 2003 (43–61), 51–2) Kail frames the contrast of absolute and epistemic modality with reference to the adequateness or inadequateness of impressions of sensation as representations of external objects. This is unfortunate since, at the fundamental explanatory level at which modal contents are determined, impressions do not stand for external objects and do not in general represent objects but

The crucial move in the sceptical realist interpretation is thus that of ascribing to Hume a distinction of absolute and epistemic modality and of articulating his Conceivability accordingly. I have already given reasons to doubt that there is a robust distinction of absolute and epistemic modalities in Hume's philosophy. Therefore, I doubt that Hume's conceivability arguments against real powers and the numerical difference of objects and perceptions can be restricted to cognitive positions. Hume's Inferentialist Naturalism explains modalities, ultimately, in terms of the contents of ideas, the conditions of their conception by the imagination, and the transitions of this latter. But this explanatory apparatus is consistent with denying that what this excludes or includes are cognitive positions rather than objects or ways the empirical world can be. Furthermore, the Kripkean distinction of absolute or metaphysical and epistemic possibilities essentially depends on rigid designation. But rigid designation presupposes non-descriptive reference and this latter collides with Hume's thorough descriptivism (as we have seen in § 2.4.3). Lastly, it is not clear what the ground and the status of Humean absolute modalities would be if they were contrasted with the epistemic ones. Kripke's absolute modalities are the expression of principles of essentialism, about identity, natural kinds, and theoretical identifications, which determine the corresponding (metaphysical, in Kripke's language) necessities. But the sceptical realist cannot accept essentialism and drop Conceivability without parting ways with Hume's philosophy.[48]

A second move one could attempt is to preserve something of a conceivability account of modality by connecting the Established Maxim with conceptions of objects kept to a minimum of content. For instance, relative ideas (Strawson) or some non-idea constituted 'notion' or 'knowledge' or 'understanding' of what would be to be acquainted with what is not a possible object of acquaintance (self, causal power) (Kail).[49] The textual basis for this move (and for the ensuing understanding of absolute modalities) is sparse, to say the least.[50] I think that the sceptical realist interpretation here faces a dilemma. Any account of modality in terms of Conceivability, both epistemological and content-constitutive, involves constraints on conceiving that contribute to explaining the modal force of its conclusions. Such constraints include non-normative ones like the objectual character of the content of conceptions (Yablo and Gregory) or their positive rather than

---

rather are objects. The focus of Kail's discussion is defending the meaningfulness of what he calls the 'Bare Thought', the thought of powers or necessity residing in the objects (which would be known a priori and whose contrary would be inconceivable). In view of the capacities for reasoning Hume includes in the imagination, I do not think this thought needs special defense. It just does not deliver knowledge or probability.

[48] See A. Mallozzi, A.Vaidya, M. Wallner, 'The Epistemology of Modality', *The Stanford Encyclopedia of Philosophy*.

[49] Strawson, *Secret Connexion*, 51; Kail, *Projection and Realism*, 34–5, 60.

[50] See, for analysis of textual evidence and discussion, Beebee, *Hume on Causation*, 173–225.

negative character (Chalmers).[51] Such constraints are present in Hume as the fact that he ascribes the modality-constituting inferences to the imagination, particularly in relation to its more limited part. This involves that conception figures in the Established Maxim, by Two Viewpoint, primarily under the guise of the mental existence of ideas, that is, of the qualities with which they exist in the mind. The more limited imagination primarily responds to the mental existence of ideas and is a function from their mental existence to the conception and modification of their contents. The qualitative individuation of ideas, their rich, sensorially based phenomenology, is thus an indispensable requirement of Hume's theory of modal content. I doubt that relative ideas or notions satisfy such requirement. Therefore, I doubt that modalities can be absolute and still be individuated or known by Conceivability in the way indicated by the sceptical realist interpretation. To escape this horn of the dilemma, the sceptical realist should make the contents of modality-identifying conceiving much more robust. Then, the threat becomes that of falling back to some sort of essentialist conception of modality: there is some sort of primitive representation of modal matters. This would fall foul of Representational Naturalism.

Furthermore, the qualitative, quasi-perceptual character of ideas can explain how we are involved in our modal imaginations in a way in which we are not with suppositions (as when we assume something for reductio) or with distinctions of reasons. This involvement, while different from credence, seems to be a mark of modal ascriptions and is neatly explained in Hume's theory of modal imagination.[52] The attempt to link conceivability with a notion of what would it be like

---

[51] D. Gregory, 'Conceivability and Apparent Possibility', in B. Hale & A. Hoffman, *Modality. Metaphysics, Logic, and Epistemology*, Oxford University Press, Oxford 2010, 319:341, 320–1. David Chalmers, 'Does Conceivability Entail Possibility?' in Gendler & Hawthorne, *Conceivability and Possibility*, 145:200, 150–152, connects modality with 'positive notions of conceivability' requiring that 'one can form some sort of positive conception of a situation'; this, in turn, 'is to imagine (in some sense) a specific configuration of objects and properties'. On his view, imagination has 'mediated objectual character': it is not strictly a propositional attitude, it is not simply supposing that P. See also M. Balcerack Jackson, 'On the Epistemic Value of Imagining, Supposing, and Conceiving', in Kind & Kung, *Knowledge through Imagination* (41–60), 45–9. To imagine is to have a cognitive attitude not toward a proposition or a sentence, but toward a specific situation or configuration of objects and properties, which 'verifies' such a proposition or sentence, thereby allowing us to imagine *that* so and so. Yablo ('Is Conceivability a Guide to Possibility?', part X) also endorses the objectual, rather than propositional, character of imagination. Propositional imagining proceeds by way of objectual imagining: by imagining an object at a certain location with certain properties, a certain situation. The object or the situation are imagined as determined, as possessing determinates for each of its determinable; but not as determinately imagined, that, with fully specified determinates. This is deeply consonant with Hume's view that imagination is objectual and partial, concrete or qualitative and incomplete. This seems important, because, by tying conceivability to partially described objects, which is something we can assume imagination allows us to do, we can make room for epistemic discoveries and for things turning out in different ways, for cognitive and real variation, which is the core of our (and Hume's) interest in modality. (Tying conceivability to fine-grained items like propositions would not do, I suppose.)

[52] Gendler insists on the crucial role of the 'engagement which distinguishes imagination from mere supposition', which is essentially connected to imaginative resistance (only when there is engagement resistance can arise) and which is difficult to pin down in its 'self-involving' character. Resistance

to be acquainted to what is not an object or impression also conflicts with Hume's modalities being *transparent* and *immediate*. In general, and especially in Hume's case, unless some special subject matter is in question, modal imagination does not include a conception of the subject of conceiving.[53] We seem to read off possibilities and necessities from the consideration of objects. We seem to encounter in experience items like causal powers, external bodies, and persistent selves, which all involve modal qualifications. There is, admittedly, an element of error in this appearance, which is at the root of scepticism and false philosophy. But modalities have unquestionable importance in ordinary and philosophical cognition. This does not sit well with the idea that conceivability is mediated by relative ideas or de se constructs.[54]

It is also important that, by partitioning Humean modalities into absolute and epistemic and by connecting absolute modalities to relative ideas or notions, the sceptical realist reading ends by calling into question the conditions of Hume's modal objectivity. In its production of modal contents, as in general in its content-productive inferences, the more limited imagination preserves the identity of the object-representing ideas it interacts with. There is a strong connection between Non-Mixture and the inferential character of how the imagination produces content and cognition. Now, the identity of ideas endued with cognitive content lies in their qualitative phenomenology. The imagination proceeds in its cognitive working by operating on qualitative ideas of objects and by producing cognitively significant changes in their roles.[55] Generalized or modalized ideas differ in conception (for how they are present to awareness) from particular and non-modalized ones. These differences realize their new cognitive imports in the natural mind. Still, such ideas preserve their core of representational contents, which secure their application to objects. Ideas without a qualitative determination

---

and engagement are closely connected and they seem connected with the productive character of imagination with regard of modality. As Gendler remarks, imaginative engagement is also a form of actual engagement, it shares ordinary conceptual repertoires and appraisals, and can result in 'novel insights about, and changed perspectives on, the actual world', T. Szabo Gendler, 'Imaginative Resistance Revisited', in *Architecture of Imagination*, 149–173, 150–1.

[53] This is also a concern in contemporary discussion of conceivability by imagination. As Yablo, 'Is Conceivability a Guide to Possibility?', remarks, I find p conceivable means: I can imagine a situation *of* which I truly believe that p—not: I can imagine a situation *in* which I truly believe that p: 'Conceiving that p is a way of imagining that p; it is imagining that p by imagining a world of which p is held to be a true description. Thus p is conceivable for me is (CON) I can imagine a world that I take to verify p'.

[54] See M. O. Fiocco, 'Conceivability, Imagination and Modal Knowledge', in *Philosophy and Phenomenological Research* 2007, 364:380, 376–7, for a discussion of two understandings, one intuitive, one pragmatic, of the grounds of modal cognition. Hume is firmly on the pragmatic, mentalist, constructivist side.

[55] Recent theorizing has recognized the importance of qualitative phenomenology as a trait of the imagination that is also relevant for modal thinking. Whatever we imagine, we imagine it, primarily, as a qualitatively specified object with properties and relations; as a situation. See A. Kind, 'Putting the Image back in the Imagination', *Philosophy and Phenomenological Research*, 62, 2001, 85:109; P. Kung, 'Imagining as a Guide to Possibility', *Philosophy and Phenomenological Research*, 83, 2010, 620:663.

would fail to have application; our modal thinking would end up being empty. Furthermore, without the qualitative individuation of modalized ideas one would be at a loss to explain the connection between the systems of reality owing to sense and memory and that owing to judgement, which is Hume's main explanatory target. The qualitatively specification of the ideas of the imagination also lends epistemic authority to the application of the Established Maxim, since such ideas are constrained by and can be compared with those that issue from sense-experience and are supported by the authority of sense and memory. To sum up: Non-Mixture, together with the individuation of ideas by their qualitative phenomenology, give a decisive contribution to the objectivity and reliability of our modal thinking. If the price for identifying a layer of realism in Hume's philosophy of modality were to connect conceivability to relative ideas or notions, rather than to qualitatively specified ideas, it would not be worth paying.[56]

In the modal realism–anti-realism debate, Hume is firmly on the non-realist side. This has been, essentially rightly, the prevalent interpretation of Hume's theory of modality by expressivist, pragmatist, projectivist, and fictionalist philosophers. But it is important to keep present that Hume's modal anti-realism is primarily addressed against representational views of modal contents: it is a theory of how such contents are supplied by the imagination. Not a theory of how such contents are applied. In this respect, Hume is firmly on the objectivist and epistemologically realist side. Furthermore, modal contents are cognitive from the start (this is true of imaginative contents generally). There is an authoritative, non-realist reading of Hume, which insists that the contents that fill up what I am calling cognitive gaps start with non-cognitive roles, associated with non-cognitive attitudes. Kemp Smith and Stroud are classic exponents of this reading; Blackburn—only to some extent—and Price—more decidedly—give philosophical articulation to it.[57] If what I am saying is on the right track, the detour via a

---

[56] In a recent, well-crafted discussion, Peter Kung has proposed a qualified defense of the role of imagination in modal epistemology that speaks to some aspects of Hume's theory. The core of the theory is the distinction, within basic sensory imagination, between basic qualitative content and assigned content, the first consisting of observational properties by which we picture in our minds things and situations, the second of labels and stipulations, simple categorizations, and specifications. By the latter, we can imagine different things in connection with the same phenomenal content. Qualitative contents are more constrained than assignment contents because they are grounded on the contents of perceptual experiences, that is, ways in which sensorial qualities are distributed in and fill up the three-dimensional scene of our environment. This sets a limit to what we can imagine sensorially. (There is no such limit to what we can suppose by way of assignments—including the impossible.) It is interesting that the elements that realize the epistemic import of imagination for modality are also elements of Hume's content-constitutive conception of imagination. See Kung, 'Imagining as a Guide to Possibility', 620–63.

[57] This applies also to Holden, 'Hume's Absolute Necessity', 403: 'On such an account, when we pronounce that a certain proposition is absolutely necessary we are giving voice to a non-representational attitude—most likely, the prescriptive attitude of insisting that the proposition in question…be treated as a non-negotiable element in our system of belief.' (See Vaidya, 'Modal Knowledge', 104–106, on the perspectives of modal empiricism and anti-realism.) As Kail, *Reality and Projection*, 111–112, puts it, Hume understands modality as a non-detective position. I would say that

practical attitude is superfluous. The role of the imagination is to instantiate in its inferences contents which are cognitive in character and as to their role, but which are not representational. This is how it is with the contents realizing modal thought and cognition. The discussion of Hume's modal constructivism should be conducted by keeping in mind the difference between the conception of cognitive but non-representational contents and the expression of non-cognitive attitudes.[58]

5.3 To Consider the Matter A Priori

Hume's theory of metaphysical modality implies that we can get to conclusions about what is possible simply by reflecting on and comparing ideas or objects, in their individuating qualities and internal relations. This makes room for 'intuition', 'demonstration', 'knowledge and certainty' (1.3.1.2), that is, for the a priori. Hume recognizes perfectly familiar domains of first-order a priori cognition: arithmetic and the simplest parts of geometry. And he recognizes and relies on a variety of 'principles' which are 'clear and self-evident' (1.2.4.22): a priori philosophical maxims. These cognitions and these principles, together with the corresponding a priori reasonings, mark a major cognitive gap in representation, which is only by sense and memory, a posteriori, and dependent on the actual presence of sensible objects. Hume closes this cognitive gap with resources provided by his account of modality: the distinction between metaphysical and physical possibility and Separability as modality-constituting principle.

5.3.1 Hume's A Priori

According to Hume, we can have a priori 'knowledge and certainty' by intuition or demonstration, depending on whether a priori truths are 'discoverable at first

---

'detective' is ambiguous between cognitive and representational: modal content is cognitive, but not representational. In fact some problems are induced in Kail's work by the lack of distinction between representation and cognition: inferential dispositions are squarely set by Kail in the non-cognitive field, because they do not aim to represent the world; but inference is hardly a non-cognitive operation of the mind. A. J. Vaidya, 'Modal Knowledge: Beyond Rationalism and Empiricism', in B. Fisher & F. Leon, eds., *Modal Epistemology after Rationalism*, Springer, London 2017 (85–114), 89.

[58] The paradigmatic version of Humean modal anti-realism is Simon Blackburn's 'Modals and Morals', in S. Blackburn *Essays on Quasi-Realism*, Oxford University Press, Oxford/New York 1993, 52:74. I appreciate, inter alia, Blackburn's commitment to understanding modal thinking and discourse as thoroughly and legitimately cognitive (see especially 66–71). This marks a difference with H. Price's sketch of the 'location' problem for modality, 'Will There Be Blood? Brandom and Hume on the Genealogy of Modals', in *Philosophical Topics*, 36, 2008, 87:97. While Price's emphasis on the inferentialist link connecting Hume and Brandom is right and important, his pragmatist tones should be somewhat muted. Hume is committed to a genuine if limited representational dimension of cognition. The content-productive role of imagination can be directly individuated and assessed in cognitive terms. Pragmatic considerations lie only in the background.

sight' or require 'enquiry or reasoning'. When the differences and resemblances of ideas are considerable, we need only engage in reflection and 'we always pronounce a first sight, without enquiry or reasoning'. Demonstration, complex a priori reasoning, is restricted to 'proportions of quantity and number' and therefore to algebra and arithmetic. These are the only domains where a priori knowledge can and must be gained 'in a more *artificial* manner', by reasoning (1.3.1.3). Hume explicitly contends that 'algebra and arithmetic [are] the only sciences, in which we can carry on a chain of reasoning to any degree of intricacy, and yet preserve a perfect exactness and certainty' (1.3.1.5). Hume denies that geometrical truths can be known with certainty or deserve the name of demonstrations, because its exact standard of equality—like the number of mathematical points in a segment—is one we cannot cognitively master and apply. This, however, does not exactly correspond to Hume's practice. Also the simplest truths of geometry can be discovered by a priori reasoning. In fact, Hume's first example of relations that 'depend entirely on the ideas, which we compare together', that is, are object of a priori reasoning, is from geometry. ''Tis from the idea of a triangle, that we discover the relation of equality, which its three angles bear to two right ones; and this relation is invariable, as long as our idea remains the same' (1.3.1.1). (I am not going to address Hume's philosophy of mathematics: see § 8.2.2 for some discussion of the imaginative processes underlying geometry.)[59]

Alongside mathematics, Hume's a priori includes multiple 'general maxims of philosophy' (3.2.6.8). Consider the various sorts of a priori principles at work in Hume's philosophy.

(1) General principles of Hume's '*Logic*', that is, principles concerning the nature of ideas and reasoning. They include the principle that 'whatever we conceive, we conceive to be existent' or that 'any idea we please to form is the idea of a being' (11.2.6.4). The principle of the particularity of the content of perceptions as of objects: 'That the mind cannot form any notion of quantity or quality without forming a precise notion of the degrees of each' (1.1.7.3). The Established Maxim and Separability: 'Whatever is clearly conceiv'd may exist; and whatever is clearly conceiv'd, after any manner, may exist after the same manner. This is one principle, which has been already acknowledg'd. Again, every thing, which is different, is distinguishable, and every thing which is distinguishable, is separable by the imagination' (1.4.5.5).[60]

---

[59] Also the distinction between intuition and demonstration, just like that between sense and memory, is not too deep. For Hume, just as for Descartes and Locke, intuitions, immediate comparisons of ideas, are the elements demonstrations are composed of. And as per the Important Footnote, reason can be exerted by employing only two ideas, without a third one as a medium (1.3.7.5 fn. 20). This is explicitly stated about causal reasoning; but it might also apply to demonstrative reason if we consider ideas of relations as the inferentially linked units. Don Garrett has pointed out to me the need for this qualification.

[60] Cummins, 'Hume on Possible Objects and Impossible Ideas', 220 strongly argues for the metaphysical—a priori and necessary—status of these principles.

(2) Maxims giving shape to Hume's *ontology of perceptions*. They include Two Viewpoints, which is based on a distinction of reason between the contents and the mental existence of perceptions. The claim that perceptions can exist independently: 'since all our perceptions are different from each other, and from every thing else in the universe, they are also distinct and separable, and may be consider'd as separately existent, and may exist separately, and have no need of any thing else to support their existence' (1.4.5.5). The claim that perceptions can exist without being perceived or appear to the mind: 'An interrupted appearance to the senses implies not necessarily an interruption in the existence. The supposition of the continu'd existence of sensible objects or perceptions involves no contradiction' (1.4.2.40). Particularism about impressions and other mental existents: 'The confusion, in which impressions are sometimes involv'd, proceeds only from their faintness and unsteadiness, not from any capacity in the mind to receive any impression, which in its real existence has no particular degree nor proportion. That is a contradiction in terms; and even implies the flattest of all contradictions, *viz.* that 'tis possible for the same thing both to be and not to be' (1.1.7.4).

(3) Principles of Hume's *ontology of objects*. One is Equivalence. Anther, the principle of nominalism: '''Tis a principle generally receiv'd in philosophy, that every thing in nature is individual, and that 'tis utterly absurd to suppose a triangle really existent, which has no precise proportion of sides and angles' (1.1.7.6). The principle that only individual particulars, unitary beings, exist: '''Tis evident, that existence in itself belongs only to unity, and is never applicable to number, but on account of the unites, of which the number is compos'd' (1.2.2.3). The principle that all distinct real existents are only contingently related: 'to consider the matter *a priori*, any thing may produce any thing, and...we shall never discover a reason, why an object may or may not be the cause of another' (1.4.5.30). The principle that the idea of identity is not that of one object:

> As to the principle of individuation; we may observe, that the view of any one object is not sufficient to convey the idea of identity. For in that proposition, *an object is the same with itself*, if the idea express'd by the word, *object*, were no ways distinguish'd from that meant by *itself*, we really shou'd mean nothing, nor wou'd the proposition contain a predicate and a subject, which however are imply'd in this affirmation. One single object conveys the idea of unity, not that of identity.' (1.4.2.26)

The principle that any individual existent is a substance: 'If instead of answering these questions, any one shou'd evade the difficulty, by saying, that the definition of a *substance* is *something which may exist by itself*; and that this definition ought to satisfy us: Shou'd this be said, I shou'd observe, that this definition agrees to every thing, that can possibly be conceiv'd' (1.4.5.5). The 'obvious' principle 'that whatever is capable of being divided *in infinitum*, must consist of an infinite number of parts' (1.2.1.2). Alternatively and better, that 'if...any finite extension be infinitely divisible, it can be no contradiction to suppose, that a finite extension contains an infinite number of parts' (1.2.2.2). The principle that 'indivisible parts, being nothing in themselves, are inconceivable when not fill'd with something real and existent' (1.2.4.2) (while it is a posteriori that this filling must consist of colour and solidity).

(4) *Epistemological* principles. The principle that truth conditions fall into two kinds: 'Truth or falshood consists in an agreement or disagreement either to the *real* relations of ideas, or to *real* existence and matter of fact' (3.1.1.9). The principle that adequate representation is the foundation of a priori and a posteriori knowledge: 'Wherever ideas are adequate representations of objects, the relations, contradictions and agreements of the ideas are all applicable to the objects' (1.2.2.1). The principle that there is no 'knowledge' of the dependence of one object on another because this 'wou'd imply the absolute contradiction and impossibility of conceiving any thing different' (1.3.6.1).

Hume proposes these principles as a priori. Given their role in the science of man, we can say that, even apart from mathematics, there is nothing trifling about a priori cognition. But, of course, the role of the a priori in Hume's philosophy threatens to be a mystery. There is a cognitive gap in object representation corresponding to the possibility of the a priori.

5.3.2 From Metaphysical Necessity to the A Priori

Hume's solution of the problem of the a priori is that inferences by Separability are the source of a priori knowledge. Metaphysically necessary contents of cognition are produced by Separability inferences of the imagination, which only depend on reflection on ideas and objects, in their individuating qualities and internal relations. Such inferences do not draw on experience but only on possession of and reflection on ideas and have metaphysically necessary true conclusions. The subject matter of cognition is not necessarily complex. The Important Footnote establishes that simple and complex contents are the same as to conception or the act of the mind that apprehends them; therefore, they are equally, potentially, subject matters of cognition. But there are still important cognitive differences. In particular, a priori cognition can only be inferential: object representation is only a posteriori, because it depends on sensibly given objects. Now, inference requires some relation of ideas or the conception of a complex idea.[61]

---

[61] Owen, *Hume's Reason*, 104: 'If relations of ideas are complex ideas, and demonstrations are a chain of related ideas, then a demonstration is really just a process that lead to the formation of a complex idea.'

The Important Footnote corrects in this respect the traditional view only as to the number of the ideas required: two are sufficient. Therefore, the condition of Separability on conceptions of ideas that can support a priori cognition is restricted to qualitatively individuated complex ideas structured by internal relations. The internal dependence of such relations of the identities of ideas is a modality-constituting constraint both on the conceptions of ideas and on the transitions of the imagination. We cannot conceive clearly of ideas standing in such relations without any change to a different conception of them, to their being differently related or not related at all, being blocked. On Hume's theory of modality, the experience of such a block amounts to the conception of the corresponding contents as metaphysically necessary. This modal conclusion only requires the apprehension and consideration of the ideas, that is, 'abstract reasoning or reflexion', without the need for 'information from experience'. Internal relations of ideas thus mediate between modality and the a priori. This is how Hume's imagination contributes to closing the cognitive gap of the a priori; and it is, of course, an important advance in his crusade against rationalism.

It is important to distinguish two different forms of Hume's abstract reasoning. As David Owen has pointed out, Hume recognizes *deductive* reasoning based on abstract reflection and comparison of ideas. *All sorts* of philosophical relations, not only the internal ones of resemblance, degree of quality, proportion, and contrariety, support reasoning based only on the contents of general ideas and their names. Thus, if I have the relevant ideas, I can suppose that As cause Bs; I can suppose that an A is present in certain circumstances and that the circumstances are right for its causing a B; in this way, I conclude to the supposition that a B will be present too. This deductive reasoning is based on the comparison of the ideas of As and Bs, of that of cause, and of that of the circumstances. We have the content of those ideas from experience. Since no further empirical information is required to form and accept the conclusion, such reasoning is a priori. However, deductive reasoning is not *demonstrative* reasoning. Both proceed by comparison and relations of ideas. But demonstrative reasoning, differently from deductive reasoning, *produces* knowledge, rather than simply transmitting what is supposed in the premises to the equally suppositional conclusions. It is a source of knowledge, of a priori knowledge. The difference depends on the fact that demonstrative reasoning proceeds by a chain of intuitions structured by internal relations of ideas, which are units of a priori knowledge (see § 11.1.2 for an examination of Hume's account of the cognitive import of the a priori). A priori reasoning is more than suppositional or stipulative; it consists in a positive exercise of conception by Separability, which individuates a chain of metaphysical necessities, and delivers a priori, categorical conclusions.[62]

---

[62] See Owen, *Hume's Reason*, 104–6. See Beebee, *Hume on Causation*, 23–4; 45–58. Deductive reasoning differs from probable reasoning in two structural respects: it *does* necessarily consist in a

On this reading, little or nothing is formal about a priori knowledge. It consists in the grasp or intuition of metaphysical necessities—of metaphysically necessary truths, articulated by internal relations of ideas—and in the capacity of connecting them in a chain leading to a conclusion. Therefore, it consists in conceptions determined by their component, object-individuating, and representing ideas and in inferences along their internal relations. Such activity is based on principles of the imagination: offline conception, transpositions of ideas, blocks, or facilitations of transition. Therefore, pace Kemp Smith, Hume's a priori reason also has little if nothing to do with '*analytic* reason', in Leibniz's and Kant's sense; or in any sense of analyticity, formal or linguistic, familiar in contemporary philosophy.[63] Occasionally Hume seems to identify demonstrative import with logical form.

> That this opinion is false will admit of an easy proof. For if such an inference may be drawn merely from the ideas of body, of motion, and of impulse, it must amount to a *demonstration*, and must imply the absolute impossibility of any contrary supposition. Every effect, then, beside the communication of motion, implies a formal contradiction: and 'tis impossible not only that it can exist, but also that it can be conceiv'd. (1.3.9.10)

comparison of ideas and it does *not* transmit or modify belief. Firstly, probable reasoning, *at the primitive level*, is the inference, grounded on experience and on its effects on imagination, from the observation of one object to the conclusion that another non-observed object is present. This inference does not consist in a comparison of ideas: in particular it does not depend on the availability of the idea of cause. Rather, its primary function is to put us in possession of this idea, as well as to give us empirical information. *Mature* probable reasoning, as we will see, does not involve the direct repeated observation of the objects it is about; but still it does not require that we compare their ideas with the idea of cause. Secondly, deductive reasoning can only be hypothetical: it can move from one cognitively detached idea to another, without altering our doxastic commitments. Probable reasoning is by construction doxastically committed: we could not engage in probable reasoning, or in reasoning a priori, or conclude to some physical necessity, without starting from and concluding to belief. (Of course, we can perform deductive reasonings with the ideas of cause and effect; but this is a different matter from probability.)

[63] For an enlightening and detailed study of the material, content-grounded, early modern concept of inference, particularly in Descartes and Locke, as well as in Hume, see Owen, *Hume's Reason*, 5–6, 91 99–110. Owen's account of Hume's theory of demonstrative reasoning and of the distinction between intuition and demonstration inference is the best available and is deeply consonant to my account of Hume's imagination. In particular, the claim that 'If relations of ideas are complex ideas, and demonstrations are a chain of related ideas, then a demonstration is really just a process that leads to the formation of a complex idea' (104; see also 112) naturally suggests a strict, reciprocal link between imaginative operations, relations of ideas, and inferential structure. See H. Smit, 'Apriority, Reason, and Induction', *Journal of the History of Philosophy*, 48, 2010, 313–43. See also Echelbarger, 'Hume and the Logicians', 147–9, who remarks that in Hume propositions and arguments amount to compound ideas and that the Important Footnote draws an explicit and important distinction between conceiving and judging, forming an argument and drawing an inference. Echelbarger also points out that Hume's focus in this area is 'to explain how human beings are capable of *acquiring the ability* for syllogistic reasoning rather than having it in their very nature': an issue of (broadly) production of content, which was foreign to the traditional and modern logicians.

However, mention of a 'formal contradiction' notwithstanding, we should not locate here, in logical form, the ground of Hume's a priori. Contradiction and absurdity are not individuated by logical principles, but directly by the inconceivability of certain combinations of contents; by violations of Separability, which in their turn depend on and are completely explained by the contents of ideas and relations as well as by the nature of the imagination. This is a cognitive and an epistemological matter, not one of logical form ('Such an inference wou'd amount to *knowledge*, and wou'd imply the absolute contradiction and impossibility of conceiving any thing different', 1.3.6.1). Much the same holds of linguistic accounts of analyticity. Hume says that our language functions as a matter of convention and gives to language an important, if somewhat undertheorized role in non-representational cognition, primarily in generality. But the explanatory role of language depends on its inclusion in the concurrence of sense, memory, and the imagination, operating as natural mental faculties. Neither object-representing perceptions nor the imagination are in any sense conventional; and both seem to shape language more than they are shaped by it. This is enough to reject the identification of Hume's a priori with linguistic conventions.[64]

5.3.3 Explaining A Priori Maxims

Once all has been said, one is left wondering whether Hume can really explain and vindicate the complexity of our a priori cognition with the sparse resources he mobilizes.[65] While this is not a task I am addressing in its full scope, I want to give two examples of how the metaphysical necessity and thereby the a priori status of the maxims of philosophy could be established by inferences of Separability in terms of one of the internal relations.

A maxim like 'Whatever we conceive, we conceive to be existent' or 'Any idea we please to form is the idea of a being' could be explained, in a Hume-friendly way, as follows. We have an idea representing an idea we have: this idea of reflection makes us acquainted with that idea as an internal perception with regard to its individuating qualities as well as to its relations, positions, and durations. Through a conception by the imagination, the idea we have of this internal

---

[64] What about the notion of a priori and analyticity as truth in virtue of conceptual inclusion? This notion, apart from the widespread doubts about it—doubts which quite reasonably hinge around how to connect at all truth with concepts *alone*—could be regimented to Hume's apparatus, by identifying concepts with sensibly given contents generalized and modalized by the imagination. In this sense, the a priori would fall in line with the analytic, but the analytic would be reduced to a combination of ideas that the imagination cannot conceive otherwise.

[65] Garrett, *Hume*, 92–3, rightly points out the difficulty of figuring out how demonstrative reasoning can be accounted for in terms of the four relations of ideas and sketches a solution in terms of relations among revival sets. I give two examples in terms of relations between reflective ideas of ideas.

perception is turned into a perfect idea. By abstract consideration of the idea of reflection and Separability, we can tell apart the individuating qualities of the internal perception from its location, position, and duration. By Two Viewpoints, we can move from the qualities that individuate the existence of the idea we are reflecting on to the content that it represents and that is borne by those qualities. By Equivalence, we come to conceive of the object that is individuated by the content of the idea. Since this inference of Equivalence is based only on the individuating qualities shared by the idea and the object, that is, on their exact resemblance in this respect, it defines an internal relation between them. On this basis, by Separability, we can conclude that it is metaphysically impossible that an idea with representational content fails to be the idea of an object. (They are only distinct by reason, which is a possible conception, an epistemic and not an absolute possibility.) But in order to have the idea of an existent or being is necessary and sufficient that we have an idea with representational content. Therefore, any (at least potentially representational) idea that we form is the idea of a being or of an existent. The maxim is known a priori, by abstract reasoning, because of its metaphysical necessity and because of the internal relation of resemblance.

To take another example: 'The mind cannot form any notion of quantity or quality without forming a precise notion of the degrees of each'. Again, we have by an idea of reflection the representation of the ideas we have of the particular quantities and qualities of an object (such ideas are considered in their contents). Abstract reflection on any of these ideas in terms of the internal relation of contrariety blocks the imagination in the attempt to conceive of an object with such quantitative and qualitative properties but without any particular degree of them. This block realizes a condition of (non-) Separability: conceiving the actual quantities and qualities of an object without any particular degree would be conceiving them as existing but excluding any particular way in which they can exist (their degrees) from existence (this is the content of the internal relation of contrariety: existence and non-existence). This is an attempt to separate the inseparable. Therefore, we know a priori that the mind cannot form any such conception (this conclusion is about mental existence and is based on Two Viewpoints). Hence, whatever object we can have an idea of, must be conceived with a precise degree of quality or quantity.

In the light of his account of the a priori, Hume can say that these maxims are known as the result of a well-disciplined, perfectly natural cognitive exercise of imagination: the modal implications of the Established Maxim, of Separability, and of internal relations of ideas. Mathematical knowledge and knowledge by intuition and demonstration of philosophical maxims are aspects of the ordinary activity of the mind. Hume's a priori maxims depend on reflection on internal relations between ideas such as: perception, object, representation, cognition, existence, identity, possibility, necessity, reality, space, time, divisibility, body, possibility, necessity, truth, reference, knowledge, and reason. The availability of these general ideas and the relevant modal inferences are explainable as operations of the imagination. It is true that Hume often introduces these maxims as commonly received or as what all accept and believe—what we would call platitudes. This expresses Hume's essential trust in common sense and in well-conducted philosophical enquiry. But it is not the ultimate ground of acceptance of such principles. A priori knowledge has its grounds in ideas and in the modal transitions of the imagination. If it is widely shared, this is as a consequence of our sharing an intellectual world of ideas created by the imagination.

Thus, we can say that with his theory of modality and of the a priori, Hume makes good two centrally important points of Book 1. One is that the mathematicians have no title to claim 'that those ideas, which are their objects, are of so refin'd and spiritual a nature, that they fall not under the conception of the fancy, but must be comprehended by a pure and intellectual view' (1.3.1.7). The other is that 'our demonstrative and probable reasonings' are included in imagination in the larger sense, as 'the faculty, by which we form our fainter ideas' (1.3.9.19 fn. 22), which also includes the more limited one. Also in the modal domain therefore, Hume's resorting to imagination is an explanatorily indispensable, cognitively liberating factor.[66]

5.4 Summary

Modality and the a priori are the second mode of conceptual thinking that Hume aims to explain with imagination. Such explanation is at work in most of the arguments of Book 1 and is one of its philosophical highpoints.

In § 5.1 I examine Hume's conceivability account of modality, summarized in the Established Maxim: 'nothing we imagine is absolutely impossible'. The explanatory-constitutive role of the imagination is based on a cognitive gap of modality, discussed in § 5.1.1. The Established Maxim responds to the non-modal character of object representation: impressions and ideas representing them are locked on actuality; their contents are not susceptible to modal variation.

In § 5.1.2 I examine the content of the Established Maxim. The imagination puts in place modal contents, in the first place, with its detached conception of ideas, which constitutes our primitive sense of possibility. This potential for offline thinking finds realization in a family of inferences of conceivability (to

---

[66] There are thus limits to likening Hume's conception of the a priori with Lewis's and Jackson's idea of 'platitudes' as the source and ground of a theoretically important, a priori claims. Noonan, *Hume on Knowledge*, 81–2, recognizes that Hume states logical (a priori) truths about impressions (the most important of which is that they must be determined in their degrees of both quantity and quality).

be understood as content-constitutive material inferences, not as deductive schemes). Jointly, they define the ways in which the imagination spans across conception and possibility. Such transitions constitute our grasp and mastery of modal contents.

§ 5.1.3 addresses the structure of the modality-constituting transitions of the imagination. Conditions on conception produce modal qualifications by their non-logical effects on the imagination. The content-structure of conceptions can ease, hinder, or block the imagination in its conceiving of ideas. The experience of such effects drives the more limited imagination to conceive of the objects of such ideas as possible or impossible. Hume identifies two principles that explain the modality-constituting transitions of the imagination. The first is Separability: the constraint on conceptions issuing from internal relations of ideas. Separability grounds the conceivability of potentially object-representing ideas. Another condition of conceivability is Determination: the channelling of imaginative transitions caused by non-representational features of ideas, like their repeated presence in experience.

§ 5.2 deals with some general aspects of Hume's philosophy of modality. In § 5.2.1 I argue that the duality of Separability and Determination is reflected in an important distinction between kinds of modality. Separability grounds metaphysical possibilities, relating to possible existence as such. Determination grounds physical possibilities, which refer to ways the empirical world can be. This distinction (crucial to Hume's account of causality) is one of the philosophical achievements of the *Treatise*. It is a tool of philosophical criticism, gives conceptual articulation to modal thinking, and defines principled possibilities of error, thus contributing to the objectivity of modal thinking.

The issue of modal objectivity is addressed directly in § 5.2.2, in terms of the distinction between absolute and epistemic possibility. I suggest that both metaphysical and physical possibility are absolute and that there is no strong sense in which Hume's modalities are epistemic. Distinctions of reasons come closest to this concept but Hume ultimately excludes them from the domain of modality. Finally, in § 5.2.3, I discuss against this background the sceptical realist interpretation of Hume, in respect of its looking for support in a Kripkean apparatus of absolute and epistemic modalities. I deny that this apparatus can be applied to Hume's philosophy of modality and that it is required by its claims to objectivity and its commitments to realism.

In § 5.3 I address Hume's stance to the a priori. Hume, as I indicate in § 5.3.1, recognizes familiar domains, like arithmetic, algebra, and the simplest parts of geometry, where we achieve a priori cognition. He also relies on a priori philosophical maxims, referring to the nature of ideas, to the ontology of perceptions, to the ontology of objects, and to epistemological principles and implications. This unveils a major cognitive gap since object representation can only be a posteriori. Hume's answer to this cognitive gap, discussed in § 5.3.2, is that Separability and metaphysical possibility are the source and the subject matter of the a priori. Inferences of Separability depend only on reflection on ideas and their internal relations and only deliver metaphysically necessary true conclusions. Metaphysical modality and a priori cognition thus entail each other and have their grounds in the imagination. Hume aims in this way to provide a naturalist account of the a priori. Finally, in § 5.3.3, I sketch a tentative, affirmative answer to the question of whether Hume's conceptual apparatus of the a priori is up to the task of explaining the a priori philosophical maxims that he himself recognizes.

PART III

A NEW SYSTEM OF REALITIES

The unity of Hume's theory of the imagination and its systematic importance for his philosophy depend on the fundamental problem it aims to solve: how our ordinary and philosophical cognitive practices and our overall worldview are possible, given the naturally necessary limits of object representation. The principles of Hume's doctrine of elements, like Two Viewpoints, Equivalence, Representation, Structural Principle, Important Footnote, and Non-Mixture, make sense in relation to that problem and to that function of the imagination. In particular, throughout Parts 2, 3, and 4 of Book 1 of the *Treatise*, Hume addresses the question of the unity of our view of reality.

Hume formulates this task of his theory of the imagination in terms of the distinction and connection of a first with a second 'system' of 'realities'. Sense and memory, the primitive and immediate form of our cognition, make available a system of realities.

> 'Tis evident, that whatever is present to the memory, striking upon the mind with a vivacity, which resembles an immediate impression, must become of considerable moment in all the operations of the mind, and must easily distinguish itself above the mere fictions of imagination. Of these impressions or ideas of the memory we form a kind of system, comprehending whatever we remember to have been present, either to our internal perception or senses; and every particular of that system, join'd to the present impressions, we are pleas'd to call a *reality*. (1.3.9.3)

Together, sense and memory present and preserve the synopsis of sensible objects and their actual order and form. But this leaves much of our ordinary and philosophical practices and our worldview unexplained. The task Hume assigns to the imagination, with the new contents it puts in place, is precisely to fill this explanatory gap.

> But the mind stops not here. For finding, that with this system of perceptions, there is another connected by custom, or if you will, by the relation of cause or

effect, it proceeds to the consideration of their ideas; and as it feels that 'tis in a manner necessarily determin'd to view these particular ideas, and that the custom or relation, by which it is determin'd, admits not of the least change, it forms them into a new system, which it likewise dignifies with the title of *realities*. The first of these systems is the object of the memory and senses; the second of the judgment.   (1.3.9.3)

By the conjunction of these two systems 'I paint the universe in my imagination, and fix my attention on any part of it I please' (1.3.9.4; see § 1.2.2).

Hume articulates this general question into two others. One concerns the fragmentary, disconnected character of object representation and the impossibility to overcome it with more information drawn from sense and memory or with idea-comparing reasoning. The other is that sensible representation and reasoning do not provide grounds for conceiving of objects as continuants, for their persistence across time and change. The first question is the focus of Hume's theory of causal content and our topic in Chapters 6 and 7. The core of Hume's theory of causal content is thus the internal link between our painting the universe in the imagination, the possibility of reasoning about matters of fact, and the possession of the idea of cause. This is the topic of Chapter 6. To the inferential dimension of the idea of cause, Hume's theory joins a modal one: to think in causal terms is to think in terms of causal necessity. Chapter 7 deals with this further, imagination-grounded aspect of causal content and with the general character of Hume's account of causation.

6
A Just Inference

> The only connexion or relation of objects, which can lead us beyond the immediate impressions of our memory and senses, is that of cause and effect; and that because 'tis the only one, on which we can found a just inference from one object to another.
>
> (1.3.6.7)

Hume's theory of causation follows the general pattern of cognitive gaps and works of imagination. But, at this stage of the argument, the pattern is more complicated. Throughout Book 1 of the *Treatise*, the individuation of cognitive gaps has recursive character. At the basic level, there is a straightforward contrast between sensible representation and conceptual thinking; and the imagination enters to close the gaps of generality and modality. The account of causation opens with the distinction between knowledge and probability and, under the heading of knowledge, introduces the a priori or 'demonstrative reason' (3.1.119 fn. 69) as a further dimension along which to individuate cognitive gaps. The imagination thus must not only *loosen* the fixed order and connection of sense and memory but also *restrict* the possibilities left open by the a priori. As we will see, also 'probable reasoning' (1.3.8.12), reasoning by comparing causal ideas sense, marks a cognitive gap: it cannot explain the inferential potentials it is based on.

Another complicating factor in Hume's account of causation is the dual role of the idea of cause in ordinary and philosophical cognition. It is the idea we apply when we *conclude by reasoning*, from the observation of an object to the future or past existence of another, unobserved one. And it is the idea that makes us conceive of distinct existents as *necessarily connected* to one another. The *inferential* and *modal* dimensions of the idea of cause jointly define the cognitive gap of causation and both depend on the more limited imagination. But no matter how strictly interrelated, they and the corresponding operations of the imagination are distinct. It is important to keep this in mind, because it shapes the structure of the argument of Part 3. Hume progresses from idea-comparing causal reasoning to idea of cause; from the idea of cause to causal necessity; from causal necessity to primitive, non-idea-comparing causal inferences; and finally reverts from the explanation of causal inference to that of causal necessity. I have divided my discussion of causation and imagination accordingly, in two parts. The first (this chapter) focuses on causal inference; the second (Chapter 7) on causal necessity.

6.1 The Cognitive Gap of Causation

6.1.1 Causal Reasoning and Causal Content: Inferring the Unobserved

The conceptual connection between the idea of cause and the character and function of causal reasoning provides the theoretical framework of Hume's account of causation. We have an ordinary practice of idea-comparing causal reasoning: a practice that Hume takes to be not only indispensable but in good epistemic order. This practice is an expression of the imagination as a whole but primarily in its idea-comparing sense. The conditions and the structure of this kind of causal inference allow us to individuate the idea of cause as we have it, as it is compared and applied in reasoning. Hume's starting points are therefore the conceptual roles of the idea of cause in the ordinary and philosophical causal reasoning. This also allows the identification of a cognitive gap in sensible representation and the a priori. Hume then proceeds to explain how such cognitive gap is closed by content-producing operations of the more limited imagination; or, equivalently, how the conceptual roles associated with the idea of cause can be realized by empirical mental operations that are neither representational nor a priori.

Even though Hume proceeds piecemeal and alternates considerations concerning modality and inference, this programme finds clear expression in the overall structure of the text. The centrepiece of Part 3 of Book 1, Sections 1.3.4–13, focused on the structure of causal inference, is preceded by a sketch of our reasoning with the idea of cause, and followed by a conclusive account of causal necessity (respectively at 1.3.2 and 1.3.14). Hume links the possibility of a certain practice of reasoning, the content and mode of the idea of cause, and certain properties and operations of the imagination. The structure of causal reasoning and its underlying inferential and imaginative conditions come first; the content of the idea of cause and the nature of causal necessity follow.[1] This is the core of Hume's Inferentialist Naturalism about causation. Hume explicitly highlights its inferentialist character by commenting on why he defined causes at the end rather than at the beginning of his account.

> This order wou'd not have been excusable, of first examining our inference from the relation before we had explain'd the relation itself, had it been possible to proceed in a different method. But as the nature of the relation depends so much

---

[1] See, for a reading along these lines Beebee, *Hume on Causation*, 60–1: 'It is not that we believe that some effect *e* will occur *because* we have an impression of *c* and already believe that *c* is a cause of *e*; rather we come to think of *c* as a cause of *e* because, on having an impression of *c*, we find ourselves inferring *e*.'; P. Kail, 'Efficient Causation in Hume', in T. A. Schmalz, ed., *Efficient Causation. A History*, Oxford University Press, Oxford 2014, 231–57.

on that of the inference, we have been oblig'd to advance in this seemingly preposterous manner. (1.3.14.30)

The relation of cause (the content of the idea of cause) depends on causal inference (on its structure and underlying conditions). This is because idea-comparing causal reasonings depend on causal ideas, the content of which consist in causal relations; but causal ideas, as to their inferential potential and modal import, depend on transitions of the imagination, in the more limited sense. I will thus approach Hume's theory of causation through his conception of idea-comparing causal reasoning. 'All kinds of reasoning consist in nothing but a *comparison*, and a discovery of those relations, either constant or inconstant, which two or more objects bear to each other' (1.3.2.2). In this way we can identify the content of the idea of cause as a complex idea of relation and show how only the transitions of the more limited imagination (by the Structural Principle) can explain that content.

Hume divides his seven kinds of philosophical relations into those that 'depend entirely on the ideas, which we compare together' and those that 'may be chang'd without any change in the ideas'. The division determines the different kinds of idea-comparing reasoning. Constant relations are the object of a priori intuition and demonstrative reasoning, delivering knowledge. Inconstant relations (contiguity and distance in space and time, identity, causation) 'cannot be foreseen by the mind'. But the relation of cause has a special position in connection with reasoning because it is the only one of the inconstant relations that supports informative inferences by comparison of ideas.

> This comparison we may make, either when both the objects are present to the senses, or when neither of them is present, or when only one. When both the objects are present to the senses along with the relation, we call *this* perception rather than reasoning; nor is there in this case any exercise of the thought, or any action, properly speaking, but a mere passive admission of the impressions thro' the organs of sensation. According to this way of thinking, we ought not to receive as reasoning any of the observations we may make concerning *identity*, and the *relations* of *time* and *place*; since in none of them the mind can go beyond what is immediately present to the senses, either to discover the real existence or the relations of objects. 'Tis only *causation*, which produces such a connexion, as to give us assurance from the existence or action of one object, that 'twas follow'd or preceded by any other existence or action; nor can the other two relations be ever made use of in reasoning, except so far as they either affect or are affected by it. (1.3.2.2)

Hume distinguishes three cases. The first is when the objects compared in terms of one of these relations are both present to the senses. This is our firmest cognitive hold on objects and the only way in which we can gain information about identity and relations of time and place. But it is not inference: we have 'perception rather than reasoning', 'a mere admission of the impressions thro' the organs of sensation'. The second case is left undescribed. I would say that reasoning or comparison by inconstant relations in the absence of the related objects is simply a comparison of perfect ideas of distinct existents. This is a deductive exercise of abstract reflection and reason, without demonstrative import, without new information, which can take all sorts of relations as its subject matter. Ideas are compared in such a way that some deductively follow from others; but without intuitive and demonstrative import. The conclusions do not depend on experience and are a priori, but do not constitute demonstrative knowledge, because the relations according to which ideas are compared do not depend only on the ideas and are not metaphysically necessary (see § 5.3.2).

In the third case, only one object is present to the senses, but the content of the idea with which we conceive of it and of its relations allows us to conclude from its presence and existence to the existence of another object, not present to us. This is the only case in which an inconstant relation can be *both* an object of reasoning *and* a source of new information and cognition. By being informative, such a reasoning is the a posteriori counterpart of demonstrative reasoning, which is productive of knowledge. It is thus deeply different from deductive reasoning, since the inferential principle lies in the content of the ideas compared (in their causal content), not in their arrangement. However, differently from demonstrative reasoning, the comparison is according to features of contents and to relations of ideas individuated only a posteriori. Causal relations are 'never discoverable merely from their ideas' and 'we receive information [about them] from experience, and not from any abstract reasoning or reflection' (1.3.1.1). In this sense, by being informative and a posteriori, such reasoning is a sort of inferential counterpart of sense and memory.[2] This is the core of Hume's concept of probability or probable reasoning: 'the mind can go beyond what is immediately present to the senses, either to discover the real existence or the relations of objects' (1.3.2.2). This is also Hume's fundamental characterization of causal reasoning.

> Here then it appears, that of those three relations, which depend not upon the mere ideas, the only one, that can be trac'd beyond our senses, and informs us of existences and objects, which we do not see or feel, is *causation*. This relation,

---

[2] There are three things to distinguish here. One is deductive inference applying causal ideas, which is a priori and cannot give any new cognition of relations of ideas or of objects. The second is probable reasoning implicitly or explicitly comparing causal ideas, which is a posteriori and can give new cognition of objects and matter of fact. The third is a certain kind of mental transition involving impressions and ideas, which first instantiates and explains causal contents. It is crucial that we distinguish these three kinds of inference; in particular, that we recognize the distinction and the relations between the second and the third. Beebee, *Hume on Causation*, 43, 64, points out that Hume's account of the origins of the idea of cause takes its start from causation as philosophical relation.

therefore, we shall endeavour to explain fully before we leave the subject of the understanding. (1.3.2.3)

Causation is the only inconstant relation of ideas that makes it possible to infer unobserved objects from observed ones, thus gaining new information. It is the principle of construction of the second system of realities. The idea of cause is the one we rely on when we engage explicitly in such construction. We can reason about the relations of space and time and of identity only because such reasoning is hiddenly causal; only by assuming that 'some secret cause' is at work (1.3.2.2).

Hume makes it very clear that this is the distinctive, constitutive feature of causal reasoning. Causal inference *is* inference to unobserved existence. 'The mind in its reasoning from causes or effects carries its view beyond those objects, which it sees or remembers' (1.3.4.1). The idea of cause must be such as to support this feature of reasoning. This determines the overall structure of Hume's argument. The elements of causal reasoning are the 'mixture of impressions, or at least of ideas of memory' and perfect ideas (1.3.4.1); the inference to the existence of an object, grounded on experience (1.3.6.1); the role of the principle of uniformity (1.3.6.4); and the nature of the beliefs which are its conclusion (1.4.7.1, 2). These elements are individuated by their roles in inferences to the unobserved. Hume puts forward 'two principles' about causation, whose acceptance would 'throw' us 'loose from all common systems'. '*There is nothing in any object, consider'd in itself, which can afford us a reason for drawing a conclusion beyond it*'; '*Even after the observation of the frequent or constant conjunction of objects, we have no reason to draw any inference concerning any object beyond those of which we have had experience* (1.3.12.20). Both principles deal with inferring the unobserved. And he summarizes the teaching of Sections 4–13 of Part 3 as explaining 'the manner, *in which we reason beyond our immediate impressions, and conclude that such particular causes must have such particular effects*' (1.3.14.1).

Causal reasoning depends on the idea of cause; more precisely, in causal reasoning we compare (together with other ideas, representing or describing objects) causal ideas: ideas of causes, of effects, of this causing that, of all events having a cause, of causes and effects being necessarily connected, of the same causes having the same effects, and so on. We can apply and compare these ideas implicitly, simply taking this or that object as causally related; or reflexively, by heeding to rules of reasoning. In any case, by applying these ideas, on the prompt of observations or 'experiments', we can draw and are entitled to conclusions concerning unobserved matters of fact. (As Hume remarks, the original, prompting impression might be lost, but we could still go on reasoning on the force of our initial 'conviction', 1.3.4.3.) Hume repeatedly claims that our 'method' of causal reasoning is ordinarily not that of explicitly collecting and rehearsing the past experience of a certain conjunction of objects (even though this is experience is the cause of our having that idea). Rather, because of our experience, we apply and compare causal ideas to judge if certain objects are causally connected. Notice that idea-comparing causal reasoning is not deductive reasoning: it is a perfectly good inference to the unobserved, based on a present impression or on an idea of memory, with which we draw a categorical, existential conclusion by application of causal ideas and by abstraction and modalization. This is how ordinary, mature causal reasoning operates to provide substantive information (1.3.12.3; 1.3.8.14).[3] Thus, there is a very tight nexus between a distinctive, indeed unique practice of reasoning and the idea of cause: the properties of causal reasoning depend on the nature of the causal ideas it compares. Only the relation of cause and effect can 'perswade us of any real existence' and only this 'perswasion' can 'give force to the other relations' (1.3.9.6). Reciprocally, with its special features, ordinary causal reasoning gives us a lead as to the properties and contents of the idea of cause and at the same time sets the problem of explaining that idea, which it presupposes.[4]

6.1.2 The Missing Idea of Cause: Necessity

Having identified the role of the idea of cause in causal reasoning (allowing inferring the unobserved), Hume proceeds to individuate a cognitive gap: the idea of cause that could support causal reasoning is neither given by sensible representation nor is it a priori. It thus may seem impossible for the natural mind to engage in 'just' and 'regular' inferences to the unobserved, as it manifestly does. Notice that Hume is assuming that causal reasoning can be in good order, a 'just inference'; this is a basic assumption of inferentialism, since it only can give determinateness to the inferential specification of contents.[5]

> To begin regularly, we must consider the idea of *causation*, and see from what origin it is deriv'd. 'Tis impossible to reason justly, without understanding perfectly the idea concerning which we reason; and 'tis impossible perfectly to

---

[3] Philosophical relations of cause and effects are concepts of causal relations: the idea of two objects related as cause and as effect, that is, with at least a minimally explicit recognition of their causal status. Mature causal reasoning is thus typically conceptual reasoning. On the other hand, present-day research points out that categorization and conceptual reasoning in general under many respects rely on causal concepts and beliefs: 'Conceptual reasoning is essential causal reasoning' (D. Danks, 'The Psychology of Causal Perception and Reasoning', in H. Beebe, C. Hitchcock, & P. Menzies, eds., *The Oxford Handbook of Causation*, Oxford University Press, Oxford 2009, 447–70, 459). This gives important support to Hume's concentration on causal cognition.

[4] Beebee, *Hume on Causation*, 7: 'But for Hume, causation and inference from the observed to the unobserved are inseparable: we come to believe that Cs are causes of Es just *because* we *instinctively* infer Cs from Es' (see also 43–4).

[5] The non-sceptical or even anti-sceptical character of Hume's account of causation is by now such a well-established interpretive conclusion that I feel I can take it for granted. See T. Beauchamp & A. Rosenberg, *Hume and the Problem of Causation*, Oxford University Press, New York/Oxford 1981, 33–76; Garrett, *Cognition and Commitment*, 83; F. Wilson, *Hume's Defense of Causal Inference*, University of Toronto Press, Toronto 1997, 191–3; Loeb, *Stability and Justification*, 38–47; Kail, *Projection and Realism*, 41–2; Beebee, *Hume on Causation*, 41, 53–5.

understand any idea, without tracing it up to its origin, and examining that primary impression, from which it arises. (1.3.2.4)

Hume moves from ordinary, good causal reasoning to the idea of cause as we understand and apply it: the first gives the guidelines for individuating the second; the second explains and validates the second. 'Let us therefore cast our eye on any two objects, which we call cause and effect, and turn them on all sides, in order to find that impression, which produces an idea of such prodigious consequence' (1.3.2.5). The 'prodigious consequence' of the idea of cause is the support it gives to inferring the unobserved, the property we have to explain. Success in individuating its 'primary impression' would make of that idea the representation of an object. Hume's first claim against this possibility is that the idea of cause is not based on any particular quality of objects, because objects can count as causes or effects independently of their sharing any quality. 'And indeed there is nothing existent, either externally or internally, which is not to be consider'd either as a cause or an effect; tho' 'tis plain there is no one quality, which universally belongs to all beings, and gives them a title to that denomination' (1.3.2.5). To count as representational, the idea of cause should thus be derived from some relation given in impressions of sense and memory (1.3.2.6). Two relational elements of the idea of cause that Hume individuates by turning it 'on all sides' indeed derive from sense and memory: contiguity in space and time; priority in time of causes on effects.

> I find in the first place, that whatever objects are consider'd as causes or effects, are *contiguous*; and that nothing can operate in a time or place, which is ever so little remov'd from those of its existence. (1.3.2.6)
>
> The second relation I shall observe as essential to causes and effects, is not so universally acknowledged, but is liable to some controversy. 'Tis that of PRIORITY of time in the cause before the effect. (1.3.2.7)

Hume offers an argument for his second claim, while he leaves the first at a phenomenological level. However, he is also non-committal about the conclusiveness of this part of his analysis. He anticipates that objects—perceptions—can be causally connected even if not spatially related (contiguity would thus be only in time). And he minimizes the importance of the priority claim: 'the affair is of no great importance' (1.3.2.8). In fact, he regards both relations as 'imperfect and unsatisfactory' if the task is to characterize the idea of cause. One reason of Hume's dismissive attitude might be simply that *another* element of causal content is both essential and non-representational. This element is *modal*.

> Shall we then rest contented with these two relations of contiguity and succession, as affording a compleat idea of causation? By no means. An object may be contiguous and prior to another, without being consider'd as its cause.

There is a NECESSARY CONNEXION to be taken into consideration; and that relation is of much greater importance, than any of the other two above-mention'd. (1.3.2.11)

Hume does not regard this modal aspect of the idea of cause as being in need of argument. He takes it for granted on the basis of our common sense distinction between causal and accidental generalizations; possibly, also of the phenomenology of our awareness of causation. This modal element thus stands in need of explanation but is under no threat of elimination. Hume also spends very little time establishing that such necessary connection does not derive from any sensibly given object or matter of fact. 'Here again I turn the object on all sides, in order to discover the nature of this necessary connexion, and find the impression, or impressions, from which its idea may be deriv'd' (1.3.2.11). The enquiry, however, does not reveal any further representational element.[6] Hume's theory of modality allows him to take a short cut here: only imagination, not representation, can unveil possibilities. Therefore, the idea of cause includes a non-representational component, a modal component of content that needs explanation.[7]

6.1.3 From Necessity to Inference

Hume does not make it clear at first how the modal component of the idea of cause is related to causal reasoning as inference to the unobserved. But the next

---

[6] Hume, at a later stage of his discussion, introduces a further representational element central for causal ideas, the constant conjunction of objects. One might wonder why he does not introduce it here (Hume anticipates that there is a limitation in this respect: he is considering only a 'single instance of cause and effect', 1.3.2.9.) I think that this is because constant conjunction is not part of our ordinary idea of cause. It is a crucial part of their explanation; it shapes causal content; but it is not something we think about when we think of causes and effects. Ordinary causal reasoning is modal: it is marked by the distinction between accidental and essential features of the coming to be of objects; rather than by constant conjunctions of resembling objects. (This is also the way Hume formulates his rules for causal judgement, 1.3.15.) Constant conjunctions come into sight only when we engage in philosophical reflection on our inferential practice. Correspondingly, Hume's two-definition of cause, which sums up his philosophical account, is framed in terms of constant conjunctions.

[7] Hume follows Malebranche in identifying the modal element of causal relations. See Malebranche, *Recherche de la verité*, Book 6, Part 2, chapter 3, 391: 'Cause veritable est une cause entre laquelle et son effet l'esprit apperçoit une liaison necessaire, c'est ainsi que je l'entens'. And in denying that we have any idea of such element drawn from the ideas of finite material or intellectual beings (what Malebranche decries as a sort of causal polytheism). 'Il n'y a donc point de forces, de puissances, de causes veritables dans le monde materiel et sensible, et il n'y faut point admettre de forms, de facultez, et de qualitez réelles pour produire des effets que les corps ne produisent point, et pour partager avec Dieu la force et la puissance qui lui sont essentielles' (Malebranche, *Recherche de la verité*, Book 6, Part 2, chapter 3, 390). Of course, Hume denies that there is any real necessary connection even in the case of God. See S. Nadler, 'Malebranche on Causation', in S. Nadler, ed., *The Cambridge Companion to Malebranche*, 112–38. Berkeley also denies that any 'necessary connexion' is given in sense-experience, which would provide a priori cognition of the relations between different objects of the same or of different senses. Or which would explain, on an a priori basis, the cognitive operations that support features of ordinary experience (for example, that visible objects are at a distance; or the apparent size of the moon when it is close to the horizon). See *New Theory*, 45, 72 (21, 28).

steps of the complex identification of the cognitive gap of causation begin to untangle the interrelation between the inferential and the modal dimensions of causal content. The failure to individuate an impression of sensation corresponding to the relation of necessary connection leaves open two options.

> Shall the despair of success make me assert, that I am here possest of an idea, which is not preceded by any similar impression? This wou'd be too strong a proof of levity and inconstancy; since the contrary principle has been already so firmly establish'd, as to admit of no farther doubt; at least, till we have more fully examin'd the present difficulty. (1.3.2.12)

Accepting the view that the idea of necessary connection is without a similar preceding impression would be relinquishing the First Principle. If no other sort of explanation of ideas were available, this would amount to leaving necessary connexion unexplained.[8]

The other option is to look for a different sort of explanation, which may or not involve some sort of impression (it does, as it finally turns out, but without making of necessary connexion the representation of an object).

> We must, therefore, proceed like those, who being in search of any thing, that lies conceal'd from them, and not finding it in the place they expected, beat about all the neighbouring fields, without any certain view or design, in hopes their good fortune will at last guide them to what they search for. 'Tis necessary for us to leave the direct survey of this question concerning the nature of that *necessary connexion*, which enters into our idea of cause and effect; and endeavour to find some other questions, the examination of which will perhaps afford a hint, that may serve to clear up the present difficulty. (1.3.2.13)

The change in style of explanation consists, in the first place, in shifting the focus of the enquiry away from the modal element of the idea of cause. A 'direct survey' (one which was inspired by the notion of object representation) would

---

[8] There is a wealth of psychological research—stemming at least from Michotte's work—establishing that we have a relatively automatic, relatively irresistible perception of causation. 'Certain judgments of causality seem to be part-and-parcel of perception, rather than something that occurs after "basic" perception has taken pale' (Danks, 'The Psychology of Causal Perception and Reasoning', 448–51. Danks' chapter is an excellent survey of this area.) This goes to some extent against Hume's basic claim that we do not observe causal connections, which rather are grounded on inference. However, two points are to be noted. The first is that Hume is perfectly comfortable with the idea that imagination simulates the experience of causation. Such simulated experience is constrained by conditions (like spatial and temporal contiguity) that contemporary research is ready to recognize. Furthermore, contextual factors seem relevant and it is doubtful that causal perception is a module (like visual perception, for instance). The second point is that it is likely that causal inference does not belong, psychologically, with causal perception ('In sum, there is a growing body of direct and indirect evidence that causal perception and causal inference are different cognitive processes', Danks, 'Psychology of Causal Perception', 457).

vainly look for a 'similar impression' for the modal element. The cognitive gap in representation corresponding to the idea of cause cannot be closed by adding further representational elements because it has modal grounds and modality is not representational *at all*. The 'other questions', which could clear up the present one, should therefore address necessary connection indirectly, by relying not on representation but on inference. This is how Hume states such questions.

> Of these questions there occur two, which I shall proceed to examine, *viz*.
>
> *First*, For what reason we pronounce it *necessary*, that every thing whose existence has a beginning, shou'd also have a cause?
>
> *Secondly*, Why we conclude, that such particular causes must *necessarily* have such particular effects; and what is the nature of that *inference* we draw from the one to the other, and of the *belief* we repose in it? (1.3.4.13–15)

Hume's fundamental move is therefore resolving the issue of the modal content of the idea of cause into that of the nature of causal inference. More precisely, in the nature of inferential *activity* or *practice*: the reasons why we 'pronounce' it necessary that any beginning of existence has a cause; why we 'conclude' that certain causes must have certain effects; the nature of the causal inferences we 'draw'.[9] This is Hume's move to Inferentialist Naturalism about causal necessity and thus about causal content in general. Hume follows the lead of the properties of ordinary, idea-comparing causal reasoning to individuate an irreducibly non-representational, modal element of the idea of cause, as we apply it. Against this background, the point of the second of the two questions is reasonably clear. The first of its two sub-questions asks for an explanation of why we ascribe necessity to the conclusions of particular causal inferences. The other asks about the nature of causal inference and of causal belief. The first finds an answer at 1.3.14, where Hume finally gives an inferentialist explanation of causal necessity. The second is addressed throughout 1.3.4–13: it is the bulk of Hume's inferentialist account of causal content. Together, they apply to causation the general pattern of Book 1: overcoming natural cognitive limits by replacing representation with inferences of the imagination.

One is left wondering, however, what the point of the first question is. Some interpreters have found it difficult or uninteresting to discuss this issue, but I think that it deserves attention. (By the way, it was what most interested Kant.)[10]

---

[9] Millican remarks that understanding 'connexion in terms of *inference*' is the 'unifying factor' of Hume's argument ('Hume, Causal Realism, and Causal Science', 574).

[10] One of the best interpretations explicitly abstains from addressing this issue, see Beebee, *Hume on Causation*, 44. As Don Garrett has pointed out to me, Hume's discussion of it also attracted enormous (negative) attention from his contemporaries, partly because it seemed to them to undermine the cosmological argument for the existence of God. It is also prominent in the charges against him in connection with the chair in Edinburgh. See, for a full analysis of 1.3.3, essentially in accord with my suggestions, Anderson, *Dogmatic Slumber*, 122–44.

I think we should regard 1.3.3: *Why a cause is always necessary*, as an indispensable complement of the analysis of the idea of cause and of the shift to inference at 1.3.2. Hume endorses the general maxim that every beginning of existence must have a cause, as an idea we compare in causal reasoning.[11] "'Tis a general maxim in philosophy, that *whatever begins to exist, must have a cause of existence*. This is commonly taken for granted in all reasonings, without any proof given or demanded' (1.3.3.1). But he asks what grounds there are for it ('For what reason we pronounce it *necessary*'). The discussion of such grounds allows Hume to take a further step in his argument and to reject—even in a case apparently favourable to it—the view that the modal force of the idea of cause is of metaphysical necessity and a priori. As an imposing tradition, some of whose exponents Hume discusses in this text (Hobbes, Clarke, and Locke), had asserted. Against this tradition, Hume denies that there is a proof a priori of this general maxim, the Causal Maxim, as I will call it.

> 'Tis suppos'd to be founded on intuition, and to be one of those maxims, which tho' they may be deny'd with the lips, 'tis impossible for men in their hearts really to doubt of. But if we examine this maxim by the idea of knowledge above-explain'd, we shall discover in it no mark of any such intuitive certainty; but on the contrary shall find, that 'tis of a nature quite foreign to that species of conviction. (1.3.3.1)

The proposition: whatever has a beginning also has a cause of existence, manifestly involves none of the relations of ideas that are scrutable a priori (1.3.3.2). Furthermore, if the necessity of a cause were metaphysical, we could establish it by Separability. But a Conceivability/Possibility inference by Separability is always available against any supposed a priori version of the Causal Maxim.

> Now that the latter proposition is utterly incapable of a demonstrative proof, we may satisfy ourselves by considering, that as all distinct ideas are separable from each other, and as the ideas of cause and effect are evidently distinct, 'twill be easy for us to conceive any object to be non-existent this moment, and existent the next, without conjoining to it the distinct idea of a cause or productive principle. The separation, therefore, of the idea of a cause from that of a beginning of existence, is plainly possible for the imagination; and consequently the actual separation of these objects is so far possible, that it implies no contradiction nor

---

[11] 'But allow me to tell you, that I never asserted so absurd a Proposition as *that any thing might arise without a Cause*: I only maintain'd, that our Certainty of the Falsehood of that Proposition proceeded neither from Intuition nor Demonstration; but from another Source. [...] There are many different kinds of Certainty; and some of them as satisfactory to the Mind, tho perhaps not so regular, as the demonstrative kind', Letter to John Stewart, February 1754, in J. Y. T. Craig, ed., *The Letters of David Hume*, 2 volumes, Oxford University Press, Oxford 2011 (1932), I, 187.

absurdity; and is therefore incapable of being refuted by any reasoning from mere ideas; without which 'tis impossible to demonstrate the necessity of a cause. (1.3.3.3)[12]

(Notice the restriction: 'so far'; the Causal Maxim might still have a different, physical kind of necessity.) This modal argument marks an important step in Hume's argument. The modal dimension of the idea of cause frustrates the a posteriori search of an impression, a sensible, representational ground for it: this is the teaching of 1.3.2. But since metaphysical necessity is a priori and our inferential practices include demonstrative reasoning, it could still be that causation is a matter for intuition and demonstration. This was in fact the dominant position in early modern philosophy. The task of 1.3.3 is to explore and reject this possibility in the most favourable case for it: the Causal Maxim, the general, sound principle that all events have a cause. (It is only later on, at 1.3.14, that Hume explicitly argues for the non-metaphysical character of the necessity of causes, see § 7.1.) In this indirect way, Hume adds another trait to the specification of the causation gap: neither sensible representation nor the a priori put in place causal necessity.[13] It is thus not surprising that, just like 1.3.2, 1.3.3 concludes with a shift from a modal question to a question about inference.

> Since it is not from knowledge or any scientific reasoning, that we derive the opinion of the necessity of a cause to every new production, that opinion must necessarily arise from observation and experience. The next question, then, shou'd naturally be, *How experience gives rise to such a principle?* But as I find it will be more convenient to sink this question in the following, *Why we conclude, that such particular causes must necessarily have such particular effects, and why we form an inference from one to another?* We shall make that the subject of our future enquiry. 'Twill, perhaps, be found in the end, that the same answer will serve for both questions. (1.3.3.9)[14]

---

[12] There is no deductive grounding for the Causal Maxim, simply because valid deductive inferences could not deliver the new cognition it contains: 'They are still more frivolous, who say, that every effect must have a cause, because 'tis imply'd in the very idea of effect. Every effect necessarily pre-supposes a cause; effect being a relative term, of which cause is the correlative. But this does not prove, that every being must be preceded by a cause; no more than it follows, because every husband must have a wife, that therefore every man must be marry'd' (1.3.3.8).

[13] The background for this argument against rationalism is what Kail (*Projection and Realism*, 84, 88–90) calls the 'Bare Thought' of what causal necessity and causal powers would be if they resided in the objects and were manifest in the simple view of them. (A 'thin notion' which 'is not itself an idea of causal power, but an understanding of what it would be to have such an idea'.) I think that the content of this conception should be identified as a true a priori conditional, issuing from abstract reflection, connecting the idea of causal necessity, that of relation of objects, and that of a priori knowledge. The conditional is coherent: it is in fact true. Since the epistemological consequent is false, the metaphysical antecedent is false: there is no necessity in the objects. Since the argument is a priori, there is no idea at all of necessity in the objects. Defending the coherence of the thought is thus required to establish the conclusion that the idea of causal necessity in re is empty.

[14] Surprisingly, Hume is not explicit about what the answer is to the first question in the text just quoted. Broadly, it is that the imaginative transition of ideas that explains all the inferential and modal

That is: if the a priori character of the Causal Maxim is discarded, what is left is to 'sink' the question concerning its ground in the general question of how the ascription of such necessity is linked to our inferential activity and its conditions. Thus, 1.4.3 opens the path to a thorough, anti-rationalist inferentialism about causal content.

> Perhaps 'twill appear in the end, that the necessary connexion depends on the inference, instead of the inference's depending on the necessary connexion
> (1.3.6.3)

6.1.4 From Inference to Experience

The next step of Hume's argument is thus to specify the nature of 'the inference': its elements, structure, and conditions. This also concludes the individuation of the causation gap, which is finally identified with a *step* of causal inference. These are the topics of 1.3.4–10.

Hume moves from a review of the diversity of elements that constitute causal inference: the 'component parts of our reasonings concerning cause and effect' (1.3.4), the 'essentially different' 'materials' of a 'mix'd and heterogeneous nature' which we employ in this 'kind of reasoning' (1.3.5.1). These structural elements, which are traceable at the levels both of idea-comparing and of more limited imagination, are identified by Hume's functional description of causal inference as inference to the unobserved.

> Here therefore we have three things to explain, *viz. First*, The original impression. *Secondly*, The transition to the idea of the connected cause or effect. *Thirdly*, The nature and qualities of that idea. (1.3.5.1)

For our present purposes, it is the second thing, the transition of ideas, which matters the most. The third one, the cognitive state in which the conclusion of the inference consists, will be examined in the context of our discussion of belief and imagination (§ 11.1.2). The first one has importance in connection with the third (the nature of the conclusions of causal reasoning) as well as in connection with the objects of such reasoning, by Non-Mixture.

> Tho' the mind in its reasonings from causes or effects carries its view beyond those objects, which it sees or remembers, it must never lose sight of them entirely, nor reason merely upon its own ideas, without some mixture of impressions, or at least of ideas of the memory, which are equivalent to impressions. (1.3.4.1)

---

features of the idea of cause also explains, and makes compelling, the Causal Maxim (1.3.14.35). Since the Causal Maxim is also a reliable guide of judgement, we are entitled to use it in causal reasoning.

With causal reasoning, we extend our cognition of objects. But 'without the authority either of the memory or sense our whole reasoning wou'd be chimerical and without foundation'. We would have only '*hypothetical* arguments, or reasonings upon a supposition' (1.3.4.2); but no anchoring in existing objects and no categorical conclusions.

The second element, 'the transition to the idea of the connected cause or effect' (1.3.5.1), is crucial for inferentialism about causal content. This transition makes us move in thought from an observed object to a non-observed one (from an impression to an idea). Spelling out this condition and searching for its natural, mental realization are the topics of 1.3.6: *Of the inference from the impression to the idea*, which, together with 1.3.14: *Of the idea of necessary connexion*, is the philosophical core of Hume's account of causation. Here Hume examines the nature of the step we take when we reason with causal ideas, that is, by comparing ideas of objects in terms of the philosophical relation of cause. This elucidation of mature causal reasoning, at last, pinpoints where and how the cognitive faculties summoned up until now (sensible representation and a priori reason) fall short of explaining our reasoning with the idea of cause. That is, where exactly, at the deepest explanatory level of the science of man, the causation gap is located.

Hume, in the first place, extends to causal inference the Separability argument he had given against the Causal Maxim.

> There is no object, which implies the existence of any other if we consider these objects in themselves, and never look beyond the ideas which we form of them. Such an inference wou'd amount to knowledge, and wou'd imply the absolute contradiction and impossibility of conceiving any thing different. But as all distinct ideas are separable, 'tis evident there can be no impossibility of that kind. When we pass from a present impression to the idea of any object, we might possibly have separated the idea from the impression, and have substituted any other idea in its room. (1.3.6.1)

The inferential step we take in causal reasoning is not sanctioned by Separability; it is not a priori, it does not express our 'penetration' in the 'essences' of objects and our discovery of 'the dependence of the one upon the other'. There is no metaphysically necessary truth grounding the inference, just as there is no dimension of metaphysical necessity in the causal relation. This means that the inferential step is a posteriori and depends on information about the contingent state of the world. "Tis therefore by EXPERIENCE only, that we can infer the existence of one object from that of another' (1.3.6.2). The task then is to explain how experience can support this inferential step. The starting point is, once again, our ordinary practice of idea-comparing causal reasoning.

> The nature of experience is this. We remember to have had frequent instances of the existence of one species of objects; and also remember, that the individuals

of another species of objects have always attended them, and have existed in a regular order of contiguity and succession with regard to them. Thus we remember to have seen that species of object we call *flame,* and to have felt that species of sensation we call *heat*. We likewise call to mind their constant conjunction in all past instances. Without any farther ceremony, we call the one *cause* and the other *effect*, and infer the existence of the one from that of the other.   (1.3.6.2)

This text is somewhat complex. The first trait of experience is that it involves only representational contents and states: impressions of sensation and ideas of memory of the qualities—species—and relations—contiguity and succession—of certain objects. In this respect, experience gives us the first system of realities. To the representations that constitute experience, however, we immediately apply ('without any farther ceremony') causal ideas and causal language ('we call the one *cause* and the other *effect*') and draw the corresponding existential inference. This is what makes such reasoning idea comparing, the work of imagination in the larger sense. The concept of experience, as it figures in ordinary, mature causal reasoning, combines the two apparently inconsistent properties of having representational content and being inferential in character. But this is as it should be if experience is to be the a posteriori ground for inference to the unobserved. Hume explicitly comments on the novelty of this conception of experience, with reference to the explanatory shift from modality to inference.

> Thus in advancing we have insensibly discover'd a new relation betwixt cause and effect, when we least expected it, and were entirely employ'd upon another subject. This relation is their CONSTANT CONJUNCTION. Contiguity and succession are not sufficient to make us pronounce any two objects to be cause and effect, unless we perceive, that these two relations are preserv'd in several instances. We may now see the advantage of quitting the direct survey of this relation, in order to discover the nature of that *necessary connexion*, which makes so essential a part of it.   (1.3.6.3)

Merging the study of causal necessity into that of causal inference has unveiled a dimension of representational content—constant conjunctions of resembling of objects—which because it comes in view only as an element of the structure of causal inferences would have escaped us if we had focused only on the idea of cause.

One might think that, once this dimension of representational content (the representational content distinctive of experience) is taken into account, an explanation of the inferential step to the unobserved is forthcoming. But right at this juncture Hume identifies a new and crucial difficulty, leading to the ultimate individuation of the causation gap.

> There are hopes, that by this means we may at last arrive at our propos'd end; tho' to tell the truth, this new-discover'd relation of a constant conjunction

seems to advance us but very little in our way. For it implies no more than this, that like objects have always been plac'd in like relations of contiguity and succession; and it seems evident, at least at first sight, that by this means we can never discover any new idea, and can only multiply, but not enlarge the objects of our mind. It may be thought, that what we learn not from one object, we can never learn from a hundred, which are all of the same kind, and are perfectly resembling in every circumstance. As our senses shew us in one instance two bodies, or motions, or qualities in certain relations of succession and contiguity; so our memory presents us only with a multitude of instances, wherein we always find like bodies, motions, or qualities in like relations. From the mere repetition of any past impression, even to infinity, there never will arise any new original idea, such as that of a necessary connexion; and the number of impressions has in this case no more effect than if we confin'd ourselves to one only. (1.3.6.3)

Hume explicitly characterizes experience and its content, constant conjunctions, as representational: it consists of impressions, delivered by sense and preserved by memory, which acquaint us with a multiplicity of objects and their properties and relations. But experience, as we have it, cannot be only representation; it is explicitly introduced as a ground of inference to the unobserved.

In all those instances, from which we learn the conjunction of particular causes and effects, both the causes and effects have been perceiv'd by the senses, and are remember'd: But in all cases, wherein we reason concerning them, there is only one perceiv'd or remember'd, and the other is supply'd in conformity to our past experience. (1.3.6.2)

However, as a representation of constant conjunctions of objects, experience does not enlarge or change the contents available to the mind. No new idea can be produced by experience, conceived in these terms. But this is precisely what is required and why experience was introduced: explaining the inferential potential of the idea of cause and, indirectly, its modal import. The cognitive gap of causation is thus finally individuated right in the structure of causal inference, which Hume had resorted to, rightly, to close it. The contents of experience do not explain our actual inferential behaviour: 'after the discovery of the constant conjunction of any objects, we always draw an inference from one object to another' (1.3.6.3); but, for all we know, this seems an impossible feat.

6.1.5 From Experience to the Imagination

Hume establishes this conclusion with one of the most influential arguments of the *Treatise*, later identified with the problem of induction. The argument is framed in terms of cognitive faculties and introduces imagination in the context of causal cognition.

> Since it appears, that the transition from an impression present to the memory or senses to the idea of an object, which we call cause or effect, is founded on past *experience*, and on our remembrance of their *constant conjunction*, the next question is, Whether experience produces the idea by means of the understanding or imagination; whether we are determin'd by reason to make the transition, or by a certain association and relation of perceptions? (1.3.6.4)

Hume's argument is that causal inference cannot be completely explained in terms of comparisons of ideas. It is not that such inferences by comparison are impossible: quite the contrary, this is how we ordinarily think in causal terms. But they cannot be explained in terms of the ideas which are compared when we engage in them. There is a hidden cognitive impossibility, a gap in the train of ideas that could explain them, which comes in view under analysis. Hume remarks that such idea-comparing inferences presuppose a certain premise (distinct from the memory of a constant conjunction and the impression of an object).

> If reason determin'd us [to make the transition], it wou'd proceed upon that principle, that instances, of which we have had no experience, must resemble those, of which we have had experience, and that the course of nature continues always uniformly the same. In order therefore to clear up this matter, let us consider all the arguments, upon which such a proposition may be suppos'd to be founded; and as these must be deriv'd either from knowledge or probability, let us cast our eye on each of these degrees of evidence, and see whether they afford any just conclusion of this nature. (1.3.6.4)

The premise is doubly problematic from the viewpoint of sense and memory, of course: it is a universal generalization and it has modal force. This problematic character is rightly of the sort that motivates Hume's turn to inferentialism. But now it turns out that the inferential solution is itself problematic, because (if we are restricted to inferences performed by imagination in the idea-comparing function) it presupposes a premise (an idea) that cannot be put in place by any idea-comparing reasoning, either a priori or a posteriori. It is a 'proposition' *unavailable* to demonstrative reason and *presupposed* by probable reasonings.[15]

---

[15] It is in this explanatory rather than in an epistemological fashion that something like the problem of induction figures in Hume's argument. There is by now a well-established interpretive tradition holding that Hume, just as he is no sceptic about causation, is no sceptic about induction. Even more to the point, Hume is not primarily interested in what we now consider the problem of induction. He is not primarily interested in justifying inductive inferences, but in explaining how they come about. See Beauchamp & Rosenberg, *Hume and the Problem of Causation*, 33–76; Garrett, *Cognition and*

It cannot be 'founded' a priori because it cannot be reached by comparison of ideas in terms of Separability.

> Our foregoing method of reasoning will easily convince us, that there can be no *demonstrative* arguments to prove, *that those instances, of which we have had no experience, resemble those, of which we have had experience*. We can at least conceive a change in the course of nature; which sufficiently proves, that such a change is not absolutely impossible. To form a clear idea of any thing, is an undeniable argument for its possibility, and is alone a refutation of any pretended demonstration against it. (1.3.6.5)

But it cannot be 'founded' by idea-comparing causal reasoning and by inference to the unobserved either, because these *already apply* this proposition, the idea that instances we have no experience of resemble those we have experienced. By its very notion, this kind of reasoning 'discovers not the relations of ideas, consider'd as such, but only those of objects': that is, inconstant relations of objects, not internal relations of ideas. Causal or probable reasoning requires that 'there be something present to the mind, either seen or rememeber'd' and that 'we infer something connected with it, which is not seen nor remember'd' (1.3.6.6). But this is possible, in an idea-comparing way, only by relying on the proposition whose grounds are in question. Therefore, this kind of reasoning, insofar as it is a 'just inference', cannot ground the relevant 'proposition'.[16]

> According to this account of things, which is, I think, in every point unquestionable, probability is founded on the presumption of a resemblance betwixt those objects, of which we have had experience, and those, of which we have had none; and therefore 'tis impossible this presumption can arise from probability. The same principle cannot be both the cause and effect of another; and this is, perhaps, the only proposition concerning that relation, which is either intuitively or demonstratively certain. (1.3.6.7)

Commitment, 91–2; Owen, *Hume's Reason*, 118–10; and for a very clear discussion, Beebee, *Hume on Causation*, 38–39, 63. I take their interpretive conclusions for granted. Of course, it is a legitimate philosophical move to turn to Hume for inspiration about how to address the problem of induction. Hume's inferences to the unobserved are inductive; the problems he raises about them have epistemological implications in his philosophy; the issues raised by Goodman and Kripke in their well-known arguments are close to Hume's concerns.

[16] As Schmitt, *Hume's Epistemology*, 146–55, forcefully argues, Hume's argument for grounding causal inference on more limited imagination assumes that causal inference is defeasibly justifying; that it is 'just'. My take on this point (which may not be Schmitt's) is as follows. Idea-comparing inferences can be just; but anyway they fail to establish the principle of uniformity. This principle is already required if causal inference is to be just. Therefore, the principle of uniformity cannot be grounded on idea-comparing just reasoning. The grounding is provided by the more limited imagination, in the guise of customary transitions.

Neither a priori nor a posteriori reasoning can deliver an idea presupposed by our inferences to the unobserved and thereby required by any account of the idea of cause.

> Thus not only our reason fails us in the discovery of the *ultimate connexion* of causes and effects, but even after experience has inform'd us of their *constant conjunction*, 'tis impossible for us to satisfy ourselves by our reason, why we shou'd extend that experience beyond those particular instances, which have fallen under our observation. We suppose, but are never able to prove, that there must be a resemblance betwixt those objects, of which we have had experience, and those which lie beyond the reach of our discovery. (1.3.6.11)

Hume is asking a constitutive-explanatory question: how can we engage in causal inferences, as inferences to the unobserved? His answer is that we will never be able to prove or to have reasons for the required extension of a represented pattern of resemblance. This lack of proof or reasons is also a cognitive or mental impossibility. Hume has a conception of reason as a cause, that is, has a causal-explanatory approach to cognition, as it is suitable to his science of human nature: 'Our reason must be consider'd as a kind of cause, of which truth is the natural effect' (1.4.1.1). The difficulty concerning the reasons or proofs for causal reasoning is thus also and correspondingly causal and explanatory: 'The same principle cannot both be the cause and the effect of another'. His arguments aim to establish that causal inference, as comparison of ideas, lacks a sufficient cause; therefore, it is physically impossible for the mind. This also completes the individuation of the causation gap. The gap opens at the juncture of the representation of constant conjunctions of objects with the inferential step to the existence of an unobserved object resembling the other, constantly conjoined ones. This step, if taken by comparison of ideas, requires the 'proposition' or 'principle' of uniformity of nature. But this proposition, being general and modal, cannot derive from an impression. Being separable and metaphysically contingent it has no a priori proof. And being presupposed by probable idea-comparing reasoning it cannot be established by it. This leaves causal inferences without an adequate cause—unless we introduce the more limited imagination.

6.2 The Nature of that Inference

The cognitive gap unveiled by the detection of the inferential limits of experience, of course, is also the discovery of a paradox, since we *do* ordinarily perform in and assess causal inferences by comparing ideas (1.4.1.1). But the paradox can be dissolved and the cognitive gap can be closed by resorting to the Structural Principle. The crucial point is that, when merging causal necessity into causal inference, we were in no way restricted to idea-comparing inferences. Imagination is the faculty of inference; but it includes, besides its idea-comparing part, the more limited imagination, inferential propensities, and transitions not reducible to the contents and relations of the involved ideas. It makes sense thus that the missing inferential potential can be explained, without assuming the proposition of the uniformity of nature, with some operation of that part of the imagination. In this way we can reconcile our ordinary engagement in the 'just inference' from causes to effects by comparison of ideas with the principle that 'no kind of reasoning can give rise to a new idea' (1.4.14.17).

6.2.1 Causation as a Natural Relation

The Structural Principle controls Hume's explanation of causal inference and of the idea of cause both regarding its inferential potential and its modal import. This is expressed in Hume's conclusive summary of his account of causal inference as the distinction between the philosophical and the natural relation of cause.

> Thus tho' causation be a *philosophical* relation, as implying contiguity, succession, and constant conjunction, yet 'tis only so far as it is a *natural* relation, and produces an union among our ideas, that we are able to reason upon it, or draw any inference from it. (1.3.6.16)

The claim delivers an important point about the levels and structure of Hume's explanation of the idea of cause. To say that causation is a philosophical relation of ideas is to say that it is a 'particular circumstance, in which, even upon the arbitrary union of two ideas in the fancy, we may think proper to compare [ideas]' (1.1.5.1). Causal reasoning that consists in comparisons of ideas is based on causation as philosophical relation, by which we are free to apply causal ideas to any object that seems fit to us. This is the work of imagination in its idea-comparing part. This is also how our ordinary practices of inferring unobserved matters of fact or of enquiring into causes proceed.[17] But reasoning with the philosophical relation of cause is not self-supporting and self-explanatory. It even turns out to be paradoxical because it involves a cognitive gap and a seeming cognitive impossibility. To explain how we can engage in idea-comparing causal reasoning and come by the idea of cause and causation as philosophical relation, Hume shifts to causation as a natural relation. A natural relation is 'that quality, by which two ideas are connected together in the imagination, and the one naturally introduces

---

[17] Beebe, *Hume on Causation*, 43, makes it clear that Hume's account aims to explain the origin of the idea of causation as philosophical relation.

the other' (1.1.5.1). As we know, certain properties of ideas—intrinsic qualities, locations in space and time, constant conjunctions—produce a 'bond of union', consisting in transitions and propensities to transitions of ideas of the more limited imagination (§ 3.2.3). These are natural relations and it is to causation as a natural relation that Hume turns for an explanation of the inferential potential of causal ideas.

> We have already taken notice of certain relations, which make us pass from one object to another, even tho' there be no reason to determine us to that transition; and this we may establish for a general rule, that wherever the mind constantly and uniformly makes a transition without any reason, it is influenc'd by these relations. Now this is exactly the present case. Reason can never shew us the connexion of one object with another, tho' aided by experience, and the observation of their constant conjunction in all past instances. When the mind, therefore, passes from the idea or impression of one object to the idea or belief of another, it is not determin'd by reason, but by certain principles, which associate together the ideas of these objects, and unite them in the imagination. (1.3.6.12)

The explanandum is, of course, the inference 'from the idea or impression of one object to the idea or belief of another'. Hume's all-important proviso—'even tho' there be no reason to determine us to that transition'—marks the cognitive gap and motivates the shift to a different level of explanation: from the content and explicit role in reasoning of causal ideas to underlying mental transitions, underdetermined by any antecedently given idea. The 'connexion of one object to another', represented by an idea, would be such a reason. Hume thus programmatically pursues an explanation of causal inference that does not rely on comparisons of ideas. A constant and uniform mental transition, not supported by reasons, is an association of ideas. 'Now this is exactly the present case': associations and transitions explain, without regress or circularity, the missing inferential step, because they operate beyond the scope of representation and of demonstrative and probable reasoning.

This association and transition are activities of the more limited imagination. At this level, the imagination responds to the contents of ideas only for how such contents are borne by the properties with which ideas exist in the mind and because of the effects that such properties have on its primitive qualities. Two Viewpoints finds one of its most important theoretical applications here. The repeated presence of perceptions to the mind and their resemblance (properties of existence) concur with qualities of the imagination to put in place transitions from one idea to another (a further property of mental existence) and the corresponding propensities. Such transitions and propensities are experienced and come to awareness as a mode of conception, as an inferential potential proper to ideas of those kinds (a property of content). Ideas 'connected together in the imagination' take the place of the 'connexion of one object to another' which sensible representation or demonstrative or probable reason could never give us. Therefore, the more limited imagination can engage in causal inferences (regular and natural inferences to the unobserved) without relying on antecedently given causal ideas.

The merging of the philosophical with the natural relation of cause is not limited to the production by the latter of the ideas required for the former. Even though Hume fails to give a detailed account of this, the natural relation of cause is the standing support of our thinking in terms of the corresponding philosophical relation. Idea-comparing causal reasoning receives explanation from its embedding in the transitions of the more limited imagination not only with regard to the availability of causal ideas but also to the shape and limits of our engagement in it. Across all our cognitive activities, the imagination operates as a single faculty, articulated by the Structural Principle. This has important consequences for Hume's understanding of causal cognition and for his response to scepticism.

6.2.2 Customary Transitions

Our present task is to see how Hume thinks this inferential potential comes about, by examining in detail the mechanism of more limited imagination that underlies causal inference and content. We have seen that this inferential potential systematically correlates with experience (observation of constant conjunction); the task is to explain how experience can put it in place. Hume remarks that, as is usually the case with the more limited imagination, such explanation must resort to a tacit, implicit operation: 'experience may produce a belief and a judgment of causes and effects by a secret operation, and without being once thought of' (1.3.8.13). The secret operation, just as in the case of general contents and meanings, is custom or habit.

> Now as we call every thing CUSTOM, which proceeds from a past repetition, without any new reasoning or conclusion, we-may establish it as a certain truth, that all the belief, which follows upon any present impression, is derived solely from that origin. When we are accustomed to see two impressions conjoined together, the appearance or idea of the one immediately carries us to the idea of the other. (1.3.8.10)

Custom explains the inferential step to the unobserved and the proposition of the resemblance of future to past. Custom, together with other empirically individuated principles of the more limited imagination (cognitive hysteresis, § 9.2.2; integration and completion of relations, § 9.3.2; shift from resemblance of actions to resemblance of ideas, § 9.3.2; reconciliation of conflicting conceptions, § 9.3.3), operates as an inferential propensity of the imagination. This propensity consists 'in bestowing a *facility* in the performance of any action or the conception of any object; and afterwards a *tendency* or *inclination* towards it' (2.3.5.1). That is, in a capacity—the facility—and in an ensuing bent—the tendency or inclination—to conceive of certain ideas dependently on the conception of certain others: the ideas being those whose observed constant conjunction is involved in the genesis of the custom. Such propensities come to awareness as expectations that an object will be followed or has been preceded by another one. But they are active at a deeper explanatory level, as certain patterns of the transitions of the more limited imagination. These patterns of transitions, the cause and structure of our expectations, rather than the expectations in themselves, make most of the explanatory work.

Custom and the more limited imagination (the part of our faculty of inference that is susceptible to effects of habituation) converge in Hume's important explanatory notion of 'customary transition'. A customary transition directs the mind from an impression or idea to a 'correlative idea' and gives rise to a 'perswasion' with that idea as its subject matter (1.3.8.11; see *E* 5.20). The customary transition is the expression of the 'propensity, which custom produces, to pass from an object to the idea of its usual attendant' (1.3.14.22; see *E* 7. 28). Or of the 'determination of the mind, which is acquir'd by custom, and causes us to make a transition from an object to its usual attendant, and from the impression of one to the lively idea of the other' (1.4.7.5). 'Custom and transition of ideas' work jointly in this explanation of causal association, that is, of the natural relation of ideas that grounds causal inference as inference to non-observed objects (1.3.8.14). It is the notion of customary transition that allows us to explain the cognitive effects of experience. Repetition per se does not change the contents that are available to the mind and thus does not directly produce any change of content, such as an inferential potential. But it has effects of habituation of the mental existence of ideas; and, by Two Viewpoints, *these* have changes in the contents of ideas, certain inferential potentials, as their effects. In this way, it is as if we learned directly from the contents of experience; while what learning there is, it is realized by its mental effects, in the indirect way just summarized.

> For supposing that in all past experience we have found two objects to have been always conjoin'd together, 'tis evident, that upon the appearance of one of these objects in an impression, we must from custom make an easy transition to the idea of that object, which usually attends it; and by means of the present impression and easy transition must conceive that idea in a stronger and more lively manner, than we do any loose floating image of the fancy. (1.3.9.16)

Once customary transitions of the more limited imagination have explained how experience can produce the inferential potentials of our ideas in the ways distinctive of causal inference, the architecture of Hume's account of this latter comes in full view.

> Had ideas no more union in the fancy than objects seem to have to the understanding, we cou'd never draw any inference from causes to effects, nor repose belief in any matter of fact. The inference, therefore, depends solely on the union of ideas.   (1.3.6.12)
>
> 'Tis not, therefore, reason, which is the guide of life, but custom. That alone determines the mind, in all instances, to suppose the future conformable to the past. However easy this step may seem, reason would never, to all eternity, be able to make it.   (A 16)
>
> We can give no reason for extending to the future our experience in the past; but are entirely determined by custom, when we conceive an effect to follow from its usual cause.   (A 21)

A customary transition that follows repeated observation or experience is the source, as a process of the more limited imagination, of the proposition or idea of the resemblance of the future with the past. In particular, the resemblance of the future with the past as a proposition ('supposition'), is linked, rather than to 'arguments', to an inferential step we tacitly take at all times ('determination to transfer').

> We may observe, that the supposition, *that the future resembles the past*, is not founded on arguments of any kind, but is deriv'd entirely from habit, by which we are determined to expect for the future the same train of objects, to which we have been accustom'd. This habit or determination to transfer the past to the future is full and perfect; and consequently the first impulse of the imagination in this species of reasoning is endow'd with the same qualities.   (1.3.12.9)[18]

---

[18] Berkeley here anticipates Hume. Constant experience, habit, results in associations of ideas and in the corresponding, immediate, and compelling propensities to judgement. The habitual connexion—say, between sensations attending ocular movements and the idea of greater and lesser distance—consists in the fact that 'the mind no sooner perceives the sensations arising from the different turn it gives the eye [...] but it withal perceives the different idea of distance, which was wont to be connected with that sensation; just as upon hearing a certain sound, the idea is immediately suggested to the understanding which custom had united to it', *New Theory*, 17 (11). These immediate transitions of the mind from one idea to another are 'sudden judgments', by which I 'forthwith conclude' what ideas are, 'by the wonted course of Nature', likely to follow what others, *New Theory*, 20, 45 (12, 20). Such ideas are 'as it were, most closely twisted, blended, and incorporated together'. This is a 'far more strict connexion' than that between words and ideas. It is so close and so strong that it is extremely difficult, in the case of words and ideas and even more in that, say, of visible and tangible objects, to separate, to discriminate between them. It is even the case that the suggested ideas 'more strongly affect us' and are 'more regarded' than those which are immediately present, *New Theory*, 51 (22). Differently from Hume, Berkeley does not equate these sudden judgments with the acquisition of new and original (non-representational) ideas but with new patterns of mental activity. Still, the anticipation of Hume's inferentialist views about content is strong. 'Sudden judgments', made without demonstration of necessity of coexistence of ideas, 'or without even so much as knowing what it is that makes them so to coexist', *New Theory*, 24–5 (12). A 'transition' between, say, visible and tangible ideas which is so 'swift and unperceived' 'that we can scarce forbear thinking them equally the immediate object of vision', *New Theory*, 145 (51). A 'sudden act of the judgment', which changes planes and, more deeply, 'diversity of colors', into solids, *New Theory*, 157–8 (54).

It is because of this transition that we can engage at all in inferences from observed to non-observed objects (one-object inferences). These are functionally causal inferences, inferences along the natural relation of cause; and the engagement in and mastery of such inferences or relation finally puts us in possession of causal ideas and opens the path to idea-comparing causal reasoning.

It is important to distinguish the different aspects of the mental process that issues from 'the influence of custom on the imagination' (1.3.16.8) and allows the closing of the gap of causal inference. The Structural Principle, Two Viewpoints, and Non-Mixture take hold of Hume's account.

(1) The customary transition has the effect of introducing a new perception in the mind: an idea, a particular existent or individual particular, individuated by its qualities, which in this way acquires new relations to the perceptions that form a mind. The new perception is resembling other ones present in the mind as impressions or ideas of memory; but it is numerically different. It exists in the mind as a perfect idea, even though it was never present as impression. It is a case of indirect or potential representation, prompted and regulated by the resemblance of these qualities to those of the constantly conjoined objects whose observation and memory operate on the more limited imagination.

(2) Alongside the production of new individual ideas, the customary transition to unobserved objects constitutes itself a deep, structural cognitive change. This customary transition is the psychological realization of the natural relation of causation and of the corresponding, primitive inferential potential; the conditions of inferences to the unobserved. Since the possibility of justly or regularly concluding to the unobserved is the distinctive feature of causal inference and of causal content, the mind through this propensity of the more limited imagination is in a position to engage in recognizable patterns of causal inference. This is the dawn of causal cognition.[19]

---

[19] There are interesting oscillations in how Hume identifies and designates the different views and roles of the same perceptions. 'There is no object, which implies the existence of any other if we consider these objects in themselves, and never look beyond the ideas which we form of them. Such an inference wou'd amount to knowledge, and wou'd imply the absolute contradiction and impossibility of conceiving any thing different' (1.3.6.1). The point here is *not* that we 'never look beyond' ideas as *mental existences*, as if we were prisoners of our perceptions. Never looking beyond ideas has rather to do with *representational contents*; with the objects represented by ideas. Thus, in this text, 'ideas' are equated with 'objects in themselves' as to their contents. Looking beyond ideas or objects in themselves thus would be to look at their mental existence. One page later Hume seems to make a similar point about the a posteriori character of causal inferences, asserting that 'probability' 'discovers not the relations of ideas, consider'd as such, but only those of objects' (1.3.6.5). Ideas considered as such are mere potentially representational contents, possible items of representation. The relations of ideas considered as such are discovered a priori. Probability discovers the relations only of objects. That is, discovers relations which involve (as one of the relata) something present to sense or to memory; that is, an object. These relations depend on the psychological apparatus of custom and transition which underlie probability in general. Therefore, in this passage, discovering relations of objects requires that the imagination interacts with perceptions also with regard of their existence.

(3) The more limited imagination proceeds in causal inference as if it had causal ideas in view, while it only moves from one idea to the other on the basis of custom as a principle of transition. Nothing here implies the causal conceptualization of objects and their relations or the application of causal ideas. Rather, such conceptualization and such application depend on the engagement at the primitive level in those customary transitions.[20] But the involved ideas, by Non-Mixture, preserve their identities as to their contents. In this way causal contents are applied to objects, just as it is in idea-comparing causal reasoning; and causation as a natural relation (which is nothing but the transitions of the more limited imagination) can be the ground of causation as philosophical relation or for our possession of the idea of cause. The inferential potential that is essential to causal reasoning and contents is already included in the customary propensities of the more limited imagination.

> We have no other notion of cause and effect, but that of certain objects, which have been *always conjoin'd* together, and which in all past instances have been found inseparable. We cannot penetrate into the reason of the conjunction. We only observe the thing itself, and always find that from the constant conjunction the objects acquire an union in the imagination.   (1.3.6.15)

Hume's genetic claims: 'All our reasonings concerning cause and effects are deriv'd from nothing but custom' (1.4.1.8) must therefore be understood with constitutive import. 'According to my system, all reasonings are nothing but the effects of custom; and custom has no influence, but by enlivening the imagination, and giving us a strong conception of any object' (1.3.13.11).

> When I examine with the utmost accuracy those objects, which are commonly denominated causes and effects, I find, in considering a single instance, that the one object is precedent and contiguous to the other; and in inlarging my view to consider several instances, I find only, that like objects are constantly plac'd in like relations of succession and contiguity. Again, when I consider the influence of this constant conjunction, I perceive, that such a relation can never be an object of reasoning, and can never operate upon the mind, but by means of

---

[20] Berkeley importantly anticipates Hume's conception of the cognitive mechanism underlying causal inference. What we have in the place of any inference of the senses, of any intuition or a conclusion supported by immediately perceived ideas, is 'an habitual or customary connexion' between ideas, a 'customary tie', an 'experimental connection', a connection 'that is entirely the result of custom and experience'. The natural (divinely ordained) language of vision must be learned; and it 'has been learnt at our first entrance into the world; and ever since, almost every moment of our lives, it has been occurring to our thoughts, and fastening and striking deeper into our minds', *New Theory*, 17, 62, 72, 104, 144 (11, 25, 28, 39, 51). This seems perfectly fitting with the analogy between connections of sense and language. What is cognitively gained by experience is thus neither a further layer of sensible ideas nor ideas of a different, intellectual sort.

custom, which determines the imagination to make a transition from the idea of one object to that of its usual attendant, and from the impression of one to a more lively idea of the other. (1.3.14.31)[21]

This is Hume's nearly conclusive statement of his account of causation. The representation of constant conjunctions can acquire an inferential potential, as it is required for probable reasoning, only by being taken up, by custom, in the primitive, customary inferential transitions of the imagination. This is the closing of the gap in causal inference and marks the crucial importance of the more limited imagination, the only mental faculty susceptible to habituation effects. This inferential potential is not reducible to any element or combination of elements of representation. What we represent, when thinking causally, is by Non-Mixture the same before and after we take the inferential step: a plurality of resembling constantly connected objects, in memory; present objects resembling the conjoined ones, in impression. Constant conjunctions have inferential weigh only in the context of custom-based transitions; the inferential step is taken on non-representational grounds.

Hume's account of causal inference, based on Two Viewpoints and the Structural Principle, has important implications for the cognitive functioning of the imagination—some of which have not been lost on contemporary research.[22] Because of custom and transitions, the more limited imagination can store, in an implicit way, in the guise of biases, empirical information and thus make sense of learning from experience. This way of collecting and keeping information derived from sense-experience (or, for that matter, from testimony: Hume has a theory of how, by what mechanism, testimony, education, and so on, operate on imagination: 1.3.9.12) differs from memory because it is not realized as a set of individual

---

[21] 'All our faculties can never carry us farther in our knowledge of this relation, than barely to observe, that particular objects are constantly conjoined together, and that the mind is carried, by a customary transition, from the appearance of one to the belief of the other. We know nothing farther of causation of any kind, than merely the constant conjunction of objects, and the consequent inference of the mind from one to another', Hume, *Enquiry*, 8. 21 (156–7).

[22] In contemporary research the processes of the imagination and its distinctive cognitive functions are frequently modelled in inferential terms. See Williamson's characterization of imagination as the offline analogue (with a mix of offline and online input) of the online updating of beliefs in the light of new information and his modelling its processes by deductive reasoning, especially on the tableaux method (Williamson, 'Knowing by Imagining', 10, 13, 14–16). Cognitive psychology has also focused of the inferential character of imaginative processes. In many respects, imagination finds its primary exercise in framing and assessing counterfactual situations. There are rules to the imaginative construction of counterfactual situations, particularly in connection with what is kept constant and what is allowed to change in deriving conclusions. Just as with Hume's observation- and regularity-based constraints on the customary transitions underlying causal connections or of persistent existence, an important source of the rules of imaginative inference is knowledge of reality, R. Byrne, 'Imagination and Rationality', in A. Kind, ed., *The Routledge Handbook of Philosophy of Imagination*, Routledge, Oxford/New York, 2016, 339–52, 341–2. Notice that such information needs not be explicit. It can operate in the way of effects of availability or familiarity. This is another point of resemblance with Hume.

representational ideas but through the mental effects of repetition, in the guise of biases. In this way, the more limited imagination can explain the cognitive input and role of experience in ways that would not be available in terms of representation. It allows us to give cognitive relevance to information that could not be encoded in individual representations.[23]

The imagination acquires this information not by discrete units but by *gradual change*. 'The past experience, on which all our judgments concerning cause and effect depend, may operate on our mind in such an insensible manner as never to be taken notice of, and may even in some measure be unknown to us' (1.3.8.13). 'As the habit, which produces the association, arises from the frequent conjunction of objects, it must arrive at its perfection by degrees, and must acquire new force from each instance, that falls under our observation' (1.3.12.2). Correspondingly, empirical information is put to work in non-representational terms; that is, not as ideas, as items of comparison, but in the guise of propensities: biases, blocks, and facilitations of conception and mental transition.[24] A propensity is, quite simply, a disposition with a very high likelihood of coming to expression in an open response. A cognitive propensity is a propensity of the mind to engage in certain activities, which, in the causal case, are inferences to existence, prompted by impressions of sense or memory. Hume collects these propensities under the label of custom, 'which proceeds from a past repetition, without any new reasoning or conclusion' (1.3.8.10). The biases of the more limited imagination, when produced by and expressive of experience of constant conjunctions, that is, as effects of custom, are the primitive counterparts of the steps of mature causal reasoning in its comparisons of ideas. In this way, experience can be an input to causal

---

[23] This property is sometimes labelled *domain specificity*. The imagination seems both to store and to put to work certain assumptions concerning what is likely to be given in actual experience. These assumptions may be based on previous learning or even have an evolutionary basis. They are like fragments of a worldview and operate as implicit constraints on thinking and belief. 'Domain-specific processes' depend, for their identification and operation, on specific organizations of content, relating to recognizable areas of experience. These contents are like parts of a naïve, widely shared, possibly species-specific manifest image. This is important for explaining the cognitive productivity of imagination, see J. Weinberg & A. Meskin, 'Puzzling over the Imagination: Philosophical Problems, Architectural Solutions', in Nichols, ed., *The Architecture of the Imagination* (175–202), 181.

[24] Also in contemporary research, real information typically operates on imagination by being implicitly encoded in biases and propensities. One could even say that imagination has as one of its primary functions rightly that of making possible for information about the world to weight in an immediate, fast, abbreviated, rough, but effective way on cognition, See, for a contrast in the cognitive role of beliefs and imaginings, N. Van Leeuwen, 'The Meanings of "Imagine" Part II: Attitude and Action', *Philosophy Compass*, 9, 2014 (791–802). The mental construction of counterfactual situations is governed, as to the selection of the changes in the facts of the real situation, by principles (which also govern the corresponding inference) that express certain assumptions about the context, without explicitly representing them (say, as occurrent beliefs). The paradigmatic way in which such assumptions bear on imagination and inference is in terms of the availability and salience of certain features of situations, that is, in terms of certain properties of mental processes, neither of which directly represent them as obtaining or as true, See R. Byrne & V. Girotto, 'Cognitive Processes in Counterfactual Thinking', in Markman et al., *Handbook of Imagination and Simulation*, 151–60, 156–7; E. Wong et al., 'The Counterfactual Mind-Set', in Markman & al., *Handbook of Imagination and Simulation*, 161–74, 168.

reasoning without circularity; together with the gradual character of cognitive changes, this shows how the limited imagination can avoid the cognitive impossibilities detected by Hume.[25]

Idea-comparing imagination is Hume's counterpart to a faculty of the understanding or reason (including the a priori). By constitutively explanatorily connecting it with imagination in the more limited sense, as parts or functions of the faculty of imagination (opposed to sense and memory, to representation of objects), Hume makes room for a fully naturalistic conception of understanding and reasoning. The imagination is so important for Hume's philosophy because it enacts or simulates the operation of reason or the understanding, without introducing any break or real difference in our cognitive nature. At the same time, the conditions and the properties of reasoning are determined (and modified with respect to the philosophical tradition) by the fact that the imagination operates as a single faculty, that its idea-comparing inferences and its primitive biases transitions are jointly at work in our cognitive activity. The Structural Principle is at work in both directions (so to say): it explains not only how we come to have causal ideas, which we can apply as concepts in idea-comparing reasoning, but also how the shape and conditions of our reasoning capacity depend on its being the expression of a faculty like Hume's imagination. Merging the two parts of the imagination in our cognitive activity is crucially important for Hume's detailed account of probable reasoning as well as for his discussion of scepticism. Only in this way, we can 'carry our view beyond those few objects, which are present to our senses' (1.4.7.3) and come to have the view of a connected universe.

6.2.3 Causal Ideas

Hume's view of the imagination as a faculty simulating or enacting a faculty of reason or understanding also allows us to answer the venerable objection that his account of the idea of cause is circular because it resorts to causal association. Now, undoubtedly, the underlying principle of association is *not* causal because it *operates* causally. *All* principles of association are causal in this sense. Rather, unless the explanation of the idea of cause involves a change of subject matter,

---

[25] One could wonder how making such steps insensible could help with this problem: after all, ideas are either available or they are not; how large is the inferential step that the mind should take without the relevant ideas should not matter. This is true only if we stick to the notion of inference as comparison of ideas (which is where the problem arises in the first place.) But if inference is a mental process which combines features of content and features of mental existence, which is what it is when imagination concurs with representation, how perceptions come to exist and succeed each other in the mind can have an independent causal role to play. "tis evident, that the qualities, which operate upon that faculty [the imagination], run so insensibly and gradually into each other, that 'tis impossible to give them any precise bounds or termination' (3.2.3.7, fn. 73): the claim is about the exact limits of possession; but it can be generalized.

there must be something in the *content* of the underlying association that makes it causal, rather than one by resemblance or contiguity. Then, the objection that Hume is helping himself with a primitive grasp of causal contents seems compelling. However, the objection betrays a neglect or misunderstanding of the Structural Principle. The crucial point is whether the causal content of the relevant natural relations or transitions involves some primitive grasp (not to say comparison) of the idea of cause. But this is not how Hume conceives of this. As we have seen, the transitions of the more limited imagination, that is, of the imagination at its deepest explanatory level, do not encode information and content in the guise of ideas but in that of biases and other ways of responding to perceptions and of changing their properties of existence and content. There is no question, at this level, of imagination grasping and comparing causal ideas in reasoning; even though such ideas ultimately spring from its transitions.

But how are we entitled, then, to identify causal contents with such biases, propensities, and transitions, since they do not involve any causal idea? The answer is that such identification is theory-based, that it depends on Hume's method of cognitive gaps and works of the imagination. In this, as in other cases, Hume proceeds from a cognitive characterization of some mode or instance of thinking which is a perfectly ordinary part of our cognitive practices and is in some respects and to some degree in good order. Like, in the present case, mature causal reasoning, the 'just inference', and the idea of cause. The second step is some argument establishing that no such mode or content can be traced to background cognitions that are non-problematic at the relevant stage of the theory. Like, in the causal case, sense and memory or the a priori. Third, Hume advances radically revisionary explanations, in terms of imagination, of such modes and contents which reinstate, with room for correction and improvement, the cognitive functions that were the starting point of the theory. Now, the primitive imaginative processes which are in theoretical equilibrium with, by being necessary and sufficient explanations for, the conditions and contents of ordinary causal reasoning are, by construction, themselves causal. In the present case, the connection that holds together idea-comparing causal reasoning and the natural relation of cause is that both allow inferring the unobserved in response to observed constant conjunctions and a present impression. In this functional equivalence and in their explanatory priority lies the causal character of the primitive transitions of the imagination; not in their including causal ideas.

This said, there is still the problem of specifying the connection between the transitions of the more limited imagination and mature causal reasoning. This latter, the conclusions of which are directed and reflective causal judgements, is made possible by our possession and mastery of a repertory of causal ideas: ideas of causes, of effects, of this causing that, of all events having a cause, of causes and effects being necessarily connected, of the same causes having the same effects and so on. The availability of such ideas determines a deep difference between the causal transitions of the more limited and the causal reasoning of the idea-comparing imagination. Quite simply, once causal ideas are available, our causal judgements and beliefs cease to be the expression of habituation effects and repeated observation and become a proper cognitive activity.

> 'Tis certain, that not only in philosophy, but even in common life, we may attain the knowledge of a particular cause merely by one experiment, provided it be made with judgment, and after a careful removal of all foreign and superfluous circumstances. (1.3.8.14)

We ordinarily engage in causal reasoning by grasping and comparing causal ideas and principles. The role of custom is only *indirect*, as Hume remarks. It embeds idea-comparing reasoning. It gives us the potential for inferring the unobserved, by grounding in the imagination the proposition of uniformity. In the case of causal judgments based on one observation, it puts us in possession of a principle of causal uniformity which we apply in belief-formation.

> Tho' we are here suppos'd to have had only one experiment of a particular effect, yet we have many millions to convince us of this principle; *that like objects, plac'd in like circumstances, will always produce like effects*; and as this principle has establish'd itself by a sufficient custom, it bestows an evidence and firmness on any opinion, to which it can be apply'd. (1.3.8.14)[26]

Hume remarks that the only form of causal reasoning we are acquainted with when 'arriv'd at the age of maturity' is the idea-comparing one (1.3.12.3). This is also because our experience typically includes contrasting cases, which demand reflection oriented by the grasp of the idea of cause.

> But this method of proceeding [the habitual determination of the mind] we have but few instances of in our probable reasonings; and even fewer than in those, which are deriv'd from the uninterrupted conjunction of objects. In the former species of reasoning we commonly take knowingly into consideration the contrariety of past events; we compare the different sides of the contrariety, and carefully weigh the experiments, which we have on each side. (1.3.12.7)

In the light of this, a full account of causal inference would require an explanation of how the customary transitions of the imagination put in place causal

---

[26] See Schmitt, *Hume's Epistemology*, 136–7: 'For Hume, probable inference is not a form of Lockean reasoning, since it does not involve a presumed connection between ideas. Rather, it is a transition, given an observed constant conjunction of impression of objects'. See, on Locke on reasoning, Owen, *Hume's Reason*, 31, 32, 34, 49, 60–1.

ideas, as they are applied in mature causal reasoning. Causal ideas have conceptual character: the reflective, careful, explicit consideration of circumstances and evidence distinctive of mature causal reasoning (both ordinary and philosophical) involves intentional directedness of thought, distinction of aspects, generalization, and mastery of modal import. These are conceptual features of thinking, which should find a place in Hume's explanation of causal content.

It is fair to say that Hume leaves the issue of how customary, imaginative transitions are turned into the contents of the causal ideas we apply in reasoning undertheorized, just as he does with how the more limited imagination embeds and gives shape to reflection and reason. Hume's account of the idea of cause, as announced at 1.3.3.9, is focused on singular causal inferences. The mental mechanism that ultimately explains causal inference and causal content only makes sense in connection with individual perceptions and beliefs. Still, the particular unions of ideas which allow us to infer causes and effects on particular occasions can in principle form, by composition and abstraction, our general conceptual grasp of causation and the different causal concepts and maxims that we apply in causal reasoning and doxastic deliberation. Hume has a complex and interesting take on causal generalizations. Mature, idea-comparing causal reasoning typically requires general ideas. It includes the grasp and the application of the general names of cause and effect ('Without any farther ceremony, we call the one *cause* and the other *effect*, and infer the existence of the one from that of the other', 1.3.6.2). In ordinary cognitive practice, the constant observation of conjunctions of resembling objects, which Hume primarily identifies in terms of ideas of memory, is bound to weigh on inference as a general idea. That is, not as a collection of ideas of memory of resembling Xs being followed by resembling Ys but as the abstract idea with the general content: all Xs are followed by Ys.[27] And in idea-comparing causal reasoning, we can proceed by directly applying causal concepts and causal rules to singular, one-object situations given in experience. In all these respects, mature causal reasoning is an exercise of conceptual cognition. And Hume's theory can explain how causal ideas can attain generality and modality, the two basic marks of conceptuality. A theory of conceptual causal content could be developed in this way, along naturalist-inferentialist lines.[28]

---

[27] I think that the Causal Maxim—every beginning of existence must have a cause—is susceptible of the same treatment, even if Hume does not tell us much about it. Of course, he denies that is grounded on demonstrative reason. And claims that we cannot be certain of it 'but from experience and observation' (1.3.14.35). However, since it is an idea or maxim with causal content; and since it can obviously have a role in reflective causal reasoning as a conceptual principle, its derivation from experience may well follow the same path as the principle of uniformity of nature.

[28] See, for a concise, brilliant presentation of Hume's account of conceptualized causal reasoning, D. Garrett, 'Hume', in Beebe, Hitchcock, & Menzies, *Oxford Handbook of Causation* (73–91), 77–81. My reading of Hume's doctrine of probable reasoning is very close to the one advanced by Garrett, *Cognition and Commitment*, 82–6, 91–2: causal and inductive inferences are instances of reasoning; can have perfectly good epistemic standing; but do not depend on higher-level reasonings. However, I think one should say that imagination, rather than reason, is the inferential faculty (see Garrett,

'Tis this latter principle, [judgement, imagination as a whole] which peoples the world, and brings us acquainted with such existences, as by their removal in time and place, lye beyond the reach of the sense and memory. By means of it I paint the universe in my imagination, and fix my attention on any part of it I please. (1.3.9.4)

6.3 Summary

Hume's account of the idea of cause is the centrepiece of Book 1 of the *Treatise*. Chapter 6 focuses on its inferentialist, imagination-based dimension.

In § 6.1 I address Hume's analysis of the idea of cause and his shifting it from representation to inference. Hume individuates the content of the idea of cause, as I show in § 6.1.1, from its role in ordinary and philosophical cognition: making possible to infer the existence of unobserved objects, to overstep with reasoning the objects we have available in representation.

This conceptual role, discussed in § 6.1.2, unveils a cognitive gap, because sense and memory lack inferential and modal import and the relation of causation is not metaphysically necessary and a priori. In § 6.1.3 I suggest that the inferentialist character of Hume's account comes to the fore in his dropping the consideration of causal necessity in favour of that of the nature of causal inference. This is also the point of his rejection of the principle that a cause is always necessary.

Hume's Inferentialist Naturalism about causality is examined through the elements, structure, and conditions of causal inference in § 6.1.4. The crucial step of Hume's analysis is the identification of experience as the ground of causal inferences. The nature of experience includes an element of representational content, the constant conjunctions of resembling objects, and inferences from one such object to another, non-observed one.

In § 6.1.5 I suggest that this at last completely identifies the causation gap, a hidden impossibility of experience-based inferences to the unobserved. Hume's extremely influential argument is that the idea of a uniform course of nature, required as a step in such inferences, can be neither from sense and memory nor from demonstrative reason; and that is presupposed by any sort of (non-deductive) reasoning. Only the imagination can put in place the missing idea.

§ 6.2 discusses the inferential mechanism with which the more limited imagination puts in place our idea of cause. § 6.2.1 introduces the distinction between causation as a natural and as a philosophical relation of ideas. The seeming cognitive impossibility of causal reasoning and of causal content is confined to the philosophical relation. The underlying transitions of the more limited

---

Cognition and Commitment, 94): the unity and the explanatory and epistemic role of reason become visible only from the perspective afforded by the inferential working of imagination.

imagination, or causation as a natural relation, allow dissolving the appearance of paradox.

In § 6.2.2 I outline how custom produces the inferential potential of the idea of cause. Experience, the repetition of ideas, cannot change their contents but only the properties and the effects of their mental existence. It can have habituation effects on the more limited imagination, consisting in a certain shape of the inferential propensities and transitions of the imagination. These change how ideas exist in the mind, that is, in certain patterns of union. This change in mental existence is also a change in their contents. In particular it comes to conception as the inferential import essential for causal content and explicit in the proposition of the uniformity of nature. Represented or possible objects come in this way to be conceived as causes and effects.

Finally, in § 6.2.3, I discuss whether Hume's account of the idea of cause is hiddenly circular, by presupposing, in the transitions of the imagination, some grasp of causal content. However, such transitions do not compare ideas but respond to their conception in terms of non-representational structuring factors, like custom. These transitions can encode information corresponding to causal contents, without these being present as ideas. The functional equivalence of such transitions with causal reasonings is the basis for individuating the former as causal.

7
That Intelligible Quality

> I do not ascribe to the will that unintelligible necessity, which is suppos'd to lie in matter. But I ascribe to matter, that intelligible quality, call it necessity or not, which the most rigorous orthodoxy does or must allow to belong to the will. I change, therefore, nothing in the receiv'd systems, with regard to the will, but only with regard to material objects.
>
> (2.3.2.4)

We now have to consider the second problematic aspect emerging from Hume's analysis of causal reasoning as inference to the unobserved and of the idea of cause: causal necessity or the '*necessary connexion*, which enters into our idea of cause and effect' (1.3.2.13). Causal necessity is explained with the Established Maxim by Determination rather than by Separability. But, to explain the modal import of the idea of cause, Hume must identify the pertinent determining principles of the imagination; and do this in such a way as to make sense of causal cognition as we have it, with its conceptual roles and conditions of justness. The modal dimension of causal content is also key to understanding Hume's overall philosophy of causation and the source of some interesting interpretive and conceptual problems.

7.1 The Missing Idea of Necessary Connexion

Part 3 of Book 1 of the *Treatise* has a pleasant chiastic structure. We move from causal necessity to causal inference and then from causal inference to causal necessity. The first step consists in the discovery that the relation of necessary connection, which is 'of much greater importance' than any other aspect of the idea of cause, should be explained with the nature and structure of causal inference. Hume then advances, as a second step, a radically revisionary conception of causal inference, based on imagination and custom. At the third step he applies his conception of causal inference to advance a revised conception of causal necessity and thereby of the overall content of the idea of cause. This is done in 1.3.14: *Of the idea of necessary connexion*, which together with 1.3.6: *Of the inference from the impression to the idea*, is the hinge of Hume's account of causation.

> Having thus explain'd the manner, *in which we reason beyond our immediate impressions, and conclude that such particular causes must have such particular effects*; we must now return upon our footsteps to examine that question, which first occur'd to us, and which we dropt in our way, *viz. What is our idea of necessity, when we say that two objects are necessarily connected together.* (1.3.14.1)

Hume's basic line of answer is that, in the light of the Established Maxim, a change in what contents we can conceive, like that consisting in the conferral of inferential potentials on ideas of objects, can have effects on the conception of the corresponding ideas and issue in their modal qualification. Hume proceeds by rehearsing and refining the arguments given in 1.3.2–6, now with a special focus on the causal necessity gap. In fact, at 1.3.14.2–14, Hume provides the much needed support for the interim conclusion of 1.3.2.12 (as the opening lines of 1.3.14 remind the reader): the idea of necessary connection is not from impressions of sensation; and integrates with it the claim that causal necessity cannot have origin in comparison of ideas. The progression of Hume's argument is not perspicuous and requires commentary.

Hume's explicit topic is the central question of the metaphysics of causation: the productive character of causes. 'There is no question, which on account of its importance, as well as difficulty, has caus'd more disputes both among antient and modern philosophers, than this concerning the efficacy of causes, or that quality which makes them be follow'd by their effects' (1.3.14.4). The view of causal efficacy that Hume takes as traditional and wants to criticize and revise is that it consists in some quality residing in the objects. 'That quality which makes them be followed by their objects' (1.3.14.3). Therefore, Hume's modal question about causation, parallel to the question of whether the inferential potential of causal inference depends on object representation, is an enquiry into the nature and grounds of causal necessity. Whether 'when we speak of a necessary connexion betwixt objects' we can 'suppose, that this connexion depends upon an efficacy or energy, with which any of these objects are endow'd' (1.3.14.14). Hume's revisionist and reductionist metaphysics of powers is that no productive quality, energy, or power is inherent to objects and that the necessity of the causal relation is mind dependent: it consists in a relation between ideas. Both causal necessity and causal inference unveil a cognitive gap and only transitions of the imagination put them in place. In this way Inferentialist Naturalism gives unity to Hume's theory of causation.

Hume's first step in individuating the modal gap of causation is to examine 'what idea we have of that efficacy, which is the subject of the controversy' (1.3.14.3). He points out that this idea cannot be defined in terms of other, plausibly related ones, because they form a network of notions with essentially the same content.

> I begin with observing that the terms of *efficacy, agency, power, force, energy, necessity, connexion,* and *productive quality,* are all nearly synonymous; and therefore 'tis an absurdity to employ any of them in defining the rest.   (1.3.14.4)

These terms or ideas cannot be defined because they give expression to a new and original dimension of content, which cannot be reduced by Non-Mixture and the First Principle to given elements. As Hume says, 'this of power' is 'a new idea' (1.3.14.17; the same holds of the equivalent ones, of course). Then, it is no wonder that the efficacy, and so on, of causes cannot be known by reason or by imagination comparing already given ideas.

> No kind of reasoning can give rise to a new idea, such as this of power is; but wherever we reason, we must antecedently be possest of clear ideas, which may be the objects of our reasoning. The conception always precedes the understanding; and where the one is obscure, the other is uncertain; where the one fails, the other must fail also.   (1.3.14.17)

Since the idea of causal efficacy is new and should be 'an object of the simplest understanding, if not of the senses' (causal ideas are in the repertory of perfectly ordinary thinkers) (1.3.14.7), the thought suggests itself that it is given representationally, in sensation or reflection. 'Since reason can never give rise to the idea of efficacy, that idea must be deriv'd from experience, and from some particular instances of this efficacy, which make their passage into the mind by the common channels of sensation or reflection.' (1.3.14.6). Hume therefore asks whether there is some 'natural production, where the operation and efficacy of a cause can be clearly conceiv'd and comprehended by the mind, without any danger of obscurity or mistake' (1.3.14.6) and advances two arguments against this possibility.

(1) The first argument is elenctic. It opens with an (expedited) review of the received opinions about the energy of causes. ('There are some, who maintain, that bodies operate by their substantial form; others, by their accidents or qualities; several, by their matter and form; some, by their form and accidents; others, by certain virtues and faculties distinct from all this.') These opinions are all rejected as 'perfectly unintelligible and inexplicable'. Hume then sets a challenge to show an instance of a cause 'where we discover the power or operating principle'. (This move is typical of Book 1: 'This defiance we are oblig'd frequently to make use of, as being almost the only means of proving a negative in philosophy', 1.3.14.7.) The failure to meet this challenge ("the small success, which has been met with in all attempts to fix this power") is the reason which 'at last oblig'd philosophers to conclude, that the ultimate force and efficacy of nature is perfectly unknown to us, and that 'tis in vain we search for it in all the known

qualities of matter' (1.3.14.8). This sceptical conclusion about the intelligibility of causation and the ensuing discussion and rejection of the ways out philosophers have explored—Occasionalism, the restriction of causal agency to God; the identification of the efficacy of secondary causes with an unknown quality—are Hume's elenctic grounds for denying that causal power resides in the objects.

(2) Hume's a priori argument hinges on what it is to conceive of a 'particular species' of power, that is, to be 'able to place this power in some particular being, and conceive that being as endow'd with a real force and energy, by which such a particular effect necessarily results from its operation' (1.3.14.13). This is an application of the all-important distinction between metaphysical and physical necessity and of the connection between the former and the a priori; therefore it is an argument that directly addresses the modal dimension of the ideas of causal power.

> (i) The starting point of the argument is what a representation of power, 'the true manner of conceiving a particular power in a particular body' (1.3.14.13), would be. The conditions of such representation are that such force or energy should be real, that is, belong as a real property to a particular object; and that it should be 'absolutely requisite' to the production of effects. This is assumed for reductio.
> (ii) These conditions have an epistemic implication: to have such representation would be to 'distinctly and particularly conceive the connexion between the cause and effect, and be able to pronounce, from a simple view of the one, that it must be followed of preceded by the other' (1.3.14.13). We would know the productive qualities in objects a priori, given only that we conceived them.
> (iii) But no such epistemic position is available. First, by Hume's conceivability account of modality, necessity can be based on the 'simple view' of objects only if it is derivable by Separability. But this falsifies the nature of causal necessity: necessity by Separability applies only to objects that are neither different nor distinguishable; but causal relations only obtain between different, distinguishable, and separable objects (see 1.4.5.30). In this way, to satisfy the epistemic implication, we would arrive to a concept of causal necessity that could not be applied to causally related objects.[1] Second, such epistemic position is in itself an impossibility.

---

[1] Later in 1.3.14 Hume responds to an objection against his positive account of causal power as mind-dependent by pointing out that the objection depends on misconstruing the idea of power or efficacy. Obscurity and error begin to take place when 'we make the terms of power and efficacy signify something, of which we have a clear idea, and which is incompatible with those objects, to which we apply it' (1.3.14.27). Here the crucial point is that ordinary thinkers and 'false philosophy' associate to the ideas of power and efficacy a meaning that is incompatible with their application to objects.

> The human mind cannot form such an idea of two objects, as to conceive any connexion betwixt them, or comprehend distinctly that power or efficacy, by which they are united. Such a connexion wou'd amount to a demonstration, and wou'd imply the absolute impossibility for the one object not to follow, or to be conceiv'd not to follow upon the other: Which kind of connexion has already been rejected in all cases. (1.3.14.13)

In this way, Hume puts to work his conclusion about causal inference (it does not deliver a priori knowledge) in the reductio of the view that causal necessity can be in the objects. (This was only indirectly proved at 1.3.3, with the rejection of the Causal Maxim, see § 6.1.3.) The epistemic, inferential gap of causation is the ground for identifying the causal modal gap in representation. Locating causal powers in objects makes their idea illusory: 'we can never distinctly conceive how any particular power can possibly reside in any particular object' (1.3.14.13). This allows Hume to conclude with complete generality: 'We never have any impression, that contains any power or efficacy. We never therefore have any idea of power' (1.3.14.11). (Notice that the dialectical import of the argument requires that an intelligible conception of causal power should be anyway available.) Together with the rejection of a source for the idea of causal efficacy in idea-comparing reasoning, this argument completes the individuation a modal cognitive gap in causal cognition.

> Thus upon the whole we may infer, that when we talk of any being, whether of a superior or inferior nature, as endow'd with a power or force, proportion'd to any effect; when we speak of a necessary connexion betwixt objects, and suppose, that this connexion depends upon an efficacy or energy, with which any of these objects are endow'd; in all these expressions, *so apply'd*, we have really no distinct meaning, and make use only of common words, without any clear and determinate ideas. (1.3.14.14)

7.2 Imagination and the Necessity of Causes

7.2.1 From Causal Inference to Necessary Connexion

This negative result should be balanced with Hume's recognition that necessary connexion is the most important relation included in the idea of cause and thus that an intelligible notion of causal necessity is required and should be possible. In this connection, the restriction, '*so apply'd*', that Hume emphasizes in the last quoted text, is crucially important. Hume is only rejecting the view that the idea of causal necessity is gained by object representation or by reasoning. There may be, however, a legitimate understanding and application of this idea, which Hume is prepared to explain and to vindicate (as he did with causal inferential potentials)—no matter how such intelligible meaning may be hidden and distorted in ordinary and philosophical discourse. Hume's explanatory task is thus also revisionary and qualifiedly vindicatory: identifying, with the conceptual resources of his conceivability account of modality, the source and right application of the idea of causal necessity and, thereby, of ideas like powers, energies, and so on. In either regard (explanatory and vindicatory), there is a strict continuity between Hume's account of causal inference and that of causal necessity. The production of the inferential potential of causal ideas by the more limited imagination is a change in the contents we can conceive. Conceivability is the general ground for the modal qualification of contents. Hume can therefore move from the conditions of causal inference to causal necessity and from the justness of the first to the intelligibility of the second.

This is why he extends the explanation of causal inference to necessary connexion. The 'simple consideration' of one or two objects, 'of which the one is the cause and the other the effect', does not allow us to 'perceive' the 'tie' that unites them and to 'pronounce, that there is a connexion betwixt them'. 'Did we never see any but particular conjunctions of objects, entirely different from each other, we shou'd never be able to form any such ideas' (1.3.14.15). Just as we could never infer the one from the other. But the conditions on conceivable contents, in regard both to connexion and inference, change as soon as we consider the repeated observation of conjunctions of objects.

> But again; suppose we observe several instances, in which the same objects are always conjoin'd together, we immediately conceive a connexion betwixt them, and begin to draw an inference from one to another. This multiplicity of resembling instances, therefore, constitutes the very essence of power or connexion, and is the source, from which the idea of it arises. In order, then, to understand the idea of power, we must consider that multiplicity; nor do I ask more to give a solution of that difficulty, which has so long perplex'd us. (1.3.14.16)

The solution is provided by Two Viewpoints. No change in content and conception would be intelligible if we were restricted to the viewpoint of the contents of ideas. But perceptions figure in the theory also for their mental existence, with properties determined, for instance, by repetition and habituation effects. These properties are at the same time content-bearing qualities and their effects on the mind have import for the conceivability of contents. The combination of Two Viewpoints with the Established Maxim allows Hume to identify the change in conception required for explaining the idea of causal necessity.

> For thus I reason. The repetition of perfectly similar instances can never *alone* give rise to an original idea, different from what is to be found in any particular instance, as has been observ'd, and as evidently follows from our fundamental principle, *that all ideas are copy'd from impressions*. Since therefore the idea of

power is a new original idea, not to be found in any one instance, and which yet arises from the repetition of several instances, it follows, that the repetition *alone* has not that effect, but must either *discover* or *produce* something new, which is the source of that idea. (1.3.14.16)

The new content of the idea of power is generated by the repetition of conjunctions of objects. Hume considers two views of such generation: as a *discovery* or as a *production*, in relation to objects and ideas. But repeated ideas, considered in their contents of for the objects they at least potentially represent, are 'multiply'd', not 'enlarg'd' or changed by their repetition. Therefore, their mere repetition cannot *discover*, represent anything new in the objects. Objects, in their turn, are distinct existences and their repeated occurrence leaves intact their distinctness. In this respect, it cannot *produce* anything new in them. (Of course, distinct objects can be causally connected; but the content of this thought is precisely what is to be explained.) 'There is, then, nothing new either discover'd or produc'd in any objects by their constant conjunction, and by the uninterrupted resemblance of their relations of succession and contiguity' (1.3.14.19). Just as repetition of representations cannot produce any inferential potential ('we can draw no inference from it, nor make it a subject either of our demonstrative or probable reasonings; as has been already prov'd', 1.3.14.17; see also 1.3.14.1), so it cannot have any modal import. Content as of causal power, in what it has of new and original, must then be produced in the ideas and discovered about them. This is a task for the more limited imagination.

7.2.2 From Necessary Connexion to the Imagination

The experience of constantly conjoined, resembling objects and what it produces and discover in our other ideas put us in possession of the problematic ideas of power and necessary connection: 'But 'tis from this resemblance, that the ideas of necessity, of power, and of efficacy, are deriv'd'. Because of their genesis and conditions, such ideas do not even *purport* to represent objects: 'These ideas, [the network of ideas of causal necesssity] therefore, represent not any thing, that does or can belong to the objects, which are constantly conjoin'd' (1.3.14.19). This is just as it should be, with Hume's apparatus of cognitive gaps, which requires us to move away from object representation. 'We must, therefore, turn ourselves to some other quarter to seek the origin of that idea' (1.3.14.19). Such 'other quarter' is the more limited imagination.

7.2.2.1 The Inferential Core
The repeated observation of constantly conjoined resembling perceptions produces a change in mental existence. It causes a new perception, a new impression that by its occurrence and character is the model for the idea of causal necessity.

> Tho' the several resembling instances, which give rise to the idea of power, have no influence on each other, and can never produce any new quality *in the object*, which can be the model of that idea, yet the *observation* of this resemblance produces a new impression *in the mind*, which is its real model. (1.3.14.20; see also 1.3.14.1: 'But upon farther enquiry I find, that the repetition is not in every particular the same, but produces a new impression.')

The explanation of causal necessity applies Two Viewpoints. Hume spells this out in the following text, which is the paradigm of his account of modality by the Established Maxim and Determination.

> For after we have observ'd the resemblance in a sufficient number of instances, we immediately feel a determination of the mind to pass from one object to its usual attendant, and to conceive it in a stronger light upon account of that relation. This determination is the only effect of the resemblance; and therefore must be the same with power or efficacy, whose idea is deriv'd from the resemblance. The several instances of resembling conjunctions lead us into the notion of power and necessity. These instances are in themselves totally distinct from each other, and have no union but in the mind, which observes them, and collects their ideas. Necessity, then, is the effect of this observation, and is nothing but an internal impression of the mind, or a determination to carry our thoughts from one object to another. (1.3.14.20; see also 1.3.14.1: 'the mind is *determin'd* by custom to consider its usual attendant')

The basis of the explanation, of course, is the same with that of generality and of causal inferential potentials. A repeated experience produces a customary transition of the more limited imagination, thus changing the propensities and the activities of the mind. Such propensities and transitions are different in the different cases. In generality, the propensity is to shift from an occurrence of one of the resembling names given to resembling ideas to the conception of one of such ideas, together with the consciousness that transitions to other resembling ideas were available and with the elicitation of counterexamples to transitions actually performed. In causal inferential potentials, it is the propensity to move from one idea (present in impression or memory) to another one, constantly conjoined to it but present in impression or memory, and to take the object represented by the second idea as existing or having existed. In causal necessity, the transition and the propensity are the same with causal inference, but it is considered in a different regard and with different general effects. The propensity to customary transitions among ideas does not matter, in the case of causal necessity, directly for the relations or unions of ideas that it produces (a potential for inference), but for how it determines the activity of the imagination and for the feeling of such determination (a channelling of conception). The description of the mental change, thus, has shifted from function (union of ideas and expectation) to phenomenology (a feeling or internal impression of determination). This influence on the imagination and the phenomenology of it are crucial for the explanation of causal necessity. "'Tis this impression, then, or *determination,* which affords me the idea of necessity' (1.3.14.1).

As has already been said, this is a paradigmatic case in which Two Viewpoints, the Structural Principle, and the cognitive flexibility of the imagination are central to Hume's explanations. Consider the following text (from the conclusive part of 1.3.14).

> When any object is presented to us, it immediately conveys to the mind a lively idea of that object, which is usually found to attend it; and this determination of the mind forms the necessary connexion of these objects. But when we change the point of view, from the objects to the perceptions; in that case the impression is to be considered as the cause, and the lively idea as the effect; and their necessary connexion is that new determination, which we feel to pass from the idea of the one to that of the other.   (1.3.14.29)

Here Hume is reverse-engineering his explanation of causal necessity: a change in viewpoint allows the distinction of two patterns of relations among what are actually the same beings and makes it possible to explain cognitive changes that would otherwise be unaccountable. One pattern involves a present object, the content of an impression, which immediately conveys the mind to the idea of another object (by a customary transition). This is a relation between contents and thus between objects; the determination of the mind to pass from the one to the other is the source of the idea of the necessary connexion of these objects or contents. This is what we think when we think in terms of causal necessity: we think of them as necessarily connected; this is the most important aspect of the idea of cause. But to explain this determination we cannot rely only on the objects or contents of the ideas. We must 'change the point of view' from objects to perceptions, moving from properties of content to properties of mental existence of the same perceptions. This is the second pattern. From this point of view, the transition of the imagination does not count as a relation of contents but as the shaping of our acts of conceiving. This channelling of the imagination and the experience of it explain how a necessary connexion is ascribed to the objects of these ideas. The modal force springs from the determination of the mind, the individuation of the modalized objects springs from the contents of the ideas, by Non-Mixture. If we only considered contents or objects, the necessity would be unexplained. If we only considered perceptions or mental existence, the ascription of necessity to certain objects would be unexplained. The transitions of the more limited imagination are the unifying principle.

With regard of causal necessity, as in the other cases, this inferentialist explanation is not only indispensable ('Without considering it in this view, we can never arrive at the most distant notion of it, or be able to attribute it either to external or internal objects, to spirit or body, to causes or effects', 1.3.14.20) but, if it succeeds, constitutive. 'This determination is the only effect of the resemblance; and therefore must be the same with power or efficacy, whose idea is deriv'd from the resemblance.' Hume makes claims of constitutive import or identity about the relations between impression, determination, and necessity. "Tis this impression, then, or *determination*, which affords me the idea of necessity' (1.3.14.1). 'Necessity, then, is the effect of this observation, and is nothing but an internal impression of the mind, or a determination to carry our thoughts from one object to another' (1.3.14.20). 'There is no internal impression, which has any relation to the present business, but that propensity, which custom produces, to pass from an object to the idea of its usual attendant. This therefore is the essence of necessity' (1.3.14.22). This is, of course, an implication of the Established Maxim: what can be clearly conceived of only in one way, excludes any other conception and possibility of the same kind.

The imaginative and inferential core of causal necessity comes into view, forcefully, in a conclusive, complex claim combining causal inference, customary transitions, and necessary connexion.

> The necessary connexion betwixt causes and effects is the foundation of our inference from one to the other. The foundation of our inference is the transition arising from the accustom'd union. These are, therefore, the same.   (1.3.14.21)

The first sentence refers to the role of causal necessity in mature causal reasoning: when we reason by comparing causal ideas, we take into account their modal dimension (we will see later that this raises some issues). We also rely on principles with modal force. Hume endorses the Causal Maxim, the necessity of a cause for any beginning of existence; and clearly assumes that it is a principle of reasoning we ordinarily, almost inescapably accept. The principle of the uniformity of nature, which is the propositional form of the inferential potential of our reasoning to the unobserved, is modal in character; and the same is certainly true of the principle of causal uniformity, which is its application in reflective causal reasoning. The second sentence refers to what makes causal inference possible, what produces the inferential potential of the idea of cause: customary transitions of the more limited imagination. Furthermore, when performing idea-comparing causal inferences we are still engaged in imaginative transitions: in our cognitive activity there is no deep divide between the former and latter (this is important for the conditions of causal cognition and for Hume's response to scepticism). The third sentence states the identity of necessary connexions and customary transitions, with the essential mediation of the Established Maxim. This verifies the hypothesis that the relation of necessary connection might depend on the inference, rather than the other way around (1.3.6.3).

7.2.2.2 The Impression of Determination

The impression of determination belongs to the mental kid of impressions of reflection, or secondary impressions, individuated by what causes them (in this case, the change that repetitions of perceptions bring about in the mind), as opposed to impressions of sensation, which are primarily individuated by the objects they present (see § 2.1). As an impression of reflection, an 'internal impression', it is a distinct mental episode and thus different from belief, which is a pure manner of conception (see *Appendix* 4). But still, as it is with any impression, it is accompanied by feeling, by a distinctive mode of conception. 'For after we have observ'd the resemblance in a sufficient number of instances, we immediately feel a determination of the mind to pass from one object to its usual attendant, and to conceive it in a stronger light upon account of that relation' (1.3.14.20).[2] It is a feeling of being determined to think or conceive of certain ideas in a certain succession. Its psychological character is thus well suited to ground necessity by the Established Maxim. This is neatly summarized in the following texts.

> Wherever, therefore, we observe the same union, and wherever the union operates in the same manner upon the belief and opinion, we have the idea of causes and necessity, tho' perhaps we may avoid those expressions. Motion in one body in all past instances, that have fallen under our observation, is follow'd upon impulse by motion in another. 'Tis impossible for the mind to penetrate farther. From this constant union it *forms* the idea of cause and effect, and by its influence *feels* the necessity. (2.3.1.16)

These claims, in particular that the internal impression *is* the determination of the mind, have been found difficult by some interpreters.[3] I would rather say that this is exactly the form that Hume's explanation of causal necessity should take. The distinction between determination and impression is only functional, of explanatory role: the first puts in place an inferential potential, the second acts as a condition on conceivability. One and the same item, a transition and a propensity to a transition of ideas, can figure in either regard. Most importantly, the propensity can only be identified, in the framework of Hume's philosophy, by its manifestations, transitions of ideas. 'I have already observ'd, that power, as distinguish'd from its exercise, has either no meaning at all, or is nothing but a possibility or probability of existence; by which any object approaches to reality,

---

[2] For a good characterization of the multiple roles of the internal impression of determination is in D. Garrett, 'Hume's Theory of Causation', in D. Ainslie & A. Butler eds., *The Cambridge Companion to Hume's Treatise*, Cambridge University Press, New York 2015 (69–100), 75–6.

[3] See Beebee, *Hume on Causation*, 146–7; Stroud, *Hume*, 80–1.

and has a sensible influence on the mind' (2.2.5.7). Such manifestations are felt, are secondary impressions. The 'essence of necessity' is the 'internal impression, or impression of reflection', which is the 'propensity, which custom produces, to pass from an object to the idea of its usual attendant' (1.3.14.22). Thus, there is nothing amiss in saying that determination and impressions are in fact the same, even though conceptualized differently. Given that they are constitutive of causal necessity, there is also nothing amiss in saying that determination and impression *are* causal necessity.

7.2.2.3 Causal Necessity and the Imagination

Hume's Determination account of causal necessity merges customary transitions with the general, Conceivability theory of modal content. This substantiates in a crucial respect the Established Maxim. A major discovery of Part 3 of the *Treatise* is precisely that the necessity of causes is physical necessity, not explained by Separability. And the reciprocal: that physical necessity is instantiated in causal relations, with which we are perfectly familiar. Thus, there are actual principles of conception—in the nature of our minds—which make this kind of modality available and applicable in an intelligible way. Hume's theory of physical necessity is premised on the claim that Separability does not restrict possibility enough to account for our cognitive practices and our worldview. 'All beings in the universe, consider'd in themselves, appear entirely loose and independent of each other' (3.1.1.22). But our view or image is one of a world of connected contingent objects, of a posteriori or external but non-accidental relations, of empirical but structural conditions. The internal impression of determination, because of the way it takes hold of our awareness, can certainly channel conception by the imagination. Therefore, it can govern inferences of Conceivability: what I have dubbed *pour cause*, Determination, as opposed to Separability. To have such impression or feeling is to be restricted in one's capacity for conceiving ideas, that is, in one's imagination. The experience of a constant conjunction produces a propensity to conceive of objects in that relation which is such 'that we cannot *without a sensible violence* survey them in any other' (1.3.11.4; my italic). The mind is determined by custom to pass from cause to effect and 'upon the appearance of the one, 'tis almost impossible for it not to form an idea of the other'. In fact, it cannot entertain '*without violence*' any other, contrasting conception (1.3.12.11; my italic). Objects, in this way, seem 'inseparable', even in the absence of 'any primary connexion betwixt the ideas' (1.3.8.13). This near impossibility of conceiving otherwise, a property of the more limited imagination grounded in custom and in internal impressions, puts in place the idea of causal necessity. ''Tis this impression, then, or *determination*, which affords me the idea of necessity' (1.3.14.1).

7.2.3 Transitions and Conceptions: Spreading in the Mind, Spreading on the Objects

7.2.3.1 Conceiving Connexions

Hume is perfectly comfortable with the idea that the manifest image, the worldview of the vulgar (that is, of any of us, most of the time) is one of entities connected by necessary causal relations and endued with powers and energies. (This view is disorderly, unsystematic: it also makes room for chance and even miracles.) The causal structure of the world is not a pragmatic or linguistic principle of organization (like in Berkeley) but what we seem to ourselves to perceive, to be given in perception or experience.

> 'Tis natural for men, in their common and careless way of thinking, to imagine they perceive a connexion betwixt such objects as they have constantly found united together; and because custom has render'd it difficult to separate the ideas, they are apt to fancy such a separation to be in itself impossible and absurd. (1.4.3.9)[4]

The empirical world immediately appears to us *as cemented*; the two systems of realities, as connected or even *as one*; objects, as powerful and *dependent* one on the other. The same holds (even though Hume does not make this point explicitly) of the conditions of causal inference: the course of nature, which is the general background for such inference, appears to us *as uniform*; the causal inferential potentials associated to the ideas of objects, *as identifying* them. When we conceive and judge of objects as causally related, when we engage in first-order, reflective causal reasoning, we seem to ourselves to be reading off causes, effects, powers, energies from our perceptual experience. The analytic starting point of Hume's account ('To consider the matter *a priori*, any thing may produce any thing', 1.4.5.30; 'All beings in the universe, consider'd in themselves, appear entirely loose and independent of each other', 3.1.1.22) is, rightly, *analytic*, gained by relatively a priori reasoning. The fixed order and connection of sense and memory is, by contrast, a layer of our actual experience.[5]

---

[4] 'The generality of mankind never find any difficulty in accounting for the more common and familiar operations of nature; such as the descent of heavy bodies, the growth of plants, the generation of animals, or the nourishment of bodies by food: But suppose, that, in all these cases, they perceive the very force or energy of the cause, by which it is connected with its effect, and is for ever infallible in its operation. They acquire, by long habit, such a turn of mind, that, upon the appearance of the cause, they immediately expect with assurance its usual attendant, and hardly conceive it possible, that any other event could result from it' (*E* 7.21).

[5] It is by now a stable interpretive position that Hume outlines and subscribes such a phenomenology of causation. See Beebee, *Hume on Causation*, 77–81, 88–9; and Kail, *Projection and Realism*,

However, the 'real model' of the idea of power and of the equivalent ones: efficacy, agency, force, energy, necessity, connexion, and productive quality is nothing but the impression or feeling of determination '*in the mind*'. Hume strongly contrasts his explanation to any other that refers to 'any new quality *in the object*, which can be the model of that idea [causal necessity]' (1.3.14.20). Still, we do have those ideas and apply them to objects and by their means we come to think and believe something about the world. Something qualitative and cognizable. 'I paint the universe in my imagination, and fix my attention on any part of it I please' (1.3.9.4). Causal ideas therefore find application (in conception, judgement, and reasoning) to the objects we are acquainted with by sense and memory. But they are essentially inferential and cannot be modelled on qualities of objects. The problem then arises of how transitions of the imagination and impressions in the mind can be the real model of ideas suitable for composing our qualitative worldview, which is, after all, a huge complex idea. Notice that this is not a problem which Non-Mixture can address: it is not a problem about the individuation of the objects which take up modal qualification, but about the phenomenology of modally qualified ideas.

Hume is perfectly aware of the importance and difficulty of this topic. His account of the idea of necessary connexion is built around the contrast between the ordinary and philosophical (*falsely* philosophical) view of causal necessity and powers as really being in the objects and his view of the internal model of the idea of causal necessity, as 'something, that exists in the mind, not in objects'. Hume duly records this contrast in terms of the paradoxical character of his account.

> I am sensible, that of all the paradoxes, which I have had, or shall hereafter have occasion to advance in the course of this treatise, the present one is the most violent, and that 'tis merely by dint of solid proof and reasoning I can ever hope it will have admission, and overcome the inveterate prejudices of mankind.
>
> (1.3.14.24)

Hume rightly doubts that his deeply revisionary doctrine that 'power and necessity' are 'qualities of perceptions, not of objects, and are internally felt by the soul,

---

108–10. The idea that imagination is involved in some sort of imaging and painting, of course, is widespread: for the Cartesians, ideas are images painted in the brain or in the imagination; imagination is active in creating images and is corporeal, as painting requires. For contemporary discussion, see A. Kind, 'Putting the Image Back in Imagination', *Philosophy and Phenomenological Research*, 52, 2001, 85–109, 98–9. It would be badly anachronistic to bring Hume into this debate. Hume's overall conception of the content of ideas, whether representational or not, straddles across the pictorial-descriptional divide. It is phenomenal, imagistic, therefore mereologically constituted; but this structure is held to bear, realize distinctive cognitive functions like apprehension, judgment, inference (see § 4.2.4). In the case of ideas of imagination, some sort of compositionality coexists with pictorial character. No matter how uneasy we can be with this match, it is Hume's own position and makes void any attempt to categorize his imagination as imagistic or not.

and not perceiv'd externally in bodies' can ever gain widespread acceptance. But his concern is certainly not for the popularity of his views. It is explanatory. The Important Footnote provides a general rationale for the step from transitions to conception. Conception is the simple act of the mind, which is common to ideas, judgements, and reasonings. In this respect, for how they are present to awareness or for their phenomenology, perceptions and transitions are on a par (their structures are different, of course). But applying the principle laid down in the Important Footnote to the case of causal transitions and causal ideas would require a complex analysis and explanation that Hume fails to provide. Hume takes the conversion of mental transitions into conceptions as a manifest phenomenon and does not attempt to reduce it to any deeper property of the mind or to specify a psychological mechanism for it. Still, just as he does for the other original qualities of the imagination, he describes its way of operating and its contribution to explaining our cognition.[6]

7.2.3.2 Spreading in the Mind

In Hume's texts we find *two* varieties and functions of spreading of ideas. One is a spreading of ideas which is *internal to the mind*, internal to the phenomenology of perceptions. The mind spreads itself or, better, spreads its transitions as conceptions of ideas, in such a way as to fill gaps in the qualitative texture of experience. The missing shade of blue is the paradigmatic example. But Hume talks of this sort of spreading also with reference to our completion of partial visual images.

> Suppose I see the legs and thighs of a person in motion, while some interpos'd object conceals the rest of his body. Here 'tis certain, the imagination spreads out the whole figure. I give him a head and shoulders, and breast and neck. These members I conceive and believe him to be possess'd of. Nothing can be more evident, than that this whole operation is perform'd by the thought or imagination alone. (*Appendix* 4)

Spreading of this sort is also involved in filling general gaps of observation or sense-experience. Phenomena of spreading seem to be involved in the perception of the size of visible objects.

> 'Tis only by experience that he infers the greatness of the object from some peculiar qualities of the image; and this inference of the judgment he confounds

---

[6] See M. Boehm, 'Hume' Projectivism Explained', in *Synthese*, Topical Collection: *Humeanisms*, 2020 https://doi.org/10.1007/s11229-020-02718-9. In her excellent discussion, Boehm points out that Hume owes an account of the mental process realizing spreading and that some suggestions can be found in the way impressions of reflection can be merged with ideas and relations of ideas (Boehm rightly considers 2.2.6.1 as a key text in this area).

with sensation, as is common on other occasions. Now 'tis evident, that the inference of the judgment is here much more lively than what is usual in our common reasonings, and that a man has a more vivid conception of the vast extent of the ocean from the image he receives by the eye, when he stands on the top of a high promontory, than merely from hearing the roaring of the waters.

(1.3.9.11)

Spreading in this case seems to consist in the merging of judgement with sensation: the ideas grounded on imagination and tacitly applied in judging are seamlessly inserted in visual experience and present themselves to the mind with a sensorial appearance. The same holds of distance: "Tis thus the understanding corrects the appearances of the senses, and makes us imagine, that an object at twenty foot distance seems even to the eye as large as one of the same dimensions at ten' (1.3.10.12). Quite generally, our view of the spatial and temporal continuity of the world, which is an aspect or a step of Hume's account of the idea of body, requires the imagination to spread ideas in the mind, as a consequence of its inferences and as a support for and a complement of them (see § 9.2.1).

'Tis evident I can never account for this phaenomenon [the delivery of a letter from a distant friend], conformable to my experience in other instances, without spreading out in my mind the whole sea and continent between us, and supposing the effects and continu'd existence of posts and ferries, according to my memory and observation. (1.4.2.20).

Spreading ideas in the mind consists in the imagination completing the field of our experience with materials qualitatively homogeneous with those delivered by sense and memory but not dependent on them for their presence and location. It is an expansion and complement of what is present to awareness. This is particularly clear in the first, second, and fourth example; but the third also seems to be of this character: sensorial clues are the main factor in determining the apparently sensible dimensions of objects. This sort of spreading appears to be an indispensable function of the imagination, in the context of cognitive gaps, as well as one which is widely recognized in contemporary theories of the imagination and perception.[7] I would suggest that such spreading of ideas in the mind is the sort of act of conception that gives best expression to the associative function of the more limited imagination and allows it to weigh on our awareness. The unions that ideas can have in the fancy (in contrast to the understanding) consist in its transitions and provide contents for its further, idea-comparing inferences. But

---

[7] For an accessible introduction to the cognitive science of the varieties of integration and organization which are at work in vision (vision is paradigmatic in the study of perceptual experience), see V. Bruce et al., *Visual Perception*, Psychology Press, Hove 1996, especially 106–70.

since, by Separability and Non-Mixture, the existence and contents of such ideas persist to be distinct, something is required to put in place the phenomenology of connected, uniform things and events. Hume introduces the spreading of ideas in the mind, in the field of experience, precisely with the function of giving to transitions of ideas psychological reality and weight as a unified system of realities. Be this as it may, this variety of spreading is not especially problematic in Hume's philosophy. Given the equivalence of inference and conception as acts of the mind, by the Important Footnote, there are no principled obstacles to think that the transitions of the imagination can result in and be present as ideas; and in the cases of filling up that Hume is considering, sense-experience and memory strongly constrain the production of ideas.

7.2.3.3 Spreading on External Objects

The other variety and function is the *spreading of ideas on external objects*, the kind of spreading that Hume introduces to explain the common assumption that causal necessity and powers are in the objects. This variety is importantly different from the first one.

> This contrary biass [viewing powers in the objects] is easily accounted for. 'Tis a common observation, that the mind has a great propensity to spread itself on external objects, and to conjoin with them any internal impressions, which they occasion, and which always make their appearance at the same time that these objects discover themselves to the senses. Thus as certain sounds and smells are always found to attend certain visible objects, we naturally imagine a conjunction, even in place, betwixt the objects and qualities, tho' the qualities be of such a nature as to admit of no such conjunction, and really exist no where. But of this more fully hereafter. Mean while 'tis sufficient to observe, that the same propensity is the reason, why we suppose necessity and power to lie in the objects we consider, not in our mind, that considers them; notwithstanding it is not possible for us to form the most distant idea of that quality, when it is not taken for the determination of the mind, to pass from the idea of an object to that of its usual attendant.   (1.3.14.25)[8]

The obvious difference between the two kinds of spreading is that, in the present case, ideas are not spread in the mind but 'on external objects' (more on the relevant notion of the external in what follows). This points to a deeper, more important difference. In the case of causal necessity, we have to combine something

---

[8] 'With regard to energies, which are exerted, without our annexing to them any idea of communicated motion, we consider only the constant experienced conjunction of the events; and as we feel a customary connexion between the ideas, we transfer that feeling to the objects; as nothing is more usual than to apply to external bodies every internal sensation, which they occasion' (*E* E.2).

internal (an internal source and constituent of content) with something *external* (qualitative, sensible objects). In Hume's account of causation, this sort of spreading—spreading *on* the objects—is introduced only in connection with causal necessity; there is no mention of it in his account of causal inference, not even in connection with the uniformity of nature. I think that this notion of spreading of the mind is Hume's naturalistic response to the straight incompatibility between the nature of the impression which is the model of causal necessity and the ordinary location of this idea in objects. The conjunction of internal impressions with external objects is inherently problematic, bordering contradiction. This is a sceptical threat that needs to be assessed.

This is made explicit, in the above-quoted text, by the fact that this sort of spreading is introduced in connection with the conjunction in place of smells or sounds to visible and tangible objects. This issue is discussed in 1.4.5, in the context of a sceptical discussion of the immateriality of the soul. Hume holds that visible objects are given in spatially extended and located impressions and represented by spatially extended and located ideas (see § 9.4.1). Smells and sounds are given in non-extended and non-located impressions and are represented by non-spatial ideas. They exist but exist nowhere (1.4.5.8, 10). Therefore, these two sorts of objects or perceptions are 'incapable of any conjunction in place' (1.4.5.11). Their qualitative features (what they present to the mind and how they exist in the mind) are incompatible. In the light of this contrast, the complex of qualities with which we experience and conceive most of the sensible objects seems to be an impossibility and our mental, cognitive position seems to be a paradox. This, however, would be the case only if the unity of the incompatible qualities were in the objects and were represented by ideas. But this is not how Hume regards the cognitive situation: rather than representing, we 'naturally imagine' such conjunction: smells and sounds located within or together with visible and tangible objects. Internal impressions and external objects are constantly conjoined in experience and the former depend on the latter ('internal impressions, which they occasion, and which always make their appearance at the same time that these objects discover themselves to the senses'); the conjunction depends on the effects of this on the imagination. But it would be difficult to explain the conjunction of incompatible qualities if the imagination operated in this case only by transposition of ideas; or even, by spreading its ideas in the mind. The opposition between the internal and the external character of those perceptions, which (we may suppose) comes out in some feature of our awareness of them, makes it difficult to see how their conjunction can result from filling up a lacuna in one experience: by construction, there are no parts of a unitary experience one can start from. This is the rationale for Hume's introduction of spreading on objects. Whatever its psychological mechanisms, by this operation of the imagination perceptions which are present as internal (phenomenally internal: olfactory or auditory) are spread on objects and in this way united with perceptions present as external (phenomenally external: visual or tactile). This change in those perceptions does not amount to their actual location or presence in space and in the visual and tactile objects: this would be impossible. But there is no such threat of impossibility here: the non-spatial qualities do not come to be present and represented in space and thus do not actually become spatial. Rather, they are only *spread* on spatial objects. Their external character is only simulated. The radically non-representational character of spreading on the objects explains the unified phenomenology and content of sensible experience, without involving our mental life in paradox and without inviting sceptical doubts.

The same holds of the spreading of ideas that explains our locating causal necessity in the objects, that is, our own, shared causal worldview. The source of the problem is, again, a contrast between internal and external: an impression, feeling, or determination '*in the mind*' is the 'real model' of power and of the necessity of causes, which in our ordinary worldview seem located in the objects. This conflict between the qualities of causal ideas and their source and application generates a paradox and supports scepticism if the modal content of causal ideas is considered representational; and even if it is explained by spreading in the mind. But the operation of the more limited imagination is different: it is turning some of its internal perceptions, secondary impressions, feelings of determination into external ones, by regarding them as properties of objects. Hume solves the paradox of causal necessity by modelling the idea of causal necessity on an internal impression (individuated not by its content but by its feeling) *and* treating such modelling not as a representation but as change in the content of ideas of objects, issuing from that feeling as some sort of projection. This reconciles the fact that we 'suppose necessity and power to lie in the objects we consider, not in our mind, that considers them' with the fact that 'it is not possible for us to form the most distant idea of that quality, when it is not taken for the determination of the mind, to pass from the idea of an object to that of its usual attendant' (1.3.14.25). The determination of the mind is not represented by the ideas modelled on it; therefore, the fact that, were it to be represented, ideas of causal necessity would be impossible is not a threat against Hume's account.[9] In ordinary cognition, causal necessity is read off the objects not by representation, but because of a 'biass' or as something we 'naturally imagine'. The internal character of the impression which is the model for causal necessity is not in conflict with its phenomenology, with powers being in view as real.[10]

---

[9] The ideas of power, necessary connexion, and so on do not *represent* the impression of determination. To represent it would be to have an idea of reflection of the occurrence of such impression. Those ideas rather express how we conceive of certain objects under the cognitive pressure of that internal impression.

[10] B. Stroud, "'Gilding or Staining" the World with "Sentiments" and "Phantasms"', in R. Read & K. A. Richman eds., *The New Hume Debate* (Revised Edition), Routledge, London/New York, 2007, (16–30), 26–9, points to a deep difficulty investing the projective account of moral, aesthetic, and causal ideas. The impressions which are spread on the world, which gild and stain the world, must

Hume detects this variety of spreading also in other cognitive situations. The ascription of all sorts of secondary qualities is 'founded neither on perception nor reason, but on the imagination', which differentiates between such qualities and pains and pleasures, even though they appear originally, to the senses, 'on the same footing' (1.4.2.13). The originally internal impressions are spread on external objects and contribute in this way to our view of sensible reality. 'So strong is the prejudice for the distinct continu'd existence of the former qualities, that when the contrary opinion is advanc'd by modern philosophers, people imagine they can almost refute it from their feeling and experience, and that their very senses contradict this philosophy' (1.4.2.13). Spreading is also—famously—involved in morals. Vice and virtue are likened to secondary qualities. 'Vice and virtue, therefore, may be compar'd to sounds, colours, heat and cold, which, according to modern philosophy, are not qualities in objects, but perceptions in the mind' (3.1.1.26). This comparison is then developed by Hume in the sketch of an account of taste in terms of spreading of the internal on the external.

> Thus the distinct boundaries and offices of *reason* and of *taste* are easily ascertained. The former conveys the knowledge of truth and falsehood: The latter gives the sentiment of beauty and deformity, vice and virtue. The one discovers objects as they really stand in nature, without addition or diminution: The other has a productive faculty, and gilding or staining all natural objects with the colours, borrowed from internal sentiment, raises, in a manner, a new creation.[11]

The two main differences between spreading in the mind and spreading on the objects are thus that the latter is at work in closing cognitive gaps that involve structural features of our worldview and point at deep cognitive impossibilities; and, relatedly, that it makes appear internal perceptions as external, as qualities of objects. But what sort of internal–external contrast is in question here? External *existence*, the continued and independent existence of bodies or matter, is not in question. This idea is the product of further, complex operations of the imagination and it cannot be assumed at this stage of the theory. The contrast between internal and external should rather be one between features with which perceptions are present to awareness. As it is often the case with issues about subjective

---

have contents or intentionality, otherwise the very need and the possibility of such spreading would not arise: simple feelings do not require nor allow any projection. But such contents and intentionality must be categorially different from anything which could be part of the world. But then it seems inconsistent to think of the resulting contents and objects, the results of the gilding and staining, as included in the world. The tension to be resolved (or which, according to Stroud, cannot be resolved) is between the presuppositions and the expected output of imaginative spreading. I am only ready to accept that there is such tension and that the notion of spreading lacks serious elaboration by Hume. However, the distinction between representational and inferential-imaginative contents and the framework of cognitive gaps and works of imagination are fitting with a psychological mechanism of objectification of inner states (and with a cognitive role for such mechanism).

[11] D. Hume, *An Enquiry concerning the Principles of Morals*, T. L. Beauchamp, ed., Oxford University Press, Oxford/New York 1998, 163 ('Appendix 1: Concerning Moral Sentiment').

experience, Hume's hold on this is not firm. Still, internal impressions must somehow be present to the mind as internal and different, in this respect, from other, external ones. To make sense of this, Hume seems to rely, in the case of morals, on their hedonic and motivational dimension; in the case of secondary qualities, on their original sameness in appearance with pains and pleasures; in the case of non-spatial perceptions, on some salient, phenomenal feature (non-extension, primarily). He provides for the internal character of the impression of determination by identifying it with a feeling. By contrast, we can say that external perceptions have qualities that somehow drive the focus of awareness away from the mind itself and from its perceptions. This can be because of their intrinsic possession of content (as opposed to hedonic and motivational states) or because of the nature of their contents (their extension and location). Spreading on the objects therefore does not involve any impossible presupposition. The contrast between internal and external, which motivates and drives this spreading activity of the more limited imagination, is phenomenal; and one which Hume's theory can provide for.[12]

Causal necessity is therefore an intelligible quality: it is intelligible in its genesis and its content does not include any inconsistency or paradox. (This, of course, once spreading has been substituted for representation.) Hume, as already hinted, does not attempt to reduce the shift from transition to conception of ideas by the imagination, or spreading of ideas in the mind and on the objects, to some simpler components or acts. But, as we have seen, he provides a functional characterization of spreading and its varieties and, with Two Viewpoints and the Important Footnote, at least the outline of its possibility for the natural mind, particularly for the more limited imagination. The idea also suggests itself of reading Hume's doctrine of spreading in terms of the notion of metacognitive experiences, as I have already proposed: the process, distinctive of and restricted to the imagination, by which a property of mental activity comes to be regarded as a property of what the mental activity is about or results from it.

7.3 Hume's Philosophy of Causation

7.3.1 The Two Definitions: Structure, Rationale, and Implications

7.3.1.1 The Complexity of Causal Content

The core of Hume's theory of causal content is the discovery that the more limited imagination, because of its susceptibility to habituation effects and customary

---

[12] Beebee, *Hume on Causation*, 146–7, suggests that we should read Hume's doctrine as if what is spread (or projected) are not internal impressions, but the underlying inferential habits. The rationale of the suggestion is to be looked for in her projectivist reading of spreading, which hinges on the notion of propositional behaviour of non-propositional states and fits inferential habits better than feelings. The problem with this suggestion is that it goes against Hume's texts and the significance he gives to the fact that it is a qualitatively internal impression that underlies our ascriptions of necessity.

transitions of ideas, concurs with representations of constant conjunctions of resembling objects to produce inferential potentials (1.3.6.2) and modally qualified contents (1.3.14.16), supporting inferences to unobserved existence. Together, they contribute to the content of the idea of cause and make possible mature causal reasoning. Hume's carefully constructed arguments notwithstanding, there are obscurities about the relations between the representational, the inferential, and the modal dimensions of causal content. Hume writes 'the constant conjunction of objects constitutes the very essence of cause and effect' (1.4.5.33); 'this multiplicity of resembling instances, therefore, constitutes the very essence of power or connexion' (1.3.14.16); *the constant conjunction of objects determines their causation* (1.3.15.1). This latter is not only an enabling factor but a constitutive dimension of the idea of cause. 'We must not here be content with saying, that the idea of cause and effect arises from objects constantly united; but must affirm, that 'tis the very same with the idea of these objects' (2.3.1.16). But necessity seems also essential to causal content: as a component of the idea of cause it is of 'greater importance' that the others (which are elements of the content of constant conjunctions) (1.3.2.11). This comes out clearly in Hume's rehearsal of the definitions of the idea of cause in Book 2. He writes that 'necessity makes an essential part of causation' (2.3.1.18) and then defines necessity just as he had defined cause.

> I define necessity two ways, conformable to the two definitions of *cause*, of which it makes an essential part. I place it either in the constant union and conjunction of like objects, or in the inference of the mind from the one to the other. (2.3.2.4)

Since in Hume's theory—which he is now summarizing—the necessary connexion is the 'foundation' of causal inference and such foundation is put in place by and consists in some 'transition arising from the accustom'd union' (1.3.14.21), the inferential potential of the idea of cause is also essential to its content. We have thus three different essential constituents of causal content; and the more limited imagination has a role with regard to at least two of them. This does not per se amount to inconsistency, but there is some interpretive work to do.

7.3.1.2 Inferentialism and the Two Definitions

This work can be done by focusing on the conclusive discussion in which Hume wants 'to collect all the different parts of this reasoning', to provide an 'exact definition' or a 'precise definition' of the relation or of cause and effect. It is enormously interesting that, in this context, Hume explicitly connects the complexity of his account of causation to its obligatory inferentialist character. He pleads guilty to having discussed the inference based on the causal relation before the relation itself. But he adds the remark that he was 'oblig'd to advance in this seemingly preposterous manner' because 'the nature of the relation depends so much on that of the inference', that he had to 'make use' of causal terms before being 'able exactly to define them, or fix their meaning' (1.3.14.30). The priority of use, of facts about the practice of causal inference and its conditions, over the identification of causal ideas and the definition of causal terms, is the paradigmatic, inferentialist order of explanation. Thus, when Hume proceeds to 'correct this fault' by providing the long expected definition of cause, we should locate this definition in the context of Inferentialist Naturalism. This is crucial for understanding his conclusive position, including the fact that he provides *two* definitions of cause.

> There may two definitions be given of this relation, which are only different, by their presenting a different view of the same object, and making us consider it either as a *philosophical* or as a *natural* relation; either as a comparison of two ideas, or as an association betwixt them. We may define a CAUSE to be 'An object precedent and contiguous to another, and where all the objects resembling the former are plac'd in like relations of precedency and contiguity to those objects, that resemble the latter.' If this definition be esteem'd defective, because drawn from objects foreign to the cause, we may substitute this other definition in its place, *viz.* 'A CAUSE is an object precedent and contiguous to another, and so united with it, that the idea of the one determines the mind to form the idea of the other, and the impression of the one to form a more lively idea of the other.' Shou'd this definition also be rejected for the same reason, I know no other remedy, than that the persons, who express this delicacy, should substitute a juster definition in its place. But for my part I must own my incapacity for such an undertaking. (1.3.14.31)

This text has been much discussed by Hume scholars. The focus of discussion has been the relations between the two definitions—and with this, whether they are definitions at all—and the extent of Hume's commitment to them. I will say something about the first point later. About the second, I only remark that, apart from challenging his opponents to propose a better one, Hume relies on his definitions as 'establish'd maxims' (1.3.14.31). The two definitions direct his further discussion of causality, at 2.3.1–2: *Of liberty and necessity*. This is commitment enough, I would say.[13]

My principal focus, however, is the joint dependence of the two definitions on Hume's inferentialism and what they say about the role of the imagination. Hume's official definiendum is 'a CAUSE', introduced as 'an object': an individual particular, standing in a causal relation. But, more properly, the two definitions

---

[13] For a balanced and insightful summary of these discussions, see Beebee, *Hume on Causation*, 94–107. Two outstanding treatments of the two definitions are Garrett, *Cognition and Commitment*, 96–117; and Millican 'Hume, Causal Realism, and Causal Science', 660–6.

aim to bring into view the complexity of the idea of cause, making explicit the distinct dimensions of causal content.[14] Hume's inferentialist account of the idea of cause is articulated in terms of the dualism of object-representing faculties and imagination, of impressions or ideas of objects and mental transitions. The idea of cause *can only* be constitutively explained and therefore *must* be defined in terms of these distinct and necessary contributions. One thing that the first definition does is to tell us in what respect the idea of cause depends on objects, or includes the representation of objects in experience. The second definition tells us in what respect the idea of cause depends on transitions of the imagination. What we have from representation are constant conjunctions of resembling objects, preserved by Non-Mixture. What we have from more limited imagination are transitions of ideas and impressions. Both are indispensable; neither is reducible to the other. This dual individuation is the only available for the idea of cause, which neither sense and memory alone nor imagination alone could produce. The representational dimension alone would lack inferential and modal import; the imaginative and inferential one would fail to connect with objects.

If the two definitions express two distinct aspects of Hume's inferentialism about the idea of cause, the problem of their extensional and intensional equivalence loses any urgency. They are not equivalent; but they need not be, because they elucidate the idea of cause with respect to the dual aspect of its mental genesis, content, and cognitive role. Hume says that the two definitions 'are only different, by their presenting a different view of the same object [the causal relation], and making us consider it either as a *philosophical* or as a *natural* relation; either as a comparison of two ideas, or an association betwixt them' (1.3.14.31). This is in line with my view that the two definitions aim to capture the necessarily dual character of causal content. The philosophical relation of cause is internally linked to the representation of constant conjunctions. Causation as a philosophical relation is a 'particular circumstance, in which, even upon the arbitrary union of two ideas in the fancy, we may think proper to compare them' (1.1.5.1). Therefore, to individuate the philosophical relation of cause, we must see in what respect or 'circumstance' we think it proper to compare ideas in mature, reflective causal reasoning (imagination in idea-comparing sense). As we will see in § 7.3.2, this comparison refers to constant conjunctions of objects and, from this viewpoint, this is what the idea of cause consists in. 'The constant conjunction of objects determines their causation' (1.3.15.1). Of course, constant conjunctions can contribute at all to causal contents only if they are involved in transitions of ideas: but they are still both an independent explanatory condition of the idea of cause and a part of its content and application. (They are what is left of the causal relation, if

---

[14] This is well captured by Strawson, *Secret Connexion*, 237: 'Our actual admittedly non-Regularity-theory concept of causation is a curious hybrid, deriving its non-Regularity-theory element from an impression or feeling in the mind.'

we abstract from the non-arbitrary union of ideas in the fancy.) The second definition can be non-problematically read in terms of the natural relation of cause: a transition and union of ideas produced by the more limited imagination, with an associated impression of determination. The two conditions on the idea of cause are conceptually different, therefore the two definitions are not intensionally equivalent; and the same objects can satisfy one without satisfying the other, so they can also diverge estensionally. But if the true point of the definitions is to articulate and summarize the inferential and imaginative account of the idea of cause, this does not matter for their tenability.

Therefore, with reference to individual objects (things or events), the two definitions require that, to count as a cause on the idea of cause we have, an object should be *both* one element of an ordered pair of constantly conjoined resembling objects *and* taken up in customary transitions of the imagination and in internal impressions of determination. In the other cases, the application of the idea of cause to that object would fail; the idea would be applied improperly. This is Hume's inferentialist framework and explains his qualifications of the two definitions. Hume remarks that first definition could be 'esteem'd defective, because drawn from objects foreign to the cause'. He says that one could 'substitute' the second definition 'in its place'. But he recognizes that also the second definition could be 'rejected for the same reason'. He is sceptical, however, that any 'juster definition' could take the place of his two. 'I think it fruitless to trouble myself with any farther enquiry or reasoning upon the subject, but shall repose myself on them as on establish'd maxims.' Hume recognizes that it is somehow problematic that the two definitions are 'drawn from objects foreign to the cause' but denies that this makes them untenable or really defective ('establish'd maxim' seems to be a term of high epistemic praise in Book 1).

To see why Hume says that his definitions could be 'esteem'd defective' (without being so), we should keep in mind that he is considering his definitions from the singularist–realist viewpoint that was more or less tacitly assumed in the philosophical tradition. That is, the view that the idea of cause can be fully understood and explained with reference to individual objects and their intrinsic properties. One way or another, as some sort of power or energy or other essential property or as an internal relation, causation was seen as residing in individual objects and as fully understandable with reference to them. With his highly revisionary definitions, therefore, Hume debunks from the inside the singularist–realist view of the idea of cause. The first definition appeals to objects foreign to the cause because whether an object is a cause is made to depend on how other objects are extrinsically related to each other and to it. The second definition makes it depend on whether and how the mind is determined to conceive the idea of it. The causal status of an individual particular is therefore extrinsic and mind-dependent. In this sense Hume's definitions have resort to objects foreign to the cause (*the* cause: *that* object considered as a cause). But this is not a sense in which they fail to individuate and specify adequately the idea of cause, on account of its necessary, inferentialist explanation. There is no other, 'juster' way of conceiving of causation.

7.3.1.3 The Ontology of Causation

Hume's two definitions thus appear to be in good order. They give the 'distinct meaning' of the idea of cause; their specification of its meaning is the 'only reasonable' one and supports 'establish'd maxims'; in short, they elucidate how causal reasoning can be a 'just inference' and causal necessity an 'intelligible quality'. Therefore, the two definitions, we should suppose, can tell us something about Hume's ontology of causation. If we can identify the *true idea* of cause—like those of space and time, of body, of mind—we can have some indication of what cause, space and time, cause and effect, body, and mind *are*. (Of course, of their empirical being: but nothing else can be intelligibly in question.) The dual nature of the idea of cause that comes into view in Hume's two definitions seems to suggest that the nature of causation, insofar as we have any title to say something about it, is also dual.[15] More particularly, in Hume's philosophy, causation as it really is includes mind-dependent as well as mind-independent aspects.

The first definition, by specifying the explanatory contribution of sensible representation to causal content, allows saying that causation is something in the objects, which does not reduce to the operations of the mind.

> As to what may be said, that the operations of nature are independent of our thought and reasoning, I allow it; and accordingly have observ'd, that objects bear to each other the relations of contiguity and succession; that like objects may be observ'd in several instances to have like relations; and that all this is independent of, and antecedent to the operations of the understanding. But if we go any farther, and ascribe a power or necessary connexion to these objects; this is what we can never observe in them, but must draw the idea of it from what we feel internally in contemplating them.   (1.3.14.28)

Hume's claim is that, since an object to which we properly apply the idea of cause must satisfy the conditions specified in the first definition, we find in this a key to understand the *independent reality* of causation: constant conjunctions do not obtain dependently on the operations of the mind; if they obtain at all, they obtain in the objects. Since Hume declares constant conjunction to be the 'very essence

---

[15] For an interpretation alert to the complex relations of the two definitions, and to the hybrid ontology and content of Hume's causes, see Beauchamp & Rosenberg, *Hume and the Problem of Causation*, 21–32; Wilson, *Hume's Defense of Causal Inference*, 15–21. Garrett, *Hume*, 133–7 addresses insightfully the issue of the two definitions on the basis on his important notion of sense-based concepts; in particular, on their systematic ambiguity between their individuation in terms of mental responses and in terms of the qualities of the input-perceptions (126).

of cause and effect', causation is a real, objective condition or state of affairs and the independent operations of objects do not fall short of being causal.[16] This is consistent with constant conjunctions *not* being all there is to the ontology of causation: it is all there is to causation *as it is in the objects*. In so far as we succeed to refer and to form true beliefs in the causal domain, we do so by satisfying the first definition. On this view, causation in the objects is a primitive and bare condition on how objects are present in the actual world. It is not reducible to any other element of reality; there are no reasons to think that is grounded on something different in kind from it (powers and so on). In the history of philosophy, this view of the reality of causation as an actual and inclusive pattern of objects has been further refined by identifying causation as 'universality', a 'perduring entity' with particular causal relations as its spatial and temporal parts; or as a qualitative character of a Lewisian world, a 'big physical object'.[17] This is a conception of causality we are familiar with, also and particularly because of its inception in Hume: some form of regularity view, the kind of view that trades the conception of causality as production of an individual by an individual with that of causality as dependence of one kind of beings on another one.[18]

The second definition also has implications for the ontology of causation. This definition, differently from the first, states a condition of mind-dependence for the proper application of the idea of cause: the objects it is applied to must be involved in customary transitions of ideas and in an ensuing internal, secondary impression. The second definition allows making an extremely strong clam about the ontology of causation, as Hume does not refrain to remark.

> Thus as the necessity, which makes two times two equal to four, or three angles of a triangle equal to two right ones, lies only in the act of the understanding, by which we consider and compare these ideas; in like manner the necessity or power, which unites causes and effects, lies in the determination of the mind to pass from the one to the other. The efficacy or energy of causes is neither plac'd in the causes themselves, nor in the deity, nor in the concurrence of these two principles; but belongs entirely to the soul, which considers the union of two or

---

[16] As is rightly remarked in D. Garrett, 'Hume', in Beebee, Hitchcock, Menzies, *The Oxford Handbook of Causation* (73–91), 84.

[17] See S. Psillos, 'Regularity Theories', in Beebee, Hitchcock, Menzies, *The Oxford Handbook of Causation* (131–57), 133. See D. Lewis, *On the Plurality of Worlds*, Blackwell, Oxford 1987, 69: 'A world is the mereological sum of all the possible individuals that are parts of it, and so are worldmates of one another.'

[18] Beauchamp & Rosenberg, *Hume and the Problem of Causation*, 80–8 carefully articulate and strongly defend this regularist insight. This is also the Humean thread in Lewis' conception of causation, as summarized in R. L. Anjum & S. Mumford, *Causation*, Oxford University Press, Oxford 2013, 18, 22. The reality of causation and of external objects is a matter of 'unknown objects', 'unobservable mechanisms and structures'; the epistemic limits in this respect are simply 'ignorance of objects'; the character of real causation is 'brute regularity *all the way down*', 'brute fact' (Winkler, 'The New Hume', 56–7, 68, 71).

more objects in all past instances. 'Tis here that the real power of causes is plac'd, along with their connexion and necessity. (1.3.14.23)

This condition of mind-dependence should not be taken to imply irrealism, illusoriness, or subjectivity (in any scepticism-inducing sense). The modal content of causal ideas does not even purport to represent objects: it is the spreading on represented objects of the experience or feeling of a compelling transition of the imagination. We have seen that the modal dimension of the idea of cause has 'true meaning' and, just as customary transitions support a 'just inference', it conveys an 'intelligible quality'. And, as we have also seen, no contradiction is involved in its combining internal and external dimensions, because the internal impression is not represented in but spread on the objects. The proper application of the idea of cause to an object, which is our only key to the ontology of causation, thus requires that that object be appropriately related to the modality-constituting processes of the imagination. The object must be included in a constant conjunction of resembling objects and, because of this and by being represented accordingly, it must be involved in customary transitions and impressions of the imagination. ('A CAUSE is an object precedent and contiguous to another, and so united with it, that the idea of the one determines the mind to form the idea of the other, and the impression of the one to form a more lively idea of the other.'). If this complex condition is not satisfied (there is no such determination of the mind with regard to such object; there is a determination but not because of the observation of its constant conjunction), the idea of cause is not properly applied (or is misunderstood). If it is satisfied, and the idea of cause finds proper application, it defines a real condition concerning objects, a way in which the empirical world can be, inclusive of relations and transitions of perceptions. Perceptions and minds, in Hume's philosophy, are ontologically on a par with objects. Mind-dependence is a relation among objects.

Modally qualified causal ideas (powers, necessary connexions, and so on), insofar as we can 'really' entertain them and 'understand our meaning in talking', in contrast with the blotched, disastrous attempts to have them represent objects and their properties, allow us saying something real, something about the empirical world, but only in a respect in which it is mind-dependent. This is the 'reasonable' or 'intelligible' kind of thought that is made available by the second definition. We can follow the vulgar in taking causal powers and energies as qualities of the objects. Only, as true philosophy and the second definition teach, with the proviso that such qualities are mind-dependent.[19] Hume takes an almost

---

[19] Strawson, *Secret Connexion*, 157–9, draws a distinction between causal powers and causal necessity, because of the 'very strong subjectivist line' Hume takes about necessity and of his (presumptive) acceptance of real causal powers in the objects. I think that this is doubly mistaken. For one thing, as I have attempted to show, Hume's account of modality is not subjectivist—it is not even epistemic, in any sense with entailments of subjectivism. Metaphysical and physical modalities are absolute. For

quietist attitude towards the mind-dependent dimension of the ontology of causes. As the 'true philosophy', which 'approaches nearer to the sentiments of the vulgar, that to those of mistaken knowledge', is ready to conclude, 'we have no idea of power or agency, separate from the mind, and belonging to causes' (1.4.3.9). But then we do have such ideas, and they express relations in which constantly conjoined objects can stand to minds. And given the proper understanding of such ideas, we can say what causation is in the objects and what in it is mind-dependent. Causal powers are not different, in this, from secondary qualities; neither are, by Hume's own lights or by ours, subjective in any way amounting to illusion or unreality. The modal dimension of the idea of cause raises no deep ontological worry and Hume's contrasting claims about the essence of causation can be to some extent reconciled.[20]

Where is my reading of Hume on causation located in the interesting taxonomy proposed by Helen Beebee? Beebee identifies three main interpretations. The first, the Traditional Interpretation, makes the positive claim that causation in the objects is a matter of temporal priority, contiguity, and constant conjunction. It also makes the negative claim that it is illegitimate to apply the idea of necessary connexion to external objects. The Projectivist Interpretation accepts the positive claim but denies the negative one: there is a legitimate way of

another one, only modal conceptions of causal powers, energies, efficacy, and connexion are available to Hume (or to anyone else I would say). Only the relevant ascriptions of necessity make sense of the contents of these ideas. These modal ideas support non-representational, inferentially individuated causal beliefs about objects, which do not require for their cognitive significance that anything like power or necessity be in the objects. Hume's combination of imagination, inferentialism, and cognitive import in the causal domain somehow escapes Strawson's attention.

[20] Of course, at 1.4.4.15 Hume draws sceptical implications from the notion of secondary qualities. But this is only on the blotched representationalist supposition of the double existence of internal perceptions and external objects. Lewis' reading of Hume's causal reductionism: 'Humean supervenience', is in general helpful. See Lewis, *Philosophical Papers*, Volume 2, Oxford University Press, New York/Oxford 1986, ix–x: 'Humean supervenience is named in honor of the great denier of necessary connections. It is the doctrine that all there is to the world is a vast mosaic of local matters of particular fact, just one little thing and then another. (But it is no part of the thesis that these local matters of fact are mental.)' We have geometry, points in spacetime, point-sized bits of matter or aether or fields, local qualities at these points. 'For short: we have an arrangement of qualities. And that is all. There is no difference without difference in the arrangement of qualities. All else supervenes on that.' Hume's causal powers supervene on matters of particular fact about objects and minds. The sceptical realist interpretation, anticipated by Kemp Smith and developed by Wright, Strawson, and Kail, takes issue with this reading. I want to remark that, textual support for the realist interpretation being scanty, the main support for it should come from some overwhelmingly important philosophical consideration. But the one advanced by Strawson, the presence in Hume's philosophy of a proto-Kripkean distinction between reference and reference-fixing, with the ensuing representational construal of relative ideas, is untenable. Even an interpreter like Wright, who does not saddle Hume with this sort of views, is bound to draw unacceptable conclusions from a realist understanding of causal powers and necessity. As he—very earnestly—remarks, the realistic interpretation is committed to ascribing to Hume 'the view that there is no ultimate ontological distinction' between causes and effects; that 'a kind of identity' holds of them (*Sceptical Realism*, 156). The realistic interpretation is discussed in Beebee, *Hume on Causation*, 73–225 and Millican, 'Hume, Causal Realism, and Causal Science', *passim*. Garrett, 'Hume on Causation', 82–97, identifies in Hume's theory of causation elements distinctive of the reductionist, projectivist and realist interpretations.

applying Hume's idea of necessary connexion to external objects. The Sceptical Realist Interpretation denies the first claim: Hume's conceptual apparatus allows describing and referring to the world in causal terms that go beyond constant conjunction. It also denies the negative claim, at least on a certain reading of it.[21] Since I accept the positive claim, I stand opposed to the Sceptical Realist Interpretation. My interpretation is also opposed to the Traditional one, because I deny the negative claim. But on this point my position, while close to that of the Projectivist Interpretation, still importantly differs from it. A basic claim is common ground: contents with special and important roles, like the inferential and modal ones of causal ideas, are non-representational; they do not consist in, nor are they explained by, reference to and description of objects. But there are different ways of developing this basic claim. An important consideration has to do with the character of the mental activity that underlies the inferential import and the modal qualification of causal ideas. There is a standing temptation in projectivism to conceive of this activity as primarily non-cognitive, of a sort that is intentionally describable (not blank) but does not primitively and immediately contribute to our cognitive capacities, to how we conceive of or reason about objects. Typically, some sort of practical engagement, some sort of stance or attitude. In my view, by contrast, the underlying mental activity is cognitive all the way down: it consists in conceptions, manners of conceptions, and inferences addressing perceptions and objects originally given in sense-experience. It is phenomenologically homogeneous with sense-experience and susceptible to compositional operations. It is animated by principles that respond under aspects and selectively to the givens of internal and external experience, by Non-Mixture. It adds in this way to representation; but it is inherently cognitive, proto-conceptual, and proto-discursive. In Hume the contrast between representational and cognitive is more important and clear-cut than that between cognitive and non-cognitive.

7.3.2 True Meaning and Wrong Application

Hume claims that 'when we talk of any being, whether of a superior or inferior nature, as endow'd with a power or force' or 'when we speak of a necessary connexion betwixt objects, and suppose, that this connexion depends upon an efficacy or energy, with which any of these objects are endow'd', our expressions 'have really no distinct meaning, and make use only of common words, without any clear and determinate ideas' (1.3.14.14). He also remarks, however, that this is because of the way they are 'apply'd'. While ''tis more probable, that these

---

[21] See Beebee, *Hume on Causation*, 108.

expressions do here lose their true meaning by being *wrong apply'd*, than that they never have any meaning' (1.3.14.14). Having studied the genesis of the idea of cause, the articulation of its content, and its specification in the two definitions, we should now take a closer look at its right application, to give its 'true meaning' or 'distinct meaning'.

In the case of the first definition, deriving conditions of correct application is straightforward. The first definition characterizes causation as a philosophical relation. The content of the philosophical relation of cause consists in constant conjunctions of resembling objects. Philosophical relations are primarily applied in reflective reasoning: they are circumstances in which we think it proper to compare ideas, even when not naturally associated. Now, reflective reasoning, including, of course, mature causal reasoning, has normative, epistemic conditions. In mature causal cognition, we can 'build an argument on one single experiment, when duly prepar'd and examin'd' (1.3.12.3). In these circumstances, causal judgements should be accepted 'after careful removal of all foreign and superfluous circumstances' (1.3.8.14). If we look at such normative conditions, at the 'careful', 'duly prepar'd and examin'd' application of causal ideas in the practice of causal reasoning, we see that Hume identifies them with reference to constant conjunctions of objects. Care, preparation, and examination should ensure that we individuate real constant conjunctions of objects, real regularities; that we search for counterexamples; that we are not misled in our observations.

This is also the main point of Hume's discussion in 1.3.15: *Rules by which to judge of causes and effects*. The rules are fixed against the background that 'Any thing may produce any thing' and the two principles '*that the constant conjunction of objects determines their causation*, and *that properly speaking, no objects are contrary to each other, but existence and non-existence*'. Imagination, also imagination in the larger sense, is unconstrained by the 'mere survey' of objects, 'without consulting experience'. Therefore, some 'general rules' are needed, by which to know when objects really have 'that constant conjunction, on which the relation of cause and effect totally depends' (1.3.15.1, 2). The first three rules instruct precisely to look for such constant conjunctions in our reasonings about causes and effects, thus summarizing the first definition. This is on the ground that "Tis chiefly this quality, [constant union] that constitutes the relation' (1.3.15.5). The fourth is the principle of causal uniformity, which is applied in one-experiment inferences and generally in mature causal reasoning; it instructs how to extend the results of 'any clear experiment', 'without waiting for that constant repetition, from which the first idea of this relation is deriv'd' (1.3.15.6). This is an indirect application of constant conjunctions, as are the fifth and the sixth rules, which also articulate the principle of causal uniformity. The seventh rule instructs how to individuate compounded causes and effects, on the basis of the constant conjunction of changes in their parts (1.3.15.9). The eighth again refers to causal uniformity and instructs how to tell whether an object is the complete cause of an effect (1.3.15.10). All these rules, directly or indirectly, are about whether our applications and comparisons of ideas of cause and effects lock onto constant conjunctions. Hume says that these rules are 'all the LOGIC, I think proper to employ in my reasoning' (1.3.15.11). This logic is the right application in reasoning of the idea of cause, as it is given expression in the first definition; it is the normative, epistemological implication of that definition.[22]

The right application of the idea of cause, by the first definition, is captured by the criterion of the constant conjunction of resembling objects. A wrong application would be the attempt to ground causal reasonings and judgement on the simple view of objects, see 1.3.3.2; 1.3.6.1; 1.3.14.13. Hume also remarks that it would be a mistake to think, as philosophers have done, that the truth of causal judgements requires more than the fact that certain objects are 'different from each other' and that they are 'constantly united' in 'experience' (1.4.5.31). This would be to think that 'nothing can be the cause of another, but where the mind can perceive the connexion in its idea of the objects' (1.4.5.31). The demand for such a perception would imply that the connexion lies in the intrinsic nature of the objects and that the truth of causal judgements is manifest in the simple view of them, a priori or a posteriori. (A priori for false philosophy; a posteriori for the vulgar view.) This would lead to first-order scepticism in the causal domain, by the denial of causation in general. 'We in reality affirm, that there is no such thing in the universe as a cause or productive principle, not even the deity itself'. It would also lead to 'the grossest impieties and absurdities' concerning human agency and responsibility, if the deity is admitted as causal principle (1.4.5.31). Rather, the true meaning captured by the first definition is simply 'that all objects, which are found to be constantly conjoin'd, are upon that account only to be regarded as causes and effects' (1.4.5.32). This is the truth-maker of causal judgements, both the singular ones that are our primary response, immediate or reflective, to one-object situations, and their generalizations (see § 12.2.2).[23]

By contrast, it is a somewhat complicated matter to spell out what right application of the idea of cause is mandated by the second definition. The second definition gives the idea of cause as a natural relation, that is, as it is constituted by transitions of the more limited imagination; and in this way it addresses its modal dimension, the idea of the necessity of causes. This is a dimension of causal content and cognition that Hume has recognized as problematic since the initial stages of his analysis of causation ('*Why we conclude, that such particular causes must necessarily have such particular effects*', 1.3.3.9). This idea is, by Hume's own lights, intelligible. However, it is not easy to say what cognitive difference is made

---

[22] See, on Hume's rules, Wilson, *Hume's Defence of Causal Inference*, 123–40.
[23] Kail, *Reality and Projection*, 114–15, remarks that there is no need to 'concede that the vast majority of causal thought is non-cognitive quasi-thought'. This includes the specification of truth conditions. See also Garrett, 'Hume on Causation', 79–80, 97.

by thinking along the lines of the second definition, that is, in terms of causal necessity. That is, what kind of activity involved in reflective, idea-comparing causal reasoning (if any) is made uniquely possible by our possession and application of causal ideas (powers, energies, necessary connexions), precisely because of their constitutive modal dimension. (This way of putting the question is owing to Barry Stroud.)

I think that a promising answer to this question is that the possession and the mastery of the idea of causal necessity is a condition for engaging at all, in a conceptually informed way, in causal reasoning. We should look back at Hume's analysis of the idea of cause and at its essential link with the functional and cognitive nature of causal reasoning: concluding to unobserved existents. I suggest that we can reflectively engage in causal reasoning, reason by comparing ideas and concluding to unobserved existence, only because we possess and apply ideas of causal necessity: the physical necessity of connections of distinct objects. When forming causal ideas, we only need to respond (with the more limited imagination) to constant conjunctions of objects. When assessing causal judgements, we only need to look at and abide by constant conjunctions of objects. But in order to engage at all in idea-comparing causal reasoning, we need to grasp and apply causal ideas in their modal dimension.

To see this, we may start from the apparently contrasting fact that Hume (in the first *Enquiry*) seems to ground causal inference on his first definition, which does not include a modal dimension.

> Similar objects are always conjoined with similar. Of this we have experience. Suitably to this experience, therefore, we may define a cause to be *an object, followed by another, and where all the objects similar to the first are followed by objects similar to the second.* Or in other words *where, if the first object had not been, the second never had existed.*[24]

This is a difficult text. It may seem to call into question the distinct theoretical role of Hume's causal necessity (and the second definition), which would be reducible to constant conjunctions (the first definition) and a counterfactual formulation. In my view, Hume here is rather refining his notion of causation in the objects and complementing rather than debunking his account of the modal dimension of the idea of cause (as per the second definition). Lewisian conceptions of causation have embraced and developed this refinement, giving accounts of causation in terms of causal dependence; of causal dependence in terms of counterfactual dependence; and of counterfactual dependence in terms of truth in descriptively individuated worlds and of a metric of closeness to the actual

---

[24] *Enquiry on Human Understanding*, 146 (7.9).

world. It would be utterly anachronistic to read such position into Hume, of course, no matter how conceptually continuous it is with his overall approach to causation. However, we can find in Hume the resources for articulating a view somehow similar to this position.[25]

It would be inadmissible in Hume's philosophy that causal necessity were part of what causation is in the objects. The counterfactual formulation puts pressure on this point; however, a consistent way of construing this passage might be the following. Assume that there is an instance of causation: that a certain object causes another one to exist or change. Then, based on the first definition, there is a mind-independent, completely general constant conjunction of objects resembling the first one and objects resembling the second one. On this assumption, we can legitimately infer that objects of the succeeding class would not exist or undergo that change, had not someone of the preceding class existed or changed. The point now is the force of this conditional: whether it amounts to Humean causal necessity. It is certainly not metaphysical necessity, which is here out of the question because the objects are perfectly separable. One might be tempted to think that, by expressing constant conjunctions of resembling objects with a counterfactual, Hume is committed to regarding the modal force of such counterfactual as physical necessity. But there are precise genetic and functional conditions on the kind of imaginative channelling that constitutes causal necessity. It must issue from customary propensities and transitions of the more limited imagination, responding to repeated observation. It must be deployed in inferences from observed to unobserved existents. Nothing of the sort is at work here. Hume assumes that there is a constant conjunction of objects and does not even mention that one such object is actually observed and involved in a customary transition. The point he is making is purely about the existence of causal relations. I think we should read the counterfactual as a non-demonstrative comparison of ideas: an implication of what is for objects to be constantly conjoined. Its necessity is thus purely deductive, which only applies to ideas, to our arrangements of ideas, with a wide scope. No comparison of ideas can licence concluding categorically to unobserved existence. Therefore, the counterfactual inference is simply an alternative way of expressing the unrestricted generality of the constant conjunctions ('in other words'), in terms of the deductive dependence (as opposed to the physical necessitation) between the ideas of objects.[26]

---

[25] See D. Lewis, 'Causation' (1973), in *Philosophical Papers*, Volume 2, Oxford University Press, Oxford-New York 1986 (159–213; the original text is at 159–72). Lewis's starting point is the text from the first *Enquiry* we are discussing, which he sees as expressing his own view of causal dependence: 'The, *e* depends causally on *c* iff, if *c* had not been, *e* never had existed. I take Hume's second definition as my definition not of causation itself, but of causal dependence among events' (167). Lewis also remarks and explains the affinity between the regularity view and his counterfactual view of causation (169).

[26] For a strictly related reading of Hume's understanding of causal counterfactuals, see Beauchamp & Rosenberg, *Hume and the Problem of Causation*, 145–51. The important point is that law like

The text just discussed therefore does nothing to dismantle the irreducibility of the modal dimension of causal ideas. Then we must clarify its cognitive role, its unique contribution to causal cognition. The crucial consideration, here, seems to be the one-object character of the cognitive situations which call for causal reasoning. In the earlier discussion of Hume's (putative) counterfactual conception of causality, we have implicitly assumed cognitive situations in which all the objects are present (observed constant conjunctions) or none is (all are only conceived). But these are not the conditions that mandate causal reasoning, where one object is present and another is inferred. (This is what makes causal cognition both inferential and informative.) Now, the crucial point is whether, in this paradigmatic kind of situation, we would be in a position to engage in idea-comparing causal reasoning with causal ideas restricted in their contents to the first definition. That is, if we could reason to the conclusion that something unobserved exists, has existed, or will exist, by comparing causal ideas with contents only as of constant conjunctions of objects and their counterfactual implications. I think that this would be impossible. Quite simply, the attempt to apply causal ideas specified in that way to situations in which only one of a pair of constantly conjoined objects is present would be frustrated by the fact that such situations are *counterexamples* to the constant conjunction and thus call into question the appropriateness of applying the idea of cause. Causal reasoning is functionally and cognitively individuated as a custom-based categorical inference to non-observed existents: as both inferential and informative. But this makes sense only in the context of one-object cognitive situations; and such situations are neither causes of nor reasons for applying an idea of cause restricted to the first definition. Hume points to this problem in the context of his account of the idea of external existence (see § 9.2.1). By contrast, if we have ideas of causal necessity, that is, causal ideas with modal force, as per the second definition, we could certainly engage in idea-comparing causal reasoning in one-object situations, on the prompt of the impression or memory of that object. The custom-based idea of the necessary connections of the two objects or of the power of the one to produce the other would enable us to contemplate and actually engage in such reasoning.[27]

I think that these considerations explain why necessity is a dimension of the explicit content of the causal idea (as it was unveiled by the analysis at 1.3.2.13): why we apply it when we reason and judge in causal terms. This comes into view also in Hume's modal formulation of the proposition of the uniformity of nature (see §7.2.1) and other principles like the Causal Maxim: any event must have a

---

regularities—constant conjunctions—provide all the mind-independent ontology that Humean counterfactuals require. (In the text I give further reasons for regarding Hume's counterfactual claim as consistent with the first definition.)

[27] Of course, we might have causes and reasons to enquire whether the situation we are in is actually a counterexample to the pertinent constant conjunction of objects. But this would require that we somehow modally qualify the constant conjunction, as something which could or should be the case.

cause (see § 7.2.2). Of course, if we reflect on and assess our causal reasoning, we must have resort to the constant conjunctions that provide its truth conditions. But the content of the ideas that give us access to such reasoning cannot but be modal. Causal inference and causal necessity are thus united not only in their foundation (customary transitions of the more limited imagination) but in the application of causal ideas in reasoning.[28] This suggestion is closely related to another one, which I have repeatedly made: idea-comparing, potentially reflective probable reason is inextricably connected, in our actual cognitive practice, with mental transitions, with the primitive inferences of the imagination. The two parts of the imagination jointly operate in causal cognition. I conclude that thinkers whose conceptual repertoire lacked the idea of causal necessity would lack a conceptual requisite for engaging in idea-comparing causal reasoning. We would share with such non-modal thinkers the same observations of constant conjunctions. Just like them, on the force of the first definition, we would consider observed constantly conjoined objects as causally connected. But differently from them, we could also form the idea of causal connections between objects which have not been observed as constantly conjoined (because in some situation only one element of the pertinent pair is present). We could think of one object as necessitating the presence of the other. This idea thus makes it possible to engage in idea-comparing reasoning that realizes the functional definition of causal reasoning: inferring unobserved existents. The non-modal thinkers are not in a position to do this. Their causal cognition is thus seriously impoverished. This appears to be a right and important application of the idea of cause as given in the second definition.[29]

---

[28] I thus find less than convincing the discussion of this topic in Beebee, *Hume on Causation*, 168–71. I would deny that the idea of necessity is the special locus for our recognition of reasons for causal inference and belief. ('In saying or thinking that the black *must* move, we conceive of ourselves as having good *reasons* for thinking that the black will move', 170.) Reasons for causal inference and judgment are sufficiently defined by the first definition, which gives their truth-makers and sets their critical standards.

[29] For a suggestion somewhat along the lines I am proposing, see Beauchamp & Rosenberg, *Hume and the Problem of Causation*, 135–43; Wilson, *Hume's Defence of Causal Inference*, 30–1. Stroud, *Hume*, 93–4, 226–9, denies that people who thought of causation according to the first definition but lacked the conceptual resources delivered by the second would have all our causal thoughts and beliefs. In particular they would lack the capacity to explicitly consider alternative possibilities and to reason in explicit modal terms. However, he also doubts that Hume has the resources to pursue effectively this line of thinking. (I am more optimistic in this regard.) This is right, as far as it goes; but perhaps is does not go far enough, because we can reiterate the question about the role of ascriptions of necessity in doxastic deliberation, as conceived by Hume. I also doubt the claim in Beebee, *Hume on Causation*, 168–71, that beings who inferred and judged only in terms of the first definition would fail to think causally. ('Because we project our habits of expectation on to the world and they do not, we think of reasoning concerning matters of fact as *causal* reasoning—as reasoning from causes and effects—while they do not', 171.) Given that the mental apparatus underlying causal necessity is a contingent feature of human nature and that the first definition captures an essential feature of causation (causation in the objects), thinking along the first definition alone is a *way* of thinking causally, not of failing to do so. Beebee, *Hume on Causation*, 139–40, also rightly remarks that this sits well with a (broadly) projectivist reading of Hume's causal content.

7.4 Summary

Causal necessity belongs to the content of the idea of cause as we have and apply it. The connection of causal modality with causal inference is inextricable and the second is explanatorily prior on the first. Still, they involve different conditions and set different explanatory tasks.

In § 7.1, I discuss Hume's individuation of the modal gap of causal cognition. The family of philosophically important ideas variously linked to causal necessity (power, energy, production, and so on) is not from sense and memory; and it is not a priori. Hume individuates the modal gap by excluding what it would be for causation to be in the objects: a metaphysical necessity, knowable a priori.

§ 7.2 discusses how Hume's theory of modality can provide an intelligible idea of causal necessity. In § 7.2.1, I argue that the difficulties with causal necessity arise only from the attempt to ground it representationally or a priori. The idea may have non-spurious content and right application, if properly understood. Hume gets to this conclusion by applying the Established Maxim to the new, imagination-based conditions on the conception of objects that constitute the inferential potential of the idea of cause. What makes this possible, discussed in § 7.2.2, is that the repeated experience of constantly conjoined objects drives the more limited imagination to engage in transitions among their ideas. This change is experienced by the more limited imagination as the compellingness of such transitions. This experience constitutes the idea that the involved objects are necessarily related. Causal necessity is perfectly intelligible as physical necessity, by conceivability and Determination.

In § 7.2.3 I address a question that Hume leaves undertheorized: how transitions of ideas and their feelings are turned into qualitative contents and conceptions of ideas. Hume recognizes this as a general possibility, but only hints at an explanation. The conversion of inferences into conceptions is by what Hume calls spreading of ideas. Hume distinguishes two sorts of such spreading. One consists in filling lacunae in the field of our experience with qualitatively continuous ideas (the Missing Shade of Blue is the example, already discussed in §3.1.1). The other, more problematic, is the attribution to objects of properties that only pertain to our experience of their ideas. Hume is aware of the difficulty of this conversion of internal experiences into features of at least potentially object-representing contents. The projectivist account of ideas of causal necessity he suggests, no matter how incomplete, has, however, been widely influential in later philosophy.

In § 7.3 I deal with general issues in Hume's philosophy of causation. In § 7.3.1 I address the complexity of causal content, in connection with the two definitions with which Hume summarizes his theory. Inferentialist Naturalism about causal content is the right context to understand the two definitions. It explains why the definitions are two, corresponding to the irreducible and indispensable representational (observed constant conjunctions) and inferential and modal (imaginative transitions) dimensions of causal content. Hume says, somewhat misguidingly, that the two definitions express causation as philosophical and as natural relation. This is true in the sense that when performing and assessing idea-comparing causal reasoning, we must consider whether we are identifying actual constant conjunctions of objects. The two definitions also deliver the ontological point that being a cause is an extrinsic and mind-dependent condition on objects. Based on this, causal inference is just and causal necessity is intelligible.

§ 7.3.2 engages with Hume's view of the right application of the idea of cause, along its two definitions. The right application of the first definition is in idea-comparing causal reasoning. Hume summarizes it in a set of rules by which to judge causes and effects. The right application of the second definition is more difficult to identify. Following other interpreters, I address this question by asking what cognitive activity is made uniquely possible by the modal dimension of the idea of cause. My tentative answer is we can engage in idea-comparing reasoning to unobserved existence, the typical form of our causal reasoning, only in virtue of our possessing the idea of the necessity of causes.

PART IV
AN EXTERNAL AND INTERNAL WORLD

The operations of the more limited imagination, which are 'so trivial, and so little founded on reason', allow us to have causal ideas, to infer the existence of unobserved objects, and to gain a view of the world as connected by physical necessity. The imagination also explains our view of objects as persisting, of independently and continuedly existing bodies and minds, and of an external and internal world.

> Nay, even to these objects [the objects 'present to our senses'] we cou'd never attribute any existence, but what was dependent on the senses; and must comprehend them entirely in that succession of perceptions, which constitutes our self or person. Nay farther, even with relation to that succession, we cou'd only admit of those perceptions, which are immediately present to our consciousness, nor cou'd those lively images, with which the memory presents us, be ever receiv'd as true pictures of past perceptions. (1.4.7.3)

The principles of the more limited imagination that produce the idea of the external and internal world are different from those that produce causal ideas. There are deep connections. The genesis of causal ideas requires that we have some sense of the unperceived existence of objects, underlying our inferences to unobserved objects. The imagination, in spreading its ideas on the objects, must be sensitive to some difference between internal perceptions and external objects. But causal contents are cognitively simpler and explanatorily more primitive than the ideas of the mind-independent existence of bodies and of the persistence of selves. Our ideas of body and matter, of self and personal identity, therefore mark a cognitive gap not only in representation and the a priori but also in causal content and cognition. The pattern of cognitive gaps and works of the imagination is recursive across Book 1 of the *Treatise*.

These cognitive gaps are marked, at a deep level, by the idea of identity. This constitutes the primary difference between Hume's account of the idea of cause and that of the ideas of material and psychical objects. For reasons which we will consider, Hume thinks that the genesis and the content of the idea of identity, as well as the role of the ideas of body and self in ordinary and philosophical cognition, are more problematic than those of the idea of cause. Hume's enquiry into the character of and the conditions for these ideas thus turns into a discussion of the sceptical threats that he sees arising in connection with them. Scepticism is a main subject matter of Part 4 of Book 1 of the *Treatise*. I address these issues in Chapters 9 and 10. In Chapter 8 I deal with the closely related, but distinct issue of the content of our spatial and temporal ideas and cognition. Relatively not only to the ideas of body and self but also to that of cause, spatial and temporal ideas are cognitively closer to the qualities and the fixed order and form of sensible objects. But Hume explains some important non-representational aspects of spatial and temporal thought with principles of the imagination that diverge from those underlying causal ideas and are at work in the production of the ideas of body and self. I have thus decided to discuss Hume's theory of the ideas of space and time right at the juncture of his theory of causation with his theory of the external and internal world.

8
The Ideas which are Most Essential to Geometry

> It appears, then, that the ideas which are most essential to geometry, *viz.* those of equality and inequality, of a right line and a plain surface, are far from being exact and determinate, according to our common method of conceiving them.
>
> (1.2.4.29)

In the carefully crafted structure of Book 1, the relations between Part 2: *Of the ideas of space and time*, and Part 3: *Of knowledge and probability*, are somewhat complicated. As interpreters have remarked, 'Hume relies heavily on the descriptions of causes and effects in purely spatiotemporal terms to substitute for the dramatic terms "necessity", "power", "force", "impact", "collision", etc.'[1] This is an overstatement, since opting out of modality is not part of Hume's programme. But certainly the spatial and temporal ordering of perceptions, the constant conjunctions of resembling objects, are cognitively more primitive than causal connections. Spatial and temporal contents are closer to sensible representation than the causal ones; these latter mark a cognitive gap in what is given spatially and temporally. This explains their position in the architecture of Book 1, immediately after the elements of Hume's philosophy in Part 1. But spatial and temporal cognition is not restricted to representation. There are crucial aspects of it, like the fundamental ideas of geometry and the ideas of an empty space and time, which only the imagination can explain. In accounting for these ideas, Hume moves even further away from sense and memory than in the case of causation. In this respect, the works by which the imagination closes the gaps in the representation of space and time as well as the resulting ideas raise issues of spuriousness. This thread connects Part 2 with Part 4: *Of the skeptical and other systems of philosophy*.

---

[1] Beauchamp & Rosenberg, *Hume and the Problem of Causation*, 200.

8.1 Representing Space and Time

8.1.1 Manners of Disposition of Visible and Tangible Objects

Hume's 'system concerning space and time consists of two parts, which are intimately connected together'. The first is that the 'idea of extension or duration' consists of a 'finite number' of 'simple and indivisible' 'parts or inferior ideas' and that space and time 'exist conformable to this idea'. The second is that 'The ideas of space and time are therefore no separate or distinct ideas, but merely those of the manner or order, in which objects exist' (1.2.4.1–2). This is the core of the *representational* content of the ideas of space and time and the background of the work of the imagination in this domain.

I will take the second part first. Hume argues for his conclusion by showing that, by the First Principle, the idea of space represents, that is, causally depends on and resembles visual impressions.[2]

> Upon opening my eyes, and turning them to the surrounding objects, I perceive many visible bodies; and upon shutting them again, and considering the distance betwixt these bodies, I acquire the idea of extension. As every idea is deriv'd from some impression, which is exactly similar to it, the impressions similar to this idea of extension, must either be some sensations deriv'd from the sight, or some internal impressions arising from these sensations. (1.2.3.2)

Internal impressions (passions, emotions, desires, aversion) are out of the question; the 'principal question', which 'decides without appeal concerning the nature of the idea', is then about the nature of the impressions of sensation conveyed to the mind by visual experience.

> The table before me is alone sufficient by its view to give me the idea of extension. This idea, then, is borrow'd from, and represents some impression, which this moment appears to the senses. But my senses convey to me only the impressions of colour'd points, dispos'd in a certain manner.... The idea of extension is nothing but a copy of these colour'd points, and of the manner of their appearance (1.2.3.4)

The impressions of touch are like those of sight as to the disposition of their parts, with the sensation of solidity presenting points in place of that of colour (1.2.3.5).

---

[2] 'No discovery cou'd have been made more happily for deciding all controversies concerning ideas, than that above-mention'd, that impressions always take the precedency of them, and that every idea, with which the imagination is furnish'd, first makes its appearance in a correspondent impression' (1.2.3.1).

The idea of time in its turn derives 'from the succession of our perceptions of every kind, ideas as well as impressions, and impressions of reflection as well as of sensation' (1.2.3.6).[3]

The impressions that give rise to the ideas of space and time are thus *complex*. They consist of individual particulars, visible and tangible points or perceptions, together with their manners of disposition: mutual position and distance or succession. 'As 'tis from the disposition of visible and tangible objects we receive the idea of space, so from the succession of ideas and impressions we form the idea of time' (1.2.3.7). The perceptions that give origin to the idea of space consist of elements that are 'so situated, as to afford us the notion of distance and contiguity; of length, breadth, and thickness'. The impressions represented by the ideas of extension and duration are, by Equivalence, complex objects: the 'extended object, or composition of colour'd points' consists in a 'disposition of points, or manner of their appearance' and is equivalent with the 'disposition of visible and tangible objects' from which 'we receive the idea of space' (1.2.3.5). It is important to specify the application of the First Principle to the ideas of space and time. The principle deals with how our cognitive nature realizes the conditions of object representation. In the case of space and time, such realization is in the phenomenal qualities of visual and tactile or, respectively, internal, introspective experience. This is of course a posteriori. The relatively a priori conclusion is that, insofar as we have representation of them by sight and touch or by introspection, space is extension (the visible and tactile disposition of a plurality of simple impressions) and time is duration (the successive disposition of ideas in internal experience). In this respect, complexity is essential to spatial and temporal objects, impressions, or presentations, and to spatial ideas or representations, as we have them. (As we will see in § 8.2.2, Hume's notion of spatial and temporal nature must be complicated in a disjunctive sense, in order to explain how the imagination produces the idea of a vacuum.)[4]

---

[3] For a clarification of the representational character of spatial and temporal contents, see L. Falkenstein, 'Hume on the Idea of a Vacuum', *Hume Studies*, 2, 2013 (131–68), 152–5.

[4] On the compound character of the impressions of space and time and the irreducible role of manner of disposition (besides colored and tangible points), see R. Newman, 'Hume on Space and Geometry', Hume Studies, 7, 1981 (also in Tweyman, *David Hume. Critical Assessments*, III, 39–59, 50: 'The idea of space is abstract because it is formed on the basis of an observed "resemblance" among impressions of extended objects, this resemblance covering both impressions of sight and touch and consisting in that disposition of points (or parts) or manner of appearance, in which they agree'). Newman also rightly contends (contra Kemp Smith) that the arrangement or disposition 'does lie "in the content" of spatial perceptions' so that spatial cognition is grounded on impressions (48). Additionally, he draws attention to the needful distinction between sensibly presented physical points—which are extended, have parts, and are divisible—and mathematical points, which are the offspring of imagination and display a projective dimension (51). It is the former, not the latter that contribute to the impressions, that are the objects of spatial thought and cognition. There is therefore no contrast between spatial minima and the essentially complex character of spatial objects. See also Falkenstein, 'Space and Time', 62–3, 67–8. However, I do not want to saddle Newman or Falkenstein with my pluralistic ontology of Hume's sensible objects; more specifically, with the purely mereological view of simple and complex impressions which I am proposing.

Even though space and time as complex impressions or objects are composed of simple elements, they can be individuated, together with the content of the ideas that represent them, only in terms of complex wholes. Neither of the elements to which we can reduce complex impressions of space and time are by themselves, as different and distinct, space or time; or can be represented as space and time. Manners of disposition, quite simply, do not exist by themselves. Simple impressions or objects have neither extension nor duration. They exist in the mind as visual, tactile, or internal perceptions without any inner, phenomenological structure or configuration. Such simples have spatial and temporal nature only because of their being coloured and solid and of their introspective manifestation. This makes them uniquely suited to constitute complex objects and impressions with extensions and durations; but it does not qualify them as extended or successive.[5] The mereological priority of simple over complex impressions does not translate into a logical priority (in Hume's sense: the nature of ideas and the understanding) or into a psychological one (the nature of our spatial awareness). As a matter of fact, it is only through careful experiments and a priori reasoning that we come to perceive and to recognize spatial minima, simple spatial ideas, and impressions (1.2.1.2–4).[6] The same holds of time. 'Five notes play'd on a flute give us the impression and idea of time; tho' time be not a sixth impression, which presents itself to the hearing or any other of the senses. Nor is it a sixth impression, which the mind by reflection finds in itself.' The mind 'only takes notice of the *manner*, in which the different sounds make their appearance' (1.2.3.10). This is of course no obstacle to regard spatial and temporal ideas as representational: complex ideas can be exact representations of complex impressions and complex impressions present complex objects; and regions of space and time are such complex objects.[7]

---

[5] Spatial and temporal minima have no extension and duration. The compositional and representational import of perceptions of space and time seems thus to hang in the air. However, the simple elements of the complex impressions of space and time still have an internal affinity with what is extended and successive. Hume remarks, in Section 5 of Part 4, that only certain perceptions and objects are susceptible to location in space: the impressions of sight and touch and visible and tangible objects. Therefore, visible and tangible elements of content seem uniquely suitable to constitute extended objects and uniquely related to space. They are potentially extended, so to say. L. Falkenstein, 'Space and Time', 61–2, remarks that extension arises from composition not as a product of the size of visible and tangible points but out of their manner of disposition. They have proto-spatial properties different from extension. See D. Jacquette, 'Hume on Infinite Divisibility', 72–3.

[6] Hume also ascribes epistemological priority to simple spatial impressions and ideas because they cannot but be adequate presentations and representations of objects, see § 8.1.2. This follows a priori on the idea of spatial minima. But, again, this condition of epistemic authority does not establish a psychological priority, a priority in immediate awareness.

[7] See D. L. M. Baxter, 'Hume on Infinite Divisibility', in *History of Philosophy Quarterly*, 5, 1988 (in Tweyman, *David Hume. Critical Assessments*, III, 16–24), 16: 'Regions of space have the structure of extended objects'. See also M. J. Costa, 'Hume, Strict Identity, and Time's Vacuum', in *Hume Studies*, 16, 1990, 1–16, 4; and, for a strong defense of the representational import of manners of disposition, see L. Falkenstein, 'Hume on Manners of Disposition and the Ideas of Space and Time', *Archiv für Geschichte der Philosophie*, 79, 1997, 179–80, especially 190–1. (See also Falkenstein, 'Space and Time' in S. Traiger, ed., *The Blackwell Guide to Hume's* Treatise, Blackwell, Oxford 2006 (59–76), 67–8.)

Hume also gives two modal, a priori arguments against the possibility of simple ideas of space and time. The first one addresses only time; the second has primary reference to space. The first argument is a paradigmatic application of Impossibility/Inconceivability.

> In order to know whether any objects, which are join'd in impression, be separable in idea, we need only consider, if they be different from each other; in which case, 'tis plain they may be conceiv'd apart. Every thing, that is different, is distinguishable; and every thing, that is distinguishable, may be separated, according to the maxims above-explain'd. If on the contrary they be not different, they are not distinguishable; and if they be not distinguishable, they cannot be separated. But this is precisely the case with respect to time, compar'd with our successive perceptions. (1.2.3.10)

There is no real difference, in temporal impressions or objects, between the manner of disposition of their elements, the pattern of succession, and the elements so disposed or succeeding. The two, therefore, cannot exist separately. There is only a distinction of reason between successive manners of appearance and the simple perceptions that appear in this way. One can attend to the first without considering the second and apply the resulting (non-representational) conception to other perceptions. This makes it possible to distinguish their respective contributions to our possession of temporal contents but falls short of the conditions for a distinct and simple idea of time. The disposition or succession is the properly temporal dimension of such impressions or objects. If there is no way to conceive of it as such, by a simple idea, there is no way in which time is conceivable by a simple idea.

> The idea of time is not deriv'd from a particular impression mix'd up with others, and plainly distinguishable from them; but arises altogether from the manner, in which impressions appear to the mind, without making one of the number. (1.2.3.10)

The second argument proceeds in the opposite direction, Conceivability/Possibility, by considering the composition of the simple elements of the complex impression of space: indivisible, visible, and tangible impressions. 'That compound impression, which represents extension, consists of several lesser impressions, that are indivisible to the eye or feeling, and may be call'd impressions of atoms or corpuscles endow'd with colour and solidity' (1.2.3.15). To see whether a separate, simple idea of space is possible, we must see what spatial contents can be formed starting by composing these simple elements. Now, in such composition, the properties of the parts that determine the spatial or extended nature of the resulting contents are kept fixed, by Non-Mixture. "Tis not only requisite, that these atoms shou'd be colour'd or tangible, in order to discover themselves to our senses; 'tis also necessary we shou'd preserve the idea of their colour or tangibility in order to comprehend them by our imagination.' Otherwise, there would be nothing for the imagination to conceive and form an idea with. 'There is nothing but the idea of their colour or tangibility, which can render them conceivable by the mind.' 'Now such as the parts are, such is the whole. If a point be not consider'd as colour'd or tangible, it can convey to us no idea; and consequently the idea of extension, which is compos'd of the ideas of these points, can never possibly exist' (1.2.3.16). The shift from only unextended, only inchoately spatial perceptions, to extended, properly spatial ones, does not involve any change in their qualities but only their composition (according to some structure or disposition). Therefore, properly spatial perceptions can only be complex, as to their existence and contents.[8]

The representational character of spatial and temporal contents also entails that perceptions of space and time are *extended* or have *duration*. Impressions of space or time are spatial or temporal objects; but then they must be extended or have duration. This claim can be extended to ideas. By Two Viewpoints, the properties of the content of perceptions must also be properties with which they exist in the mind. Therefore, if there are impressions that present spatial objects and ideas that represent them, these ideas must exist in the mind with extension and duration. 'The first notion of space and extension is deriv'd solely from the senses of sight and feeling; nor is there any thing, but what is colour'd or tangible, that has parts dispos'd after such a manner, as to convey that idea' (1.4.5.9). From this follows that some perceptions, those of the sight and feeling, have 'parts' 'so situated with respect to each other, as to form any figure or quantity'; and that the 'whole' is so related to 'other bodies' 'as to answer to our notions of contiguity or distance' (1.4.5.10). Perceptions with spatial contents are spatial mental objects as well.

> That table, which just now appears to me, is only a perception, and all its qualities are qualities of a perception. Now the most obvious of all its qualities is extension. The perception consists of parts. These parts are so situated, as to afford us the notion of distance and contiguity; of length, breadth, and thickness. The termination of these three dimensions is what we call figure. This figure is moveable, separable, and divisible. Mobility, and separability are the distinguishing properties of extended objects. And to cut short all disputes, the very idea of extension is copy'd from nothing but an impression, and consequently must perfectly agree to it. To say the idea of extension agrees to any thing, is to say it is extended. (1.4.5.15)

---

[8] See on imagination and time and space, Rocknak, *Imagined Causes*, 138–41.

A parallel claim holds of the representation of time: only perceptions that really have duration, as successions of simple perceptions, can present and represent time.

8.1.2 Finite Divisibility and Adequate Representation

Hume can make good his theory of spatial and temporal representation only if he can secure the visible and tangible simple elements it postulates, on the side of objects (impressions) and of perceptions (ideas). He addresses this problem in the first part of his system, concerning the finite divisibility of space and time. Hume joins in this way a longstanding debate in the history of metaphysics, but I will only discuss the role of finite divisibility in spatial and temporal representation.[9] Hume's views combine (i) an argument for the finite divisibility of the perceptions of space and time with (ii) an argument for the finite divisibility of space and time themselves.

(1) Hume proposes an a priori argument against the infinite divisibility of the ideas of space and time. The first premise of the argument is the assumedly self-evident fact 'that the capacity of the mind is limited, and can never attain a full and adequate conception of infinity' (1.2.1.2). The second premise is the a priori one that 'whatever is capable of being divided in infinitum, must consist of an infinite number of parts, and that 'tis impossible to set any bound to the number of parts, without setting bounds at the same time to the division'. From these premises, by Impossibility/Inconceivability, Hume draws the 'induction' that 'the *idea*, which we form of any finite quality, is not infinitely divisible' and that by distinctions and separations 'we may run up this idea to inferior ones, which will be perfectly simple and indivisible'. 'In rejecting the infinite capacity of the mind, we suppose it may arrive to an end of the division of its ideas.' The a priori conclusion about the limit to the division of ideas of extensive magnitudes finds a counterpart in the a posteriori limits of our natural capacities of conception by imagination. ''Tis therefore certain, that the imagination reaches a *minimum*, and may raise up to itself an idea, of which it cannot conceive any sub-division, and which cannot be diminished without a total annihilation' (1.2.1.3).

Ideas of the imagination which are such that they would cease to exist, that is, to be in the mind, if they were further divided, are simple and indivisible mental existents. By Two Viewpoints, the contents they bear are also simple or indivisible: minimal spatial or temporal contents. Therefore, both as to their existence

---

[9] See, for the historical background, the 'Editors' Annotations' to Sections 1 and 2 of Part 2, in the Norton & Norton edition of the *Treatise*. For a good discussion of the relations between visible and tangible minima, finite divisibility of space and time, and representational adequacy, see M. Frasca-Spada, *Space and the Self in Hume's Treatise*, Cambridge University Press, Cambridge 1998, 38 ff., 54–5.

and as to their contents, spatial and temporal ideas cannot be divided without limit. Hume makes a similar point about impressions, to establish that finite divisibility is a matter of the original way in which spatial and temporal perceptions and contents are given. "'Tis the same case with the impressions of the senses as with the ideas of the imagination. Put a spot of ink upon paper, fix your eye upon that spot, and retire to such a distance, that at last you lose sight of it; 'tis plain, that the moment before it vanish'd the image or impression was perfectly indivisible' (1.2.1.4). Just before vanishing from awareness, before its disappearance from the mind, an impression is not susceptible of further distinction and separation. Therefore, it is a minimal visible and tangible object, simple and indivisible. The limits of discrimination of visual and tactile experience and conception make available the minimal perceptions (as to mental existence and content) postulated by Hume's account of the representation of space and time.[10]

Finite divisibility is a claim in Hume's 'logic', without implications for natural philosophy. Hume is ready to recognize that by reflection on and reasoning about empirical information we can think that objects presented and represented by minimal impressions or ideas can still be of different sizes.

> When you tell me of the thousandth and ten thousandth part of a grain of sand, I have a distinct idea of these numbers and of their different proportions; but the images, which I form in my mind to represent the things themselves, are nothing different from each other, nor inferior to that image, by which I represent the grain of sand itself, which is suppos'd so vastly to exceed them. (1.2.1.3)

Hume endorses the conclusion that we can draw from the conceivability of objects smaller than those we represent by minimal perceptions: 'sound reason convinces us that there are bodies *vastly* more minute that those, which appear to the senses' (1.2.4.24). We can judge the sizes of objects and conclude that there are objects which are smaller than some we perceive or conceive by vanishing perceptions. We take the 'impressions of those minute impressions, which appear to the senses, to be equal or near equal to the objects'; and we find 'by reason, that there are other objects vastly more minute' (1.2.1.5). This contrast between conclusions of 'sound reason' about the real sizes of objects and the lessons drawn from vanishing ideas might seem to make these latter spurious. In this way, the

---

[10] Ainslie, 'Adequate Ideas and Modest Scepticism in Hume's Metaphysics of Space', in *Archiv für Geschichte der Philosophie*, 92, 2010 (39–67), 45–6, rightly remarks Hume's illustrations of the finite divisibility of the ideas of space and time involve the distinction and connection of the viewpoints of their contents ('awareness-of-content') and of their existence in the mind ('mental objects'). As Jacquette points out, finite divisibility is a natural or formal property of the visual field, which characterizes any mental presentation of space ('Hume on Infinite Divisibility and Sensible Extensionless Indivisibles', in *Journal of the History of Philosophy*, 34, 1996 (61–78), 66–8), no matter what we can conclude by experience and reason about the size of objects. See Frasca-Spada, *Space and Self*, 51–2.

role of vanishing perceptions in Hume's argument for finite divisibility would be called into question and the argument itself would be debunked.

Hume is undeterred. He says that is only a 'false reason' that seems to persuade us 'that there are bodies *infinitely* more minute' than what appears to the senses (1.2.4.24). On the one hand, moving from '*vastly* more minute' to '*infinitely* more minute' is obviously a misstep. Therefore, there are no implications here against the *conclusion* of finite divisibility. More interestingly, the contrast between the real sizes of objects and the minima of spatial conceivability does not invalidate Hume's *arguments* for that conclusion. This is because the contrast between ideas of the size of objects we form by reflection and apply in reasoning and our indivisible spatial impressions and ideas is not a difference between clear and distinct and obscure and confused perceptions. It is a contrast between different modes of cognition relating to spatial and temporal objects.[11] There is an *epistemological* difference between the judgements of size we make on the basis of immediate appearances and those we form by reflection and reasoning. The first judgements, based on sense and imagination, are reliable only to some extent and susceptible to reflective correction. But this does *not* mean ('we too hastily conclude') that our minimal impressions and ideas fail to present and represent minimal objects or that there are objects 'inferior to any idea of our imagination or impression of our senses' (1.2.2.5). This would not be a limit but a flaw in what spatial and temporal contents we have available. We would not have ideas and impressions identifying spatial and temporal minima, so that we could not perceive or conceive such minima, so that no content could be attached to the claim of finite divisibility.

By contrast, according to Hume, we do have perceptions appropriate to present and represent minimal parts of extensions and successions, whatever these turn out actually to be. 'This however is certain, that we can form ideas, which shall be no greater than the smallest atom of the animal spirits of an insect a thousand times less than a mite' (1.2.1.5). These minimal perceptions are perfectly appropriate for representing and conceiving unextended parts of space and non-successive parts of time. 'What consists of parts is distinguishable into them, and what is distinguishable is separable. But whatever we may imagine of the thing, the idea of a grain of sand is not distinguishable, nor separable into twenty, much less into a thousand, ten thousand, or an infinite number of different ideas' (1.2.1.3). We are susceptible to errors of judgements concerning size, to doxastic shortcomings. But this is the *only* defect of our spatial cognition. 'The only defect of our senses is, that they give us disproportion'd images of things, and represent as minute and uncompounded what is really great and compos'd of a vast number of parts' (1.2.1.5). But the simple, minimal elements that compose these objects are perfectly and soundly representable and conceivable, by way of our simple

---

[11] See Ainslie, 'Adequate ideas and Modest Scepticism', 49–51.

and indivisible perceptions. They can be wrongly applied in our empirical enquiries; but they exactly represent the minima we need to represent. In this respect, there is no cognitive gap in Hume's representation of time and space.

Relatedly, Hume makes clear that the phenomenon of vanishing impressions has not to do with the physical conditions of visual perception (a matter of natural philosophy) but with the character of visual experience and content (a matter of 'logic'). "'Tis not for want of rays of light striking on our eyes, that the minute parts of distant bodies convey not any sensible impression; but because they are remov'd beyond that distance, at which their impressions were reduc'd to a minimum, and were incapable of any farther diminution' (1.2.1.4). Intervening on the causal conditions of perception (with 'a microscope, or a telescope') would simply change the threshold at which impressions are present as minimal; it would rearrange our visual field; but it would leave the naturally necessary minimal character of its elements intact, as to their logical features and to their phenomenology.[12]

(2) The argument for finite divisibility allows Hume to establish that minimal spatial and temporal ideas successfully represent minimal spatial and temporal objects. In principle, the ideas of space and time can be representational since they are spatial and temporal in their qualities of mental existence; such qualities are content bearing; and in this way they can correspond to spatial and temporal objects or impressions. We can have a proof that they exactly represent such objects if we consider minimal ideas of space and time (these Hume has already introduced and defended). We can be 'certain' that nothing is 'more minute' than a minimal idea with spatial content ('of a part of extension'). Therefore, we can be confident that anything we discover by this 'least idea' is 'a real quality of extension'; more precisely, it is a real minimal constituent of extension. These ideas successfully represent objects. The argument is a priori and the condition of representation is not one of causal dependence of ideas on impressions. However, indirectly, there is a causal ground to representation since the minimal size of ideas depends on the nature of our visual experience. As all spatial objects can be composed out of such minimal objects or point, spatial ideas can in general be at least potential representations. In this way, a fortiori, they are in general clear and distinct and provide an appropriate input to the Established Maxim.

This is how Hume extends, by a priori modal inferences, the claim of finite divisibility from the ideas of space and time to space and time themselves.

---

[12] Hume's discussion of finite divisibility is mostly about space. He remarks that the same arguments hold of time; and adds another one, based on its successive nature. "'Tis certain then, that time, as it exists, must be compos'd of indivisible moments. For if in time we could never arrive at an end of division, and if each moment, as it succeeds another, were not perfectly single and indivisible, there would be an infinite number of co-existent moments, or parts of time; which I believe will be allow'd to be an arrant contradiction' (1.2.2.4).

> Wherever ideas are adequate representations of objects, the relations, contradictions and agreements of the ideas are all applicable to the objects; and this we may in general observe to be the foundation of all human knowledge. But our ideas are adequate representations of the most minute parts of extension; and thro' whatever divisions and subdivisions we may suppose these parts to be arriv'd at, they can never become inferior to some ideas, which we form. The plain consequence is, that whatever *appears* impossible and contradictory upon the comparison of these ideas, must be *really* impossible and contradictory, without any farther excuse or evasion. (1.2.2.1)

Hume's argument is, quite simply, the following. Suppose our ideas are adequate representations of the most minute parts of extension. Then we may proceed, firstly, by Impossibility/Inconceivability: (1) ideas of space and time are spatial and temporal in their mental existence; (2) no spatial and temporal idea is possible in the natural mind that is inferior to the minimal ones; (3) therefore we can conceive of nothing inferior to such ideas. Then, by Inconceivability/Impossibility, we can conclude that, since nothing inferior to the minimal ideas of space and time is conceivable, no object of that sort is possible. An infinitely divisible spatial content cannot be conceived; spatial conceptions are clear and distinct; therefore infinitely divisible spatial and temporal objects cannot exist.

> Every thing capable of being infinitely divided contains an infinite number of parts; otherwise the division would be stopt short by the indivisible parts, which we should immediately arrive at. If therefore any finite extension be infinitely divisible, it can be no contradiction to suppose, that a finite extension contains an infinite number of parts: And *vice versa*, if it be a contradiction to suppose, that a finite extension contains an infinite number of parts, no finite extension can be infinitely divisible.   (1.2.2.2)[13]

An infinitely divisible space is inconceivable by clear representational ideas. Because of inconceivability, 'no finite extension is capable of containing an infinite number of parts; and consequently...no finite extension is infinitely divisible'. Infinite divisibility of space is metaphysically impossible. By contrast, by Conceivability/Possibility: (1) minimal spatial and ideas: visible and tangible or introspective minima, can be formed in the mind; (2) the qualities with which

---

[13] See, for discussion and a defense of Hume's claim, T. Holden, 'Infinite Divisibility and Actual Parts in Hume's *Treatise*', Hume Studies, 28, 2002, 3–25. Holden rightly remarks that the well-known objections to Hume's doctrine (carefully rehearsed in J. Franklin, 'Achievement and Fallacies in Hume's Account of Finite Divisibility', Hume Studies, 20, 1994, 85–101: an independently interesting work) hold only on the assumption that Hume is 'raising a purely *mathematical* challenge' to infinite divisibility, rather than an 'objection to the infinite divisibility of *physical quantities with concrete, actual parts*' (7).

they exist also bear contents as of objects; (3) minimal spatial and temporal objects are possible. Since space and time cannot exist in any other way, this is how they actually exist. The idea of an extension composed out of indivisible 'inferior ideas' is perfectly conceivable (again, on Hume's exactly representing minimal ideas). 'Consequently 'tis possible for extension really to exist conformable to it' (1.2.2.9). More pointedly: "Tis therefore possible for space and time to exist conformable to this idea [finite divisibility]; And if it be possible, 'tis certain they actually do exist conformable to it; since their infinite divisibility is utterly impossible and contradictory' (1.2.4.1).[14] Our representational cognition of space and time is therefore comprehensive and deep. The lack of simple impressions of space and time is more than compensated by the representational import of minimal spatial and temporal perceptions and by the claim of finite divisibility.[15]

8.2 Imagining Space and Time

This robust representational layer of spatial and temporal content is embedded in the general framework of cognitive gaps and works of imagination. There are ideas with spatial and temporal contents, part of our ordinary and philosophical cognition, which object representation does not explain. These gaps in spatial and temporal representation can be closed only by the more limited imagination. The works of the imagination, in this domain, go beyond abstraction and generality and diverge from those underlying causal content.

---

[14] Hume's discussion of finite divisibility is mostly about space. He remarks that the same arguments hold of time; and adds another one, based on its successive nature. "Tis certain then, that time, as it exists, must be compos'd of indivisible moments. For if in time we could never arrive at an end of division, and if each moment, as it succeeds another, were not perfectly single and indivisible, there would be an infinite number of co-existent moments, or parts of time; which I believe will be allow'd to be an arrant contradiction' (1.2.2.4).

[15] See, for a good discussion of the representational import of the simple ideas of space and time, Ainslie, 'Adequate Ideas and Modest Scepticism', 54–63. This is of course a point of major contrast between Hume and Kant: see H. Allison, *Custom and Reason in Hume*, Clarendon Press, Oxford 2008, 59–60, 103–11, 205–9. I limit myself to two remarks. Hume's doctrine of space and time, including its metaphysical implications, addresses space and time as they appear to the mind, their sensible, phenomenal constitution. This is the ultimate source of any content we can entertain (this is well pointed out by Ainslie, 'Adequate Ideas and Modest Scepticism', 41; see also Baxter, 'Hume's Theory of Space and Time', 116–20). But in Book 1 appearance is not a subjective condition. It is, primitively, the presence of sensibly specified and individuated individual particulars: an 'Edenic world' (Chalmers) with primary and secondary qualities. This is different from Kant's view of sensible intuitions, which includes an essential element of subjectivity: sensation as the perception of how the subject is affected in experience. This idea, which recalls some positions in the rationalist tradition, is significantly absent in Hume. Hume has a more objective, third-personal view of sensible cognition than Kant.

8.2.1 An Abstract Idea of Time and Space

One question is easily dispatched. We have only particular spatial and temporal impressions, but we have general ideas of space and time and apply them in reflection and reasoning. Hume can explain this with his theory of abstraction. In the case of space, we start from an impression of sensation, the 'extended object, or composition of colour'd points, from which we first receiv'd the idea of extension' (1.2.3.5). Suppose the points are of 'a purple colour': this is how the object appears 'in every repetition of the idea'. But the experience of other colours, green, red, and black, and of their different compositions, together with the observed resemblances in their dispositions allow us, given cognitive detachment, to 'found an abstract idea merely on that disposition of points, or manner of appearance, in which they agree'. There is only a distinction of reason between points and manners of disposition; but this is necessary and sufficient for abstraction and generalization. This process can be extended across the sensorial modes of sight and touch. ('Nay even when the resemblance is carry'd beyond the objects of one sense, and the impressions of touch are found to be similar to those of sight in the disposition of their parts; this does not hinder the abstract idea from representing both, upon account of their resemblance", 1.2.3.5).[16]

The same account holds of the general idea of time. 'The idea of time, being deriv'd from the succession of our perceptions of every kind, ideas as well as impressions, and impressions of reflection as well as of sensation, will afford us an instance of an abstract idea, which comprehends a still greater variety than that of space, and yet is represented in the fancy by some particular individual idea of a determinate quantity and quality' (1.2.3.6). General ideas of space and time are not problematic. The general spatial and temporal cognition they make possible is correlated with spatial and temporal representations and forms the background of Hume's account of the idea of cause.

8.2.2 The Definitions and Demonstrations of Geometry

Other gaps in spatial and temporal representation raise more serious problems. Hume addresses them indirectly at 1.2.4–5, when discussing some 'objections' to his 'system'. Such objections deal with the contrasts between finite divisibility and certain presumed geometrical demonstrations; and between the nature of the

---

[16] Therefore, as remarked by Allison, *Custom and Reason*, 48, Hume's stance on the Molyneux Question would be closer to Leibniz's than to Locke's. An abstract idea of space formed on particular tactile ideas could represent newly encountered objects of sight and allow us to recognize them as the same with objects of touch with which we are familiar.

ideas of space and time and the ideas of an empty space and time, which we seem to need and possess. The objections indicate genuine cognitive gaps in the representation of space and time and raise serious conceptual challenges to Hume's theory. It is thus incumbent on Hume not only to disarm the objections but also to explain how they arise and, given that the objections point to important conceptual roles in our cognition of space and time, what ideas actually perform such roles.

8.2.2.1 The Cognitive Gap of Geometrical Equality

Hume has a dual agenda in his discussion of the ideas of geometry. He wants to debunk some objections against finite divisibility that seem warranted by geometrical practice. And he wants to explain how we come to have the ideas that really support that practice. This is required to achieve the first aim, since that explanation removes a misunderstanding concerning geometrical demonstrations that is the source of the objections. But it is also a theoretical requirement on its own since Hume's account of spatial representation might seem to make a mystery of geometry.

Hume leaves unspecified what geometrical objections to the doctrine of finite divisibility he has in mind. We find in the text that he is addressing some sort of 'geometrical demonstration for the infinite divisibility of extension' (1.2.4.32).[17] But the general outline of his discussion is clear enough. Hume points out that the principal definitions of geometry—those of surface, line, and point—are 'favorable', 'conformable' to the doctrine of finite divisibility (1.2.4.8). 'A surface is defin'd to be length and breadth without depth: A line to be length without breadth or depth: A point to be what has neither length, breadth nor depth. 'Tis evident that all this is perfectly unintelligible upon any other supposition than that of the composition of extension by indivisible points or atoms' (1.2.4.9). Such definitions involve the idea of 'termination' and terminations are inconceivable and impossible without indivisible parts. 'A surface terminates a solid; a line terminates a surface; a point terminates a line; but I assert, that if the ideas of a point, line or surface were not indivisible, 'tis impossible we shou'd ever conceive these terminations' (1.2.4.14). Hume's plan is to use the definitions in order to reject the presumed demonstrations of the infinite divisibility of extension ('defend the definitions, refute the demonstrations', 1.2.4.8).

---

[17] For an illustration of the objections Hume could have had in mind, see 1.2.4.30: 'How can he [any mathematician] prove to me, for instance, that two right lines cannot have one common segment? Or that 'tis impossible to draw more than one right line betwixt any two points?' Hume's challenge focuses on what one can (reasonably) see as geometrical challenges to finite divisibility. See C. D. Broad, 'Hume's Doctrine of Space', *Proceedings of the British Academy*, 46, 1961; Garrett, *Cognition and Commitment*, 74–5; Franklin, 'Achievements and Fallacies', 89–90; Falkenstein, 'Space and Time', 64; Baxter, 'Hume's Theory of Space and Time', 123 fn. 31.

> Thus it appears, that the definitions of mathematics destroy the pretended demonstrations; and that if we have the idea of indivisible points, lines and surfaces conformable to the definition, their existence is certainly possible: but if we have no such idea, 'tis impossible we can ever conceive the termination of any figure; without which conception there can be no geometrical demonstration. (1.2.4.16)

Hume also gives a completely general argument to the effect that no geometrical demonstration could establish a conclusion like infinite divisibility. ('But I go farther, and maintain, that none of these demonstrations can have sufficient weight to establish such a principle, as this of infinite divisibility', 1.2.4.17.) This is because of the epistemological weakness of geometrical demonstrations. 'When geometry decides any thing concerning the proportions of quantity, we ought not to look for the utmost precision and exactness. None of its proofs extend so far.' This epistemological weakness, in turn, depends on the nature of the ideas we apply in geometrical practice. Such ideas 'are not exact' and the corresponding maxims 'not precisely true' (1.2.4.17). 'The ideas, which are most essential to geometry, *viz.* those of equality and inequality, of a right line and a plane surface, are far from being exact and determinate, according to our common method of conceiving them' (1.2.4.29).

The source of the inexactness and imprecision is that the ideas of geometry, 'according to our common method of conceiving', that is, *as they are applied in our geometrical practice*, cannot be grounded in representation. On Hume's representational conception, the essential ideas of geometry would be as precise and exact as one may want.

> There are few or no mathematicians, who defend the hypothesis of indivisible points; and yet these have the readiest and justest answer to the present question ['what they mean when they say one line or surface is EQUAL to, or GREATER, or LESS than another?', 1.2.4.18]. They need only reply, that lines or surfaces are equal, when the numbers of points in each are equal; and that as the proportion of the numbers varies, the proportion of the lines and surfaces is also vary'd. (1.2.4.19)

This idea of equality is representational, because it is caused by and resembles simple impressions, pairs of sensible objects, or individual parts of perceptions. (Counting is such a pairing.) It exactly represents the relations of size of regions of space. However, this is *not* an idea of equality that can support our actual geometrical practice.

> But tho' this answer be just, as well as obvious; yet I may affirm, that this standard of equality is entirely useless, and that it never is from such a comparison we

determine objects to be equal or unequal with respect to each other. For as the points, which enter into the composition of any line or surface, whether perceiv'd by the sight or touch, are so minute and so confounded with each other, that 'tis utterly impossible for the mind to compute their number, such a computation will never afford us a standard, by which we may judge of proportions. (1.2.4.19)

Thus, the demonstrations of geometry lack the epistemic force to debunk the claim of finite divisibility, which underlies geometrical definitions. In judging of proportions, equality of size, linearity, and planarity, we cannot use the standard provided by the representational content of geometrical ideas ('enumeration of the minute indivisible parts'), which would make our geometrical demonstrations exact. This is because of the natural fact of our insufficient powers of discrimination. The supporters of infinite divisibility cannot even devise such an exact standard or have resort to the congruity of figures, which also presupposes finite divisibility (1.2.4.20–1). Therefore, geometricians proceed on principles 'too coarse to afford any such subtle inferences as they commonly draw' (see 1.2.4.25, 27), like those concerning infinite divisibility. (And, of course, if they had available precise and exact ideas of size, this would be only because space is *finitely* divisible.) (1.2.4.31). But our geometrical practice thus seems to lack adequate support in ideas. This opens a cognitive gap corresponding to the 'foundation of mathematics' (1.4.2.22).

8.2.2.2 Closing the Gap: Geometrical Equality

Thus Hume has an explanatory problem to solve. He makes claims about the imprecision and coarseness of the ideas of geometry: 'But tho' its [the mind's] decisions concerning these proportions be sometimes infallible, they are not always so; nor are our judgments of this kind more exempt from doubt and error, than those on any other subject' (1.2.4.23). But such claims go together with the claim that its first principles are 'certain and infallible' (1.2.4.31). He adds that while geometry 'fails of evidence in this single point' (the pretended demonstrations of infinite divisibility) 'all its other reasonings command our fullest assent and approbation' (1.2.4.32). Hume's position about geometrical cognition is thus complex—even apart from the question of whether it is analytic or synthetic, which does not sit well with his philosophical framework.[18]

Hume is a sceptical realist about geometry. He talks of the 'justest' answers to questions concerning sizes and proportions (1.2.4.19); of the 'accurate and exact

---

[18] Hume's grounds of necessity and apriority, therefore of demonstrative import, are internal relations of ideas and Separability, neither of which are well understood in terms of meaning or concept-inclusion. Thus, mathematical truths can be demonstratively known and, on this standard, still be synthetic. This means that the analytic–synthetic distinction does not cut much ice in the philosophy of Book 1. (Thanks to Don Garrett for prodding me on this issue.)

standard' of equality and of any proportion (1.2.4.31); of the 'order' and 'rule' that are ' peculiar and essential' to a right line (1.2.4.30), as matters which are real but 'perfectly unknown' to us (1.2.4.25). As Hume says, 'even upon the system of indivisible points, we can only form a distant notion of some unknown standard to these objects' (1.2.4.25). Then, upon that system, at least a notion of an unknown but real and accurate standard of spatial and temporal properties is available. (No such standard is available upon the system of infinite divisibility.) Nothing of this sort is possible with causal powers, external existence, and personal identity, where there are no objects of representation, no sensible particulars to be ignorant of. By contrast, no matter how feeble our grasp and how limited our capacity for discriminating and enumerating spatial objects, we can know that they stand in certain real relations of size we cannot determinately know.

The cognitive gap of geometry correspondingly differs from those underlying causation, existence of body, and personal identity, by being primarily epistemic. The reason why our geometrical reasonings are not explained by the representation of geometrical objects is not that there can be no such representation. Representations of visible and tangible points are perfectly possible and all other geometrical objects are composed of them. The gap opens only because our natural capacities for discriminating minute objects are limited. Sceptical-sounding texts like 1.2.4.30 should be read in this key. When challenging the geometrician to produce a proof that two right lines cannot have a common segment, Hume contrasts the relevant definitions (the order and the rule with which points are taken) with 'the standard from which we form the idea of a right line'. He doubts whether 'there is any such firmness in our senses or imagination, as to determine whether such an order is violated or preserv'd'. This is an epistemic and even psychological gap, not a logical gap (in Hume's sense); it is a fact about the capacity for discrimination of our minds that does not call in question the existence and genuineness of geometrical contents.

Within the limits of our capacities for discrimination, the commonly used geometrical ideas or standards are in part representational. We have reliable perceptions, that is, sensible representations, of the size and proportions of certain objects, when those are different and large enough. 'There are many philosophers, who refuse to assign any standard of equality, but assert, that 'tis sufficient to present two objects, that are equal, in order to give us a just notion of this proportion. All definitions, say they, are fruitless, without the perception of such objects; and where we perceive such objects, we no longer stand in need of any definition' (1.2.4.22). Hume subscribes to this ('To this reasoning I entirely agree'). The 'only useful notion of equality is deriv'd from the whole united appearances and the comparison of particular objects'. And this is reliably a matter of sensible representation. The eye or rather the mind can determine 'at one view' the proportions of bodies, 'without examining or comparing the number of their minute parts', when, for instance 'the measure of a yard and that of a foot are presented'. Judgements based on such two-objects situations are 'in many cases certain and infallible'.

Still, there *is* a cognitive gap at the roots of geometry and Hume *has* explanatory work to do to mediate the definitions of geometry with its demonstrations. This is because the conception and the standard of equality which can actually be provided by our spatial representation are too restricted in scope to support our geometrical practice. Therefore, the ideas of geometry, if they are to support our 'assent and approbation' of ordinary geometrical reasonings, must tap non-representational sources of content, that is, the imagination. 'The first principles are founded on the imagination and senses: The conclusion, therefore, can never go beyond, much less contradict these faculties' (1.2.4.31). The senses contribute with the 'general appearance' of objects. The imagination contributes with the production of a more comprehensive and more accurate standard of equality (relative to the judgements we can actually make on the basis of the senses). Hume's explanation of how this standard, this idea of equality, is produced, is somewhat complex.

First. At the basic explanatory level, the level that is occupied in the causal case by the effects of repeated experience on the more limited imagination, we find an *idea-comparing* activity of imagination in the larger sense, that is, probable reasoning about our judgements of size, with which we reflect on and correct our immediate, appearance-based judgements. 'We frequently correct our first opinion by a review and reflection; and pronounce those objects to be equal, which at first we esteem'd unequal; and regard an object as less, tho' before it appear'd greater than another' (1.2.4.23). Geometrical reasoning is primarily a deliberate engagement in comparisons of ideas. This exercise requires, firstly, cognitive detachment from the impressions of the sizes and proportions of objects; and, then, the combination of the corresponding perfect ideas in new, possibly counterfactual assessments of sizes. It also requires forming the abstract, general idea of measure, which has mental reality only as a particular idea and is physically real as an instrument. 'Nor is this the only correction, which these judgments of our senses undergo; but we often discover our error by a juxta-position of the objects; or where that is impracticable, by the use of some common and invariable measure, which being successively apply'd to each, informs us of their different proportions.'

Second. The effective, applicable standard of geometrical equality applied in this reflective activity of assessment and correction can be explained by our very engagement in this practice and by its iteration, which starts from the general appearance of objects but is not restricted to it. This move from practice to content is paradigmatically inferentialist.

> There are therefore three proportions, which the mind distinguishes in the general appearance of its objects, and calls by the names of *greater, less* and *equal.*

> But tho' its decisions concerning these proportions be sometimes infallible, they are not always so; nor are our judgments of this kind more exempt from doubt and error, than those on any other subject. We frequently correct our first opinion by a review and reflection; and pronounce those objects to be equal, which at first we esteem'd unequal; and regard an object as less, tho' before it appear'd greater than another. (1.2.4. 23)

(The issue of the iteration of reasoning is crucial for Hume's discussion of scepticism: see 1.4.1: *Of scepticism about reason* and § 11.3.1 for discussion.) To explain how the idea of a standard of equality emerges in the iteration of geometrical reasoning (which it supports in its progress), Hume resorts to the effects of such iteration on imagination in the more limited sense. The elements of Hume's account are thus the same as those of his explanation of causal inference; but their explanatory order is reversed. Our practice of idea-comparing geometrical reasoning has habituation effects on the mind, that is, on the more limited imagination; and these effects lead us to conceive an idea of geometric equality that goes beyond the general appearance of objects.

> When therefore the mind is accustom'd to these judgments and their corrections, and finds that the same proportion which makes two figures have in the eye that appearance, which we call equality, makes them also correspond to each other, and to any common measure, with which they are compar'd, we form a mix'd notion of equality deriv'd both from the looser and stricter methods of comparison. (1.2.4.24)

As it is in general with Inferentialist Naturalism, the Structural Principle has a fundamental role; Hume's imagination is one faculty, the faculty of fainter and changeable ideas; its articulation into comparisons of ideas and primitive transitions allows us to explain the complexities of its production of content.

Third. The customary transition determined by the repeated acts of comparison, reflection, and correction is from perceived to unperceived equality. It is an extension of the equality that two figures 'have in the eye', which is the only one we are directly acquainted with, to one which is beyond our capacities for discrimination. These cases, per se, would be out of the scope of the primitive idea of equality. But by the repeated practice of reflection and correction we come to apply the primitive idea beyond its nature. This application is involved in the iteration and at the same time supported by it: per Hume's Inferentialist Naturalism, a customary transition of the imagination, caused by our practice of explicitly reasoning with the idea of equality, gives support from the inside to an extension of such reasoning, by providing the ideas it needs to compare. This transition is conceived by us as a change in the content of the idea of equality, as a *mixed idea* of geometrical equality, which combines the loose but manifest and immediately available comparison of figures with a stricter but only mediated one. (This also holds of the related ideas of rightness and planarity.) The content of this idea is dual because it combines a representational with an inferential dimension. It derives from the inferential activity of the imagination both in its idea-comparing and in its more limited sense.

This allows us to reason with an idea of equality that is not restricted to object representation but does not involve any cognitive impossibility (like counting indivisible points). This idea closes the gap between the definitions of geometry, which are in principle representational and rely on finite divisibility, and its demonstrations, which cannot apply the exact, representational idea of equality. The mixed idea of equality makes it possible, by its application, to proceed reflectively in the assessment and correction of our judgements of size, as if we had an exact standard of equality (equality as number of point). While its content and existence in fact depend only on the practice of correcting judgements of size and express the ensuing transitions of the imagination. This has epistemological consequences: the mixed idea makes geometry inclusive and accurate while limiting its aims of precision. (This, it will be remembered, was Hume's response to the objection he is discussing.) 'Our appeal is still to the weak and fallible judgment, which we make from the appearance of the objects, and correct by a compass or common measure' (1.2.4.29). Within these limits, however, our geometrical cognition is reliable. This is, quite simply, because in this domain (proportions of size) there is a perfectly adequate layer of representations and truth-conditions, even though our access to it is partial. 'When geometry decides any thing concerning the proportions of quantity, we ought not to look for the utmost precision and exactness. None of its proofs extend so far. It takes the dimensions and proportions of figures justly; but roughly, and with some liberty. Its errors are never considerable; nor wou'd it err at all, did it not aspire to such an absolute perfection' (1.2.4.17).

8.2.2.3 The Illusion of Perfect Equality

Hume's more limited imagination has by contrast a primary position in the explanation of the illusion of having an idea of equality different from the mixed one: the idea of a perfectly accurate and effective standard of equality. This supposition underlies the philosophical illusion that we can attain perfect precision and exactness in geometry. (That geometry is on a par with arithmetic and algebra.) Hume's explanation consists in steps the imagination takes beyond the mixed idea ('But we are not content with this', that is, with the 'mix'd notion of equality', 1.2.4.24).

First. We tend to make a certain error in reasoning. From the correct conclusion ('sound reason') that there are 'bodies vastly more minute' that those that appear to the sense we falsely infer ('a false reason wou'd perswade us') that there are bodies 'infinitely more minute' (1.2.4.24). This makes us think that 'we are not possess'd of any instrument or art of measuring, which can secure us from all error and uncertainty'.

Second. This conclusion induces a *conflicted state of mind* about the idea of such instrument or art. On the one hand, 'we are sensible that the addition or the removal of one of these minute parts, is not discernible either in the appearance or measuring'; on the other, 'we imagine, that two figures, which were equal before, cannot be equal after this removal or addition'. To assuage this conflict, we 'suppose some imaginary standard of equality, by which the appearances and measuring are exactly correct'd, and the figures reduc'd entirely to that proportion'. Hume introduces here a principle of the more limited imagination that recurs in Part 4, *Reconciliation*: a conflict in our views generates a cognitive tension and the imagination operates to resolve or ease the conflict by forging a reconciling idea. This propensity and the transition to the conflict-resolving idea is crucial in the explanation of the idea of identity, in this case, of perfect geometrical equality (see also §§ 9.3.4 and 10.2.3); while it has no place in Hume's account of causal content. The operation of this principle of the more limited imagination is complemented by that of another principle, *Hysteresis* or cognitive inertia. 'But tho' this standard be only imaginary, the fiction however is very natural; nor is any thing more usual, than for the mind to proceed after this manner with any action, even after the reason has ceas'd, which first determin'd it to begin.' Also this principle is involved in the explanation of identity: it explains the direction taken by the transitions with which imagination responds to cognitive dissonance. (Reconciliation and Hysteresis are further discussed in §§ 9.2.2 and 9.3.4.)

Third. Differently from the mixed notion of equality, however, the idea of a perfect standard is spurious. 'This standard is plainly imaginary. For as the very idea of equality is that of such a particular appearance corrected by juxta-position or a common measure, the notion of any correction beyond what we have instruments and art to make, is a mere fiction of the mind, and useless as well as incomprehensible' (1.2.4.24). The contrast with the mixed notion is striking. Not all ideas produced by the imagination are imaginary, mere fictions. Whether they are or not depends, on the one hand, on properties of the underlying processes of the imagination and, on the other, on the conceptual and epistemic roles of putative ideas in our cognitive practices. This polarity of conditions and their theoretical equilibrium determine the cognitive status and the epistemic value of the ideas produced by the imagination. In the present case, the idea of a perfect standard of equality is based on a bad inference and has no regular and just application in geometrical practice (it is rather a source of error). The propensities of the imagination that underlie the idea: Reconciliation and Hysteresis, differently from customary inferential propensities issuing from repeated experience, do not correlate well with representation and are not indicators of representational adequateness. The imagination, in producing this idea, loses contact with the conditions which require the application of a standard of equality and, with this, any reference to spatial representation.

This leaves the mixed idea of equality intact and secures the good standing of all the 'other reasonings' of geometry. 'As the ultimate standard of these figures is deriv'd from nothing but the senses and imagination, 'tis absurd to talk of any perfection beyond what these faculties can judge of; since the true perfection of any thing consists in its conformity to its standard' (1.2.4.29). (See also 1.3.1.6, about the high degree of exactness of geometrical conclusions: 'its mistakes can never be of any consequence'.) Therefore, the mixed notion of equality, which allows geometry to take so many steps beyond the general appearance of objects, has non-illusory, non-spurious content, different from but correlated with our observation of objects.[19] This clearly evidences the structure of the explanatory work of Hume's imagination: different conceptual roles and epistemic statuses in the domain of geometry are aligned with the different nature of the underlying principles of imagination and with different elements of representational cognition. It is only by searching explanatory equilibrium between these factors that the relevant imaginative principles and their content-constitutive work can be individuated.

8.2.3 A Vacuum or Pure Extension

The second cognitive gap depends on Hume's identification of spatial and temporal representational contents with manners of disposition of visible or tangible points or of internal perceptions. Hume makes clear what is missing. 'We can form no idea of a vacuum, or space, where there is nothing visible or tangible' (1.2.5.1). We 'really' have no idea of 'time without any changeable existence' (1.2.5.28). Hume's language and rhetoric point in the direction of illusion of content and of elimination of spurious ideas. There is 'nothing more common' than the fact that we 'deceive' ourselves about the 'reality' of some idea, in particular, that of a vacuum (1.2.5.22). We 'falsly imagine' that we can 'form' the idea of vacuum (1.2.5.14). We 'fancy we have that idea [of "time without changeable existence"]' (1.2.5.29). 'We are apt to confound our ideas, and imagine we can form the idea of a time and duration, without any change or succession' (1.2.5.29). Such language is unparalleled in the account of causation or, for that matter, of

---

[19] The same account holds of time. 'This appears very conspicuously with regard to time; where tho' 'tis evident we have no exact method of determining the proportions of parts, not even so exact as in extension, yet the various corrections of our measures, and their different degrees of exactness, have given us an obscure and implicit notion of a perfect and entire equality' (1.2.4.24). And of other cognitive domains—music, painting, mechanics—where we entertain notions of a perfect standard without being able to tell where we derive them from.

geometrical equality, where indictments of spuriousness are restricted to the idea of a perfect standard of equality. But Hume's intellectual position is uneasy. The identification of space and time with arrangements of visible and tangible objects brings him close to Berkeley's and Leibniz's relational conceptions of space and time. By contrast, the philosophical tradition Hume sees as closest to him, that is, Locke's and Newton's, non-problematically admits absolute space and time and the possibility of vacuum; in fact, it requires them.[20] Hume could not fail to be aware of this conflict and he implicitly recognizes it in a footnote added in the *Appendix*, where he expresses his agreement with the 'Newtonian philosophy', but only if 'rightly understood; adding that in this philosophy 'a vacuum is asserted" (1. 2. 5. 26, fn. 12). This suggests that, while the idea of spatial and temporal vacuum conflicts with the conditions of temporal and spatial representation, it differs from the idea of a perfect standard of equality because it has a place and a role in our best natural philosophy. In this sense, there is an important cognitive gap to fill. Hume must not only dismantle the illusion that we represent extension without matter and duration without change but also explain what ideas actually perform, if only under a deep revision, important, non-illusory cognitive roles supposedly associated to representations of a vacuum.[21]

8.2.3.1 The Missing Idea of a Vacuum

Hume's attack on the idea of a vacuum takes the form of an enquiry into the 'nature and origin of several ideas' (1.2.5.5). Its main result is that we have no impressions, either simple or complex, which the idea of a vacuum can correspond to; and therefore no representation of it. Not simple impressions: 'The idea of utter darkness can never be the same with that idea of a vacuum.' Utter darkness delivers no visual impression; it has no visual qualities or phenomenology, that is, no mental existence, and thus no content. It is 'merely the negation of light, or more properly speaking, of colour'd and visible objects'. In utter darkness, just like in congenital blindness, one 'has no idea either of light or darkness'. The same is true of unimpeded motion: a flying man, 'supported in the air' and 'softly convey'd along by some invisible power', who, for the same reason, would lack the relevant sensations, could not have the idea of space and extension. Thus, 'darkness and motion, with the utter removal of every thing visible and tangible, can never give us the idea of extension without matter' (1.2.5.7).

---

[20] See, for an enlightening discussion of Hume's 'Newtonianism', Y. Hazony & E. Schliesser, 'Newton and Hume', in P. Russell, ed., *The Oxford Handbook of Hume*, Oxford University Press, New York 2016 (673–707).

[21] In my discussion I follow Hume in concentrating on the idea of an empty space. The explanation of the genesis and illusory character of the idea of a time without change (at 1.2.5.28–9) raises partially different problems, particularly regarding with the idea of identity. I address them in § 9.4.1, in connection with Hume's account of the idea of existence of body.

This also holds of complex impressions, darkness, and motion 'mix'd with something visible or tangible'. In this case, visual or tactile objects *are* present to the mind and there is no absence of perceptions (as to their existence and contents). To address this issue, Hume resorts to an interesting if problematic distinction between two kinds of impressions and ideas of the distance between visible and tangible objects. One coincides with the impression and the idea of the extension interposed between the objects; the other has a radically different kind of source and its content is not an extension. There are circumstances, like those we are now to consider, in which by perceiving a distance we do not perceive an extension. This is a complicated point, but Hume's treatment of the idea of a vacuum crucially depends on the viability of the idea of unextended distance. Here is my reconstruction of how Hume tries to make it good.

(1) Two bodies can visually appear separated by an extension even though there are no individual visible things placed between them (my spread fingers are perfectly separated by the blue colour of the sky if I hold my hand before me) (1.2.5.8, lines 1–6). A corresponding claim holds of the objects of our feeling (1.2.5.9, line 11). The absence is of a concrete particular, a visible body; but of course, there is a visual impression and an object, the stretch of blue sky.

(2) We can now suppose that 'amidst an entire darkness, there are luminous bodies presented to us, whose light discovers only these bodies themselves, without giving us any impression of the surrounding objects' (1.2.5.8). We can also suppose 'something to be perceiv'd by the feeling; and after an interval and motion of the hand...another object of the touch to be met with' (1.2.5.9). Such objects are visually and tangibly present as separated or distant, as numerically distinct by their distance (1.2.5.10, lines 18–21).

It might seem that the two cases are similar and that in the second we perceive an extension without anything visible (a limiting case of the first), a pure extension.

(3) However, entire darkness does not operate like a non-thing-like visual impression (the empty blue sky). The presence of luminous bodies leaves intact the supposition that they appear in utter darkness: 'all the rest continues as before, a perfect negation of light, and of every colour'd or visible object' (1.2.5.11). This is true 'of the very distance, which is interposed betwixt them; that being nothing but darkness'. We have no visual perception of this distance, just as a blind man would not have it (1.2.5.11 lines 33–5). We have no visual impression separating the luminous bodies and thus no visual impression of their separation or distance.

(4) Therefore, that we perceive objects separated or distant without any interposing object, without their distance being 'any thing color'd or visible', does not mean that 'there is here a vacuum or pure extension' (1.2.5.10), even though this is 'our natural and familiar way of thinking' (1.2.5.11). The impressions of these objects and of their manner of disposition in fact do not convey any idea of

extension at all. (This means that impressions of manners of disposition must be somehow qualified to generate such contents and ideas.)

(5) However, as it is intuitive, we do have an impression and an idea of the spatial disposition (pattern, manner of appearance) of these luminous bodies. But we have the impression and the idea of the distance between such bodies only from 'the manner they affect our senses'. 'The angles, which the rays of light flowing from them, form with each other; the motion that is requir'd in the eye, in its passage from one to the other; and the different parts of the organs, which are affected by them' (1.2.5.12).

(6) The crucial point is that this sort of spatial impression (the impression of a distance and of a non-successive manner of disposition) is not the impression of an extension. Any proprioceptive impression that gives us such an idea of the distance, or manner of disposition, is 'simple and indivisible'. But a perception of distance between the two bodies that is 'without parts, without composition, invariable and invisible', 'dark and undistinguishable' cannot give us the idea of extension and a fortiori, of an empty extension, of a vacuum.

Hume grants that, if we had an impression of extension in the specified circumstances, it would be the impression of a vacuum, of an extension without matter. Therefore, it is crucial to see whether he has warrant to talk of 'two kinds of distance' (1.2.5.17); in particular, whether proprioception gives us an impression of a distance that, by not being visible and tangible, is not the impression of an extension.[22] This may well seem difficult. The soundness of Hume's argument, within his own philosophical framework, depends on (3): the presence of luminous bodies does not alter the fact that they appear in utter darkness and does not afford a visual perception of their distance; and on (6): proprioceptive impressions are simple in phenomenology and content and thus do not convey an idea of extension. I think that (5) can be granted to Hume: proprioceptive impressions are plausibly enough related to the perception of spatial properties and different enough from visual and tactile impressions that they make room for spatial qualities and contents different from but related to the visual or tactile ones. Spatial experience can take up a disjunctive character.

---

[22] The proprioceptive character of the way in which the senses are affected by the two visible and tangible point-like bodies comes out clearly in the second condition, 'the motion that is requir'd in the eye, in its passage from one to the other'. Hume later came to reject, perhaps on Berkeley's prompt, the first condition: 'The first [error] may be found in Book 1, page 42–3, where I say, that the distance betwixt two bodies is known, among other things, by the angles, which the rays of light flowing from the bodies make with each other. 'Tis certain, that these angles are not known to the mind, and consequently can never discover the distance', *Appendix*, 22; see Berkeley, *New Theory*, 12 (10). However, if such angles were known to the mind, this would be by some sort of proprioceptive sensation, say, of muscular tension in the eyes. By contrast, I doubt that much sense can be made, in proprioceptive terms, of the third condition, "the different parts of the organs, which are affected by them'. But this is true also of any visual or tactile interpretation.

Interpreting Hume's problematic, somewhat messy discussion of these issues requires disentangling how different sensorial modes contribute to the content of this complex perception of distance. Taking (3) first, the question to be asked is why adding two visible objects to utter darkness, a 'perfect negation of light', would *not* determine a visual impression of extension (1.2.5.11 lines 26–30). We would certainly have the visual experience of two distinct point-like luminous bodies in some spatial relation; why not the impression of an extension (consisting of the two bodies and of what is between them)? This question is difficult, in Hume's framework, because of his relational conception of space or extension: why are the relations we visually perceive between the two luminous bodies insufficient to generate the idea of an extension, of distance as a stretch of extension? One cannot appeal to the fact that utter darkness is no visual perception, because, quite simply, the two luminous bodies have changed the visual field. (We may still have no visual perception of darkness; but we perceive two non-successive luminous points.)

Hume *seems* to concede that we have a visual perception of distance in such a case: "tis evident, that when only two luminous bodies appear to the eye, we can perceive, whether they be conjoin'd or separate; whether they be separated by a great or small distance; and if this distance varies, we can perceive its increase or diminution, with the motion of the bodies' (1.2.5.10). But this is *only* 'our natural and most familiar way of thinking', 'which we shall learn to correct by a little reflection' (1.2.4.11). In fact, it is rightly the illusion that we have the idea of a vacuum. And one of the conclusions of reflection is that in cases like this we do *not* judge of distance by visual or tactile perceptions but by different, proprioceptive ones (1.2.5.12). Thus, Hume's claim is that a visual experience like the one just specified is *not* the visual perception of a distance, even though a distance is perceived. Under this disjunctive perspective, it is spatial but does not issue in an idea of extension (which would be an *empty* extension).

This is a very strong claim. To make sense of it, we should begin with asking how adding more visual phenomenology and content, say, by turning utter darkness into a coloured background, would alter the nature of visual perception so dramatically that we would then come to perceive distance *visually* and thereby to have an impression and idea of extension. (Keep in mind that the change (a) must be in the relations or manners of dispositions of objects and (b) must depend on this phenomenological addition alone.) A speculative but Humean answer could avert to the essential connection between extension and divisibility. What is missing from the visual field or scenario consisting of darkness and point-like luminous bodies are *parts*—the divisibility of what separates the simple bodies. What is gained by turning what separates the simple luminous objects into something 'colour'd and visible', a stretch of colour, is the possibility of distinguishing and dividing it, and the visual field or scenario, into parts.[23] Once introduced, the coloured background—now a visual, *seen* object—turns the invisible and indivisible separation or distance between the point-like objects into something we can distinguish parts into and thus take measures on. This property of a visual impression thus makes of a distance an extension: the *first kind* of impression of distance, divisible, composed, extended, and visible or tangible. Without such a coloured background, we only have visual experience of scattered points, with no extension interposed. It is in this sense that, by contrast, a complex impression with visual elements can be 'without parts, without composition, invariable and indivisible' (1.2.5.11); thereby, not an extension at all. This is not the visual experience of a distance: indivisible distance is no visual distance and no experience of an extension; therefore it is not the impression of a vacuum.[24]

This account of the impression of luminous bodies in the dark identifies the distinct contributions of visual impressions to our overall experience. When we are actually having such experience we in fact perceive 'whether [the luminous bodies] be conjoin'd or separate; whether they be separated by a great or small distance; and if this distance varies, we can perceive its increase or diminution, with the motion of the bodies'. However, this perception of distance is not visual but only proprioceptive.

> The sole difference betwixt an absolute darkness and the appearance of two or more visible luminous objects consists, as I said, in the objects themselves, and in the manner they affect our senses. The angles, which the rays of light flowing from them, form with each other; the motion that is requir'd in the eye, in its passage from one to the other; and the different parts of the organs, which are affected by them; these produce the only perceptions, from which we can judge of the distance. (1.2.5.12)

The combination of visual perception and proprioception delivers the *second kind* of distance: an invisible and intangible one, distinct from the visible and tangible one which arises from visual or tactile perceptions of regions of space. The distinct contribution of proprioception is that it allows us to have a sense of how far apart the luminous points are and of how their distance changes.[25] Hume regards

---

[23] See Baxter, 'Hume's Theory of Space and Time', 142. Broad, 'Hume's Doctrine of Space', 6, suggests the useful term 'stretch'.

[24] This can at least in part answer a critique levelled against Hume's vacuum by Falkenstein, 'Hume on the Idea of a Vacuum', 146. Falkenstein objects that the fact that there is no difference between how the relations and situation of two objects are perceived in utter darkness or against a coloured background leaves no room for a difference as to whether a distance or extension is perceived. My answer is that something entailed by a visual impression of an extension or distance, that its content or object be divisible, is not satisfied.

[25] There are thus three cognitive conditions to distinguish. When we have the visual impression of a spatial object or region of space, defined by its visible and tangible constituents and by their manner

this kind of perception of distance as unveiling something about spatial objects of sense. 'Thus, if it be ask'd, whether the invisible and intangible distance, interpos'd betwixt two objects, be something or nothing: 'Tis easy to answer, that it is something, viz. a property of the objects, which affect the senses after such a particular manner' (1.2.5.26 fn. 12, added in the *Appendix*).[26] However, it is *not* the impression of an *extension*: it is not distance as a stretch of space that we can partition and measure. Hume remarks, about the proprioceptive perceptions that give us this idea of distance: 'But as these perceptions are each of them simple and indivisible, they can never give us the idea of extension' (1.2.5.12). But, in the present case, this is not a defect of the content borne by perceptions. The proprioceptive impression of a distance is not supposed to be divisible, to have parts and a metric. It is not an extension: extension is necessarily complex, proprioceptive impressions, simple. Proprioception is different in kind, in sensorial mode, from vision and touch. The impressions, the affections of our senses that bring to awareness the distance of the objects have intensive, not extensive magnitude; they are not extended and give us no idea of extension. Hume also sketches a positive distinction between the two kinds of distance.

> If it be ask'd, whether two objects, having such a distance betwixt them [an invisible and intangible one], touch or not: It may be answer'd, that this depends upon the definition of the word, touch. If objects be said to touch, when there is nothing sensible interpos'd betwixt them, these objects touch: If objects be said to touch, when their images strike contiguous parts of the eye, and when the hand feels both objects successively, without any interpos'd motion, these objects do not touch. (1.2.5.26 fn. 12, added in the *Appendix*)

The objects separated by the invisible and intangible distance do not touch, in the sense that they are not visually or tactilely continuous. However, the lack of visual

---

of disposition, we have an impression of extension and the distances between its parts are determinable and measurable by visual or tactile means. This is visible and tangible distance. If the impression of distance is proprioceptive, in combination with simple impressions of visible or tangible bodies in utter darkness, we have the impression and can form the idea of a non-extended, invisible, and intangible distance. These are the two kinds of distance. If in the second condition we abstract from the contribution of proprioception keeping firm the content of visual experience, there is no perception of distance of any kind.

[26] This is missed in the otherwise interesting discussion in M. Boehm, 'Filling the Gaps in Hume's Vacuums', *Hume Studies*, 38, 2012 (79–99). Boehm holds (81, 85–6) that the invisible and intangible distance is no distance at all; and that this is the only way in which, in the perceptual condition of two point-like bodies appearing in utter darkness, we fail to have the perception of an extension. I think that this suffers from a confusion between what is true of the contribution of visual perception to our overall experience in that circumstance and what is true of the experience itself, which also includes proprioception. Hume's talk of an 'imaginary distance' and of a 'fictitious distance' refers, respectively, to the lack of any impression of distance in a situation of unimpeded motion (equivalent to the visual experience of utter darkness and point-like luminous bodies) (1.2.5.13) and to the false attribution to vision of the proprioceptive impression of distance (1.2.5.23). Neither tell against our having by proprioception the impression and the idea of an invisible, intangible, indivisible distance.

or tactile impressions is not itself an impression, therefore no sensible object is interposed between the objects. Therefore, in this sense, the objects touch. If we feel a tension between these two claims, we should remark that, in another respect, something sensible is interposed between the objects: we have proprioceptive impressions of a distance associated to the visual and tactile one of the two objects. In this respect, the two objects can be said not to touch and we have a positive idea of their distance.

To sum up. There are two different kinds of impressions and, correspondingly, of ideas of 'two kinds of distance' (1.2.5.17): the visible, tangible one delivered by the visual and tactile perceptions of a coloured and solid extension and the invisible, intangible, dark one delivered by proprioceptive perceptions and by the visual or tactile impressions of coloured and solid points. Both are spatial, but only in a disjunctive sense. Neither gives the idea of a vacuum, of extension without matter: the first, because it is not without matter; the second, because it is not the idea of an extension. Therefore, the idea of a vacuum cannot derive from any of the representational sources we have of spatial content.

Hume's distinction of the two ideas of distance has been heavily criticized.[27] Certainly, even on my somewhat speculative reconstruction, it suffers of serious, perhaps unredeemable, lack of detail. However, I think that Hume is onto something. The distinctive contribution of proprioception to spatial cognition is a recognized fact.[28] Hume seems to be groping after something like the distinction between a topological and a metric notion of distance. *Very* approximately, the first is a notion and a measure only in terms of numbers of objects and their order: in the present case, two distinct objects would be at one remove from one another; of three objects, the first would be at two removes from the third; and so on. The second is the standard understanding of distance as measured in space or extension. This only imperfectly fits with Hume's text. Hume wants the first kind of distance to be susceptible of degree, as greater or small in an intensive sense, also between only two objects. Still, it is a gesture in the direction of what might have been at the back of his mind.

8.2.3.2 We Falsely Imagine We Can Form such an Idea
Hume explains the illusion that we have an idea of a vacuum with a complex interaction of the more limited imagination with ideas of these two kinds of

---

[27] See Falkenstein 'Hume on the Idea of a Vacuum', 143–5. However, by distinguishing the different sensorial modalities and the different perceptions involved in this doctrine, one can disambiguate the ways in which something sensible is or is not interposed between the two objects, so that they touch or not. Furthermore, proprioceptive distance is perceivable only between visually or tangible objects. Therefore, Hume runs no danger of having to say that sounds or smell touch.

[28] See F. De Vignemont, 'Bodily Awareness', in *The Stanford Encyclopedia of Philosophy* (especially Section 4). See, for a discussion in the cognitive science (and literature), A. G. Renault et al., 'Does Proprioception Influence Human Spatial Cognition? A Study on Individuals With Massive Deafferentation', *Frontiers in Psychology*, 2018; 9.1322 10.3389/fpsyg.2018.01322.

distance.[29] Such interaction is mediated by the similarities between the two sorts of disjunctively spatial contents. 'There is a close relation betwixt that motion and darkness, [those which convey the idea of an unextended distance] and a real extension, or composition of visible and tangible objects' (1.2.5.14). Hume individuates three relations that can affect the imagination and explain its merging of the two ideas. One is association by resemblance. The manner in which two visible objects affect proprioception is the same when they appear in utter darkness and when they are separated by space filled with visible objects. The case is the same with the sensation of motion (1.2.5.15). The second and the third relation are directly and, respectively, indirectly causal. Experience teaches that two bodies separated by an invisible and intangible distance, which appear to the senses with the same arrangement as two separated by a certain extension consisting of visible objects, can receive between them the same extension, without impulse or penetration. (The same holds of feeling and sensation of motion.) 'That is, in other words, an invisible and intangible distance may be converted into a visible and tangible one, without any change in the distant objects' (1.2.5.16). This is a physical possibility established by causal reasoning. Lastly, an association by causation can ground a judgement of resemblance. The two kinds of distance appear to have nearly the same effects on every natural phenomenon. 'For as all qualities, such as heat, cold, light, attraction, &c. diminish in proportion to the distance; there is but little difference observ'd, whether this distance be mark'd out by compounded and sensible objects, or be known only by the manner, in which the distant objects affect the senses' (1.2.5.17). Hume explicitly regards the first of these two relations as one of causation and the second as one of resemblance, grounded on causal uniformity: same effects-same causes. ('As the first species of distance is found to be convertible into the second, 'tis in this respect a kind of cause; and the similarity of their manner of affecting the senses, and diminishing every quality, forms the relation of resemblance', 1.2.5.21.)

The second and the third relation are thus structured by principles of the imagination we have not yet met in our discussion. (At least explicitly: spreading might be reconstructed as involving them.) One is *Resemblance*: the inclination of the imagination to confound resembling ideas. 'For we may establish it as a general maxim in this science of human nature, that wherever there is a close relation betwixt two ideas, the mind is very apt to mistake them, and in all its discourses and reasonings to use the one for the other' (1.2.5.19). The other, which reinforces the first, is the inclination to merge the similarity of the actions of the mind with that of its ideas, *Act/Idea Resemblance*. 'We may in general observe, that wherever the actions of the mind in forming any two ideas are the same or resembling, we are very apt to confound these ideas, and take the one for the other' (1.2.5.21).

---

[29] See, on the role of imagination or mediate perception, Boehm, 'Filling the Gaps', 85–6; Falkenstein, 'Hume on the Idea of a Vacuum', 147–50.

(These properties are explanatorily important—'Of this we shall see many instances in the progress of this treatise'—and mark the continuity of Part 4 of the Treatise with Part 2; see § 9.3.4.) The effect of these principles is a transition, based on resemblance and causation, from the idea of the invisible and intangible, 'topological' distance to that of the metric, visible and tangible one. This pattern of the imagination explains 'why the one has so often been taken for the other, and why we imagine we have an idea of extension without the idea of any object either of the sight or feeling' (1.2.5.19).[30] Hume proposes a very qualified physiological explanation of this error, in terms of the motion of spirits along the traces in the brain (1.2.5.20). However, the most relevant level of explanation is mental. Only the mental faculty of the imagination, which is uniquely responsive to principles like Resemblance and Act/Idea Resemblance, can explain how we come by the idea of a vacuum.

Hume makes explicit that what he has explained is a 'mistake'; the illusion that we have the idea of a vacuum. This is because—their relations and association notwithstanding—the two ideas of distance are incompatible in their fundamental contents (as to an essential property, divisibility, of the objects they represent). Therefore, the propensity to move from the one to the other, the transition which connects them in the mind, cannot make them coexist in one state of mind without deeply altering their contents. What happens is that we merge them in one perception, which combines the invisible and intangible distance represented by the one with the extended and divisible extension, which is the content of second. Imagination enacts the idea of an empty space rightly by neglecting the differences between the two ideas. 'And this likewise is the reason, why we substitute the idea of a distance, which is not consider'd either as visible or tangible, in the room of extension, which is nothing but a composition of visible or tangible points dispos'd in a certain order' (1.2.5.21). But the idea thus produced is spurious, is only imaginary. Failing to notice the transition, we end by thinking we have an idea we cannot really have.[31]

---

[30] The discussion of this explanation in Falkenstein, 'Hume on the Idea of a Vacuum', 155–63 is marred by the assumption that the idea of a vacuum that we take ourselves to have is grounded on the association between a visual experience of utter darkness and visible points and a fully coloured one (see 155, 157). This neglects the fact that Hume's explicitly refers to the associative relations between the proprioceptive and the visual experience of distance. On the other hand, Falkenstein is right that Hume does not specify enough how the visual clues we have in utter darkness are connected with proprioceptive experience (156, 159). This is the basic shortcoming of Hume's theory, in my view: the most serious lacuna in how imagination can explain the idea of a vacuum we really have. But perhaps it is remediable, at least in principle. It may be true that the visual content of the experience of utter darkness (the luminous bodies) is too indeterminate to guide the movements of the eye and other conditions of proprioception. (I have likened it to the position and the relations of objects in optical illusions.) But one might suggest that proprioception can feedback and help to determine the overall content of that experience; that the movements of our eyes and the feelings of muscular tension, starting from partial and ambiguous visual clues, can fix the spatial content we have available.

[31] Hume proposes a related but different account of the illusion of having the idea of time without change. This is discussed in § 10.2.1.

8.2.3.3 A Vacuum is Asserted

However, there is more to Hume's account of the idea of a vacuum than an exercise in error theory. Hume's account is embedded in the discussion of three objections to the claim that we have no such idea. The objections are drawn, respectively, from the common knowledge that the idea of a vacuum is disputed; from the metaphysical claim that it is a consequence of the conceivability of the annihilation of a part of matter; and from the metaphysical point, which is of relevance for natural philosophy, that a vacuum seems required for the possibility of motion (1.2.5.2–4). Hume's responses to these objections are important because they show that, aside from unveiling an illusion of content, he wants his theory to make good a role that the idea of a vacuum has in ordinary and philosophical cognition.

Hume's general response is that the objections are based on the confusion between the two kinds of distance he has taken care to disentangle. This defangs the objections. However, at least the second and the third of them raise genuine, conceptual challenges to Hume's theory. We may say that longstanding disputes about the vacuum only prove that we can deceive ourselves about the reality of an idea, 'especially when by means of any close relation, there is another idea presented, which may be the occasion of their mistake' (1.2.5.22). But the second objection requires a different treatment. Hume recognizes the metaphysical possibility that a part of matter be annihilated while the surrounding bodies remain at rest. This might seem to entail the possibility of an empty space. But if this were a possibility, then an empty space would be a priori conceivable; a priori, a part of space could be separated from any matter. But then we would have the idea of an empty space. To avoid a contradiction, one should show that we can conceive of what is left by annihilation: for instance, if such annihilation takes place in a chamber and the walls are at rest, 'the chamber must be conceiv'd much in the same manner as at present, when the air that fills it, is not an object of the senses' (1.2.5.23). However, such conception fails to be the idea of an empty space. In order to suppose and conceive the condition of annihilation-and-rest, we do not need such an idea. Therefore, this conception does not entail the possibility of a vacuum.

Hume's disjunctive conception of space provides for such a conception of the empty chamber. 'This annihilation leaves to the eye, that fictitious distance, which is discover'd by the different parts of the organ, that are affected, and by the degrees of light and shade; and to the feeling, that which consists in a sensation of motion in the hand, or other member of the body' (1.2.5.23). That is: post-annihilation, the space inside the chamber is conceived by an idea of distance or separation (between the walls) that combines proprioceptive and visual or tactile clues. This is not the idea of an extension; therefore it is not the idea of a vacuum, and therefore it is not the basis for a Conceivability/Possibility inference concerning a vacuum. But it is sufficient for the conceivability and thereby for the possibility of the annihilation of matter. This idea is fictitious only because and insofar as it is taken to be one of a visible extension; that is, because and insofar as it is taken for a visual or tangible idea of a vacuum inside the room. But beyond this error, it is an idea, grounded on a distinct complex impression, which can make a cognitive difference, by allowing us to conceive, if not to represent, what would be for everything inside the chamber to be annihilated. This idea, in this role, is an appropriate content of thought. This conception of the annihilation of a part of matter does not even aim to represent or make us conceive of an empty extension and is the ground for the metaphysical possibility of annihilation.

Hume also denies that the possibility of motion entails the possibility of a vacuum and thus the conceivability of an empty extension. Hume is committed to give a revisionary account of the possibility of motion, an issue of great concern for natural philosophy; in particular for Newtonian philosophy.[32] To this end, he extends to motion the account given of the conceivability of annihilation: motion can be conceived as the annihilation and recreation of an object, without alteration of the surrounding bodies (1.2.5.24). This satisfies the Established Maxim, secures the conceivability, and thereby the metaphysical possibility of motion ('This suffices to satisfy the imagination, and proves there is no repugnance in such a notion', 1.2.5.24), without implying the possibility of a vacuum. However, this is not enough to satisfy the demands of natural philosophy. One should explain and vindicate not only the conceivability and the metaphysical possibility that bodies be so situated as to receive body between them, without alteration, but also the corresponding physical possibility. The conditions of possibility of motion, on a revised notion of it, must be at least potentially part of empirical reality. To this effect, Hume resorts to experience and causal reasoning.

> Afterwards experience comes in play to persuade us that two bodies, situated in the manner above-describ'd, have really such a capacity of receiving body betwixt them, and that there is no obstacle to the conversion of the invisible and intangible distance into one that is visible and tangible. However natural that conversion may seem, we cannot be sure it is practicable, before we have had experience of it. (1.2.5.24)

The idea of invisible and intangible distance can be put to work in natural philosophy because experience allows and compels us to regard that kind of distance as a potential for receiving body, for being occupied by some body. This is the modal, causal principle which is presupposed by the physical possibility of motion. More precisely: natural philosophy seems to need the idea of an extension which can receive extended bodies, without penetration or annihilation. We

---

[32] See, for a careful reconstruction, J. E. McGuire, 'Body and Void and Newton's De Mundi Systemate', *Archive for History of Exact Sciences*, 3, 1966 (206–48).

do not have this idea; we have neither the representation nor the conception of an unoccupied extension. But we have the idea of an unextended distance and we draw on the basis of experience the conclusion that such distance has the power to take in an extended body. This belief we have from causal inference; it is owing to imagination; its content individuates not only a metaphysical but a physical possibility. This is, of course, restricted to the inferences we can draw from 'the *appearances* of objects to our senses, without entering into disquisitions concerning their real nature and operations' (1.2.5.26, fn. 12). But this is exactly the restriction that is pertinent for empirical cognition and experimental reasoning. In this way, the association by causation of the two kinds of distance—the key concept is the *causal* one of 'power of receiving body'—and the cognitive possibilities that the imagination opens for conception and reasoning are put to service to Newtonian philosophy, if only in a key of modest scepticism.

> If the Newtonian philosophy be rightly understood, it will be found to mean no more. A vacuum is asserted: That is, bodies are said to be plac'd after such a manner, as to receive bodies betwixt them, without impulsion or penetration. The real nature of this position of bodies is unknown. We are only acquainted with its effects on the senses, and its power of receiving body. Nothing is more suitable to that philosophy than a modest skepticism to a certain degree. (1.2.5.26 fn. 12)[33]

8.3 Summary

Next to a universe cemented by causal necessity, the ideas of persisting and independent bodies and selves, of an external and internal world, are a fundamental structure of our worldview. These ideas are produced by the more limited imagination, but by principles different from the causal ones.

Spatial and temporal ideas are closer to sensible representation than causal ideas. However, Hume's account of how imagination produces them resorts to the idea of identity, which is prominent in the account of body and self and a source

---

[33] 'Si omnes omnium corporum particulae solidae sint ejusdem densitatis, neque sine poris rarefieri possint, vacuum datur', Newton, *Principia*, Book III, Proposition VI Theorem VI, Corollary 4. ('If all the solid particles of all bodies have the same density and cannot be rarefied without pores, there must be a vacuum', I. Newton, *Mathematical Principles of Natural Philosophy*, University of California Press, Oakland 1999, 456.) See, for discussion, Hazony & Schliesser, 'Newton and Hume', 683–6. I agree that Hume aims, also in this domain, to curb Newton's and the Newtonians' epistemological enthusiasm. But, still, his commitment is not in any way to cast doubt on the foundations of Newton's mechanics, but to provide a different, better understanding of them, by redefining the relevant ideas. To make good Newton's assertion of a vacuum without introducing a representation or anyway an idea of it.

of scepticism. This is why I address Hume's treatment of space and time together with that of the external and the internal world.

§ 8.1 studies the representational dimension of the ideas of space and time. In § 8.1.1, I discuss how space and time are sensibly given or, reciprocally, how ideas can represent space and time as impressions or objects. Hume's account is by the First Principle and in terms of visual and tactile impressions and of internal experience. The qualities primitively identifying their contents are extension, for space, and duration, for time. Hume's basic claim is that space and time are present and represented as complex impressions or objects, consisting in simple impressions and manners of disposition. Neither sort of constituents can exist by itself as space or time. Individual, simple objects or impressions are without extension and duration. Manners of disposition cannot exist at all by themselves. Complexity is therefore essential to space and time and their exact representations. By Two Viewpoints and Equivalence, perceptions with spatial and temporal contents exist in the mind with extension and duration.

In § 8.1.2 I show how Hume's Representational Naturalism about space and time is complemented and completed by the thesis of their finite divisibility. Complex impressions and ideas of space and time presuppose simple constituents. Indivisible spatial and temporal simples are representable and thereby conceivable, because spatial and temporal perceptions at the threshold of visibility and tangibility or of introspective awareness are indivisible and without extension or duration. Their spatial and temporal nature consists in the qualities making them susceptible to composition into extensions and durations: colour, solidity, and being introspectable. The finite divisibility of spatial and temporal ideas secures that they are exact representations of their objects and, by a chain of inferences by the Established Maxim, that space and time are themselves only finitely divisible.

§ 8.2 discusses how this robust layer of representational, spatial, and temporal content is still marked by gaps that only the imagination can close. Hume individuates the gaps from our cognitive practices. The topic of § 8.2.1 is that the fundamental ideas of our practice of geometry (equality, rightness, planarity) are not object representing. Spatial representation supports the definitions of geometry; but ideas of equality conforming to such definitions (in terms of number of indivisible points) overstep our capacities of discrimination and have no application. This cognitive gap has a sceptical realist character: we lack cognitive capacities for representing objects that are in principle individuable. Only inexact ideas of equality find application in geometrical practice. The imagination produces such ideas because of our activity of measuring sizes of objects and checking and correcting our measures. The habituation effects of this idea-comparing practice drive the more limited imagination to conceive an idea of equality of size beyond what we can observe. Further iterations by the imagination of this process explain how we come to have the illusory idea of a perfect standard of equality, which is the source of ungrounded objections against finite divisibility. In this account, Hume introduces principles of the more limited imagination, like Reconciliation and Hysteresis, which differ from causation.

Finally, § 8.2.2 deals with the cognitive gap of the ideas of an empty space and time. Hume argues that vacuum is simply the absence of any content and quality, not any visual or tactile impression. We cannot have any representation of it. The same is true if simple visible and tangible objects are added. However, the imagination can produce a non-representational idea of a spatial vacuum. Hume distinguishes between two representations of distance: by vision and by proprioception. The first gives us an idea of distance as extension; but there is no such impression in the case in discussion. The second gives us an idea of distance, also when only visible or tangible simples are present. But it is not the idea of an extension. Hume's distinction of the two kinds of distance is problematic, but it explains the production of the idea of vacuum by the imagination. Because of the resemblances between their ideas (in a disjunctive sense, both are spatial), the imagination is disposed to mistake the non-extended distance we can represent for an extended. This puts in place the idea of an extension without objects or of a vacuum. While Hume seems bent on unveiling the illusory character of this idea, he is also aware of its endorsement by Locke and Newton. He thus seems ultimately to propose a complex revisionary account of the idea of a vacuum, up to the tasks it has in natural philosophy.

9
The World as Something Real and Durable

> Here then I am naturally led to regard the world, as something real and durable, and as preserving its existence, even when it is no longer present to my perception.
>
> (1.4.2.20)

In Hume's *Treatises*, 1.4.2: *Of scepticism with regard to the senses* is the longest and conceptually and interpretively the most difficult section of Book 1. Its main topic is how we come by the idea of a real and durable world and the distinction between an external and an internal world. It forms a close-knit unity with 1.4.3: *Of the antient philosophy*, which is dedicated to the idea of material substance and to the unity of bodies, and with the challenging 1.4.4: *Of the modern philosophy*, which is dedicated to the distinction of primary and secondary qualities and to the conception of matter. The reasons why this section is so complicated are principally two. One is the complexity of the background of cognitive gaps and of operations of the imagination against which Hume casts his explanation of this kind of ideas. The second source of complication is that the idea of external existence is present in ordinary and philosophical cognition with different contents and in different forms: a vulgar, a false philosophical, and a true philosophical one. Furthermore, more deeply, differently than with the idea of cause (or the ideas of space and time), the idea of external existence is not associated to an easily recognizable conceptual role in ordinary and philosophical cognition. It is rather an 'implicit faith', something we take 'for granted in all our reasonings'. Therefore, on all the three relevant sides—the cognitive background, the conceptual roles, the principles of the imagination—the task of achieving the right, inferentialist theoretical equilibrium is, in this case, more complex and more difficult. The sceptical concerns that Hume makes explicit already in the title of the section mirror this difficulty and complexity.

9.1 The Missing Idea of Body

9.1.1 The Principle Concerning the Existence of Body

Hume variously characterizes the subject matter of 1.4.2: 'existence of body' (1.4.2.1), 'external existence' (1.4.2.2), 'real and corporal existence' (1.4.2.9), 'distinct continu'd existence' (1.4.2.15), 'external objects' (1.4.2.19), 'the world as something real and durable' (1.4.2.20), 'existence of all external bodies' (1.4.2.23), 'real existence, of which we are insensible' (1.4.2.24), 'real body or material existence' (1.4.2.38), and 'contin'd existence of matter' (1.4.2.43). The idea of body or external existence that Hume aims to explain is thus extremely diverse and robust. It is the idea of a material, external world, in contrast with the internal world of our perceptions. This is certainly a major cognitive structure of our worldview (1.4.7.3), which Hume regards as a non-negotiable feature of it.

> Nature has not left this to his choice, and has doubtless esteem'd it an affair of too great importance to be trusted to our uncertain reasonings and speculations. We may well ask, *What causes induce us to believe in the existence of body?* but 'tis in vain to ask, *Whether there be body or not?* That is a point, which we must take for granted in all our reasonings.   (1.4.2.1)

The only legitimate questions we can raise in connection with the 'principle concerning the existence of body' are about the 'principles of human nature' which account for it (1.4.2.2). These are content-explanatory questions, rather than epistemological or (in a traditional sense) metaphysical. The explanation of the idea of external existence is under two theoretical constraints, which spring from Hume's general philosophy:

(a) The idea must be *qualitatively specifiable*; it must allow us to conceive of and to individuate external existents in qualitative, sensorial ways. We have no other idea of existence but that of individual sensible particulars or impressions of sensation; this a posteriori constraint is inherited by the idea of external existence, body or matter.

(b) Correspondingly, objects we ascribe external existence to or conceive as bodies cannot differ, as to their individuating features from the corresponding perceptions (impressions of sensation and object-representing ideas).

> Now since nothing is ever present to the mind but perceptions, and since all ideas are deriv'd from something antecedently present to the mind; it follows, that 'tis impossible for us so much as to conceive or form an idea of any thing specifically different from ideas and impressions.   (1.2.6.8)[1]

---

[1] See Garrett, 'Naturalistic Theory', 305, for a discussion of Hume's claim that external objects are perfectly conceivable but not as specifically different from perceptions. See also A. Butler, 'Hume on Believing the Vulgar Fiction of Continued Existence', *History of Philosophy Quarterly*, 27, 2010 (237–54), 244–5.

We can think of external existence in cognitively significant ways only in terms of qualities that are the same in kind with those that individuate our perceptions, together with the recognition of different relational properties.

> The farthest we can go towards a conception of external objects, when suppos'd *specifically* different from our perceptions, is to form a relative idea of them, without pretending to comprehend the related objects. Generally speaking we do not suppose them specifically different; but only attribute to them different relations, connections and durations. But of this more fully hereafter. (1.2.6.9)

The reference forward—given in a footnote—is to 1.4.2, where Hume remarks: 'For as to the notion of external existence, when taken for something specifically different from our perceptions, we have already shown its absurdity' (1.4.2.2; 'For we may well suppose in general, but 'tis impossible for us distinctively to conceive, objects to be in their nature any thing but exactly the same with perceptions', 1.4.2.56). This is crucial for any interpretation of 1.4.2. Hume seems to regard that way of conceiving of 'an object, or external existence' (1.4.5.19) as a non-starter. He labels that 'notion' as an 'absurdity' (1.4.2.2). On closer inspection, this must be importantly qualified. We can form an idea of specifically different external existence. But this is only if we leave it empty, 'without pretending to comprehend the related objects' (1.2.6.9). To understand this important restriction on the cognitive import of the relative idea of external existence, we should look at what Hume says about it elsewhere: to have this idea is 'to conceive an external object merely as a relation without a relative' (1.4.5.19). This is not impossible: we can certainly entertain, by a distinction of reason, the idea, say, of relations like _is larger than_ or _ is smaller than_, without filling the blank spaces with the ideas of objects, one of which it is larger or smaller than another. But, as we have seen, distinctions of reasons fail to establish absolute possibilities; they are rather what corresponds, in Hume's philosophy, to our epistemic possibilities: possible conceptions with no implications for possible existence and for belief (§ 5.2.2).[2]

But we are not restricted to relative ideas of external existents. Specific difference or sameness, difference or sameness of nature, is difference or sameness of

---

[2] Why then do we have such ideas? I think that Hume is merely recording the fact that we have them and explaining and limiting their content. See Kail, *Reality and Projection*, 59–61: in a broad sense, the interpretation of our conception of external objects as same in nature and existence/different in locations, durations, and connexions is right. But I think that this is not what relative ideas *are*; but what they are *not*. Relative ideas are the conceptions we form when we assume that external objects are specifically different: these conceptions afford no real understanding; only relations without a relative. If we do *not* frame such relative ideas and do not suppose external objects to be specifically different, then we conceive external objects as same in nature with perceptions. See K. Winkler, 'Hume on Scepticism and the Senses', in D. Ainslie & A. Butler, eds., *The Cambridge Companion to Hume's* Treatise, Cambridge University Press, Cambridge 2015, 135–64, 136–9; Ainslie, *True Scepticism*, 104–5.

individuating qualities. In the case of external objects and internal perceptions, the specific sameness or sameness of nature is the sameness of their qualitative specifications, of their phenomenal, sensorial characters. This follows from Equivalence, holds of objects in general, and thus of external objects. What allows us to think of external existence in a cognitively significant way and not only by relative ideas is the extrinsic character of what marks the internal–external difference: locations, durations, and connections. This is the fundamental ontological insight of Hume's theory of external existence. It comes clearly into sight in Hume's articulation of the idea of external existence along the two dimensions of continued and distinct existence. Continued existence is a matter of different durations: the existence of perceptions is interrupted; individual perceptions come and cease to be with our awareness of them. The concept itself of body is of something that exists both when it is perceived and when it is not. Continued existence, a property of duration, captures the primitive, immediate point of the idea of body. 'The opinion of the *continu'd* existence of body' is 'prior to that of its *distinct* existence, and produces this latter principle' (1.4.2.23).[3] The idea of distinct existence includes an insight concerning their locations and connections. 'Under this last head [distinct existence] I comprehend their situation as well as relations, their *external* position as well as the *independence* of their existence and operations' (1.4.2.2). Hume regards the two aspects of external existence as 'intimately connected' and such that 'the decision of the one question decides the other' (1.4.2.2).[4] Together, they define the 'only questions, that are intelligible on the present subject', '*viz.* why we attribute a CONTINU'D existence to objects, even when they are not present to the senses; and why we suppose them to have an existence DISTINCT from the mind and perception?' (1.4.2.2).

This is, in the barest outlines, the content of Hume's 'principle concerning the existence of body' and the explanatory task of 1.4.2. Most of what Hume wants to say about the content of the idea (and the underlying ontology) of external existence descends from this fundamental assumption about how to conceive of it and of its difference from the internal.

---

[3] 'I have already observ'd, that there is an intimate connexion betwixt those two principles, of a *continu'd* and of a *distinct* or *independent* existence, and that we no sooner establish the one than the other follows, as a necessary consequence. 'Tis the opinion of a continu'd existence, which first takes place, and without much study or reflection draws the other along with it, wherever the mind follows its first and most natural tendency' (1.4.2.44).

[4] Hume seems in this way to suggest that the two specifications of the existence of body are logically equivalent. Taken in abstract, they are not (an entity might have external, independent, and interrupted existence). But if we restrict these specifications to the connections between mind and objects, Hume's point goes through. 'For if the objects of our senses continue to exist, even when they are not perceiv'd, their existence is of course independent of and distinct from the perception; and *vice versa*, if their existence be independent of the perception and distinct from it, they must continue to exist, even tho' they be not perceiv'd' (1.4.2.2).

9.1.2 The Cognitive Gap of External Existences

Hume argues that the idea of body is missing from sensible representation and a priori knowledge; and that probable reasoning is not sufficient to produce it. Just like with the idea of cause, the individuation of the gap and of the corresponding works of the imagination is progressive: it is complete only once the coherence and the constancy of perceptions have been discovered as the closest antecedents of the idea of body. Hume identifies this cognitive gap by enquiring 'whether it be the *senses, reason*, or the *imagination*, that produces the opinion of a *continu'd* or of a *distinct* existence' (1.4.2.2).

9.1.2.1 The Senses

The senses are the ultimate source of the qualitative features that individuate particular existents and of the manners of conception that tell apart real from merely possible existence. But they cannot account for the difference between the idea of existence and that of external existence, understood as continued and distinct existence or as body. This is Hume's final statement of his position.

> Thus to resume what I have said concerning the senses; they give us no notion of continu'd existence, because they cannot operate beyond the extent, in which they really operate. They as little produce the opinion of a distinct existence, because they neither can offer it to the mind as represented, nor as original.
> (1.4.2.11)

Two points require attention. One is the modal character of the notion of external existence, which is explicit when he adds, about the senses: 'because they cannot operate beyond the extent, in which they really operate'. The senses cannot produce the idea of external existence because it includes the thought that objects could exist in conditions different from those in which they actually exist and are observed, while sensible cognition is locked on actuality. This feature is a common one in Hume's arguments for cognitive gaps in sense and memory: ideas with modal aspects cannot be explained by object representation. The second is the distinction between the senses (supposedly) giving the idea of external existence 'as represented' and 'as original'. By Two Viewpoints, impressions of sensation can be considered either as 'images and representations' or as 'distinct and external existences' (1.4.2.3). Hume denies *both* that they can deliver the idea of distinct existence as an object, as a content they represent, *and* that they exemplify it with the properties of their own existence.

First. As to their contents, impressions of sensations are not images of something distinct, or independent, or external, because they are not images or representations of *anything at all*: 'they convey to us nothing but a single perception, and never give us the least intimation of any thing beyond' (1.4.2.4). Impressions of sensation are neither ideas nor impressions of reflection (insofar as these latter include a cognitive dimension). If impressions of sensation can be regarded as representing something (rather than being sensibly present objects), it is only by a causal inference and an empirical enquiry; not simply by their appearance and our grasp of them. 'When the mind looks farther than what immediately appears to it, its conclusions can never be put to the account of the senses; and it certainly looks farther, when from a single perception it infers a double existence, and supposes the relations of resemblance and causation betwixt them' (1.4.2.4). To look farther, to infer a double existence, is to think that objects could be different from their impressions. This is a thought we cannot have got by the senses, which have neither inferential nor modal import.

Second. Hume also denies that impressions of sensation are present in the mind as having distinct existence (that is, with external position and independence of operations). That our awareness of them can present their distinct existence 'as original'. 'If our senses, therefore, suggest any idea of distinct existences, they must convey the impressions as those very existences, by a kind of fallacy and illusion' (1.4.2.5). Hume sketches three arguments in support of this claim, all based on his fundamental assumption that external existence is conceivable not in terms of the 'nature' but of the 'relations and situation' of existents. 'Now if the senses presented our impressions as external to, and independent of ourselves, both the objects and ourselves must be obvious to our senses, otherwise they cou'd not be compar'd by these faculties. The difficulty, then, is how far we are *ourselves* the object of our senses' (1.4.2.5). The first and the second argument are relatively a priori and invest the possibility that impressions be present to the senses as external to ourselves:

(1) The idea of self or person either belongs to the 'most profound metaphysics' or (as it is present 'in common life') is 'never very fix'd or determinate'. In either regard, it is 'absurd' to think that 'the senses can ever distinguish betwixt ourselves and external objects' (1.4.2.6).

(2) All impressions, external and internal, considered as mental episodes ('as impressions or perceptions') appear 'in their true colours' (1.4.2.7). All actions and sensations of the mind, being known to us 'by consciousness', 'must necessarily appear in any particular what they are, and be what they appear'. This, of course, only refers to mental existence ('every thing that enters the mind, being in *reality* a perception') and to how mental existence appears to awareness (''tis impossible any thing shou'd to *feeling* appear different'). 'Feeling' here stands for creature consciousness, which as we by now know is a badly undertheorized aspect of Hume's philosophy. This would also apply to their 'situation and relations': but perceptions, present *as such* to awareness, cannot appear as external; they rather

appear as or are phenomenally internal (even though Hume has no real account of this internal phenomenology).
(3) Besides enquiring 'whether 'tis possible for the senses to deceive us', Hume also asks 'whether they really do so' (1.4.2.8). Hume has in mind an inference like the following: our own body belongs to us; our body appears in our visual experience; some visual impressions appear external to our body; therefore they appear external to ourselves. To 'prevent this inference' Hume remarks that it is not easier to explain why impressions are ascribed 'a real and corporeal existence' when they present our body than in any other case. Sounds, tastes, and smell are regarded as continued and independent qualities without appearing to the senses as situated externally to the body; distance or 'outness' is not manifest to the senses immediately but only by 'a certain reasoning and experience' (1.4.2.9).[5]

9.1.2.2 Reason

We can take for granted that intuitive or demonstrative reason cannot produce the idea of body, because it cannot produce *any* new idea at all. But Hume must also enquire whether the idea of external existence or body can issue from probable or causal reasoning. Hume's claim is that it cannot. He supports his claim with two arguments:

(1) So basic a belief as that of 'objects independent of the mind' cannot be grounded on rational arguments 'known to very few' (mostly philosophers) (1.4.2.14). Furthermore, there is a radical contrast between the opinions of the vulgar and those of the philosophers in this domain. 'For philosophy informs us, that every thing, which appears to the mind, is nothing but a perception, and is interrupted, and dependent on the mind; whereas the vulgar confound perceptions and objects, and attribute a distinct continu'd existence to the very things they feel or see' (1.4.2.14). This latter opinion is 'entirely unreasonable' and empirically false and it cannot proceed from the understanding.
(2) Specifically about causal inferences, both of the idea-comparing and of the more limited imagination.

To which we may add, that as long as we take our perceptions and objects to be the same, we can never infer the existence of the one from that of the other, nor

---

[5] Notice that this does not affect the fact that impressions of sensation present existents or real particulars; but only that they present the idea of a body. It is not the representation of existence or reality—via fixed order and force and vivacity—that comes here in question, but the idea of continued and distinct existence.

> form any argument from the relation of cause and effect; which is the only one that can assure us of matter of fact. Even after we distinguish our perceptions from our objects, 'twill appear presently, that we are still incapable of reasoning from the existence of one to that of the other: So that upon the whole our reason neither does, nor is it possible it ever shou'd, upon any supposition, give us an assurance of the continu'd and distinct existence of body. (1.4.2.14)

It is directly a priori that there is no idea-comparing inference from the existence of our perceptions to the external existence of objects, assuming they are the same: only causal inference can conclude to existence or actuality and causal inference can connected only ideas of different, distinct existents. As a relatively a priori matter and with reference to the transitions of the more limited imagination, no such inference is possible, no matter whether its objects are different. Causal inference can only be based on past experience and the constant conjunction of two beings which 'are always present at once to the mind'.

> But as no beings are ever present to the mind but perceptions; it follows that we may observe a conjunction or a relation of cause and effect between different perceptions, but can never observe it between perceptions and objects. 'Tis impossible, therefore, that from the existence or any of the qualities of the former, we can ever form any conclusion concerning the existence of the latter, or ever satisfy our reason in this particular. (1.4.2.47)

On either account therefore, causal reasoning fails to explain our idea of existence of body. This conclusion, together with the one about the senses, points to a cognitive gap corresponding to the idea of external existence.

9.1.3 Refining the Individuation of the Gap

This, however, still falls short of a complete individuation of the gap.

For one thing, Hume's Inferentialist Naturalism postulates that some cognitive role be determined for the missing ideas. This is essential to identify, under revision, their authentic contents as well as the principles and operations of the imagination appropriate to close the gaps. General ideas, distinctions of reasons, the foundations of mathematics, the idea of extension without matter and duration without change, and the idea of cause exemplify this pattern. By contrast, Hume is less than clear about what exactly is the 'great importance' of the 'principle concerning the existence of body'. He only talks, in connection with belief in body, of an 'implicit faith' and of an 'implicit confidence' as our natural cognitive condition, which philosophical reflection and scepticism can only occasionally disturb (1.4.2.56). And he says that it is 'a point, that we must take for granted in all our reasonings' (1.4.2.1). I will suggest (see § 9.2.1) that one conceptual role for the idea of external existence is the support it gives to causal reasoning dealing with external objects; and therefore, to our engagement in and commitment to causal reasoning in general. But this conceptual role is defined in a context that falls short of addressing the whole scope of our thought of a real and durable world.

Aside from its modal characterization, up to now Hume has not identified in a detailed way the antecedents of the idea of body in background contents and cognitions (as he does, in the case of space and time, with the manners of disposition of sensible minima and, in the causal case, with observed constant conjunctions). Or, equivalently, in what precise respects the content of that idea is out of the grasp of our representation and reasoning. This he does right at the start of his enquiry into the operations of the more limited imagination that produce the idea of external existence.

> Since all impressions are internal and perishing existences, and appear as such, the notion of their distinct and continu'd existence must arise from the concurrence of some of their qualities with the qualities of the imagination; and since this notion does not extend to all of them, it must arise from certain qualities peculiar to some impressions. (1.4.2.15)

The peculiar qualities that allow contrasting 'the impressions, to which we attribute a distinct and continu'd existence, with those, which we regard as internal and perishing' (1.4.2.15), identify with more precision the cognitive gap of external existence. Quite simply, if the idea of external existence requires the concurrence of the imagination with such qualities, differently from other properties of perceptions, then they indicate the closest our perceptions may come to the idea of external existence and, thereby, narrow to a minimum the identification of the missing elements. Hume individuates such qualities in properties of the content and of the existence of perceptions that manifest, at the same time, interruptions and some sort of continuity: constancy and coherence.

Constancy consists in the resemblance and fixed order with which objects appear to the senses, across the interruption of their perceptions. Impressions are and appear interrupted and perishing; but their contents are constant, strictly resembling.

> Those mountains, and houses, and trees, which lie at present under my eye, have always appear'd to me in the same order; and when I lose sight of them by shutting my eyes or turning my head, I soon after find them return upon me without the least alteration. My bed and table, my books and papers, present themselves in the same uniform manner, and change not upon account of any interruption in my seeing or perceiving them. (1.4.2.18)

Constancy is a property of representational content that, by Two Viewpoints, is also a property with which impressions and ideas exist in the mind and operate on the imagination. Coherence is also a property of content, which complements constancy; but it is more complex and non-representational. 'This constancy, however, is not so perfect as not to admit of very considerable exceptions. Bodies often change their position and qualities, and after a little absence or interruption may become hardly knowable' (1.4.2.19). Even in this case, however, we ascribe continued and distinct existence to the impressions, that is, to the objects they present, because of the coherence of their changes.

> But here 'tis observable, that even in these changes they [bodies] preserve a *coherence*, and have a regular dependence on each other; which is the foundation of a kind of reasoning from causation, and produces the opinion of their continu'd existence. (1.4.2.20)

Thus, coherence is an inferential and modal property of the content and existence of perceptions, which has its source in the imagination. At the same time and no less than constancy, it is 'one of the characteristics of external objects', of the content of the idea of body (1.4.2.20).

The combination of these properties of the content and existence of perceptions with their interrupted appearance drives the more limited imagination in producing the idea of external world, as a matter of relations, connections, and durations of ideas. The cognitive gap of external existence is therefore individuated in two ways, corresponding to two mutually exclusive properties of perceptions: coherence and constancy. In Hume's account of causation, only one property of perceptions, their constant conjunction, interacts with the more limited imagination in producing causal contents and, in this way, locates the corresponding cognitive gap at the step from constant conjunction to causal thinking. The account of body or external existence, by contrast, has two such properties, coherence and constancy, which differ by being representational and, respectively, non-representational and provide two ways of individuating the corresponding cognitive gap. This makes (together with Hume's reticence about the role of the idea of external existence) for the complications of the latter account. Still, I think that it is possible to give a unitary and interesting reading of Hume's position, along inferentialist and imagination-oriented lines.

9.2 Imagining a Real and Durable World: Coherence and Spreading

The exclusion of the senses and of reason leaves only one possible explanation for the idea and belief of external existence. 'That opinion must be entirely owing to the IMAGINATION: which must now be the subject of our enquiry' (1.4.2.14). The role of imagination and the specific content of the idea will be different depending on whether the imagination concurs with the coherence or the constancy of interrupted perceptions.

9.2.1 'Spreading out in my mind the whole sea and continent'

The importance of the coherence account lies in the link it forges between causal inference and the idea of external existence. Its core is that, in most cases, causal inferences compellingly incline the imagination to ascribe continued existence to its objects, the causes and effects. Without this, a cognitive gap would open in such inferences. Still, this ascription is a distinct operation of the more limited imagination, the principles of which are not reducible to the causal ones.

To explain how coherence contributes to the opinion of external existence, Hume proceeds from a fact about ordinary causal cognition: 'coherence and regularity' in appearance is 'of somewhat a different nature' in 'those internal impressions, which we regard as fleeting and perishing' and in 'bodies' (1.4.2.20). In either case, coherent and regular appearances are the ground for causal inference and belief. 'Passions', no less than bodies, are 'found by experience to have a mutual connexion with and dependence on each other'. But in their case, 'in order to preserve the same dependence and connexion, of which we have had experience', that is, to engage in causal inference, it is not necessary 'to suppose, that they have existed and operated, when they were not perceiv'd'. Contrast with this the case where we reason about what we take as external objects. 'The case is not the same with relation to external objects. Those require a continu'd existence, or otherwise lose, in a great measure, the regularity of their operation' (1.4.2.20). With the regularity of operation of external objects, the content and the possibility of causal reasoning are in great measure would be lost.[6] This is a difference within our practice of causal reasoning, in the light of different suppositions concerning the objects of reasoning, that is, whether they are external objects, bodies, or internal impressions, like passions (and, I would say, perceptions considered as such). The cognitive gap that opens between the coherence of perceptions and causal reasoning, if such perceptions are considered as external but not as continuedly existent or as bodies, puts the mind under a pressure to frame such an idea. By contrast, if the objects of causal reasoning are conceived as internal, we are under no pressure to assume that they have continued existence in order to draw causal conclusions (we may still be propense to suppose that some continuant is present: but it is the underlying self, not the individual perceptions, see § 10.2.3).

---

[6] See Loeb, *Stability and Justification*, 184–6, fn. 10 and 11.

Once again, some utterly primitive awareness of an internal/external distinction is tacitly presupposed, like in the account of causal necessity (internal impressions spread on external objects).

The coherence account thus only makes sense in a context of causal ideas and causal reasoning. It is only within an ongoing practice of causal cognition that we come to ascribe continued existence to objects, in the way just sketched.[7] However, the operations of the imagination that put in place the idea of continued existence are different from those that put in place causal ideas. Their distinction and combination comes out clearly in Hume's beautiful example of the porter and the letter (1.4.2.20). The example is one of integration of the first with the second system of realities. 'I am here seated in my chamber with my face to the fire; and all the objects, that strike my senses, are contain'd in a few yards around me.' My cognitive ken is restricted to the 'information' from 'my senses and memory'; it is limited to present and past objects, not giving 'any testimony to the continuance of their being'. It is restricted to elements of the first system. The noise of a door opening and the sight of a porter advancing into the chamber alter the cognitive situation. (The porter is bringing a letter from a distant friend.). 'This gives occasions to many new reflections and reasonings': reflections and reasonings connecting coherently my present perceptual condition with elements of the second system: unobserved entities and relations. The unseen motion of the door and the noise I heard; the quality of gravity, the presence of the porter in the chamber, and my not having observed him mounting the stairs; my holding the letter from a friend 'two hundred leagues distant', and the unobserved ways and means of its delivery ('posts and ferries, according to my memory and observation'). Under the natural supposition that all these are objects and not perceptions, these data seem to go against the observed regularities, the coherence of perceptions and experience, which ground our causal cognition.

> To consider these phaenomena of the porter and letter in a certain light, they are contradictions to common experience, and may be regarded as objections to those maxims, which we form concerning the connexions of causes and effects. I am accustom'd to hear such a sound, and see such an object in motion at the same time. I have not receiv'd in this particular instance both these perceptions.
> (1.4.2.20)

Therefore, in a case like the present one, the effects of custom on the imagination and our confidence in such causal relations should be diminished. (I have commented on this when discussing the cognitive role of causal necessity, § 7.3.2.)

---

[7] The causal background of the coherence account is rightly emphasized in Price, *Hume's Theory of the External World*, 50–3. See, for discussion, Rocknak, *Imagined Causes*, 115–22.

Since such a case is perfectly ordinary ('there is scarce a moment of my life, wherein there is not a similar instance presented to me'), our general confidence in causal reasoning should be seriously dinted. But also in cases like this we immediately and unhesitatingly draw the relevant causal inferences, without noticing any contradiction. The conclusion Hume draws from this is that the customary transitions underlying causal reasoning must operate jointly with some other principle of the imagination and with new content it produces: the continued existence of objects. 'The present phenomenon is a contradiction to all past experience, unless the door, which I remember on the other side of the chamber, be still in being.' Unless I assume that 'the stairs I remember be not annihilated by my absence', the presence of the porter in my room violates the law of gravity. And 'without spreading out in my mind the whole sea and continent' and supposing its 'continued existence', I cannot account for a letter of a distant friend being in my hands. In all these cases, I must 'suppose the continu'd existence of objects, in order to connect their past and present appearances, and give them such an union with each other, as I have found by experience to be suitable to their particular natures and circumstances'. That is, I cannot engage in perfectly ordinary causal inferences, in which I apply the idea of causal powers, without assuming that objects exist unperceived. 'And this supposition, which was at first entirely arbitrary and hypothetical, acquires a force and evidence by its being the only one, upon which I can reconcile these contradictions' (1.4.2.20). The idea of continued existence (an essential and primary dimension of the idea of a real and durable world) makes it possible, in circumstances like the present ones (causal reasoning on the assumption that it deals with external objects), to avoid 'contradictions' to 'common experience' and to engage in causal reasoning.[8]

This marks the cognitive gap that the coherence account of the idea of body is meant to close. It is a gap that can only be individuated in relation to causal cognition; but the missing and needful idea is that of the continued existence of causally connected objects. In this case, rightly because of the strict connection with causal cognition, the idea of external existence has a significant cognitive role: supporting the force and the justness of causal inferences. By what mental mechanism do we move, then, from the thought of causally connected objects to that of their continued and distinct existence?

---

[8] This layer in Hume's theory of causality complicates in some measure its relation to Kant's. In the *Second Analogy*, Kant objects to (something like) Hume's account of causation that it helps itself with the idea of objective succession of events, which could only be derived from the concept of cause. However, as we have just seen, Hume holds, not a priori but as a matter of empirical fact, that the idea of cause can be applied with complete generality only if one assumes that we are confronted with an objective world of continuants. The two ideas—causality and objective existence—are instantiated together in the natural mind.

9.2.2 The Hysteresis of the Imagination

Hume explicitly denies that the idea of cause and the idea of continued existence are grounded on the same inferential principles of the more limited imagination. 'But tho' this conclusion from the coherence of appearances may seem to be of the same nature with our reasonings concerning causes and effects; as being deriv'd from custom, and regulated by past experience; we shall find upon examination, that they are at the bottom considerably different from each other' (1.4.2.21). Hume's characterization of this difference is that, in the case of external existence, the 'inference' depends on custom 'in an indirect and oblique manner'. This is because custom can only derive from the regular succession of perceptions ('nothing is ever present to the mind, besides its own perceptions') so that it is 'impossible, that any habit shou'd ever be acquired otherwise than by the regular succession of these perceptions' and that it 'should ever exceed that degree of regularity'. Therefore, custom 'can never be a foundation for us to infer a greater degree of regularity in some objects, which are not perceiv'd; since this supposes a contradiction, *viz.* a habit aquir'd by what was never present to the mind'. But the inference to continued existence from the coherence of objects is precisely 'in order to bestow on the objects a greater regularity than what is observ'd in our mere perceptions'. We come to 'suppose' that the objects continue to exist, in their connexion, even when unperceived. But our 'extending' in this way custom and reasoning cannot be the 'direct and natural effect' of constant repetition. The 'co-operation of some other principles' is thus required.

This may seem puzzling. What Hume says about indirect and oblique grounding in custom and experience seems insufficient to mark a deep difference between causal inference and inference to continued existence. As we know, mature causal reasoning typically has only indirect and oblique grounds in custom. The consideration that in inferring continued existence we extend the regularities observed in experience also seems to cut little ice. Causal inferences are by construction ampliative of observed regularities. One-object situations are paradigmatic of causal reasoning. And one-experiment conclusions are perfectly ordinary. Lastly, causal reasoning is not restricted to completely constant conjunctions, as Hume's discussion of the probability of causes amply testifies. These difficulties can be answered. The case of probabilities versus proofs is completely different from that of inference to continued existence. In this latter case, we do not have contrasting experiments that condition resulting inferential habits; we consider circumstances in which a coherent experience and an established inferential would seem to be contradicted.[9] Projecting in the future regularities observed in the past is obviously different from projecting a greater degree of

---

[9] Loeb, *Stability and Justification*, 182-4, rightly warns against assimilating inference to continued existence to the probability of causes.

regularity than has been observed.[10] And that inferences to continued existence arise from custom in an indirect and oblique way does not entail that they arise in the same way as one-experiment causal conclusions.

I think that something more substantive could be said for Hume's position. We should look more closely at the 'greater degree of regularity' which is our aim 'whenever we infer the continu'd existence of the objects of sense from their coherence, and the frequency of their union' (1.4.2.21). To begin, we may ask what form the required 'greater degree of regularity' takes. The answer is the form of 'objects of sense', in contrast with 'our mere perceptions'. The inference responds to missing or interrupted perceptions ('the turning around of our head, or the shutting of our eyes') and concludes to objects of sense that, by existing unperceived, are more regular than perceptions and make it possible to reason causally in the domain of the external. This greater regularity is achieved by a dual cognitive *change*: the burden of regularity is shifted from perceptions to objects and objects are taken to exist unperceived or continuedly. That is, such greater degree of regularity, as it is required for causal inferences, involves a change in the way we conceive of the causally related items: from their being equivalently describable as perceptions or objects to their necessary description as external existents, bodies. This change of conception constitutes the element of indirectness or obliqueness hinted to by Hume: customary transitions are mediated by a different idea of the involved items. Nothing of the sort is required by the customary transitions supporting causal content. Correspondingly, such transitions, our inferences to the unobserved, have for conclusion that something, qualitatively identified, exists. That it exists as described, what does not make a difference as to whether to regard it as perception or object; and that it necessarily exists as described. No further qualification of its existence is necessary, legitimate, and available on this ground. By contrast, continued existence is not existence simpliciter; it is a modification of the idea of something existing. It must be established by a separate inference, by a separate transition of the imagination. Hume is thus right that the two inferences are 'considerably different' and that the idea of continued existence 'must arise from the co-operation of some other principles' (1.4.2.21).[11]

The further, indirectly customary principle of the more limited imagination that Hume introduces to explain this conception of causal relata as bodies is the following. 'I have already observ'd, in examining the foundation of mathematics, that the imagination, when set into any train of thinking, is apt to continue, even when its object fails it, and like a galley put in motion by the oars, carries on its

---

[10] See Winkler, 'Scepticism about the Senses', 152–3.
[11] Loeb, *Stability and Justification*, 186, restricts his attention to the gappiness of observed regularities. I think that this is Hume's starting point, but not all there is to the more regularity issue. A reading closer to the one I am proposing is in Price, *External World*, 52–7.

course without any new impulse' (1.4.2.22). This principle was already at work in the production of the idea of a perfect standard of equality. Price, on the authority of Hume's text, calls it the *inertia* of imagination.[12] I prefer to call it the *Hysteresis* of imagination, to highlight that the bias of the imagination depends on its previous history of learning.[13] This principle of the more limited imagination, together with its propensity to spread its transitions as ideas in the mind, increases the coherence of appearances with the opinion of continued existence.

> Objects have a certain coherence even as they appear to our senses; but this coherence is much greater and more uniform, if we suppose the objects to have a continu'd existence; and as the mind is once in the train of observing an uniformity among objects, it naturally continues, till it renders the uniformity as compleat as possible. The simple supposition of their continu'd existence suffices for this purpose, and gives us a notion of a much greater regularity among objects, than what they have when we look no farther than our senses. (1.4.2.22)

9.2.3 'A principle too weak to support so vast an edifice'

This looks like a rather successful attempt at linking and at the same time marking off the idea of cause and the idea of body, with the underlying principles of the imagination. We have then to explain why Hume does not stop at the coherence account and moves on to give a profoundly different one, related to the constancy of impressions. Hume concludes the coherence account with the following remark.

> But whatever force we may ascribe to this principle [the hysteresis of imagination], I am afraid 'tis too weak to support so vast an edifice, as is that of the continu'd existence of all external bodies; and that we must join the *constancy* of their appearance to the *coherence*, in order to give a satisfactory account of that opinion. (1.4.3.23)

This is all he has to say about a puzzling twist in the argument of 1.4.2.[14] It is somewhat difficult to grasp Hume's point. What Hume certainly says is that Hysteresis and thereby the coherence account is too weak; that it is too weak

---

[12] Price, *External World*, 54.

[13] Hume's description of Hysteresis and of its role find counterparts in contemporary research. It is one of the mechanisms involved in our framing notions of the continuity and stability of experience and its objects. This also holds of other applications of it, like motivational biases: it is important for Hume's theory of the passions, as well as for the explanation, say, of the relevance of sunken costs and of the possibility of practical consistency. See: S. Grossberg, ed., *The Adaptive Brain I: Cognition, Learning, Reinforcement, and Rhythm I*, North Holland, Amsterdam/New York 1987.

[14] See Loeb, *Stability and Justification*, 187–93.

relatively to the vastness of the edifice of external existence, of a real and durable world; and that the constancy account allows remedying to this weakness. He does not say that the coherence account is incorrect; that the constancy account must replace the coherence one; that the problem with the coherence account lies elsewhere than in Hysteresis. Mention of the vastness of the edifice of external existence and the reference to Hysteresis are the keys to a solution of the puzzle; but this requires some interpretive work.

A first consideration is that Hysteresis operates within the bounds of causal reasoning. One could doubt that the idea of continued existence can in this way be applied to all the objects. Not all objects figure in our experience as connected in regular successions; while belief in continued existence certainly extends to objects simply given in sense and memory and is not reducible to the feeling of presence or reality that attends impressions of sensation. We have, so to say, a completely general sense of immersion in a world of independent continuants, which the coherence account fails to explain.[15] Still, this does not seem a forceful reason to complement the coherence account with one based on a different principle. Our worldview is formed by the union of the first and of the second system of realities; that is, by connecting observed and unobserved object by causal relations. Insofar as we have at least this idea of the unity of reality, there seem not to be limits of principle to our ascriptions of continued existence.

Rather than looking at any restriction of the scope of application, we should look at the imaginative principle underlying the coherence account, Hysteresis. Hysteresis and Spreading in the mind explain how we come to apply the idea of continued existence to certain objects, in order to support our causal reasonings involving them. Customary transitions are pursued beyond what we have observed and the application of the idea of continued existence makes this possible. But this does not explain how the new idea of continued existence becomes available. Hysteresis is not a mental process that can firstly instantiate such an idea. Per se, Hysteresis is only the customary propensity of the imagination to pursue in certain customary transitions of ideas beyond their original conditions. It is a second-order customary transition, which involves our causal customary transitions; that is, which shapes the way we engage in them. But then, it is related to the idea of continued existence not because it puts it place but rather because the application of this idea is an easy and compelling way of pushing further our customary transitions. The idea of continued existence must be independently available in order to be applied or, anyway, to be taken in the scope of the operations of Hysteresis.

---

[15] This is the solution proposed for the puzzle in Loeb, *Stability and Justification*, 191. Price, *External World*, 65–7, denies that there is any deep difference between the coherence and the constancy account since both have to do with resemblances of series of perceptions.

The problem with this is not that there is a flaw of circularity in the coherence account.[16] Hume would certainly have regarded circularity as an error and the coherence account as incorrect. I think that Hume is concerned rather with an explanatory limit of the coherence account. The vastness of the edifice of the real and durable world is a matter not only of width but also of depth. The coherence account explains how the application of the idea of body is required for causal reasoning and how it naturally follows from principles related to those underlying causal ideas. This gives substance to Hume's claim that the idea of body must be taken for granted in all our reasonings. It tells us, also, how such idea, no matter how imperfect in its structure and grounding, can be appropriately applied. But the idea itself has not yet been given grounds in human cognitive nature. To overcome the limits of the coherence account and to provide a fundamental, constitutive explanation for the idea of a real and durable world, this latter should be addressed in connection with a more primitive layer of background cognition, a deeper one than causal reasoning. This is precisely what Hume does with the constancy account and what explains its structure, in particular its taking its start from a representational property of sensible objects and impressions, their resemblance; rather than from how constantly connected perceptions weigh on imagination and inference. The constancy account therefore neither replaces nor is subsumed under the coherence one; it is its theoretical complement; and it is the only context in which we can fundamentally explain the idea of a real and durable world.[17]

9.3 Imagining a Real and Durable World: Constancy and Identity

Hume makes remarks on the fundamental position as well as on the problematic character of the constancy account. He writes that 'the constancy of perceptions has the most considerable effect on the opinion of continued existence' (1.4.2.56). The explanation of how an 'inference' of imagination instantiates the idea of external existence, starting from constant impressions of sensation rather than from coherent ideas and causal inference, involves a 'very profound reasoning' (1.4.2.23). At the same time, the constancy account is 'attended with the greatest

---

[16] See Ainslie, *True Scepticism*, 73–4.

[17] Loeb, *Stability and Justification*, 177, 179–80, 186–7, proposes a complex argument to establish that (a) the ascription of identity is dispensable; (b) the coherence account gives an adequate account of the idea of continued existence; and (c) Hume joins the constancy to the coherence account to explain in terms of imagination, rather than of understanding, the false vulgar belief of continued existence. Loeb also contends that the constancy account could be subsumed under the coherence account. I think that what I say about the different aims and backgrounds of the two accounts raises a serious difficulty against these claims. Attempting to reconstruct the vulgar belief without having recourse to constancy and identity simply leaves unexplained its distinctive content.

difficulties' (1.4.2.56). This 'profound reasoning' casts the explanation of persisting and independent objects in terms of a discussion of the idea of identity and of how it is formed from materials afforded by our experience of time. As we will see, the structure and genesis of this idea are inherently complex. The constancy account also focuses on the relations between perceptions and objects, on the ontology of external and internal existence: how objects can be both individuated by the qualities of perceptions *and* thought of as persisting across their interruptions *so that* they can count as bodies or matter. This is, again, something missing from the coherence account, which leaves such ontology untouched (while presupposing some grasp of it). The constancy account thus bears most of the constitutive-explanatory burden of our idea of a real and durable world. It also makes room for the sceptical problems that Hume sees as arising from our idea of external existence.

Hume gives a 'short sketch or abridgment' of his 'system'. It consists in the constancy of impressions ('We find by experience, that there is such a *constancy* in almost all the impressions of the sense, that their interruption produces no alteration of them', 1.4.2.35); in our propensity to regard them 'as individually the same' because of their resemblance; in the manifest fact that such perceptions are interrupted; and in our supposing and believing that they are 'connected by a real existence, of which we are insensible' (1.4.2.24). He correspondingly distinguishes four explanatory tasks in the constancy account.

> In order to justify this system, there are four things requisite. *First*, To explain the *principium individuationis*, or principle of identity. *Secondly*, Give a reason, why the resemblance of our broken and interrupted perceptions induces us to attribute an identity to them. *Thirdly*, Account for that propensity, which this illusion gives, to unite these broken appearances by a continu'd existence. *Fourthly* and lastly, Explain that force and vivacity of conception, which arises from the propensity. (1.4.2.25)

The four tasks fall naturally in two steps: the first and the second deal with how the idea of identity of perceptions arises out of the constancy and interruptions of perceptions. The third and the fourth deal with how the idea of identical perceptions is changed into the idea and belief of continued existence. The more limited imagination is in either case the main explanatory factor.

9.3.1 The Cognitive Gap of Perfect Identity

The 'principle of identity' is not given in sensible representation. It does not come from a priori and a posteriori reason either: identity is not an internal relation and thus is not susceptible to demonstration; and probable reasoning presupposes that its ideas and objects be different and distinct. Hume's identification of this cognitive gap is directly a priori, from a conceptual analysis of the paradigmatic 'proposition' of identity: *an object is the same with itself* (1.4.2.26). This proposition gives expression to the relation of identity 'in its strictest sense' as applied to 'constant and unchangeable objects' (1.1.5.4).

Now, the 'view' of 'any one object'—the at least potential representation of an object—'is not sufficient to convey the idea of identity', as expressed in the paradigmatic statement (1.4.2.26). The idea expressed by 'object' must be distinguishable from that meant by 'itself'. Otherwise 'we really shou'd mean nothing, nor wou'd the proposition contain a predicate and a subject, which however are imply'd in this affirmation'. But no such distinction, which would amount to a difference and to a separation, is conveyed by that idea. The idea of 'one single object conveys the idea of unity, not that of identity'. The representation of a 'multiplicity of objects' cannot convey the idea of identity either. 'The mind always pronounces the one not to be the other, and considers them as forming two, three, or any determinate number of objects, whose existences are entirely distinct and independent' (1.4.2.27). In this case, it is the condition of sameness included in the content of the 'proposition' that is not satisfied.

> Since then both number and unity are incompatible with the relation of identity, it must lie in something that is neither of them. But to tell the truth, at first sight this seems utterly impossible. Betwixt unity and number there can be no medium; no more than betwixt existence and non-existence. After one object is suppos'd to exist, we must either suppose another also to exist; in which case we have the idea of a number: Or we must suppose it not to exist; in which case the first object remains at unity. (1.4.2.28)

It is impossible to *represent* identity by ideas of one object or of a number of objects. But, of course, we *do* have that idea: identity is the 'most universal' of all philosophical relations 'being common to every being, whose existence has any duration' (1.1.5.4). Therefore, there is a cognitive gap in correspondence to the idea of identity and the problem is how we come to have it, what its source and nature are.[18]

---

[18] The gap of perfect identity dovetails with the 'difficulty' that, according to Baxter's important discussion, motivates Hume's account: 'The difficulty is raised by the clear fact that identity is something we can be unsure about. We are able to think of two things while leaving it open whether or not they are identical.... As Hume puts it, the idea of identity must be an idea of "a medium betwixt unity and number"... This difficulty is what motivates Hume to give the principle of identity as steadfastness yet with duration' (*Hume's Difficulty*, 48–9; see 51–4). Such difficulty manifests a gap of conception, which calls for partial remedy in imagination. ('The idea [the fictional idea of perfect identity] is at root contradictory and confused, but it seems to Hume to be the only one we have that will do.') Baxter is right that Hume's difficulty, or the identity gap, is different from Frege's Puzzle (59). Frege's problem is about the informativeness of true statements of identity. Hume's problem is about the very conceivability of the contents of such statements.

To explain how the gap of identity is filled, Hume exploits the a priori connection between time and identity and reverts to his theory of temporal ideas. 'To remove this difficulty, let us have recourse to the idea of time or duration' (1.4.2.29). Hume more particularly reverts to his account at 1.2.5 of how the imagination produces the idea of an empty time or time without change. There is a cognitive gap corresponding to the idea of a time without change; the operations of the imagination that fill this gap are close in kin with those that give us the missing idea of identity.

Temporal ideas consist of successions of perceptions, that is, of representations of changes. The idea of time then can be applied to unchangeable objects 'only by a fiction of the imagination, by which the unchangeable object is suppos'd to participate of the changes of the co-existent objects, and in particular of that of our perceptions' (1.4.2.29). Such fiction is not difficult to reconstruct ('we can easily point out those appearances, which make us fancy we have that idea', 1.2.5.28). 'We may observe, that there is a continual succession of perceptions in our mind'. Because of this, the idea of time (the general idea abstracted from particular instances of such internal observation) is always present to us. This steady presence turns itself (by habituation) into a propensity to apply the idea of time beyond the conditions that give rise to it. The principles of the more limited imagination here at work are the same that Hume introduces in the coherence account of continued existence: Hysteresis and Spreading in the mind. 'When we consider a steadfast object at five-a-clock, and regard the same at six; we are apt to apply to it that idea in the same manner as if every moment were distinguish'd by a different position, or an alteration of the object' (1.2.5.29). By this application, we spread in the mind the succession of our perceptions; that is, we spread it in the interval between the two appearances of the steadfast object, as we do with the two kinds of distance. The interval, which being without changes observable in the object is not duration (just like the proprioceptive distance is not extension), is spread with ideas of changes and in this way takes up the appearance of a duration. The two appearances of the object 'seem equally remov'd as if the object had really chang'd'. (This is repeated at 1.4.2.29.) Like in the case of empty space, we fail to distinguish the imagined from the perceived duration because they have the same causal and modal properties. 'To which we may add, what experience shews us, that the object was susceptible of such a number of changes betwixt these appearances; as also that the unchangeable or rather fictitious duration has the same effect upon every quality, by encreasing or diminishing it, as that succession, which is obvious to the senses.' (1.2.5.29). We think in modal and causal terms, that is, by the faculty of imagination; but we take ourselves to represent what we think. This puts in place new content.[19]

---

[19] See the discussion in Costa, 'Hume, Strict Identity, and Time's Vacuum'; and in Baxter, *Hume's Difficulty*, 43–7.

320   THE WORLD AS SOMETHING REAL AND DURABLE

This explanation of empty time is applied to the idea of perfect identity: an object persisting without change. (Hume only thinks of identity as diachronic; synchronic identity he discusses, briefly, under the heading of simplicity in 1.4.3.) This fiction of the imagination gives us 'a notion of identity' from 'a single object, plac'd in front of us, and survey'd for any time without our discovering in it any interruption of variation' (1.4.2.29). The core of the explanation is the transition from the mutually inconsistent representational *ideas* of unity and number (which are involved in the content of the proposition of identity) to two different but consistent *viewpoints* on one unchanging object. The more limited imagination makes available these different viewpoints by spreading ideas of changes in the unchangeable appearance of the object. Taking either of such viewpoints does not alter the representation we have of that object (by Non-Mixture, the object-representing content of the idea stays the same). The distinction they allow us to make is only one of reason. But if we can have the non-representational idea of this *one* unchanging object as being *in time*, by taking on it two distinct time-related perspectives, the imagination can form a further, new idea of it, one with the content required for the thought of its identity.

> For when we consider any two points of this time, we may place them in different lights: We may either survey them at the very same instant; in which case they give us the idea of number, both by themselves and by the object; which must be multiply'd, in order to be conceiv'd at once, as existent in these two different points of time: Or on the other hand, we may trace the succession of time by a like succession of ideas, and conceiving first one moment, along with the object then existent, imagine afterwards a change in the time without any *variation* or *interruption* in the object; in which case it gives us the idea of unity.
>
> (1.4.2.29)

The two perspectives made available to the imagination by Two Viewpoints and by the spreading of duration in the perception of an unchanging object produce the content of the idea of identity. Hume is describing a very complex and multi-layered operation of the imagination, which I will try to reconstruct proceeding bottom up.

(1) At the bottommost level, we have the representation, that is, the impression, of an unchanging object. This impression is not temporal. As mental episode it exists in a temporal context, that is, it is included in and therefore corresponds to a stretch of the flux of perceptions, which is the mind. But it does not itself change and is not present to awareness as a succession; therefore, it has no duration; and, by Two Viewpoints, it does not present or represent any temporal content, any object having duration.[20]

---

[20] Price finds fault with the very notion of an 'unchanging sense-impression', in this way challenging the constancy account at its very root (and thereby denying that it importantly differs from the

(2) Because of Hysteresis and Spreading in the mind, the imagination spreads our awareness of real successions of our perceptions, our successive ideas, in the unchanging perception of the object. Therefore, it forms the idea of it as having duration, an idea with multiplicity and change for content. (The spreading is in the mind, in a stretch of awareness without duration, like in the case of a spatial vacuum.)

(3) This opens a new cognitive possibility. 'On any two points of this time', of the imagination-produced duration of one unchanging object, two perspectives can be taken. One is considering them in their succession or flow. The other is considering them at the same instant, that is, from one fixed point and as two fixed points. These two perspectives allow us to draw a distinction of reason between two aspects of the unchanging object, one of unity and one of multiplicity.

Thus the principle of individuation is nothing but the *invariableness* and *uninterruptedness* of any object, thro' a suppos'd variation of time, by which the mind can trace it in the different periods of its existence, without any break of the view, and without being oblig'd to form the idea of multiplicity or number.

(1.4.2.30)

The represented object and its idea do not actually change. This makes it so that, by considering it as if it were successive or changing, the condition (explicit in the 'principle of identity') that an object is the *same* with itself comes to have content and application. No break of view, no multiplicity of contents, is involved by the articulation of the principle of individuation (this would not be possible with changing objects, that is, with variable series of perceptions). But, still, the principle of identity can be articulated by a distinction of reason between the object and *itself*, through the consideration of it at two points in time. In this way, by the availability of the two viewpoints, the idea of one object being the same with itself makes a difference to our thinking. Invariableness 'thro' a suppos'd variation of time' (as imagined) bears on our thinking differently from invariableness per se (as represented). The difference between the two viewpoints is only epistemic, not modal. It is *epistemically* possible to distinguish the ideas expressed by 'object' and 'itself' (which are *absolutely* one and the same), as it is required by the content of the 'proposition' of identity. 'Here then is an idea, which is a medium betwixt unity and number; or more properly speaking, is either of them, according to the view, in which we take it: And this idea we call that of identity'

coherence account) (*External World*, 46–7). Our awareness is rather of a series. However, Price's arguments are inconclusive. The possibility of an interruption of our awareness fails to establish that our awareness is not of one unchanging object (consists of one unchanging perception). Impressions are a-modal in their contents; it is not part of the content of our experience and it is not relevant to it that what we experience could be different.

(1.4.2.29). The distinction only defines an epistemic possibility: no separation, therefore no different existences are involved; which is just as it should be, since it is the idea of the identity of an object with itself that is in question.

This idea is obviously and explicitly non-representational. It is the result of an operation of the imagination: distinguishing and taking in turn viewpoints that do not represent different properties of an object, over the product of another process of the imagination: an unchanging object with duration. There are no differences in representation between the idea of *one* object and the idea of *one object which is the same with itself*. But there is an epistemic difference in the views we can have of that object and it is this difference that forms the content of the idea of identity. The availability to the mind of the two viewpoints, the possibility of taking them in turn, constitutes the idea of identity. 'By this means we make a difference, betwixt the idea meant by the word, *object*, and that meant by *itself*, without going to the length of number, and at the same time without restraining ourselves to a strict and absolute unity' (1.4.2.29).[21]

9.3.2 The Cognitive Gap of Imperfect Identity

The next question on Hume's explanatory agenda is: 'Why the constancy of our perceptions makes us ascribe to them a perfect numerical identity, tho' there be very long intervals betwixt their appearance, and they have only one of the essential qualities of identity, viz. *invariableness*' (1.4.2.31). A constant perception is

---

[21] This begins to answer to Baxter's important consideration: 'Hume's account explicitly involves a fiction. Thus, he has not given an account that strictly speaking resolves the difficulty. He has only explained how we generate an idea that seems to resolve it.... Hume has explained how we come up with an idea that involves switching between the view of something as one and the view of some things as many, but he has not explained how we represent something viewed as one and the things viewed as many as the same thing(s). That, however, was the original problem' (*Hume's Difficulty*, 66–7). Hume's account, however, is precisely that the shift between the two viewpoints allows us to conceive of the same object as one and as many, without having to entertain the conception and the metaphysical possibility that the object be distinct from itself. Baxter underplays the complexity and resourcefulness of Hume's account of how ideas allow us to conceive of objects. In particular, the possibility that inferential transitions, like the shift from one viewpoint to the other, allow us to think significantly of what we cannot represent (an object being the same with itself, understood, as Hume does, as an a posteriori matter). (This is related, I think, to a point made by D. Garrett, 'Difficult Times for Humean Identity?', *Philosophical Studies*, 2009, 146, 435–43, 438). In this regard, Baxter's useful conceptual and interpretive distinction between 'what there is which a representation represents' and 'what a representation represents there as being' (*Hume's Difficulty*, 3) does not go far enough, because representing should be itself resolved into either reference to and acquaintance with individual particulars or detached, general, and modal conception of qualitatively specified conditions. It is of course a different matter—and one that cannot be addressed here—whether Hume's apparatus helps to overcome the Kripke-inspired difficulty about conceiving a posteriori identities pointed out by Baxter (83–92). What is at issue is whether epistemic and metaphysical possibilities can be so divorced as to make possible representing something as the same or as different (as when we are uncertain what of these alternatives is the case). Hume's extremely flexible apparatus of Conceivability and of distinctions of reasons is of help here. In the case of identity, we can conceive a distinction that is not a difference and separation and that defines an epistemic and not a metaphysical possibility.

not an unchanging object, because it is interrupted. The application of the idea of identity to constant perceptions therefore fails to satisfy the conditions Hume has set for the individuation of this idea. He marks this fact by presenting his discussion as the search for the 'source of the error and illusion with regard to identity, when we attribute it to our resembling perceptions, notwithstanding their interruption' (1.4.2.32). Identity, insofar as we apply it to constant (not unchanging) perceptions or objects, is only 'imperfect identity' (1.4.6.9). There is an aspect of cognitive spuriousness, absent from the idea of perfect identity, which infects the constancy account and the content of the idea of body.

Hume explains imperfect identity with a principle of the more limited imagination that makes it so that we 'mistake one idea for another', the idea of constancy for that of identity. This principle, like Hysteresis, extends the transitions of the imagination and its production of ideas beyond their original conditions (in this case, the invariability and uninterruptedness of a perception). But it differs from that principle in an important respect: it does not proceed, even indirectly and obliquely, from past experience. It is rather an expression of the concurrence of imagination with resemblance, the simplest, most general, and most primitive property of impressions that acts as a principle of association. And it depends on resemblance on account of a property that his latter does *not* share with contiguity and causation. 'Of all relations, that of resemblance is in this respect the most efficacious; and that because it not only causes an association of ideas, but also of dispositions, and makes us conceive the one idea by an act or operation of the mind, similar to that by which we conceive the other.' 'For a general rule', 'whatever ideas place the mind in the same disposition or in similar ones, are very apt to be confounded' (1.4.2.32). We have already encountered this principle, *Act/Idea Resemblance*, when discussing Hume's account of the idea of a perfect standard of equality. In the present case, the 'circumstance' underlying the confusion (which, as Hume remarks, is 'of great moment') is the resemblance between constancy and identity and between the mental acts that involve them. The transitions of the imagination can respond not only to properties of content and mental existence of perceptions but also to properties of mental actions.

(1) We start from the 'view' of 'any object which preserves a perfect identity', that is, from a perception, the 'thought' of an object that we 'suppose' to 'continue the same for some time', with any change lying 'only in the time', that is, in the change and succession of other perceptions that we also have in view (1.4.2.33).

(2) To this unchanging perception corresponds a 'disposition' of the mind, a mode of mental activity in which the 'faculties of the mind repose themselves', taking 'no more exercise, than what is necessary to continue that idea', 'which subsists without variation and interruption'; scarce any feeling accompanies the passage from one moment to another in this mental activity.

(3) A disposition of the mind resembling this can be caused by and correspond to a 'succession of related objects', which 'is consider'd with the same smooth and uninterrupted progress of the imagination', with 'little alteration on the mind', so that we seem engaged in 'the continuation of the same action' (1.4.2.34).
(4) 'The very nature and essence of relation is to connect our ideas with each other, and upon the appearance of one, to facilitate the transition to its correlative.' 'The continuation of the same action is an effect of the continu'd view of the same object.' There is thus a systematic shift or transition from ideas to dispositions or mental acts and then to ideas.[22]
(5) This transition ends up by adding to the invariableness of perceptions (strict similarity) their uninterruptedness, or identity. 'The thought slides along the succession with equal facility, as if it consider'd only one object; and therefore confounds the succession with the identity' (1.4.2.34; see 1.4.2.35 fn. 39; 1.4.6.6).

To sum up:

An easy transition or passage of the imagination, along the ideas of these different and interrupted perceptions, is almost the same disposition of mind with that in which we consider one constant and uninterrupted perception. 'Tis therefore very natural for us to mistake the one for the other. (1.4.2.35)

This transition is a clear instance of the production of content and cognitive change by the more limited imagination. There is a complex, even baffling structure of mental contents and actions ('somewhat abstruse, and difficult to comprehend', 1.4.2.35 fn. 39): 'two relations, and both of them resemblances, which contribute to our mistaking the succession of our interrupted perceptions for one identical object'. The mutual influence of the resemblance of perceptions and of actions obviously is neither an instance of a priori nor one of a posteriori reasoning (it neither expresses Separability nor Determination by repeated observation and custom). If our cognitive faculties were restricted to the senses and memory, or to a priori and a posteriori reason, this cognitive structure would be mysterious and its outcomes unintelligible.[23]

---

[22] As Hume remarks, about the very closely related matter of the unity of bodies, the 'easy transition' is the 'effect, or rather the essence of the relation' - in this case, of the synchronic identity of perceptions or objects (1.4.3.3).
[23] Hume's account of the fundamental ideas of 'antient philosophy'—'*original* substance or matter' (which is assumed to be an 'unknown something'); '*substantial form*'; '*accidents*'; '*occult qualities*'—in 1.4.3 is strictly related to the constancy account but subtly and tellingly different from it. The 'unreasonable and capricious' 'fictions' of ancient philosophers 'have a very intimate connexion with the principles of human nature' (1.4.3.1). Also in this case, the idea of body 'as ONE thing, and as continuing the SAME under very considerable variations' is grounded on 'collections form'd by the mind of

9.3.3 From Imperfect Identity to Continued and Distinct Existence

From the idea of the (imperfect) identity of constant perceptions, the imagination moves to that of objects that exist continuedly and distinctly and to the corresponding belief. (These are, respectively, the third and the fourth thing required by Hume's 'system'.) This is Hume's explanation of how we come to have the idea of external existence that, according to the coherence account, we apply in most cases to causally related objects.

9.3.3.1 The Opposition of Two Principles

The core of Hume's explanation is that the transition to the idea of continued existence is produced by a cognitive conflict unclenched by the attribution of identity to constant perceptions. We ascribe to our perceptions, to our 'images', a 'perfect identity'. But these images are 'interrupted', are not continuedly present to awareness. 'But as the interruption of the appearance seems contrary to the identity, and naturally leads us to regard these resembling perceptions as different from each other, we here find ourselves at a loss how to reconcile such opposite opinions' (1.4.2.36). The strict similarity of perceptions and their interrupted

---

the ideas of the several distinct qualities, of which objects are compos'd, and which we find to have a constant union with each other' (1.4.3.2). The explanation of the idea of substance is in many respects the same with the constancy account; the differences emerge when Hume doubles the explanation of diachronic identity with that of synchronic identity or simplicity of body. 'We entertain a like notion with regard to the *simplicity* of substances, and from like causes' (1.4.3.5). The similarity in the presence to the mind of 'an object perfectly simple and indivisible' and one 'whose *co-existent* parts are connected together by a strong relation' induces a similarity in the 'action of the mind, in considering these two objects'. In both cases, there is facility of conception, a 'single effort of thought, without change or variation'. This is the transition of the imagination between the different parts of the 'compound object'. This produces the idea of such object as a simple thing. 'Hence the colour, taste, figure, solidity, and other qualities, combin'd in a peach or melon, are conceiv'd to form *one thing*'. Differently from the constancy account, however, these 'primary and more natural notions' are contrasted not with the equally primary and natural awareness of the interruption or variation of perceptions, but with a more explicit and reflective shift to considerations of separability. 'But the mind rests not here. Whenever it views the object in another light, it finds that all these qualities are different, and distinguishable, and separable from each other.' This is just as it should be, since Hume's task here is not to explain the primitive content of the idea of body, but a philosophical doctrine, which is grounded on abstract reflection. The contrast between the natural notion of the simplicity of the body and the reflective one of its diversity 'obliges the imagination to feign an unknown something, or *original* substance and matter, as a principle of union or cohesion among these qualities, and as what may give the compound object a title to be call'd one thing, notwithstanding its diversity and composition.' (1.4.3.5). This, again, is superficially resembling but deeply different from the constancy account. This latter directly identifies continuants with perceptions construed in terms of the fiction of the identity of constant impressions. Ancient philosophy, by contrast, identifies continuants with unknown, imperceptible substrata, with perceptible qualities figuring as substantial forms and accidents (1.4.3.6–7). This is because no constant (strictly resembling) content of individual perceptions can provide support for a direct ascription of external existence. The relation between the different qualities that compose the compound object is only their regular conjunction. In this respect, ancient philosophy is closer to the coherence account (but still more reflective than this latter). It is also close to the account of personal identity in 1.4.6. I draw attention to this in order to emphasize the fine-grainedness and flexibility of Hume's recourse to the imagination. On the similarities and the differences between the idea of continued existence and the idea of substance see Loeb, *Stability and Justification*, 150–1.

'manner of appearance' have opposite effects on the imagination. 'The smooth passage of the imagination along the ideas of the resembling perceptions makes us ascribe to them a perfect identity. The interrupted manner of their appearance makes us consider them as so many resembling, but still distinct beings, which appear after certain intervals' (1.4.2.36). This is a conflicted cognitive state, in which the mind is under opposed, representational, and inferential pressures to regard perceptions as the same and as different.

Reconciliation, the principle with which the imagination responds to conflicted cognitive states and to the need to ease them, was part of the processes of the imagination underlying the idea of a perfect equality of size (§ 8.2.2). This is no surprise since such perfect equality is identity of size. The coherence account also introduces the pressure to avoid a contradiction as the source of the attribution of external existence to causally connected, unperceived objects. But the cognitive situations are very different. In the coherence account, the contradiction is what we end up with, when we reason in causal terms without assuming the unperceived existence of causally related external objects. In the present case, the conflict is immediate and primitive, between the representation of constancy, on the one hand, and the identifying transitions of the imagination, on the other. Furthermore, the opposition between the identity of resembling perceptions and their interrupted appearance has for background the supposition, shared by 'all the unthinking and unphilosophical part of mankind, (that is, all of us, at one time or other)', that 'perceptions' are 'their only objects'; that the 'very image, which is present to the senses' is the 'real body'. Because of this supposition, the easing of the cognitive conflict can only take the form of a view of objects as continuedly and distinctly existing, rather than that of a dualism of perceptions and objects. Or, as we can say, of a conception of external existence as a distinction only extrinsic (relations, durations, locations) between perceptions and objects. This conception has its difficulties; but it is also one to which, as we will see, the true philosophy of external existence comes close.

9.3.3.2 How to Reconcile Such Opposite Opinions

'The perplexity arising from this contradiction produces a propension to unite these broken appearances by the fiction of a continu'd existence, which is the *third* part of that hypothesis I propos'd to explain' (1.4.2.36). This fiction is produced by the imagination in order to reconcile a conflict of views. It is not that the contradiction or opposition per se demands reconciliation. But the reconciliation is motivated by the uneasiness, by the unpleasantness and unsettledness of a conflicted state of mind. 'Nothing is more certain from experience, than that any contradiction either to the sentiments or passions gives a sensible uneasiness, whether it proceeds from without or from within'. Because of the 'opposition' between identity and interruption, the mind must be 'uneasy' and 'will naturally seek relief from the uneasiness' (1.4.2.37). Note that Reconciliation adds a further trait to Hume's imagination, which is also relevant for contemporary discussions: the susceptibility of imagination to be motivated, without the complications that this would raise for other cognitive states, like reasoning or belief.

The motivational pressure to find relief from this sort of cognitive dissonance is constrained by the conceptual and psychological features of the conflict. For one thing, the background of the conflict is the supposition that the very images are the real objects: it is against this background that a reconciliation must be sought. This means in particular that here, as everywhere else in 1.4.2, the explanandum are the relations, connections, situations, and durations that mark off perceptions and bodies. For another one, the opposed principles are 'contrary', so that 'relief' can be looked for only in 'sacrificing the one to the other'. In this respect, there is an asymmetry between them. The 'smooth passage of our thought along our resembling perceptions' and the ensuing ascription of identity are stronger than our awareness of their interrupted character (Hume seems to take this as a datum). In this way, we end up supposing that 'our perceptions are no longer interrupted, but preserve a continu'd as well as an invariable existence, and are by that means entirely the same'. This step beyond the identification of constant perceptions gives origin to the idea of continued existence, the idea of objects, individuated by the same qualities with perceptions, continuedly and distinctly existing (existing with different relations, locations, and durations from perceptions, but the same with them).

> This propension to bestow an identity on our resembling perceptions, produces the fiction of a continu'd existence; since that fiction, as well as the identity, is really false, as is acknowledg'd by all philosophers, and has no other effect than to remedy the interruption of our perceptions, which is the only circumstance that is contrary to their identity. (1.4.2.43; I discuss the falsity of this fiction later)

As ordinary thinkers, we 'not only *feign* but *believe* this continu'd existence'. Explaining the source of such belief is the 'fourth member of this system' (1.4.2.41). The attitude of belief is in general explained by the transmission of force and vivacity of conception along some relation in which impressions stand to ideas. The relevant relation here is resemblance. 'Our memory presents us with a vast number of instances of perceptions perfectly resembling each other, that return at different distances of time, and after considerable interruptions' (1.4.2.42). This gives us a propensity to consider these interrupted perceptions as the same and to connect them by continued existence. 'Here then we have a propensity to feign the continued existence of all sensible objects; and as this propensity arises from some lively impressions of the memory, it bestows a vivacity on that fiction; or in other words, makes us believe the continue'd existence of body'

(1.4.2.41; the concept of belief will be discussed in Chapter 11). This is a 'consistent system, which is perfectly convincing' (1.4.2.43).[24]

Hume's constancy account of the idea of continued existence is, in a nutshell, the following: 'When the exact resemblance of our perceptions makes us ascribe to them an identity, we may remove the seeming interruption by feigning a continu'd being, which may fill those intervals, and preserve a perfect and entire identity to our perceptions' (1.4.2.40). Once this idea and these beliefs are available, we can apply them to objects that are 'perfectly new to us', on grounds of resemblance and by 'analogy and reasoning' (1.4.2.42). Just as it is with causal ideas, the idea of continued existence, constitutively explained with the constancy account, can be applied in implicit or explicit more or less reflective reasoning; primarily, if not exclusively, in causal reasonings that require spreading in our minds ideas as continuedly existing objects.

9.4 The External World: Perceptions, Bodies, Qualities

Even though Hume is not giving a full-scale metaphysics of the 'real and durable' world, the individuation and constitutive explanation of its idea, based on the imagination, can provide a clue to the ontology of bodies, of their relations with perceptions, and of the divide between existence within and without the mind. By discussing these topics, I can also complete the outline of the ontology of Humean perceptions given in § 2.2.3.[25]

---

[24] See, on the mechanism of formation of the belief in continued existence, Loeb, *Stability and Justification*, 145–6. Loeb acutely remarks that, while in the causal case repetition and custom are responsible for both contents and for assurance, in the case of belief in body they are only responsible for the attitude.

[25] Hume's ontology of perceptions can be interestingly contrasted with an argument in the first of Berkeley's *Dialogues* (153–6). Hylas introduces, against the conclusion that 'all sensible qualities are alike to be denied existence without the mind', the following consideration: 'One great oversight I take to be this: that I did not sufficiently distinguish the object from the sensation. Now though this latter may not exist without the mind, yet it will not follow that the former cannot'. Adding: 'The sensation I take to be an act of the mind perceiving; beside which, there is something perceived; and this I call the object'. Berkeley—Philonous—answers to this consideration by addressing the 'distinction between sensation and object' taken in its full generality: 'If I take you right, you distinguish in every perception two things, the one an action of the mind, the other not'. Berkeley's argument is not crystal clear, but his aim seems to be to establish that, at least in the case of ideas of sense (as opposed to ideas of imagination), no such distinction holds. Therefore, at least in this case, no appeal can be made to the act–object distinction in order to prevent the unacceptable—both to Hylas and to Philonous—conclusion that a perception could exist in an unthinking substance. 'So that if there was a perception without any act of the mind, it were possible such a perception should exist in an unthinking substance'. Hylas objects that this is impossible. Berkeley's and Philonous's counter-objection is that sensations, not including any 'volition', being 'altogether passive', do not include any act of the mind. Therefore, on the act–object distinction proposed by Hylas, these sensations or perceptions could exist in an unthinking substance, what all parts recognize as a 'plain contradiction'. Putting into brackets the deeply questionable volitionist interpretation of the act–object distinction, Berkeley seems to assume that, if such distinction could be applied to ideas of sense, the existence of perceptions—qua objects, not qua acts—without the mind would be conceivable. He also thinks that this is

9.4.1 Perceptions without the Mind, Objects within the Mind

The crucial and most complicated question in Hume's ontology of external existence is that of the relations between perceptions and continuedly and distinctly existing objects or bodies. The idea of a real durable world goes beyond anything licensed by Two Viewpoints and Equivalence. The former principle gives expression to a distinction of reason and only defines an epistemic possibility. But, right now, the question is of the real relations between inner and outer, between perceptions and bodies (1.4.7.3). It is a matter of absolute, not of epistemic possibility. Equivalence, in turn, gives expression to the idea of existence simpliciter: the being or presence of a sensible particular. This is a condition on the ontology of objects and perceptions much weaker than continued and distinct existence. The idea of external existence is a substantive structure of our worldview. It is not about objects in general but bodies. What is necessary and sufficient for the existence of objects in general (their equivalence with impressions) may still be necessary but is not sufficient for bodies.

Hume specifies the content of the idea of a real and durable world, in the light of its production by the imagination, with two claims.

The first is that continuedly and distinctly existing objects or bodies are specifically the same with perceptions (impressions of sensation and ideas representing them): that they are individuated by the same qualities that also individuate such perceptions. This is a condition on the idea of external existence, a constraint on the ideas we can have of bodies, which descends from Equivalence and from the fact that the idea of existence is abstracted from our ideas of sensible particulars and has the conception of some such particular as its content. We can conceive of bodies in a cognitively robust way (so as to conceive their absolute possibility and to form beliefs about them) only under a qualitative specification; relative ideas of external existence neither imply absolute possibility nor support belief.

The second, much stronger and inherently more controversial claim, is that bodies and perceptions are numerically identical; that the same beings can be

---

unacceptable. (See K. Winkler, in *Berkeley. An Interpretation*, Clarendon Press, Oxford 1989, 4–6, 7–9, who finds this text problematic. He suggests that Berkeley's argument is ad hominem; and that it is consistent with some form of the act–object distinction. I doubt of the first claim; and the second might be consistent with my point, that there is more to Hume's perceptions in the way of the act–object distinction than what Berkeley admits. See also R. Muehlmann, 'Strong and Weak Heterogeneity in Berkeley's New Theory of Vision', in S. H. Daniel ed., *New Interpretations of Berkeley's Thought*, Humanity Books, Amherst 2008 (121–44), 141–2.) Now, without postulating an actual filiation from this text, Hume's ontology of perceptions, in primis impressions, seems to take up the alternative that Berkeley discards: the ideas of sense admit of an act–object distinction; they include acts of awareness—the sensations—distinct from their object. In Hume's theory, this takes the form of Two Viewpoints and of the equivalence of impressions with objects of sense. In the light of these alternative identifications, the fact and the mode of the existence in the mind of perceptions is contingent and a posteriori. Perceptions can exist unperceived: their esse is not percipi. (See J. P. Wright, *Hume's A Treatise of Human Nature. An Introduction*, Cambridge University Press, Cambridge 2009, 67).

continuedly and distinctly existing things and perceptions existing in the mind. This claim concerns not only how we can conceive in general of existence and therefore a fortiori of external existence but specifically what is to exist as a body, as a part of a real durable world. Of course, as any conclusion we can draw about the reality of causation, of the external world, of the mind, it is based on the idea we have of the existence of bodies. But such idea is now considered not only as to what produces it and makes it conceivable, but as to what it unveils about the reality of objects, directly or by implication; that is, as to the relevant absolute possibilities. Hume is aware of the problematic character of this claim. He explicitly addresses this issue at a crucial step of the constancy account, the application of Reconciliation to the contradiction between the identity and the interruptions of constant perceptions.

> But here the interruptions in the appearance of these perceptions are so long and frequent, that 'tis impossible to overlook them; and as the *appearance* of a perception in the mind and its *existence* seem at first sight entirely the same, it may be doubted, whether we can ever assent to so palpable a contradiction, and suppose a perception to exist without being present to the mind. (1.4.2.37)

The reconciliation is attempted with the new idea of the continued and distinct existence of perceptions. The problem, however, seems to resurface, because of the contradiction between the immediate, interrupted appearance of our perceptions; the identity ('at first sight') of the existence and of the appearance of perceptions to the mind; and the ascription of continued and distinct existence to them, as per the constancy account. The supposition that a perception can exist without the mind thus seems to involve a contradiction. At the same time, this is what, according to Hume, we ordinarily say of the continued and distinct existence of perceptions.

> 'Tis also certain, that this very perception or object is suppos'd to have a continu'd uninterrupted being, and neither to be annihilated by our absence, nor to be brought into existence by our presence. When we are absent from it, we say it still exists, but that we do not feel, we do not see it. When we are present, we say we feel, or see it. (1.4.2.38)

Hume is here speaking in the voice of the vulgar but also, as we will see, of true philosophy. Most importantly, he explicitly denies that this view involves any contradiction. 'The supposition of the continu'd existence of sensible objects or perceptions involves no contradiction. We may easily indulge our inclination to that supposition' (1.4.2.40). To begin sorting this out, we should consider that 'absence' and 'presence', in the last quoted text, stand for the different relations, connections, and durations, which constitute the internal–external difference.

The crucial point is that, if such relations, connections, and durations were non-separable from the specifically identical perceptions and objects, the contradiction between continued existence and interrupted appearance would arise. Perceptions and objects would be numerically *distinct*. Perceptions and objects could not be the same across the divide between presence to and absence from the mind, just as they could not persist across a change in their individuating qualities. The change from presence to absence to the mind would be identity altering. By asserting the numerical identity of perceptions and bodies, we would attempt to separate what is inseparable (the relations, &c, and their subjects). We would attempt to conceive of some entities as existing without (some of) their conditions of individuation. Imagination itself could not overcome this contradiction, since it violates the conditions of conceivability by Separability.

Hume's response to this difficulty is drastic. It is to deny what 'at first sight' seems to be certainly true, that 'the *appearance* of a perception in the mind and its *existence*' are 'entirely the same' (1.4.2.37). In order to establish this point, Hume argues that the relations, connections, and durations that make the difference between inner or mental and outer or bodily existence are extrinsic and metaphysically contingent. This is a crucially important move that completes the specification of the content of the idea of external existence and defines Hume's ontology of bodies and perceptions. It is best understood as an argument of Separability: the relations, connections, and durations that differentiate internal and external existence are separable from their objects, be they bodies or perceptions; therefore, it is metaphysically possible for these objects (for the same beings) to exist internally or externally, as bodies or perceptions. This is no deep metaphysical divide. This comes out in the two questions with which Hume articulates his argument.

> *First*, How we can satisfy ourselves in supposing a perception to be absent from the mind without being annihilated? *Secondly*, After what manner we conceive an object to become present to the mind, without some new creation of a perception or image; and what we mean by this *seeing*, and *feeling*, and *perceiving*?
> (1.4.2.38)

The background here is the modal and a priori one (based on the simple consideration of the idea of a perception) that perceptions are independent existents, are substances, in the minimal sense in which Hume accepts and endorses this notion: 'something which may exist by itself' (1.4.5.5). On this basis, Hume gives relatively a priori answers to both questions. The a posteriori element is his conception of mind. 'What we call a mind, is nothing but a heap or collection of different perceptions, united together by certain relations, and suppos'd, tho' falsely, to be endow'd with a perfect simplicity and identity' (1.4.2.39; in a footnote, he refers forward to his discussion of personal identity at 1.4.6). This is a posteriori insofar as it is a belief based on introspective experience and on probable inference. (Hume also gives a priori arguments for this position, see § 10.1.2; but we can do with the weaker, a posteriori ones.) Existence in the mind is conceived, correspondingly, as distinct and separable perceptions standing in certain metaphysically contingent, non-internal relations with others (in such a way that they form a heap or bundle). Then, a priori, it is metaphysically possible that perceptions exist without such relations; the relations, connections, and durations that constitute their internal existence, their appearance, are separable from them. An unperceived perception is a metaphysical possibility.

> Now as every perception is distinguishable from another, and may be consider'd as separately existent; it evidently follows, that there is no absurdity in separating any particular perception from the mind; that is, in breaking off all its relations, with that connected mass of perceptions, which constitute a thinking being. (1.4.2.39)[26]

The same a priori argument gives an answer to the second question.

> If the name of perception renders not this separation from a mind absurd and contradictory, the name of object, standing for the very same thing, can never render their conjunction impossible. External objects are seen, and felt, and become present to the mind; that is, they acquire such a relation to a connected heap of perceptions, as to influence them very considerably in augmenting their number by present reflections and passions, and in storing the memory with ideas. The same continu'd and uninterrupted being may, therefore, be sometimes present to the mind, and sometimes absent from it, without any real or essential change in the being itself. (1.4.2.40)

What is metaphysically possible, here, is not simply that objects be somehow joined with the mind. This might simply be a way to describe the intentional relation between the mind and its objects, by way of seeing, feeling, or perceiving. What Hume says is that it is metaphysically possible for an object to be joined with the mind without the creation of a new perception or image, that is, simply as the perception *and* the object that *it is* and because of its inclusion in the causal connection of the mind. External objects or bodies can stand in the relations, connections, and durations that make them to be internal to the mind, in the only intelligible conceivable way in which we can think of this.[27]

---

[26] This is also one of his main points in the discussion of materialism and dualism at 1.4.5.

[27] V. C. Chappell, 'Hume on What There Is', Royal Institute of Philosophy, 5, 1972 in Tweyman, ed., *David Hume. Critical Assessments*, Volume 3, 77–87) sketches an ontology of Humean perceptions not too different from the one I have proposed: a perception 'is (A) something that is perceived, (B)

We can and should be suspicious of Hume's blunt treatment of issues of intentionality and of subjective consciousness. Still, his picture of the idea of continued, independent, and external existence, and its parsimonious metaphysical implications, has some attractions. Bodies, individuated by their qualities, can be seen or felt and thus exist in the mind (count as perceptions). Perceptions, individuated by their contents, can externally exist with their qualities (count as bodies). Therefore, there is neither specific difference nor numerical distinction between bodies and perceptions: they are 'the very same thing'. Internal existence is not metaphysically necessary for perceptions (therefore their appearance is not all there is to their existence) just as external existence is not metaphysically necessary to objects. This is neatly summarized by Hume as follows.

> The same continu'd and uninterrupted Being may, therefore, be sometimes present to the mind, and sometimes absent from it, without any real or essential change in the being itself. An interrupted appearance to the senses implies not necessarily an interruption in the existence. (1.4.2.40)

This goes beyond anything warranted by Two Viewpoints and Equivalence. The modal dimension of Hume's argument and of this conclusion is crucial. No change in conception and in being takes place across the divide of perceptions and objects: existing within or without the mind is a metaphysical possibility for the same object. In either regard, existence is not appearance. My conclusion is that Hume proposes a viable ontology of bodies and perceptions, hinging on their specific and numerical identity. One might object that Hume is only giving voice to the vulgar view of external existence. But true philosophy can be closer to the vulgar view than to false philosophy. And, while there is an error in the vulgar view, it is not that of asserting the identity of perceptions and bodies but of mistaking the nature of the relevant modalities (see § 9.5.1). Most importantly, the metaphysical contingency of the locations, durations, and connections that constitute the difference between presence to and absence from the mind, is required by the conception of the mind as bundle or flux of perceptions, which is a non-negotiable part of Hume's science of human nature.[28]

---

something that represents something or has content, and (C) a particular' (78). Differently from Chapell, however, I think that Hume draws, by and large, the right distinctions between (A) and (B). I also doubt that there is a contrast between a 'Lockean' ontology in Parts 1, 2, of Book 1 of the *Treatise* and a 'trans-Berkelyan', phenomenalist one in Part 4. The theory of perceptions as particulars, of external objects, and of properties developed in Part 4 essentially provides the metaphysical support for the ontology of perceptions; integrates rather than replacing the views about mind, content, and objects put forward in the preceding parts of Book 1. (This of course is not to say that such metaphysical support is free from problems.)

[28] Rocknak, *Imagined Causes*, 173–6 rightly remarks that, even though it is part of his discussion of the vulgar view, these claims express Hume's own ontology of external existence.

9.4.2 Bodies Existing with the Qualities of Impressions

The metaphysical possibility that perceptions exist as bodies is mirrored in Hume's conception of the properties with which bodies exist. This is put forward in Section 1.4.4: *Of modern philosophy*, a notoriously difficult text, which I will consider only for what it tells about the content of the idea of body.[29]

The 'fundamental principle' of modern philosophy is that colours, sounds, tastes, and so on are 'nothing but impressions in the mind, deriv'd from the operation of external objects, and without any resemblance to the qualities of the objects' (1.4.4.3). Hume's discussion of this principle and of its implications has the form of an antinomy. The first side of the antinomy is a causal argument, regarded by Hume as 'satisfactory', in support of the principle. The argument is 'deriv'd from the variations of those impressions, [secondary qualities] even while the external object, to all appearance, continues the same' (1.4.4.3). Examples of such variations are cases in which the conditions of our body or environmental factors change our sense-perceptions without a change in the objects. 'Instances of this kind are very numerous and frequent'. From these observations, Hume draws a causal inference—an inference that applies and compares the idea of cause—to a conclusion 'as satisfactory as can be imagined'. The argument is in three steps:

(1) 'When different impressions of the same sense arise from any object, every one of these impressions has not a resembling quality existent in the object' (1.4.4.4).
(2) We accept causal uniformity: 'From like effects we presume like causes.'
(3) 'Many of the impressions of colour, sound etc. are confest to be nothing but internal existences, and to arise from causes, which no way resemble them. These impressions are in appearance nothing different from the other impressions of colour, sound, etc.'
(4) 'We conclude, therefore, that they are, all of them, deriv'd from a like origin.'

The further conclusion of modern philosophy is that these qualities are removed 'from the rank of continu'd independent existences' (1.4.4.5). Primary qualities: extension and solidity, and figure, motion, gravity, and cohesion, are 'the only *real* ones, of which we have any adequate notion'. These qualities are the

---

[29] See the important suggestion in Noonan, *Hume on Knowledge*, 82: 'To appreciate Hume's confidence that he has here hit upon a logical truth, [about the determinateness of impressions] it is important to recall the point that impressions for Hume are not representations of other (external) things, as even ideas of sensation are for Locke; and are themselves (the only) possessors of both primary and secondary qualities. Thus, to deny the determinateness of impressions, for Hume, is to acknowledge indeterminacy *in the world*.'

principles of the material universe, of the 'elements and powers of nature', 'of which we can form the most distant idea'. I do not see why Hume should not find this cosmological conclusion, and possibly the argument leading to it, as satisfactory.[30]

The second side of his antinomy is a 'very decisive' objection. The objection is that by the satisfactory conclusion of modern philosophy 'instead of explaining the operations of external objects' we 'utterly annihilate all these objects, and reduce ourselves to the opinions of the most extravagant scepticism' (1.4.4.6). If secondary qualities are 'merely perceptions', primary ones are also; and 'nothing we can conceive is possest of a real, continu'd, and independent existence; not even motion, extension and solidity, which are the primary qualities chiefly insisted on' (1.4.4.6). Hume argues for this side of the antinomy a priori, by way of conceptual analysis of the ideas of motion, extension, and solidity. The idea of motion is inconceivable alone and 'necessarily supposes that of a body moving'. In this way it 'must resolve itself into an idea of extension or solidity' (1.4.4.7). The idea of extension can only be conceiv'd 'as compos'd of parts, endow'd with colour or solidity' (1.4.4.8). Since 'colour is excluded from any real existence', its reality depends on that of the idea of solidity. The idea of solidity, in turn, is that of two bodies, 'which being impell'd by the utmost force, cannot penetrate each other' (1.4.4.9). But since bodies can be conceived neither in terms of secondary qualities nor in terms of solidity, we are left without resources for conceiving of bodies at all. Hume regards this argument as 'entirely conclusive'. 'Upon the whole [we] must conclude, that after the exclusion of colours, sounds, heat and cold from the rank of external existence, there remains nothing, which can afford us a just and consistent idea of body' (1.4.4.10). Hume draws from the consideration of the two arguments a famously sceptical conclusion.

> Thus there is a direct and total opposition betwixt our reason and our senses; or more properly speaking, betwixt those conclusions we form from cause and effect, and those that persuade us of the continu'd and independent existence of body. When we reason from cause and effect, we conclude, that neither colour,

---

[30] Loeb, *Stability and Justification*, 221–3 and Ainslie, *True Scepticism*, 201–5 deny that the argument to the conclusion is satisfactory. Loeb claims that the generalizing step (resembling effects, resembling causes) ignores differences, which may be relevant, between impressions. For instance, phenomenal differences. However, Hume's argument is a form of the Argument from Illusion, so that the relevant resemblance between impressions is their self-imposing, qualitative manifestation to awareness. Arguments from Illusion are perhaps answerable: but no particular answer can be non-problematically relied upon. Ainslie claims that Hume does not endorse the argument of modern philosophers, because he is unproblematically committed to mind–body causation; because he is not committed to the view that we are always aware of our inner perceptions; and because he regards our beliefs about internal perceptions as equally in need of explanation as those about external bodies. I am not sure that these are grounds strong enough for the conclusion that Hume does not accept the principle of modern philosophy (or the related conclusion about the falsity of the vulgar belief), as he says he does.

sound, taste, nor smell have a continu'd and independent existence. When we exclude these sensible qualities there remains nothing in the universe, which has such an existence. (1.4.4.15)

Hume reprises and amplifies this conclusion in the final assessment of the results of Book 1, with particular reference to the principles and products of imagination (in a footnote to this text Hume refers back to 1.4.4).

'Tis this principle, ['the imagination, or the vivacity of ideas'] which makes us reason from causes and effects; and 'tis the same principle, which convinces us of the continu'd existence of external objects, when absent from the senses. But tho' these two operations be equally natural and necessary in the human mind, yet in some circumstances they are directly contrary, nor is it possible for us to reason justly and regularly from causes and effects, and at the same time believe the continu'd existence of matter. (1.4.7.4).

The opposition is between the causal inference leading to the conclusion that secondary qualities exist only in the mind and the idea and belief of continued and distinct existence, the contents of which can only consist of such qualities (colour, feeling).

The lesson that Hume draws from the arguments and from this conclusion is somewhat elusive. The argument is 'satisfactory' and the objection is 'decisive'. But this is just how it should be with an antinomy, of course; and to make good a corresponding claim of scepticism. I think that it is interesting that Hume does not press against modern philosophy or against the objection the point of the psychological unsustainability of an extravagantly sceptical conclusion. He actually does not seem to regard either the satisfactory conclusion or the entirely conclusive objection as per se sceptical at all. What is problematic, what is indeed a 'manifest contradiction' (1.4.7.4), is their combination. In this regard, I would suggest that, as it is the case with Kant's antinomies, the root of the manifest contradiction seems to be some sort of error of presupposition. This is a reconstructive reading; but Hume's text is in need of reconstruction. It is interesting that the arguments for two sides of the antinomy are logically so different, being respectively a posteriori and a priori. The argument for the principle of modern philosophy is a sound instance of causal reasoning, to the conclusion that impressions of secondary qualities are unreliable indicators of the properties of bodies (anyway, less reliable than those of primary ones). It is physically possible that the body, individuated by its primary qualities, remain the same, while our experience of it, in terms of secondary qualities, changes. This is an empirical claim, which Hume certainly endorses, given its importance for modern physics. By contrast, the conclusion about our loss of the idea of external existence, based on the inseparability of primary and secondary qualities in the content of the idea of body, is a relatively a priori claim in 'logic', the theory of ideas and understanding. The extravagant sceptical conclusion follows only on the false presupposition that the empirical conclusion bears on the definition of the content of the idea of body. Or, that the consideration of the causation of sense-impressions determines their role in the genesis of contents. On this basis, the physical possibility of a divergence between primary and secondary qualities ends by individuating the content of the idea of body; while, in that regard, there is only a distinction of reason between them. We could say that the manifest contradiction derives from mistaking for metaphysical possibilities concerning primary and secondary qualities what are physical possibilities concerning the relations between bodies and bodies and minds.

These seem to be the 'circumstances' in which the two accounts, and the two natural and necessary operations of the imagination, conflict and give rise to sceptical troubles. That is, the supposition that excluding secondary qualities from natural philosophy is to exclude them from the content of our idea of body and thereby of continued and distinct existence. While, given the specific sameness of perceptions and bodies, their ideas must share the same individuating qualities, and the content of the idea of external existence must be conceived of in terms of primary and secondary qualities. In some respects, we have encountered a similar situation in Hume's discussion of finite divisibility. When discussing of visible minima, Hume remarks that we can say, on the basis of causal reasoning, that some bodies are much smaller than the bodies that are presented by our minimal visual impressions. But that this is consistent with denying that they are infinitely smaller, meaning by this that, were they made visible, they would still be presented by our minimal impressions. The first is a claim in natural philosophy, the second a claim in logic (the theory of ideas). This also defines the true philosophy of primary and secondary qualities. From the perspective of Hume's own theory, the manifest contradiction is rightly what should be expected, if one fails to make the right distinctions between the two arguments. And one can commit consistently to the two arguments, by dropping any attempt to combine them, or to exclude the one in favour of the other, just as one should do in the case of minimal visual impressions.[31]

On this reading, the argument of 1.4.4 has no sceptical implications against the a posteriori, empirical claim that secondary qualities have a more limited

---

[31] My conclusions come close, if by a different interpretive route, to Ainslie, *True Scepticism*, 204–5. See also Price, *External World*, 106: the manifest contradiction is between the causal or scientific and the supplementary (that is, content–constitutive) employment of imagination. One could suggest that the contradiction can also be resolved by a consideration of the Structural Principle. The argument of modern philosophy relies on idea-comparing reasoning. The decisive objection is at the level of how the more limited imagination constitutes the idea of body.

cosmological and informational role than the primary ones. What we know from empirical enquiry about the causation of experience tells us that sight and feeling are more reliable indicators of properties in the environment than olfactory or auditory sensorial modes, because of their causal patterns and in normal conditions. But equally, it has no sceptical implications against the a priori claim of Hume's logic or about the nature of ideas, that the ideas of bodies or matter merge in their contents primary and secondary qualities. Furthermore, if bodies exist with both sorts of qualities, which are also the qualities that constitute internal perceptions, then they can exist internally, in the mind, with all their qualities, without any essential change and without the need for a new perception. Furthermore, again, conflating considerations about the causation of sense-impressions and their role in the constitution of mental content is a root of a false philosophy of external existence, hinging on causal relations and resemblance between numerically different perceptions and objects (see § 9.5.1).

9.5 Scepticism with Regard to the Senses

For Hume, as we have seen, the identity of perceptions and bodies is metaphysically possible and is what we can conceive a priori about external existence. But he also connects this view to his explanatory target: 'I here account for the opinions and belief of the vulgar with regard to the existence of body; and therefore must entirely conform myself to their manner of thinking and expressing themselves'. This is because the idea of external existence is instantiated, in the first place, in our compelling sense of immersion in a real and durable world. The view that the shoe now sensibly present to me is the shoe that would exist unobserved seems to be part of this ordinary attitude of realism. But the status of the vulgar belief in body is precarious; and with it, the status of belief in body in general. One of Hume's initial arguments for identifying the source of belief in body in the imagination is that the 'sentiment' of the vulgar that 'the very things they feel or see' have 'distinct continu'd existence' is 'entirely unreasonable' and therefore cannot proceed from the understanding (1.4.2.14). Hume has frequent resort, with respect of the idea of external existence and in the context of the constancy account, to talk of 'error', 'deception', and 'illusion' (1.4.2.32, 1.4.2.56). He also contends that the 'fiction of a continued existence' and the 'identity' of resembling perceptions are 'really false, as is acknowledg'd by all philosophers, and has no other effect than to remedy the interruption of our perceptions, which is the only circumstance that is contrary to their identity' (1.4.2.43). And of course, the title of 1.4.6 and its opening and closing, in their arguments and rhetoric, manifest a strong concern for sceptical issues. There are opposing conceptual pressures on the numerical identity of objects and perceptions and, in this respect, on the idea of external existence.

9.5.1 The Vulgar and the Philosophical Belief

Hume distinguishes, in the concluding part of 1.4.2, two forms of belief in body and of the corresponding idea. The vulgar belief makes no distinction between perceptions and objects, perceptions are taken just to be bodies: 'a single existence'. The philosophical belief is based on the difference, distinction, and separation of internal perceptions and external objects and on their relations of causation and resemblance: 'a double existence and representation' (1.4.2.31).

It is crucial to understand the exact relationship between the two forms of belief. The philosophical belief is a response to the empirical falsehood of the vulgar belief: experiment and observation show, on causal grounds, that perceptions have no independent and therefore no continued existence. Confronted with the empirical evidence of the mind-dependent being of perceptions and unable to reject the natural opinion of the continued existence of bodies, philosophers resort to the view that bodies and perceptions are different kinds of existents. Hume claims that, this opposition notwithstanding, the philosophical belief is derivative on the vulgar one. 'There are no principles either of the understanding or fancy, which lead us directly to embrace this opinion of the double existence of perceptions and objects, nor can we arrive at it but by passing thro' the common hypothesis of the identity and continuance of our interrupted perceptions' (1.4.2.46). This is because of its mental genesis: the philosophical belief is possible only on the basis of the cognitive effects that constancy has on the imagination; as well as of the elements of its content, the identity of perceptions, and continued existence. The explanation of the idea of external existence by the imagination also decides of the different forms of the corresponding belief.

> Were we not first perswaded, that our perceptions are our only objects, and continue to exist even when they no longer make their appearance to the senses, we shou'd never be led to think, that our perceptions and objects are different, and that our objects alone preserve a continu'd existence. *The latter hypothesis has no primary recommendation either to reason or the imagination, but acquires all its influence on the imagination from the former.* (1.4.2.46)

Reason, the idea-comparing imagination, cannot primarily recommend the hypothesis of double existence, because we can never observe a conjunction of objects and perceptions and therefore can never infer the existence of objects from perceptions (1.4.2.47). And Hume denies that the more limited imagination could engage in a transition from interrupted perceptions to distinct, if resembling, persisting objects, without the intermediate steps (themselves owing to the imagination) of the identity of perceptions and of their own continued existence as bodies (1.4.2.48). This is the vulgar belief. A little reflection and few experiments show that perceptions have only mind-dependent existence. Thus, philosophers, who except for a 'few extravagant sceptics' hold fast to the idea of body, 'change their system' (1.4.2.47) and generate a 'new hypothesis' (1.4.2.51). In order to reconcile the identity and the interruption of constant perceptions in terms of continued existence, they draw a distinction 'betwixt perceptions and objects, of which the former are supposd to be interrupted, and perishing, and different at every return; the latter to be uninterrupted, and to preserve a continu'd existence and identity' (1.4.2.46).

The vulgar and the philosophical belief are therefore two varieties of the constancy account. They are based on mental mechanisms that are mostly the same and stand in a clear relation of explanatory ordering. A principle of the more limited imagination that underlies the philosophical belief but is not mentioned in connection with the vulgar one is *Completion*: the propensity of the more limited imagination to add one relation to another in order to complete the union of perceptions.

> The relation of cause and effect determines us to join the other of resemblance; and the ideas of these existences being already united together in the fancy by the former relation, we naturally add the latter to compleat the union. We have a strong propensity to compleat every union by joining new relations to those which we have before observ'd betwixt any ideas   (1.4.2.55)

The two kinds of belief differ in regard of to how the more limited imagination implements Reconciliation: the distinction of the existence and the appearance of perceptions ('The interruption consequently extends not beyond the appearance, and the perception or object really continues to exist, even when absent from us', 1.4.2.50) or the double existence of perceptions and objects.

What we have just seen dooms the philosophical belief. Both beliefs are flawed. The vulgar belief is empirically false, as 'a very little reflection and philosophy' can unveil (1.4.2.44). Experiments and reasoning make us perceive that the doctrine of the independent existence of our perceptions is 'contrary to the plainest experience'. The 'experiments' are cases of psychophysical causation and standard fare in the sceptical discussions of the senses: double vision; the difference between real and apparent size; alterations in perception because of alterations in the organs of sense; and 'an infinite number of other experiments of the same kind; from all which we learn, that our sensible perceptions are not possest of any distinct or independent existence' (1.4.2.45). The philosophical belief reacts to the falsity of the vulgar one. But Hume firmly denies that it provides a sound alternative to the vulgar one. This is completely explicit and no amount of interpretive manoeuvring can change the situation. 'This philosophical system, therefore, is the monstrous offspring of two principles, which are contrary to each other, which are both at once embrac'd by the mind, and which are unable mutually to destroy each other' (1.4.2.52). The two principles are the propensities of the more limited imagination, which make us conceive of resembling and interrupted perceptions as identical and continuedly existing; and representation and idea-comparing reasoning, which tell us that they are different and separable.

The epistemic position of the philosophical system is in fact *worse* than that of the vulgar belief. 'But however philosophical this new system may be esteem'd, I assert that 'tis only a palliative remedy, and that it contains all the difficulties of the vulgar system, with some others, that are peculiar to itself' (1.4.2.46). The 'difficulties' that are common to the two beliefs are those inherent to imperfect identity, which is their common source in the constancy account. Insofar as the identity of constant perceptions is imperfect because it is false—and it is false, 1.4.2.43—the philosophical belief, whose content is causally based on imperfect identity, is based on a false assumption; just as the vulgar one is. Of course, the philosophical belief does not include the empirically false claim that what exist continuedly are our perceptions. But this does not make things better for it, because it is 'loaded with this absurdity, that it at once denies and establishes the vulgar supposition' (1.4.2.56). Philosophers reject the view that our resembling perceptions are identical and uninterrupted: what is the same and uninterrupted are bodies, which are different beings from perceptions. In this, they reject the vulgar belief. But they tacitly assume the identity and uninterruptedness of perceptions in order to give content to the double existence claim. They 'have so great a propensity to believe them [the perceptions] such [uninterrupted and the same], that they arbitrarily invent a new set of perceptions, to which they attribute these qualities. I say, a new set of perceptions: For we may well suppose in general, but 'tis impossible for us distinctly to conceive, objects to be in their nature any thing but exactly the same with perceptions' (1.4.2.56). In this, they accept the vulgar supposition. Therefore, philosophers end up by affirming and denying that perceptions are 'identically the same, and uninterrupted'.

I think that this absurdity is rooted in a fundamental modal error. Philosophers mistake the physical necessity that perceptions exist dependently on certain, actual causal connections for a metaphysical necessity. In this way, they exclude that perceptions can exist distinctly and continuedly; that the very same beings can exist both with and without the different relations, connexions, and durations that constitute continued and independent existence. This has the consequence that they miss the metaphysical possibility of a divergence between the appearance and the existence of perceptions, as an intelligible way of reconciling the conflict between identity and interruption of perceptions; and they plunge in the absurdity of double existence. Alternatively, philosophers might conceive of external objects merely by relative ideas. But this would fail to establish even the appearance of a metaphysical possibility. It is interesting that this kind of modal error is the same with one that Hume regards as widespread among the vulgar and therefore as natural and expectable (it has a counterpart in causal cognition): mistaking a difficulty or determination to conceive for absolute inconceivability (1.4.3.9). By contrast, if one takes into account the difference in kind of modality, the denial of the physical possibility of independently existing perceptions is perfectly consistent with the affirmation of their metaphysical possibility; in this way, the numerical identity of perceptions and objects is not restricted to the vulgar belief. The vulgar belief has an implicit grasp of the right metaphysical possibilities concerning the existence of body, or matter: the same things can be present to or absent from the mind. But, on the other hand, it is blind to the fact that the external existence of perceptions and the internal existence of bodies are only metaphysical possibilities. That there is physical necessity to existence within the mind (presence) or without the mind (absence), because of their consisting in different causal connections. The simple psychophysical experiments show precisely that perceptions can physically only exist dependently on their causal conditions, that is, on the mind (the other perceptions they are bundled with). This is an empirical error, an error in psychophysics; but it involves no absurdity.

9.5.2 The Sceptical Malady and Hume's Realism

The roots of the empirically false vulgar belief in body are intertwined with those of the absurd philosophical belief. Such 'confusion of groundless and extraordinary opinions', of 'error and falsehood' (1.4.2.56) is an obvious source of scepticism. In fact, the dialectic of vulgar and philosophical belief expands into a more fundamental one between implicit faith and sceptical doubt concerning external existence. Hume addresses this issue at the very end of 1.4.2.

> Having thus given an account of all the systems both popular and philosophical, with regard to external existences, I cannot forbear giving vent to a certain sentiment, which arises upon reviewing those systems. I begun this subject with premising, that we ought to have an implicit faith in our senses, and that this wou'd be the conclusion, I shou'd draw from the whole of my reasoning. But to be ingenuous, I feel myself *at present* of a quite contrary sentiment, and am more inclin'd to repose no faith at all in my senses, or rather imagination, than to place in it such an implicit confidence.   (1.4.2.56)

The inclination to scepticism springs from the consideration of the operations of the more limited imagination that underlie belief in body in all its forms. The sceptical, epistemological concerns ('How can we justify to ourselves any belief we repose in them?', 1.4.2.56) are grounded on features of the content of our ideas and of its production by the imagination. Sceptical threats are endemic to human cognition, on Hume's account of it, because the pattern of cognitive gaps and works of imagination forces deep revisions of the content and application of our most common ideas. Still, there are differences in Hume's attitude to the idea of external existence and to other products of the imagination, like general and modal ideas, the ideas of space and time, the foundations of mathematics, the idea of cause and of causal necessity, possibly even the ideas of an empty space and time. These differences can be explained with the character of the corresponding operations of the imagination and with the kind of cognitive role associated to the missing ideas. The cognitive role of the idea of continued and distinct existence, as we have seen, is well determined only in relation to causal reasoning about external objects. But, as Hume remarks, the idea of a real and durable world is 'so vast an edifice' that its application cannot be restricted to causal reasoning. The explanation of the idea of body, in its turn, involves a stratification of principles of the imagination, some of which, like Act/Idea Resemblance and Reconciliation, mark a radical deviation from representation and reasoning. Both principles condition the change and transposition of ideas on factors like the what-is-it-like of mental activity or the tensions issuing from having conflicting views. Differently from custom-based inferential propensities, or even from Separability and Determination (which specify ultimately content-responsive conditions of conceivability), these principles are not well correlated with object representation and comparison of ideas. They may have further, important cognitive roles; but of an indirect, inherently more problematic character. This divergence between what we can conceive and believe and what we can represent or conclude to in reasoning is the source of the sceptical troubles about a real and durable world.

Hume's response to such sceptical threats draws, in turn, on properties of the more limited imagination. Hume turns against the sceptic the trivial character of the principles of imagination involved in the idea of body that had invited scepticism in the first place. This is an argumentative line that Hume exploits in 1.4.1 and rehearses and generalizes in 1.4.7 (see § 11.3.1 for further discussion). Reflection and reasoning unveil the trivial character of the principles of the imagination underlying many of our ideas, their lack of the credentials from sensible representation or reason; in this way, they open the door to scepticism. However, because of the influence of these principles on our imagination, we do not respond steadily or monotonically to reflection and argument. A stance of reflection and reasoning in opposition to the propensities and transitions of the imagination, that it, a sceptical stance, is unsustainable. 'Sceptical doubt' with respect both to reason and the senses is a 'malady, which can never be radically cur'd, but must return upon us every moment', if only at intervals (1.4.2.57). The remedy is not reflection, which only increases our doubts (it is their source). 'Carelessness and in-attention alone can afford us any remedy. For this reason I rely entirely upon them; and take it for granted, whatever may be the reader's opinion at this present moment, that an hour hence he will be persuaded there is both an external and internal world.'[32] Carelessness and inattention are possible and expectable because reflection goes against the grain of the more limited imagination. They support our idea and belief of external existence precisely because they give rein to the propensities on which these are based. In this way, the imagination is both the cause and the remedy of sceptical doubt about the continued and distinct existence of sensible objects (this is how we should understand Hume's 'scepticism about the senses').

However, there is more to Hume's response to scepticism about the senses. Carelessness and inattention must be viable: they must bring us back to a position that we can cognitively sustain. The reconciliation and the reiteration of our conflicted cognitive states should converge on some sort of partial, intelligible equilibrium. In this respect, the main consideration is the consistency of the vulgar idea and belief of external existence: 'the supposition of the continu'd existence of sensible objects or perceptions involves no contradiction', so that 'we may easily indulge our inclination to this supposition' (1.4.2.40). Under this guise, as we ordinarily have it, the idea of external existence is a real cognitive possibility and can put limits to scepticism. By contrast, the philosophical belief is false philosophy. It marks a progress on the vulgar opinion because it recognizes the vulgar error of thinking that perceptions, as matter of physical possibility, can exist mind-independently. But the philosophical belief is untenable, because it mistakes for a metaphysical possibility what is at most an epistemic possibility: a relative idea of what exits without the mind. The interesting question is what the true philosophy of external existence is. Quite obviously, it is Hume's own, with its central claims. The idea of continued and distinct existence is a product of the imagination. External objects and internal perceptions are qualitatively the same, their difference consisting in locations, connections, and durations. Those locations, connections, and durations are separable from their objects, so that the very same things can exist within the mind (perceptions) or without it (bodies). On these grounds, once the right distinctions have been drawn, we can take an attitude of 'indolence and indifference' with regard to metaphysical disquisitions (as Don Garrett has pointed out to me), as well as to the errors of the vulgar.

True philosophy marks a progress over the vulgar opinion, just as false philosophy does, because it denies that it is physically possible for perceptions to exist independently. It also marks a progress on false philosophy because it does not entertain the idea of the double existence of perceptions and objects. Then, in what respect is true philosophy closer to the sentiments of the vulgar than to false philosophy? Quite simply, in respect of their sharing, even though in a

---

[32] 'Our propensity to this mistake is so great from the resemblance above-mention'd, that we fall into it before we are aware; and tho' we incessantly correct ourselves by reflection, and return to a more accurate method of thinking, yet we cannot long sustain our philosophy, or take off this biass from the imagination. Our last resource is to yield to it, and boldly assert that these different related objects are in effect the same, however interrupted and variable' (1.4.6.6).

respectively unreflective or reflective manner, the views that internal perceptions are numerically identical with external objects, that appearance is not all there is to the existence of perceptions, or that the inner-outer distinction is no deep metaphysical divide. What the true philosophy adds to the vulgar opinion is the reflective understanding of the conditions of our possessing the idea of external existence.[33] I would thus suggest that the imagination, as it is involved in the production of the idea of continued and distinct existence, may have epistemic virtues; and that, insofar as the conception of that idea licensed by Hume's 'true philosophy' is sound, the vulgar belief, which comes close to it, is valuable too.

It will be objected that Hume declares the vulgar belief false and that its falsity invests the view that perceptions can exist independently of the mind; that is, it invests the thesis of the numerical identity of perceptions and objects. But the vulgar belief, as we have seen, is *empirically* false: it is false on a point of psychophysics, about the empirical, physically necessary conditions of having perceptions. In our nature, internal experiences or perceptions causally depend on bodily and environmental conditions. By ignoring or overlooking this fact, as they are likely to do in their insouciance about natural philosophy, the vulgar embrace a false empirical conception of sense-perception and expose themselves to confutation by philosophy, true and false (the experiments considered by Hume are standard in the sceptical tradition).[34] But this leaves intact the claim of the numerical identity of perceptions and objects. This doctrine of true philosophy and this grain of truth of the vulgar belief identify a metaphysical possibility.

One will also object that Hume is committed to the double existence of perceptions and external objects and the causal dependence of the first on the second by his recognition that impressions of sensation could be caused by bodies (by bodies in the environment or by our own body). Original impressions 'without any antecedent perception arise in the soul, from the constitution of the body, from the animal spirit, or from the application of objects to the external organs' (2.1.1.1; see also 1.3.5.2).[35] The metaphysical possibility of such causal relations requires that bodies and impressions are distinct, different, and separable beings. ('As long as we take our perceptions and objects to be the same, we can never infer the existence of the one from that of the other, nor from any argument from the relation of cause and effect', 1.4.214). But this remark can be countered. Hume explicitly *denies* that the philosophical belief provides the resources for a causal theory of sensible representation ('Even after we distinguish our perceptions from our objects, 'twill appear presently, that we are still incapable of reasoning from the existence of the one to that of the other.') By contrast, Hume *has* such a theory

---

[33] For a discussion along these lines, see Loeb, *Stability and Justification*, 210–11.
[34] See Price, *External World*, 113–16; Stroud, *Hume*, 111; Ainslie, *True Scepticism*, 106–8.
[35] See for instance Kail, *Reality and Projection*, 106; Garrett, *Hume*, 104; Ainslie, *True Scepticism*, 144–5.

available, without having to resort to the double existence of bodies and perceptions. This causal theory is advanced right in the course of the constancy account. The mind is nothing but a heap or collection of different perceptions, united by causal relations. Every perception can exist separately from any other; therefore it can exist (in the guise of a body) without any mind. Reciprocally, any body can be conjoined with a mind and be present to it, without the creation of a new perception. These possibilities simply consist in the onset of causal relations between different beings that are bodies *and* perceptions and that can compose or fail to compose minds or heaps of perceptions (1.4.2.39–40). Hume therefore construes the sensible representation of bodies in causal terms. But the causal connections that matter are those that connect perceptions, which also are bodies, into a heap or bundle, a mind. The distinct existence postulated by the metaphysical possibility of causation is that of the individual perceptions or bodies, not that of two classes of beings, perceptions and bodies. This schematic account, which does not involve any sort of 'funky' (non-efficient) causation, makes room for the natural-philosophical study of sensible representation.[36] As Hume says, the causation of impressions of sensation is not a matter for moral philosophy. 'As these [impressions of sensation] depend upon natural and physical causes, the examination of them wou'd lead me too far from my present subject, into the sciences of anatomy and natural philosophy' (2.1.1.2; see 1.1.3.1).

Hume's scepticism about the senses, that is, the radical limits he imposes, on content-theoretical and naturalistic grounds, on what we can represent and conclude by reasoning about bodies, is, however, consistent with a commitment of realism about the external world. Hume can uphold a position of empirical realism. Insofar as our empirical enquiries into the causes of sense-experience are successful, we can form correct beliefs about bodies and external existence in general and about how sense-perception represent them. Our empirical information about these processes and their reliability may well be limited; but they involve no metaphysical or epistemological mystery. Hume's moral philosophy, the science of human nature, complements empirical realism, the (qualifiedly reliable) the natural-philosophical enquiry into the objects and conditions of sense-experience, with a position of non-sceptical realism. The metaphysical possibility that the same things exist within and without the mind is equivalent, as we have seen, to a deep, metaphysical distinction of existing and appearing, of *esse* and *percipi*. And this is the core insight of Hume's realism about the external world. In light of Hume's ontology of perceptions and bodies, nothing bars us from forming a consistent idea of a world existing continuedly and independently

---

[36] See Ainslie, *True Scepticism*, 204, fn. 20. The inclusion of perceptions in the causally connected heap of a mind is a simple mereological matter. Nothing but efficient causation is needed for grounding such inclusion. See Price, *External World*, 120–1 (on the difference between a selective and a generative theory of the physiology of sensation); Loeb, *Stability and Justification*, 210–11.

of us. The real and durable world is specifically the same with our perceptions: the qualities of sense-experience are the qualities with which bodies and matter exist as well as the condition of their conceivability and metaphysical possibility. (This position of monism or radical empiricism was not lost on James and Russell.)[37] There are grounds for scepticism about the external world only insofar as we look for some sort of representation of it or we attempt to derive its existence by reasoning. But once the true, non-representational content of the idea is recognized, our cognitive limits with respect to the world as real and durable turn out to be consistent with our having a conceivable idea of body and external existence, which does not fall short of establishing their metaphysical possibility. And of our possibly having true beliefs about what exists without the mind, what exists as distinct from what appears.[38]

9.6 Summary

The difficulty of Hume's theory of the external world depends on its complex background of cognitive gaps and operations of the imagination, on the different forms its idea takes, and on the elusiveness of its indispensable role in our cognition. This is also the root of Hume's sceptical concerns in this area.

§ 9.1 deals with the individuation of the corresponding cognitive gap. In § 9.1.1 I specify how only a qualitative idea of external existence (like that of a body) is clearly and distinctly conceivable and define a possible existence. The idea of external existence has relational character, consisting in the conditions of continued and independent existence of perceptions. These are the focus of Hume's account. § 9.1.2 discusses how such idea is missing from sensible representation. The modal dimension of the ideas of continued and distinct existence is crucial. Hume also denies that a priori or probable reason can be the source of the idea of external existence. The first because it is no source of ideas at all; the second because the conditions of causal inference are not satisfied. Only the imagination can put that idea in place.

The cognitive gap of external existence is refined in § 9.1.3. The interrupted character of perceptions is inconsistent with continued existence. Since the perceptions that we come to regard as externally existing are those that exhibit

---

[37] Hume outlines a highly original, naturalistic conception of the mind–world relations—one which is interesting in its own and deeply relevant both for Kant's philosophy and for forms of neutral monism. I have in mind, of course, views like those voiced by W. James in section 6 of his 'Does 'Consciousness' exist?' or in section 2 of 'How Two Minds can Know One Thing' (see *Essays in Radical Empiricism*, Dover, New York 2003 (1912), 14–18, 67–9) or by B. Russell (*The Analysis of Mind*, Allen and Unwin, London 1978 (1921), 25–6, 101–6, 124–36.
[38] See, for a critical discussion, Allison, *Custom and Reason*, 243–5.

constancy or coherence, the cognitive gap of body is finally individuated at the juncture of interruption and of constancy or coherence of perceptions.

§§ 9.2 and 9.3 discuss how the imagination produces the idea of body. § 9.2.1 shows how the coherence of perceptions links causal inference and external existence. Causal inferences, if taken to be about objects and not perceptions, compel the imagination to ascribe continued existence to the objects they are about. Otherwise, the scope of causal reasoning would be extremely restricted. The idea of body thus has a role in the context of causal cognition, but it is based on different principles of the imagination. In particular, as I show in § 9.2.2, the coherence account of the idea of body depends on Hysteresis, the cognitive inertia of the more limited imagination. The imagination produces a double cognitive change, shifting the burden of coherence from perceptions to objects; and to objects conceived as existing continuedly. Finally, in § 9.2.3, I discuss Hume's remark that the coherence account cannot fully explain our idea of the external world. I suggest that this points to the need for a further layer of explanation: coherence explains how we apply the idea of external existence to objects; not how we come to have it in the first place.

This is the task of the constancy account, discussed in § 9.3. In §§ 9.3.1 and 9.3.2 I address the first part of the constancy account, the idea of identity, perfect and imperfect, which the imagination applies to constant, interrupted perceptions. The idea of identity is non-representational and not derived from reason. Hume gives an analysis of the relation of identity as mediating unity and number; and explains it with his philosophy of time. The imagination can apply the idea of time beyond its representational limits, to unchanging objects. On this basis, it can occupy two viewpoints on such objects, considering them both as one and as multiple. This possibility comes to conception as the idea of identity across time. Then, the imagination can apply this idea, as imperfect identity, to interrupted but resembling objects. This transition badly correlates to representation and to causal reasoning.

The second part of the constancy account, discussed in § 9.3.3, is the transition from the imperfect identity of perceptions to the idea and belief of external existence. Hume explains this transition with the cognitive conflict between the represented interruption and the inferred identity of perceptions; the tension and uneasiness arising from such conflict; and the function of the imagination of reconciling such conflict by producing a suitable idea. This function is constrained by the underlying, persisting object-representing content of ideas. The reconciling idea takes the form of bodies: objects individuated by the same qualities with perceptions, but existing continuedly and distinctly. The same transition, conveying with the vividness of memory, explains belief of external existence.

In § 9.4 I discuss Hume's ontology of mental existence. The crucial questions, in § 9.4.1, are the relations between perceptions and bodies. I suggest that, for Hume, perceptions and bodies are numerically identical. The same being can exist within and without the mind; external or internal existence are metaphysically contingent conditions. This view entails and is entailed by Hume's conception of the mind as bundle or flux of perceptions. In § 9.4.2 I discuss an implication of the numerical identity of perceptions and bodies: bodies and perceptions can only exist with the same kinds of qualities; perceptions exist only with primary and secondary qualities; such qualities are inseparable also in bodies. This is consistent with inseparable entities being included in different causal connections; such difference is a physical possibility. This is the grain of truth of the modern philosophy of matter, which otherwise brings to sceptical conclusions.

Finally, in § 9.5, I discuss some difficulties with Hume's theory of the external world. As I point out in § 9.5.1, Hume distinguishes a vulgar from a philosophical belief of external existence. They differ as to whether perceptions and bodies are held to be numerically identical or different. Hume clearly holds that the philosophical belief is derivative on the vulgar one and a variant of the constancy account. Besides, the epistemic status of the philosophical belief is worse than that of the vulgar one. This latter is empirically false, since it neglects that it is causally, physically necessary for perceptions to exist in the mind. But the philosophical idea of the double existence of bodies and perceptions is inconsistent, a metaphysical impossibility.

In § 9.5.2 I take up the issue of scepticism. The modal errors underlying the two sorts of belief in body motivate radical sceptical doubts about the external world. Hume's response draws on the more limited imagination: the kind of reflection that opens the door to scepticism does not have a steady influence on the natural mind. But Hume also aims toward a viable, if unsteady cognitive position. In this respect, true philosophy is closer to the vulgar belief than to false philosophy, precisely because of its conception of external existence and of its commitment to a difference between appearance and existence of perceptions.

10
A Mind or Thinking Person

> The only question, therefore, which remains, is, by what relations this uninterrupted progress of our thought is produc'd, when we consider the successive existence of a mind or thinking person?
>
> (1.4.6.17)

Without the imagination, we would not confront with an external world; we would not attribute any existence to objects, 'but what was dependent on the senses'; we would 'comprehend them entirely in that succession of perceptions, which constitutes our self or person' (1.4.7.3). The same holds of 'our self or person': 'Nay farther, even with relation to that succession, we cou'd only admit of those perceptions, which are immediately present to our consciousness, nor cou'd those lively images, with which the memory presents us, be ever receiv'd as true pictures of past perceptions' (1.4.7.3). Hume's claim is condensed but we can articulate it as follows. Based on what we can represent of our perceptions by immediate consciousness we could admit or receive, that is, be aware of, only the present ones. To overstep by reflective representation the boundaries of present internal experience, we would have to receive or admit ideas of memory as true pictures or representations of past perceptions. But we cannot have such perceptions present at the same time and we cannot take some as representing some of the others. Any extension of our internal cognition beyond our present perceptions and any more comprehensive idea of our self or person therefore can only depend on the imagination. The internal world is not different from the external one; the distinction of the two systems of realities holds in both cases. Hume's account of the idea of self and personal identity thus proceeds from the identification of a gap in the representation we have by reflection (introspection, internal experience) of our perceptions and relies on the imagination to turn such representation into the conception of an 'internal world' (1.4.2.57) or 'intellectual world' (1.4.5.1). Or to turn it into an idea of our mind as a self or thinking person, identical across time and the succession of perceptions. (I will refer to it as the idea of self and personal identity.)[1]

---

[1] See, on the paradoxical character (in Hume's philosophy) of our practice of talking about people as single beings, T. Penelhum, 'Hume on Personal Identity', *The Philosophical Review*, 64, 1955 (in V. C. C. Chappell, *Hume. A Collection of Critical Essays*, Macmillan, London 1966 (213–39, 214)).

10.1 The Missing Ideas of Soul and Self

Throughout 1.4.5: *Of the immateriality of the soul*, and in the first part of 1.4. 6: *Of personal identity*, Hume argues on a priori and a posteriori grounds that reason and representation by reflection fail to put in place two ideas that seem central for understanding 'our internal perceptions, and the nature of the mind' (1.4.5.1): *thinking substance* and *self and personal identity*. However, the arguments and their targets and aims are different. In 1.4.5 Hume addresses the tradition, culminating in Descartes and his successors, which conceives the mind as a substance and, on the prevalent assumption of its immateriality, regards it as immediately present and better known than the body. In 1.4.6 he addresses the ideas of self and personal identity and implicitly targets Locke and the discussions issuing from his ground-breaking theory of personal identity.[2] Since Hume recognizes the need for a positive, productive role of the imagination only in relation to this latter, my discussion of thinking substance will be summary.

10.1.1 The Soul as Substance

The arguments in 1.4.5 focus on traditional metaphysical issues about thinking substance and are essentially negative, aiming to establish that there can be no idea of immaterial or material thinking substance or soul. Differently than in the case of personal identity, however, Hume does not search for an alternative, revisionary identification of the missing idea. As a purely philosophical fiction, it is well lost. Hume's criticism of philosophical views 'concerning the material or immaterial substances, in which they suppose our perceptions to inhere' (1.4.5.2) is at different levels and in different regards. He denies that we can have at all an idea of mind *as substance*: the claim that we have this idea is inconsistent, because it postulates that perceptions are not substances (so that they inhere in the thinking substance) but in this way leaves us without resources for conceiving at all of the 'substance of our minds' (1.4.5.3). 'For how can an impression represent a substance, otherwise than by resembling it? And how can an impression resemble a substance, since, according to this philosophy [the claim that perceptions inhere to a substance], it is not a substance, and has none of the peculiar qualities or characteristics of a substance?' This point can be put positively. Hume has a legitimate, thin notion of substance, answering to the conditions for counting as an existent or object, which comes to expression in Separability: 'a substance is

---

[2] See U. Thiel, *The Early Modern Subject*, Oxford University Press, Oxford 2011, for a detailed reconstruction of this background.

something which may exist by itself' (1.4.5.5). This definition, he observes, 'agrees to every thing, that can possibly be conceiv'd; and never will serve to distinguish substance from accident, or the soul from its perceptions'. It is thus inconsistent to apply the legitimate notion of substance, grounded on Separability, to distinguish a mental substance from non-substantial perceptions.

Hume's a priori arguments target the idea of thinking substance also from the viewpoint of its exhaustive and exclusive categorization as either material or immaterial. Given the concept of thinking substance as what perceptions necessarily belong to, and given what we know about perceptions, the soul as substance *must* be material or immaterial but it *cannot* be either. The argument builds on a claim already discussed: the 'maxim', which he says goes against the opinion of metaphysicians and (apparently) against the principles of human reason, that '*an object may exist, and yet be nowhere*'. Hume also adds that this is not only a possibility but a fact: 'the greatest part of beings do and must exist after this manner' (1.4.5.10). Hume has in mind perfectly natural beings (objects), that is, 'all our perceptions, except those of the sight and feeling'. These perceptions stand with others of the same kind and with the perceptions of sight and feeling in relations of causation and contiguity in time of appearance. The 'illusion' of their spatial location has its roots in these relations. However, considered in themselves, in their existence, these perceptions are 'utterly incapable' of location and 'exist without a place'. Given this, no substance in which they inhered could be material: 'in this view of things, we cannot refuse to condemn the materialists, who conjoin all thought with extension' (1.4.5.15). However, by the same argument, one must also reject the position of the immaterialists, 'who conjoin all thought with a simple and indivisible substance'. The perceptions of sight and touch are, in virtue of their representational role and content, extended: just as the objects they are or can be. By Two viewpoints, this is also a property of the qualities with which they exist.[3] 'And to cut short all disputes, the very idea of extension is copy'd from nothing but an impression, and consequently must perfectly agree to it. To say the idea of extension agrees to any thing, is to say it is extended' (1.4.5.15). The anti-materialist argument can therefore be reversed: 'The freethinker may now triumph in his turn; and having found there are impressions and ideas really extended, may ask his antagonists, how they can incorporate a simple and indivisible subject with an extended perception?' (1.4.5.16). Therefore, the idea of mind as substance is neither that of a material nor that of an immaterial substance. Thus, it has no genuine content.

---

[3] The role of the a priori conditions of representation or objecthood in this context is emphasized in the discussion of the mutual reducibility of the philosophy of Spinoza and of the doctrine of the immateriality and simplicity of a thinking substance (1.4.5.18–28).

10.1.2 Selfless Perceptions

While the idea of thinking substance is only to dismiss, the idea of self and personal identity requires a different treatment. In fact, it is only in connection with this latter idea that we can talk of a cognitive gap rather than of a target for scepticism. This depends on important differences between the ideas of soul and self. (Hume in this may have taken a lead from Locke. As we will see, the dialectics with Locke's theory of personal identity is crucial for understanding Hume.)

While the idea of soul is anchored on a flawed philosophical conception of substance, the idea of self or person includes a range of ordinary and philosophical forms and commitments, with different degrees of metaphysical involvement.

> Thus we feign the continu'd existence of the perceptions of our senses, to remove the interruption; and run into the notion of a *soul*, and *self*, and *substance*, to disguise the variation. But we may farther observe, that where we do not give rise to such a fiction, our propension to confound identity with relation is so great, that we are apt to imagine something unknown and mysterious, connecting the parts, beside their relation; and this I take to be the case with regard to the identity we ascribe to plants and vegetables. And even when this does not take place, we still feel a propensity to confound these ideas, tho' we are not able fully to satisfy ourselves in that particular, nor find any thing invariable and uninterrupted to justify our notion of identity. (1.4.6.6)

The idea of self is not necessarily the philosophical one of a strictly identical and simple mind. We can also conceive of it as an unknown and mysterious, nondescript principle of unity, like that of living beings, to which we somehow ascribe related perceptions as parts. It can even consist simply in an imaginative propensity to identify related perceptions: this latter, while not being manifest per se, is its actual, primitive content.

Self and personal identity ('which has become so great a question in philosophy, especially of late years in *England*') are certainly of concern for philosophers. But a view of ourselves as persons and a sense of our identity across time and change are also certainly aspects of the manifest image. The idea of self is ordinarily applied, first- or third-personally, in reflection and introspection and in imagination ('when I enter most intimately into what I call *myself*', 1.4.6.3; 'suppose we cou'd see clearly into the breast of another, and observe that succession of perceptions, which constitutes his mind', 1.4.6.18). As Hume remarks, it is an idea we have in 'common life', even though it is 'never very fix'd nor determinate' (1.4.2.6). This is important because the theoretical pattern of cognitive gaps and works of imagination presupposes, as we know, that the contents and cognitions to be explained have a firm place and some role in our cognitive practices and worldview. A too restrictive concentration on philosophical ideas, with the sceptical worries they inevitably raise, would severely restrict the import of Hume's discussion.[4]

Therefore, just as one cannot seriously ask whether there are bodies, one cannot seriously ask whether one is a self or person. Only on occasion, in abstract reflection, and against the background of this 'implicit faith', we can ask questions, in particular causal questions, about this idea and belief. A missing idea of self or personal identity, in contrast to that of thinking substance, would be a cognitive gap which needs closing by the imagination.

Hume's discussion of this cognitive gap, in the opening sentences of 1.4.6, draws our attention to a philosophical position.

> There are some philosophers, who imagine we are every moment intimately conscious of what we call our SELF; that we feel its existence and its continuance in existence; and are certain, beyond the evidence of a demonstration, both of its perfect identity and simplicity. The strongest sensation, the most violent passion, say they, instead of distracting us from this view, only fix it the more intensely, and make us consider their influence on *self* either by their pain or pleasure. To attempt a farther proof of this were to weaken its evidence; since no proof can be deriv'd from any fact, of which we are so intimately conscious; nor is there any thing, of which we can be certain, if we doubt of this. (1.4.6.1)

Hume says that we do not have 'any idea of *self*, after the manner it is here explain'd' (1.4.6.2). He gives four arguments to this effect:

(1) One argument is relatively a priori. Based on the First Principle and on the philosophical concept of self (a conscious, simple, identical subject), it is a priori that we have no such idea, because no impression can have such nature and content. 'It must be some one impression, that gives rise to every real idea. But self or person is not any one impression, but that to which our several impressions and ideas are suppos'd to have a reference' (1.4.6.2). This is a different application of an argument given in 1.4.5 against the idea of thinking substance.

(2) Another argument, also resorting to the First Principle and to the concept of self, is a posteriori. 'If any impression gives rise to the idea of self, that impression must continue invariably the same, thro' the whole course of our lives; since self is suppos'd to exist after that manner. But there is no impression constant and invariable. Pain and pleasure, grief and joy,

---

[4] See, for a survey of the roles of the idea of self, D. Garrett, 'The Idea of Self in Hume's *Treatise*', forthcoming in P. Kitcher, ed., *Self: History of a Concept*, Oxford; Oxford University Press.

passions and sensations succeed each other, and never all exist at the same time. It cannot, therefore, be from any of these impressions, or from any other, that the idea of self is deriv'd; and consequently there is no such idea' (1.4.6.2).

(3) A straightly a priori argument rejects the traditional, philosophical conception of the relations between perceptions and mind. 'But farther, what must become of all our particular perceptions upon this hypothesis? All these are different, and distinguishable, and separable from each other, and may be separately consider'd, and may exist separately, and have no need of any thing to support their existence. After what manner, therefore, do they belong to self; and how are they connected with it?' (1.4.6.3; this argument was already present in 1.4.5). Hume does not endorse this view of the relations between mind and perceptions and the argument is therefore only ad hominem.

(4) Lastly, a posteriori, there is the content of our ordinary introspective experience, where nothing unitary and persistent is found.

> For my part, when I enter most intimately into what I call *myself*, I always stumble on some particular perception or other, of heat or cold, light or shade, love or hatred, pain or pleasure. I never can catch *myself* at any time without a perception, and never can observe any thing but the perception. When my perceptions are remov'd for any time, as by sound sleep; so long am I insensible of *myself*, and may be truly said not to exist.   (1.4.6.3)
>
> There is properly no *simplicity* in it at one time, nor *identity* in different.   (1.4.6.4)

What all this excludes is that we have an impression of our self or that the self is an object, a particular represented by an idea of reflection. Reflection is a species of the genus representation. The content and the very existence of ideas of reflection depend on the presence of their objects, perceptions with their properties and relations. Perceptions, considered as objects or in their mental existence, have the force and vivacity of impressions (1.3.8.15). Ideas resembling internal perceptions are caused by their existence. Reflection is thus the representation of the succession of our perceptions. Ideas of reflection make it possible for us to represent a posteriori our inner or mental life, as it is before and independently of any operation of the imagination. This comes out clearly from a text where Hume nails his arguments with the customary challenge to philosophers or metaphysicians.

> If any one upon serious and unprejudic'd reflection, thinks he has a different notion of *himself*, I must confess I can reason no longer with him. All I can allow him is, that he may be in the right as well as I, and that we are essentially

different in this particular. He may, perhaps, perceive something simple and continu'd, which he calls *himself*; tho' I am certain there is no such principle in me. (1.4.6.3)

If, counterfactually, one had by reflection a different notion of its own self from the one we all have, this would indicate a *real difference* between us. There *would be* something simple and continued in them, while *there is* nothing of the sort in us. Hume is committed to regarding ideas of reflection as delivering what we really are as thinking beings. The actual content of such representation is a plurality of individual perceptions, which neither individually nor collectively can be regarded as constituting an individual, identical self. Still, we *do* have an idea of self and personal identity, as it is manifest in our very engagement in reflection, 'when I enter most intimately into what I call *myself*'. We can think meaningfully of ourselves, even though Hume is careful not to commit as to the nature of the target of this thinking ('what I call *myself*'). This capacity for meaningful thinking about oneself involves that we have a descriptive, qualitative, non-representational idea of our self and personal identify. Hume is ready to recognize that we have this idea and tells it apart from spurious, merely verbal disputes about personal identity.

> Thus the controversy concerning identity is not merely a dispute of words. For when we attribute identity, in an improper sense, to variable or interrupted objects, our mistake is not confin'd to the expression, but is commonly attended with a fiction, either of something invariable and uninterrupted, or of something mysterious and inexplicable, or at least with a propensity to such fictions.
> (1.4.6.7; see also 1.4.6.21)

We are not restricted to the ungrounded and inconsistent philosophical idea of self. But since no idea *at all* of self or mind is provided by reflective representation, Hume's arguments reveal the existence of a gap in representation and reason, in correspondence to this idea.

10.2 Imagining the Self and Personal Identity

10.2.1 Identity of Successive Perceptions

Ideas of reflection provide us with a representation of ourselves, as we really are.

> I may venture to affirm of the rest of mankind, that they are nothing but a bundle or collection of different perceptions, which succeed each other with an inconceivable rapidity, and are in a perpetual flux and movement.... The mind

is a kind of theatre, where several perceptions successively make their appearance; pass, re-pass, glide away, and mingle in an infinite variety of postures and situations.... The comparison of the theatre must not mislead us. They are the successive perceptions only, that constitute the mind; nor have we the most distant notion of the place, where these scenes are represented, or of the materials, of which it is compos'd. (1.4.6.4)

A succession of perceptions is all we represent of our minds when we 'most intimately' enter in ourselves. No separable impression and idea of self is part of such representation. This representation—the mind as a bundle, or flux, or theatre of perceptions—is not supposed by Hume to explain our idea of self and personal identity and it does not even exhaust what we can truly say about minds. It is only how ideas of reflection represent ourselves. This sets the stage for the work of the imagination, which produces an idea of self and personal identity we can and we do have, as opposed to the philosophical illusion of a perfectly identical and simple self.[5] Hume explicitly remarks that the bundle, flux, or theatre of perceptions exhausts the content of our idea of self *only if* we insulate and suspend the natural propensity to imagine its simplicity and identity: 'whatever natural propension we may have to imagine that simplicity and identity' (1.4.6.4). What we represent of ourselves by entering most intimately in ourselves is thus only the first, necessary step of a progression through which we come to conceive of our own persistence. The problem then becomes that of individuating and describing the 'propension' of the imagination that gives rise to the idea of self.

This is a very complex interpretive and conceptual issue. It is convenient to begin addressing it from how Hume himself states his question.

What then gives us so great a propension to ascribe an identity to these successive perceptions, and to suppose ourselves possest of an invariable and uninterrupted existence thro' the whole course of our lives? (1.4.6.5)

As this text makes clear, there are two parts to Hume's account of how imagination produces the idea of self: ascribing identity to successive perceptions; imagining (supposing) our self, continued and identical across time. The relations between these two parts are far from clear in the text, even though a consistent reading of it is possible. I begin with examining Hume's conception of what makes us ascribe identity to the successive perceptions we are acquainted with in reflection.

1.4.6 contains Hume's most detailed discussion of how the imagination produces the ideas of perfect and imperfect identity. I have already introduced

---

[5] For a summary of the idea of self that is Hume's explanatory target, see Strawson, *Evident Connexion*, 68.

materials from 1.4.6 when discussing Hume's constancy account of the idea of body (see § 9.3.1–2). The main explanatory principle is a 'biass of the imagination', a non-logical, topic-relative principle of the more limited imagination. We have the 'distinct idea of an object, that remains invariable and uninterrupted thro' a suppos'd variation of time': identity or sameness. 'We have also a distinct idea of several different objects existing in succession, and connected together by a close relation'. This gives us a 'notion of *diversity*' (1.4.6.6). These ideas are 'perfectly distinct, and even contrary' but we ordinarily confound the one with the other. The principle at work is Act/Idea Resemblance.

> That action of the imagination, by which we consider the uninterrupted and invariable object, and that by which we reflect on the succession of related objects, are almost the same to the feeling, nor is there much more effort of thought requir'd in the latter case than in the former. The relation facilitates the transition of the mind from one object to another, and renders its passage as smooth as if it contemplated one continu'd object. This resemblance is the cause of the confusion and mistake, and makes us substitute the notion of identity, instead of that of related objects. However at one instant we may consider the related succession as variable or interrupted, we are sure the next to ascribe to it a perfect identity, and regard it as invariable and uninterrupted. (1.4.6.6)

The resemblance of the action of the imagination composes with the relations among successive perceptions to facilitate the imaginative transition from diversity to identity. This propensity operates tacitly ('before we are aware'). It is susceptible to correction by 'reflection' and by a 'more accurate method of thinking'. Still, we cannot 'take off this biass from the imagination', or even resist it for long (1.4.6.6). As Hume conclusively summarizes his account of the identity of successive perceptions, 'our notions of personal identity, proceed entirely from the smooth and uninterrupted progress of the thought along a train of connected ideas, according to the principles above-explain'd' (1.4.6.16).[6]

In the case of self and personal identity, the imaginative grounds of the ideas of perfect and imperfect identity are all the more visible in the wide array of features underlying our ascriptions of identity. As Hume says, to explain personal identity 'as it regards our thought or imagination', that is, the content of this idea, 'we must take the matter pretty deep, and account for that identity, which we attribute to plants and animals; there being a great analogy betwixt it, and the identity of a

---

[6] Since he is accounting for our idea of self in general, Hume seems to have to grant this method of thinking also to ordinary thinkers, as well as a sensitivity to the 'absurdity' of identifying different objects. This may look suspicious (he also talks, in this context, of 'our philosophy'). However, he seems to assume that the internal experience of our own existence as a collection and succession of perceptions is common to humankind (1.4.6.4); this gives at least some support to the idea that reflection and correction are ordinarily accessible.

self or person' (1.4.6.5). Hume here obviously has Locke's theory in mind: the identity of persons is patterned on that of living beings. But at the same time he radically revises it, even subverting its aims. Locke's ground-breaking analysis of individuation and identity for masses of matter, plants and animals, artefacts, human beings, and persons bases each variety of identity on an individuating, general idea, a 'Sortal',[7] which allows counting objects according to some distinctive character.[8] This is to make it so that such 'relations and ways of comparing', including identification, are 'well founded, and of use to the Understanding'.[9] Hume has resort to a corresponding taxonomy of ideas or criteria of identity: material objects, living beings, artefacts, selves or persons, but with the aim of highlighting the non-representational, non-rational aspects of the works of imagination and, at the same time, their indispensable content-constitutive role.

The different ideas of imperfect identity—relating to masses of matters, animals and vegetables, artefacts, and minds—are all produced by 'an easy transition of the imagination' from one distinct idea to another, in so far as this 'act of the mind' resembles that 'by which we contemplate one continu'd object' (Act/Idea Resemblance) (1.4.6.7). Thus, the 'perfect identity' of a 'mass of matter', the parts of which are 'contiguous and connected', depends on such parts continuing 'uninterruptedly and invariably the same', no matter how the whole or the parts change of place. But we ascribe identity to masses of matter also on different conditions. Even though the addition or subtraction of 'some very *small* or *inconsiderable* part' 'absolutely destroys the identity of the whole', we go on considering the mass of matter as the same (1.4.6.8). Even when the change is 'considerable', one may not withhold identity because 'we must measure the greatness of the part, not absolutely, but by its *proportion* to the whole' (1.4.6.9). And while a 'change in any considerable part of a body destroys its identity', 'where the change is produc'd *gradually* and *insensibly* we are less apt to ascribe to it the same effect' (1.4.6.10). What explains that we can and do conceive of the identity of material bodies in these divergent ways is that the thought of identity springs from the more limited imagination, rather than from ideas of objects, and so it can respond to representationally and rationally irrelevant clues.

> 'Twill be impossible to account for this, but by reflecting that objects operate upon the mind, and break or interrupt the continuity of its actions not according to their real greatness, but according to their proportion to each other: And therefore, since this interruption makes an object cease to appear the same, it must be the uninterrupted progress of the thought, which constitutes the imperfect identity. (1.4.6.9)

---

[7] Locke, *Essay*, 3.3.15 (417).   [8] Locke, *Essay*, 2.27.7 (332).
[9] Locke, *Essay*, 2.27.2 (329).

Hume takes the same approach to the identity relations underlying the identity of living beings and artefacts, which overstep what could be concluded from the ideas we have of them. 'In a very few years both vegetables and animals endure a *total* change, yet we all attribute identity to them, while their form, size, and substance are entirely alter'd' (1.4.6.12). Hume explains the extended application of the idea of identity or even, in this case, of imperfect identity (across *total* change) not with some special feature of the contents of our ideas but with the concurrence of such ideas with the imagination. 'There is, however, another artifice, [besides the biases linked to the size, proportion, and gradualness of changes] by which we may induce the imagination to advance a step farther' (1.4.6.11). Such artifice or, better, artifices are the supposition of 'a reference of the parts to each other, and a combination to some *common end* or purpose' (1.4.6.11) (in the case of artefacts); or of a 'sympathy of parts', which 'bear to each other, the reciprocal relation of cause and effect' (1.4.6.12) (in the case of living beings). This can superficially resemble Locke's account of the identity of the same sorts of beings, which is based on the vital or functional organization that holds together their parts.[10] But what is different is the role played by this kind of characterization. In Locke it expresses, if only in an epistemically limited way, the nature of these objects and provides a real foundation for understanding their identities. In Hume it explains the 'easy transition of the imagination' that is all there is to the content of our ideas of imperfect identity (1.4.6.11).[11] The upshot is thus that our thought of the (imperfect) identity of our perceptions is owing to the more limited imagination.

10.2.2 The True Idea of the Human Mind

Having explained the identity of successive perceptions with Act/Idea Resemblance, Hume asks, as the 'only question' that remains, 'by what relations this uninterrupted progress of our thought is produc'd, when we consider the successive existence of a mind or thinking person?' (1.4.6.17). That is, what relation between our ideas of reflection—the ideas we have of we 'successive existence' as mind or thinker, of the flux of perceptions that we call ourselves—drives the identifying transitions of the imagination. Hume takes into consideration two such

---

[10] Locke, *Essay*, 2.27.4 (330–1).

[11] A further respect in which only the imagination can explain the scope and character of our ascriptions of identity is the following. 'Where the objects are in their nature changeable and inconstant, we admit of a more sudden transition, than wou'd otherwise be consistent with [identity]' (1.4.6.14). What explains this is that the imagination stores implicit empirical information. 'What is natural and essential to any thing is, in a manner, expected; and what is expected makes less impression, and appears of less moment, than what is unusual and extraordinary. A considerable change of the former kind seems really less to the imagination, than the most trivial alteration of the latter; and by breaking less the continuity of the thought, has less influence in destroying the identity' (1.4.6.14).

relations: resemblance and causation. Imagination concurs in radically different ways with resembling and with causally associated ideas of internal perceptions; but only causation can provide the right account of the idea of self and personal identity.

The resemblance account takes the matter deeper than the causation one because it grounds the identifying transition of the imagination on a relation between ideas that is immediately available to representation by reflection. Ideas of reflection represent internal perceptions; resembling internal perceptions are represented by resembling ideas of reflection; the imagination proceeds easily along resembling ideas of refection and conceives of them as ideas of one, identical object (relations of resemblance 'convey the imagination more easily from one link to another, and make the whole seem like the continuance of one object', 1.4.6.18). This is the counterpart to the exact similarity of impressions, which is the basis of the constancy account of body. Given the representational character of resemblance, which mirrors the qualitative properties of ideas of reflection, is not surprising that Hume casts the resemblance account both in a third and in a first-personal perspective. Hume opens the discussion explicitly in third personal perspective: 'suppose we cou'd see clearly into the breast of another, and observe that succession of perceptions, which constitutes his mind or thinking principle' (1.4.6.18).[12] The conclusions drawn from this impersonal, external observation are then extended to the first-personal perspective. 'The case is the same whether we consider ourselves or others'. The main task of the account is therefore to explain how internal perceptions come in general to be so resembling, while variable because successive, that the ideas of reflection representing them are also resembling. Hume resorts, again, to a representational faculty, memory (the primitive faculty of making copies of perceptions; not judgemental memory, which is here one of the explananda). Supposing the man whose mind or succession of perceptions we are observing 'always preserves memory of a considerable part of past perceptions', ''tis evident that nothing cou'd more contribute to the bestowing a relation on this succession amidst all its variations'. Memory is the faculty by which we 'raise up the images of past perceptions'. Since 'an image necessarily resembles its object', memory would determine the 'frequent placing of these resembling perceptions in the train of thought' (1.4.6.18). Therefore, even though the identifying transition is owing to the imagination, the causal condition for it, the resemblance of successive perceptions and of the ideas representing them, is brought about by memory. 'In this particular, then, the memory not only discovers the identity, but also contributes to its production, by producing

---

[12] Notice that third-personal cognition of another's mind is not problematic for Hume. Our access to the minds of other is limited and indirect, inferential. But within such limits, the true idea of the human mind, a system of causally and functionally connected perceptions, is such that we can have probable cognition of it. The problems for Hume theory rather come from the side of a first-personal idea of our mind or self.

the relation of resemblance among the perceptions' (1.4.6.18). In this way, Hume's resemblance account makes an implicit reference to Locke's theory of personal identity, which, as it was prevalently understood in the first decades of the Eighteenth century England, ascribed to consciousness a productive role with regard to personal identity and identified consciousness with memory: personal identity extends so far as memory extends.[13]

It is thus interesting (and an aspect of his critical attitude to Locke's theory of personal identity) that Hume does not stop at the resemblance account. Hume points out that if memory produced the idea of personal identity, even with the concurrence of imagination, the scope of our judgements of personal identity would be intolerably restricted.

> For how few of our past actions are there, of which we have any memory? Who can tell me, for instance, what were his thoughts and actions on the first of *January* 1715, the 11th of *March* 1719, and the 3d of *August* 1733? Or will he affirm, because he has entirely forgot the incidents of these days, that the present self is not the same person with the self of that time; and by that means overturn all the most establish'd notions of personal identity? (1.4.6.20)

If memory produced the idea of personal identity by producing resemblance between internal perceptions and ideas of reflection, no extension of the idea of self would be possible. But it is in the nature of the transitions grounded on resemblance that they can only take in their scope objects which are or have been observed. They associate ideas in two-object situations, without conferring any further inferential potential to those ideas. The further effects on the imagination of these transitions are limited in the same way. Therefore, the idea of self and personal identity that springs from the resemblance account cannot be applied beyond what ideas of memory we have. "Twill be incumbent on those, who affirm that memory produces entirely our personal identity, to give a reason why we can thus extend our identity beyond our memory' (1.4.6.20). This was, of course, the basis of Berkeley's and Reid's objection of intransitivity to Locke's theory of personal identity: we may now lack memory of some our past actions which at an earlier stage of our life we still remembered and we may now have memory of actions of ours at that earlier stage. This makes it so that, if personal identity is produced by memory, I may be and not be the same with myself across time. Memory is not transitive across life-stages while personal identity is.[14] Hume,

---

[13] See Thiel, *Early Modern Subject*, 153–89.
[14] 'The persons in A and B are the same, being conscious of common ideas by supposition. The person in B is (for the same reason) one and the same with the person in C. Therefore, the person in A is the same with the person in C, by that undoubted axiom, *Quae conveniunt uni tertio convenient inter se*. But the person in C hath no idea in common with the person in A', G. Berkeley, *Alciphron; or, the Minute Philosopher*, Dialogue 7, in *The Works of George Berkeley*, A. C. Fraser, ed., Volume 2,

however, seems rather interested in the cognitive gap that in this way opens between the idea of self and personal identity issuing from the resemblance account, with its relying on memory, and our ordinary cognitive practice with the idea of self and personal identity.

Hume's own explanation of identifying transitions resorts, by contrast, to causal relations between perceptions. 'Our self or person' is constituted by a 'chain of causes and effects', (1.4.6.20). Hume's general account of causation applies non-problematically to the flux of perceptions. Perceptions are 'different existences' (1.6.3.19) and this—not being contrary the ones to the others—is all that is required for objects to possibly be causes and effect (1.4.5.32). We also represent, with our ideas of reflection, constant conjunctions of internal perceptions and actions of the mind (2.3.1.5-9). This associates the ideas of reflection of internal perceptions by making easy, indeed compelling, the transitions or inferences of the imagination among them. In this way we come to conceive and believe that successive perceptions (the objects of ideas of reflection, not the ideas themselves) are causally connected. The constant conjunction of distinct existents and the inference of the mind are the only conditions for the application of the idea of cause in reasoning. This latter, therefore, can be performed with regard to our internal no less than to our external experience (2.3.1.16).

The shift from resemblance to causation determines an important change in the structure of the explanation of the idea of self and personal identity. In the resemblance account, the identifying transitions of the imagination are borne by relations that hold directly among individual, successive perceptions and consequently by the ideas of reflection representing them. The relations are those of resemblance between perceptions and their copies in memory: a resemblance represented by ideas of reflection and borne by them. The idea of mind that is at work in the resemblance account of is simply the primitive, representational one of a bundle or flux of perceptions. The imagination, in unifying this bundle along the relation of resemblance among ideas of reflection, cannot take any step beyond the perceptions that are actually so related: the perceptions copied by ideas of memory and the ideas of reflection that represent such perceptions and ideas. Transitions of the imagination based on resemblance do not confer any

---

Clarendon Press, Oxford 1901, 335 (A, B, and C are 'parts' of a 'space of time' during which one person is conscious of its ideas). 'There is another consequence of this doctrine, which follows no less necessarily, though Mr. Locke probably did not see it. It is, that a man may be, and at the same time not be, the person that did a particular action.' (The well-known example of the flogged boy, the brave officer, and the old general follows: the general remembers being the officer, the officer being the boy, but the general has forgotten everything about his life as a boy. On Locke's theory, the boy is the same with the officer.) 'Whence it follows, if there be any truth in logic, that the general is the same person with him who was flagged at school. But the general's consciousness does not reach so far back as his flogging, therefore, according to Mr. Locke's doctrine, he is not the person who was flogged. Therefore the general is, and at the same time is not, the same person with his who was flogged at school', T. Reid, *Essays on the Intellectual Powers of Man*, B. Brody, ed., The MIT Press, Cambridge (Mass.) and London 1969, 357-8. See Thiel, *The Early Modern Subject*, 210-21.

new inferential potential to ideas. By contrast, the causal-associative operations of the imagination produce a different, non-representational idea of the mind as a causal system, possibly with features of common ends and causal sympathy (like in living beings and artefacts), which is then susceptible to the identifying transitions of the imagination. The role of memory in this case is different. Rather than being the cause of a relation (resemblance) represented by ideas of reflection, it is itself an aspect of reflective representation. By reflection, we can represent our perceptions and their resemblances; we keep memory of this, in this way coming to represent their constant conjunctions; the memory of these constant conjunctions, in its turn, has effects on the imagination, as per Hume's theory of causal content, and makes us conceive of the internal perceptions as causally connected.

Hume gives expression to the different role of memory in the two accounts by saying that in the second 'memory does not so much *produce* as *discover* personal identity, by showing us the relation of cause and effect among our different perceptions' (1.4.6.20). In this way, we come by a non-representational and inferentially rich idea of our minds.

> The true idea of the human mind, is to consider it as a system of different perceptions or different existences, which are link'd together by the relation of cause and effect, and mutually produce, destroy, influence, and modify each other. Our impressions give rise to their correspondent ideas; and these ideas in their turn produce other impressions. One thought chaces another, and draws after it a third, by which it is expell'd in its turn. (1.4.6.19)

This 'true idea of the human mind' makes an important addition to the representational idea of the mind as flux or bundle of perceptions. This idea is consistent with that of the mind as bundle (since Separability is consistent with causal connectedness; metaphysical contingency with physical necessity) but obviously it is not entailed by it, because it adds to it the factual condition that certain perceptions are constantly conjoined and the inferential one of their relations in the mind. As a causal idea, it is different from and irreducible to any content primitively given in reflection; and can enjoy the good epistemic standing, the justness, of proofs. Something true about the human mind would be missing if one considered only individual perceptions and their relations.[15] It is this idea of the mind that underlies the capital discussion of perceptions and minds at 1.4.2.38–9. (Hume may here be hinting to considerations of reference to a common end and of causal sympathy when he talks of perceptions that 'influence, and modify each other'.) In this way, the causation account is characterized by a more complex

---

[15] Missing this difference is the main shortcoming of Galen Strawson's detailed discussion of Section 6 and of the *Appendix*. See Strawson, *Evident Connexion*, 33–4, 45–7, 48, 53–5, 120.

cognitive background of the underlying imaginative processes and of the resulting idea of self.[16]

The causation account does not face the problems that beset the resemblance account. Constant conjunctions among internal perceptions are represented by reflection, preserved by memory, and causally reconceived by imagination. This confers an inferential potential to the true idea of the human mind and makes completely standard patterns of causal reasoning about the succession of our perceptions possible. This reasoning can take place in internal experience just as in a putative third personal observation of a flux of perceptions. Once we have the relevant causal ideas and inferences, the corresponding ideas of identity follow by further transitions of the imagination and we can apply them in forming beliefs about our self and our personal identity that go beyond the conditions that give rise to it in the first place. 'But having once acquir'd this notion of causation from the memory, we can extend the same chain of causes, and consequently the identity of our persons, beyond our memory' (1.4.6.20). Therefore, by our practice of probable reasoning, we can judge of our identity at times and in circumstances of which we have no memory. This might be seen as an implicit response to Berkeley's (and later Reid's) objection of intransitivity. Both on the resemblance and on the causation account, the idea of self and personal identity is produced by the imagination operating on ideas of reflection. But in the second case the mechanism of production of that idea allows us to apply it also at times of our lives of which we retain no memory. In this way, the conditions for an objection of intransitivity are removed, without having to assume the reality or the idea of a simple and identical self. On the whole then, we may say that the causal account is the one Hume endorses.[17]

---

[16] The relations between the proposed explanations of the idea of self and those of the idea of body are complex. The causation account of self is analogous to the coherence account of body because both operate on a causal conception of objects and, respectively, perceptions. The resemblance account, by contrast, recalls the constancy account by being based on the representational property of resemblance. However, differently from the coherence account of body and like the constancy one, the causation account of the self includes ascriptions of identity and is the more comprehensive in its scope. Furthermore, the causation account primitively instantiates the idea of self or personal identity, rather than applying it to certain causal circumstances; and in this, again, it is different from the coherence account. Apart from their relying on the same biases of the imagination, there is no obvious mapping of the imaginative operations underlying the idea of self to those underlying the idea of body. These differences might point to a reason why, according to Hume, the intellectual world seems to be free of the contradictions of the natural one.

[17] Hume also remarks that the imaginative genesis of the idea of self deprives us of a 'just standard' for assessing questions concerning personal identity, because 'the easiness of the transition may diminish by insensible degrees' (1.4.6.21). This, however, does not deprive the idea of self of content. Hume does declare such disputes as 'merely verbal'; but adding: 'except so far as the relation of parts gives rise to some fiction or imaginary principle of union'. Within the limits of non-representational, imaginative content, the idea of self is in order. T. Penelhum, 'Hume on Personal Identity', 646–7, who holds that we owe the idea of self to a mistake, recognizes that Hume's language is not always consistent with his error-theoretical reading.

10.2.3 The Same Thinking Person

The conclusive step of Hume's account, the transition from the true idea of the human mind and the imperfect identity of successive perceptions to the idea of self and personal identity, requires integration and careful discussion. Causally connected internal perceptions have independent existence but 'we suppose the whole train of perceptions to be united by identity'. The imperfect identity of the successive perceptions we have explained with Act/Idea Resemblance, based on the causal connections that unite them in the true idea of the human mind. But this is clearly an interim conclusion, or a lemma in the explanation, since the (imperfect) identity of perceptions one with another falls short of individuating the content of the idea of self and personal identity (along the spectrum of the forms that this idea can take, 1.4.6.6). At this stage, Hume resorts again to properties of the more limited imagination. The explanation of the transition to the idea of self and personal identity depends, in the first place, on 'whether it be something that really binds our several perceptions together, or only associates their ideas in the imagination? That is, in other words, whether in pronouncing concerning the identity of a person, we observe some real bond among his perceptions, or only feel one among the ideas we form of them?' (1.4.6.16). Hume's answer, of course, is the second. The understanding never observes any real connexion among objects, even in the causal union of internal perceptions. 'For from thence it evidently follows, that identity is nothing really belonging to these different perceptions, and uniting them together; but is merely a quality, which we attribute to them, because of the union of their ideas in the imagination, when we reflect upon them' (1.4.6.16). A transition of the imagination is therefore the cause of the idea of self: 'it follows, that our notions of personal identity, proceed entirely from the smooth and uninterrupted progress of the thought along a train of connected ideas' (1.4.6.16).

The key to this further transition and construal of identity (in line with the constancy account of the idea of body) is the imperfect character of the identity ascribed to variable internal perceptions. The perceived variability of the flux of perceptions is the same with the distinctness of its component perceptions and thus is in tension with their imagined identity. 'The identity, which we attribute to the human mind, however perfect we may imagine it to be, is not able to run the several different perceptions into one, and make them lose their characters of distinction and difference, which are essential to them' (1.4.6.16). This induces cognitive instability and uneasiness. The causation account of the idea of self and personal identity follows also in this the pattern of the constancy account. The 'biass' of the imagination to take related perceptions as the same conflicts with 'reflection', by which we recognize their variable character. The bias prevails but leaves a lingering cognitive uneasiness, which triggers Reconciliation.

Our last resource is to yield to it, and boldly assert that these different related objects are in effect the same, however interrupted and variable. In order to justify to ourselves this absurdity we often feign some new and unintelligible principle, that connects the objects together, and prevents their interruption or variation. Thus we feign the continu'd existence of the perceptions of our senses, to remove the interruption; and run into the notion of a *soul*, and *self*, and *substance*, to disguise the variation. (1.4.6.6)

This is the genesis and the nature of our actual, fictional but non-spurious (conceivable and applicable) idea of self and personal identity.

We should pay attention to a difference between the causation account of the idea of self and the constancy account of the idea of body. The difference is in the phenomenological features of perceptions that they involve: respectively, interruption and variation (1.4.6.6). A lack of perceptions is not itself experienced and represented, as Hume makes clear in his analysis of the idea of a vacuum. But we can experience and represent that certain perceptions, individuated by their contents (as of this or of that object), are not anymore present to us and have been substituted by others. In the constancy account, the interruption of perceptions is balanced, in its concurrence with the imagination, by the exact similarity of their contents. The resemblance of ideas and of the corresponding acts of conception explains, by Act/Idea Resemblance and then by Reconciliation, that we form the idea of something existing continuedly and distinctly. This disguises the interruption of the perceptions. This also determines the nature of the idea of such a continuant. The contents of the perceptions are exactly resembling. By Non-mixture, this secures a qualitative homogeneity across the transitions of the imagination and identifies the particular conceived to exist continuedly and independently. It is a particular that has the same qualities with the constant perceptions. This corresponds to Hume's a priori conception of body or external existence: something indiscernible from perceptions but with different relations, durations, and locations, or with continued and independent existence. In this way, the constancy account of external existence disguises the interruptions of perceptions by directly reifying them.

In the case of the self, by contrast, the representational background is the experience of an uninterrupted flux of variable perceptions. 'Thus we feign the continu'd existence of perceptions of our senses, to remove the interruption; and run into the notion of a soul, and self, and substance, to disguise the variation' (1.4.6.6). What we internally experience is an ever-changing succession of perceptions. This is how perceptions exist in the mind; reflective representation gives them as they actually exist. As any other representational idea, they are caused by and exactly resemble impressions: the impression, here, is the mental existence itself of successive, different perceptions (1.3.8.15). The variations in the flux of perceptions are balanced, in the concurrence with imagination, by the causal relations holding among perceptions and by Completion, the propensity of the imagination to complete relations with other relations. Therefore, differently than in the constancy account, the imagination does not disguise the variation of successive perceptions by directly reifying their contents (they are qualitatively different). In a sense, it cannot disguise variation at all, because, differently than interruption, it is a positive, substantive content of representation. The idea of self and personal identity is correspondingly different from that of body; and, with it, the idea of the internal world is different from that of the external one. The idea of self does not consist of some internal perception, continuedly and distinctly existing. The outcome of the imaginative process is rather that the train of causally connected perceptions constitutes the 'successive existence of a mind or thinking person' (1.4.6.17). It is only in this indirect way that we can consistently think of them as identical; that we can 'yield' to the compelling inclination of the imagination to conceive them as the same. In other words, the reconciliation of the contradiction between the identity ascribed to perceptions and their observed variation consists in the imaginative production the idea of one persisting self, with such perceptions as its successive parts. The 'whole train' of perceptions is conceived as one thinking person, composed by them. While all there is and can be represented and truly believed are successive perceptions and their occurrence in a causal complex (a human mind, according to the true idea of it). It is this understanding the identity of distinct, successive perceptions as their mereological union in a thinking person, without any metaphysical remainder, that forms the core of Hume's internal world.[18]

---

[18] For a careful discussion of these matters, from which I have learned, see A. Waldow, 'Identity of Persons and Objects', *The Journal of Scottish Philosophy*, 8, 2010, 147:167. As I attempt to show in § 10.3.2, this conception of the internal character of perceptions might be too weak to support the cognitive roles Hume ascribes to the idea of self. The structure of this step in the cognitive working of imagination can be likened John Perry's notion of the relation of temporal or spatial unity of the parts of an object of a certain kind. Perry distinguishes such relation from identity: if the object of which *a* is a part is identical with that of which *b* is a part, then *a* and *b* stand in the relation of unity (J. Perry, *Identity, Personal Identity, and the Self*, Hackett, Indianapolis/Cambridge 2002, 38–9). Hume's imagination, so to say, reverse-engineers this nexus: in order for variable perceptions, which we cannot conceive as identical, to have at least the relation of temporal unity, we must imagine a temporally identical object they are the parts of. There is also some analogy with the notion of the 'I-relation' that holds 'between the several stages of a single continuant person', D. Lewis, 'Survival and Identity', in A. O. Rorty, ed., *The Identities of Persons*, University of California Press, Berkeley/Los Angeles/London 1979, 17–40, 21. But we should not saddle Hume with any anticipation of four-dimensionalism. Quite simply, Hume combines the view that souls, selves, minds, persons are temporal entities (they are successions of changes, not steadfast objects) with the causal account of their nature and the Reconciliation-based account of their identity. Nothing in this suggests the four-dimensionalist point that objects persist by being extended in time (perduring). At any given moment, all there is of a self or person is present. (S. Shoemaker, 'Personal Identity: a Materialist's Account', in S. Shoemaker & R. Swinburne, eds., *Personal Identity*, Blackwell, Oxford 1984, 67–132, 74–5, remarks that the idea of personal identity in terms of a unity-relation between temporal stages does not commit to four-dimensionalism.) M. Jacovides, 'Hume's Vicious Regress', *Oxford Studies in Early Modern Philosophy*, 5, 2010, (247–97), rightly remarks that Hume follows Locke in considering a persisting thing as composed of different constituents over time. Also Locke cannot be considered a four-dimensionalist.

This is the idea of the self and personal identity that we can and do have, as opposed to the one that the philosophers only imagine they have; and as opposed to what we discover or represent of ourselves, a flux of perceptions, which is not self or a person at all.

> In this respect, I cannot compare the soul more properly to any thing than to a republic or commonwealth, in which the several members are united by the reciprocal ties of government and subordination, and give rise to other persons, who propagate the same republic in the incessant changes of its parts. And as the same individual republic may not only change its members, but also its laws and constitutions; in like manner the same person may vary his character and disposition, as well as his impressions and ideas, without losing his identity. Whatever changes he endures, his several parts are still connected by the relation of causation. (1.4.6.19)

This idea of self is also the one that best fits with our worldview. It is systematically connected with our understanding of minds and living beings.

> And here 'tis evident, the same method of reasoning must be continu'd, which has so successfully explain'd the identity of plants, and animals, and ships, and houses, and of all the compounded and changeable productions either of art or nature. The identity, which we ascribe to the mind of man, is only a fictitious one, and of a like kind with that which we ascribe to vegetables and animal bodies. It cannot, therefore, have a different origin, but must proceed from a like operation of the imagination upon like objects. (1.4.6.15)

Furthermore, it supports the convergence of the passions with the imagination.

> And in this view our identity with regard to the passions serves to corroborate that with regard to the imagination, by the making our distant perceptions influence each other, and by giving us a present concern for our past or future pains or pleasures. (1.4.6.19)

Hume seems in this way to have closed the cognitive gap of self and personal identity.[19]

---

[19] An interpretation close to the one I propose is advanced in Loeb, *Stability and Justification*, 148–52. I am indebted to his discussion. The difference between Hume's account of body and of self is neatly summarized by M. J. Green: 'When I attribute identity over time to external objects I have perceptions that can give content to my belief in their identity over time.... But what gives content to the idea of a temporally extended self?' ('The Idea of a Momentary Self and Hume's Theory of Personal Identity'), *British Journal for the History of Philosophy*, 7, 1999, 104–22, 109). The solution of the problem, however, does not seem to me to lie in Hume's tacit assumption of an ordinary idea of a momentary self (as Green suggests, 110–11) but in articulating the idea of self in terms of successive

10.3 Hume's Recantation

It thus comes as a surprise that in the *Appendix* to the *Treatise* Hume engages in a recantation of the account of self he had proposed in the text.

> I had entertain'd some hopes, that however deficient our theory of the intellectual world might be, it wou'd be free from those contradictions, and absurdities, which seem to attend every explication, that human reason can give of the material world. But upon a more strict review of the section concerning *personal identity*, I find myself involv'd in such a labyrinth, that, I must confess, I neither know how to correct my former opinions, nor how to render them consistent.
> (*Appendix* 10)

The nature and source of Hume's concerns—the map indicating the entrance and the exit of the labyrinth—are famously elusive. I will address this much discussed interpretive issue, highlighting what it tells us about some limits of the content-productive function of the imagination.

10.3.1 The Labyrinth

In the *Appendix* Hume engages in a discussion of the 'arguments on both sides'— which turn out to be respectively the pars destruens and the pars construens of the original account. Hume still fully endorses the first side but only partially the second one. The first side consists in the arguments 'that induc'd me to deny the strict and proper identity and simplicity of a self or thinking being' (*Appendix* 10). These are arguments for rejecting the philosophical idea of self and in general any idea of the self purporting to represent it as an object. We are familiar with these arguments.

Hume claims, in the first place, that we have 'no impression of self or substance, as something simple and individual' (*Appendix* 11). This hints to his a posteriori argument. The second argument is the a priori, canonic one in terms of Separability. It is metaphysically possible that perceptions exist independently; therefore, it cannot be a priori and necessary that they inhere to a substance or a self. 'Whatever is distinct, is distinguishable; and whatever is distinguishable, is separable by the thought or imagination. All perceptions are distinct. They are, therefore, distinguishable, and separable, and may be conceiv'd as separately existent, and may exist separately, without any contradiction or absurdity' (*Appendix* 12). The dependent existence of perceptions is only a physical

---

parts and persisting wholes. Still, Green's focus on consciousness as the basis of such idea and the comparison of Hume and Locke is right and important.

necessity: this is a leading thought of 1.4.6. Hume complements this argument with supporting considerations drawn from the ontology of perceptions and objects. First: the 'doctrine of the philosophers' is that all that is present to me (this table, that chimney) are 'particular perceptions'. The 'doctrine of the vulgar' is that this table and that chimney, that are present to me, 'may and do exist separately'. This doctrine 'implies no contradiction'. It can thus be extended without contradiction to all our perceptions and supports their distinct existence (*Appendix* 13). The second consideration is that, since all ideas of objects derive from preceding perceptions, no proposition can be intelligible with regard of objects that is not also with regard to perceptions. 'But 'tis intelligible and consistent to say, that objects exist distinct and independent, without any common *simple* substance or subject of inhesion. This proposition, therefore, can never be absurd with regard to perceptions' (*Appendix* 14).

The third argument is based on the a posteriori fact that when one turns his or her reflection on oneself, one perceives oneself always and only with one or more perceptions. The 'composition' of these perceptions forms the self. Given this a posteriori fact, it is a priori that if we considered a mind with only one perception ('reduc'd even below the life of an oyster', *Appendix* 16), we would conceive of nothing else but that perception; and certainly not, besides it, of a self or substance. The addition of other perceptions would not make any difference in this regard. The conception of the annihilation of the self, following upon death, is nothing but that of the extinction of all particular perceptions, which therefore are the same with the self. This is a further application of Conceivability and Separability.

The fourth argument, extremely succinct, sets a sort of dilemma. If the self were the same with substance, the question whether it would subsist under a change of substance would not be intelligible. But Hume, together with Locke, seems to regard such a question as intelligible. If self and substance are distinct, however, it should be possible to conceive of their difference. But the only conception we have of either is in terms of particular perceptions. So, we cannot have the idea of the self as the same with or different from a substance. So, we cannot conceive at all of the self as substance or as an object (*Appendix* 18).

This takes us to the conclusion of 1.4.6 (with more emphasis on the concept of substance), here rehearsed. 'Philosophers begin to be reconcil'd to the principle, *that we have no idea of external substance, distinct from the ideas of particular qualities*. This must pave the way for a like principle with regard to the mind, *that we have no notion of it, distinct from the particular perceptions*' (*Appendix* 19). There can be no distinct representational content to the idea of self; only that of imaginatively changed and transposed ideas of reflection. This is to deny 'the strict and proper identity and simplicity of a self or thinking being' (*Appendix* 10). Hume explicitly endorses this conclusion: 'so far I seem to be attended with sufficient evidence'. When airing his doubts about his own positive account of the idea of self, Hume remarks that 'nothing but the seeming evidence of the preceding reasonings [the negative arguments] cou'd have induc'd me to receive it' (*Appendix* 20).[20]

The second side is the positive account of the idea of self. Since Hume explicitly endorses the negative side, troubles are likely to arise here, either in the positive account itself or in its relations to the negative one. Hume, however, is far from clear about what such troubles are. The background is the conclusion of the negative arguments: 'having thus loosen'd all our particular perceptions' (*Appendix* 20; that is, having reduced the idea of self to separable particular perceptions), the task is that of explaining 'what makes us attribute to them a real simplicity and identity'. This requires explaining the 'principle of connexion, which binds them together'. Hume then gives this description of the explanation given in 1.4.6.

> If perceptions are distinct existences, they form a whole only by being connected together. But no connexions among distinct existences are ever discoverable by human understanding. We only *feel* a connexion or determination of the thought, to pass from one object to another. It follows, therefore, that the thought alone finds personal identity, when reflecting on the train of past perceptions, that compose a mind, the ideas of them are felt to be connected together, and naturally introduce each other. (*Appendix* 20)

This is a fair summary of the argument of 1.4.6.16. Loose perceptions form a whole because the imagination associates in its transitions their ideas of reflection. In this way, the train of perceptions that composes a mind comes to be conceived as a whole, as one self or person. The defectiveness of Hume's account, however, is not yet in sight. In fact, Hume still appears to be endorsing his original account. 'The present philosophy, therefore, has so far a promising aspect.' (*Appendix* 20). However, the text of the *Appendix* gives at this point an important indication of what are Hume's concerns. In the original theory, right at this juncture (in fn. 89 to *Appendix*, 20 he refers back to 1.4.6.16),[21] Hume goes on asking, as the only question which remains, what relations produce the uninterrupted progress of thought that produces our idea of personal identity proceeds; and answers with the causation account. In the *Appendix* it is precisely the causation account that is dismissed, because Hume avows not to be in a position to explain how and why loose perceptions come to form a whole. Which is what he had done with the causation account.

---

[20] Why 'seeming evidence'? Has Hume some doubts about the negative side? As I argue later, the negative side might fail to identify and engage with some aspects of the idea of self, as we have it, which should have been taken into account.

[21] See J. Ellis, 'The Contents of Hume's Appendix and the Source of his Despair', *Hume Studies*, 32, 2006 (195–231), 201–2.

> But having thus loosen'd all our particular perceptions, when I proceed to explain the principle of connexion, which binds them together, and makes us attribute to them a real simplicity and identity; I am sensible, that my account is very defective... But all my hopes vanish, when I come to explain the principles, that unite our successive perceptions in our thought or consciousness. I cannot discover any theory, which gives me satisfaction on this head. (*Appendix* 20)

The 'original account', which is 'very defective', is the causation account, as a whole or in some of its elements. The interim conclusion that a cognitive shift is required from the representation of successive perceptions to the idea of their unity in a mind or person and that this requires a transition along ideas and the feeling of it, is not called in question. However, if no theory of how this is done, alternative to the causation account, is available, a cognitive gap is left, and no explanation of how the idea of self is produced is available.

This locates the defect but does not identify it, since Hume fails to say what precisely disqualifies the causation account from explaining the unity of successive perceptions in a thinking person. In fact, the conclusion of the discussion of the *Appendix* risks muddying the waters even more.

> In short there are two principles, which I cannot render consistent; nor is it in my power to renounce either of them, viz. *that all our distinct perceptions are distinct existences*, and *that the mind never perceives any real connexion among distinct existences*. Did our perceptions either inhere in something simple and individual, or did the mind perceive some real connexion among them, there wou'd be no difficulty in the case. (*Appendix* 21)

Hume's point is clear but not really helpful. The first principle excludes that the self is a substance to which perceptions inhere. The second principle excludes that real connections between perceptions can be represented. Rejecting one or the other of the principles would be sufficient, respectively a priori and a posteriori, for having the idea of an identical self. But neither can be rejected, because of Hume's general philosophical commitments. Therefore, this text does not tell us what is wrong with the original argument. Hume is voicing a deep, principled pessimism about his own theoretical position (in this area). Moreover, since the idea of renouncing either principle is put forward in a spirit of paradox or for reductio, he is implicitly insisting that any solution (if one could be had) should keep in place the apparatus of imaginative inferences and production of ideas that is distinctive of Hume's philosophy overall.

There is no sign that Hume, no matter how he despairs of finding a solution, has in mind anything like debunking his own philosophy, as he would do, if he were to introduce a representational idea of self. He explicitly presents the problem he is addressing in the *Appendix* as tractable within his own philosophical framework, even though he is not able to solve it at present.

> For my part, I must plead the privilege of a sceptic, and confess, that this difficulty is too hard for my understanding. I pretend not, however, to pronounce it absolutely insuperable. Others, perhaps, or myself, upon more mature reflections, may discover some hypothesis, that will reconcile those contradictions.
>
> (*Appendix* 21)

There is no need to thicken the mystery by supposing that Hume is dissatisfied with the basic principles of his own philosophy.[22]

10.3.2 United in our Thought or Consciousness

On the basis of what we have just seen, I think that we should look for a solution to the interpretive puzzle raised by the *Appendix* that identifies the problem with 1.4.6 as a deep and serious one;[23] does not call in question the general principles of Hume's philosophy (the problem with 1.4.6 is local); leaves in place as much as possible of the account of personal identity in 1.4.6; and makes room for Hume's hesitant claim that the problem is tractable.[24]

We can begin by distinguishing *metaphysical* and *psychological* readings of the difficulty of the *Appendix*. The source of the problem, in the first case, is located in Hume's ontology of mind: it is his dim realization that something in what

---

[22] Notice that Hume neither retracts the claim of the similarity of the explanation of the identity of plants, animals, and artifacts with that of persons, nor includes the former in the retraction of this latter. Thus, insofar as the idea of self and personal identity shares its features with that of living beings and their identity, Hume must still be satisfied with his explanation. And this was an important theme in 1.4.6.

[23] See Strawson, *Evident Connexion*, 117. Still, I propose what has been called a conservative solution to the problem. A conservative reading is also recommended by the fact that in the *Abstract* (written before the *Appendix* but after 1.4.6) Hume reiterates his overall position, sharpening its anti-Cartesian and anti-substantialist point. 'I shall conclude the logics of this author with an account of two opinions, which seem to be peculiar to himself, as indeed are most of his opinions. He asserts, that the soul, as far as we can conceive it, is nothing but a system or train of different perceptions, those of heat and cold, love and anger, thoughts and sensations; all united together, but without any perfect simplicity or identity. *Des Cartes* maintained that thought was the essence of the mind; not this thought or that thought, but thought in general. This seems to be absolutely unintelligible, since every thing, that exists, is particular: And therefore it must be our several particular perceptions, that compose the mind. I say, *compose* the mind, not *belong* to it. The mind is not a substance, in which the perceptions inhere. That notion is as unintelligible as the *Cartesian*, that thought or perception in general is the essence of the mind' (*Abstract* 28).

[24] See, for a list of criteria for an adequate interpretation of the *Appendix*, D. Garrett, 'Rethinking Hume's Second Thoughts about Personal Identity', in J. Bridges, N. Kolodny, & Wai-Hung W., eds., *The Possibility of Philosophical Understanding: Essays for Barry Stroud*, Oxford University Press, New York 2012 (15–42), 23; another list is drawn in Ainslie, *Hume's True Scepticism*, 248–51. With differences, there is a basic convergence among these lists and with the one I propose.

individual perceptions are and how they compose minds makes it impossible to form the idea of self as described in 1.4.6.[25] In the second case, the source is in some of the mental principles at work in connecting perceptions, centrally in the principles of association, which Hume discovers to be insufficient to generate the idea of the self. I am more inclined to the second kind of interpretation, since Hume's sparse ontology of perceptions seems non-negotiable. But the psychological interpretation should be articulated in a *content-theoretical* sense. My reading will focus on the contents of the ideas involved, as explanantia and explananda, in the theory of 1.4.6 and on the content-constitutive aspects of the operations of the imagination. It is only with this focus, I think, that the pieces of the puzzle fall into place.[26]

The important interpretive choice, against this background, is between two ways of articulating Hume's problem with the content of the idea of self and personal identity. One is to consider it as Hume's recognition that in 1.4.6 he had provided a *flawed* account of the *right* idea of self and personal identity; and that he has no alternative account of that idea. The other is as Hume's recognition that the account provided in 1.4.6 was *right* for producing a certain idea of self and personal identity but that that idea was in some important respect *flawed*; and that he had no right account for a corrected idea of self.[27] I think that one should opt for the second view as more conservative. It focuses on the explanatory target rather than on the explanatory method. It promises to be local, because the controversial features of the idea of self and personal identity are likely to be special to them. (This might not be the case with a defect in the explanatory apparatus.) It points to a deep and serious problem. Therefore, the focus of my interpretation is on the respects in which the idea of self and personal identity successfully established in 1.4.6 falls short of being satisfactory, in terms of Hume's own assumptions about it; and why Hume finds no way to make it right. The idea is consistent; and it is one that can be produced by imagination. Thus, the problem is not one of spuriousness of content, as it is with the philosophical idea of the simple and identical self. It must depend on the conceptual roles that the idea of self and personal identity perform in our ordinary cognitive practices. It must be a failure in achieving explanatory equilibrium between representational elements, operations of imagination, and conceptual roles.

My suggestion is that the idea of self and personal identity on which 1.4.6 focuses lacks the *first-personal* dimension that implicitly or explicitly marks the conceptual roles Hume ascribes to it. The claim is not the obvious one that this

---

[25] See Garrett, 'Rethinking Hume's Second Thoughts', 24.
[26] See Ellis, 'Contents of Hume's Appendix', 198–9, 217–26: 'Hume's problem, I will explain, concerns the relation between the contents of perceptions along which the mind proceeds with an easy transition, on the one hand, and the contents of those ideas the mind sometimes subsequently invents, on the other.' The problem arising from that relation is different in my interpretation from Ellis's.
[27] See Ellis, 'Contents of Hume's Appendix', 224–5.

idea should be applicable with reference to oneself. Rather, it is that by having this idea and applying it to ourselves, we can achieve an immediate and direct view of our internal world (perceptions, mind, person) *as our own*; a view, a recognition, a presence of *ourselves as and to ourselves*. The first thing to show then is that Hume ascribes first-personal features to the roles associated to the idea of self.[28]

(a) The phenomenology of our ordinary experience, our manifest image, is primarily that of being immersed in a world of causally connected, persisting, things and events, which includes bodies and minds. Also the phenomenology of our internal experience is that of a flux or a theatre: something we look at as spectators. There are, however, hints of a subjective phenomenology, which somehow suggest a first-personal stance. One such hint comes from Hume's rejection of the claim that that external existence is manifest to the senses. Hume argues against this position by remarking that our immediate experience only reveals perceptions as perceptions, as internal beings. 'For since all actions and sensations of the mind are known to us by consciousness, they must necessarily appear in every particular what they are, and be what they appear. Every thing that enters the mind, being in *reality* a perception, 'tis impossible any thing shou'd to *feeling* appear different. This were to suppose, that even where we are most intimately conscious, we might be mistaken' (1.4.2.7). Such intimate consciousness seems to be first personal; and Hume makes of it a general aspect of our cognition. Something like a first-personal stance is also suggested by the conception or feeling of the action of the mind, which is an (under theorized) aspect of memory. 'In thinking of our past thoughts we not only delineate out the objects, of which we were thinking, but also conceive the action of the mind in the meditation, that certain *je-ne-scai-quoi*, of which 'tis impossible to give any definition or description, but which every one sufficiently understands' (1.3.8.16)

(b) The first-personal aspects of the idea of self and personal identity multiply in Book 2, published together with Book 1 and forming a strict unity with it. In Book 2 that idea is considered in connection with the passions and

---

[28] I follow Don Garrett's discussion in 'The Idea of Self'. The difficulty I am trying to focus on is a form of the missing subject of consciousness, which should be there in order to make sense of important aspects Hume's own philosophy. As McNabb famously put it: 'How can a series of conscious states be aware of itself as a series?' (McNabb, *Hume*, 152); see, for a wisely cautious discussion, T. Penelhum, 'Hume's Theory of the Self Revisited', in *Dialogue*, 1975 (in Tweyman, *David Hume. Critical Assessments*, Volume 3, (640–74), 665, 670–1). Hume lacks a proper theory of consciousness and this harms his theory at many points—from the fallibility of impressions to the account of what is for objects to be present to consciousness to the analysis of the falsity of the vulgar belief in body to the conception of internal perceptions. In some respects, the difficulty in the *Appendix* is one of lack of a subject of consciousness; even though it has distinctive features. See, along these lines, Stroud, *Hume*, 130–3; for an opposite reading, W. Robison, 'Hume of Personal Identity', in *Journal of the History of Philosophy*, 1974 (in Tweyman, *David Hume. Critical Assessments*, Volume 3 (687–703), 696–7).

our concern for ourselves. In particular, the idea of self is the object of the indirect passions of pride and humility. It is part of the mental working that constitutively individuates, produces, and allow us to feel, recognize and, at one remove, classify such passions. It is not only a 'natural' but also an 'original' property of these passions (2.1.3.2). ''Tis always self, which is the object of pride and humility; and whenever the passions look beyond, 'tis still with a view to ourselves, nor can any person or object otherwise have any influence upon us' (2.1.3.2; see 2.1.5.3; 2.1.5.5). The idea of self, as the object or part of the content of these passions, is that individuated and explained in 1.4.6: a 'succession of related ideas or impressions' (2.1.2.2); the 'connected succession of perceptions, which we call *self*' (2.1.2.3). However, in relation to its role in eliciting, structuring, and driving passions, Hume brings into view an important, first-personal aspect of it: its affording us a sense of ourselves, an intimate—immediate and proprietary—consciousness of *ourselves* being *that* succession of perceptions. 'That succession of related ideas and impressions, of which we have an intimate memory and consciousness' (2.1.2.2). 'The immediate *object* of pride and humility is self or that identical person, of whose thoughts, actions, and sensations we are intimately conscious' (2.2.1.2). The first-personal aspect of the idea of self is explicit and prominent.

(c) This explains the phenomenon of sympathy and, thereby, of moral approval. ''Tis evident, that as we are at all times intimately conscious of ourselves, our sentiments and passions, their ideas must strike upon us with greater vivacity than the ideas of the sentiments and passions of any other person' (2.2.2.15). It also seems to be the way in which imagination and cognition can have a bearing on motivation and action. 'There is an easy reason, why every thing contiguous to us, either in space or time, shou'd be conceiv'd with a peculiar force and vivacity, and excel every other object, in its influence on the imagination. Ourself is intimately present to us, and whatever is related to self must partake of that quality' (2.3.7.1). Perhaps, awareness of this first-personal dimension motivates Hume, already in 1.4.6, to tell apart the account of the idea of self with regard to thought and imagination, which regards its content and is the deepest layer of Hume's theory, from its application in the theory of passions and motivation, where first-personal considerations are prominent.

In order to answer this question [about the propensity to ascribe identity to successive perceptions], we must distinguish betwixt personal identity, as it regards our thought or imagination, and as it regards our passions or the concern we take in ourselves. The first is our present subject; and to explain it perfectly we must take the matter pretty deep. (1.4.6.5)

Since, on the other hand, the idea of self and personal identity with regard of thought and imagination converges with that which is involved in the passions, we can legitimately require that it support all the relevant cognitive functions, including the first-personal ones.[29] Hume thus fully recognizes the first-personal aspect of the idea of self. In fact, he regards them as part of what supports the philosophical illusion of the perception of a strictly simple and perfectly identical self. ('The strongest sensation, the most violent passion, say they, instead of distracting us from this view, only fix it the more intensely, and make us consider their influence on *self* either by their pain or pleasure', 1.4.61.)

There may be signs that Hume had this first-personal aspect of the idea of self and personal identity in the back of his mind when criticizing his own earlier account. It is interesting that, when rehearsing the original account in the *Appendix*, Hume resorts to the Lockean apparatus of consciousness. He summarizes his account in one sentence. 'It follows, therefore, that the thought alone finds personal identity, when reflecting on the train of past perceptions, that compose a mind, the ideas of them are felt to be connected together, and naturally introduce each other' (*Appendix* 20). He then remarks, about the character of his account.

> However extraordinary this conclusion may seem, it need not surprise us. Most philosophers seem inclin'd to think, that personal identity *arises* from consciousness; and consciousness is nothing but a reflected thought or perception. The present philosophy, therefore, has so far a promising aspect.   (*Appendix* 20)
>
> But all my hopes vanish, when I come to explain the principles, that unite our successive perceptions in our thought or consciousness. I cannot discover any theory, which gives me satisfaction on this head.   (*Appendix* 20)

Now, that personal identity arises from consciousness was, if not what most philosophers thought, certainly what Locke did. However, it was *not* what Hume himself thought in 1.4.6, where there is barely any mention of consciousness. (Its only mention is at 1.4.6.1, to describe the philosophical position Hume is criticizing.) That consciousness goes unmentioned in 1.4.6 is one indication of the deep contrast between Locke's and Hume's theories of personal identity. To put it *very* summarily, Locke rejects any grounding of personal identity on the identity of a thinking substance. But he is also a non-reductionist: what constitutes the identity of persons is something with personal character that strictly remains the

---

[29] J. McIntyre, 'Hume and the Problem of Personal Identity', in D. F. Norton & J. Taylor, *The Cambridge Companion to Hume*, Cambridge University Press, Cambridge 2009, 177:208, 190–5, argues that the idea of self involved in Book 2 is the same with the one established in 1.4.6. (She identifies the problem in the *Appendix* in a different way from how I am proposing.) I agree that Hume's programme is precisely that of explaining indirect passions, self-concern, and sympathy, with that idea; and that this is explicit in the text. But still the first-personal aspects of the role of the idea of self, that also are present in the text, are not amenable to that idea.

same across time. Locke identifies this ground of identity in the sameness of first-personal consciousness. A person is 'a thinking intelligent being, that has reason and reflection, and can consider itself as itself, the same thinking thing in different times and places; which it does only by that consciousness which is inseparable from thinking, and, as it seems to me, essential to it: it being impossible for any one to perceive, without perceiving that he does perceive'.[30] Hume, as we have seen, disconnects the idea of self and personal identity from that of a thinking substance. But, in contrast with Locke, he is a reductionist about personal identity: nothing with personal character or pertaining to self is identical across time; the idea of self and personal identity is that of a causal system of successive perceptions, identified and unified by transitions of the imagination.[31] It is not by accident therefore that Hume carefully avoids resorting to the notion of consciousness and even using the term in 1.4.6. Essentially, just as there is nothing in Locke's theory with the role of Hume's imagination, there is nothing in Hume's theory with the role of Locke's consciousness.[32]

It is thus surprising that, in the *Appendix*, Hume likens, if only by allusion, his own account of personal identity to one giving a constitutive role to consciousness. He does this in the context of the attempt to clarify, in the first place to himself, what is amiss with his account. All his hopes vanish, when he attempts in vain to explain the principles that should unite successive perceptions in our thought or consciousness. I would also suggest that the change in the phrasing of the method of explanation ('*arises* from consciousness') is functional to the change in the explanatory aim ('unite our successive perceptions in our thought or consciousness'). I think it is highly unlikely that, in resorting to the language of consciousness, Hume was unaware of the prominence he was giving to the first-personal dimension of consciousness in the constitution of self and personal identity, along Lockean lines.[33] It is as if Hume were now alert to a new desideratum, a new explanatory target for a theory of personal identity. Such desideratum is prominent in Locke's concept of consciousness and something Hume himself fully recognizes: connecting the idea of self and personal identity to the first person.[34]

---

[30] Locke, *Essay*, 2.27.9, 335.
[31] In the discussion of the identity of artefacts (1.4.6.11) and of the confusion of numerical and specific identity, for instance, of sounds (1.4.6.13), Hume recognizes that something is the same across variation: 'the common end, in which the parts conspire' and, respectively, the cause which produced the sounds. This latter is clearly insufficient for any ascription of identity. One could hesitate about the former since it has a Lockean ring. However, Hume makes well clear that the supposition of a common end does not mark some otherwise unnoticed feature of identity but simply 'affords an easy transition of the imagination from one situation of the body to another'.
[32] The deep differences between Locke's and Hume's conceptions of consciousness are well discussed in Ainslie, *Hume's True Skepticism*, 117–28, 190–7.
[33] See, for instance, Locke, *Essay* 2.27.9, 335.
[34] In the original account, this first-personal dimension might have escaped Hume because he was reading Locke on personal identity through glasses provided by Butler or Berkeley, as a memory

This change in the explanatory target raises, by Hume's own light, difficulties for the explanation. It is interesting that the imagination now drops out from the explanans, from the underlying mental processes. 'Imagination' only occurs once in the part of the *Appendix* that deals with personal identity. This might be because Hume somehow recognizes that it does not put in place the right content for the explanandum, the idea of self and personal identity. All this is, of course, far from decisive. Hume might be simply rephrasing his preceding views. However, his point might also that the principles of imagination at work in 1.4.6 can explain how ideas of reflection of successive perceptions come to be felt as ideas of the successive parts of one thinking being. But they do not explain how they come to be united in one consciousness, if this is to be *my* consciousness; and in this way how we come to be immediately conscious of internal perceptions as belonging *to ourselves*, of *our own presence* throughout such perceptions.[35]

I think that Hume, in the *Appendix*, is reckoning with a limit (or what he has come to see as a limit) of the content-productive capacities of the imagination. The content of the idea of self and personal identity, as we apply it in our worldview and common life, includes a first-personal dimension. Entertaining and applying to oneself that idea allows having intimate consciousness of oneself as oneself and being immediately present to oneself. The transitions of imagination along related ideas of reflection make us conceive of the perceptions these latter represent as one persisting thinking person. This unity of perceptions is present to the mind, to our awareness; but this is *not* the same with having present the unity of successive perceptions *as ourselves*; with the consciousness of that unity, thinking being, as *us*. There is a *gap* between the idea of a series of internal perceptions conceived, by way of imaginative operations, as the successive existence of one thinking person *and* any idea whose content is the unity of perceptions in *our* thought or *our* consciousness; their composing *our self*. This essentially first-personal self-presence, this grasp of oneself (qua a series of internal perceptions) as oneself (in an intimate, first-personal mode) is not explained in the causation account. Hume might have come to a dim recognition that the idea of self and personal identity he had succeeded in individuating and explaining at 1.4.6 was missing a crucial element. The idea had the right explanation but its content was not the right one. Furthermore, Hume suspected that he could not derive such dimension with the apparatus of 1.4.6.[36]

---

theorist. Besides dropping any reference to consciousness, he criticizes memory (which he would have taken as the same with consciousness) as productive of personal identity because of its restricted scope and implicit circularity. One might *conjecture* that the Lockean language of the *Appendix* follows on Hume's realization that Locke was not a memory theorist, after all; and that Locke's grounding of personal identity on consciousness harboured an insight (the first-personal character) that he (Hume) also shared.

[35] Green, 'The Idea of Momentary Self', 113–14, notices the Lockean tones in the *Appendix*.
[36] See V. Mascarenhas, 'Hume's Recantation Revisited', *Hume Studies*, 27, 2001, 279: 300, 289–90; Winkler, '"All is Revolution in Us"', 24–7.

10.3.3 A Difficulty too Hard for my Understanding

Suppose this is Hume's problem in the *Appendix*. Why is this difficulty so hard? Why does Hume not see any way in which imagination can generate such an idea of self and personal identity? Answers to questions of this sort are bound to be highly speculative, given that Hume does not make clear what problem he has in mind. Still, something can be suggested, along the lines just explored. It is crucial to see whether, on Hume's principles, an idea of self and personal identity affording intimate self-consciousness could be explained without assuming a representation in reflection of our self.

The last step of Hume's explanation, as we know, is the feeling of a smooth imaginative transition by Act/Idea Resemblance along ideas of reflection of our perceptions, related in a causal 'system', a mind; together with the enactment by Reconciliation of the unity of the perceptions represented by such ideas into a persisting thinking person. This deep cognitive change allows us to think of an internal world, consisting of perceptions. But this does not seem to put in place anything we would be immediately, intimately conscious of as ourselves or the first-personal character of the idea of self or personal identity. All imagination does is to add two relations to ideas of reflection already related to each other: a relation of imperfect identity and a compositional relation. The same is true of the preceding step, at which internal perceptions are causally connected by transitions of the imagination along the constantly conjoined ideas of reflection we have of them. These customary transitions among ideas of reflection and their projection on internal perceptions do not seem to confer any first-personal character to the resulting idea. They do not appear to instantiate and spread on the flux of internal perceptions anything like the idea that that flux is *ourselves*, rather than the successive existence of *one* thinking being. The true idea of the human mind is not per se the idea of our own mind.[37]

This, however, may not be decisive. Perhaps we should re-examine the premises of the aforementioned argument. Because of their inferential and projective character and of Non-mixture, the operations of imagination leave intact the object-representing contents of antecedently given ideas. The problem with imperfect identity, for instance, depends precisely on the preservation of the contents of the associated ideas, which individuate distinct existents. Now, in the case at hand, the associated ideas are ideas of reflection. One could thus suggest that ideas of reflection, because of their nature and role, have some sort of

---

[37] In work in progress, I suggest that Hume's imagination, in Book 2 of the *Treatise*, has a sort of centred, de se character, which is an aspect of how it operates, when it interacts with the passions and contributes to them. But this de se character does not seem to have any ground in the explanation proposed by Hume in 1.4.6. Besides, one may doubt that such centred character amounts to anything like the immediate consciousness of oneself. This point would require a detailed treatment that I cannot provide here.

first-personal content and represent internal perceptions as *ours*, while failing short of representing *our self*. This is a tempting thought—but one we should resist, as Hume wisely does.

We can consider two alternative ways in which reflection could represent the flux of perceptions as our own flux of perceptions. First. It could be by an element of representational content borne by reflection. But this would amount to considering the self as an object of representation, distinct from individual perceptions and related to them. This is not a possibility in Hume's framework. Second, it could be that successive perceptions represented by reflection are, just because of this, apprehended as belonging to ourselves, not just as composing one mind and one person (this would be, so to say, an original quality of reflection). However, this is to misunderstand the cognitive nature of reflection and of its ideas. Reflection is a species of representation. Its contents are determined by its objects, that is, by internal perceptions and their properties. This takes us back to the first option: unless internal perceptions are really related to our self and we have by reflection the idea of our self and of this relation, our ownership of them cannot be part of their reflective representation. Anything different would mean that reflection alters the nature of its objects; that it is not representational. There is no other option therefore but to connect a presumptively first-personal character of ideas of reflection with a perception of our self. This is unacceptable for Hume, so we are stuck with a dramatic explanatory lacuna.

One last point. By construction, the idea of self and personal identity stands in causal relations to the ideas of reflection and to the internal perceptions that contribute to its content. This is sufficient to determine indexically, by way of such causal connection, of which mind such idea of self and personal identity is the idea: the mind or causally connected bundle that they compose together. That mind is also the person that persists the same across time. Now, I might well be (it is physically possible that I am) *that* mind. The idea of self and personal identity I come to have could then be the idea of me, of myself. But this indexical construal of the idea of self does not advance us a step toward the intimate and immediate consciousness of ourselves. This indexical or reflexive individuation and reference of the idea of self would only be de re: in virtue of the fact that I am that mind. The point is that, in order to be first personal in its content, the idea not only should be *of me* but should somehow make myself present to me *as myself* (as Locke puts it). But it is precisely this way of being present to oneself that seems to be out of the reach of reflection and of the transitions of the imagination.[38]

Thus, we have here a very deep problem. But is it also a problem that Hume *might* have considered tractable, as he seems to imply? My interpretation suggests

---

[38] Thanks to Don Garrett for pressing me on this point. I add that, if de se character counts as first personal, such reflexive individuation would not be de se. (If, as I suspect, Lewis' de se is not properly first personal, then it can well be de se; but Hume's problem then would remain.)

that it is, discounting the overall speculative character of this as of any reading of the *Appendix*. More particularly, Hume had available a way out of *this* labyrinth. Hume's difficulty arises if the first-personal aspects of the idea of self and personal identity are identified with elements of its content; that is, if the intimate consciousness of oneself that such idea should make possible consists in the representation, by that idea, of a special object with some special property—oneself. It would be precisely Hume's realization that this is the only way he has open that brings to a halt his attempts to explain the idea of self.[39] However, Hume was in a position to explain the first-personal dimension of the idea of self not by resorting to some element of the object-representing content of ideas of reflection but to a *manner of conception*. A model for this would be provided by his account of the sense of reality associated to impressions, of what distinguishes belief from mere conception and, even more to the point, of the sense of pastness associated to reminiscence (1.3.8.16). This manner of conception would be distinctive of ideas of reflection, as a non-representational mark of their representing internal perceptions, and would be transmitted along the transitions of imagination (like the other manners of conception). First-personal or intimate consciousness of oneself would not be realized as a self-standing, contentful perception; so, it would be perfectly consistent with Hume's rejection that we have any idea of the self. I am not aware that Hume entertains this possibility.[40] The conceptual and interpretive problem of the *Appendix* seems to indicate a difficulty in Hume's theory of the imagination and in his general philosophy: the difficulty of making sense of and making room for a subjective dimension in thinking and cognition, in connection with both mental activities and mental contents, and in ways consistent with radical naturalism. We have tracked this difficulty at different stages of Hume's overall argument: the right understanding of Two Viewpoints; the possibility of errors in impressions of sensation; the primitive grasp of an

---

[39] J. McIntyre, 'Hume's Underground Self', (1993) in Tweyman, *David Hume. Critical Assessments*, Volume 3, 718–29, suggests that Hume's later conception of the self is essentially the same with the earlier one, that is, that of a composite unity; but that the issue of the generation of its idea by imagination is replaced by attention to its implications for religion. This continuity is prominent in a passage from the *Dialogues*: 'A mind, whose acts and sentiments and ideas are not distinct and successive; one, that is wholly simple, and totally immutable; is a mind, which has no thought, no reason, no will, no sentiment, no love, no hatred; or in a word, is no mind at all. It is an abuse of terms to give it that appellation; and we may as well speak of limited extension without figure, or of number without composition' (D. Hume, *Dialogues concerning Natural Religion*, J. Gaskin, ed., Oxford University Press, Oxford 1993, 61).

[40] However, Strawson (*Evident Connexion*, 136–7) very helpfully quotes from a 1746 letter to Lord Kames where Hume, commenting one of Kames' *Essays* (published five years later: Henry Home, Lord Kames, *Essays on the Principles of Morality and Natural Religion*, 1779 (1751), ed. by M. C. Moran. Online Library of Liberty, 2005), remarks: 'I likt exceedingly your Method of explaining personal Identity as more satisfactory than any thing that had ever occurr'd to me.' Strawson suggests that Hume might have had in mind Kames's view that the origin of the idea of a persisting self is 'an original feeling, or consciousness of himself, and of his existence, which for the most part accompanies every one of his impressions and ideas'. I develop this hint in "Hume's Third Thoughts on Personal Ideatity", *Hume Studies*, forthcoming.

internal–external distinction; and now the first-personal dimension of the idea of self. But it is fair to say that this problem is still with us.

10.4 Summary

The idea of self and personal identity gives unity and stability to our introspective experience, defining an internal world that is the counterpart to the real, durable, external one.

In § 10.1 I examine Hume's argument that the ideas of soul and self not are not representational. As I point out in § 10.1.1, the idea of soul as substance does not properly mark a cognitive gap, because it is only a philosophers' fiction, without significant cognitive roles and thus only well lost. By contrast, in § 10.1.2, the idea of self and personal identity has a variety of needful cognitive roles in common life. One cannot seriously ask whether one is a self or thinking person. Hume gives a priori, relatively a priori, and a posteriori arguments for identifying a gap in correspondence with this idea. In particular he remarks that reflection represents our minds only as a bundle or flux of perceptions.

In § 10.2 I study the production of our idea of self and personal identity by the imagination. The imagination operates on the represented flux of perceptions, in § 10.2.1, forming the idea of the identity of internal perceptions and then that of the self that persists across their succession. (This is somewhat similar to the constancy account of body.) The crucial explanatory factor is the shift of the imagination from the resemblance of its acts to that of its ideas, which makes us ascribe identity to successive perceptions.

§ 10.2.2 discusses how Hume's integrates his account with the individuation of the relation that supports the identifying transitions of the imagination. Somewhat analogously to his theory of body, Hume distinguishes two such relations. One, representational, is resemblance: the resemblance of internal perceptions produced by the inclusion in their flux of ideas of memory. The resemblance account (like the constancy account) builds on a deep, representational layer of contents. However, Hume regards it as flawed or at least insufficient. If the identity of perceptions were restricted to such as we have memory of, the ensuing idea of self would fall short of its roles in ordinary cognition. By contrast, successive internal perceptions related by causation define the true idea of the human mind, as a bundle of different perceptions connected as causes and effects. This is the idea of the mind at work throughout the *Treatise*. Because of the inferential potential of causal ideas, the corresponding idea of self does not face problems of restricted application.

In § 10.2.3 I study how causally connected perceptions and identifying transitions of the imagination produce the idea of self and personal identity. Like in the constancy account, Hume resorts to the cognitive tensions of imperfect identity and to Reconciliation. Hume's explanation is sparing in detail. A crucial point is that the representational antecedent of the work of the imagination is not the interruption of perceptions but the variation of their continuous flux. The reconciling idea of a continuant therefore is not that of a persisting object with the qualities of resembling perceptions, but that of an entity of which the flux of perceptions constitutes the successive existence and parts. This is our actual idea of self and personal identity.

In§ 10.3 I address the interpretive problem of Hume's recantation of his own theory of self in the *Appendix* to the *Treatise*. § 10.3.1 attempts to individuate the nature and grounds of Hume's concerns, which are famously elusive. Hume still denies that we have an impression and representation idea of self. He still endorses his general style of explanation: transitions of the imagination along distinct and related ideas of our perceptions. Hume finally says that the problem is with the unity of perceptions in our thought and consciousness but fails to identify it with precision.

In § 10.3.2 I sketch a solution to this interpretive puzzle, aiming to keep together the seriousness of the problem with its being restricted to the theory of self and personal identity. My focus is whether the content of the idea of self, by the causation account, is up to the conceptual roles that Hume ascribes to that idea. I suggest that what Hume's theory fails to put in place is the first personal dimension of the idea of self: the immediate consciousness that the self we have the idea of is our own self. Hume recognizes the role of first-personal considerations, especially but not exclusively in connection with the passions. This is therefore a serious cognitive gap.

Finally, in § 10.3.3, I argue that the problem this cognitive gap raises is indeed serious for Hume's philosophy. Interestingly, in the *Appendix*, the imagination almost drops out of the picture. Hume seems to have encountered a limit in the explanatory import, radically impersonal, of perceptions and imagination, representation, and inference. The imagination, working in third-personal, mereological ways, cannot instantiate a properly subjective dimension of thinking and cognition.

PART V

THE IMAGINATION OR UNDERSTANDING, CALL IT WHICH YOU PLEASE

I have so far discussed how the imagination contributes to Hume's 'logic' with respect of the 'nature of our ideas' (how it shapes 'new original' ideas) as well as with respect to the 'principles and operations of our reasoning faculty' (how it makes possible idea-comparing inferences). But the work of Hume's imagination is to explain not only conceptual change but also the possibility of substantive cognitive achievements. This is another important respect in which Hume's imagination takes up the role of the understanding or reason. Also in this respect, the pattern of Hume's analysis and arguments is the unveiling of cognitive gaps and their closure by operations of the imagination.

Two topics are prominent. The first and most fundamental cognitive gap is the difference itself between conception and cognition: what differentiates and connects the conception of an idea and a cognition with that idea for content. The difference between having ideas and having cognitions, as we know from the Important Footnote, cannot be accounted for in terms of elements of object-representing content or of acts of the understanding individuated by such elements. The general problem with this view is that it would draw a wedge between what we conceive and what we have cognition of, by believing or judging. Hume claims that philosophers have failed to come to terms with the nature of cognition, or even to recognize that there is an explanatory task in this area.

> This operation of the mind, which forms the belief of any matter of fact, seems hitherto to have been one of the greatest mysteries of philosophy: tho' no one has so much as suspected, that there was any difficulty in explaining it. For my part I must own, that I find a considerable difficulty in the case; and that even when I think I understand the subject perfectly, I am at a loss for terms to express my meaning. (1.3.7.7)

Hume addresses this cognitive gap with a general distinction between the contents of ideas, both object-representing and issuing from imagination, and their manner of conception, the feeling with which they are present to the mind. He then puts forward his theory of belief, by discussing what manner of conception constitutes cognitive import, as well as what natural state of mind realizes cognition by probable inference. This is the subject matter of Chapter 11 and, as it will turn out, the Structural Principle takes centre stage here.

The second main topic is the cognitive gap individuated by the possibility of epistemic differences between the principles and operations of the natural mind: in particular the possibility that the principles and works of the imagination have different epistemic values. We recognize and master such epistemic differences in our ordinary and philosophical cognitive practice. And they are presupposed by Hume's philosophy as a whole; in particular but not exclusively in connection with its foundational ambitions. But in the framework of Hume's philosophy they raise a special difficulty, as it has been repeatedly pointed out by the interpreters, because of its strong naturalistic commitments. It is not immediately clear how to reconcile the naturalistic viewpoint afforded by Hume's imagination with the roles and concepts of epistemic value and authority. Hume explicitly identifies this problem rightly in connection with the fundamental position of the imagination in the mind. This deep cognitive gap is at the core of Hume's conception of the imagination as understanding and explains how scepticism has such an important position in Book 1 of the *Treatise*. This is the topic of Chapter 12.

11
One of the Greatest Mysteries of Philosophy

> What then is this *belief*? And how does it differ from the simple conception of any thing? Here is a new question unthought of by philosophers.
>
> (*Abstract* 17)

It is important to keep in mind that, under the label of belief, Hume addresses two distinct, if strictly related, questions. The first concerns belied as the *attitude* of acceptance or taking true, in relation to certain ideas, which is a common constituent of all kinds of cognitive states (whether issuing from the senses, from a priori or a posteriori reason, or from imagination in the more limited sense) and marks off cognition from conception. I will refer to the attitude of belief as 'assent'. The second question concerns belief as a distinctive kind of *mental state* (composed, as any other cognitive state, of cognitive content and assent), which is the mental, natural realization of the cognitive and epistemic condition of probability, as distinct from sense and memory and from knowledge. While internally connected—belief as a mental state is explained as the extension of assent to non-representational and non-a priori conceptions—these questions afford two distinct perspectives on cognition and should be considered separately. In either case, Hume identifies a cognitive gap and addresses it with his theory of the imagination. Also here, alongside the conception of non-object-representing contents, Hume's imagination takes up roles usually ascribed to the understanding (judgement, doxastic deliberation).

11.1 Belief as Attitude: Assent

11.1.1 The Cognitive Gap of Assent

Hume's core insight is that having cognition of something is different not only from *ignoring* but also from only *conceiving* it. The contrast between conception and cognition is the important one for our present discussion: cognitions are mental conditions—perceptions—which are composite in ways not matched by any complexity of object-representing or imagination-based contents. Hume's general problem is that the difference between conception and cognition cannot be explained by any further and distinct element of content and, in general, by any comparison or addition of ideas to those we already entertain. This impossibility indicates a cognitive gap. The gap is general and deep, because belief as assent is a common factor of mental states as different as memory and judgement: The belief, which attends our memory, is of the same nature with that, which is deriv'd from our judgments' (1.3.13.20). It is, in fact, the general distinctive mark of all cognitive states. By the Important Footnote, assent realizes in our cognitive nature the crucial a priori connection between cognition and truth (which Hume fully endorses).

> But if we compare together all the phaenomena that occur on this head, we shall find, that truth, however necessary it may seem in all works of genius, has no other effect than to procure an easy reception for the ideas, and to make the mind acquiesce in them with satisfaction, or at least without reluctance. (1.3.10.6)
>
> Whether we consider a single object, or several; whether we dwell on these objects, or run from them to others; and in whatever form or order we survey them, the act of the mind exceeds not a simple conception; and the only remarkable difference, which occurs on this occasion, is, when we join belief to the conception, and are perswaded of the truth of what we conceive. (1.3.7.5, fn. 20)

Hume individuates the cognitive gap of assent by excluding that reality can be represented and truth can be denoted by a distinct element of content (as if it were one of the qualities with which objects are present in sensation). This would require a common element in the contents of all impressions, a reality-and truth-mark, so to say; but, a posteriori, no such common element is observable. Furthermore, a priori, we can always form a detached conception of the contents of impressions of sensation, a perfect idea of their objects; if the apprehension of reality and the mark of truth consisted in a further element of object-representing contents, no such detached conception or perfect idea of impressions or objects would ever be possible. There would always be a difference in content between impressions and ideas. The mental nature of assent, given its function, is thus a problem.

Hume's general response to the cognitive gap of assent, is to identify the differentia of cognition with respect of conception not as an element of content (some element of what is present, represented, or thought with perceptions) but with a manner of conception of presentations, representations, and thoughts. This is the same line he had taken with the idea of existence (see § 2.4.1): with how we represent the existence of something, as opposite to its mere possibility. Thus, having rehearsed his conception of existence as the simple conception of any separable object (conceiving God as existent is nothing different from conceiving God), Hume makes this claim about belief as assent.

> But I go farther; and not content with asserting, that the conception of the existence of any object is no addition to the simple conception of it, I likewise maintain, that the belief of the existence joins no new ideas to those, which compose the idea of the object. When I think of God, when I think of him as existent, and when I believe him to be existent, my idea of him neither encreases nor diminishes. But as 'tis certain there is a great difference betwixt the simple conception of the existence of an object, and the belief of it, and as this difference lies not in the parts or composition of the idea, which we conceive; it follows, that it must lie in the *manner,* in which we conceive it.   (1.3.7.2)[1]

The manner of conception, in the case of the representation of existence as well as in that of the corresponding assent, is marked by force of vivacity: a lively and forceful conception. Hume makes well clear that assent is not the *effect* of a forceful and lively manner of conception but *is* that very manner of conception. 'Here we must not be contented with saying, that the vividness of the idea produces the belief: We must maintain that they are individually the same' (1.3.9.17). Hume's most extended and deepest discussion of the nature of assent is in the *Appendix*. (Both in its text and in the passages that he instructs to insert at places in the main text.) The discussion is articulated in two parts. In the first Hume insists that assent, our 'conviction and assurance' (Appendix 3), cannot consist in the addition of the idea of reality or existence to the simple conception of an object. This is because we have no distinct idea of existence and because of the involuntary character of belief ('if belief consisted merely in a new idea, annex'd to the conception, it wou'd be in a man's power to believe what he pleas'd', Appendix 2). The alternative is to consider assent as consisting 'merely in a certain feeling or sentiment; in something, that depends not on the will, but must arise from certain determinate causes and principles, of which we are not the masters.' In the second part of his discussion Hume raises a question not addressed in the main text, that is, whether assent might not consist 'in some impression or feeling, distinguishable from the conception. It does not modify the conception, and render it more present and intense; It is only annex'd to it, after the same manner that *will* and *desire* are annex'd to particular conceptions of good and pleasure' (Appendix 4). This is interesting because Hume is addressing a possible ambiguity in his view of assent. Discarding the explanation of assent by an idea added to a simple conception leaves the possibility that assent as feeling be itself a distinct

---

[1] As Owen, *Hume's Reason*, 158–9, remarks, Hume's claim that his account of belief addresses 'a new question unthought of by philosophers' seems to be connected with the central position that he ascribes to that account in the anti-rationalist programme of Book I.

impression; a distinct mental episode, accompanying simple conceptions; but not an idea. Assent would not *be* but rather *bear* the phenomenology of reality.[2]

Hume's response to this alternative view is doubly interesting. He is ready to recognize that *some* attitudes have the character of distinct impressions; but they are not cognitive but conative, desire or will, associated only to specific contents, goods, or pleasures. Conative states have thus a different mental structure from cognitive ones. Hume also clarifies in what sense assent is a manner of conception. A manner of conception is not a new episode added to an idea. It is a pure *modification* of conception, which only changes how contents are present to awareness, without adding any distinct perception to those already existing in the mind. The arguments with which Hume supports this position—evidence from internal experience, explanatory sufficiency, availability of causal grounding— aim to establish that assent 'varies and 'modifies' the ideas present to the mind, 'in a certain manner', 'but produces no act of the mind, distinct from this peculiarity of conception' (Appendix 4). Assent is nothing 'but a firmer conception, or faster hold, that we take of the object' (Appendix 5). This is an important, distinctive feature of cognitive states, the core of Hume's contrast between belief and desire (and it is obviously connected to Non-Mixture). Since manners of conception do not consist in distinguishable contents and separable mental episodes, they allow Hume to close the cognitive gap of the difference of cognition form conception.

The *Appendix* marks a change also in regard of the phenomenology and the mental functions of assent: a shift from a narrower characterization centred on force and vivacity of conception to a more subtle and nuanced one centred on feeling, on how ideas *feel*.[3] Feeling is taken to be inclusive of force and vivacity but is not identified with them. Right at the close of the *Appendix*, Hume remarks that the claim that two ideas of the same object can only be different by their different degrees of force and vivacity is an error. 'I believe there are other differences among ideas, which cannot properly be comprehended under these terms. Had I said, that two ideas of the same object can only be different by their different *feeling*, I shou'd have been nearer the truth' (Appendix 22). This is also the point of the example of trying to remember some circumstance.

> As soon as the circumstance is mention'd, that touches the memory, the very same ideas now appear in a new light, and have, in a manner, a different feeling from what they had before. Without any other alteration, beside that of the feeling, they become immediately ideas of the memory, and are assented to. (1.3.5.4)

---

[2] Garrett, *Hume*, 137, rightly remarks that belief is not an impression of reflection.
[3] To grasp this shift it is recommendable to read in a row the whole text of the *Appendix*, including the texts which were to be inserted here and there in Book 1. It is conveniently published in Volume II of the Norton & Norton edition, 674–84.

Hume seems to substitute the earlier mention of force and vivacity with the catch-all formula of feeling to achieve a more articulated characterization of the attitude, associating other features to the manner of conception that tells apart cognition from conception.

> An idea assented to *feels* different from a fictitious idea, that the fancy alone presents to us: And this different feeling I endeavour to explain by calling it a superior *force*, or *vivacity*, or *solidity*, or *firmness*, or *steadiness*. This variety of terms, which may seem so unphilosophical, is intended only to express that act of the mind, which renders realities more present to us than fictions, causes them to weigh more in the thought, and gives them a superior influence on the passions and imagination.   (1.3.7.7)

This is also what Hume says in the main text of the *Appendix*.

> Now that there is a greater firmness and solidity in the conceptions, which are the objects of conviction and assurance, than in the loose and indolent reveries of a castle-builder, every one will readily own. They strike upon us with more force; they are more present to us; the mind has a firmer hold of them, and is more actuated and mov'd by them. It acquiesces in them; and, in a manner, fixes and reposes itself on them.   (Appendix 3)[4]

This much richer description of assent is the substance under the label of feeling. This characterization of assent has been criticized as a sleigh of hand to avoid the consequences of an excessively narrow understanding of what it is to assent to an idea. I think that it marks a progress. For one thing, there is no reason to restrict phenomenology to intrinsic qualities, like force and vivacity, in contrast with essentially relational ones, like solidity, firmness, or steadiness. These latter actually seem to capture an aspect of how believed ideas feel. For another thing, more importantly, Hume's leading idea in the *Appendix* seems to be that the substantive characterization of assent as feeling mirrors the cognitive roles of this attitude and of belief as a mental state.[5]

---

[4] 'We may make use of words, that express something near it. But its true and proper name is *belief*, which is a term that every one sufficiently understands in common life. And in philosophy we can go no farther, than assert, that it is something *felt* by the mind, which distinguishes the ideas of the judgment from the fictions of the imagination. It gives them more force and influence; makes them appear of greater importance; infixes them in the mind; and renders them the governing principles of all our actions' (1.3.7.7).

[5] For a legendarily uncharitable reading of Hume's theory of belief, see A. Flew, Hume's Philosophy of Belief, Routledge & Kegan Paul, London 1961, for instance 98–103. But examples, also more recent examples, could be multiplied. Some echoes of Wittgensteinian misgivings about Hume's mentalistic conception of belief are found in Pears, *Hume's System*, 50–1.

11.1.2 Assent, Sensible Representation, and the A Priori

Against the general background of the identification of assent with a manner of conception or feeling of fixedness, Hume proceeds to show such cognitive import is caused in the different kinds of cognition. Sensible representation, realized in impressions of sensation and ideas representing them, is marked, as a fact of our cognitive nature, by forceful and lively conception, by a feeling of presence or reality (see § 2.4.1). This is the distinctive phenomenology of perceptions of this kind, the mark of their being the only primitively representational ones. This explains how we can be acquainted with something as real and, correspondingly, apprehend its perception as true.

> Thus it appears, that the *belief* or *assent*, which always attends the memory and senses, is nothing but the vivacity of those perceptions they present; and that this alone distinguishes them from the imagination. To believe is in this case to feel an immediate impression of the senses, or a repetition of that impression in the memory. (1.3.5.7)

The two aspects of sensible representation are independent: we can conceive the same objects in different manners; in particular, with perfect ideas which include all their properties or qualities but do not represent them as real. Having object-presenting and -representing contents and feeling them as real or true are conceptually different conditions. Still, one cannot actually grasp any content in impression of sensation or with an idea of memory without also having the feeling of their reality and assenting to them as real. Both conditions are explained by the fundamental condition of sensible representation (in impression or by ideas): that its objects are actually present, given to experience. This is well captured by Kemp Smith: 'Belief is *native* to sense-perception; independently of any process of inference, it carries us to matter of fact and existence'.[6] Sense and memory are (respectively) the same with and as close as possible to sensible reality; this gives them a unique cognitive role and a privileged epistemic position; this also explains their essential dimension of assent.

> To believe is in this case to feel an immediate impression of the senses, or a repetition of that impression in the memory. 'Tis merely the force and liveliness of the perception, which constitutes the first act of the judgment. (1.3.5.7)

The 'first act of judgment' is the primitive assent that accompanies the contents given in impression or by ideas of memory. The conditions for objects to be

---

[6] Kemp Smith, *Philosophy of Hume*, 112 (see also 122–3). See Rocknak, *Imagined Causes*, 34–5, 37–8, on impressions as natural (states of) belief.

present to the mind or to be represented by it are also those for the 'first act of the judgment', for our assent to their reality. It is only the feeling of the reality of objects that explains our internal demonstratives: *This such*; and demonstrative import is essential to Hume's representation. Of course, the content of an impression can be detached from the impression itself and turned into a perfect idea. But this is precisely a shift from sensation and memory to imagination.[7]

The attitude of assent requires some discussion in the case of a priori knowledge. Also in this case, cognition or, more precisely, *knowledge* is explained by the distinction and combination of the properties of its content (including the modal force that goes with its articulation by internal relations of ideas) with the attitude of assent. The conditions and the explanation of assent are clear, like in the case of sense and memory.

> I therefore ask, Wherein consists the difference betwixt believing and disbelieving any proposition? The answer is easy with regard to propositions, that are prov'd by intuition or demonstration. In that case, the person, who assents, not only conceives the ideas according to the proposition, but is necessarily determin'd to conceive them in that particular manner, either immediately or by the interposition of other ideas. Whatever is absurd is unintelligible; nor is it possible for the imagination to conceive any thing contrary to a demonstration.
>
> (1.3.7.3)

The easy answer refers to the structure of awareness of contents articulated by internal relations of ideas and thereby by Separability. In the text just quoted, Hume mixes considerations relating to the modal force of ideas and to our assent to them, which should be told apart at least conceptually and explanatorily. But this is not difficult. The modal force of contents, in the case of internal relations of ideas, is explained by Hume with a block of the imagination in its attempt to conceive separately of two internally related ideas or to conceive of two incompatible ones as united (respectively, a mountain without a valley and a square circle). This block bears on the mind as a distinct, internal impression. But what explains, in the present case, the feeling or manner of conception of assent? Hume does not give an answer (he does not even seem to acknowledge the question). I would suggest that inferences and conceptions of ideas structured by Separability ('according to the proposition') are present to awareness in a manner or with a feeling marked, if not by '*force, or vivacity*', certainly by '*solidity, or firmness, or steadiness*', which Hume (in the *Appendix*) equates with assent. Metaphysical

---

[7] For the distinction, in the area of perceptual experience, between belief as the assent-component involved in the 'immediate presence of impressions' and belief as the 'native conviction that there are enduring physical objects'—a distinction which is completely missed by Kemp Smith—see M. Hodges, J. Lachs, 'Hume on Belief' (1976) in Tweyman, *David Hume. Critical Assessments*, I, 144–53, 152.

necessities are known a priori, are 'clear and self-evident'. By Two Viewpoints, apriority, clearness, and self-evidence are properties of contents but also properties of how ideas exist in the mind; and it makes full sense that what is conceived a priori (independently of anything else), clearly (openly, not implicitly), and self-evidently (in Hume's sense of self-manifesting) is present in the mind in a forceful and lively manner, even though it is an idea and not an impression. Therefore, it is very likely to be assented to; perhaps, it is such that assent to it is a natural necessity. By Two Viewpoints, the same idea which considered in its content is the object of modal qualification, considered 'as real perception in the mind, of which we are intimately conscious' is present with 'force and vivacity', which comes to expression in our assent to that modal content. Hume calls 'certainty' this kind of assent to necessary truths, with reference both to its psychological force and to its epistemic status. Also in the case of intuition and demonstration, that is, of knowledge, the explanation of the attitude of assent is thus non-problematic ('The answer is easy') because it is a consequence of the pertinent kind of content and of what is to grasp it.[8]

11.1.3 Imagination, Probability, and Assent

It is more complicated to see how a forceful and lively manner of conception or a feeling can close the gap of cognitive import in the case of probability, of cognition by causal inference. For one thing, the contents of probability are contingent and a posteriori; therefore their structure is not such as to make it physically necessary to conceive them with force and vivacity. For another one, they are inferentially grounded and susceptible to modal variation. Therefore, probable cognition does not depend on the reality of its objects and does not include the sense of their reality. Its subject matter are perfect ideas. Against this background, it is not clear how to explain the assent to ideas with contingent contents that we have in absentia (as in the case of the existence of unperceived objects). A basic fact about the second system of realities is that we assent to the reality of its contents, we judge them to be true; and such contents, and in this way our assent and our cognition, go well beyond the limits of sense and memory and of the a priori. We then need an explanation of assent, and of the difference between conception and cognition, for probability; that is, for most of our cognitions.

Regrettably, Hume's explanation of assent to probable conclusions is restricted to its character of force and vivacity. It is only advanced in the main text and it is not further discussed in the *Appendix*. It would perhaps not be impossible to extend his explanation to the richer conception of assent; but it is not something I

---

[8] See Owen, 'Scepticism with Regard to Reason', 111 and fn. 25.

will attempt to do. Hume's explanation resorts, in a special way, to the imagination; in particular to a distinctive kind of imaginative transition. The contents and the assent of probable cognition are generated along distinct causal paths, that is, by distinct transitions of the more limited imagination; however, such transitions typically, as a matter of natural fact, proceed in parallel.

> I wou'd willingly establish it as a general maxim in the science of human nature, that when any impression becomes present to us, it not only transports the mind to such ideas as are related to it, but likewise communicates to them a share of its force and vivacity. (1.3.8.2)

To spell this out: the conditions of probability (of probable, one-object reasoning) include a customary transition involving certain ideas and the presence of an impression of sensation or idea of memory with the right contents. The former is required for generating of the inferential potentials supporting probable reasoning, the second, for actualizing such potentials on certain occasions and individuating their particular conclusions. The two conditions are obviously separable and even causally independent: the inference can take place without the impression (as in some cases of idea-comparing causal reasoning) and the impression can occur by itself. But, given that they are jointly satisfied, we conclude to the idea of an unobserved existent. (As we know, it is precisely the turning of this transition into conception, a work of the more limited imagination, which produces the involved causal ideas.) If such a transition among ideas is engaged, it is reliably accompanied by a transition of the imagination of a different sort. The impression, together with the activation of the customary inferential propensity, cause the mind to engage in a distinct transition, conveying the force and vivacity of conception, or the feeling of the present impression or idea of memory, to the conclusion of the transition of ideas. This other transition produces our assent to the idea that forms that conclusion, thus explaining how such conclusion can be a cognition rather than merely a conception. Besides being distinct, the two transitions are structurally different. The inferences that put in place the new original ideas forming the contents of probable reasoning are complex, in terms of Two Viewpoints. They involve the concurrence of perceptions and of imagination in regard both of contents and of mental existence: changes in existence count also as changes its content, that is, in the cognitive role of ideas and their bearing on other perceptions. By contrast, the transmission of feeling from impressions to ideas has a quasi-mechanical character. Given the occurrence of an impression and an extant pattern of transition of ideas, the force and vivacity of the former is almost hydraulically conveyed to the associated ideas. ('The vividness of the first conception diffuses itself along the relations, and is convey'd, as by so many pipes or canals, to every idea that has any communication with the primary one', 1.3.10.7.)

Hume sketches some 'experiments' to support his account of assent to probable contents. The experiments aim to establish that the enlivening or transmission of force and vivacity is influenced by properties of resemblance, of contiguity, and of causal connectedness of the relevant objects (1.3.8.3–11). One of the conclusions of the experiments is that a crucial explanatory principle of our assent to an idea is custom. Since custom (as well as the other mentioned principles) can only influence the more limited imagination, this also establishes that assent to probability is grounded on imagination (1.3.8.10).[9] Hume draws a sharp contrast between reasoning and custom as the source of assent. If assent, as 'act of the mind', were only annexed, 'by the original constitution of our natures', 'to a reasoning and comparison of ideas', no significant role could be played by custom: 'it cou'd never supply the place of that comparison, nor produce any act of the mind, which naturally belong'd to that principle' (1.3.9.17). Reciprocally, the fact that assent depends on custom is evidence of its stemming from the imagination. The same consideration explains other features assent takes up in the context of probability. One is that it is a matter of degree, it can be weaker and stronger. This is different from assent in the case of a priori knowledge, which is not susceptible to variation. The fact that assent can be tacit, unreflective, and still forceful is explained most naturally if assent is indirectly caused by custom. The fact that resemblance and contiguity can 'augment the conviction of any opinion, and the vivacity of any conception' (this is the effect of their making mental transitions easier) is 'no inconsiderable argument, belief is nothing but a lively idea related to a present impression' (1.3.9.8).[10]

Conversely, the fact that assent is caused by the imagination explains how resemblance and contiguity can induce deep-seated biases: our conviction that

---

[9] Custom and thereby the imagination, the more limited imagination, are also Hume's explanation of the effects of education on belief. The same mechanism—a past repetition, without any new reasoning and conclusion, influencing conception and modulating assent—can underlie widely different cognitive episodes. There are 'other kinds of custom'. Custom, which is responsible for all belief and reasoning, 'may operate upon the mind in invigorating an idea after two several ways'. One kind of custom arises from experience of constant conjunction. The other arises from the repetition of a 'mere idea', as it takes place in education. ('All those opinions and notions of things, to which we have been accustom'd from our infancy, take such deep root, that 'tis impossible for us, by all the powers of reason and experience, to eradicate them', 1.3.9.17.) The 'habit' produced by education can prevail on that which 'arises from the constant and inseparable union of causes and effects'. It is the source of 'more than one half of those opinions, that prevail among mankind'; its principles 'over-balance those, which are owing either to abstract reasoning or experience'. Its maxims are frequently contrary to reason and different in different times and places, 'tho' in reality it be built almost on the same foundation of custom and repetition as our experience or reasonings from causes and effects' (1.3.9.19). Hume puts forward his account of education—of how assent can be induced by education—as further proof of his general explanation of belief ('As liars, by the frequent repetition of their lies, come at last to remember them; so the judgment, or rather the imagination, by the like means, may have ideas so strongly imprinted on it, and conceive them in so full a light, that they may operate upon the mind in the same manner with those, which the senses, memory or reason present to us', 1.3.9.19).

[10] For a valuable summary of belief-producing processes, highlighting the room they leave for deliberate belief-formation, see L. Falkenstein, 'Naturalism, Normativity, and Scepticism in Hume's account of Belief', Hume Studies, 1997, 23, 1 (29:72), 32–42.

causal relations could be inferred from the apparent qualities of causes and effects; our mistaking our inferences from the apparent to the real size of objects for data of sensation (1.3.9.10–11). Assent by testimony is owing to resemblance, that is, to the sensitivity of assent to resemblance between the ideas which are the meaning of the words uttered in reporting some fact and the (presumptive) fact itself. This explains why human testimony is overrated (1.3.9.12). Assent can also be weakened or destroyed by lack of resemblance ('As belief is an act of the mind arising from custom, 'tis not strange the want of resemblance shou'd overthrow what custom has establish'd, and diminish the force of the idea, as much as that latter principle encreases it', 1.3.9.13.) Our implicit incredulity about the future state is a point in case. In a somewhat related key, the imaginative ground of assent explains why and how assent is influenced by positive and negative emotions.

> When any affecting object is presented, it gives the alarm, and excites immediately a degree of its proper passion; especially in persons who are naturally inclined to that passion. This emotion passes by an easy transition to the imagination; and diffusing itself over our idea of the affecting object, makes us form that idea with greater force and vivacity, and consequently assent to it, according to the precedent system. (1.3.10.4)[11]

The irreducible role of the imagination in the generation and in the modulation of assent to probability is at its clearest in Hume's treatment of the probability of chances (1.3.11). Here, again, we have to do with a cognitive gap. The problem raised by the probability of chances—our assessment of the likelihood of exhaustive and mutually exclusive classes of events, like the outcomes of throwing a pair of dice—is how the idea of a superior chance can be produced if chance is understood as the absence of causes (1.3.11.4). Hume's solution is that the mind produces the idea of a superior or inferior number of chances by a combination of indifference and causal inference and on this basis comes to form and fix its assent (1.3.11.6). Hume resorts to the basic elements of constant conjunctions and of custom, which determine transitions of ideas and transitions of feeling. But to overcome the difficulty raised by the contrasting assumption of indifference he outlines a sort of hydraulics of assent, which makes sense if cognitive activity responds to properties and relations not only of contents but of mental existence, as it is characteristic of Hume's imagination. The transition of feeling that forms our assent to causal ideas is divided equally among the events, the

---

[11] Hume proposes a similar explanation of the effects of belief on imagination, on our readiness to entertain ideas and to conceive them in a forceful manner, a topic of special importance for aesthetics: ''Tis evident, that poets make use of this artifice of borrowing the names of their persons, and the chief events of their poems, from history, in order to procure a more easy reception for the whole, and cause it to make a deeper impression on the fancy and affections. The several incidents of the piece acquire a kind of relation by being united into one poem or representation; and if any of these incidents be an object of belief, it bestows a force and vivacity on the others, which are related to it' (1.2.10.7).

different, unperceived but conceived possible objects of our customary transitions. Then, it is unified in proportion to the numbers of objects. The vivacity of ideas is proportional to the degree of the associated feeling and this generates the corresponding degrees of assent (1.3.11.12). The cognitive complexity of probabilistic reasoning and of degrees of belief is thus realized in mental processes of a quasi-mechanical, even hydraulic character, where both ideas and manners of conception are channelled, distributed, and reunited. This mental activity is ascribed by Hume to the more limited imagination, as a further transition of it. 'This may lead us to conceive the manner, in which that faculty enters in all our reasonings' (1.3.12.22).

> Now let any philosopher make a trial, and rendeavor to explain that act of the mind, which we call *belief*, and give an account of the principles, from which it is deriv'd, independent of the influence of custom on imagination, and let his hypothesis be equally applicable to beasts as to the human species; and after he had done this, I promise to embrace his opinion. (1.3.16.8; see *Abstract* 21)

11.2 Belief as a Mental State

11.2.1 The Missing State of Belief

It is regrettable that Hume has not kept more clearly distinct belief as attitude from belief as mental state and the tasks he correspondingly addresses in his theory of belief. Still, he makes reasonably clear that belief must be explained also as state of mind. 'The idea of an object is an essential part of the belief of it, not the whole. We conceive many things, which we do not believe' (1.3.7.1). In the Important Footnote Hume remarks that the 'only remarkable difference' between judgement (an episodic, occurrent belief) and conception is found 'when we join belief to the conception, and are perswaded of the truth of what we conceive'. This constitutes a sui generis, complex 'act of mind', which is different both from the simple conception and from the feeling of persuasion. The same comes out from Hume's official definition of belief.

> So that as belief does nothing but vary the manner, in which we conceive any object, it can only bestow on our ideas an additional force and vivacity. An opinion, therefore, or belief may be most accurately defin'd, A LIVELY IDEA RELATED TO OR ASSOCIATED WITH A PRESENT IMPRESSION. (1.3.7.5)

What is here defined is belief as 'opinion', that is, as a complete cognitive state. Since it is defined in terms of its components, an idea and a manner of conception (issuing from an impression by an association or transition), it is clearly neither of them individually. Hume remarks that this state, which is 'only a strong and steady conception of any idea', 'approaches in some measure to an immediate impression'. Impressions are complete mental states, consisting of the combination of content and of manner of conception.[12] Our ordinary cognition mostly is realized in states of belief. This is true not only of causal reasoning. The 'propension to bestow an identity on our resembling perceptions', which produces the 'fiction of a continu'd existence', also 'causes belief by means of the present impressions of the memory; since without the remembrance of former sensations, 'tis plain we never shou'd have any belief of the continu'd existence of body' (1.4.2.43). The same, it could be suggested, holds of our cognition of self and personal identity, which is caused as a belief by the force and vivacity of our ideas of reflection together with the unifying and identifying transitions of the imagination. It is also of belief in this sense, as mental state, not only of assent, that Hume says that 'has never yet been explain'd by any philosopher' (1.3.7.5 fn. 20).

The special explanation of assent for the case of probability is also the explanation of a special mental state, belief, which is the realization of probability in human nature and would be otherwise missing. To see that belief as a cognitive state is different from the mental states which realize object-representation or a priori knowledge and, barring the more limited imagination, it marks a cognitive gap, we have to consider what properties it derives from the functional requirements of probability and of the second system of realities.

In the first place, probability and the generation of our worldview require that some cognitive states be possible independently of the presence of their objects and of the truth of their contents. The pertinent cognitive situations are one-object: if no cognitive state were possible offline, without entailing the presence of the particular that forms its object or the internal relations of ideas that structure its content, probable reasoning and much of ordinary and philosophical cognition would be impossible.

In the second place, if we are to engage in probability and form our worldview, a thoroughly inferential cognitive state is required. That is: a state the full individuation and explanation of which is not exhausted by contents given in experience or by internal relations of ideas; but which necessarily involves what certain

---

[12] This comes out clearly in the *Appendix*: 'They [the conceptions object of assent; the states of belief] approach nearer to the impressions, which are immediately present to us; and are therefore analogous to many other operations of the mind.' (Appendix 3). 'When any object is presented, the idea of its usual attendant immediately strikes us, as something real and solid. 'Tis *felt*, rather than conceiv'd, and approaches the impression, from which it is deriv'd, in its force and influence' (Appendix 9). The functional equivalence of belief with impressions is one of the main claims in Hume's discussion of the influence of belief on the passions, in 1.3.10. See, on the similarities between impressions and belief, Owen, *Hume's Reason*, 163–7, 172–4. However, I am not sure that in the *Appendix*' Hume lessens the analogy between belief and impressions. He seems rather to make it more complex and comprehensive: belief as assent is *not* a separate impression as feeling; belief as a mental state *approaches* impressions as state. See the distinction between 'Elementary belief' and 'Causally-produced belie' in Rocknak, Imagined Causes, 38–9.

mental transitions *add* to the contents we have and to our corresponding persuasions.

In the third place, a state whose content is susceptible to generality and modal qualification. This, again, is required to gain cognition by reasoning in one-object situations.

In the fourth place, this thoroughly inferential state should be possible in relation to contents that are contingent and a posteriori. The distinctive feature of probable reasoning is concluding to real existence or matter of fact; this is also the very stuff of our worldview. But in Hume's philosophy, real existence and matter of fact can only be contingent and apprehended a posteriori.

This minimal functional description of the mental states that naturally realize probability and our worldview identifies the fundamental features of Hume's belief. Even on this sketched characterization, it is clear that neither sensible representation nor a priori reason issue and come to expression in mental states like those just specified: with general and modally qualified contents; a posteriori as to content and assent; non-object dependent; susceptible to deliberation and to preference. Intuition and demonstration have general and modal contents, like belief, while the contents of sense and memory are only particular and non-modal. But sense and memory are a posteriori, as to their contents and assent; and their contents are contingent (even though they are not represented as such). This is like belief, while intuition and demonstration, which share their inferential character with it, are only a priori and necessary. Both sense and memory and intuition and demonstration are object dependent: their existence requires the presence of the objects or the obtaining of the relations of ideas which are their subject-matter. Belief can be offline. Therefore, by Hume's taxonomy of cognitive kinds and of the mental states realizing them, the state of belief is sui generis and, if our cognitive states were restricted to sensible representation and a priori reason, an important kind of cognition would fail to have mental realization. By contrast, Hume's account of assent can be extended to explain how a mental state like belief is possible. What explains assent to contents neither given in impressions of sensation nor necessitated by internal relations of ideas also explains how a mental state can have the cognitive properties of Hume's belief. If the imagination can engage in feeling-conveying transitions concurrently with its transitions among ideas, states with the features of Hume's belief can be pervasive in our mental lives, as they actually are.[13]

---

[13] The importance of distinguishing knowledge from probability and belief as assent from belief as mental state comes clearly in sight from an epistemological perspective. In this regard there are some ambiguities, even confusions, in Schmitt's otherwise excellent account of Hume's epistemology. Schmitt rightly recognizes that Hume draws a radical contrast between knowledge and probability. Since this contrast is also a psychological one, it counts as a contrast between knowledge (as mental state) and belief (the kind of state that psychologically realizes probable cognition) (*Hume's Epistemology*, 11). He also rightly recognizes that knowledge and belief share 'a positive epistemic status with respect to which causal inference is not wholly inferior to demonstration' (*Hume's*

11.2.2 Imagination, Belief, and Doxastic Deliberation

How does Hume's individuation and explanation of belief as mental state fit with its functional description in terms of probable cognition? In particular how does the nature and structure of belief, as it issues from the imagination, explain that, differently from sense-impressions and intuitions and demonstrations, it is susceptible to doxastic deliberation? Doxastic deliberation is central among our current cognitive practices. It is thus important to see how states of belief can be reflectively formed and revised—also because this is a crucial respect in which Hume's imagination takes up the role of the understanding.

Hume addresses causal reasoning at different levels. Firstly, states of causal belief are primitively instantiated as customary, compelling transitions of the more limited imagination; they are typically implicit and may come to expression primarily in action (like stopping short at the bank of a river, 1.3.8.13).

> 'Twill here be worth our observation, that the past experience, on which all our judgments concerning cause and effect depend, may operate on our mind in such an insensible manner as never to be taken notice of, and may even in some measure be unknown to us. (1.3.8.13)

At this level, states of causal belief are common to humans and animals, as a sort of instinct of inclination or tendency.

Epistemology, 16; this is when our beliefs have the epistemic status of proofs). But then some ambiguities and confusions emerge. The epistemic status that Schmitt regards as common to knowledge and proofs (well-grounded causal beliefs) is that of justified belief: 'a status, justified belief, spanning knowledge and probability' (*Hume's Epistemology*, 18). But Schmitt seems to take belief, in this case, as a mental state that is one constituent of knowledge (which is in turn a composite state of mind). This comes out clearly from his identification of knowledge and the 'products of causal inference' as 'both (with appropriate qualifications in the case of causal inference) justified, true beliefs' (*Hume's Epistemology*, 16–17) and his explicit reference to the 'mid-twentieth-century identification of knowledge with justified true belief' (*Hume's Epistemology*, 17 and fn. 31). This, however, cannot be correct. The inspiration of the JTB analysis is precisely to build knowledge out of a mental state of belief plus the metaphysical condition of truth and the epistemic one of justification (see T. Williamson, Knowledge and its Limits, Oxford University Press, Oxford 2000, 27–33). But then there would be no contrast of mental nature between knowledge and probability—both would be mentally realized as beliefs. What is truly, mentally common to knowledge and probability is not any mental state (their natures are contrary) but simply the manner of conception of assent, which is not itself a perception or mental state; as well as their fidelity or veracity. It is our assent or commitment to an idea that stands for justification. This is not JTB but an aspect of Hume's Leibniz-inspired program of remedying to the neglect of probabilities in the systems of logic (*Abstract* 4). Regrettably, Schmitt radically underplays the theoretical role of belief as assent (see *Hume's Epistemology*, 100 fn. 6). For an extremely interesting account of Hume's place in the tradition of Oxford Realism and the rejection of the analysis of knowledge in terms of a mental state of belief plus other conditions, see M. Marion, 'Oxford Realism: Knowledge and Perception', I and II, British Journal for the History of Philosophy, 8, 2, 2000 (299–338) and 3, 2000 (485–519), 309–10, 313–14.

To consider the matter aright, reason is nothing but a wonderful and unintelligible instinct in our souls, which carries us along a certain train of ideas, and endows them with particular qualities, according to their particular situations and relations. (1.3.16.9)

But belief is not restricted to this primitive, instinctive form, even though belief-formation cannot completely part ways from the underlying activity of the more limited imagination. By the Structural Principle, more limited and idea-comparing imagination are parts of the same faculty, whose activity can easily progress from the one to the other. Still, once we have causal ideas, and master our application of them (by generalizing and modally qualifying their contents), we can engage in idea-comparing, reflective, and conceptually informed belief-formation. This is our actual, ordinary practice of forming causal beliefs. Hume remarks that doxastic deliberation replaces exposition to repeated observation as the guise of our ordinary practice of causal inference.

'Tis worthy of remark on this occasion, that tho' the species of probability here explain'd be the first in order, and naturally takes place before any entire proof can exist, yet no one, who is arriv'd at the age of maturity, can any longer be acquainted with it. (1.3.12.3)

As mature causal reasoners, we form causal beliefs not because conditioned and impelled by repeated experiences but by comparing the ideas we have of objects as causes and effects and of the corresponding inferential potentials. Reflective or deliberate belief-formation explains that we can have a belief or make a judgement in presence of limited experience, even of a single case, by keeping into account and comparing contrary cases; by assigning weighs to evidence.

'Tis certain, that not only in philosophy, but even in common life, we may attain the knowledge of a particular cause merely by one experiment, provided it be made with judgment, and after a careful removal of all foreign and superfluous circumstances. (1.3.8.14)

The ideas and the principles compared in this doxastic activity are produced in the ways we are familiar with. For instance, the idea of causal uniformity, *'like objects, plac'd in like circumstances, will always produce like effects'*, has the support of 'many millions' of observations. Also its application in reasoning is bounded and supported by the propensities of the imagination (see § 11.3.2). But the way this principle contributes to reflective, deliberate belief-formation is different from the implicit or tacit one in which it is formed. 'Nay we find in some cases, that the reflection produces the belief without the custom; or more properly speaking, that the reflection produces the custom in an *oblique* and *artificial* manner' (1.3.8.14). In the production of a belief, reflection can substitute the operation of experience and custom with the application of a principle summarizing them. The principle, not the present transition of ideas, is habitual or customary.

In this way, the nature and structure of belief as mental state makes it uniquely suitable to doxastic deliberation. We have no elbowroom in connection with the contents of sense and memory because their ideas are locked on the contents of impressions and the impressions are locked on actuality. Nor do we have it in regard of the contents of a priori knowledge because internal relations of ideas and Separability impose a necessary structure to our thoughts. Furthermore, the presence to awareness of the objects or impressions of sensation and of the ideas of memory is inseparable from assent to them (the reality of these contents, which consists in their manner of conception, is constitutive of our acquaintance and demonstrative thoughts). And the internal relations that form the content of a priori truth, also compel our assent and leave no room for cognitive alternatives. (As we will see, given our cognitive nature, we cannot but deliberate about intuitive and demonstrative conclusions; but this is precisely what reduces knowledge to probability, see § 11.3.1.) Therefore, there is no cognitive deliberation in sense and memory and a priori knowledge (intuition and demonstration). By contrast, the contents of states of belief are perfect ideas standing in non-intuitive or demonstrative inferential connections. Such inferential connections depend on experience and on the transitions of the imagination, which charge the ideas of objects with distinctive inferential potentials and modal qualifications. But this structure of content and its causal influence on the mind still leave the imagination 'free to conceive both sides of the question'; in both cases [incredulity and assent] the conception of the idea is equally possible and requisite' (1.3.7.3). Because of this, the idea-comparing imagination can perfectly well form inferences in an offline context, and on the basis of generalized and explicitly modal causal ideas. (The bounds to idea-comparing reasoning are set by the more limited imagination, § 11.3.2; but within such limits, the idea-comparing imagination is in charge.) Furthermore, in the case of belief, assent rather than being produced directly by the presence of objects, is mediated by transitions of ideas. The transitions of the imagination conveying the force and vivacity of impressions follow the path of transitions along ideas. But these latter do not have the necessity of those grounded on internal relations. Therefore, the nature of belief, by making room for deliberation about causal conceptions and causal inferences, makes it possible to deliberately confer and withdraw assent. (This is not the same as believing at will since doxastic deliberation is along the lines of causal contents and embedded in the more limited imagination.) What we do, when we engage in mature reasoning about non-demonstrative matters, is to form, assess, and revise beliefs.

An important case in which probable cognition requires us to engage in doxastic deliberation is that of belief-formation in presence of a contrariety of experiences. This 'hesitating belief for the future' (1.3.12.6), this 'reasoning from conjecture' (1.3.11.3), is our ordinary cognitive lot. Hume denies that this kind of belief-formation generally is by way of an imperfect habit and transition, which we follow immediately and without reflection. 'But this method of proceeding we have but few instances of in our probable reasonings; and even fewer than in those, which are deriv'd from the uninterrupted conjunction of objects' (1.3.12.7). The common way of forming causal beliefs in the presence of a contrariety of experience is by 'deliberation'. 'In the former species of reasoning we commonly take knowingly into consideration the contrariety of past events; we compare the different sides of the contrariety, and carefully weigh the experiments, which we have on each side: Whence we may conclude, that our reasonings of this kind arise not *directly* from the habit, but in an *oblique* manner; which we must now endeavour to explain' (1.3.13.7). Engaging in this indirect kind of belief-formation requires awareness of distinctions of correctness between different patterns of inference, responding to the same corpus of (variable) experience. As Hume remarks, in the 'second species of probability' 'we reason with knowledge and reflection from a contrariety of past experiments' (1.3.12.13).

Hume proposes a detailed explanation of this form of doxastic deliberation. Our hesitating beliefs concerning individual events are formed in three steps. The first step is the customary and immediate belief that the future resembles the past; that like causes are followed by like effects. This is the source of the cognitive dynamics that animates all this mental transition. 'This habit or determination to transfer the past to the future is full and perfect; and consequently the first impulse of the imagination in this species of reasoning is endow'd with the same qualities' (1.3.12.9). The second step has to do with the objects of this primitive, implicit belief. Consideration of our experience makes us aware of its contrary nature: it 'offers us a number of disagreeing images in a certain order and proportion'. 'The first impulse, therefore, is here broke into pieces, and diffuses itself over all those images, of which each partakes an equal share of that force and vivacity, that is deriv'd from the impulse' (1.3.12.10). This is the mental, imaginative ground of our belief that if these events happen again, they happen in the same proportion as in the past. The third step is running over these ideas 'in order to form a judgment concerning one single event, which appears uncertain' (1.3.12.11). This is done by drawing together the images presented by the experience which agree one with the other. The agreeing images unite together and render the idea they have in common stronger than those of contrary events. It is right in this context that Hume says that in this species of probability 'we reason with knowledge and reflection' (1.3.12.13).[14]

---

[14] In its emphasis on concepts, reflection, judgment, my reading of single-experiment causal reasoning differs from Schmitt's (*Hume's Epistemology*, 179–80; but see 191–2, where doxastic deliberation comes more into view).

Relatedly, general rules, which are extensions and explications of ideas produced by the imagination, can regulate and even produce beliefs. Hume advances this important view in a text added in the *Appendix*, in connection with the attitude of assent. He points out, in the first place, that the feeling that constitutes assent is not always emotionally or sentimentally charged. The feeling is primarily recognizable by its own (admittedly almost ineffable) phenomenology, rather than by its charge and effects. This is contrasted with the character of poetry.

> But how great soever the pitch may be, to which this vivacity rises, 'tis evident, that in poetry it never has the same *feeling* with that which arises in the mind, when we reason, tho' even upon the lowest species of probability. The mind can easily distinguish betwixt the one and the other; and whatever emotion the poetical enthusiasm may give to the spirits, 'tis still the mere phantom of belief or perswasion. (1.3.10.10)

This makes room for the notion of a forceful feeling or assent that does not amount to psychological coercion.

> Where the vivacity arises from a customary conjunction with a present impression; tho' the imagination may not, in appearance, be so much mov'd; yet there is always something more forcible and real in its actions, than in the fervors of poetry and eloquence. The force of our mental actions in this case, no more than in any other, is not to be measur'd by the apparent agitation of the mind.
> (1.3.10.10)

There is *calm* assent just like there are *calm* passions (see 2.3.8.13). And calm assent seems to mediate the more limited and the idea-comparing imagination, just as calm passion mediates desire with what we have of rational control on our conduct. The notion of calm assent, just like that of calmness in passions, points to a reflective and deliberative dimension in the genesis of states of belief (or of passions); to a more complex cognitive structure, which essentially includes rules.

> I cannot forbear observing, that the great difference in their feeling proceeds in some measure from reflection and *general rules*. We observe, that the vigour of conception, which fictions receive from poetry and eloquence, is a circumstance merely accidental, of which every idea is equally susceptible; and that such fictions are connected with nothing that is real. This observation makes us only lend ourselves, so to speak, to the fiction: But causes the idea to feel very different from the eternal establish'd persuasions founded on memory and custom. They are somewhat of the same kind: But the one is much inferior to the other, both in its causes and effects. (1.3.10.11)

General rules are involved not only in the genesis but also in the reflection, correction, and deliberation about assent and its degrees.

> A like reflection on *general rules* keeps us from augmenting our belief upon every encrease of the force and vivacity of our ideas. Where an opinion admits of no doubt, or opposite probability, we attribute to it a full conviction; tho' the want of resemblance, or contiguity, may render its force inferior to that of other opinions. 'Tis thus the understanding corrects the appearances of the senses, and makes us imagine, that an object at twenty foot distance seems even to the eye as large as one of the same dimensions at ten. (1.3.10.12)

The feeling that constitutes assent therefore is not something ultimate, immediate, and unexplainable; and it is permeable to our recognition of its different circumstances, accidental or real, and of the normative implications of such differences.

In this way, states of belief, as individuated, characterized, and explained by Hume, can be and often are the result of doxastic deliberation, in which we assess our cognitive activity and conclude whether or not to accept certain beliefs in the light of general rules. General rules, in their turn, are formed by the imagination.[15]

> Shou'd it be demanded why men form general rules, and allow them to influence their judgment, even contrary to present observation and experience, I shou'd reply, that in my opinion it proceeds from those very principles, on which all judgments concerning causes and effects depend. Our judgments concerning cause and effect are deriv'd from habit and experience; and when we have been accustom'd to see one object united to another, our imagination passes from the first to the second, by a natural transition, which precedes reflection, and which cannot be prevented by it. (1.3.13.8)

Notice how it is precisely because of their being grounded and embedded in the imagination that causal beliefs can be formed by doxastic deliberation. Hume's account of belief as a mental state and of belief-formation mirrors the distinction between natural and philosophical relations and, more deeply, the Structural Principle. Imagination turns representations into propensities and transitions of ideas and transitions of ideas into complex ideas. Once ideas with the pertinent, new contents become available, we can reflectively apply them as concepts in reasoning. Reasoning by comparison of ideas and doxastic deliberation are the work of the whole imagination, inclusive of its more limited part. They are

---

[15] See J. Lyons, 'General Rules and the Justification of Probable Belief in Hume's *Treatise*', Hume Studies, 27, 2001 (247–77).

naturalistic, psychological operations. The reflective character of probable cognition dovetails with Hume's naturalistic conception of belief as mental state. This completes the explanatory programme of 1.3.2–10: giving a fundamental explanation of mature, idea-comparing, reflective causal reasoning. (The analysis of the idea of cause and of reasoning with that idea is the starting point of Hume's account.) The imagination explains probable cognition, at the primitive and at the reflective level, as to its contents, assent, and mental states. In all these respects, the faculty of the imagination replaces (or reduces) the understanding. This view is not unfamiliar to us. There is talk of 'constructive imagination': imagination as a capacity for forming novel representations and for eliciting cognitive states in relation to them.[16] There is also talk of imagination as the faculty of simulation: simulation of other minds: the viewpoints, attitudes, and contents entertained by others; as well as of one's own mental states: what would it be to occupy a certain cognitive or affective position. Hume's theory of belief relies on the insight that the imagination can simulate mental states. More precisely, that it can make it as if we were having impressions of sensation or ideas of memory, while we have none; or as if we possessed a faculty of understanding and reasoning with ideas of contingent existents, while this is not part of our cognitive nature. Hume's imagination, in this way, can provide well-supported, safe cognition of reality, about potential affordances in the environment, about how to assess different hypotheses, by developing alternative scenarios which keep fixed selected aspects of reality.[17]

11.3 Scepticism and the Imagination

The nature of assent and of belief and their grounds in the imagination are also central to Hume's general treatment of scepticism. The crucial consideration, here, is that, by the Structural Principle, idea-comparing and more limited imagination actually operate together, as the whole faculty of the imagination. Abstract reflection and reasoning, or the understanding, depend on the more limited imagination for their conceptual dimensions and for their ideas. And the comparison of ideas in which reasoning consists takes place in the context and with the limits of our cognitive nature, primarily as it is marked by the more

---

[16] N. Van Leeuwen, 'The Meanings of "Imagine" Part I: Constructive Imagination', in Philosophy Compass, 8/3, 2013, 220–30-2: 'Constructive imagination is often not much of a departure from reality at all; rather, it is a selective playing with elements of ideas already accepted as representing reality.' Van Leeuwen rightly remarks that Hume is best understood as talking of constructive imagination, 224–5. See also N. Van Leeuwen, 'The Meanings of "Imagine" Part II: Attitude and Action', 2014, 5: some imaginings weakly aim at truth (include truth-tracking mechanisms).

[17] This characterization of how imagination can contribute in a unique way, as a distinctive 'method' for knowing what would happen in certain circumstances is owing to T. Williamson, 'Knowing by Imagining', in Kind (ed.) *Knowing by Imagination*, 2016, 1–8.

limited imagination. It is this circumstance that set limits to the sceptical concerns issuing from reflection and reasoning.

11.3.1 Hume's Sceptical Concerns: Sources and Varieties

Hume's confrontation with scepticism should be read in the context of the necessary limits of object-representation and of demonstrative and probable reason and of the corresponding with which the imagination produces contents and cognitive changes. Serious sceptical concerns arise from the discovery, by philosophical reflection, that certain conceptual modes of thinking (like our grasp of possibility and necessity), certain important structures of our worldview (like causal connections, external existence, or personal identity), and certain cognitive states and activities (like belief or judgement, doxastic deliberation, and reasoning) cannot be explained in terms of representation of objects or as issuing from reason. Concerns with scepticism therefore map the fundamental architecture of Hume's philosophy in Book 1.

> Almost all reasoning is there reduced to experience; and the belief, which attends experience, is explained to be nothing but a peculiar sentiment, or lively conception produced by habit. Nor is this all. When we believe any thing of *external* existence, or suppose an object to exist a moment after it is no longer perceived, this belief is nothing but a sentiment of the same kind. Our author insists upon several other sceptical topics; and upon the whole concludes, that we assent to our faculties, and employ our reason only because we cannot help it. (*Abstract* 27)

Philosophical reflection discovers gaps in the sources and the contents of many of our ideas, beliefs, and cognitive capacities. However, philosophical reflection and idea-comparing reasoning in general (as we know by now) cannot close the gaps they individuate. It is rightly the combination of the discovery by reason of the naturally necessary limits of our thought and cognition and of the impossibility for demonstrative or probable reason to overcome those limits and explain and reinstate our ordinary and philosophical practices that gives rise to serious scepticism.[18]

---

[18] The centrality of religious concerns for Hume's scepticism is a central theme in Paul Russell's book, *The Riddle of Hume's Treatise*, Oxford University Press, Oxford/New York 2008. I feel pressed to say something about how I stand with regard to this work, especially on account of its crucial thesis that 'there is no proper or convincing way to explain Hume's sceptical and naturalistic motivations that is *entirely independent* of his irreligious aims and objectives' (273). My position on these matters hinges on two key qualifications in the text just quoted, 'motivations' and 'entirely independent'. I certainly agree with the view that the relations and the tensions of scepticism and naturalism (what Russell calls the 'riddle of Hume's *Treatise*') is an important interpretive question raised by Hume's masterpiece. I also agree that this underlying structure of the *Treatise* is connected with irreligious

Only the imagination allows the natural mind to close its necessary cognitive gaps. In this way, Hume's shifting much of the burden of thought and cognition from sensibility and the understanding to the imagination explains both the surge of sceptical doubts (sense-experience and idea-comparison fail to account for perfectly ordinary and genuine steps in thinking and cognition) and how it is possible to respond to them (the imagination can explain and vindicate such steps without being representational or reducible to idea-comparison). Concern with scepticism is integral to Hume's philosophy in Book 1. Support for sceptical doubts comes directly from the science of human nature, in the guise of probable reasonings concerning our cognitive faculties. But probable cognition of the nature of our mind also explains why such sceptical doubts do not issue in the impossibility of our ordinary and philosophical cognitive practices or in their utter epistemological devaluation. Sceptical doubts are genuine and legitimate, given the nature of our mind and cognition; but they can also be overturned, as they must be. Hume's conclusive position is one of 'modest', not of radical scepticism (1.2.5.26 fn. 12).[19] In this way, Hume's confrontation with scepticism has a dialectical and constructive role: it makes salient how different the natural working of mind and cognition is from what philosophers have long held; how a reformation of philosophy is needful and helpful.[20]

---

motivations, with Hume's criticism of and opposition to religion. In this way, the interpretation of the *Treatise* cannot be entirely independent of the irreligious consideration; and we should keep well present Russell's accurate tracking of irreligious implications of Hume's philosophy. But motivations—even theoretical motivations—do not exhaust philosophical positions; they may leave them undetermined. The specific conceptual resources: principles about mind, content, cognition, which Hume summons and applies in his arguments for certain conclusion are largely independent of the motivations underlying such conclusions. This is not only on dialectical grounds (why should the holder of the opposite, philosophical-religious positions be bothered by tailor-made argumentative steps?), but on account of the complete generality and conclusiveness which go with systematic philosophy as such (and the *Treatise* is a philosophical system, if any there is). Therefore, I am confident that I can accept Russell's *Whys* and still keep asking some important *Hows*. For instance, I can accept Russell's point that the sceptical side of the *Treatise* is preparatory (via the stern criticism of theological doctrines) to the constructive project of a science of man (269); and that the 'dynamic nature' of Hume's scepticism (the progress from radical to moderate scepticism) is the key to solving the riddle of the *Treatise* (270; see also 173); and still ask *how* this program is viable at all; *what* conceptions of content, mind, and cognition support and make possible this dynamics. My concentration on the unity and structure of imagination and on its production of mental contents (with privileged reference to rationalist philosophies and, proleptically, to Kant) responds to this sort of explanatory concern.

[19] See Qu, *Hume's Epistemological Evolution*, 12, 19 fn. 28, 100. Hume does not recognize any serious threat of first-order scepticism. See, on Hume's dialectical use of scepticism, Garrett, *Cognition and Commitment*, 208.

[20] My understanding of Hume's scepticism is influenced by Ainslie, *Hume's True Scepticism*, 14–15, 37–9 (the reflective activity of philosophical reasoning brings havoc to the natural functioning of our cognitive faculties but undermines itself and dooms scepticism itself), 219, 240 (the limits of philosophy in its attempt to fundamentally justify our cognitive capacities). Ordinary cognition is sheltered from scepticism by the very fact that it does not engage in any enquiry into the conditions and the mental mechanisms that underlie its worldview; and this seems true of natural philosophy as well. It is sheltered from what Ainslie has aptly called 'reflective interference'. Hume, however, is no quietist in his own philosophical work. Thanks to the theory of imagination, he has a general, theoretical response to cognitive gaps and sceptical concerns: in the context of the science of man, naturalism, genuine contentfulness, and some epistemic positions can be preserved, if representationalism is duly restricted.

To begin exploring the complex relations between scepticism and the imagination, it is convenient to distinguish in Hume's philosophy two main varieties of sceptical concerns. (I know I am adding in this way to an already crowded taxonomy.)

- (1) The limits of representation and of idea-comparing reason, discovered reflectively, unveil the apparent *impossibility* of certain cognitive contents and capacities. This has been the main theme of the present work: the ideas of geometry, causal reasoning and the idea of cause, the idea of external existence, of matter, and of self and personal identity turn out to be impossible, under the very natural assumption that they should be derived either from experience of objects or from reason. Not all these issues of possibility are explicitly addressed by Hume *as sceptical*: most notably, he makes almost no mention of scepticism in the context of his theory of causation. But our idea and belief of external existence, both vulgar and philosophical, are explicitly regarded as a source of scepticism as 1.4.2.57 (see § 9.5.2). The same holds of our inconsistent philosophical conception of matter at 1.4.4.6 and of our idea of self and personal identity, as explained at 1.4.6 (see Appendix 10). Even the account of causal necessity is characterized as a paradox and thus, at least implicitly, as a source of scepticism (1.3.14.24; 1.4.7.5). Some of Hume's discussions of scepticism about our cognitive *possibilities* deal with even more general and fundamental subject matters: the possibility of forming beliefs in a reflective way (1.4.1: *Scepticism with regard to reason*); the possibility of choosing doxastic principles (1.4.7: the Dangerous Dilemma). This form of scepticism belongs to the philosophy of mind rather than to epistemology. It involves epistemological arguments but only to establish a claim about the mind and its cognitive capacities, a claim that counts as sceptical only because of its apparent entailments of impossibility.
- (2) Hume's responses to the sceptical questions concerning the possibility of cognitive contents and states resort to properties of imagination as a natural mental faculty. Their general character is that the impossibilities unveiled by reflection are, to a certain extent, only *apparent*: there are bounds to rational reflection; within such bounds, we can cognitively proceed without concerns of possibility. However, this also means that, within such bounds, questions can arise about the justness or regularity of the principles of our cognition, in particular the principles and operations of the imagination. That is, *given* that the imagination succeeds in putting in place cognitive contents and capacities that would otherwise appear out of our reach and in particular, given that belief-formation by reflection and reasoning has been made possible, we can have doubts about the *authority* of the imagination. Such doubts are part of our ordinary and philosophical

cognitive practice and, if left unanswered, they turn into sceptical concerns. The possibilities left open for our natural mind to work are consistent with its operating in epistemically good, bad, right, or wrong ways. Hume, correspondingly, is not shy, also in Book 1 of the *Treatise*, of giving at least an outline of the epistemology of the natural mind, of the epistemic value of its works. While epistemology is not his primary philosophical focus, it is still a crucial theoretical constraint on the science of human nature, which must be in a position to account for the epistemic distinctions it postulates (also because of its foundational aims). Now, rightly in connection with the imagination, I think we can detect in Book 1 a distinctively epistemological strand of sceptical concerns: concerns about how equally natural cognitive states, all issuing from the imagination, can have different epistemic values; about what is to be epistemically valuable at all; and about whether and how we ought to follow reason, given that we *can* follow it. The discussion of these sceptical issues is an important part of Hume's epistemology in Book 1. Therefore, scepticism concerning authority and the responses to it are nested, in Hume's philosophy, in scepticism about possibility and the responses to it. It is interesting that, while the imagination, conceived according to the Structural Principle, is Hume's solution to scepticism about possibility, it is rather part of the problem in the case of scepticism about authority.[21]

11.3.2 Reflection, Imagination, and the Possibility of Belief

Hume's general treatment of sceptical arguments of impossibility and the complex relation between scepticism and the imagination are well in sight in the much maligned but important 1.4.1: *Of scepticism with regard to reason*. I follow David Owen in identifying the aim of Hume's discussion as explaining how reasoning, demonstrative and probable, and reflective belief-formation are possible at all, rather than providing a justification of demonstrative and probable reason (this would either make it pointless or doom it to failure). Hume is

---

[21] My distinction between scepticism about possibility and scepticism about authority, as distinct kinds of sceptical concerns addressed by Hume, bears some resemblance to that between epistemological and conceptual scepticism in R. J. Fogelin, Hume's Skepticism in the Treatise of Human Nature, Routledge and Kegan Paul, London, 1985, 6: 'An epistemological skeptic accepts a system of belief as intelligible, but challenges the supposed grounds for these beliefs. A conceptual skeptic challenges the very intelligibility of a system of beliefs.' However, the challenge to intelligibility of beliefs, that is, of the ideas forming their contents, should be embedded in the pattern of cognitive gaps and works of imagination, as an aspect of Hume's overall account of mind and cognition. As Fogelin rightly remarks, this is much more important for understanding Hume's philosophy than any anticipation of the logical-positivist concern for meaningfulness.

addressing a sceptical question, but one concerning possibility, not authority.[22] Hume's discussion develops his supposition that we ordinarily form many of our beliefs by way of doxastic deliberation. The sceptical argument he considers has the form of a reductio of such a supposition and targets the possibility that assent be preserved across probable reasoning and rational reflection. Since probable reasoning (as opposed to deductive reasoning) involves assent and culminates in belief (demonstrative reasoning, in our practice, reduces to probable reasoning), the ultimate sceptical target is the possibility of reasoning as such.

Hume's discussion proceeds by the following steps.

First. Hume contrasts the different mental nature and epistemic status of knowledge and probability with how they figure in our cognitive practices. Hume's distinction refers in the first place to philosophical cognition. 'In all demonstrative sciences the rules are certain and infallible; but when we apply them, our fallible and uncertain faculties are very apt to depart from them, and fall into error' (1.4.1.1). Once this is recognized, it is incumbent on us to 'form a new judgment, as a check or controul on our first judgment or belief'. We must take into account our fallibility, 'enlarge our view to comprehend a kind of history of all the instances, wherein our understanding has deceiv'd us' and engage in reflection and deliberation concerning our claims to intuitive and demonstrative knowledge. Within this reflective context, we in fact embed intuitive and demonstrative knowledge in a context of probability, of causal reasoning and belief.

> Our reason must be consider'd as a kind of cause, of which truth is the natural effect; but such-a-one as by the irruption of other causes, and by the inconstancy of our mental powers, may frequently be prevented. (1.4.1.1)

The embedding of knowledge within probability must be conceived according to their difference in kind. Knowledge and belief are 'of such contrary and disagreeing natures, that they cannot well run insensibly into each other'; they cannot 'divide' and they 'must be either entirely present, or entirely absent'. Knowledge and probability are different cognitive kinds, marked by different properties of content, different relations between content and assent, and different epistemic value (a priori and a posteriori; certainty and at most proof). But in the context of our cognitive practice, because of its naturalistic, reflective, and corrective character, no claim to knowledge can be other than one to probability. Knowledge, within philosophical practice, is replaced by reasoned belief. This takes place also in ordinary cognition, which includes engagement in doxastic deliberation. 'I suppose, there is some question propos'd to me, and that after revolving over the impressions of my memory and senses, and carrying my thoughts from them

---

[22] See D. Owen, 'Scepticism with regard of Reason', 101–34.

to such objects, as are commonly conjoin'd with them, I feel a stronger and more forcible conception on the one side' (1.4.1.9). The 'strong conception' which 'forms my first decision' is examined in view of the possibility of error and of the fact that our judgement is 'regulated by contrary principles or causes, of which some lead to truth, and some to error'. This seems a perfectly ordinary way of proceeding in cognition: it is how merchants check their accounts (1.4.1.3). Therefore, whatever follows from engagement in doxastic deliberation and from the replacement of knowledge with probability, applies across the board to human cognition.[23]

Second. 'Since therefore all knowledge resolves itself into probability, and becomes at last of the same nature with that evidence, which we employ in common life, we must now examine this latter species of reasoning, and see on what foundation it stands' (1.4.1.4). This examination is, of course, directed by Hume's own conception of probability and is itself an instance of probable reasoning. We are under the same obligation to correct judgements of probability as we are to correct judgements of knowledge. This correction calls in question the 'authority' of such judgements 'judgments even with ourselves', because of our consciousness of past errors. 'Here then arises a new species of probability to correct and regulate the first, and fix its just standard and proportion' (1.4.1.5). Why a *new species*? Because its subject matter is different: doxastic deliberation is not about the objects of the initial judgement but about the judgement itself and is based on 'the nature of our understanding, and our reasoning from the first probability'. This second-order judgement leaves some space for error; this is recognized and, within a context of doxastic deliberation, the 'reflex act of the mind' is iterated.

> Having thus found in every probability, beside the original uncertainty inherent in the subject, a new uncertainty deriv'd from the weakness of that faculty, which judges, and having adjusted these two together, we are oblig'd by our reason to add a new doubt deriv'd from the possibility of error in the estimation we make of the truth and fidelity of our faculties. (1.4.1.6)

Such iteration is a matter of *epistemic obligation*: we ought to address this issue at every step, 'if we wou'd closely pursue our reason'. And when deliberating doxastically, when engaged in mature probable reasoning, we typically also aim to abide by our reason. (Hume's discussion therefore presupposes that we are ordinarily aware of epistemic distinctions and aim to abide by them. I discuss this in Chapter 12.) The sceptical threat of impossibility arises precisely from the psychological consequences of iterated or recursive doxastic deliberation: by abiding

---

[23] All this is rightly pointed out in Owen, 'Scepticism with Regard to Reason', 105–6, 110–12. Owen also rightly claims that Hume appears to accept this first step, as an instance of consequent scepticism, 108.

to this rational prescription we end up weakening our assent to the initial judgement and making belief-formation impossible.

> But this decision, tho' it shou'd be favourable to our preceeding judgment, being founded only on probability, must weaken still further our first evidence, and must itself be weaken'd by a fourth doubt of the same kind, and so on *in infinitum*; till at last there remain nothing of the original probability, however great we may suppose it to have been, and however small the diminution by every new uncertainty. (1.4.1.6)

This establishes, on apparently compelling epistemological and psychological grounds ('this is a doubt, which immediately occurs to us'), the sceptical conclusion.

> When I reflect on the natural fallibility of my judgment, I have less confidence in my opinions, than when I only consider the objects concerning which I reason; and when I proceed still farther, to turn the scrutiny against every successive estimation I make of my faculties, all the rules of logic require a continual diminution, and at last a total extinction of belief and evidence. (1.4.1.6)

Since the premises and the conclusions of probable reasoning consist of states of belief, the necessary extinction of assent entails the impossibility of probable reasoning, in any reflective or deliberative context; since we cannot reflectively engage in demonstrative but only in probable reasoning, we are left with no reason at all.

Hume's sceptical argument is puzzling and has given rise to an interpretive debate. If it is interpreted in terms of probability theory, that is, in terms of our formal concepts of likelihood, it is susceptible to internal and external objections. One can object that Hume neglects the possibility that our iterated doubts and corrections converge to a limit very close to the initial assessment. In fact, the probability we ascribed in our initial judgement might be increased. (We might have initially underestimated how likely true its content is.) But there is also room for objecting to the very idea of calling in question the initial assignment of probability. Once the initial judgement is assigned a probability, which is grounded on all the relevant circumstances, it seems inappropriate to say that doubts and reflections on the reliability of our faculties should call it in question. They should have already been computed in the initial probability or we should have regarded that assignment as defective. On this reading, Hume's appeal to 'all the rules of logic' seems ungrounded. But there are no compelling reasons to take Hume's argument as a formal one in the theory of probability.[24]

---

[24] See, for discussion, Fogelin, *Hume's Skepticism*, 17–20. Hume had available a version of the argument (referring to testimony) based on probabilistic considerations (see F. Wilson, 'The Origins of

On the force of the text and of the nature of Hume's sceptical concerns, which express the effects that commonly accepted epistemic commitments and doxastic engagements have on our cognitive possibilities, the argument for reductio should rather be given a strictly epistemological reading. (This is consistent with its conclusion being one of impossibility.) The epistemological considerations that are prominent in the argument are *safety from error* and *epistemic responsibility*. These are strictly epistemological aims, which make perfect sense in the context of doxastic deliberation and are not reducible to probability in our formal sense. It is helpful, in interpreting Hume's argument, to keep in mind one lesson from the Lottery Paradox.[25] Part of the point of the Lottery Paradox is that the concept of rational belief cannot be understood in terms of probability, because we are rationally entitled to give different epistemic treatment, when assessing the claim that we know that a lottery ticket is not a winner, to the extremely small probability that the ticket is actually the winner and to the larger probability, once we have testimony that the ticket did not win, of some error in broadcasts and so on. Epistemological considerations do not abide only by considerations of probability if complex aims like safety from error and epistemic responsibility are taken into account. It is somehow in this irreducibly epistemological sense that we should understand Hume's argument and its composition of uncertainties. Hume's language is epistemological: he talks of 'doubt' grounded on the recognition of the 'different degrees of authority' of our opinions, 'in proportion to the degrees of our reason and experience'; and of 'all the rules of logic'—the rules of mature probable reasoning—requiring the iteration of such doubt.[26] Against this background, Hume's argument is best understood, as Owen proposes, in terms of a progressive widening of the margin of error with which we reflectively undertake our doxastic commitments.[27] A maximally wide margin of error—at 50/50—means that we do not give or withdraw assent to a certain idea. In Hume's philosophy, the mental counterpart to this is that the assent included in the initial judgement is completely eroded. And without assent, it is not just that our beliefs are unwarranted: they become completely impossible as states of mind.

Hume's Sceptical Argument against Reason' History of Philosophy Quarterly, 2, 3, 1985 (323–35) (in Tweyman, *David Hume. Critical Assessments*, Volume 1, 253–66). This version *has* the flaws ascribed to Hume's argument. Even if Hume was actually acquainted with this version, this would be consistent with his proposing a different one. See also Qu, *Hume's Epistemological Evolution*, 105–6.

[25] See Williamson, *Knowledge and its Limits*, 58–9.

[26] See, for the strictly epistemic character of what here Hume means by rules of logic, and of the whole sceptical argument against reason, Garrett, *Cognition and Commitment*, 226–8; *Hume*, 223–6 (reading the argument in terms of the contrast between 'seemly' and 'overconfident' beliefs is particularly helpful).

[27] I draw on the valuable discussion in Owen, 'Scepticism with regard to Reason', 113–17. Hume extends his sceptical argument and his response to it to the issue of testimony (1.3.13.4 and fn. 24). Belief by testimony is under threat of extinction and can be retained for reasons having nothing to do with the iteration of probabilities (see Owen, 'Scepticism with Regard to Reason', 121–3).

Third. The conclusion of impossibility is the starting point of Hume's response to the sceptical argument. More precisely, it is used for his own reductio of an unstated premise of the 'argument': that belief is a 'simple act of the thought'; that it issues from and consists in 'mere ideas and reflections' (1.4.1.8). This reductio is, again, a probable reasoning.

(a) The conclusion of the sceptical argument is not in fact believed and the erosion of assent does not follow, even for those who consider and accept the argument.

> Shou'd it here be ask'd me, whether I sincerely assent to this argument, which I seem to take such pains to inculcate, and whether I be really one of those sceptics, who hold that all is uncertain, and that our mentjudgment is not in *any* thing possest of *any* measures of truth and falshood; I shou'd reply, that this question is entirely superfluous, and that neither I, nor any other person was ever sincerely and constantly of that opinion. (1.4.1.7)

(b) This is not because of a flaw in or of a faulty understanding of the argument, but because of a deep fact about our cognitive nature and belief in general. 'Nature, by an absolute and uncontroulable necessity has determin'd us to judge as well as to breathe and feel.' We cannot countenance the belief expressed in the conclusion of the argument because it goes against our cognitive nature, against our faculty of belief, also as expressed in reflection and doxastic deliberation.

(c) Since the rational force of the argument is naturally and in principle ineffective against our capacity to form and preserve assent, forming and preserving assent cannot be ultimately by reason. This is put forward by Hume as the aim of his discussion.

> My intention then in displaying so carefully the arguments of that fantastic sect, is only to make the reader sensible of the truth of my hypothesis, *that all our reasonings concerning causes and effects are deriv'd from nothing but custom; and that belief is more properly an act of the sensitive, than of the cogitative part of our natures.* (1.4.1.8)

Belief-formation, as understood by the sceptic, that is, as an exercise of reason alone, of 'reason unlimited',[28] *would be impossible*. Since we still continue to believe, forming and revising our beliefs reflectively and deliberately, we can 'safely conclude' that our 'reasoning and belief is some sensation or peculiar manner of conception', which the kind of iterated reflection deployed in the sceptical

---

[28] As aptly dubbed in Schmitt, *Hume's Epistemology*, 321.

argument cannot destroy. This is, after all, the intended point of 1.4.1: Scepticism with regard *to reason*.[29]

Fourth. Hume still owes an explanation of how we can engage at all in doxastic deliberation, as we manifestly do. The iteration of doubt, reflection, and correction would have its effects no matter whether belief is of a rational or sensible nature. "Tis therefore demanded, *how it happens, that even after all we retain a degree of belief, which is sufficient for our purpose, either in philosophy or common life?*' (1.4.1.9). The point of shifting belief to the imagination, therefore, is not that in this way the erosion of assent can be resisted but that the iteration of doubt and correction is prevented. Because of a property of more limited imagination, no such iteration actually threatens belief.

> I answer, that after the first and second decision; as the action of the mind becomes forc'd and unnatural, and the ideas faint and obscure; tho' the principles of judgment, and the ballancing of opposite causes be the same as at the very beginning; yet their influence on the imagination, and the vigour they add to, or diminish from the thought, is by no means equal. Where the mind reaches not its objects with easiness and facility, the same principles have not the same effect as in a more natural conception of the ideas; nor does the imagination feel a sensation, which holds any proportion with that which arises from its common judgments and opinions. (1.4.1.10)

Assent is preserved because of the Structural Principle and of the role of the more limited imagination in belief-formation. Doxastic deliberation *would* iterate, if it were the activity *only* of the understanding operating on ideas; that is, *only* of the idea-comparing part of the imagination. But mature belief-formation, doxastic deliberation, is an operation of the imagination *as a whole*: the parts of imagination can be conceived separately and thus can possibly exist separately, but they actually work jointly. This means that, even when it operates in its reasoning capacity, the natural mind works differently from reason as understood by philosophers (psychologically undescribed). In its reflective employment, inclusive of probable reasoning, the imagination is still susceptible to the biases and limitations that characterize it in its more limited sense.

In particular it is susceptible to a sort of *cognitive attrition*, antagonist to the principle of Hysteresis. Causal factors like the complication of its contents make it

---

[29] Ainslie, *Hume's True Scepticism*, 28–9, 35–6, rightly identifies Hume's aim in 1.4.1 as finding support for his conception of belief in the fact that we do not believe the sceptical conclusion and that only his conception of belief can explain this fact. This holds generally of Hume's engagement with sceptical issues: 'Hume uses our reactions to sceptical challenges—our incapacity to believe their conclusions despite finding no error in their reasoning—as evidence in favour of his model of the mind' (219). (This dovetails with my reading of Hume's discussion of scepticism about reason as focused on possibility rather than on authority: only the first kind of argument would license a conclusion in the philosophy of mind.) See also Owen, 'Scepticism with regard to Reason', 119.

progressively more difficult for the imagination to engage in comparisons of ideas. This principle—I will refer to it as *Attrition*— makes for phenomena of *intransitivity* that would be out of place if the reflective and idea-comparing part of the imagination were self-standing. Iterated doxastic deliberation, as it figures in the argument, is probable reasoning in which we compare ideas of beliefs (as states of mind) and of the processes leading to them. These ideas progressively embed more and more ideas of beliefs and of their relations so that their contents become more and more complicated. But such reasoning has to be handled by the natural faculty of the imagination. Because of this, it can happen that though we have been able to form beliefs about beliefs and so on for n times, we may not be able to form the nth + 1, even though the task is the same. Our probable reasoning does not operate as calculus. But if the complication of contents hinders and then halts the transitions of ideas, it hinders and then halts the transmission of assent, which has the same causes. Therefore, the effect of Attrition on idea-comparing imagination is to set an upper bound to the iterations of doxastic deliberation about our beliefs or judgements.

> No wonder, then, the conviction, which arises from a subtile reasoning, diminishes in proportion to the efforts, which the imagination makes to enter into the reasoning, and to conceive it in all its parts. Belief, being a lively conception, can never be entire, where it is not founded on something natural and easy. (1.4.1.11)

Assent included in the conclusions of iterated higher-order doxastic deliberation becomes progressively weaker and vanishes before it can completely erode the assent included in our initial judgement (the first-order judgement) and in its successive, first corrections.[30] But this does not mean that we fail to engage in doxastic deliberation. Rather, Hume's faculty of reasoning and doxastic deliberation is bounded and can operate within such bounds, rightly because it is grounded and embedded in the more limited imagination. Such bounds or limitations are what make it possible. The limits are per se trivial and only express a brute fact about more limited imagination. But in the context of imagination operating as one faculty, they have a positive, indispensable cognitive role, stabilizing assent so as to make it susceptible of differential or strengthening, a possibility presupposed by any engagement in reasoning and doxastic deliberation.[31]

---

[30] See Owen, 'Scepticism with Regard to Reason', 119–21, 125.

[31] One cannot but be reminded of the discussion of the backward induction paradox. The possibility of cooperation in a finitely iterated Prisoners Dilemma, where the initial non-cooperative choice is dictated by reasoning backwards from the maximizing choice of defecting at the final iteration, is based on the difficulty for rational agents to achieve and preserve common knowledge of their rationality. This may be owing to mistakes or to bounded rationality and is important in real life situations. Some limitation of our rational capacities thus seems to make possible avoiding the sub-optimal strategy of all defecting from the first round. See K. Binmore, 'Rationality and Backward Induction' Journal

The imagination and the Structural Principle therefore are the key to Hume's discussion of the argument for scepticism about reason. Hume's response seems to have the right features. It is coherent with the nature of the sceptical argument: a problem of possibility raised by the working of our mental, cognitive faculties is solved by giving a different account of such faculties and their working. It preserves, against (the threat of) '*total* scepticism' (1.4.1.7), our ordinary and philosophical cognitive practices, making sense of our inclination and commitment to test and correct our judgements and procedures (like algebraists and merchants do all the time). It is, importantly, a solution that has the desirable feature of endorsing a 'modest scepticism' (1.2.5.26 fn. 12) or a 'moderate scepticism' (1.4.3.10). In the present case, such modesty and moderation consist precisely in the revisionary account of the conditions of reflective and reasonable belief-formation, which are tracked down to a non-representational and non-exclusively idea-comparing faculty like the imagination.[32]

Lastly, the revisionary account proposed by Hume also explains how the very idea of dismantling reasoning by way of reasoning can be entertained and requires a response like the one he gives. Hume contrasts his own analysis and solution of the sceptical doubt about reason with the 'expeditious way, which some take with the sceptics, to reject at once all their arguments without enquiry or examination' (1.4.1.12). The (purported) rejection hinges on this claim: 'If the sceptical reasonings be strong, say they, 'tis a proof, that reason may have some force and authority: if weak, they can never be sufficient to invalidate all the conclusions of our understanding' (1.4.1.12). Hume's reply is that the 'argument is not just' and that, if 'sceptical reasonings' were possible at all, they 'wou'd be successively both strong and weak, according to the successive dispositions of the mind'; and thus would effectively destroy the force of reason. Hume's *defence* of the possibility of 'sceptical reasonings' has the same character of his *rejection* of their conclusion of impossibility. In either case, Hume's point is that the underlying conception of reason is mistaken. In particular, the 'expeditious' rejection depends on conceiving of belief-forming reasoning as 'a simple act of the thought, without any peculiar manner of conception, or the addition of a force and vivacity' (1.4.1.8). The supposition that a successful argument against reason would preserve its 'force and authority' and an unsuccessful one would not 'invalidate' its conclusions, that is, that in no case reason can be called into doubt by reasoning, only takes into account reasoning as comparison of ideas. On this view, all there is to the understanding and reason are ideas internally related by their contents or externally

---

of Economic Methodology, 4, 1997 (23–41); R. Aumann, 'Rationality and Bounded Rationality', in Games and Economic Behavior, 21, 1997 (2–14); R. Sugden, The Economics of Rights, Cooperation, and Welfare, Blackwell, Oxford 1986.

[32] 'The central idea is that a satisfactory equilibrium is achieved through the *balancing* of causal factors. The demands of the understanding are important, for without them there would be no way to distinguish between a reasonable belief and sheer superstition. Yet a belief must always be a vector of these demands in conjunction with other causal influences', Fogelin, *Hume's Skepticism*, 21.

related by probability (causal relations); and to take one or more step in reasoning is to conceive of and follow some such relations of ideas. Therefore, no activity of reasoning, no comparison of ideas, can call in question the authority of reason, the relations of ideas that form its structure. Sceptical reasonings would thus be inherently paradoxical.

But Hume denies that reasoning is only an act of thought and that it can be explained by comparisons of ideas alone. More in particular, reasoning by comparison of ideas must be embedded in the structure of the imagination; it must be considered in the light of how the imagination conveys and fixes manners of conception, or assent. From this viewpoint, it is possible to think of reasoning activity, including sceptical reasonings, in terms of a cognitive dynamics in which assent is added to and subtracted from ideas so that the force with which ideas and their relations are present in the mind can be changed.

> Reason first appears in possession of the throne, prescribing laws, and imposing maxims, with an absolute sway and authority. Her enemy, therefore, is oblig'd to take shelter under her protection, and by making use of rational arguments to prove the fallaciousness and imbecility of reason, produces, in a manner, a patent under her hand and seal. This patent has at first an authority, proportion'd to the present and immediate authority of reason, from which it is deriv'd. But as it is suppos'd to be contradictory to reason, it gradually diminishes the force of that governing power, and its own at the same time; till at last they both vanish away into nothing, by a regular and just diminution. (1.4.1.12)

The same kind of cognitive dynamics, owing to the embedding of idea-comparison in the more limited imagination, can explain both how assent can be preserved across doxastic deliberation and how sceptical reasonings are available to us, even though, ultimately, without posing any real threat of impossibility.

> The sceptical and dogmatical reasons are of the same kind, tho' contrary in their operation and tendency; so that where the latter is strong, it has an enemy of equal force in the former to encounter; and as their forces were at first equal, they still continue so, as long as either of them subsists; nor does one of them lose any force in the contest, without taking as much from its antagonist. 'Tis happy, therefore, that nature breaks the force of all sceptical arguments in time, and keeps them from having any considerable influence on the understanding.
> (1.4.1.12)

11.3.3 The Dangerous Dilemma

The complex relation between Hume's imagination and scepticism about the possibility of cognitive contents and capacities is also in view in Hume's culminating discussion of scepticism at 1.4.7: *Conclusion of this book* (again, my discussion is selective, and focused on the role of the imagination). In that section, before moving to the dialectic of alternating moods unclenched by reflection on the scepticism-conducive traits of our cognition—Hume's *crise sceptique*—and to its denouement in a resolution to re-engage in philosophy in a truly sceptical spirit (Books 2 and 3 are the output of this renewed philosophical effort, 1.4.6.23), Hume lists and discusses four main sources of sceptical concern. The *first* is rather a general characterization of the nature of sceptical issues in Book 1. The cognitive condition 'common to human nature' is that our assent to any reasoning depends on 'experience' and 'habit' operating 'upon the imagination' so as to make us 'form certain ideas in a more intense and lively manner'. It is because of this that 'imagination, or the vivacity of ideas' is the foundation of 'memory, senses, and understanding' (this is a text I have discussed repeatedly) (1.4.7.3). Hume remarks that a 'principle so inconstant and fallacious' can be expected to 'lead us into errors, when implicitly followed (as it must be) in all its variations' (1.4.74), thus paving the way for the discussion of other sceptical concerns. The *second* and the *third* sources address particular problematic ideas and beliefs. These are the paradoxical implications of two of Hume's most important doctrines in Book 1, the inconsistency between causal reasoning and belief of external existence, on the one hand, and the explanation of the ideas of causal necessity and efficacy, on the other. Both issues had already been introduced and briefly discussed by Hume, respectively, at 1.4.4.15 and at 1.3.14.24 (see §§ 7.2.3 and 9.4.2); even though their connection with scepticism is made fully explicit only in the present context.

What I am interested in right now is the *fourth* sceptical consideration, which takes one step further Hume's engagement with scepticism about possibility. This consideration builds on the discussion of scepticism about reason in two distinct but correlated ways. In the first place, it relies on and extends the conclusion that sceptical reasonings (or even only sceptical concerns about some of our problematic beliefs) fail to have any lasting effect on our capacities for reasoning and belief. The 'deficiency of our ideas' (exemplified by the conflict between causal reasoning and belief of external existence; or by the internal source of causal necessity) is not 'perceiv'd in common life' (Hume refers to our ignorance of the 'ultimate principle' of causal conjunctions; but the point can be easily generalized), because of an 'illusion of the imagination' (1.4.7.6). The illusion is owing to the imaginative mechanism of spreading, together with Attrition and the ensuing intransitivities in imagination-based reasonings dealing with multiple and increasingly complex ideas. In the second place, and most importantly, the conclusion of the discussion at 1.4.1 now becomes the basis of a different sceptical problem. The problem concerns whether and how we can make a reflective choice of the principles of our doxastic deliberations and take epistemic responsibility for it. Suppose that the availability and stability of beliefs with problematic contents and of the corresponding reasonings are owing to illusions, or trivial properties, of the imagination. This gives rise to a question concerning 'how far we ought to yield to these illusions' (1.4.7.6). This is the Dangerous Dilemma that ultimately drives the sceptical crisis of 1.4.7.

> This question is very difficult, and reduces us to a very dangerous dilemma, which-ever way we answer it. For if we assent to every trivial suggestion of the fancy; beside that these suggestions are often contrary to each other; they lead us into such errors, absurdities, and obscurities, that we must at last become asham'd of our credulity. Nothing is more dangerous to reason than the flights of the imagination, and nothing has been the occasion of more mistakes among philosophers. (1.4.7.6)

Here imagination is the more limited imagination, of course. But we cannot embrace the second horn of the dilemma, relying only on idea-comparing imagination, because of the problem of erosion of assent.

> But on the other hand, if the consideration of these instances makes us take a resolution to reject all the trivial suggestions of the fancy, and adhere to the understanding, that is, to the general and more establish'd properties of the imagination; even this resolution, if steadily executed, wou'd be dangerous, and attended with the most fatal consequences. For I have already shewn, that the understanding, when it acts alone, and according to its most general principles, entirely subverts itself, and leaves not the lowest degree of evidence in any proposition, either in philosophy or common life. (1.4.7.7)

Only trivial properties or the illusions of imagination, only the more limited imagination, make it possible to fix assent in a way suitable to our having beliefs. But then the problem arises of how we can draw a distinction between the illusions or trivial properties we should rely upon and those we should not; and in what circumstances and to what extent we should accept or reject any of them.

> What party, then, shall we choose among these difficulties? If we embrace this principle, ['no refin'd or elaborate reasoning is ever to be receiv'd'] and condemn all refin'd reasoning, we run into the most manifest absurdities. If we reject it in favour of these reasonings, we subvert entirely the human understanding. We have, therefore, no choice left but betwixt a false reason and none at all. (1.4.7.7)

The Dangerous Dilemma is a sceptical problem that unifies different first-order sceptical concerns about possibility. It is not about some particular issue but about the possibility of our use of reason in general. In this sense, it is a sort of second-order sceptical problem, which calls in question Hume's own response to scepticism, by addressing its consistency with the very possibility of philosophy and of rational commitment. If we are confined to the choice between a false reason (the trivial suggestions of the fancy) and no reason at all (the self-subverting understanding), as Hume's response to scepticism about reason makes it seem we are, we in fact have *no choice at all* concerning our cognitive conduct; no choice of a method of reasoning. While not only do we take ourselves to have such choice, it is the aim of Hume's philosophy as a whole to promote a 'reformation' of philosophy by recommending an experimental method of reasoning across all our ordinary and philosophical cognition.[33]

As I have suggested, sceptical problems of possibility are correlated to cognitive gaps and to the content-constituting operations of the imagination; therefore, they are an integral part of Hume's philosophy. But sceptical problems need to be answered, just as cognitive gaps demand closure. Hume gives to the Dangerous Dilemma the same general kind of response he had given to its immediate antecedent, scepticism about reason. The imagination enters only to a limited extent into the kind of reasonings that support the Dilemma, which include the consideration of the iterated correction of our judgements of probability.

> For my part, I know not what ought to be done in the present case. I can only observe what is commonly done; which is, that this difficulty is seldom or never thought of; and even where it has once been present to the mind, is quickly forgot, and leaves but a small impression behind it. Very refin'd reflections have little or no influence upon us; and yet we do not, and cannot establish it for a rule, that they ought not to have any influence; which implies a manifest contradiction. (1.4.7.7)

In this way, the second-order sceptical threat posed by the Dangerous Dilemma is addressed with a second-order application of Attrition. This application, of course, does not remove the Dilemma: Attrition, as expressing a trivial principle of the imagination, is actually a condition for it. But because of Attrition, that is, by living by the imagination, we can live with the Dangerous Dilemma without risking the epistemic and cognitive paralysis that would follow from its consideration and from the attempt to solve it in one way of the other. And this common sense position is buttressed by the correct understanding of mind and cognition, in particular of how the imagination operates. Our pre-theoretical indifference to this sceptical concern thus finds a counterpart and a rationale in Hume's science of human nature. The possibility of doxastic deliberation, of

---

[33] Garrett, *Cognition and Commitment*, 208 (see also 214–15), summarizes the Dangerous Dilemma in a way that highlights its dealing with an issue of cognitive possibility: 'the inability of reason alone to defend any satisfactory principle for determining which seemingly trivial belief-influencing features of the imagination to accept and which to reject'. (This is consistent with the Dangerous Dilemma *also* raising doubts about the authority of reason, *within* the limits in which it is a possible faculty of ours.)

reflective-belief-formation and belief-revision, is secured within the bounds that are set to reflection and reasoning by the real nature of these mental operations, that is, their issuing from the imagination conceived according to the Structural Principle. Within these bounds, we can engage in mature, reflective probable reasoning. In much the same way, we are not blocked in our choice of a method of reasoning by the consideration of the false reason/no reason alternative, because such consideration does not take hold, persistently and consistently, of our reflection; and does not bear, persistently and consistently, on our engagement in cognition. And this is because reflection and cognition, including those involving the Dangerous Dilemma, are functions of the imagination as a whole faculty (and not only of the more limited or the idea-comparing imagination). Therefore, by treating the understanding as the imagination, Hume can define a safe space, a space of possibility for doxastic deliberation and cognitive agency and responsibility. This is also the space for raising questions (possibly with sceptical implications) of epistemic value and authority.

11.4 Summary

The imagination takes up roles otherwise ascribed to the understanding and reason in connection not only with conceptual change but also with substantial cognitive achievements and with epistemic value and authority.

In § 11.1 I address the difference between conception and cognition, which Hume thinks the other philosophers have left unexplained. This is the point of his theory of belief as the attitude of accepting for true, or assent. As I show in § 11.1.1, Hume identifies a gap between conception and cognition across all the forms of this latter: sense and memory, a priori knowledge, and probability. Hume's core insight is that conception and cognition do not differ by elements of representational content. Hume closes this gap by identifying assent with a manner of conception: a lively and forceful conception of ideas. This manner of conception is not a distinct perception but only a way in which perceptions are present to awareness. Its phenomenology is as a feeling of force, firmness, solidity, steadiness, and influence of ideas.

§ 11.1.2 deals with assent in sense and memory and in demonstrative reason. In the first case assent is the feeling of presence of objects, which is part of the nature of impressions of sensation and ideas of memory. Content and manner of conception, in sensible representation, are conceptually distinct but, by physical necessity, jointly instantiated. Also in the case of a priori knowledge assent is causally determined by the content of ideas. Not by its presence as object, however, but its structure (internal relations), which confers to conception the firmness and solidity that constitute assent.

In § 11.1.3 I show how the imagination takes centre stage in explaining assent in the case of probable cognition. Hume explains assent to probability with a distinctive kind of transition of the imagination, conveying to perfect ideas the force and vivacity of impressions of sensation or ideas of memory. Distinct, structurally different, transitions produce the inferential potential of causal contents and the assent that turns causal conceptions into causal judgements. The assent-constituting transitions are customary; since only the more limited imagination is susceptible to repetition effects, probable cognition is thoroughly a product of the imagination.

In § 11.2 I apply Hume's theory of assent to his individuation of the mental state, belief, which realizes probability in our nature. § 11.2.1 discusses the cognitive gap marked by this mental state. Probability, like any other form of cognition, is a composite of content and assent. The resulting mental state is belief (as opposed to sense and memory, on the one hand, and knowledge, on the other). Beliefs compose most of our ordinary cognition and cannot be explained with object representation or the a priori. They combine features inconsistent with either, being non-object dependent, thoroughly inferential, susceptible to generalization and modal qualification, with contingent and a posteriori contents. The state of belief is therefore the primary cognitive expression of the imagination.

It is remarkable (see § 11.2.2) how Hume's individuation of belief and its nature fits with the requirements of doxastic deliberation, which is our ordinary, mature form of probable cognition. Humans and animals share primitive states of belief. Reflective-belief formation does not completely part ways with its primitive form. Still, the nature of belief makes it uniquely susceptible to doxastic deliberation, because of the content-constitutive role of customary transitions and of the guidance that idea-comparisons provide for the conveyance of assent. This is a deep functional contrast with sensible representation and a priori knowledge. Belief-formation in presence of conflicting evidence and general rules are perfectly ordinary examples of such doxastic deliberation.

In § 11.3 I address the relations between Hume's imagination and scepticism. Hume's confrontation with scepticism, discussed in §11.3.1, is an offspring of the natural limits of object representation and of reason. Philosophical reflection discovers cognitive gaps but cannot close them with further representation and reasoning. This requires productive operations of the imagination and entails deep revisions of the nature and contents of our ideas. Hume's confrontation with scepticism is thus a central aspect of his reformation of philosophy. Hume addresses two different, nested kinds of scepticism. One arises from the apparent impossibility of certain, ordinary contents and cognitions. Imagination can make up for such missing cognitive possibilities. But in regard of its operations, further sceptical doubts arise concerning the epistemic authority of the imagination and our titles to epistemic rationality.

In § 11.3.2 I discuss Hume's paradigmatic discussion of scepticism about cognitive possibility: scepticism about reason. This much-discussed text addresses the possibility of probable reasoning and reflective-belief formation. The sceptical doubt hinges on how iterated reflection, mandated by principles of fallibility and of epistemic responsibility, seems to erase our assent to any proposition. We could not form beliefs by doxastic deliberation and this would disrupt our ordinary cognitive practices. Hume's response resorts to the nature of assent and of belief. If belief-formation by idea-comparison is embedded in the imagination as a whole, the intransitivities of the more limited imagination set bounds to the iterations of reflection, because of the increasing complexity of ideas. This makes possible our ordinary practice of reasoning (but only on a deep revision of its character).

Finally, in § 11.3.3, I examine another case scepticism about cognitive possibility: the Dangerous Dilemma, which summarizes the sceptical threats raised by Hume's own philosophy. The Dilemma builds on the conclusion of scepticism about reason: only a trivial property of the imagination, its susceptibility to intransitivities, enables reflective reasoning. This is the basis for a further question: whether, in choosing principles of doxastic deliberation, we should rely on the more limited imagination or commit to idea-comparing reasoning. Since neither option is viable, we have a sceptical problem of possibility, arising from Hume's own response to scepticism. And if we had no choice of a method of reasoning, the very aim of Hume's philosophy would be frustrated. At this level, again, Hume's response is that the imagination can only enter to a limited extent into scepticism-inducing reflections.

12
The Ultimate Judge of All Systems of Philosophy

> To talk therefore of objections and replies, and ballancing of arguments in such a question as this, is to confess, either that human reason is nothing but a play of words, or that the person himself, who talks so, has not a capacity equal to such subjects.
>
> (1.2.2.6)

Hume's epistemology, even the question of whether there is anything like an epistemology in Hume, is a notoriously complicated topic. Here I will address it only from the viewpoint of Hume's theory of the imagination; but it is rightly from this viewpoint that some of the most interesting conceptual and interpretive problems come in view. To put it in a nutshell: the ideas we compare and the judgements we form in the context of doxastic deliberation, as well as the corresponding reasoning activities, are owing to the imagination. The imagination, understood in terms of inferentialist naturalism and the Structural Principle, produces the general, modal, inferential import of mental contents and acts. The reflective assessment of the epistemic status of our beliefs (as we have seen in the discussion of scepticism about reason) is itself a case of idea-comparing probable reasoning, of doxastic deliberation. Furthermore, it is an important thesis of Hume's general philosophy that normative ideas, such as are compared in epistemic assessments, are not object representing *at all*. Whatever bearing on cognition they have, it must be owing to the imagination. Therefore, as Hume remarks, the imagination is the ultimate judge not only of all systems of philosophy but also of all our cognitive engagements in general.

In this way, two problems arise. The first is that the imagination is also the *source* of all the systems of philosophy and all the cognitive efforts that take us beyond sense and memory (and, in a different respect, intuition and demonstration). Therefore, the threat is that the imagination turn out to be judge *in sua re* and that, with this, the validity or integrity of any 'critical examination' of our beliefs be called into question. The second problem is that Hume conceives of the imagination, programmatically and systematically, as a thoroughly naturalistic faculty. Its processes and outputs are all causally explainable on the basis of empirical information about the properties of perceptions and the original principles of mental activities. Then a problem clearly arises concerning the grounds of normative, epistemic distinctions among equally natural mental processes and conditions. The very possibility of such distinctions seems to be either called into question or to require us to resort to non-naturalistic principles. (This is of course a fundamental problem in early modern and modern philosophy and one that in many respects is still with us.) These problems sum up to a cognitive gap, which raises a difficulty for Hume's theory of the imagination. A difficulty that Hume recognizes and addresses explicitly.

12.1 The General and More Established Properties of the Imagination

Hume's arguments in Book 1 of the *Treatise* involve epistemological distinctions in multiple ways and at multiple levels. The science of man has explicit foundational aims, put forward in the *Introduction*: 'In pretending therefore to explain the principles of human nature, we in effect propose a compleat system of the sciences, built on a foundation almost entirely new, and the only one upon which they can stand with any security' (*Introduction* 6). After the complex, critical and constructive dialectic of the sceptical crisis in the *Conclusion* of Book 1, Hume hedges but reiterates his foundational ambitions. 'We might hope to establish a system or set of opinions, which if not true (for that, perhaps, is too much to be hop'd for) might at least be satisfactory to the human mind, and might stand the test of the most critical examination' (1.4.7.14). Book 1, including the theory of the imagination, must therefore put in place the epistemological buttress of the 'tribunal of human reason' (*Introduction* 1). Quite generally, epistemological distinctions and epistemic commitments are also an aspect of our ordinary and philosophical cognitive practices. Mature probable reasoning and our various sorts of belief concerning matters of fact are susceptible to and typically directed by rules that express epistemic distinctions. Correspondingly, some of the explanations in Hume's science of human nature involve not only the availability but also the grasp or the awareness of some of such distinctions: the explanatory weight borne by the susceptibility of general conclusions to counterexamples is a point in case.[1] Explaining how such normative considerations are possible is thus not only a matter of consistency but also a crucial, substantive task for Hume's philosophy. Quite expectably, this task is marked by a cognitive gap; but, as we will see, individuating and closing this gap raises complex conceptual problems in Hume's philosophy.

---

[1] See, for discussion, Owen, *Hume's Reason*, 205–6; and (with reference to causal inference) Schmitt, *Hume's Epistemology*, 146–67.

12.1.1 An Unjust Blame?

Hume is aware of the difficulties raised, in his philosophy, by the aim of keeping together the fundamental cognitive role of the imagination and the possibility of the epistemic distinctions that his own theory recognizes or even postulates. He gives an explicit, second-order formulation of such difficulty in an important text. (The context is Hume's critical discussion of ancient and modern philosophy, at 1.4.3–4, which focuses on the concept of substance and on the distinction of primary and secondary qualities and concludes with rejecting the claims of modern philosophers to any superiority over the ancient ones.)

> But here it may be objected, that the imagination, according to my own confession, being the ultimate judge of all systems of philosophy, I am unjust in blaming the antient philosophers for makeing use of that faculty, and allowing themselves to be entirely guided by it in their reasonings. In order to justify myself, I must distinguish in the imagination betwixt the principles which are permanent, irresistable, and universal; such as the customary transition from causes to effects, and from effects to causes: And the principles, which are changeable, weak, and irregular; such as those I have just now taken notice of. The former are the foundation of all our thoughts and actions, so that upon their removal human nature must immediately perish and go to ruin. The latter are neither unavoidable to mankind, nor necessary, or so much as useful in the conduct of life; but on the contrary are observ'd only to take place in weak minds, and being opposite to the other principles of custom and reasoning, may easily be subverted by a due contrast and opposition. For this reason the former are received by philosophy, and the latter rejected. One who concludes somebody to be near him, when he hears an articulate voice in the dark, reasons justly and naturally; tho' that conclusion be deriv'd from nothing but custom, which infixes and enlivens the idea of a human creature, on account of his usual conjunction with the present impression. But one, who is tormented he knows not why, with the apprehension of spectres in the dark, may, perhaps, be said to reason, and to reason naturally too: But then it must be in the same sense, that a malady is said to be natural; as arising from natural causes, tho' it be contrary to health, the most agreeable and most natural situation of man. (1.4.4.1)

This important and complex even somewhat tormented text requires a careful reading. Hume seems to be pursuing two distinct, strictly interrelated lines of thought. The first, which opens the text, concerns whether the fundamental, systematic, and constructive cognitive role of imagination leaves any room for criticism of philosophical positions. At the end of 1.4.3: *Of the antient philosophy*, Hume reproaches the 'Peripatetics' for having been 'guided by every trivial propensity of the imagination', just as children and poets (excusably) do; and asks rhetorically: 'But what excuse shall we find to justify our philosophers in so signal a weakness?' (1.4.3.11). The objection that opens the text addresses precisely this demand for justification. If imagination is the judge of all systems of philosophy, philosophers are justified in following its propensities, because in this way they ipso facto abide by its judgements. (This point can be extended to ordinary cognitive practices.) To justify himself in his criticism, Hume must in his turn explain how, even though imagination is the source of all systems of philosophy and of all ordinary cognitive performances and therefore is judge of itself, it still makes sense to ask whether one ought to accept or to reject its principles (in philosophy and in common life). If this did not make sense, ancient and modern philosophy, all sorts of cognitive positions, being the offspring of imagination, would be epistemologically on a par.

The second, strictly connected, line of thought emerges at the end of the text and addresses generally and directly the issues of naturalism and normativity. Equally natural causal processes underlie regular and non-regular reasonings. But if this is so, then, from the naturalistic perspective of Hume's philosophy, any normative distinction seems either arbitrary or inconsistent. The mind and its properties, activities, and outputs are things, processes, and facts of nature. When reasoning to a sound conclusion one 'reasons justly and naturally'. But when forming an unsound opinion one still may be said 'to reason, and to reason naturally too'. In this second case, 'natural' is used in a 'sense' in which 'a malady is said to be natural'. But of course maladies *are* perfectly natural 'as arising from natural causes'. Thus, Hume seems to run the risk of losing the point of his analogy: the naturalizing analogy between epistemic correctness and health. He ends by saying something awkward like that some natural conditions are 'most natural' to man (1.4.4.1; see 1.4.3.8: 'The whole system, [of ancient philosophy] therefore is entirely incomprehensible, and yet is deriv'd from principles as natural as any of those above-explained'). Notice that, since the imagination is the common natural cause of all sorts of cognitions, the two lines of thought—how can the imagination be the judge of itself and still be a judge; how can naturalism differentiate in normative terms equally natural processes—ultimately converge. What here comes into view is one of the philosophically most interesting themes in Hume's theory of the imagination.[2]

On my reading, Hume's treatment of these issues, inextricably connected with his discussion of scepticism, is in three steps; better, it involves three aspects that

---

[2] Hume rightly remarks that the common-sense distinction between careful and rash judgement raises the same problem as the epistemic distinctions between principles of the imagination. 'According to my system, all reasonings are nothing but the effects of custom; and custom has no influence, but by inlivening the imagination, and giving us a strong conception of any object. It may, therefore, be concluded, that our judgment and imagination can never be contrary, and that custom cannot operate on the latter faculty after such a manner, as to render it opposite to the former' (1.3.13.11).

must turn out to be coherent. The first is Hume's search for *naturalistic identifications* with properties of the imagination of the normative, epistemic distinctions deployed in ordinary and philosophical cognition. The second is the specification of the *character* of such epistemic distinctions. The first and the second aspects are, of course, mutually dependent: the character of epistemic distinctions regulates and validates their naturalistic identifications; the identifications with properties of the imagination gives to such distinctions a foothold in our cognitive nature. Third and finally, the *possibility* (consistently with what we know about the nature of our minds) that ideas with such content and character have normative import, value, and authority. Unless this possibility is established, both the identification of the epistemically important properties of the imagination and the characterization of epistemic ideas or concepts hang in the air; and with them the title of the imagination to judge our claims to cognition. I think that Hume has important things to say in all the three respects and that this is one of the achievements of his philosophy.[3]

12.1.2 The First Question: 'Principles, which, however common, are neither universal nor unavoidable in human nature'

Hume's first step in addressing these issues is to look for some natural properties of the imagination that can realize the normative distinctions postulated by the science of man and provide content for the corresponding ideas. The imagination is a fundamental, natural cognitive faculty. If no property of it could be a plausible naturalistic candidate for the realization of epistemic distinctions, for giving content to epistemic ideas, Hume's philosophy would face a serious challenge. On a certain view of Hume's general philosophy, the very idea of tracking down epistemic distinctions to natural properties of cognitive faculties, primarily, of the imagination, may seem suspicious. Epistemic distinctions are normative, distinctions in the value of our thoughts and beliefs. They are about what we ought to think and believe. But Hume, as a general and well-known point of his philosophy, denies that any object we can represent, reason about, or judge or believe truly, any existence or matter of fact, can individuate and ground any normative distinctions. The point of Section 3.1.1: *Moral distinctions not deriv'd from reason*, is precisely this. 'The operations of human understanding divide themselves into two kinds, the comparing of ideas, and the inferring of matter of fact'; 'were virtue discover'd by the understanding, it must be an object of one of these

---

[3] See, for a very insightful discussion of 1.4.4.1 in the context of Hume's epistemology in the *Treatise* and as expressive of Hume's account of and commitment to certain grounds of epistemic distinctions, L. Loeb, 'Epistemological Commitment in Hume's *Treatise*', *Oxford Studies in Early Modern Philosophy*, 6, 2011 (309–47), 313–16, 341–5. See also 341, 346, for very helpful summaries of the epistemic distinctions endorsed by Hume in the *Treatise*.

operations'. But it cannot be such an object (3.1.1.18). This claim about normativity seems to extend to distinctions of epistemic value and authority. The idea of identifying epistemic distinctions with natural properties of the imagination and, in this way, determining their contents with reference to certain objects and properties (perceptions, mental activities) seems to contrast with this claim. However, this would be the case only if such identifications were a priori: the internal relations between epistemic ideas and ideas of natural properties (of the imagination) would make them inseparable and would leave no options but to regard them as necessarily the same. But there is no pressure, in Hume or generally, to regard the identifications of epistemic distinctions with properties of the imagination as a priori. Rather, everything in Hume's philosophical framework (and in some of our most authoritative ones) pushes in the opposite direction: it is only physically necessary for epistemic distinctions to find realization in this or that property of the imagination. It is a necessity only for our nature, which springs from its metaphysically contingent constitution. The two sets of considerations, epistemic and naturalistic, remain conceptually, as to their characters, perfectly distinct; at the same time, we come to see in what ways and under what conditions the normative qualifications of thought and cognition can gain a foothold in our cognitive nature.[4]

Hume is thus on safe philosophical ground when he refers down the distinction between reasonable and unreasonable inferences and beliefs to one between the principles (and operations, and outputs) of the imagination. That is, the distinction between those that are 'permanent, irresistible, and universal', like customary causal transitions and those that are 'changeable, weak, and irregular', like the torment or fear of spectres (1.4.4.1). Or the 'principles of human nature' that have 'intimate connexion' with the 'unreasonable and capricious' 'fictions' of ancient philosophy (1.4.3.1). Again, some principles of the imagination are 'solid, permanent, and consistent' and others 'however common, are neither universal nor unavoidable in human nature' (1.4.4.2). These distinctions also come out in the *Conclusion* of Book 1. The 'trivial suggestions of the fancy', which are often 'contrary to each other' and lead us into 'errors, absurdities, and obscurities', as well as into philosophical mistakes, are to be kept apart from the 'general and more established properties of the imagination' which are the true nature and constitution of the 'understanding' (1.4.7.7).

Hume in this way begins to justify his criticism of ancient and modern philosophy by connecting different naturalistic properties of the imagination with normative differences in their operations. The connection thus established is

---

[4] On the role of a posteriori identifications in a naturalistic account of normativity, see A. Gibbard, *Meaning and Normativity*, Oxford University Press, Oxford 2012, 26–35 (of course, the literature is enormous; I only refer to Gibbard's work because it is the work I learned most from). The issue is discussed, under the heading of the 'indicator interpretation' of the 'criterion' proposed at 1.4.4.1, by Schmitt, *Hume's Epistemology*, 296–9.

descriptively rich. It is based on our ordinary understanding of such normative distinctions and on a posteriori information concerning the natural mind. It allows us to individuate what natural properties of the imagination underlie epistemically privileged kinds of reasonings and beliefs, just as other natural properties of perceptions and the mind underlie the authority of sense and memory and the certainty of knowledge. Hume explicitly individuates these properties as realizing the differences between good and bad, acceptable and objectionable, fit and unfit reasonings and beliefs, and in this way as fixing the reference of our common sense and philosophical epistemic ideas.

> The opinions of the antient philosophers, their fictions of substance and accident, and their reasonings concerning substantial forms and occult qualities, are like the spectres in the dark, and are deriv'd from principles, which, however common, are neither universal nor unavoidable in human nature. The *modern philosophy* pretends to be entirely free from this defect, and to arise only from the solid, permanent, and consistent principles of the imagination. Upon what grounds this pretension is founded must now be the subject of our enquiry.
> (1.4.4.2)

This also begins to explain how we come to master ordinary and philosophical epistemic distinctions or, equivalently, how we come to apply such distinctions to objects: we can recognize, in perfectly naturalistic ways, what mental episodes or principles bear the relevant epistemic properties, simply by checking whether they have the relevant natural properties. Since these a posteriori identifications, and thereby our mastery of epistemic ideas, are a form of probable reasoning, this begins to clarify how the imagination can non-paradoxically be the ultimate judge of all systems of philosophy. By the imagination we can identify and recognize a posteriori the naturalistic differences that make for certain epistemic differences; in this way, by the imagination, we can differentially assess the principles, processes, and outputs of the imagination itself.

12.1.3 Rules of Judgement

This is also the background of Hume's discussion at 1.3.15: *Rules by which to judge of causes and effects*, which is explicitly normative and epistemological. 'According to the precedent doctrine, there are no objects, which by the mere survey, without consulting experience, we can determine to be the causes of any other' (1.3.15.1). 'Since therefore 'tis possible for all objects to become causes or effects to each other, it may be proper to fix some general rules, by which we may know when they really are so' (1.3.15.2). Hume holds that such rules refer to and are realized in natural properties of the mind or imagination. 'Here is all the *Logic* I think proper to employ in my reasoning; and perhaps even this was not very necessary, but might have been supply'd by the natural principles of our understanding' (1.3.15.11). These rules, no matter how difficult in their application, are easily accessible in their contents by observation, reflection, and inference from the relevant operations of the imagination. ('All the rules of this nature are very easy in their invention, but extremely difficult in their application.') Hume, elsewhere, remarks that these rules, 'by which we ought to regulate our judgment concerning causes and effects', 'are form'd on the nature of our understanding, and on our experience of its operations in the judgments we form concerning objects' (1.3.13.11). That is, the different ways in which the imagination operates in judgement or belief formation, which depend on its different principles, are what we must look at in forming epistemic rules. Such reference fixing determines the content and the application of all the rules which the imagination forms in forestalling the effects of rashly formed rules. It is the key to Hume's view of how general rules are related to the contrasts between custom and judgement (1.3.13.9) or judgement and imagination (1.3.13.11).

> Thus our general rules are in a manner set in opposition to each other. When an object appears, that resembles any cause in very considerable circumstances, the imagination naturally carries us to a lively conception of the usual effect, tho' the object be different in the most material and most efficacious circumstances from that cause. Here is the first influence of general rules. But when we take a review of this act of the mind, and compare it with the more general and authentic operations of the understanding, we find it to be of an irregular nature, and destructive of all the most establish'd principles of reasonings; which is the cause of our rejecting it. This is a second influence of general rules, and implies the condemnation of the former. (1.3.13.12)

The opposition and the second influence of general rules makes room for the normative qualification of imagination-based, natural cognitive activities. It is essential for such qualification that the principles of such activities be contrasted in such respects as to bear opposite normative features. At the same time, such contrast is drawn from experience and probable reasoning about natural properties of the imagination. These are what we refer to when we think in epistemic, normative terms. It is in this guise that the 'more general and authentic operations of the understanding' contribute to the epistemic competence that Hume's philosophy postulates and aims to promote. Some of the natural properties of the imagination realize epistemic distinctions and the imagination is positioned to recognize them in forming and applying epistemic rules. Notice that while reflection is certainly involved in the explanation of how we manage to think and to refer in terms of normative, epistemic ideas, it is not what constitutes such content. Such ideas do not issue from and are not grounded in reflection; they do not derive normative import from passing some reflective test. Such import is rather constituted by a posteriori naturalistic identifications and (as we will see) by a priori considerations about the character of normative distinctions as well as by a naturalistic, sentimentalist account of value and obligation. Reflection has a role only as a cognitive tool, a form of abstract and of probable reasoning, which allows us to explore and connect these considerations.[5]

12.2 Reasonable Foundations of Belief

We are not yet able to solve the difficulty set by epistemic distinctions. A posteriori naturalistic identifications of epistemic distinctions do not exhaust the account of epistemic normativity. What is further required is a specification of the character of the relevant distinctions: what kinds of normative differences they make; what normative concepts (general normative ideas) they involve. Without such a specification, it would not even be possible to identify a posteriori the relevant, general, and more authentic operations of the understanding. A first task is to establish whether the normative distinctions that Hume accepts are specifically epistemic or rather of some other, possibly pragmatic character. I discuss this and defend an epistemic interpretation in §12.2.1. I then proceed to discuss Hume's specifically epistemic distinctions. I think that for Hume it is a priori that truth is the fundamental epistemic consideration, spanning across knowledge and important kinds of belief. Truth-related epistemic assessments can be extended to some strictly non-truth-apt beliefs, to cognitive faculties, and to cognitive subjects in terms of what we would call reliability and entitlement (§ 12.2.2). Lastly, I suggest that a further, distinct, and somehow vague epistemic consideration, important for Hume's epistemology of imagination, has to do with objectivity and with cognitive improvement (§12.2.3).

12.2.1 The Test of the Most Critical Examination

At first sight, the distinction between 'permanent, irresistible, and universal' and 'changeable, weak, and irregular' principles seems to be of a pragmatic character. 'The former are the foundation of all our thoughts and actions, so that upon their removal human nature must immediately perish and go to ruin. The latter are neither unavoidable to mankind, nor necessary, or so much as useful in the

---

[5] For an opposite, deeply interesting but ultimately in my opinion unsatisfactory view, see A. Baier, *A Progress of Sentiments*, Harvard University Press, Cambridge (Mass.)/London, 1991, 97–100. Like every other Hume scholar, I have learned much from Baier's masterful work and particularly from her interpretation of Hume's views of normativity in terms of reflexivity. But I have come to the conclusion that success in reflexivity is evidence for, rather than constitutive of, normative import.

conduct of life' (1.4.4.1). The normative significance of the different principles and works of imagination seems to depend on their effects on our survival and well-being. Principles that are permanent, irresistible, universal, and unavoidable are better than principles that are changeable, weak, and irregular because they are at least 'useful in the conduct of life'. Now, this sort of line of thinking is certainly present in Book 1. Naturalism in Hume's philosophy is cashed out also at something like a biological level; traces of what we would call an adaptive conception of mind, cognition, emotion, and action are detectable. A pragmatic-naturalistic perspective seems thus to provide a compelling interpretation of the ground of Hume's distinction between principles of imagination.[6]

However, Hume's normative distinctions among cognitive principles are also recognizably epistemic. The general and established principles of the imagination are the 'foundation of all our thoughts and actions'. This foundational role, also considered pragmatically, involves correct cognitions of things and relations. But there is something more: while pragmatic considerations are salient, the diversity of the criteria of Hume's distinctions should not be neglected. Think of the following contrasts: 'permanent, irresistible, and universal' and 'changeable, weak, and irregular', 'unavoidable', and '[not] necessary, or so much as useful'. While the contrast between weak and irresistible principles points in a psychological direction, and that between unavoidable and non-necessary principles in a pragmatic direction, those between permanence and changeability or between universality and irregularity admit and support an epistemic reading. Permanent or stable and universal principles of idea and belief formation seem to put us in a better position to reason about and gain cognition of matters of fact, because they allow us to individuate and exploit conditions which are not accidentally related to objects. Solid, permanent, and consistent principles of the imagination seem thus to be valuable in an epistemic sense. The pragmatic consequences of the different principles of the imagination thus are one but not the only source of normative distinctions between mental episodes and processes.

The application to ancient and modern philosophy of the distinctions drawn at 1.4.4.1 is also epistemic in intent. The identification of the natural principles of the imagination that explain the ideas of substance or original matter, substantial form (1.4.3.6), accidents (1.4.3.7), and occult qualities (1.4.3.8) opens the way to a *criticism* of the corresponding beliefs as 'unreasonable and capricious' (1.4.3.1). Such criticism also addresses the epistemic shortcomings of vulgar and philosophical 'opinions' about the identity and simplicity of bodies. The vulgar opinion that we perceive a connection between objects we observe to be constantly united turns out to be false on philosophical reflection, by a priori considerations of

---

[6] See, for a careful discussion and criticism of the pragmatic interpretation of Hume's views concerning the normativity of cognitive activities and state, K. Schafer, 'Curious Virtues in Hume's Epistemology', *Philosophers' Imprint*, 14, 1, 2014 (1–20), 4–10.

Separability and by the a posteriori discovery of the effects of repeated experienced (1.4.3.9). Philosophers, in their turn, fail to draw from their observations the 'just inference' that we have only mind-dependent ideas of power or agency. Missing this 'just conclusion', because of a misunderstanding of the idea of power, they engage in a misguided and frustrating search, based on false existential presuppositions, for the qualities in which power consists. ('For what can be imagin'd more tormenting, that to seek with eagerness, what for ever flies us; and seek for it in a place, where 'tis impossible it can ever exist?', 1.4.3.9.) The invention of 'wholly insignificant and unintelligible' terms like *'faculty'* and *'occult quality'* reflects this epistemic rather than pragmatic error. Hume's answer to this predicament, his 'moderate skepticism', is itself a distinctly epistemological position (1.4.3.10). Also Hume's discussion of the 'fundamental principle' of modern philosophy ('the opinion concerning colours, sounds, tastes, smells, heat and cold; which it asserts to be nothing but impressions in the mind, deriv'd from the operation of external objects, and without any resemblance to the qualities of the objects', 1.4.4.3) is distinctly epistemological. Hume pays most attention to show how this opinion, joined to his own account of our ideas of external objects, leads to the 'most extravagant skepticism' of denying that anything we conceive has 'a real, continu'd, and independent existence' (1.4.4.6). What dooms ancient and modern philosophy is not just that their views fail to contribute in a necessary or even useful way to the survival of our species. It is also and primarily that such views derive from false beliefs and flawed steps of reasoning and are inherently unreasonable. This holds of the whole of Part 4, which is largely dedicated to the epistemological criticism of philosophical ideas: the intellectual nature of reasoning and belief, the double existence of perceptions and objects, the relations between perceptions and the mind, the immaterialist and materialist metaphysics of the mind, the perfectly simple and identical self.[7]

The epistemic character of Hume's normative distinctions between principles and operations of the imagination is pervasive. The normative requirements on the inferential working of abstraction are in terms of truth and falsehood of conclusions (1.1.7.8). Intentional directedness is individuated in terms of pertinence of ideas to topics of discourse (1.7.7.15). The standard of the adequateness of ideas is in terms of representation and of contribution to knowledge (1.2.2.1). The

---

[7] This marks a difference with Berkeley, who insists that sense-experience, the 'language of nature', or the 'universal language of the Author of Nature', is structured and regulated in terms of (God's concern for) what contributes the 'benefit or injure' of our own bodies, *New Theory*, 59 (24). The ultimate explanation of the regularities, of the rules, of the order and connexion displayed by ideas of sense, and of the very fact that there is any such regularity at all, is pragmatic or teleological. The 'use and end of sight' explains the principles, the reach, and the conditions of correctness of vision, *New Theory*, 87 (34). The same pragmatic rationale supports and limits our attempts to know the laws of nature, the rules which connect ideas of sense and determine the order of *rerum natura*. Knowledge of the laws of nature gives us 'a sort of foresight, which enables us to regulate our actions for the benefit of life'. Knowledge of nature consists in 'sure and well-grounded predictions, concerning the ideas we shall be affected with, pursuant to a great train of actions', *Principles*, 31, 59 (86, 94).

enquiry into the nature of spatial ideas determines the truth-conduciveness, fallibility, and exactness of the branches of mathematics (1.2.4.17, 22–3; 1.3.1.3–6). The deviations of spirits along the traces of the brain determine errors in reasoning, because of the use of ideas related to but with a somewhat different content from that which the survey demanded (1.2.5.20). The correct account of the idea of vacuum vindicates the use made of this idea by the Newtonian philosophy (1.2.5.26 fn. 12). The differences in the otherwise similar mental causes of education and experience or probable reasoning—repeated impressions as opposed to the repetition of ideas; 'an artificial and not a natural cause'—make it so that 'its maxims are frequently contrary to reason, and even to themselves in different times and places' (1.3.9.19). The difference in degree of evidence between knowledge, proof, and probability is straightforwardly epistemological (1.3.11.2). The features that mark off unphilosophical probability from the other species of probability are mostly and primarily epistemological. Some have to do with its grounds in experience. 'When we have not observed a sufficient number of instances, to produce a strong habit; or when these instances are contrary to each other; or when the resemblance is not exact; or the present impression is faint or obscure.' The same with the pattern of mental transitions, as when 'the inference [is] deriv'd from general rules, and yet not conformable to them' (1.3.13.19). This last one is an interesting case. Hume seems to have in mind an inference that is caused by certain rules without being justified by them.

Finally, in his conclusive assessment of the achievements of Book 1, Hume admits that 'perhaps' truth is 'too much to be hop'd for'—in this way, however, recognizing that it would be the appropriate criterion of assessment. But being 'satisfactory to the human mind' and (especially) standing 'the test of the most critical examination' or (possibly) the 'examination of the latest posterity' are perfectly good epistemological aims, which dovetail with the general epistemological ambitions of the *Treatise*. 'For my part, my only hope is, that I may contribute a little to the advancement of knowledge, by giving in some particulars a different turn to the speculations of philosophers, and pointing out to them more distinctly those subject, where alone they can expect assurance and conviction. Human Nature is the only science of man; and yet has been hitherto the most neglected' (1.4.7.14). We can thus safely conclude that the kind of normativity that suits Hume's imagination is also and essentially of epistemic.[8]

12.2.2 The Truth and Fidelity of our Faculties

Against this background, it is unsurprising that the primary epistemic consideration in Hume's *Treatise* is that of truth and of the truth-related notion of 'fidelity' (reliable truth-conduciveness): 'the estimation we make of the truth and fidelity

---

[8] See Garrett, *Hume*, 152–4.

of our faculties' (1.4.1.6); or 'the veracity or deceitfulness of our understanding' (1.4.1.1).[9] Hume's concept of truth is the classical one of correspondence or agreement between ideas and their objects. Truth is firmly embedded in the representational relation as providing foundations for cognition in general.

> Truth is of two kinds, consisting either in the discovery of the proportions of ideas, consider'd as such, or in the conformity of our ideas of objects to their real existence. (2.3.10.2)
>
> Reason is the discovery of truth or falshood. Truth or falshood consists in an agreement or disagreement either to the *real* relations of ideas, or to *real* existence and matter of fact. Whatever, therefore, is not susceptible of this agreement or disagreement, is incapable of being true or false, and can never be an object of our reason. (3.1.1.9)

Notice that Hume in these texts is *not* contrasting a coherence with a correspondence concept of truth. Hume has no coherence concept of truth. He has a theoretical role for the coherence of perceptions and its bearing on mental states. But such role is essentially mediated by the transitions of imagination; it is content-generating, not truth-making. Truth is *agreement* of representational ideas with something *real*: either *real* relations of ideas, considered as such, or *real* existence of objects and matter of fact. Truth is correspondence in either case; what differs is what ideas correspond to. Objects in their real existence or matters of fact are objects in impression or in memory: ideas are true if they agree with impressions, in terms of the representational relation. Also ideas which are only potentially representational are susceptible to truth or falsehood. They are true if they turn out to agree with objects present in sense-experience, even though they do not derive from impressions of these objects; they are false if they do not agree with anything empirically given: the golden mountain. Real relations or proportions of ideas 'consider'd as such' are relations that ideas have in their mental existence because of their contents: their connexion and repugnance. These relations are no less real than those of objects of sense. They are not given as impressions but in reflection. But Hume remarks that perceptions considered in their mental existence (it is in this sense that ideas are *considered as such*) or as actual episodes are present and represented with force and vivacity of conception, not dissimilarly from impressions (1.3.8.15). Thus, the conditions for the cognitive

---

[9] I regard Schmitt's discussion of the essential and central role of truth in Hume's account of cognitive value as conclusive (see *Hume's Epistemology*, 33, 102–4, 108–9). Notice, however, that this is consistent with recognizing an epistemic role for other features of cognitive states, in particular, as I try to show at § 12.2.3, for properties of invariance or stability (in a broad sense). Schmitt, *Hume's Epistemology*, 1 fn. 2, 24, lists the stability account among the alternatives to his veritistic account, recognizing that the textual support for it is 'impressive'. I think that this can be made consistent by recognizing that both truth and features of stability are required for the generation of cognitive pleasure, entailed by epistemic approval and thereby by epistemic value.

import of ideas are also satisfied in this case.[10] This conception of truth has a fundamental epistemological application. It is the subject matter and the proper domain of reason ('Reason is the discovery of truth or falsehood'). And it is the fundamental and most general epistemic consideration.

> Wherever ideas are adequate representations of objects, the relations, contradictions and agreements of the ideas are all applicable to the objects; and this we may in general observe to be the foundation of all human knowledge. (1.2.2.1)

The concept of truth applies to episodic mental states. But we can also make sense along Humean lines of the epistemic status of cognitive processes and even of cognitive faculties, with the truth-related notion of fidelity. An important suggestion comes from Hume's claim that reason is a fallible cause of truth. 'Our reason must be consider'd as a kind of cause, of which truth is a natural effect; but such-a-one as by the interruption of other causes, and by inconstancy of our mental powers, may frequently be prevented' (1.4.1.1). The epistemic value of reason, of cognitive processes in general, is that of reliably producing truth, where reliability consists in the high probability that the conclusions of rational processes are true.[11] This is the key to Hume's taxonomy of cognitive faculties. A priori reason is maximally reliable, because the truth of intuitions and demonstrations consists in their agreement with internal relations of ideas, which are metaphysically necessary and a priori; and the awareness of such relations is causally necessary and sufficient for our assent. In this way, a priori reason is a cause of truth that enjoys the status of maximal reliability. (It is the reliability, not the logical structure of knowledge, which I am specifying in these terms: reliability is a matter of causation, not of simple relations of ideas.)[12]

---

[10] For a good discussion of Hume's theory of truth see G. J. Nathan, 'A Humean Pattern of Justification', *Hume Studies*, 9, 2, 1983 (in Tweyman, ed., *David Hume. Critical Assessments*, Volume 1 (183–97), 184–90. Nathan reconstructs Hume's theory in terms of the two kinds of truth-conditions; he rightly individuates in Hume a distinction between semantic and epistemic considerations about truth; he also recognizes that impressions and ideas of memory have an import of truth in either sense (although his reading of the representational role of impressions is different from mine). However, his discussion of sense and memory would have benefited from drawing a distinction, also in the case of real existence, between knowledge (which these capacities can deliver) and belief (inferential, imaginative belief).

[11] On truth and reliability as the basic contents of Hume's epistemic distinctions see Beebee, *Hume on Causation*, 71–4. Still, locating Hume in the contemporary epistemological landscape is not a straightforward matter. Contemporary reliabilism attempts to provide an answer to Gettier cases and to reinstate an account of knowledge in terms of belief, truth, and some further normative notion. But Hume treats belief and knowledge as different kinds of cognition. His problem is not establishing how belief can sum up to knowledge, once it is joined with other conditions, but how, at what conditions, states of belief can imitate or approximate states of knowledge.

[12] Schmitt, *Hume's Epistemology*, 69–76, identifies the epistemic status of knowledge with infallibility, that is, necessary reliability. But it is important to fix properly the modalities: the production of a cognitive state by reason is by construction a causal matter; therefore the likelihood of its producing truth cannot exceed the certainty of proof. But the degree of reliability of a faculty also depends on the antecedent likelihood that the states of the kind it produces be true. In the case of a priori reason, their truth is necessary.

The authority of sense and memory is closest to that of a priori knowledge and is also of epistemic in character ('veracity'). This is the crucial text in this regard.

> Thus it appears upon the whole, that every kind of opinion or judgment, which amounts not to knowledge, is deriv'd entirely from the force and vivacity of the perception, and that these qualities constitute in the mind, what we call the *belief* of the existence of any object. This force and this vivacity are most conspicuous in the memory; and therefore our confidence in the veracity of that faculty is the greatest imaginable, and equals in many respects the assurance of a demonstration. (1.3.13.19)

Hume is here explicitly making an epistemological point: what equals in many respects the assurance of a demonstration is our confidence in the truth of the contents we grasp. In the case of memory (and the senses), such confidence is produced by the presence of objects in impressions of sensation and by the retention of such impressions as ideas of memory. Therefore, it is a reliable indicator of truth. The reason why Hume places the faculty of sense and memory almost at the same level with a priori reason is that the epistemically important mental structure of sense and memory is closer to that of knowledge than to that of belief. States of sense and memory are caused by the contingent existence of the sensible objects that form their contents, both as what they present and in relation to the attitude of assent. Even though truth here is metaphysically contingent and a posteriori, there is a connection between truth and the very possibility of sense and memory. Therefore, if our faculty of sense and memory functions properly, nothing else is required for the truth of what they deliver. This marks their epistemic value. Their reliability does not have the force of demonstration, because senses and memory are of contingent matters; but it sums up to a very high probability or proof.[13]

12.2.3 Truth, Imagination, and Belief

We must now see whether and to what extent the epistemic criteria of truth and fidelity hold beyond knowledge, sense, and memory. Hume's talk of truth as

---

[13] Schmitt, *Hume's Epistemology*, 74–5, remarks that Hume seems to extend knowledge to 'all actions and sensations of the mind', which are 'known to us by consciousness', and 'must necessarily appear in every particular what they are, and be what they appear' (1.4.2.7). As Schmitt also suggests, this is best understood as the distinction and the necessary correspondence, in any such mental episode, of the '*reality*' of perceptions with their appearing to '*feeling*'. This would require a more complex articulation of mental existence in terms of the intrinsic, phenomenal individuation of mental episodes and in the subjective experience of them, our being 'most intimately conscious' of them. A theme that is only liminally present in Hume. (Introspective reflection is only the a posteriori representation of the perceptions.)

agreement of our ideas to real existence or objects should be taken with some latitude, as including the distinctive, specifically imaginative mental state of belief. Hume claims that our 'judgment of causes and effects', that is, episodic causal beliefs, has reference 'to truth and reason' and that this constitutes their cognitive character, marking their mental difference from the passions (2.3.3.6). Against this background, Hume's theory makes for highly differentiated ascriptions of truth-aptness to beliefs. Particular beliefs issuing from probable reasoning, which are about what follows what or what precedes what, about unobserved particular existents, are non-problematically truth-apt. They identify physical possibilities and are a posteriori; we have ideas of their truth-conditions based on experience; and these ideas, together with their manners of conception, form their overall contents. General judgements of what follows from what or of what precedes what (probable generalizations) can be considered as truth-apt because of the alignment that Hume's abstraction establishes between general contents and the corresponding particular ideas. Particular and quantified judgements of successions of events, however, do not exhaust causal cognition. We must also consider judgements framed in explicitly causal terms, in terms of concepts such as causal power, causal efficacy, or necessary connexion. The problem with those judgements is that such ideas are essentially modal and therefore, on Hume's conception of modality, cannot be individuated, even compositionally, by objects or properties of objects. Truth-conditions, insofar as they can be assigned to components of the content of these judgements, fail to extend to their overall content (this is clear from the two definitions of cause and of necessity). Therefore, we cannot regard probability as all and homogeneously truth-apt: this will depend on the nature of the contents assented to; but certainly most of our probable beliefs are truth-apt or can be aligned to truth-apt ones. Furthermore, explicitly modal causal judgments can be easily translated into general and particular judgments regular successions of objects.

Correspondingly, Hume brings the consideration of fidelity or veracity to bear on the belief-producing processes of the imagination and on the epistemic value of the imagination as a faculty. He extends the epistemological ordering of our cognitive faculties from a priori reason or sense and memory to probability or causal reasoning, the paradigmatic cognitive operation of the imagination.

> The next degree of these qualities [force and vivacity of perception, 'confidence in the veracity' of a faculty] is that deriv'd from the relation of cause and effect; and this too is very great, especially when the conjunction is found by experience to be perfectly constant, and when the object, which is present to us, exactly resembles those, of which we have had experience. But below this degree of evidence there are many others, which have an influence on the passions and

imagination, proportion'd to that degree of force and vivacity, which they communicate to the ideas. (1.3.13.19)

Even though it is mixed with considerations about the force and vivacity of assent, Hume's point here is the epistemic status of the cognitive processes of the imagination. This comes very clearly from an important text, closely related to the present one, where he explicitly articulates the degrees of evidence of the faculty of probable reason in epistemological terms.

> Those philosophers, who have divided human reason into *knowledge and probability*, and have defin'd the first to be *that evidence, which arises from the comparison of ideas*, are oblig'd to comprehend all our arguments from causes or effects under the general term of probability. But tho' every one be free to use his terms in what sense he pleases; and accordingly in the precedent part of this discourse, I have follow'd this method of expression; 'tis however certain, that in common discourse we readily affirm, that many arguments from causation exceed probability, and may be receiv'd as a superior kind of evidence. One wou'd appear ridiculous, who wou'd say, that 'tis only probable the sun will rise to-morrow, or that all men must dye; tho' 'tis plain we have no further assurance of these facts, than what experience affords us. For this reason, 'twould perhaps be more convenient, in order at once to preserve the common signification of words, and mark the several degrees of evidence, to distinguish human reason into three kinds, viz. *that from knowledge, from proofs, and from probabilities*. By knowledge, I mean the assurance arising from the comparison of ideas. By proofs, those arguments, which are deriv'd from the relation of cause and effect, and which are entirely free from doubt and uncertainty. By probability, that evidence, which is still attended with uncertainty. (1.3.11.2)

As this text makes clear, the difference between proofs and probabilities is epistemological: it is a difference with regard of doubt and uncertainty. Proofs and probabilities are thus not different kinds of mental states: they are different positive degrees of the epistemic value of belief-formation within the faculty of probability. The difference is of reliability, of doubt and uncertainty left open by reasoning, based on the causal circumstances of the production of belief (the mental state, not only the attitude): the constancy of the experience, the resemblance of the objects. It is a difference in how likely it is that the judgements we form are true. In some cases (proofs) the epistemic value issuing from probable reasoning can be nearly as good as that of knowledge and, we may add, of sense and memory: this is the case of causal arguments 'entirely free from doubt and uncertainty'. In other cases (probabilities), it is not. Probable reason, sense and memory, and a priori reason thus are different as faculties, because of their structure and conditions; but they can be close in terms of the degree of their epistemic value. This is another indication of the reliabilist orientation of Hume's epistemology.[14]

To some extent, the same strategy applies outside of probability to inferential and a posteriori beliefs about external existence and personal identity. In both cases we are perfectly able to form particular beliefs that it would be hard, for Hume and for ourselves, not to consider truth-apt. I have in mind particular beliefs about the distinct and continued existence of objects (the door of my chamber, the stairs of my house, the seas and continents of the Earth) which figure in Hume's coherence account of the idea of external existence and actually are its conclusions (1.4.2.20; see § 9.2.1). Or particular beliefs concerning our existence 'on the first of January 1715, the 11th of *March* 1719, and the 3d of *August* 1733', which (having no memory of our actions) we form by application of the causal idea of the mind and of the idea of its identity across change (1.4.6.20; see § 10.2.2). Belief formation in these cases (as Hume makes explicit with reference to the coherence account of the idea and belief of body) involves probable reasoning. But the contents of the involved ideas and the principles underlying their production and the conveyance of assent include elements and aspects that diverge from the causal ones. Still, at least in connection with particular beliefs like those just mentioned, there seems to be no obstacle to talk of truth-conditions. However, Hume's epistemic assessment of the belief-producing processes of the imagination in domains like external existence and personal identity is very different from that of probability, as shown by his concern for sceptical problems in this area. This seems to be because such processes—except in some cases—are unlikely to produce true or even truth-apt beliefs. Vulgar beliefs in body, insofar as their contents include a conception of perceptions as empirically

---

[14] The focus of Hume's epistemology is not on cognitive subjects. But if truth and fidelity are its key notions, thinkers can also be conferred epistemic status. The right notion for this extension could be that of the *entitlement* subjects have to certain cognitive states and operations, on account of facts about the conditions and structures of these latter and without having access to these facts or understanding their role as reasons. We are typically entitled to accept our sense perceptions or some simple calculations or inferential steps. Such acceptance is epistemically in good order, simply because of the reliability of these cognitive operations; but we do not typically access and understand the relevant reasons. (See T. Burge, 'Content Preservation', *Philosophical Review*, 102, 1993, (457–88); T. Burge, 'Perceptual Entitlement', *Philosophy and Phenomenological Research*, 67, 2003, (503–48); for discussion, A. Casullo, 'What is Entitlement?', *Acta Analitica*, 22, 2007, (267–79).) This sits well with Hume's general perspective on mind and cognition. The imagination includes a very primitive level of cognition and connects it with more reflective and explicit operations. Hume's epistemology can address not only the vulgar but also children and even animals. Our basic mental and cognitive faculties are *animal* but can still be epistemically assessed (1.3.16). But Hume is also perfectly comfortable with the idea that our cognitive positions often descend from reflection and deliberation on our beliefs and reasonings. This opens the path, in Hume's philosophy, to a further layer of epistemic assessment of cognitive subjects, which we can more properly understand in terms of justification and epistemic responsibility. Entitlement does not immediately translate into epistemic justification and responsibility, because the second involves the reflective viewpoint of a thinker deliberating on her cognitive positions; and Hume is not shy of resorting to this epistemic viewpoint, particularly in the context of normatively informed explanations and of the discussion of sceptical threats.

the same with external objects, are false. Philosophical beliefs, which involve the notion of double existence, do not even achieve truth-aptness, because in this respect they fail to individuate any metaphysical possibility. Something along these lines holds of the processes of the imagination underlying the idea and belief of personal identity. Also in this case, the vulgar beliefs are by and large tacit; but insofar as they make explicit and robust ascriptions of identity and simplicity, they are not truth-apt; and the explicit philosophical idea of a strictly simple and identical self does not individuate a metaphysical possibility. The sensitivity of the imagination to repetition and its customary transitions explain why probable reasoning and probability in general has more fidelity than other, equally imagination-grounded, cognitive processes (starting from education).[15] This is because custom is responsive in a rather direct way to repeated observation, which delivers representations of objects and is unquestionably truth-apt. By contrast, the other principles of the imagination, like Hysteresis, and especially Completion, Act/Idea Resemblance, and Reconciliation, diverge from sensible representation in ways not guaranteed to preserve even truth-aptness.

12.2.4 The Improvement of the Human Mind

The cognitive work and the epistemic bearing of Hume's imagination extend beyond the limits of truth and fidelity—even though these remain the crucial epistemic considerations. Ordinary, non-representational ideas like mixed equality, empty space and time, powers, continuedly and distinctly existing objects, and persisting persons have roles in our ordinary cognition and in our system of realities which are not exhausted by truth and fidelity. While this makes them the principal target of sceptical concerns, it is important to take note of this further layer of Hume's epistemic assessment of such problematic ideas and beliefs.

The cognitive role I have in mind is that of complementing probable reasoning in the construction of a unified system of realities. A view of connections and powers as in the objects, a view of bodies and minds as identical, exerts a strong pull on our minds to regard the world as a whole, as unitary, and as stable across diversity and variation of viewpoints. Throughout Book 1 Hume identifies and explains different ways in which the imagination produces an inclusive and unified view of the world. Some such cases are the following: the Missing Shade of Blue (1.1.1.10); the simulation of a whole intellectual world of ideas (1.1.7.15);

---

[15] At 1.3.9.16 Hume distinguishes between 'two kinds of custom', one based on experience and one on education. In either case, the effects of custom are an easy transition of ideas and transmission of force and liveliness; that is, states of belief. But it is only in the first case that custom determines contents which can figure in a just idea-comparing inference, because they are aligned to the objects that prospectively figure in causal relations. Education, whose 'maxims are frequently contrary to reason, and even to themselves' 'is never upon that account recogniz'd by philosophers', 1.3.9.19.

space and time posited in the absence of objects (1.2.5.25, 28); the filling up of inconstant perceptions (1.4.2.35); the unification of variable secondary ideas (1.4.6.16); the inner–outer distinction (1.4.7.3). The unifying function is not restricted to causal contents and beliefs. In fact, one of Hume's most famous texts in this vein, the cement-of-the-universe passage, refers to all the principles of association, not only to causation.

> These principles of association are reduced to three, *viz. Resemblance*; a picture naturally makes us think of the man it was drawn for. *Contiguity*; when *St. Dennis* is mentioned, the idea of *Paris* naturally occurs. *Causation*; when we think of the son, we are apt to carry our attention to the father.
>
> 'Twill be easy to conceive of what vast consequence these principles must be in the science of human nature, if we consider, that so far as regards the mind, these are the only links that bind the parts of the universe together, or connect us with any person or object exterior to ourselves. For as it is by means of thought only that any thing operates upon our passions, and as these are the only ties of our thoughts, they are really *to us* the cement of the universe, and all the operations of the mind must, in a great measure, depend on them.
>
> (*Abstract* 35)

The cement of the universe and the unity of the operations of the mind are secured by all three principles of association. They support and moderate together the 'empire of the imagination', its 'great authority over our ideas' (*Abstract* 35). This is not to neglect the differences between these principles and the priority of causation. But we must keep in mind that each of them, even the unruly and unreliable principle of resemblance, seems to make a distinctive contribution to the unified view of the world. These insights concerning these kinds of operations of the imagination come together in an all-important text from the *Conclusion* of Book 1, from which I have been quoting piecemeal, when introducing the productions of content by the imagination.

> Without this quality, by which the mind enlivens some ideas beyond others (which seemingly is so trivial, and so little founded on reason) we cou'd never assent to any argument, nor carry our view beyond those few objects, which are present to our senses. Nay, even to these objects we cou'd never attribute any existence, but what was dependent on the senses; and must comprehend them entirely in that succession of perceptions, which constitutes our self or person. Nay farther, even with relation to that succession, we cou'd only admit of those perceptions, which are immediately present to our consciousness, nor cou'd those lively images, with which the memory presents us, be ever receiv'd as true pictures of past perceptions. The memory, senses, and

understanding are, therefore, all of them founded on the imagination, or the vivacity of our ideas.   (1.4.7.3)[16]

The quality mentioned at the opening, as the closing makes clear, is the vivacity of ideas, a central function of the imagination. The three operations of the imagination in which the text is articulated are, respectively, the extension of assent to unobserved matters of fact by probable reasoning; the distinction of objects external to the mind from perceptions internal to it; the conception of the mind as persisting through successive perceptions. In this context, there is no contrast between the first and the other two operations, even though probability has an epistemic status lacking from the ideas of body and self; all of the three operations have a crucial constructive role.

This general cognitive function of the imagination is epistemologically important. It supports our engaging in good, mature reasoning, in deliberate, reflective belief formation, according to the rules that Hume has introduced at 1.3.15. It supports the aims of detaching our reasoning and judgement from particular standpoints and fixing on the circumstances that objectively matter in a certain situation, so that we may lock on real and not apparent matters of fact. Since engaging in mature probable reasoning is epistemically valuable because truth-conducive, also a unified view of the world, while not truth-apt, is epistemically valuable, because it favours the fidelity of our cognitive efforts. Hume certainly seems to praise epistemic objectivity and realism.

> In the operation of reasoning, the mind does nothing but run over its objects, as they are supposed to stand in reality, without adding any thing to them, or diminishing any thing from them. If I examine the *Ptolomaic* and *Copernican* systems, I endeavour only, by my enquiries, to know the real situation of the planets; that is in other words, I endeavour to give them, in my conception, the same relations, that they bear towards each other in the heavens. To this operation of the mind, therefore, there seems to be always a real, though often an unknown standard, in the nature of things; nor is truth or falsehood variable by the various apprehensions of mankind. Though all human race should for ever

---

[16] Kant was certainly acquainted with this text from the *Treatise*, 1.4.7, that had been translated by Hamann and published, even though without attribution to Hume, in 1771; see G. Hatfield, 'Introduction' to Kant, *Prolegomena*, xvii, fn. 16. One is left wondering why he held the view that Hume's sceptical concerns (as he characterized them in *Prolegomena*, 10, for instance) were restricted to causation. A possible answer is that Kant regarded the a priori dimension of space and time and the synthetic character of mathematics as his first discovery and fundamental innovation with respect to Hume; and Hume's views concerning these matters are not present in 1.4.7. P. Guyer, *Knowledge, Reason, and Taste. Kant's Response to Hume*, Princeton University Press, Princeton 2008, 6–7, remarks, in connection with 1.4.7, that Kant might not have been able to fathom from it the extent and depth of Hume's doubts—or of Hume's Problem. He adds that Kant's response to Hume's account of causation can be extended to that of external objects and of the self.

conclude, that the sun moves, and the earth remains at rest, the sun stirs not an inch from his place for all these reasonings; and such conclusions are eternally false and erroneous.[17]

More generally, progress toward a more stable and objective view of reality seems to constitute an improvement of the human mind, in cognition no less than in evaluation and in moral judgement. This seems especially fitting to the nature and roles of a faculty like Hume's imagination, which is primarily a faculty of *cognitive change*.[18] This casts further light on Hume's a posteriori identification of epistemic distinctions with principles of imagination bearing certain naturalistic properties: those 'permanent, irresistible, and universal' as opposed to 'changeable, weak, and irregular' ones. The permanence, irresistibility, and universality of the principles of imagination are a plausible mental realization of the epistemic value of objectivity, of invariance of cognition or judgement across a wide range of individual, accidental circumstances and mental dispositions.[19]

12.3 Love of Truth

12.3.1 The Second Question: 'In the same sense, that a malady is said to be natural'

I thus conclude that Hume succeeds in negotiating a distance between the imagination as a judging and as a judged faculty. However, this conclusion hangs in the air, unless we make room for normative considerations within Hume's naturalistic background. This is the second question raised by Hume at 1.4.4.1: How can naturalistic philosophy (the science of human nature) make sense of

---

[17] 'The Sceptic' (1742), in D. Hume, *Essays Moral Political, and Literary*, E. F. Miller, ed., Liberty Fund, Indianapolis 1985 (158–80), 164. A powerful case for Hume's scientific realism is made in D. Landy, *Hume's Science of Human Nature. Scientific Realism, Reason, and Substantial Explanation*, Routledge, New York/London 2018. For two, excellent and articulated introductions to Hume's relation to Newton and Newtonian philosophy, see Hazony & Schliesser, 'Newton and Hume'); D. Tamás, 'Hume's Science of Mind and Newtonianism' (2019), in E. Schliesser and C. Smeenk, *The Oxford Handbook of Newton*, Oxford Handbooks Online, 10.1093/oxfordhb/9780199930418.013.19.

[18] See G. Currie, 'Imagination and Learning', in Kind, *Handbook of Imagination*, 407–19.

[19] This can remind us of the distinction between reasoning *from* an interpretation and reasoning *to* an interpretation, where the latter fixes the domain of objects and concerns that define a reasoning problem. The distinction is strictly related to that between system 1 and system 2 processes, also because reasoning to an interpretation is expression of a credulous stance and reasoning from an interpretation of a sceptical one (see Stenning & van Lambalgen, *Human Reasoning*, 11, 20–1, and especially 126). This interpretive function, which is distinct from truth- or validity-related considerations, might suggest a way of understanding the objectivity-conferring operations of Hume's imagination.

epistemic differences between cognitive principles that count as equally natural because of their issuing from the imagination? In discussing Hume's a posteriori identifications and the contents and character of epistemic distinctions, I have taken for granted the *normative force* of such distinctions and of concepts like truth, fidelity, and cognitive improvement. Hume's second question concerns precisely this normative force. The point and role of epistemic distinctions and concepts is not exhausted by the descriptive features that fix their reference and by their a priori characterization: also their dimension of value and authority requires explanation. Fixing the reference and the character of epistemic distinctions allows us to say whether certain ideas and beliefs are regular or irregular, erroneous or accurate. But not what the epistemic *badness* of such errors or irregularities or the *goodness* of the opposite positions consist in; why epistemic rightness and wrongness *matter*; why we *ought* to avoid error and are under an *obligation* to pursue reason. We have not yet explained the possibility of epistemic normativity.[20]

In Hume's philosophy, there is *no a priori* connection of the reference of epistemic (or moral) distinctions with their normative force. The latter is not scrutable from the former, from what we refer to with such distinctions. And cognitive differences are not in their turn scrutable from differences in epistemic value. Therefore, if we had *cognition at all* of epistemic values, it could only be a posteriori. But then, it would be a mystery how cognitive differences can have any normative, epistemic force. Quite simply, all cognitive principles and operations, a posteriori and naturalistically understood, are normatively on a par. As Hume remarks, a malady is a perfectly natural phenomenon, 'as arising from natural causes'. In this sense, it is as natural as health. But then we are left wondering how illness and health can be 'contrary' to one another, since they only differ as natural facts, just like two pieces of rock differ in their chemical composition. The second question is therefore how to make sense of epistemic values and distinctions in the context of Hume's naturalism about thought and cognition (which comes to full expression in the theory of the imagination). Epistemic normativity indicates a gap in our cognition in general. Hume's recognition and treatment of the parallel problem in the domain of morals is one of the greatest achievements of his philosophy. But, as we have seen, at 1.4.4.1 he recognizes it also in connection with thought and the imagination. Regrettably, Hume's treatment of this latter question is deeply elusive. We have to look elsewhere, in Book 2 and 3, to find a theoretical pattern that can cast light on epistemic value.

---

[20] See Garrrrett, *Hume*, 147: 'Part of Hume's naturalism lies in his general unwillingness to accept any normativity as explanatorily basic *tout court*: if some things have value of a specific kind, it should be explicable how there is such a kind of value and how things come to be valued in relation to it.'

12.3.2 The Cognitive Gap of Value and Hume's Naturalistic Sentimentalism

Hume's fundamental answer to the gap of normativity is that one can be a naturalist about value and rightness, so as to draw normative distinctions between equally natural objects, by becoming a sentimentalist. If value and rightness can be explained as a natural phenomenon without reducing them to a priori or a posteriori descriptive differences, that is, without assuming that values are representable or inferentially cognizable, naturalism and normativity may be consistent. Explaining values with our sentiments is Hume's way of making them consistent with naturalism. This is Hume's well-known conclusion from his vain search of a priori or a posteriori grounds in the objects for moral distinctions.

> The vice entirely escapes you, as long as you consider the object. You never can find it, till you turn your reflection into your own breast, and find a sentiment of disapprobation, which arises in you, towards this action. Here is a matter of fact; but 'tis the object of feeling, not of reason. It lies in yourself, not in the object.
> (3.1.1.26)

Hume's basic ideas here are the following:

(1) Oughts are grounded on a deeper normative level, which is to be understood in terms of value.
(2) This deeper level is not descriptive but only and ultimately evaluative: descriptions must be complete before values can be conceived of and ascribed.
(3) The deepest normative level is one of observer evaluation: an affectively charged response to non-evaluative ideas and beliefs.
(4) The affectively charged response does not consist in a manner of conception, but in a distinct feeling of pleasure or pain, giving rise to a sentiment of approval, of praise or blame.
(5) Sentiments of approval may or may not bear on action, call us to act. If they do, they constitute oughts and authority.
(6) Obligation is the form that ought or authority take when the possibility of acting on them depends on our endorsement of them, typically under the guise of a rule or principle.[21]

---

[21] This is loosely based on 3.1.1–2. For a very good interpretation and discussion of Hume's theory of value see R. Cohon, *Hume's Morality. Feeling and Fabrication*, Oxford University Press, Oxford 2008; Garrett, *Hume*, 147–51.

For our present concerns, two philosophically important lessons to draw from this sketch of Hume's account of value, ought, and obligation are:

(a) Value is a natural phenomenon but cannot be accounted for in cognitive terms: it is not represented or inferred but felt; the ground of the differences of value is not restricted to causal and functional properties of the objects but must include the different responses of suitably placed and disposed subjects. Value thus individuates a gap in cognition in general.
(b) Such gap can be closed rightly because the subjective responses that constitute differences of value are not simple manners of conceptions but distinct impressions. A simple manner of conception, like assent, would be essentially cognitive and modify the overall content and role of our cognitive states; but value-constituting responses are distinct perceptions, feelings, or passions, which make it so that the ensuing distinctions of value are not cognitive. Non-Mixture does not ensure the sameness of normative and non-normative contents, because something else than a further element of content or a manner of conception is added to ideas.

If we can extend this theoretical apparatus from Book 3 to Book 1 of the *Treatise*, it can provide an account of epistemic normativity consistent with Hume's naturalism, by explaining how equally natural principles and operations of the imagination could have different epistemic values. It would do this by resorting to the perfectly natural fact of our subjective responses, feelings, and sentiments. Together with the a posteriori identifications and the specification of the character of epistemic distinctions, this would close the overall gap of the epistemic normativity of thought and cognition. Hume's sentimentalism about value, in certain respects, converges with his inferentialism about content. Both sentiments and the imagination are called upon to close major gaps in cognition. Both theories are firmly focused on our minds and their responses, not on features of the objects presented or represented by perceptions. Both inferentialism and sentimentalism can do their work only against the background of our ordinary competence with reasoning and belief formation or with evaluation and praise or blame. Ultimately, the test of Hume's sentimentalist explanations of values or of his inferentialist explanations of ideas is whether their naturalistically based conclusions are in equilibrium with our established first-order moral and cognitive practices.

12.3.3 The Satisfaction We Derive from the Discovery of Truth

To explain epistemic value and rightness we must individuate the sentiments of epistemic praise and blame; and to individuate those sentiments, we must identify and characterize the corresponding feelings of pleasure and pain. Hume leaves this complex set of questions seriously undertreated.[22] We can, however, gather some information from Section 2.3.10: *Of curiosity, or the love of truth*, where Hume outlines the phenomenology of cognitive pleasure jointly with its objects and the features of those objects that cause it. Hume's talk of love of truth suggests applying to the sentiments of epistemic approval his general pattern of explanation for indirect passions (which include love, alongside pride, humility, and hate). This cannot be strictly correct as it stands because, in Hume's complex construal of such passions, combining ideas of objects and properties and causes of passions together with distinct and associated pleasurable or painful impressions, the object can only be 'some thinking person' distinct from the subject of the passion (2.2.1.5; '*self-love*' is not love 'in a proper sense', 2.3.1.2). However, Hume remarks that this 'passion' or 'affection' is 'of so peculiar a kind, that 'twou'd have been impossible to have treated of it under any of those heads, which we have examin'd without danger of obscurity and confusion' (2.3.10.1; this is the final Section of Book 2 and Hume is referring to his own classification of the passions). I think this supports extending to love of truth, even though its objects are actions or states of mind, the explanatory apparatus of the indirect passion of love. I will therefore look for the *objects* and the *causes* of the sentiments of epistemic approval together with the distinctive *qualities* of the related feelings of pleasure and pain.[23]

As Hume's discussion at 2.3.10 makes well clear, the generic *object* of epistemic approval is truth (this might well be extended to truth-related notions, like proof,

---

[22] See Owen, *Hume's Reason*, 205–23 for a clear statement of the problem and discussion: the issue of the grounds of our preference for reason (against education, for instance) is the core of Hume's theory of warrant, of his epistemology (that Owen regards as best developed in the first *Enquiry* than in the *Treatise*). Owen's solution hinges on Hume's account and vindication of preference for philosophy over cognitive apathy and superstition (at 1.4.7 and in Section 10: *Of miracles*, of the *Enquiry*) as more pleasing and useful, to ourselves and to others (212). Epistemic approval is thus essentially the same as moral approval (220, 223). The focus of Loeb, *Stability and Justification*, is the relation between cognitive easiness and cognitive stability. See also Garrett, *Hume*, 155–6, 159–62: we derive pleasure in connection with truth from the exertion of genius in a matter of importance; also settling belief in a matter of interest is pleasant. There is much to say for Loeb's proposal: the character of our approving manner of conception or feeling with regard to truth, justness, regularity, falsehood, error, seems to be that of a sense of fittingness and of stability (close to our sense of truth, of our assent to truth). As we will see, it is closer to aesthetics than to ethics.

[23] Thanks to Don Garrett for prompting me to clarify this point. Love of truth is discussed in Schmitt, *Hume's Epistemology*, 381–5, but only as the goal of philosophy. Schmitt does not seem to address the issue of the grounds of epistemic value. I think that my approach, focused on the conditions and structure of epistemic approval and value is different from but can easily converge with the one, focused on the psychology and motivation of epistemically good (and bad) reasoning and on epistemic virtue, which is proposed in Schafer, 'Curious Virtues', 17–20. M. Ridge, 'Epistemology Moralized: David's Hume Practical Epistemology', *Hume Studies*, 29, 2003 (165–204), 178–84, 189, proposes an account of Hume's view of the justification of the understanding modelled (as the one I propose) on his conception of moral justification. However, while Ridge explicitly substitutes moral (or practical or pragmatic, 178–9) justification, I read Hume as preserving such epistemic character, by applying to cognitive states and capacities a general conception of sentimentalist approval and value.

probability, and veracity). But this claim is qualified by Hume in important ways. In the first place, as he remarks, the 'satisfaction, which we sometimes receive from the discovery of truth, proceeds not from it, merely as such, but only as endow'd with certain qualities' (2.3.10.2). Hume makes this comment with reference to a priori truth, the 'discovery of the proportions of ideas, consider'd as such' (2.3.10.2). But he tacitly extends it to a posteriori truth, the 'conformity of our ideas of objects to their real existence' (2.3.10.2). 'The same theory, that accounts for the love of truth in mathematics and algebra, may be extended to morals, politics, natural philosophy, and other studies, where we consider not the abstract relations of ideas, but their real connexions and existence' (2.3.10.11). His argument is that truths of the same nature may give or fail to give pleasure or satisfaction (2.3.10.2). To identify and explain epistemic sentiments, their objects must therefore be individuated in more stringent ways.

Hume's starting point, in a somewhat tortuous discussion, is that the 'first and most considerable circumstance requisite to render truth agreeable, is the genius and capacity, which is employ'd in its invention and discovery' (2.3.10.3, see 2.3.10.7). It is this 'stretch of thought or judgment' that 'of all other exercises of the mind is the most pleasant and agreeable' and elicits epistemic approval (2.3.10.3). Hume also remarks that 'the truth we discover must also be of some importance'; otherwise we turn our attention 'to what is more useful and important' (2.3.10.4). A third observation is that the object of epistemic approval must involve a 'degree of success in the attainment of the end, or the discovery of that truth we examine' (2.3.10.7). Hume remarks that the pleasure we feel for an 'action or pursuit' gives rise, 'by the natural course of affections', to a 'concern for the end itself' and to uneasiness if we fail to achieve it (2.3.10.7). Hunting or gaming are examples of this phenomenon (2.3.10.8–9). This point reinforces Hume's general line of thought, that truth is necessary but not sufficient to explain and identify the object of epistemic sentiments. What we epistemically approve of is a whole state or action of the mind, which we take as a discovery of truth. Such state calls for praise because of the properties of its content (truthfulness) and as a mental exercise or episode (difficult, important, to some extent successful).

But to gain an account of epistemic approval, we must consider not only what objects such sentiment is addressed to but also the qualities of its objects it selectively responds to; that is, the *causes* of the feelings of pleasure and pain which are its affective grounds. Some indications come from the text we are discussing. Hume takes some pains to specify that the contribution of the importance of truth (he even talks of usefulness) to the pleasure we take in its discovery is only partially and not ultimately pragmatic. Hume recognizes a 'contradiction' between the concern of philosophers for the importance of the truths they enquire after and their lack of 'public spirit' (2.3.10.4). Hume's first answer to this difficulty is that the imagination can put in place a measure of sympathy with the 'interests of humanity' without any actual kindness (2.3.10.5). Since he himself recognizes that 'such a remote sympathy is a very slight foundation for a passion, and that so much industry and application, as we frequently observe in philosophers, can never be deriv'd from so inconsiderable an original' (2.3.10.6), he suggests a second, *non-pragmatic* explanation of the contribution of the importance of truth to cognitive pleasure. This contribution is strictly connected to the nature of the basic object of cognitive pleasure, the action of the mind.

> If the importance of the truth be requisite to compleat the pleasure, 'tis not on account of any considerable addition, which of itself it brings to our enjoyment, but only because 'tis, in some measure, requisite to fix our attention. When we are careless and inattentive, the same action of the understanding has no effect upon us, nor is able to convey any of that satisfaction, which arises from it, when we are in another disposition.   (2.3.10.6)

Immediately after, in discussing the similarities between hunting and philosophy, Hume also remarks: 'the utility or importance [of the end: a game of choice, truth] of itself causes no real passion, but is only requisite to support the imagination' (2.3.10.8). Thus, the contribution of the importance of truth to cognitive pleasure is *cognitive* and *imagination related*: fixing our attention or supporting the imagination in its grasp and acceptance of some idea as true. But why does such fixing of the attention constitute a pleasant experience?[24] A suggestion comes from what Hume says, almost incidentally, in a digression at the end of the section, when discussing how love of truth can be divorced from our pleasure for mental activity. Hume here resorts to belief as assent.

> It has been prov'd at large, that the influence of belief is at once to inliven and infix any idea in the imagination, and prevent all kind of hesitation and uncertainty about it. Both these circumstances are advantageous. By the vivacity of the idea we interest the fancy, and produce, tho' in a lesser degree, the same pleasure, which arises from a moderate passion. As the vivacity of the idea gives pleasure, so its certainty prevents uneasiness, by fixing one particular idea in the mind, and keeping it from wavering in the choice of its objects.   (2.3.10.12)

Assent contributes to a feeling of pleasure associated to cognition, to belief as mental state and knowledge, both positively, by fixing attention, and negatively, by preventing the focus of our minds to waver.

---

[24] I read Hume as regarding fixing of attention as a *constituent* of cognitive pleasure. Something inherently cognitively pleasant. What Hume remarks at 2.3.10.10—attention *causes* pleasure by making us take interest in the vicissitudes of a course of action and thus deriving satisfaction (although mixed with pain) from it—seems to apply to what he is there discussing, the pleasures of gaming. Even though an extension to philosophical practice would not be farfetched.

'Tis a quality of human nature, which is conspicuous on many occasions, and is common both to the mind and body, that too sudden and violent a change is unpleasant to us, and that however any objects may in themselves be indifferent, yet their alteration gives uneasiness. As 'tis the nature of doubt to cause a variation in the thought, and transport us suddenly from one idea to another, it must of consequence be the occasion of pain. (2.3.10.12)

Doubting is painful. Even though Hume is here discussing a partially different phenomenon, what he says about how assent contributes to cognitive pleasure converges with and explains how fixed attention or well-supported imagination can contribute to it. The cause of cognitive pleasure is the fixedness and stability of the action of the mind in its achieving truth (of course, truth as we understand and recognize it). These qualities in the states of mind cause our sentiments of epistemic approval, by causing such pleasure.[25]

Finally, we must specify the *impression* or *feeling* of pleasure that is the primitive basis of the evaluative dimension of epistemic distinctions. The quality of this feeling is sui generis. The qualities of pleasures and pains can be highly specific, in relation to the nature of their objects and of the qualities that cause them ('A good composition of music and a bottle of good wine equally produce pleasure; and what is more, their goodness is determin'd merely by the pleasure. But shall we say upon that account, that the wine is harmonious, or the music of a good flavor?', 3.1.2.4). In particular the pleasure we take in true and important cognition because of its fixedness and stability is different from moral pleasure, just as this latter is different from the pleasure given by a sip of good wine. Moral pleasure is a satisfaction of a 'peculiar kind' felt in response to an 'action, or sentiment, or character' (its objects: character is primary) (3.1.2.3–4). The causes of such pleasure are, by way of our sympathetic identification, the effects of the character of a person on the pleasures or pains of those who are directly affected by it ("tis therefore from the influence of characters and qualities, upon those who have an intercourse with any person, that we blame or praise him', 3.3.1.17). Our feelings

---

[25] This subject matter is masterfully discussed in Loeb, *Stability and Justification*. Some examples in Hume's text, aside from 2.3.10, follow. At 1.2.4.7 he equates 'unsteadiness' of imagination and the senses with an 'infirmity' and 'uneasiness'. At 1.3.9.6–8 he contrasts causation with resemblance and contiguity because of their lack of determination. Such relations are felt to be loose and uncertain. I would suggest that this difference in feeling makes for a difference in cognitive pleasure or easiness. At 1.3.10.6, Hume remarks that truth and reality only procure an easy reception for ideas—and therefore, I would say, are pleasurable. Hume remarks that the 'disagreement of ideas, consider'd as copies, with those objects, which they represent' is a 'contradiction' (2.3.3.5). The recognition of such a contradiction cannot fail to give us a painful feeling. Of course, fixedness, stability, and achievement of truth are not the only sources of pleasure we can derive from mental activity. We feel a satisfaction also from adding relations to relations, thus completing the union of objects and ordering them (1.4.5.12). This source of cognitive pleasure is not restricted to cognition but, certainly, when recognizing truth we make an addition to the relations in which our ideas stand.

of moral pleasure and pain are vicarious for the feelings of the subjects involved; therefore they are vicarious feelings of mental or bodily benefit or harm. This is the what-is-it-like of moral sentiments and it seems perfectly distinct from that of epistemic sentiment (even bracketing, insofar as it is possible, their different objects and causes).

I would say that cognitive pleasure rather resembles aesthetic pleasure. What is common to the two kinds of pleasure and sentiment are their dwelling on order, construction of parts, form, and structure (2.1.8.2). They focus on genius or mental exercise, force, power of imagination; our relishing the correspondence of parts, a consistent and uniform whole.[26] I am not denying that epistemic sentiments include heterogeneous features both as to their qualitative phenomenology and as to the features of their objects. In particular epistemic sentiment has a pragmatic dimension. I pointed to this fact at § 13.2. But the same is true of aesthetic sentiment. Hume insists that there is a pragmatic dimension to aesthetic pleasure: 'Our sense of beauty depends very much on this principle; [sympathy] and where any object has a tendency to produce pleasure in its possessor, it is always regarded as beautiful.' But this is 'considerable a part' of 'beauty'; not the whole of it (3.3.1.8). Hume tentatively distinguishes beauty of interest and beauty of form ('a beauty of interest, not of form, so to speak', 2.2.5.16); sympathy is causally involved in the first, not in the second. Something like this distinction could be applied to epistemic value.

Hume thus gives at least the outline of a sentimentalist explanation of epistemic value and authority. Epistemic sentiment is love of truth attentively pursued and grasped, achieved by a steady and unimpeded action of the imagination. Love of truth is caused by a pleasant feeling, the feeling of the stability and fixedness of our cognitive action. And love is approval, praise, what makes true cognition valuable. Since love is also a motivating sentiment (as we will see), what we approve of in this way is not only something valuable but something which can have authority on our thought and cognitive activity.[27]

---

[26] See 'Of tragedy' (1757), in Hume, *Essays* (216–25) 1985, 219, 222; and 'Of the standard or taste' (1757), in Hume, *Essays* (226–49), 240. See D. Townsend, *Hume's Aesthetic Theory*. Taste and Sentiment, Routledge, London/New York 2001, 152, 166, 184–5.

[27] The feeling that forms the sentiment of epistemic approval resembles and is linked with but perfectly distinct from belief-as-assent. Both are part of our sensitive nature; but they still differ from one another in their mental nature. When we assent to or believe an idea, we take it as true and conceive of it as fixed, stable, real, weighty, and so on. Therefore, states of belief, because of their manner of conception, are prime candidates as causes of cognitive pleasure. 'Belief must please the imagination by means of the force and vivacity which attends it; since every idea, which has force and vivacity, is found to be agreeable to that faculty' (1.3.10.7). But still the feeling of assent is not a sentiment of epistemic approval. These latter is a distinct impression a secondary one; assent is only a manner of conception.

12.4 Oblig'd by Our Reason

12.4.1 The First Source of All Our Enquiries

Sentimentalism is thus Hume's naturalistic alternative to normative cognitivism and closes the gap which value opens in cognition in general. This thesis also promises an explanation of epistemic motivation. If epistemic approval or love of truth resembles the indirect passion of love, then we naturally have a desire for true and important cognitions: because of the original constitution of the mind, love is constantly accompanied by benevolence, by a desire directed to its object, even though it is distinct from it (2.2.6.5–6). Love for truth and epistemic approval are by physical necessity motivating (this comes out clearly in Hume's equating love for truth with curiosity). As Hume says, this is the 'first source of all our enquiries' (2.3.10.1); and it is a source that somehow connects cognitive activity with the grasp and endorsement of epistemic values.

This kind of motivation to cognitive activity—epistemic motivation—can take different forms, depending on the role taken by epistemic distinctions. Epistemic values can be articulated and expressed in the guise of rules or principles of reasoning, like *'that like objects, plac'd in like circumstances, will always produce like effects'* (1.3.8.14); or like the 'rules by which to judge of causes and effects', rules 'by which we may know' whether objects are 'really' 'causes or effects to each other' (1.3.15.2). These principles express and systematize our approval of beliefs and of belief-formation processes in relation to truth and fidelity, that is, in epistemic terms; and we can be motivated to cognitive activity accordingly. But the apprehension of and motivation by such principles can be different in different cases. They may simply summarize and facilitate the natural working of the imagination and of our cognitive pleasures and passions, which in the main could proceed by themselves. This is suggested at 1.3.15.11, rightly in reference to the rules of causal judgement: 'Here is all the LOGIC I think proper to employ in my reasoning; and perhaps even this was not very necessary, but might have been supply'd by the natural principles of our understanding.' Since the rules are modelled on (some of) the natural principles of our understanding, what Hume means is that their representation and acceptance as rules 'was not very necessary'. In this case, epistemic motivation is only tacitly at work in our cognitive activity. This kind of epistemic motivation is important in Hume's philosophy. A prime example is offered by his explanation of generality. As we have seen, a crucial component of that explanation is the recognition and acceptance of counter-examples as invalidating our reasoning to a certain conclusion. The ideas that fail to agree with the general conclusion (formed on a particular idea) not only 'immediately crowd in upon us', but 'make us perceive the falshood of this proposition' (the conclusion), even though it is true of the particular idea with which it is formed (1.1.7.8). This capacity or custom, which is crucial for Hume's account of our 'partial consideration' of ideas (generalization), involves the recognition of an epistemic flaw; and, on the way to this, a somewhat complex epistemic distinction between truth-conditions. But this is primarily a matter of the structure of our cognitive process, rather than of our grasp of and the commitment to a rule.

But epistemic motivation also finds expression in the epistemic agency that we exercise in reflective, mature causal reasoning and doxastic deliberation about proofs and probabilities. In this case, we explicitly represent and endorse epistemic principles and resort to them in such a way that the belief is produced by 'reflection' and only 'in an *indirect* and *oblique* way' by customary transitions. This is the case of one-experiment causal inferences (which we engage with not only in philosophy but 'even in common life'): 'we may attain the knowledge of a particular cause merely by one experiment, provided it be made with judgment, and after a careful removal of all foreign and superfluous circumstances' (1.3.8.14). The aim of this cognitive engagement is explicitly epistemic: attaining knowledge; and the conditions for this are in their turn explicitly epistemically characterized: 'with judgment'; 'removal of all foreign and superfluous circumstances'. The rules of epistemic value that allow the satisfying of these cognitive conditions are thus reflectively and deliberatively followed. Another example is the explanation of the idea of geometrical equality. As we have seen, it is a 'mix'd notion of equality' that is employed in our geometrical practice. This idea is that of a 'particular appearance' (the equality of two figures 'to the eye') but 'corrected by juxta-position or a common measure' (1.2.4.24). This idea depends for its genesis and structure on the recognition of the inexactness of our judgements of size as a cognitive *flaw* that calls for their iterated tests and corrections. ('We frequently correct our first opinion by a review and reflection; and pronounce those objects to be equal, which at first we esteem'd unequal... And even this correction is susceptible of a new correction, and of different degrees of exactness, according to the nature of the instrument, by which we measure the bodies, and the care which we employ in the comparison', 1.2.4.23.) The best explanation of this iteration seems to be our awareness that this inexactness is an error and our caring for its correction (both can be iterated beyond our actual capacities for comparing and correcting).

Epistemic motivation can also consist in the direct recognition of an epistemic *ought* and thus take the form of an epistemic *obligation*. This is the case if the corresponding cognitive activity is possible *only* because of the recognition and acceptance of the pertinent epistemic values and rules. I think that this kind of epistemic motivation underlies and explains the cognitive process involved in scepticism about reason. In this way, it completes Hume's account of that sceptical reasoning and his response to it. (But it is in sight also in the iteration driving us to the imaginary idea of equality of size.) Engagement in this kind of iterated reflection and doxastic deliberation seems to be motivated and made possible only by our acceptance of a general epistemic principle, a principle amounting to the recognition of the inherent fallibility of our faculties as an epistemic defect and to the demand for its rectification. In this case, as Hume explicitly recognizes, our cognitive activity is motivated by something like an obligation of reason.

> Having thus found in every probability, beside the original uncertainty inherent in the subject, a new uncertainty deriv'd from the weakness of that faculty, which judges, and having adjusted these two together, we are oblig'd by our reason to add a new doubt deriv'd from the possibility of error in the estimation we make of the truth and fidelity of our faculties. (1.4.1.6)

What is distinctive of this epistemic pattern of cognitive activity is that it is motivated neither by the cognitive constraints of the doxastic situation (like in one-experiment probable inferences) nor by the detection of some particular cognitive flaw (like in the account of the idea of geometrical identity, at least at the first stages). Rather, it is motivated only by the recognition and endorsement of a general epistemic principle: errors of our cognitive faculties deserve correction. This epistemic principle is general in the sense that it is not 'deriv'd from the nature of the object' (one of our particular judgements) but 'from the nature of the understanding' (1.4.1.5). It is only the very thought of possibility of error and of its epistemic disvalue that motivates us to engage in correcting any judgement of probability and to iterate such correction. 'This is a doubt, which immediately occurs to us, and of which, if we wou'd closely pursue our reason, we cannot avoid giving a decision' (1.4.1.6).

This strictly epistemic motivation, our 'being oblig'd by reason', fits with the recursive character of the sceptical reasonings about reason. No matter what epistemic status we ascribe to any of our particular probable judgements, if we aim to remedy to the fallibility of our faculties, we ought to check and correct it. At any step, we are motivated to engage in doxastic deliberation, because of the consideration that this is in general the epistemic thing to do. This is also in line with Hume's concept of obligation and motivation by obligation, as it is articulated in Book 3, Part 2 of the *Treatise*: *Of justice and injustice*. At its barest core, Hume's conception of obligation is that of a motivation that cannot be accounted for in terms of individual aims and actions but only of (more or less tacit) self-interested commitment to some general practice and of the (more or less tacit) consideration of the merit of that practice (see 2.1.6.9; 3.2.1.8; 3.2.1.17; 3.2.2.23; 3.2.5; 3.2.8.3–9; 3.2.9.4).[28] The grounding value can be a consideration of

---

[28] On the concepts of normative motivation and of obligation in Hume, see T. Magri, 'Natural Obligation and Normative Motivation in Hume's *Treatise*', *Hume Studies*, 22, 1996 (23–254). Hume gives full articulation to these concepts at 3.2, in his theory of the artificial virtues, see T. Magri, 'Hume's Justice', in Ainslie & Butler, *Cambridge Companion to Hume's* Treatise (301–32).

self-interest or of moral merit (as in the case of rules of justice); or it can be an epistemic consideration relating to truth, fidelity, or cognitive improvement (as in the case of recursive checks and corrections of probable reasonings). What is distinctive of the obligation of reason is that nothing but the consideration of a general principle and of its epistemic merit can explain why we would engage in a certain pattern of reasoning (and come under threat from scepticism about reason). At the same time, the obligation of reason, just as the obligation of self-interest and moral obligation, has a natural character. This pattern of motivation, in general and in the epistemic case, can be accounted for in terms of more primitive elements of Hume's philosophy: the sentimentalist theory of value and the production of general rules by the imagination. Since it can in this way be ascribed to the sensitive and imaginative part of the mind, the obligation of reason is susceptible to their constraints and limits as expressed in particular by the Structural Principle. This completes Hume's argument that the sceptical arguments against the possibility of reasoning (scepticism about reason and the Dangerous Dilemma) are no actual threat against our reflective belief-forming practices.

12.4.2 The Title of Reason

Hume blocks the sceptical threat against the possibility of reasoning and of reflective cognition in general by pointing to a mistake of presupposition in the sceptical arguments he discusses at 1.4.1 and 1.4.7. Idea-comparing reasonings, inclusive of the obligation of reason to reflect on and to correct our beliefs, do not take place in a mental vacuum but are embedded in the natural faculty of the imagination. In this context—which is marked by the Structural Principle—they do not iterate in the ways supposed by the sceptic and the conclusions of impossibility which, in the case of scepticism about reason, primarily target assent and doxastic deliberation and, in that of the Dangerous Dilemma, epistemic agency and responsibility in general, do not follow. Hume's conclusion against scepticism about possibility is thus that, within bounds fixed by the nature of our mental faculties, assent, probable reasoning, doxastic deliberation, and epistemic agency and commitment (by choosing belief-forming principles and methods) are possible. However, within these bounds of possibility, a different sort of sceptical concern might arise. Given the character of our natural reasoning faculty, the equivalence of the understanding with the imagination, and the unity of idea-comparing and more limited imagination, one might doubt of the epistemic value of our cognitive capacities and of the rightness of their conclusions. While not impossible for us, probable reasoning and doxastic deliberation might lack epistemic justness, rightly because of their mental nature. The Dangerous Dilemma might be replicated, but with reference to the authority, not to the possibility, of our cognitive capacities. This would be because of the solution just given to the problem of possibility: a trivial and inherently non-truth-related property of the imagination. Our *actual* exercise of reflection and doxastic deliberation would thus still fall under the scope of *false reason* rather than *no reason at all*. If it is a false reason that is put in place, supported, and bounded by the more limited imagination; if this is our actual and natural faculty of reasoning, then it seems questionable that it has any epistemic authority (value and rightness). Within the bounds set to the sceptical doubts about the possibility of reason and of epistemic agency by the nature of our reasoning faculty, another sceptical concern seems to arise. Quite generally, in Hume's arguments in Book 1, Part 4, the boundaries between scepticism about cognitive possibility and about epistemic authority are somewhat fuzzy. This is particularly true of Hume's culminating discussion of scepticism at 1.4.7: *Conclusion of this book*, to which I now revert.[29]

In that text, Hume deals (inter alia but centrally) with the epistemic conditions of our use of reason (of reason as it is actually within our reach, as a way of working of the imagination) in probable reasoning and doxastic deliberation. The elements of his discussion are by now familiar. In some respects, the narrative format chosen by Hume at 1.4.7, somewhat on the pattern of Descartes' *Meditations*, is not of help. Immediately after having stated his response to the problem of possibility raised by Dangerous Dilemma ('this difficulty is seldom or never thought of; and even where it has once been present to the mind, is quickly forgot'), Hume introduces the further step of his discussion with a narrative of alternating moods of intellectual despair and indifference. The narrative concludes with a renewed engagement in philosophy and focuses on the psychological temper that is favourable to philosophy, in the face of scepticism and superstition. More narrowly, on the motivations that are appropriate for engaging in or returning to philosophy: 'curiosity to be acquainted with the principles of moral good and evil' and 'concerning truth and falsehood, reason and folly'; as well as the 'ambition' 'of contributing to the instruction of humanity' (1.4.7.12). This seems to be in some ways once more a problem about the *possibility* (the psychological possibility) of cognition, at least, of philosophical cognition, rather than one about the authority of its principles; and it is not immediately clear how it can dig new epistemological ground. Even though, as we have seen, motivational considerations are germane to Hume's broached epistemology in the *Treatise*. The passional root of the sentiment of epistemic approval, love of truth, is also naturally motivating and explains our sense of epistemic ought, the basis of the role of epistemic rules in causing and guiding doxastic deliberation.

---

[29] See, for an excellent characterization of the epistemological dimension of Hume's discussion of scepticism at 1.4.7 (including the Dangerous Dilemma), D. Garrett, 'Hume's Conclusions in "Conclusion of this Book"', in Traiger, *Blackwell Guide to Hume's Treatise* (151–75), 166–8.

However, it is not difficult to see through Hume's narrative and rhetoric and detect the outlines of his conclusive discussion of scepticism about the authority of reasoning capacities as we actually have them.

> In all the incidents of life we ought still to preserve our scepticism. If we believe, that fire warms, or water refreshes, 'tis only because it costs us too much pains to think otherwise. Nay if we are philosophers, it ought only to be upon sceptical principles, and from an inclination, which we feel to the employing ourselves after that manner. Where reason is lively, and mixes itself with some propensity, it ought to be assented to. Where it does not, it never can have any title to operate upon us. (1.4.7.11)

This is what Garrett has aptly called the *Title Principle*: the epistemic title of reason to operate upon us; its epistemic authority; or reason, as it 'ought to be assent to'.[30] Hume's formulation of the principle is terse, even condensed. But it is not difficult to give articulation to it through its conceptual components and to connect it to Hume's overall conception of epistemic normativity. I propose to identify three dimensions of the Title Principle, which are individually necessary and jointly sufficient to explain the authority of reason or why we ought to assent to it.

First, *reason*. Hume's conception and characterization of reason is the same throughout the *Treatise*: functionally, it is the immediate or mediate comparison of ideas in terms of their contents and dependently on internal relations or on the external relation of causation; causally, it is a natural and fallible cause of true cognitions, ultimately, of proofs and probabilities. This is also its epistemic force, based on the overall conception of epistemic normativity that I am ascribing to Hume. Insofar as we reason, we engage in a well-defined kind of cognitive activity or inference which reliably but fallibly tracks truth. This recommends it to our assent, because of the nature of our epistemic praise and blame; and thus in part determines why we ought to assent to it.

Second, *where it is lively*. Idea-comparing inferences are epistemically as good as the ideas they compare: if such ideas are not susceptible to truth or too ill defined to allow for truth-conductive comparisons, comparing them does not cause truth either. Now, ideas abiding by the First Principle, caused by and resembling impressions of sensation or the experience of the flux of perceptions, have the authority of object-representation, of reference and truth. But, as a matter of natural necessity, representation, either sensible or reflective, is severely limited.

---

[30] See Garrett, *Hume*, 229–31; Qu, *Hume's Epistemological Evolution*, 117: 'Hume's resolution to excessive scepticism in THN 1.4.7 turns on the Title Principle'. My reading of the Title Principle is close to the one proposed by P. Kail, 'Hume's "Manifest Contradiction"', *Royal Institute for Philosophy Supplement*, 78, 2016 (147–60).

Only imagination-produced ideas explain the scope of our ordinary and philosophical cognition, which crucially includes comparisons of ideas. Insofar as we can make any general claim of justness and regularity with regard of our cognition, it will depend on the justness and regularity of the ideas produced by the imagination and, at one remove, of its idea-producing operations. It is in this way, as epitomizing the cognitive and epistemic embedding of reasoning in the imagination, that the liveliness of reason contributes to its title to operate upon us. In the context of 1.4.7, when specifying the fundamental role of the imagination with regard to our cognition in general ('The memory, senses, and understanding'), Hume identifies it with 'the vivacity of ideas' (1.4.7.3). Reason, or the comparison of ideas, is lively when it deals with the contents and manners of conception, with the ideas and beliefs, stemming either from representation or from the best operations of the imagination. This has epistemic import, contributing not only to the explanation but to the authority of reason (we ought to assent to it) insofar as representation and imagination have truth and fidelity. Now, sense and memory (and we can extend this to internal reflection) have 'in many respects the assurance of a demonstration' (1.3.13.19). And when the ideas produced by the imagination have causal contents, they are susceptible to a 'very great' degree of 'confidence' or 'assurance' or 'evidence' (and to different, progressively lower ones) (1.3.13.19). These notions are ambiguous between a cognitive and an epistemic import; certainly, the second is not excluded.

Third, *mixes itself with some propensity*. In the context of the narrative of 1.4.7, the propensities in question are the passions that motivate Hume's return to philosophy: curiosity and ambition. It is not immediately clear, however, how this motivational role can have epistemic import, contributing to our oughts with regard to reasons, as distinct from its explanatory import and to our interest for philosophy. But a plausible interpretation delivering an epistemic role is close at hand. As we have seen, the passion of curiosity or love of truth is the root of epistemic value and rightness. Love of truth is constituted by our pleasure in achieving some important and non-obvious truth. This is, in turn, what constitutes our approval of true and important cognitions. Love of truth, furthermore, because of the nature of our minds, includes a desire for true and important cognitions, our being motivated to achieve them. Love of truth is therefore a propensity that contributes to constituting, in Hume's sentimentalist and naturalistic framework, the epistemic value and authority of reason.[31]

---

[31] For a different reading of the Title Principle see Qu, *Hume's Epistemological Evolution*, 127–31, 147–66. Qu equates the liveliness of reason with the vivacity of assent and the propensity with which it mixes with the passions of curiosity and ambition. While this is certainly attuned to the immediate context of 1.4.7.11 (Hume's own *crise sceptique*), I think that we should not lose sight of the general import of Hume's discussion, which is, in my view, the convergence of scepticism with regard of mental content (possibility) and with regard of epistemology (authority). Furthermore, as I have remarked, at 1.4.7.3, somewhat surprisingly, Hume equates *all* the work of the imagination, including its content-productive one, with the vivacity of ideas. And love of truth is the basis of Hume's sentimentalist

Overall therefore the Title Principle effectively establishes, on the basis of Hume's own epistemological views and of his conception of mind and cognition, the conditions at which we ought to assent to reason. Such conditions deprive of authority sceptical *idea-comparing reasonings* (insofar as they must be supported by the imagination) and act as an epistemic sieve on the propensities of more limited imagination (insofar as they must be approved for truth and fidelity).[32] In this way, it counters the sceptical doubts concerning the authority of reason, which persist also within the bounds of possible natural reason. It is the epitome of Hume's response to scepticism concerning epistemic authority. Hume has serious, even dramatic doubts concerning the 'reasonableness', not to say the 'obligation', to engage in complex cognitive tasks; as well as concerning the 'prospect' of arriving in this domain 'at truth and certainty' (1.4.7.10). The Title Principle defends such reasonableness, conditions such obligation (reason *ought* to be assented to), and articulates and supports that prospect. As Hume's answer to the ultimate sceptical threats raised by the Dangerous Dilemma, it summarizes and involves the different strands of his conception of epistemic normativity in the *Treatise*. Since the different dimensions of the Title Principle depend on or are in strict relation to properties and operations of the imagination, this establishes and qualifies, against excessive scepticism, the moderate but good epistemic standing of the imagination itself.[33]

---

account of epistemic value. Correspondingly, on my wider and conjunctive reading (conjunction of three *epistemic* conditions), the Title Principle is more fitting as an answer to scepticism about authority. Idea-comparing reason is a natural cause of truth; idea-producing and assent-conveying imagination is at least locally truth-conducive; and love of truth is the suitable ground for epistemic approval and value. These are conclusions of the science of human nature and their consideration gives grounds for recognizing and accepting not only the authority of reason, but the Title Principle itself.

[32] See Garrett, 'Hume's Conclusions', 169–70: 'In effect, the Title Principle excises from the domain of assent-worthy reasoning precisely the reason-undermining iterations of the probability of causes.'

[33] My vindication of Hume's epistemology in the *Treatise* is qualified. I agree with Qu, *Hume's Epistemological Evolution*, 117–18, that Hume would ultimately have reason to become dissatisfied with his response to scepticism in the *Treatise*; and more generally that there are deep epistemological differences between Hume's *Treatise* and the first *Enquiry*—differences which amount to an improvement in terms of systematicity, explicitness, and substantive content (177–8). Hume's later and more mature epistemology, which Qu aptly characterizes as '"internalist reliabilism" or "benign bootstrapping", leveraging our faculties (trusted by default) in order to obtain a justification (via reflexive investigation) for these faculties themselves' (179, 185; see also 212–14) is only dimly anticipated in the *Treatise* (also on the reading I am giving of Book I). This brings much order and clarity to Hume's attempted reformation of philosophy, in his response to scepticism, and in the method of his own philosophy (for an instance, see Qu's discussion of the stronger resources that the first *Enquiry* can muster against the sceptical argument of 1.4.1, 233–6). At the same time, we should pay attention (as certainly Qu does, in a careful and systematic way, see, for instance, 231) to the very different philosophical programmes Hume is pursuing in the two works and, correspondingly, to the different position that epistemology occupies in them. Echoing a widespread interpretive orientation, Qu remarks that 'in contrast with the *Treatise*, where the psychological project was front and centre, in the *Enquiry*, the epistemological project takes the leading role' (43). In general, the focus of the *Treatise* is descriptive, that of the *Enquiry*, normative. This is broadly correct, but it does not go deep enough. As I have attempted to show, Book 1 of Hume's *Treatise* and the theory of the imagination that is fundamental to it are theoretically unified by the problem of (recursive) cognitive gaps and of the production of non-representational cognitive contents, such as can make place for different varieties of a priori and non-a

12.5 Summary

In this final chapter, I address the role of the imagination in Hume's epistemology. The science of human nature has explicit epistemic, foundational aims. The explanations it proposes often involve our grasp of epistemic distinctions. It is thus a crucial question whether epistemic considerations and commitments are consistent with the overarching cognitive role of Hume's imagination.

§ 12.1addresses the first of two questions about naturalism, normativity, and the imagination identified in § 12.1.1: whether the imagination, by producing the non-representational ideas compared in epistemic assessment, is judge in sua re. In § 12.1.2, I outline the first step of Hume's response to this problem: his naturalistic identifications of epistemic distinctions. Being a posteriori, such naturalistic identifications do not threaten the irreducibility of normative contents. At the same time, they allow fixing the reference of the judgements of the imagination on its own operations. This deflates the worry that the imagination is judge in sua re. The same, sophisticated naturalist approach to epistemic rightness comes to expression, discussed in § 12.1.3, in the explicitly normative general rules that Hume sets for causal judgement.

In § 12.2, I deal with the second step of Hume's response: the character of the relevant normative distinctions. As I claim in § 12.2.1, the kind of normativity Hume has in mind is specifically epistemic. While he does not refrain from associate pragmatic values (even in adaptive terms) to the general, stable, solid

---

priori inferential cognitions. Within Hume's naturalistic framework, this problem has a crucial descriptive dimension. But it would be an error to think that the conclusions of this descriptive (empirical) enquiry only have normative *applications*, that they are only normatively *relevant*. Hume's problem in Book 1 is that of the constitutive conditions of contents that have inherent normative, epistemic properties (truth and fidelity); properties the normative import of which can be explained in a naturalistic fashion. (That the conditions of possibility are naturalistic rather than, say, transcendental, does not make a difference in this respect.) If these are the aims of Hume's theory, then, at least in its intentions, it straddles the border between descriptive and normative concerns. Seen in this light, the theoretical shift from the *Treatise* to the first *Enquiry* is not one from a descriptive to a normative project, but rather one from one descriptive *and* normative project to a different one. Qu is perfectly right that Hume's epistemology is in various respects different in the two works. I would only complement this remark with the claim that epistemological concerns in the *Treatise* are primarily *meta-epistemological*: rather than proposing epistemological principles and arguing for them, Hume asks how such principles and arguments are available at all to our cognitive nature. Epistemological commitments are derivable from this enquiry, rather than being a primary or even independent theoretical target. This is why the epistemological change marked by the first *Enquiry*, where epistemology becomes a philosophical topic on its own and a central one, is correlated with the marginalization of the philosophy of mind and with the total eclipse of the imagination. Why Hume opted for this complex change is too large an interpretive question to be addressed in a footnote. Taking a hint from Hume's own words in the letter to Gilbert Elliot of Minto, 1751 ('By shortening & simplifying the Questions, I really render them much more complete', quoted in Qu, *Hume's Epistemological Evolution*, 11), I would regard that change as issuing not only from dissatisfaction with the epistemology of Book 1 but also from the awareness of some foundational weaknesses in the overall project in Book 1. Possibly the unresolved relation between subjective experience and objective perceptions and principles of the imagination that I have been highlighting.

principle of the imagination, the epistemic considerations are certainly present and unreducible.

The fundamental epistemological considerations are for Hume—see § 12.2.2—those of truth and reliability. Hume has a concept of truth as correspondence, firmly embedded in his theory of representation and reference. The epistemic role of truth can be extended from cognitive episodes to processes and faculties, in terms of their truth-conduciveness. Reason (on Hume's revised notion of it: reasoning as operation of the whole faculty of the imagination) is a fallible cause of truth. Hume's epistemic taxonomy of kinds of cognition is also in terms of certainty or likelihood of truth.

The problematic case, discussed in § 12.2.3, is that of belief. Hume marks the contrast between beliefs and passions in terms of truth-aptness. Against this background, he makes for highly differentiated ascriptions of truth-aptness. Particular beliefs about non-observed objects issuing from probable reasoning are non-problematically truth-apt. The same holds for the corresponding general judgements. By contrast, explicitly causal, modalized causal judgements have truth-conditions only modulo to their translation in potentially object-representing terms, as per the two definitions of cause. Also particular beliefs concerning bodies and personal identity seem to be truth-apt. This is because their dependence on probable reasoning brings them close to causal ones. But the corresponding processes of the imagination are unreliable and open to sceptical doubt.

In § 12.2.4, I suggest that some non-truth-apt ideas like mixed equality, a vacuum, external existence, and an identical person seem to have epistemically valuable cognitive roles. Such roles are of complementing causal reasoning in constructing a unified image of the world. This is epistemically valuable, since it supports probable reasoning and contributes to our detaching ourselves from particular viewpoints and fixing on the circumstances that objectively matter for judgement. This is an improvement of the human mind.

§ 12.3 discusses how Hume's account of the normative force of epistemic distinctions. This is the second question raised by Hume (§ 12.3.1): how naturalistic philosophy can make sense of differences of epistemic value between equally natural cognitive states and activities. Since for Hume there is no a priori connection between natural features of cognition and value and authority, we have here a gap in our cognition in general.

Hume does not address systematically this issue in his theory of mind and cognition. But, as I attempt to show in § 12.3.2, his general approach is the same with his account of practical normativity: one can reconcile normativity with naturalism by dropping cognitivism and opting for sentimentalism about value and authority. Notice that this requires understanding the relevant sentimental responses as separable impressions of reflection, not as manners of conception, which could only be cognitive.

In § 12.3.3, I attempt to extend this apparatus to epistemic normativity by focusing on Hume's account of curiosity or love of truth. This account applies the explanatory pattern of indirect passions (like pride or love) to cognitive states. Epistemic values express sentiments of epistemic praise and blame, produced by feelings of pleasure and pain caused by certain properties of cognitive states: truth, difficulty, salience, and success. The imagination has an important role, because cognitive pleasure consists in the stability of its conceptions and transitions, which are in their turn caused by the properties of its contents and states. Cognitive pleasure is sui generis: it has a distinctively aesthetic quality. Epistemic value consists in the sentimental response to mental states and actions, based on cognitive pleasure and pain.

§ 12.4 addresses the authority of epistemic distinctions on our cognitive conduct. In § 12.4.1, I point out that epistemic approval resembles the indirect passion of love; this latter is naturally motivating; epistemic motivation should therefore not be a mystery. We have a natural desire for true and important cognitions. Epistemic motivation may be implicit, tacit. But it can also be explicit and reflective and even come out as an obligation to reason, grounded only on general principles of epistemic merit. Finally, in § 12.4.2, I discuss Hume's view of the rightful claims of reason on our cognitive conduct. Given that the imagination sets limits to our engagement in reflection, within such bounds it makes perfect sense to say that reason is entitled to operate on us; that we ought to assent to it. Hume's explanation of the authority of reason follows the pattern of his general view of epistemic normativity. Considering the role inferences have in that pattern, together with sentimentalism, this is another respect in which the imagination takes up the role of reason.

APPENDIX

Principles of Hume's Theory of the Imagination

I list here the principles I have resorted to in my interpretation (and, occasionally, reconstruction) of Hume's philosophy of the imagination in Book 1 of the *Treatise*. Some of them are explicitly proposed and endorsed by Hume, sometimes in the form of a maxim or principle; some are more or less implicitly at work in his analyses and arguments. While it is not easy to tell them neatly apart, I have distinguished such principles from the general conclusions that Hume draws from their application: the concept of custom or the claim about the metaphysical possibility of perceptions existing unperceived, for instance, fall in the second category. I list the principles in the order in which I have introduced them in my text. Each principle is accompanied by a statement of its content and point (when possible, in the form of a quotation), by references to the relevant texts of the *Treatise*, and by a reference to where in my text it is introduced and discussed.

(1) *Two Viewpoints* Perceptions and activities of the mind figure in and contribute to Hume's doctrine of elements and in his explanations of ideas and mental capacities in two different regards: for their mental existence, how they are in the mind; and for their contents, what they present and represent. Mental processes can be considered from either viewpoint. See 1.3.14.29; 1.4.2.3. See §§ 2.2.1–2.

(2) *Equivalence* Impressions of sensation and objects of sense have the same properties of content; the general appearance that determines what an impression presents is the same with that which individuates the presented object. The inference from the properties of the second to those of the first is good (but not that from the properties of the first to those of the second). See 1.4.5.20. See § 2.2.4.

(3) *First Principle* 'All our simple ideas in their first appearance are deriv'd from simple impressions, which are correspondent to them, and which they exactly represent' (1.1.1.7). See §§ 2.3.1–2

(4) *Representation* 'Ideas always represent their objects or impressions; and *vice versa*, there are some objects necessary to give rise to every idea', 1.3.14.6 (the quantification is restricted to ideas which represent objects or impressions). See §§ 2.4.4; 3.1.1; 4.1.2 fn. 6.

(5) *Second Principle* 'The same evidence follows us in our second principle, *of the liberty of the imagination to transpose and change its ideas*', 1.1.3.4. See also 1.3.5.3: it is 'a peculiar property of the memory to preserve the original order and position of its ideas'; by contrast, 'the imagination transposes and changes them, as it pleases'. See § 3.2.1.

(6) *Structural Principle* 'When I oppose the imagination to the memory, I mean the faculty, by which we form our fainter ideas. When I oppose it to reason, I mean the same faculty, excluding only our demonstrative and probable reasonings. When I oppose it to neither, 'tis indifferent whether it be taken in the larger or more limited sense, or at least the context will sufficiently explain the meaning', 1.3.9.19 fn. 22. See §§ 3.3.1–3.

(7) *Non-Mixture* 'Ideas never admit of a total union, but are endow'd with a kind of impenetrability, by which they exclude each other, and are capable of forming a compound by their conjunction, not by their mixture', 2.2.6.1. See § 3.4.1.
(8) *Important Footnote* 'Whether we consider a single object, or several; whether we dwell on these objects, or run from them to others; and in whatever form or order we survey them, the act of the mind exceeds not a simple conception', 1.3.7.5, fn. 20. See § 3.4.3.
(9) *Established Maxim* ''Tis an establish'd maxim in metaphysics, *That whatever the mind clearly conceives includes the idea of possible existence*, or in other words, *that nothing we imagine is absolutely impossible*', 1.2.2.8. See §§ 5.1.1–2.
(10) *Separability* 'We have observ'd, that whatever objects are different are distinguishable, and that whatever objects are distinguishable are separable by the thought and imagination. And we may here add, that these propositions are equally true in the *inverse,* and that whatever objects are separable are also distinguishable, and that whatever objects are distinguishable are also different', 1.1.7.3. See § 5.1.3.
(11) *Determination* Modal qualifications which are part of our regular cognitive practices but not explained by Separability express a felt constraint on conception that does not depend on internal relations of ideas. See 1.3.14.20: 'Necessity, then, is the effect of this observation, and is nothing but an internal impression of the mind, or a determination to carry our thoughts from one object to another'. See §5.1.3.
(12) *Spreading in the Mind* The imagination can close gaps open in the phenomenology of sensible representation by filling them with materials that are homogeneous with sense and memory but depend, for their transposition and location, on its transitions. See *Appendix* 4: 'Suppose I see the legs and thighs of a person in motion, while some interpos'd object conceals the rest of his body. Here 'tis certain, the imagination spreads out the whole figure. I give him a head and shoulders, and breast and neck'. See § 7.2.3.
(13) *Spreading on the Objects* The imagination can close gaps open between objects present in sensible representation as external (spatial) and properties present as internal. ''Tis a common observation, that the mind has a great propensity to spread itself on external objects, and to conjoin with them any internal impressions, which they occasion, and which always make their appearance at the same time that these objects discover themselves to the senses', 1.3.14.12. See § 7.2.3.
(14) *Hysteresis* '"I have already observ'd, in examining the foundation of mathematics, that the imagination, when set into any train of thinking, is apt to continue, even when its object fails it, and like a galley put in motion by the oars, carries on its course without any new impulse"' 1.4.2.22. See § 9.2.2.
(15) *Act/Idea Resemblance* 'For a general rule [...] whatever ideas place the mind in the same disposition or in similar ones, are very apt to be confounded'; 'Of all relations, that of resemblance is in this respect the most efficacious', 1.4.2.32. See § 9.3.2.
(16) *Reconciliation* 'Any contradiction either to the sentiments or passions gives a sensible uneasiness, whether it proceeds from without or from within'; because of the 'opposition' between opposite conceptions, the mind must be 'uneasy' and 'will naturally seek relief from the uneasiness', 1.4.2.37. See §§ 9.3.4; 10.2.3.
(17) *Completion* 'When objects are united by any relation, we have a strong propensity to add some new relation to them, in order to compleat the union. [...] We feel a

satisfaction in joining the relation of contiguity to that of resemblance, or the resemblance of situation to that of qualities', 1.4.5.12. See § 9. 5. 1.
(18) *Attrition* 'Where the mind reaches not its objects with easiness and facility, the same principles have not the same effect as in a more natural conception of the ideas; nor does the imagination feel a sensation, which holds any proportion with that which arises from its common judgments and opinions', 1.4.1.10. See § 11.3.1.

Bibliography

D. Ainslie, 'Adequate Ideas and Modest Scepticism in Hume's Metaphysics of Space', *Archiv für Geschichte der Philosophie*, 92, 2010 (39-67)
D. Ainslie, *Hume's True Skepticism*, Oxford University Press, New York 2015
D. Ainslie & A. Butler, eds., *The Cambridge Companion to Hume's Treatise*, Cambridge University Press, New York 2015
H. Allison, *Custom and Reason in Hume*, Clarendon Press, Oxford 2008
A. Anderson, *Kant, Hume, and the Interruption of Dogmatic Slumber*, Oxford University Press, New York 2020
R. L. Anjum & S. Mumford, *Causation*, Oxford University Press, Oxford 2013
R. Aumann, 'Rationality and Bounded Rationality', *Games and Economic Behavior*, 21, 1997 (2-14)
M. Balcerack Jackson, 'On the Epistemic Value of Imagining, Supposing, and Conceiving', in Kind & Kung, eds., *Knowledge through Imagination* (41-60)
A. Baier, *A Progress of Sentiments*, Harvard University Press, Cambridge (Mass.)/London, 1991
D. L. M. Baxter, 'Hume's Theory of Space and Time in its Skeptical Context', in Norton & Taylor, eds., *Cambridge Companion to Hume* (1993), 105-46
D. L. M. Baxter, 'Hume on Infinite Divisibility', *History of Philosophy Quarterly*, 5, 1988 (in Tweynman, *David Hume. Critical Assessments*, Volume 3, 16-24)
D. L. M. Baxter, *Hume's Difficulty. Time and Identity in the* Treatise, Routledge, Abingdon 2008
T. Beauchamp & A. Rosenberg, *Hume and the Problem of Causation*, Oxford University Press, New York/Oxford 1981
H. Beebee, *Hume on Causation*, Routledge, London/New York 2006
H. Beebee, C. Hitchcock, & P. Menzies, eds., *The Oxford Handbook of Causation*, Oxford University Press, Oxford 2009
G. Berkeley, *A Treatise Concerning the Principles of Human Knowledge* (1710, 1734), in *Philosophical Works*, M. R. Ayers, ed., Dent, London 1975 (63-127)
G. Berkeley, *Three Dialogues between Hylas and Philonous* (1713, 1734), in *Philosophical Works*, M. R. Ayers, ed., Dent, London 1975 (131-207)
G. Berkeley, *Alciphron; or, the Minute Philosopher*, in *The Works of George Berkeley*, A. C. Fraser, ed., Volume 2, Clarendon Press, Oxford 1901
G. Berkeley, *An Essay towards a New Theory of Vision* (1709, 1732), in M. R. Ayers, ed., *Philosophical Works*, Dent, London 1975 (3-59)
D. Bernstein et al., 'False Memories: The Role of Plausibility and Autobiographical Belief', in Markman et al., *Handbook of Imagination*, 89-102
K. Binmore, 'Rationality and Backward Induction', *Journal of Economic Methodology*, 4, 1997, 23:41
S. Blackburn 'Modals and Morals', in S. Blackburn, *Essays on Quasi-Realism*, Oxford University Press, Oxford/New York 1993, 52:74
N. Block, O. Flanagan, & G. Güzeldere, *The Nature of Consciousness*, The MIT Press, Cambridge (Mass.) 1998

M. Boehm, 'Filling the Gaps in Hume's Vacuums', *Hume Studies*, 38, 2012 (79–99)
M. Boehm, 'Hume's Foundational Project in the *Treatise*', in *European Journal of Philosophy*, 24, 2016 (55–77)
M. Boehm, "Hume' Projectivism Explained", in *Synthese*, Topical Collection: Humeanisms, 2020 https://doi.org/10.1007/s11229-020-02718-9
R. Brandom, *Making It Explicit*, Harvard University Press, Cambridge (Mass.) 1994
R. Brandom, *Articulating Reasons*, Harvard University Press, Cambridge (Mass.) 2000
R. Brandom, *Between Saying & Doing*, Oxford University Press, Oxford 2008
M. Brandt Bolton, 'Berkeley and Mental Representation', in S. H. Daniel ed., *New Interpretations of Berkeley's Thought*, Humanity Books, Amherst 2008, 77–106
C. D. Broad, 'Hume's Doctrine of Space', *Proceedings of the British Academy*, 46, 1961
J. Broughton, 'Explaining General Ideas', in *Hume Studies*, 26, 2, 2000 (279–89), pp. 287–8
J. Broughton, 'Impressions and Ideas', in S. Traiger, ed., *The Blackwell Guide to Hume's Treatise*, Blackwell, Oxford 2006 (43–58)
V. Bruce et al., *Visual Perception*, Psychology Press, Hove 1996
T. Burge, 'Two Kinds of Consciousness', in Block, Flanagan, & Güzeldere, *The Nature of Consciousness*, The MIT Press, Cambridge (Mass.) 1998 (427:433)
T. Burge, 'Content Preservation', *Philosophical Review*, 102, 1993, 457:488
T. Burge, 'Perceptual Entitlement', *Philosophy and Phenomenological Research*, 67, 2003, 503:548
A. Butler, 'Hume on Believing the Vulgar Fiction of Continued Existence', *History of Philosophy Quarterly*, 27, 2010 (237–54)
R. Byrne & V. Girotto, 'Cognitive Processes in Counterfactual Thinking', in Markman et al., *Handbook of Imagination and Simulation*, 151–60
R. Byrne, 'Imagination and Rationality', in Kind, ed., *Handbook of Philosophy of Imagination*, 339–52
A. Casullo, 'What is Entitlement?', *Acta Analitica*, 22, 2007, 267:279
David Chalmers, 'Does Conceivability Entail Possibility?' in Gendler & Hawthorne, eds., *Conceivability and Possibility*, 145:200
D. Chalmers, 'Perception and the Fall from Eden', in Szabó Gendler & Hawthorne, eds., *Perceptual Experience* (49–125)
D. Chalmers, *Constructing the World*, Oxford University Press, Oxford 2012
V. C. C. Chappell, ed., *Hume. A Collection of Critical Essays*, Macmillan, London 1966
V. C. Chappell, 'Hume on What There Is', *Royal Institute of Philosophy*, 5, 1972 (in Tweyman, ed., *David Hume. Critical Assessments*, III, pp. 77–87)
V. Chappell. 'Locke's Theory of Ideas', in *The Cambridge Companion to Locke*, edited by V. Chappell, Cambridge University Press, Cambridge 1994, (26–55), 31–5
J. Church, 'Perceiving People as People', in Kind & Kung, *Knowledge by Imagination* (160–84)
S. Clarke, *A Demonstration of the Being and Attributes of God: More Particularly in Answer to Hobbes, Spinoza, and their Followers*, James Knapton, London 1705
R. Cohon, *Hume's Morality. Feeling and Fabrication*, Oxford University Press, Oxford 2008
R. Cohon & D. Owen, 'Hume on Representation, Reason, and Motivation', *Manuscrito*, 20, 1997, 47–76
M. J. Costa, 'Hume, Strict Identity, and Time's Vacuum', *Hume Studies*, 16, 1990, 1–16
T. M. Costelloe, 'Hume's Phenomenology of the Imagination', *The Journal of Scottish Philosophy*, 5, 2007, 31–45
T. M. Costelloe, *The Imagination in Hume's Philosophy*, Edinburgh University Press, Edinburgh 2018

J. Cottingham, R. Stoothoff, & D. Murdoch, eds., *The Philosophical Writings of Descartes*, 2 volumes, Cambridge, Cambridge University Press 1984–1985

J. Y. T. Craig, ed., *The Letters of David Hume*, 2 volumes, Oxford University Press, Oxford 2011 (1932)

T. Crane, ed., *The Contents of Experience*, Cambridge University Press, Cambridge 1992

T. Crane, 'The Nonconceptual Content of Experience', in Crane, ed., *The Contents of Experience* (136–57)

P. D. Cummins, 'Hume on the Idea of Existence', *Hume Studies*, 17, 1, 1991 (in Tweyman, ed., *David Hume. Critical Assessments*, III, pp. 98–117)

P. D. Cummins, 'Hume on Possible Objects and Impossible Ideas', in Easton, ed. *Logic and the Workings of the Mind*, 211–27

D. Cunning, 'Descartes. Modal Metaphysics', in *The Stanford Encyclopedia of Philosophy* https://plato.stanford.edu/entries/descartes-modal/

G. Currie, 'Imagination and Learning', in Kind, *Handbook of Imagination* (407–19)

D. Danks, 'The Psychology of Causal Perception and Reasoning', in Beebe, Hitchcock, & Menzies, *Oxford Handbook of Causation*, (447–70)

M. Davies & L. Humberstone, 'Two Notions of Necessity', *Philosophical Studies*, 38, 1980, (1–30)

M. Della Rocca, 'Essentialism versus Essentialism', in Gendler & Hawthorne, *Conceivability and Possibility*, 223:252

The Philosophical Writings of Descartes, 2 volumes, J. Cottingham, R. Stoothoff, & D. Murdoch, eds., Cambridge, Cambridge University Press 1984–1985

R. Descartes, '*Meditationes de Prima Philosophia*', in *Oeuvres de Descartes*, C. Adam, & P. Tannery, eds., Volume 8, Vrin, Paris 1983

R. Descartes, '*Traité de l'Homme*', in *Oeuvres de Descartes*, C. Adam, & P. Tannery, eds., Volume 11, Vrin, Paris 1996 (3–215)

R. Descartes, 'Treatise of Man', in J. Cottingham, R. Stoothoff, & D. Murdoch, eds., *The Philosophical Writings of Descartes*, Volume 1, Cambridge University Press, Cambridge 1984–1985 (81–110)

R. Descartes, *Meditations on First Philosophy*, M. Moriarty, ed., Oxford University Press, Oxford/New York 2008

R. Descartes, *Principles of Philosophy*, in *The Philosophical Writings of Descartes*, Volume 1 (179–291)

F. De Vignemont, 'Bodily Awareness', in *The Stanford Encyclopedia of Philosophy* https://plato.stanford.edu/entries/bodily-awareness/

K. Durlann, 'Hume's First Principle, his Missing Shade, and his Distinctions of Reason', *Hume Studies*, 22, 1996, 105–21

P. A. Easton, ed., *Logic and the Workings of the Mind: The Logic of Ideas and Faculty Psychology in Early Modern Philosophy*, Ridgeview, Atascadero 1997

C. Echelbarger, 'Hume and the Logicians', in P. Easton, ed., *Logic and the Workings of Mind*, 137–51

J. Ellis, 'The Contents of Hume's Appendix and the Source of his Despair', *Hume Studies*, 32, 2006 (195–231)

G. Evans, *The Varieties of Reference*, Oxford, Clarendon Press 1982

J. St. B. T. Evans, 'In two minds: Dual-process accounts of reasoning', *Trends in Cognitive Science*, (7 (10) 2003, 454–9

S. Everson, 'The Difference between Feeling and Thinking', *Mind*, 97, 1988 (in Tweyman, *David Hume. Critical Assessments*, Volume 1 (10–23)

L. Falkenstein, 'Naturalism, Normativity, and Scepticism in Hume's account of Belief', *Hume Studies*, 1997, 23, 1 (29:72)

L. Falkenstein, 'Hume on Manners of Disposition and the Ideas of Space and Time', *Archiv für Geschichte der Philosophie*, 79, 1997, 179–80

L. Falkenstein, 'Space and Time', in S. Traiger, ed., *The Blackwell Guide to Hume's Treatise*, Blackwell, Oxford 2006 (59–76)

L. Falkenstein, 'Hume on the Idea of a Vacuum', *Hume Studies*, 2, 2013 (131–68)

M. O. Fiocco, 'Conceivability, Imagination and Modal Knowledge', *Philosophy and Phenomenological Research* 2007, 364:380

A. Flew, *Hume's Philosophy of Belief*, Routledge & Kegan Paul, London 1961

J. Fodor, *The Elm and the Expert*, The MIT Press, Cambridge (Mass.) 1994

J. Fodor, *Hume Variations*, Oxford University Press, Oxford 2003

R. J. Fogelin, 'Hume and the Missing Shade of Blue', *Philosophy and Phenomenological Research*, 45, 1984, 263–71

R. J. Fogelin, *Hume's Skepticism in the Treatise of Human Nature*, Routledge & Kegan Paul, London, 1985

R. Fogelin, *Hume's Skeptical Crisis*, Oxford University Press, Oxford/New York 2009

J. Franklin, 'Achievement and Fallacies in Hume's Account of Finite Divisibility', *Hume Studies*, 20, 1994, 85–101

M. Frasca-Spada, *Space and the Self in Hume's Treatise*, Cambridge University Press, Cambridge 1998

D. Garrett, *Cognition and Commitment in Hume's Philosophy*, Oxford University Press, New York/Oxford 1997

D. Garrett, 'Hume's Naturalistic Theory of Representation', *Synthese*, 2006, 152, 301–19

D. Garrett, 'Hume's Conclusions in "Conclusion of this Book"', in Traiger, *Blackwell Guide to Hume's Treatise*, 151–75

D. Garrett, 'Hume', in Beebe, Hitchcock, & Menzies, *Oxford Handbook of Causation* (73–91)

Don Garrett, 'Difficult Times for Humean Identity?', *Philosophical Studies*, 2009, 146, 435–43

D. Garrett, 'Rethinking Hume's Second Thoughts about Personal Identity', in J. Bridges, N. Kolodny, & Wai-Hung W., eds., *The Possibility of Philosophical Understanding: Essays for Barry Stroud*, Oxford University Press, New York 2012 (15–42)

D. Garrett, 'Hume's Theory of Causation', in Ainslie & Butler eds., *Cambridge Companion to Hume's Treatise*, (69–100)

D. Garrett, *Hume*, Routledge, London/New York 2015

D. Garrett, 'The Idea of Self in Hume's *Treatise*', forthcoming in P. Kitcher, ed., *Self: History of a Concept*, Oxford University Press, Oxford

T. Gendler & J. Hawthorne, 'Introduction', in Gendler & Hawthorne, eds., *Conceivability and Possibility*, 1:70

T. Szabo Gendler, 'Imaginative Resistance Revisited', in Nichols, ed., *Architecture of Imagination*, 149–173

T. Gendler & J. Hawthorne, eds, *Conceivability and Possibility*, Clarendon Press, Oxford 2002

B. Gertler, *Self-Knowledge*, Routledge, London/New York 2011

A. Gibbard, *Meaning and Normativity*, Oxford University Press, Oxford 2012

A. Goldman, *Simulating Minds*, Oxford University Press, Oxford/New York 2006

A. Goldman, 'Imagination and Simulation in Audience Responses to Fiction', in Nichols, ed., *Architecture of the Imagination* (41–56)

D. Gregory, 'Conceivability and Apparent Possibility', in B. Hale & A. Hoffman, eds., *Modality*

M. Grene, 'The Objects of Hume's *Treatise*', *Hume Studies*, XX, 2 1994, 163–77

M. J. Green, 'The Idea of a Momentary Self and Hume's Theory of Personal Identity', *British Journal for the History of Philosophy*, 7, 1999, 104–22

S. Grossberg, ed., *The Adaptive Brain I: Cognition, Learning, Reinforcement, and Rhythm I*, North Holland, Amsterdam/New York 1987

P. Guyer, *Knowledge, Reason, and Taste. Kant's Response to Hume*, Princeton University Press, Princeton 2008

B. Hale & A. Hoffman, *Modality. Metaphysics, Logic, and Epistemology*, Oxford University Press, Oxford 2010

J. Hakkarainen, 'The Materialist of Malmesbury and the Experimentalist of Edinburgh. Hume's and Hobbes' Conceptions of Imagination Compared', *Hobbes Studies*, 17, 2005, 72–107

J. Hakkarainen, 'Hume as Trope Nominalist', *Canadian Journal of Philosophy*, 42, 2012, 55:66

G. Hatfield, 'Descartes' Physiology and its Relation to his Psychology', in J. Cottingham ed., *The Cambridge Companion to Descartes*, Cambridge University Press, Cambridge 1992, 335–70

G. Hatfield, 'The Workings of the Intellect: Mind and Psychology', in P. A. Easton, ed., *Logic and the Workings of the Mind: The Logic of Ideas and Faculty Psychology in Early Modern Philosophy*, Ridgeview, Atascadero, 1997 (21–45, pp. 26 ff.)

G. Hatfield, 'Introduction', in Kant, *Prolegomena* (ix–xxxiv)

Y. Hazony & E. Schliesser, 'Newton and Hume', in P. Russell, ed., *The Oxford Handbook of Hume*, Oxford University Press, New York 2016 (673–707)

M. A. Hight, *Idea and Ontology. An Essay in Early Modern Metaphysics of Ideas*, Pennsylvania State University Press, University Park 2008

M. Hodges & J. Lachs, 'Hume on Belief' (1976) in Tweynman, ed., *David Hume. Critical Assessments*, I, 144–53

T. Holden, 'Infinite Divisibility and Actual Parts in Hume's *Treatise*', *Hume Studies*, 28, 2002, 3–25

T. Holden, 'Hume's Absolute Necessity', *Mind*, 123, 2014 (377–413)

H. Home & Lord Kames, *Essays on the Principles of Morality and Natural Religion*, 1779 (1751), ed. by M.C. Moran. Online Library of Liberty, 2005. http://oll.libertyfund.org/titles/1352

D. Hume, *Essays Moral Political, and Literary*, E. F. Miller, ed., Liberty Fund, Indianapolis 1985

D. Hume, *Dialogues concerning Natural Religion*, J. Gaskin, ed., Oxford University Press, Oxford 1993

D. Hume, *An Enquiry Concerning Human Understanding*, T. L. Beauchamp, ed., Oxford University Press, New York 1999

D. Hume, *An Enquiry concerning the Principles of Morals*, T. L. Beauchamp, ed., Oxford University Press, Oxford/New York 1998

D. Hume, *A Treatise of Human Nature* (also includes: *An Abstract of A Book, A Letter from a Gentleman*), D. F. Norton & M. J. Norton, eds., 2 Volumes, Clarendon Press, Oxford 2007

P. Kail, 'Conceivability and Modality in Hume', *Hume Studies*, 29, 2003, 43–61

P. Kail, *Projection and Realism in Hume's Philosophy*, Oxford University Press, Oxford 2007

P. Kail, 'Efficient Causation in Hume', in Schmalz, ed., *Efficient Causation. A History*, 231–57

P. Kail, 'Hume's "Manifest Contradictions"', *Royal Institute for Philosophy Supplement*, 78, 2016 (147–60)

I. Kant, *Critique of Pure Reason*, Palgrave, London 2003

I. Kant, *Prolegomena to any Future Metaphysics*, Cambridge University Press, Cambridge 2004
C. Kemp, 'Two Meanings of the Term "Idea": Act and Content in Hume's Treatise', *Journal of the History of Ideas*, 61, 2000, 675:690
N. Kemp Smith, *The Philosophy of David Hume*, Palgrave Macmillan, New York 2005 (1941)
A. Kind, 'Putting the Image back in the Imagination', *Philosophy and Phenomenological Research*, 62, 2001, 85:109
A. Kind, 'The Heterogeneity of Imagination', *Erkenntniss*, 78, 2013:4–159
A. Kind, 'Imagining under Constraints', in Kind & Kung, eds., *Knowledge through Imagination*, Oxford University Press, Oxford 2016, 145–59
A. Kind, ed., *The Routledge Handbook of Philosophy of Imagination*, Routledge, Oxford/New York 2016
A. Kind & P. Kung, eds., *Knowledge through Imagination*, Oxford University Press, Oxford 2016
T. Kjeller Johansen, *The Powers of Aristotle's Soul*, Oxford University Press, Oxford 2012
B. Kment, 'Counterfactuals and the Analysis of Necessity', *Philosophical Perspectives*, 20, 2006, 237:302
B. Kment, 'Varieties of Modality', in *The Stanford Encyclopedia of Philosophy* https://plato.stanford.edu/entries/modality-varieties/
S. Knuuttila, *Modalities in Medieval Philosophy*, Routledge, London/New York 1983
E. J. Kremer, 'Arnauld on Ideas as a Topic in Logic', in Easton, ed., *The Workings of Mind*, 65–82
T. Kroedel, 'Counterfactuals and the Epistemology of Modality', *Philosophers' Imprint*, 12, 12, July 2012
P. Kung, 'Imagining as a Guide to Possibility', *Philosophy and Phenomenological Research*, 83, 2010, 620:663
P. Kung, 'You Really Do Imagine It', *Nous*, 50, 2016, 90:120
M. Jacovides, 'Hume's Vicious Regress', *Oxford Studies in Early Modern Philosophy*, 5, 2010, 247:297
D. Jaquette, 'Hume on Infinite Divisibility and Sensible Extensionless Indivisibles', *Journal of the History of Philosophy*, 34, 1996 (61–78)
W. James, *Essays in Radical Empiricism*, Dover, New York 2003
I. Johansson, 'Hume's Ontology', *Metaphysica*, 13, 2012 (87–105)
P. N. Johnson-Laird & U. Hansson, 'Counterexamples in Sentential Reasoning', *Memory & Cognition* 2003, 31, 7 (1105–13)
M. Johnston, 'The Function of Sensory Awareness', in Szabo Gendler & Hawthorne, eds., *Perceptual Experience* (260–90)
D. Landy, 'Hume's Impression/Idea Distinction', *Hume Studies*, 32, 1, 2006 (119–40)
D. Landy, *Kant's Inferentialism. The Case against Hume*, Routledge, New York/Oxford 2015
D. Landy, *Hume's Science of Human Nature. Scientific Realism, Reason, and Substantial Explanation*, Routledge, New York/London 2018
P. Langland-Hassan, 'On Choosing what to Imagine', in Kind & Kung, *Knowledge through Imagination*, Oxford University Press, Oxford 2016, 61–84
P. Langland-Hassan, *Explaining Imagination*, Oxford University Press, Oxford 2020
S. Laurence & E. Margolis, 'Abstraction and the Origin of General Ideas', *Philosophers' Imprint*, 12, 2012 (1–22)
D. Lewis, 'Survival and Identity', in A. O. Rorty, ed., *The Identities of Persons*
D. Lewis, *On the Plurality of Worlds*, Blackwell, Oxford 1987
D. Lewis, 'Causation' (1973), in D. Lewis, ed., *Philosophical Papers*, Volume 2, Oxford University Press, Oxford/New York 1986 (159–213)

D. Tycerium Lightner, 'Hume on Conceivability and Inconceivability', *Hume Studies*, 23, 1, 1997, 113–32

J. Locke, *An Essay Concerning Human Understanding*, P. H. Nidditch, ed., Clarendon Press, Oxford 1975

L. Loeb, *Stability and Justification in Hume's Treatise*, Oxford University Press, 2002

L. Loeb, 'Epistemological Commitment in Hume's *Treatise*', *Oxford Studies in Early Modern Philosophy*, 6, 2011 (309–47)

E. J. Lowe, 'Experience and its Objects', in Crane, ed., *The Contents of Experience* (79–104)

J. Lyons, 'General Rules and the Justification of Probable Belief in Hume's *Treatise*', *Hume Studies*, 27, 2001 (247–77)

D. Macbeth, 'Inference, Meaning, and Truth in Brandom, Sellars, and Frege', in B. Weiss & J. Wanderer, *Reading Brandom. On Making It Explicit*, Routledge, London 2010 (197–212)

T. Magri, 'Natural Obligation and Normative Motivation in Hume's *Treatise*', *Hume Studies*, 22, 1996 (23–254)

T. Magri, 'Hume's Justice', in Ainslie and Butler, *Cambridge Companion to Hume's Treatise* (301–32)

N. Malebranche, *De la Recherche de la Verité. ou l'on traite de la Nature de l'Esprit de l'homme, et de l'Usage qu'il en doit faire pour éviter l'erreur dans les sciences*, Pralard, Paris 1678 (fourth edition) https://gallica.bnf.fr/ark:/12148/bpt6k10414993/f424.item

N. Malebranche, *The Search after Truth*, T. M. Lennon & P.J. Olscamp, eds., Cambridge University Press, Cambridge 1997

A. Mallozzi, A. Vaidya, M. Wallner, 'The Epistemology of Modality', *The Stanford Encyclopedia of Philosophy* https://plato.stanford.edu/entries/modality-epistemology/

M. Marion, 'Oxford Realism: Knowledge and Perception', I and II, *British Journal for the History of Philosophy*, 8, 2, 2000 (299–338) and 3, 2000 (485–519)

Markman et al., *Handbook of Imagination and Mental Simulation*, Psychology Press, New York 2009, 197:210

V. Mascarenhas, 'Hume's Recantation Revisited', *Hume Studies*, 27, 2001, 279:300

C. Maund, 'Hume's Treatment of Simples', *The Philosophical Review*, 1935 (now in Tweynman, ed., *David Hume. Critical Assessments*, I, pp. 75–89)

J. E. McGuire, 'Body and Void and Newton's De Mundi Systemate', *Archive for History of Exact Sciences*, 3, 1966 (206–48)

J. McIntyre, 'Hume's Underground Self', 1993, in Tweyman, *David Hume. Critical Assessments*, Volume 3, 718–29

J. McIntyre, 'Hume and the Problem of Personal Identity', in D. F. Norton & J. Taylor, *Companion to Hume*, 177–208

D. G. C. McNabb, *David Hume. His Theory of Knowledge and Morality*, Blackwell, Oxford 1966 (1951)

R. McRae, 'The Import of Hume's Theory of Time', *Hume Studies*, 6, 1980 (in Tweyman, *David Hume. Critical Assessments*, volume 3, 25–34)

F. S. Michael, 'Why Logic Became Epistemology: Gassendi, Port Royal and the Reformation of Logic', in Easton, ed., *Logic and the Workings of the Mind*, 1–20

P. Millican, 'Hume, Causal Realism, and Causal Science', *Mind*, 118, 2009 (647–712)

P. Millican, 'Hume's Fork and his Theory of Relations', *Philosophy and Phenomenological Research*, 95, 2017, (3–65)

J. Morreall, 'Hume's Missing Shade of Blue', *Philosophy and Phenomenological Research*, 42, 1982, 407–15

W. E. Morris, 'Belief, Probability, Normativity', in Traiger, ed., *The Blackwell Guide to Hume's Treatise*, 77:94

R. Muehlmann, 'Strong and Weak Heterogeneity in Berkeley's *New Theory of Vision*', in S. H. Daniel ed., *New Interpretations of Berkeley's Thought*, Humanity Books, Amherst 2008, pp. 121:144

M. J. Murray, 'Pre-Leibnizian Moral Necessity', *The Leibniz Review*, 14, 2004, 1:28

S. Nadler, 'Malebranche on Causation', in Nadler, ed., *Companion to Malebranche*, 112–38

S. Nadler, ed., *The Cambridge Companion to Malebranche*

G. J. Nathan, 'A Humean Pattern of Justification', *Hume Studies*, 9, 2, 1983 (in Tweynman, ed., *David Hume. Critical Assessments*, I, pp. 183–97)

R. Newman, 'Hume on Space and Geometry', *Hume Studies*, 7, 1981 (in Tweyman, *David Hume. Critical Assessments*, III, pp. 39–59)

I. Newton, *Mathematical Principles of Natural Philosophy*, University of California Press, Oakland 1999

S. Nichols, 'Imaginative Blocks and Impossibility', in Nichols & Stich, *The Architecture of Imagination*

S. Nichols, *The Architecture of Imagination*, Clarendon Press, Oxford 2006

H. W. Noonan, *Hume on Knowledge*, Routledge, London 1999

D. F. Norton & J. Taylor, *The Cambridge Companion to Hume*, Cambridge University Press, Cambridge 2009

D. Owen, *Hume's Reason*, Oxford University Press, Oxford 1999

D. Owen, 'Hume and the Mechanics of Mind', in D. F. Norton & J. Taylor, *The Cambridge Companion to Hume*, Cambridge University Press, Cambridge 2009

C. Peacocke, *A Study of Concepts*, The MIT Press, Cambridge, Mass. and London 1992

D. Pears, *Hume's System. An Examination of the First Book of his Treatise*, Oxford University Press, New York 1990

T. Penelhum, 'Hume on Personal Identity', *The Philosophical Review*, 64, 1955 (in Chappell, *Hume*, 213–39)

J. Perry, *Identity, Personal Identity, and the Self*, Hackett, Indianapolis/Cambridge 2002

H. H. Price, *Hume's Theory of the External World*, 1940 (in *The Collected Works of H.H. Price*, Volume 1, Thoemmes Press, Bristol 1996, 3–228)

H. Price, 'Will There Be Blood? Brandom and Hume on the Genealogy of Modals', *Philosophical Topics*, 36, 2008, 87:97

H. Price, 'Expressivism for Two Voices', in J. Knowles & H. Rydenfelt, eds., *Pragmatism, Science, and Naturalism*, Lang, Frankfurt am Main 2011 (87–113)

H. Price, *Naturalism without Mirrors*, Oxford University Press, New York 2011

S. Psillos, 'Regularity Theories', in Beebe, Hitchcock, & Menzies, *Oxford Handbook of Causation* (131–57)

Qu, Hsueh, 'Hume on Mental Transparency', *Pacific Philosophical Quarterly*, 98, 2017 (576–601), 577–82

Qu, Hsueh, *Hume's Epistemological Evolution*, Oxford University Press, New York 2020

W. V. O. Quine, 'Epistemology Naturalized', in W. V. O. Quine, *Ontological Relativity and Other Essays*, Columbia University Press, New York/London 1969 (69–90)

T. Reid, *Essays on the Intellectual Powers of Man*, B. Brody, ed., The MIT Press, Cambridge (Mass.)/London 1969

R. Read & K. A. Richman, eds., *The New Hume Debate* (Revised Edition), Routledge, London/New York, 2007

A. G. Renault et al., 'Does Proprioception Influence Human Spatial Cognition? A Study on Individuals With Massive Deafferentation', *Frontiers in Psychology*, 2018; 9.1322 10.3389/fpsyg.2018.01322

M. Ridge, 'Epistemology Moralized: David's Hume Practical Epistemology', *Hume Studies*, 29, 2003 (165–204)

J. R. Roberts, *A Metaphysics for the Mob*, Oxford University Press, Oxford 2008

W. Robison, 'Hume of Personal Identity', (1974) in Tweyman, David Hume. Critical Assessments, Volume 3 (687–703), 696–7

S. Roca-Royes, 'Conceivability and De Re Modal Knowledge', *Nous*, 45, 2011, 22:49

S. Rocknak, *Imagined Causes: Hume's Conception of Objects*, Springe, Dordrecht/New York 2013

A. O. Rorty, ed., *The Identities of Persons*, University of California Press, Berkeley/Los Angeles/London 1979

D. Rosenthal, 'A Theory of Consciousness' (1990), in Block, Flanagan & Güzeldere, *Nature of Consciousness*, (729–53)

B. Russell, 'On Propositions' (1919), in *Logic and Knowledge. Essays 1901–1950*, Allen and Unwin, London 1956 (285–319)

B. Russell, *The Analysis of Mind*, Allen and Unwin, London 1978

P. Russell, *The Riddle of Hume's Treatise*, Oxford University Press, Oxford 2008

L. Sanna et al., 'Hard to Imagine: Mental Simulation, Metacognitive Experiences, and the Success of Debiasing', in Markman & al., *Handbook of Imagination*, 197:210

K. Schafer, 'Curious Virtues in Hume's Epistemology', *Philosophers' Imprint*, 14, 1, 2014 (1–20)

K. Schafer, 'Hume's Unified Theory of Mental Representation', *European Journal of Philosophy*, 23, 4, 2015 (978–1005)

E. Schliesser, 'Hume's Missing Shade of Blue Considered from a Newtonian Perspective', *Journal of Scottish Philosophy*, 2, 2004 (164–75)

E. Schliesser, 'Two Definitions of Causation, Normativity, and Hume's Debate with Newton', *Journal of Scottish Philosophy*, 5, 2007 (83–101)

T. A. Schmalz, ed., *Efficient Causation. A History*, Oxford University Press, Oxford 2014

F. Schmitt, *Hume's Epistemology in the Treatise*, Oxford University Press, Oxford 2014

S. Sedivy, 'Hume, Images and Abstraction', *Hume Studies*, 21, 1, 1995 (117–34)

L. Shen-yi & T. Gendler, 'Imagination', *Stanford Encyclopedia of Philosophy* https://plato.stanford.edu/entries/imagination/

S. Shoemaker, 'Personal Identity: a Materialist's Account', in S. Shoemaker & R. Swinburne, *Personal Identity*, Blackwell, Oxford 1984

J. Smalligan Marušić, 'Does Hume Hold a Dispositional Account of Belief?', *Canadian Journal of Philosophy*, 40, 2010 (155–84)

A. H. Smit, 'Apriority, Reason, and Induction', *Journal of the History of Philosophy*, 48, 2010, 313–43

P. Snowdon, 'How to interpret "direct perception"', in Crane, ed., *The Contents of Experience* (48–78)

P. Steembakkers, 'Spinoza on the Imagination', in L. Nauta & D. Pätzold, eds., *The Scope of the Imagination; 'Imaginatio' between Medieval and Modern Times*, Peters, Leuven 2004, 175:193

K. Stenning & M. van Lambalgen, *Human Reasoning and Cognitive Science*, The MIT Press, Cambridge (Mass.)/London 2008

G. Strawson, *The Secret Connexion*, Oxford University Press, Oxford 1989

G. Strawson, *The Evident Connexion*, Oxford, Oxford University Press 2011

P. Strawson, 'Imagination and Perception' (1971), in R. C. S. Walker, ed., *Kant on Pure Reason*, Oxford University Press, Oxford 1982 (82–99)

B. Stroud, *Hume*, Routledge, London 1977

B. Stroud, "'Gilding or Staining' the World with 'Sentiments' and 'Phantasms'", in R. Read & K. A. Richman eds., *The New Hume Debate* (Revised Edition), Routledge, London/New York, 2007, (16–30)

R. Sugden, *The Economics of Rights, Cooperation, and Welfare*, Blackwell, Oxford 1986

T. Szabó Gendler and J. Hawthorne, *Perceptual Experience*, Clarendon Press, Oxford 2006 (49–125)

D. Tamás, 'Hume's Science of Mind and Newtonianism', (2019), in E. Schliesser and C. Smeenk, *The Oxford Handbook of Newton*, Oxford Handbooks Online, 10.1093/oxfordhb/9780199930418.013.19

U. Thiel, *The Early Modern Subject*, Oxford University Press, Oxford 2011

D. Townsend, *Hume's Aesthetic Theory. Taste and Sentiment*, Routledge, London/New York 2001

S. Traiger, ed., *The Blackwell Guide to Hume's Treatise*, Blackwell, Oxford 2006

S. Tweyman, ed., *David Hume. Critical Assessments*, 6 volumes, Routledge, London/New York, 1995

M. Tye, 'Nonconceptual Content, Richness, and Fineness of Grain', in Gendler & Hawothorne, eds., *Perceptual Experience* (504–30)

A. J. Vaidya, 'Modal Knowledge: Beyond Rationalism and Empiricism', in B. Fisher and F. Leon, eds., *Modal Epistemology After Rationalism*, Springer 2017 (85–114)

J. J. Valberg, 'The Puzzle of Experience', in T. Crane, ed., *The Contents of Experience*, Cambridge University Press, Cambridge 1992 (18–47)

L. Van Boven et al., 'Temporally Asymmetric Constraints on Mental Simulation', in Markman et al., *Handbook of Imagination*, 131–47

N. Van Leeuwen, 'The Meanings of "Imagine" Part I: Constructive Imagination', *Philosophy Compass*, 8, 2013 (220–30)

N. Van Leeuwen, 'The Meanings of "Imagine" Part II: Attitude and Action', *Philosophy Compass*, 9, 2014 (791–802)

A. Waldow, 'Identity of Persons and Objects', *The Journal of Scottish Philosophy*, 8, 2010, 147:167

W. Waxman, *Hume's Theory of Consciousness*, Cambridge University Press, Cambridge 1994

J. Weinberg & A. Meskin, 'Puzzling over the Imagination: Philosophical Problems, Architectural Solutions', in Nichols, ed., *The Architecture of the Imagination* (175–202)

J. Wilbanks, *Hume's Theory of the Imagination*, Nijoff, The Hague 1968

T. Williamson, *Knowledge and its Limits*, Oxford University Press, Oxford 2000

T. Williamson, *The Philosophy of Philosophy*, Blackwell, Oxford 2007

T. Williamson, 'Knowing by Imagining', in Kind & Kung, eds., *Knowledge through Imagination* (113–23)

F. Wilson, 'The Origins of Hume's Sceptical Argument against Reason', *History of Philosophy Quarterly*, 2, 3, 1985 (323–35) (in Tweynman, *David Hume. Critical Assessments*, Volume 1 253–66)

F. Wilson, *Hume's Defense of Causal Inference*, University of Toronto Press, Toronto 1997

K. P. Winkler, *Berkeley. An Interpretation*, Clarendon Press, Oxford 1989

K. Winkler, '"All is Revolution in Us": Personal Identity in Shaftesbury and Hume', *Hume Studies*, 26, 2000, 3:40

K. P. Winkler, 'The New Hume', in Read & Richman, eds., *The New Hume Debate*, (52–87)

K. P. Winkler, 'Berkeley and the Doctrine of Signs', in *The Cambridge Companion to Berkeley*, K. Winkler ed., Cambridge University Press, Cambridge 2005, 125–65

K. Winkler, 'Hume on Scepticism and the Senses', in Ainslie & Butler, eds., *Cambridge Companion to Hume's Treatise*, 135–64

B. Winters, 'Hume on Reason', *Hume Studies*, 5, 1979, 20–35 (in Tweyman, ed., *David Hume. Critical Assessments*, I, 229–40)

R. P. Wolff, 'Hume's Theory of Mental Activity', *Philosophical Review*, 69, 1969 (in Tweyman, ed., *David Hume. Critical Assessments*, III, pp. 158–75)

E. Wong et al., 'The Counterfactual Mind-Set', in Markman et al., *Handbook of Imagination and Simulation*, 161-74

J. P. Wright, *The Sceptical Realism of David Hume*, Minnesota University Press, Minneapolis 1983

J. P. Wright, 'Hume's Causal Realism', in Read & Richman, *The New Hume Debate*, (88-99)

J. P. Wright, *Hume's A Treatise of Human Nature. An Introduction*, Cambridge University Press, Cambridge 2009

S. Yablo, 'Is Conceivability a Guide to Possibility?', *Philosophy and Phenomenological Research*, 53, 1993, 1-42

Analytical Index

For the benefit of digital users, indexed terms that span two pages (e.g., 52–53) may, on occasion, appear on only one of those pages.

Act/Idea Resemblance 292–3, 301
Attrition 419–20, 425–6
Animal cognition
   Shared with humans 427, 446n.14
   As evidence for Hume's theory 69n.8
A priori
   As cognitive gap 179
   Theoretical roles: Mathematics and maxims 176–9, 182–4
   And Separability 179–80
   And relations of ideas 181, 191
   And metaphysical necessity 181
   Non-analytic 181–2
   And demonstrative knowledge 182, 189, 279–80
Association
   Theoretical role 79–80
   Principles 79–80
   And transitions of the imagination 82–4
   As a sort of attraction 82–3
   As cement of the universe 84–5

Belief
   As a philosophical mystery 141–2
   As attitude and as state 389
   Belief as assent 389–93
   Conception/cognition gap 389–90
   Assent as manner of conception 390–1
   Force, vivacity, feeling 391–3
   Assent versus desire 391–2
   Assent in sense, memory, and knowledge 394–6
   Transitions of feeling and the imagination 397–9
   Belief as mental state 400–1
   Functional description 401–2
   Cognitive gap of belief as mental state 402
   Belief, inference, imagination 403–5, 408–9

Causal Maxim 198–200
Causal uniformity 219, 232, 253–4
Causality
   As idea 189–91, 193–4

Causal inference and causal necessity 189, 198, 201, 203, 207–8, 227–8
Idea of cause and inference to the unobserved 191–4
As cognitive gap 194–6
Inference and experience 197–8, 202–3
Imagination and experience 203–7, 209–10
Idea of cause and causal necessity 223–4, 227–8
Cognitive gap of causal necessity 200, 223–7
Causal necessity and imagination 228–32
Only one kind of causal necessity 168–9
Two definitions of cause 243–6
Natural and philosophical relation of cause 208–9
Causality in the objects 248–9
Mind-dependent causality 249–51
Cognitive role of causal necessity 254–8
Cognitive biases 89–90, 108–9, 157–8, 215–17, 398–9
Cognitive gaps
   And the content-productive role of the imagination 7–10, 12, 67–8, 99, 274, 411
   Necessary to our cognitive nature 7, 63, 72–3
   Taxonomy 70–2, 242–3
   Individuation by cognitive functions 101–2, 143–4, 147, 149–52, 190, 218, 299, 306–7, 317–18, 353–4, 375
   Recursive individuation 189, 201
   And paradox of naturalism about cognition 88–9, 93, 95–6, 207–8
   And skepticism 15–16, 342–3, 425
Completion 340
Conceptual thinking
   Modes of conceptual thinking 21, 72, 113, 136, 141
   In ordinary cognition 70–1, 190, 193–4, 219–20, 275–6
   Conceptual thinking as cognitive gap 21, 72–3, 136, 189
   As product of the imagination 6–7, 12, 14, 134, 137–8, 147, 409–10

Consciousness
  As experience, awareness, and presence 25, 33, 126–7, 134, 157, 350
  State and creature consciousness 33–5, 37–8
  Infallible 33, 50–1, 304–5, 376
  Hume's difficulty with consciousness 32, 34–5, 242–3, 274n.15, 304–5, 333, 382–4, 443n.13
Content
  Missing mental contents 7–9, 70
  Dualism of representational and inferential contents 67–8, 102–4, 147, 245–6
Custom
  Fundamental content-productive principle 121–2
  Only imagination susceptible to custom 211, 214–15, 398–400, 422–3, 446–7
  Revival of custom 123
  Customary transitions 121–2, 128, 211, 247, 250, 256, 281–2, 315, 397
  Customary propensities 89, 135–6, 214, 256
  Inferential custom 123, 130, 135–6
  Indirect roles of custom 219, 312–13, 404–5, 460
  And content-production 211, 213–15, 232
  And assent 398–9, 404–5

Distinctions of reason
  As cognitive gap 132–4
  As mode of conceptual thinking 131–2
  And imagination 134–5
  And epistemic modality 169–71

Epistemic improvement 450
Equivalence 43
Established Maxim 142
Existence
  And conception of object-representing ideas 51–2, 105, 163
  As manner of conception 53–4
  External existence qualitatively the same with perceptions 300–1
Experience
  As representation by memory 202–3
  As inferential potential 202, 204
  As cognitive gap 204
External world
  As body or matter 299–302
  As cognitive gap 303, 306–8, 311
  Coherence account and imagination 308–14
  Cognitive role of the coherence account 309–10
  Limits of coherence account 315–16
  Constancy account 316–17, 325–6, 328
  Cognitive role of the constancy account 316
  Perceptions persisting as bodies 329–33
  Bodies existing as perceptions 334–7
  Vulgar and philosophical belief 339–40

Feeling
  And thinking 25, 52–3
  Roles as manner of conception 24, 53, 56, 62, 142, 230–1, 392, 458
First Principle 44
  Relatively a priori 50
  Aimed to taxonomy and not exclusion 49

Generality
  As change in content and cognitive gap 113–18
  And resemblance and naming 120–1
  And inference and imagination 119–26
  Roles in reasoning and counterexamples 128, 130–1

Human nature
  Original principles of our minds 13, 19, 28–9, 46–7, 70, 84
  And physical necessity 50, 73, 207
  As foundation of the sciences 10–11, 13, 97–8, 467
  And the reformation of philosophy 11, 13
Hysteresis 283

Ideas
  And impressions 23–5
  Of memory and of imagination 24, 54
  Perfect ideas 78–9
  As contents and as mental episodes 21
  And possible existence 43
  Taxonomy by kinds of contents 48–9
  No primitive intellectual ideas 73
Identity
  As cognitive gap 318, 322–3
  Analysis of the proposition of identity 317–18
  Identity, time, and imagination 316–17, 319–22
  Imperfect identity 322–3
Imagination
  Cognitive but not object representing 9, 54, 63, 67–8, 79, 87–8, 144–5
  In a larger sense 87–8, 184, 203, 280
  In a more limited sense 87, 89–90, 95–6, 191
  As one faculty 89–91, 129, 210, 217, 416, 419–20, 425–6
  Simulation, completeness, and reason 10, 137–8, 217–18, 240–1, 408–9, 412–13, 447–8
  Structure of the production of content 29–31, 138–9
  And cognitive change and agency 7–8, 76, 91–2, 98–9, 108, 132–3, 324, 425–6, 450

Important Footnote 104–5
Impressions
  Of sensation and reflection 23–4
  As primitive presentations 26–8
  As actual sensible objects 36–8
  Dual theoretical role 25–8
Inference
  Imagination as faculty of inference 9, 85, 87–8, 97–8, 101–2, 207–8, 211, 421
  As comparison of ideas 18, 87–9, 101–2, 180, 191, 224, 408–9, 421–2
  As transition of ideas 9, 16–17, 82–3, 87–8, 97–8, 101–2, 109, 157, 211, 231, 313, 393
  Formal and material 99–103
  And production of content 1–3, 9, 12, 67, 96–9, 109, 211, 231–2, 408–9
  And conception 219–20
  Inferential potentials 123–4, 191, 207–11, 214–15, 259, 427
  One-object inferences 192–3
Inferentialist Naturalism 99
Inner/outer divide 329, 331, 345
Intentionality
  Restricted to the imagination 136
  Simulates intellectual ideas and agency 137–8

Knowledge
  As species of cognition 141, 176–7, 183–4, 189, 443, 445–6
  As mental state 180–1, 191, 389, 395–6, 405, 414–15
  And adequate representation 179, 273

Manifest image: Powers and continuants 25–6, 235, 315, 338, 353–4, 376
Memory
  As object-representing faculty 9, 24, 37–8, 50–1, 53–5, 69, 77–8, 187
  Feeling of pastness 376
Mind
  As bundle of perceptions 166–7, 331–3, 357
  True, causal idea of the mind 345–6, 364–5
Missing shade of blue 63–7
Modality
  As mode of conceptual thinking 141
  As cognitive gap 144–5
  Conceivability by imagination as constitutive account 143–4, 152, 157–8, 162
  Inferences of conceivability 146–52
  Separability 153–5, 157
  Determination 159–60
  Metaphysical and physical 163–6, 202, 224, 226, 234, 341–2, 370–1

Absolute and epistemic 167–71, 182–3, 185, 321–2, 329, 344

Naturalism
  As philosophical programme 10–11, 13, 15, 50, 73, 452–3
  Science of human nature 10–13, 25, 50, 333, 346–7, 411
  Structure of philosophical naturalism: concepts and facts 50, 72, 162, 389
  Paradox of naturalism and new contents 29–31, 72–3, 93, 95–6, 122, 126–7, 207–8, 240–1
  Experimental method of reasoning 10–11
  Moral and natural philosophy 26–8, 52
New Hume Interpretation 59–61, 171–5
Non-Mixture 97
Normativity
  As a cognitive gap 14, 432–4, 437, 450–1
  Normative aims of science of human nature 467
  Epistemically grounded explanations 102–3, 129, 253, 406, 408, 430
  And imagination as ultimate judge 429–32
  And imagination as natural faculty 432
  A posteriori identifications 433–5
  And sentimentalism 429, 452–3
  Epistemic normativity 437–40
  Structure of epistemic evaluation 453–8

Objects
  Pluralism 39–40
  Simple and complex 40–1
  Minimal ontology 37–8, 61–2
  As sensible particulars 37, 114, 139, 316
  As contents of perceptions 41–2, 46

Perceptions
  As substances 21–2, 40–1, 351–2, 370–1
  As activities 21–2
Probability
  As species of cognition 189, 192, 401–2, 439–40
  As mental state 389, 396–8
  Imagination and probability 397–8
  Degrees of probability 398–400, 439–40, 444
  Probabilities and proofs 445–6
  Probability of chances 399–403
  Doxastic deliberation 404–6

Reality
  Representation of reality by feeling 50–1, 53
  Systems of realities 63–4, 71–2, 80, 193, 203, 238–9, 310, 315

Reason
  Not an object-representing faculty 9, 12, 225, 412
  And comparison of ideas 18, 108–9, 339–40, 464
  And the imagination 14, 85–8, 209–10, 217–18, 387, 404, 408–9, 418–19, 422
  A priori 181, 189, 192, 324
  Probable 191, 205–6, 257–8, 324, 416, 445
  As cause of truth 207, 442
  Truth as object of reason 397
  Obligation of reason 415–16, 450–1, 460–1
  Title of reason 464–6
Reasoning
  Idea-comparing 18, 88–9, 148, 191, 207, 398, 408–10, 422
  Deductive reasoning 146, 180, 191–2, 256, 397
  Demonstrative reasoning 89–90, 176–7, 180, 191–4, 413–14
  Probable reasoning 87–8, 90–1, 95–6, 169, 190, 192, 206, 215, 397
  Mature causal reasoning 202, 216–20, 404
  Reasoning with contrary experiences 406
  Reasoning with one experience 219, 312–13, 460
Reconciliation 283
Reference
  As extraneous denomination 58
  And existence 56–8
  Only by description 58–9
  Inner demonstratives 56–7, 394–5
Reflection
  As representation of internal perceptions 353–7, 361–2, 381–2
  Abstract or philosophical reflection 15, 59–60, 182–3, 191–2, 271, 343–4, 409–10, 425–6
Relations of ideas
  As structures of thought and cognition 82–3, 90–1, 156–7, 180–1, 183–4, 191–2, 253, 395, 441–2
  Natural and philosophical 31, 91–3, 180, 209, 217–18
Relatively a priori claims 50, 72, 115, 141, 235, 265, 304, 336–7, 384
Reliability 442–3
Representation 47
Representation/imagination continuities 97–8, 342–3, 446–7
Representation of objects
  Primitive cognitive input 7–8, 26–7, 39–40, 43, 46, 48, 62, 97–8
  Not confused or obscure 12, 73–5, 111, 137–8, 271

Only of impressions of sensation 32, 37–8, 41–2, 44–5, 47–8
  Only of sensible objects 43, 46–7, 51–2
  Only of particular objects 37–8, 56–7, 68, 115, 119
  Only object dependent 41–2, 47, 50–1, 69, 79–80
  Non-modal 55–6, 143–4, 402
  Non-conceptual 69–71
Representational Naturalism 72
General rules
  And imagination 407–9
  Rules of judgment 253–4, 439–40
  Conflict and Correction 435–7

Self and Personal Identity
  As cognitive gap 144–5, 350–2
  Roles in thought and in the passions 375–8
  Different forms in ordinary cognition 353
  Selfless perceptions 355–6
  Identification of successive perceptions 357–60
  Account by resemblance 361–3
  Account by causation 363–5
  Personal identity as composition 366–8
  Difficulty with intimate consciousness 379–80
Skepticism
  And cognitive gaps 15, 72–5, 95–6, 254, 346–7, 410
  And philosophical reflection 306–7, 342–3, 410, 418–19
  And the limits of the imagination 16, 343–4, 411, 421
  About possibility 412, 425
  About authority 412–13, 462–3
Second Principle 75
Space and time
  As representations of complex impressions 264–6
  As perceptions with extension and duration 268–9
  Finite divisibility 269–74
  As cognitive gaps 274, 276–9, 284–5
  Imagination and geometry 280–2, 284
  Imagination and empty space and time 286–91
  Illusions of content and cognitive roles 282–4, 291–3, 295–6
Spreading in the mind 237
Spreading on external objects 239
Structural Principle 86–7

Theoretical equilibrium in the science of
    man 218, 283–4, 375, 453
True Philosophy
    Close to ordinary cognition 333,
        344–5
Truth
    As correspondence 440–2

Truth-aptness 443–4, 446–7
    And epistemic normativity 440–3
Two Viewpoints 28
    As distinction of reason 28–9
    And explanation of content-production 101–2

Uniformity of nature 205–7, 219, 232

Index of Names

For the benefit of digital users, indexed terms that span two pages (e.g., 52–53) may, on occasion, appear on only one of those pages.

Ainslie, Donald 3–4, 25–6, 35n.20, 120n.8, 149n.15, 233n.2, 270n.10, 271n.11, 274n.15, 301n.2, 316n.16, 337n.31, 345nn.34–35, 345n.36, 379n.33, 411n.20, 419n.29, 461n.28
Allison, Henry 274n.15, 275n.16, 347n.38
Anderson, Abraham 8n.16, 198n.10
Anjum, Rani 249n.18

Balcerak Jackson, Magdalena 173n.51
Baxter, Donald 40n.25, 266n.7, 274n.15, 276n.17, 289n.23, 318n.18, 319n.19, 322n.21
Beauchamp, Tom 16n.24, 194n.5, 205n.15, 242n.11, 248n.15, 249n.18, 256n.26, 258n.29, 263n.1
Beebee, Helen 156n.28, 157n.29, 172n.50, 180n.62, 190n.1, 192n.2, 194nn.4,5, 198n.10, 205n.15, 233n.3, 235n.5, 243n.12, 245n.13, 249nn.16–17, 251–2, 251n.20, 258nn.28–29, 442n.11
Berkeley, George 60n.49, 68n.7, 74n.16, 83n.28, 113–17, 127n.12, 143–4, 196n.7, 212n.18, 214n.20, 235, 287n.22, 328n.25, 364n.15, 380n.35, 439n.7
Bernstein, Daniel 161n.34
Blackburn, Simon 143n.3, 145nn.11,12, 175–6
Block, Ned 34n.16
Boehm, Miren 13n.22, 166n.37, 237n.6, 290n.26, 292n.29
Bolton, Marta 74n.16
Brandom, Robert 99nn.45–46, 100nn.47,49–51, 101nn.51–52, 102n.54, 143n.3, 176n.58
Broad, Charles 276n.17
Broughton, Janet 24n.4, 35n.20, 119n.7
Bruce, Vicki 238n.7
Burge, Tyler 35n.18, 446n.14
Butler, Annemarie 233n.2, 300n.1, 301n.2, 461n.28
Byrne, Ruth 215n.22, 216n.24

Chalmers, David 30n.12, 38n.23, 57n.42, 172–3, 274n.15
Chappell, Vere 332n.27, 350n.1
Church, Jennifer 104n.61
Clarke, Samuel 168–9
Cohon, Rachel 452n.21
Costa, Michael 266n.7, 319n.19
Costelloe, Timothy 3–4, 77n.20
Cottrell, Jonathan 3–4
Crane, Tim 38n.22, 55n.39, 57n.42, 69n.8
Cummins, Philip 158n.31
Cunning, David 143n.2
Currie, Gregory 450n.18

Danks, David 194n.3, 197n.8
Davies, Martin 56n.40
Della Rocca, Michael 143n.2
Descartes, René 30n.12, 61n.51, 74n.14, 77n.21, 78n.22, 93n.41, 99–102, 107n.64, 131n.16, 142–3, 154n.27, 157–8, 177n.59, 181n.63, 351, 463
De Vignemont, Frederique 291n.28
Durland, Karànn 66n.4, 67n.6

Easton, Patricia 29n.11, 56n.41, 74n.14, 158n.31
Echelbarger, Charles 56n.41, 181n.63
Ellis, Jonathan 374n.22, 375n.27, 376n.28
Evans, Gareth 61n.51
Evans, Jonathan 93n.40
Everson, Stephen 24n.4

Falkenstein, Lorne 265nn.3,4, 266n.5,7, 276n.17, 289n.24, 291n.27, 292n.29, 293n.30, 398n.10
Fiocco, Marcello 174n.54
Flanagan, Owen 34n.16
Flew, Anthony 393n.5
Fodor, Jerry 55n.38, 80n.24, 85n.30
Fogelin, Robert 65n.3, 413n.21, 416n.24, 421n.32
Franklin, Julian 273n.13, 276n.17
Frasca Spada, Marina 269n.9, 270n.10

INDEX OF NAMES

Garrett, Don 3–4, 41n.26, 49n.32, 50n.33, 64n.1, 78n.22, 88n.34, 103–4, 122–3, 124n.9, 151n.17, 153n.20, 168n.40, 169n.43, 177n.59, 182n.65, 198n.10, 205n.15, 220n.28, 233n.2, 245n.13, 248n.15, 249n.16, 251n.20, 254n.23, 278n.18, 300n.1, 322n.21, 344, 345n.35, 354n.4, 375nn.25,26, 378n.29, 383n.40, 392n.2, 411n.19, 417n.26, 425n.33, 440n.8, 452n.21, 454nn.22–23, 463n.29, 464, 466n.32
Gendler, Tamar 4n.13, 30n.12, 55n.39, 143nn.2–3, 145n.11, 173nn.51,52
Gertler, Brie 57n.42
Gibbard, Allan 143n.3, 434n.4
Girotto, Vittorio 216n.24
Goldman, Alvin 138n.19
Green, Michael 372n.20, 380n.36
Gregory, Dominic 145n.11, 172–3
Grene, Marjorie 37n.21
Grossberg, Stephen 314n.13
Güzeldere, Guven 34n.16

Hakkarainen, Jani 39n.24, 93n.41
Hale, Bob 173n.51
Hansson, Uri 130n.14
Hatfield, Gary 61n.51, 74n.14, 77n.21, 449n.16
Hawthorne, John 30n.12, 55n.39, 143nn.2–3, 145n.11, 173n.51
Hazony, Yoram 285n.20, 296n.33, 450n.17
Hight, Marc 32n.14
Hodges, Michael 395n.7
Holden, Thomas 40n.25, 142n.1, 149n.15, 152n.19, 175n.57, 273n.13
Home, Henry Lord Kames 383n.40
Humbertsone, Lloyd 56n.40

Jacovides, Michael 369n.19
Jacquette, Dale 266n.5
James, William 347n.37
Johansson, Ingvar 22n.1
Johnson-Laird, Philip 130n.14
Johnston, Mark 55n.39, 69n.8

Kahneman, Daniel 161n.34
Kail, Peter 35n.18, 61n.51, 144n.10, 171n.47, 172–3, 175n.57, 190n.1, 194n.5, 200n.13, 235n.5, 251n.20, 254n.23, 301n.2, 345n.35, 464n.30
Kant, Immanuel 8, 12, 55n.38, 73–5, 137n.18, 198–9, 274n.15, 311n.8, 410n.18, 449n.16
Kemp, Catherine 28n.9
Kemp Smith, Norman 2–4, 18, 24n.4, 53n.35, 72–3, 82n.27, 88n.34, 95, 175–6, 181, 251n.20, 265n.4, 394, 395n.7

Kind, Amy 4, 96n.44, 107n.64, 174n.55, 215n.22, 235n.5
Kitcher, Patricia 354n.4
Kjeller Johansen, Thomas 77n.21
Kment, Boris 143n.4, 145n.13, 166n.38
Knuuttila, Simo 143n.2
Kremer, Erland 29n.11
Kripke, Saul 143n.2, 167n.39, 171, 205n.15, 322n.21
Kroedel, Thomas 145n.13
Kung, Peter 96n.44, 104n.61, 145n.11, 173n.51, 174n.55, 174n.56

Lachs, John 395n.7
Landy, David 27n.8, 50n.34, 57n.42, 58n.43, 67n.6, 70nn.9–10, 77n.20, 131n.15, 136n.17, 450n.17
Langland-Hassan, Peter 75n.17, 90n.38, 96n.44, 102n.53
Laurence, Stephen 119n.7
Leibniz, Gottfried 74n.14, 99n.45, 168–9, 402n.13
Lewis, David 249nn.17–18, 251n.20, 256n.25, 369n.19
Lightner, Tycerium 149n.15, 152n.18
Locke, John 31n.13, 65n.3, 81n.25, 91–2, 99–102, 113–14, 119, 143–4, 177n.59, 181n.63, 198–9, 219n.26, 298, 334n.29, 351, 353, 360, 360n.10, 364n.15, 369n.19, 371, 372n.20, 378–9, 380n.35, 382
Loeb, Louis 3–4, 90n.37, 139n.20, 194n.5, 309n.6, 312n.9, 313n.11, 314n.14, 315n.15, 316n.17, 324n.23, 328n.24, 335n.30, 345n.33, 346n.36, 372n.20, 433n.3, 454n.22, 457n.25
Lowe, Edward 69n.8
Lyons, Jack 408n.15

Macbeth, Danielle 101n.51
Magri, Tito 461n.28
Malebranche, Nicolas 29n.11, 93n.41, 94n.42, 196n.7
Mallozzi, Antonella 172n.48
Margolis, Eric 119n.7
Marion, Mathieu 402n.13
Mascarenhas, Vijay 381n.37
McGuire, James 295n.32
Morreall, John 66n.5
Muehlmann, Robert 328n.25
McNabb, D.G.C. 35n.20, 378n.29
Meskin, Aaron 11n.21, 216n.23
Millican, Peter 13n.22, 59n.47, 61n.51, 144n.10, 149n.15, 150n.16, 151n.17, 152n.18, 169n.43, 198n.9, 245n.13, 251n.20
Mumford, Stephen 249n.18
Murray, Michael 168n.41

INDEX OF NAMES

Nadler, Stephen 196n.7
Newman, Rosemary 265n.4
Newton, Isaac 65n.2, 284–5, 296n.33, 298, 450n.17
Nichols, Shaun 11n.21, 138n.19, 161n.33, 216n.23
Noonan, Harold 72n.13, 184n.66, 334n.29
Norton, David 86n.32, 269n.9, 379n.30, 392n.3
Norton, Mary 86n.32, 269n.9, 392n.3

Owen, David 3–4, 56–7, 79n.23, 80n.24, 81n.26, 100n.48, 104–5, 106n.63, 157n.29, 179n.61, 180, 181n.63, 205n.15, 391n.1, 396n.8, 401n.12, 413–14, 415n.23, 417, 419n.29, 420n.30, 430n.1, 454n.22

Peacocke, Christopher 26n.7
Pears, David 58n.43, 393n.5
Penelhum, Terence 350n.1, 368n.18, 378n.29
Perry, John 369n.19
Price, Henry 70n.11, 175–6, 310n.7, 313–14, 313n.11, 315n.15, 320n.20, 337n.31, 345n.34, 346n.36
Price, Huw 99n.46, 101n.52, 102n.54, 104nn.59–60, 143n.3, 145n.11
Psillos, Stathis 249n.17

Qu, Hsueng 16n.26, 33n.15, 411n.19, 416n.24, 464n.30, 465n.31, 466n.33
Quine, Willard 70n.11

Read, Rupert 46n.31, 58n.44, 241n.10
Reid, Thomas 85n.30, 364n.15
Renault, Alix 291n.28
Richman, Kenneth 46n.31, 58n.44, 241n.10
Ridge, Michael 454n.23
Roberts, John 74n.16
Roca-Reyes, Sonia 169n.44
Rocknak, Stefanie 3–4, 62n.52, 72n.12, 268n.8, 310n.7, 312n.9, 394n.6, 401n.12
Rosenberg, Alexander 194n.5, 205n.15, 249n.18, 256n.26, 258n.29, 263n.1
Rosenthal, David 34–5
Russell, Bernard 69n.8, 312–13
Russell, Paul 285n.20, 410n.18, 450n.17

Sanna, Lawrence 161n.34
Schafer, Karl 9n.20, 46n.30, 103n.57, 104n.60, 131n.15, 165n.36, 438n.6, 454n.23
Schliesser, Eric 65n.3, 66n.5, 92n.39, 285n.20, 296n.33, 450n.17
Schmitt, Frederick 87–8, 206n.16, 219n.26, 406n.14, 409n.16, 418n.28, 430n.1, 434n.4, 441n.9, 442n.12, 443n.13, 454n.23

Sedivy, Sonia 128n.13, 131n.15
Shen-yi, Liao 4n.13
Shoemaker, Sidney 369n.19
Smit, Houston 181n.63
Snowdon, Paul 38n.22, 57n.42
Spinoza, Baruch 78n.22, 99n.45, 168n.42, 352n.3
Steembakkers, Piet 78n.22
Stenning, Keith 93n.40, 450n.19
Stewart, John 199n.11
Strawson, Galen 59–60, 59n.45, 60n.50, 172–3, 246n.14, 250–1nn.19–20, 357n.5, 365n.16, 374n.24, 383n.40
Strawson, Peter 4n.13, 137n.18
Stroud, Barry 2–4, 18, 46n.31, 53n.35, 175–6, 233n.3, 241n.10, 254–5, 258n.29, 345n.34, 375n.25, 378n.29

Tamàs, Demeter 450n.17
Thiel, Udo 351n.2, 362n.14, 364n.15
Townsend, Dabney 458n.26
Traiger, Saul 24n.4, 266n.7, 463n.29
Tversky, Amos 161n.34
Tweyman, Stanley 24n.4, 88n.35, 90n.36, 265n.4, 266n.7, 332n.27, 378n.29, 383n.39, 395n.7, 416n.24, 442n.10

Valberg, Jerome 55n.39, 57n.42
Vaidya, Anand 143n.2, 172n.48, 175n.57
Van Boven, Leaf 161n.34
Van Lambalgen, Michiel 93n.40, 450n.19
Van Leeuwen, Neil 216n.24, 409n.17

Waldow, Anik 369n.19
Wallner, Michael 172n.48
Waxman, Wayne 24n.4, 35n.20, 53n.36, 95, 117n.5, 120n.8
Weinberg, Jonathan 11n.21, 216n.23
Wilbanks, Jan 7n.15, 8n.17
Williamson, Timothy 35n.18, 96n.44, 102n.53, 145n.11,13, 215n.22, 402n.13, 409n.17, 417n.25
Wilson, Fred 194n.5, 248n.15, 254n.22, 258n.29, 416n.24
Winkler, Kenneth 58n.44, 60nn.48–49, 68n.7, 74n.16, 114n.1, 116n.2, 249n.18, 301n.2, 313n.10, 328n.25, 381n.37
Winters, Barbara 88n.35
Wolff, Robert 90n.38
Wong, Elaine 216n.24
Wright, John 3–4, 29n.11, 41n.26, 60nn.49–50, 93n.41, 95, 251n.20, 314n.13, 328n.25

Yablo, Stephen 145n.11, 172–3, 174n.53